EDNA HEALEY

Coutts&Co

1692–1992

The Portrait
of a
Private Bank

A John Curtis Book
Hodder & Stoughton
LONDON SYDNEY AUCKLAND

British Library Cataloguing in Publication Data
A catalogue record for this book
is available from the British Library

ISBN 0-340-55826-1
Copyright © Coutts & Co. 1992
First published in Great Britain 1992

Published by Hodder and Stoughton,
a division of Hodder and Stoughton Ltd,
Mill Road, Dunton Green, Sevenoaks, Kent TN13 2YA
Editorial Office: 47 Bedford Square, London WC1B 3DP

Designed by Cinamon and Kitzinger, London

Typeset by Rowland Phototypesetting Ltd,
Bury St Edmunds, Suffolk

Printed in Great Britain by
Butler and Tanner Ltd, Frome and London

Endpapers: The Chinese wallpaper, painted in watercolour on mulberry paper, which was given to Thomas Coutts by Earl Macartney on his return in 1794 from his mission as Britain's first Ambassador to China. It now hangs in the boardroom of Coutts & Co.

This book is dedicated to all the librarians and keepers of archives who hold our history in caring hands, and especially to the archivists of Coutts & Co., who guard with dedication a priceless heritage.

Contents

Contents

Illustrations

Caleb Whitefoord in his distinctive Garrick wig

Sir Thomas Lawrence by Landseer

Henry Fuseli – a self-portrait, c.1779 (*National Portrait Gallery*)

George III by Sir Thomas Lawrence

Georgiana, Duchess of Devonshire (*Fotomas Library*)

Cartoon of the secret marriage of the Prince of Wales and Mrs Fitzherbert (*Mary Evans Picture Library*)

Portrait of Sir Edmund Antrobus

HEICS *Thomas Coutts* from a painting by W. J. Huggins

Sir Francis Burdett by Sir Thomas Lawrence, 1793 (*National Portrait Gallery*)

'The Three Graces': Susan, Fanny and Sophia, the three daughters of Thomas and Susannah Coutts, by Angelica Kauffmann (*Harrowby Mss Trust, Sandon Hall*)

A draft letter from Thomas Coutts to Lord Minto, 24 November 1800, showing his wandering handwriting

Thomas Coutts's house at 1 Stratton Street

Edmund and Gibbs Antrobus, nephews of Sir Edmund Antrobus (*Amesbury Abbey*)

Sir Coutts Trotter, partner from 1793 to 1837 (*private collection*)

Edward Marjoribanks junior, partner from 1838 to 1877

Andrew Dickie, the first clerk to become a partner in 1827

Harriot Mellon as Volante, her most successful role

Between pages 296 and 297

Portrait of Harriot Coutts by Sir William Beechey

Part of a love letter from Thomas to Harriot, with the mark of his lips on it

Bust of Thomas Coutts by Nollekens (*by courtesy of Hon. C. J. A. N. Money-Coutts*)

The garden of Holly Lodge, Harriot's villa in Highgate

Watercolour portrait of Sir Francis Burdett by William Ross (*National Portrait Gallery*)

William Matthew Coulthurst, partner in the Bank from 1827 to 1877

A page of neatly written Bank accounts from Edward Marjoribanks's memoirs

59 Strand – the old 'Shop', 1885

The banking hall, 59 Strand, around 1900

Angela Burdett as a young girl, by her old friend Masquerier

The Duke of Wellington with his grandchildren (*Stratfield Saye/Courtauld Institute of Art*)

Sir James Brooke, Rajah of Sarawak (*Mary Evans Picture Library*)

Charles Dickens

Queen Victoria on horseback, 1849 (*Mary Evans Picture Library*)

Engraving of Louis Philippe, one of the Bank's French royal customers

Princess Victoria Mary of Teck, later Queen Mary (*Mansell Collection*)

Letter from David Livingstone from the Zambezi, 20 February 1862

George Robinson by W. W. Ouless

Frederick Augustus Shannon, the Bank's confidential agent who handled its affairs in France

A vividly illustrated South American share bond, 1878

Between pages 392 and 393

Some of the memorabilia in the archives at Coutts & Co.: the famous golden guinea, given to Thomas Coutts by a well-wisher; the gold snuffbox presented to Andrew Dickie by Louis Philippe; a display case in the garden court recalling Victorian life in the Bank

The 1871 Christmas card from Baroness Burdett-Coutts and Mrs Brown

Photo from the *Walrus* album, 1879, showing the Baroness with her future husband Ashmead Bartlett, Henry Irving, Mr Tennant and Admiral and Mrs Gordon (*Mansell Collection*)

Lord Archibald Campbell in Highland dress

Henry Ryder, fourth Earl of Harrowby

William Rolle Malcolm

Sir George Marjoribanks

An architectural drawing for the new Bank at 440 Strand, 1903

The banking hall of 440 Strand in the early twentieth century

Charles Cockman and Charles Adcock, two twentieth-century members of staff

Lord Sandon and Sir Seymour Egerton side by side at their desks at Coutts & Co. (*The Hulton-Deutsch Collection*)

Edith and Osbert Sitwell, grateful customers of the Bank (*The Hulton-Deutsch Collection*)

Sir Jasper Ridley by Leonard Applebee, director of the Bank from 1921 to 1951

A. J. Robarts, the present Managing Director and a descendant of the Robarts banking family

Sir David Money-Coutts, the present Chairman of the Bank

Cartoon of the Queen opening the new bank at 440 Strand, 1978

Chantrey's statue of Thomas Coutts

The atrium and garden court of the new bank

Unless otherwise stated, all the photographs are from the Coutts & Co. Archives and are reproduced with their kind permission.

Partners and Directors of Coutts & Co.
descended from John Campbell and Thomas Coutts,

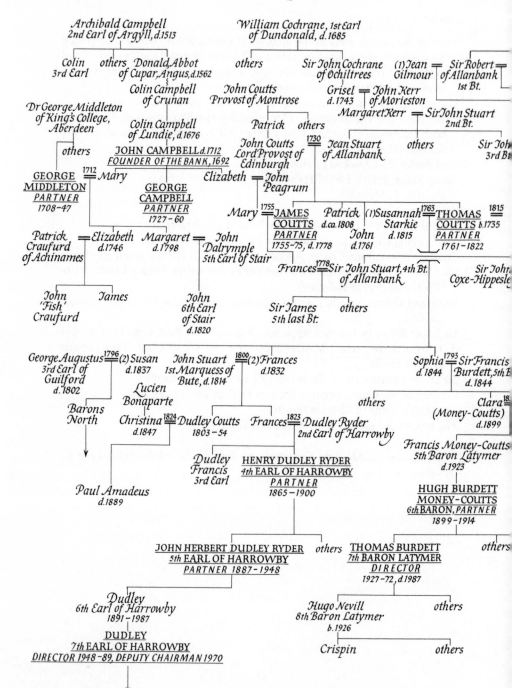

and the Marjoribanks Family

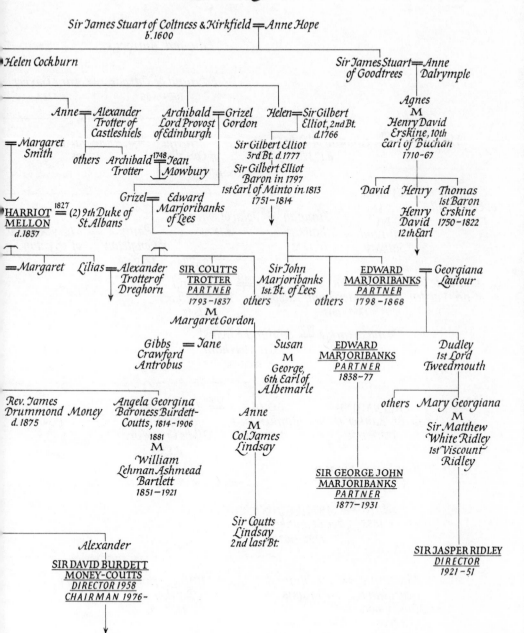

Sir James Stuart of Coltness & Kirkfield = Anne Hope
b. 1600

Sir James Stuart = Anne
of Goodtrees   Dalrymple

Helen Cockburn

Anne = Alexander   Archibald = Grizel   Helen = Sir Gilbert   Agnes
Trotter of   Lord Provost   Gordon   Elliot, 2nd Bt.   M
Castleshiels   of Edinburgh   d.1766   Henry David
                                                              Erskine, 10th
Margaret   others Archibald 1748 Jean   Sir Gilbert Elliot   Earl of Buchan
Smith   Trotter   Mowbury   3rd Bt. d.1777   1710-67
                                             Sir Gilbert Elliot
                        Grizel = Edward   Baron in 1797
                                 Marjoribanks 1st Earl of Minto in 1813
HARRIOT 1827 = (2) 9th Duke of of Lees   1751-1814   David Henry Thomas
MELLON   St. Albans   1st Baron
d.1837   Henry Erskine
                                                                 David   1750-1822
                                                                 12th Earl

Margaret Lilias = Alexander SIR COUTTS   Sir John   EDWARD   = Georgiana
                   Trotter of TROTTER   Marjoribanks MARJORIBANKS   Latour
                   Dreghorn   PARTNER   1st.Bt. of Lees PARTNER
                               1793-1837   others   others 1798-1868
                               M
                         Margaret Gordon,
              Gibbs = Jane   Susan   EDWARD   Dudley
              Crawford   M   MARJORIBANKS   1st Lord
              Antrobus   George,   PARTNER   Tweedmouth
                                  6th Earl of 1838-77
                                  Albemarle
Rev. James   others Mary Georgiana
Drummond Money Angela Georgina   M
d.1875   Baroness Burdett- Anne   Sir Matthew
                Coutts, 1814-1906 M   White Ridley
                     1881   Col. James   1st Viscount
                     M   Lindsay   Ridley
                William
                Lehman Ashmead   SIR GEORGE JOHN
                Bartlett   MARJORIBANKS
                1851-1921   PARTNER
                                  1877-1931
                                  Sir Coutts
                                  Lindsay
          Alexander   2nd last Bt.
          SIR DAVID BURDETT   SIR JASPER RIDLEY
          MONEY-COUTTS   DIRECTOR
          DIRECTOR 1958   1921-51
          CHAIRMAN 1976-

The Antrobus Family

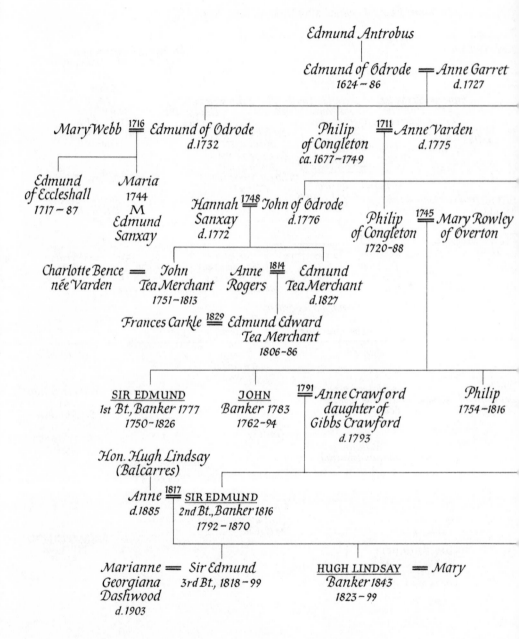

Edmund Antrobus

Edmund of Odrode = Anne Garret
1624 – 86   d.1727

Mary Webb ⚌1716 Edmund of Odrode   Philip ⚌1711 Anne Varden
                d.1732   of Congleton   d.1775
                                          ca. 1677–1749

Edmund   Maria   Hannah ⚌1748 John of Odrode
of Eccleshall   1744   Sanxay   d.1776   Philip ⚌1745 Mary Rowley
1717 – 87   M   d.1772   of Congleton   of Overton
                    Edmund   1720-88
                    Sanxay

Charlotte Bence = John   Anne ⚌1814 Edmund
née Varden   Tea Merchant   Rogers   Tea Merchant
                1751–1813   d.1827

        Frances Carkle ⚌1829 Edmund Edward
                             Tea Merchant
                             1806-86

SIR EDMUND   JOHN   ⚌1791 Anne Crawford   Philip
1st Bt., Banker 1777 Banker 1783   daughter of   1754–1816
1750 – 1826   1762-94   Gibbs Crawford
                                      d.1793

Hon. Hugh Lindsay
(Balcarres)

Anne ⚌1817 SIR EDMUND
d.1885   2nd Bt., Banker 1816
           1792 – 1870

Marianne = Sir Edmund   HUGH LINDSAY = Mary
Georgiana 3rd Bt., 1818 – 99 Banker 1843
Dashwood   1823 – 99
d.1903

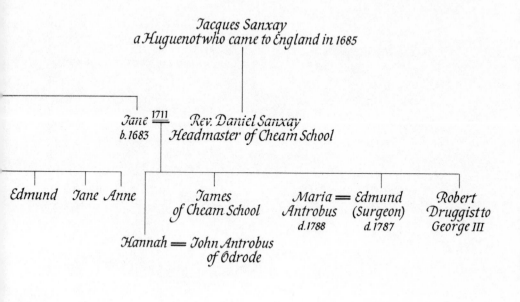

Jacques Sanxay
a Huguenot who came to England in 1685

Jane $\overset{1711}{=\!=\!=}$ Rev. Daniel Sanxay
b.1683 | Headmaster of Cheam School

Edmund Jane Anne   James   Maria = Edmund   Robert
                          of Cheam School Antrobus (Surgeon)   Druggist to
                                           d.1788   d.1787   George III

              Hannah = John Antrobus
                       of Odrode

Thomas   Mary   Jane   Frances
d.in China   d. 1828

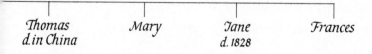

(1) Jane, da. = Gibbs Crawford $\overset{1832}{=\!=\!=}$ (2)Charlotte Crofton
of Sir Coutts Trotter   1793–1861   d.1839

Robert Crawford = Emily   John Edward
1830–1911   1831– 45

Acknowledgments

So many people have helped me during my long years of research that I cannot hope to mention them all, but they are remembered with my grateful thanks.

Her Majesty The Queen has graciously permitted publication of extracts from papers in the Royal Archives at Windsor. I am greatly indebted to Mr Oliver Everett and the Registrar, Lady de Bellaigue, for their advice.

Sir David Money-Coutts, Mr Julian Robarts and the directors of Coutts & Co. have from the beginning given me every possible encouragement and assistance. Their archivist, Barbara Peters, has been beyond praise. Without her knowledge and patience and the cheerful help of her assistants, Tracey Earl, Shirley Merry and Jackie Pearce, this book could not have been written. Miss Veronica Stokes, Barbara Peters's predecessor, gave me great help in the early part of my work. I am particularly grateful for the transcripts of documents in Scottish museums which she made during her long and dedicated service to the Bank.

I have much appreciated the help of many of the directors and staff of Coutts & Co., whose reminiscences have brought the past to life. In particular, the Earl of Harrowby, Sir Seymour Egerton, Mr Chris Horne and Mr Charles Musk kindly recorded their memories.

I was privileged to have access to so many family papers. The Duke of Devonshire and his archivist at Chatsworth, the Duke of Wellington and Lord Latymer gave me permission to quote from documents in their possession. Sir Philip Antrobus received me most kindly at Amesbury and lent me unpublished memoirs.

I should like to thank the Chairman of the Royal Bank of Scotland, who has given me permission to quote from its records, and especially to the archivist, Miss Christina Robertson, for her exceptionally helpful assistance.

So many people in Scotland have given me guidance: Dr Sheila Brock of the National Museum of Scotland, Mr George Dalgleish, Dr Philipson of the University of Edinburgh, the Director and staff of the Museum of

xvii

Montrose, the Reverend Lawrence Whitley of the Old Kirk Montrose, and Mrs Mary Fleming, who owns Provost Coutts's old house there.

I owe particular debts of gratitude to Professor Roseveare and Lord Briggs, who patiently read early drafts of this book and gave me invaluable advice.

I should like to thank Mr Douglas Matthews, Librarian of the London Library, and his staff for all their friendly help.

My secretary, Mary Morton, has dealt with a mountain of manuscript with exceptional competence: my warmest thanks are due to her, and to Jean Osborne, who typed some of the early chapters.

I thank most warmly John Curtis and Linda Osband, who have patiently guided me through the maze of 300 years of history.

Above all I wish to express my love and thanks to my family. Jenny and Derek, Tim and Jo, Cressida and my sister Doreen have encouraged me through long years of research. But my greatest debt is to my husband, Denis, who has been a source of knowledge and inspiration and whose love has been my constant support.

Preface

This is a portrait rather than a history, since to condense into one volume all the rich diversity of a bank, 300 years old, would be a sheer impossibility. In the archives of Coutts & Co. alone, there are racks upon racks of great ledgers, box upon box of letters, memorabilia and priceless relics of the past, to say nothing of those intriguing, unclaimed boxes marked '*Oubliette*'. Each holds in itself enough material for a book. There are also voluminous records of Coutts & Co. in the major libraries of Scotland and England and in the archives of Windsor Castle, Chatsworth, Sandon Hall and many other great houses, as well as in libraries in Britain, America, Canada and France. In this book, therefore, I have concentrated on the lives of the men and women who made, and are making, this Bank, setting them in their time and place.

The Bank's history begins with goldsmiths and the birth of modern banking and continues through three centuries of wars, and economic and political crises, to the changed world of 1992 and the single European market in the global village. There are four parts. Part One: 1692–1750; Part Two: 1750–1837; Part Three: 1837–92, and Part Four: 1892–1992.

Part One begins in 1692 with the Scottish goldsmith, John Campbell, in his shop in the Strand. Most of the chief players in the Bank's early history were Scots, so the scene is set not only in London but also in Scotland in 1692, especially in Edinburgh, Aberdeen and Montrose. From these towns came three men who were to create the early Bank: John Campbell, descendant of the Earl of Argyll, trained in Edinburgh. His successor, George Middleton, who directed the Bank from 1708 to 1747, was brought up in Aberdeen. Thomas Coutts, who dominated Coutts & Co. from the 1760s until his death in 1822, owed much to his ancestors, the Provosts of Montrose, and to his father, John Coutts, Provost of Edinburgh.

Middleton survived the money madness of the South Sea Bubble and the Mississippi affair of 1719–20. The letters during this period, especially those to and from John and William Law, are a unique and sometimes moving record of one of the most dramatic episodes in financial history.

In Part Two the scene shifts back to Scotland during the 1745 Jacobite rebellion in which Provost John Coutts, then a director of the Royal Bank of Scotland, was deeply involved. The Jacobite theme runs for more than half a century in the background of the history of the Bank.

In 1755 Provost Coutts's son, James, married Campbell's granddaughter and brought the Coutts name to the Bank in the Strand. It was his brother, Thomas, who reorganised the business and set the principles and standards that have lasted until today. It was he who pursued and kept powerful customers; above all it was he who established a special relationship with King George III and his sons, so introducing the recurring theme in the Bank's history – Coutts & Co., the royal bank. This he achieved at a time of exceptional turbulence during the American War of Independence, the French Revolution, the Anglo-French Wars, and the rise and fall of Napoleon.

Thomas Coutts's private life is a part of banking history. He made two secret marriages, the first to Susannah, the nursemaid of his brother's daughter, and the second to the entrancing actress, Harriot Mellon, to whom he left his fortune and who, transformed into the Duchess of St Albans, was the most extraordinary partner the Bank would ever know. Two of his daughters by his first wife married the sons of great ministers. Susan became the wife of the Earl of Guilford, son of Lord North; Fanny married the Marquess of Bute, son of the Earl of Bute, friend of George III. His youngest daughter, Sophia, married Sir Francis Burdett MP, whose radical politics distressed the banker, damaged the reputation of his Bank, and caused the loss of his most important customer, King George III.

In the first decade of the nineteenth century the counterpoint between Burdett and the banker reflects in human terms the conflict between the values of the eighteenth and those of the nineteenth centuries, between Thomas Coutts's world of patronage and order and Burdett's disturbing ideas of liberty and reform. Thomas, lonely, ill and pained by this conflict, withdrew from the daily management of the Bank, seeking consolation with Harriot and relying on his three partners, Edmund Antrobus, Coutts Trotter and Edward Marjoribanks. These three men, vital to the survival of the Bank, have hitherto been hidden in Thomas's shadow.

Before joining Thomas Coutts, Edmund Antrobus had founded the stockbroking firm which was to become James Capel & Co. His brother John's son continued his work and his family provided partners till the end of the nineteenth century. Edward Marjoribanks joined Coutts & Co. as a young man in 1798 and worked there until his death in 1868. His descendants were still helping to run the Bank in the mid-twentieth century. Coutts Trotter, godson of Provost John Coutts, brought expertise from the Navy Department and his nephew established his own dynasty in James Capel & Co., a firm which has been closely linked with Coutts & Co. ever since.

The Bank also owed much to two remarkable clerks, Andrew Dickie and George Robinson, both of whom became partners and between them spanned a century.

Thomas Coutts died in 1822 and Part Two, which ends with the death of Harriot in 1837, marks the passing of their world.

Part Three opens with the accession of Victoria to the throne and Thomas's granddaughter, Angela Burdett-Coutts, to her inheritance, both dedicated and serious young women. I have dealt with Angela's life in more detail in *Lady Unknown*; here I concentrate on her relationship with Coutts & Co. She was the public face of the Bank; her immense wealth, the recognition of her great charitable work, her known friendship with Queen Victoria and her children and with other European royal families, added prestige and created confidence in the Bank. Her friendship with Charles Dickens, her love affair with the Duke of Wellington, her support of Rajah Brooke, her astonishing marriage in old age bring into vivid life the contradictions of the Victorian period. She was the epitome of the age, involved in every field of innovation and discovery – in town planning, in trade and industry, in science, education and religion.

To keep a private bank afloat at this period needed more than phil-anthropy and good will. Part Three deals with the challenge to the private banks of the growing joint stock banks and with successive 'Black Mondays' and 'panics'. It was old Edward Marjoribanks, the senior partner, who kept the Bank steady, especially in the years 1830–48 when the railway mania made and destroyed the fortunes of many of their customers, when revol-utions rocked Europe and when Chartist demonstrations threatened the Bank's security. Nor did the problems disappear after the early 1850s, even though the Great Exhibition of 1851 ushered in a period of growing prosperity.

The 1870s brought a succession of honours to Angela Burdett-Coutts which brought reflected glory to the Bank. She was made a Baroness in 1871, later a Freeman of the Cities of London and Edinburgh, and was honoured by the Turners' and Clothworkers' Guilds. Part Three ends with her marriage to her young secretary, Ashmead Bartlett, and its effect on the Bank. Because of a clause in the will of the Duchess of St Albans, Angela should have lost her whole inheritance by marrying an alien, but in order to avoid a lawsuit, she was allowed to keep part. Her sister Clara succeeded to the inheritance. At the age of forty-five she had married the Reverend James Money and, in obedience to the will, added Coutts to her name – so introducing the intriguing and appropriate name 'Money-Coutts'.

Part Four begins a new era. The second centenary of the Bank coincided with an important development in its history. The Baroness's marriage, the deaths of the old partners, and the shock of the Baring crash in 1890 made change necessary. In 1892 Coutts & Co. became a company with unlimited liability, a small number of stockholders holding the capital in various proportions.

The story of the Bank changes in mood with the new century. Coutts & Co. opened its accounts to the public, but old traditions remain. As the Duc d'Aumale once wrote to William Rolle Malcolm, '*Messrs Coutts – c'est le confessional.*' The brilliant Malcolm and his son, Ronald, brought a new professionalism to the Bank and guided it into the modern world of banking.

In 1904 Coutts & Co. moved to new premises across the Strand, from 59 on the south side to 440 on the north. The premises at 440 were further transformed in 1978 into the splendid glass-fronted modern building designed by Frederick Gibberd.

Part Four inevitably lacks some of the colour and romance of the earlier history: the private lives of the Bank's partners no longer have the same importance. So I have called up some of the voices of the directors, clerks and members of staff who, in their recollections and memoirs, report on the Bank's survival through two world wars, the arrival of the first lady clerks and the introduction of computers.

Part Four also deals with the successful battle of Coutts & Co. to keep its identity – and its royal customers – in the fast-moving world of modern banking. In 1914 the directors – as they were now styled – took over the City bank Robarts, Lubbock & Co. and kept its premises at 15 Lombard Street. By amalgamation with this bank, the origins of which go back to 1772, they gained for the first time a seat in the Clearing House. It has not been possible to give as much space to Robarts, Lubbock & Co. as that bank deserves, since few of its records survive, but some account is given of Abraham Robarts and of Sir John Lubbock, who was perhaps the last of the giants among bankers.

The affiliation of Coutts & Co. in 1920 to the National Provincial Bank, which in 1969 merged with the Westminster & District Bank to form the National Westminster Bank, caused much heart-searching among the customers of Coutts & Co. Through a period of change, the Bank in the Strand has survived as an independent unit within the group, retaining its own identity – and its royal customers. From the days of the sailors of Montrose, the Coutts family has been outward-looking with Scottish contacts throughout the world. This tradition was carried on by Thomas Coutts and Angela Burdett-Coutts, who also set her mark on every continent. Today Coutts & Co. is once again moving to take on an even greater role in the wider world.

In October 1990 the National Westminster Bank plc asked Coutts &

Co. to develop a worldwide private banking network. As a result, three of the private banks owned by NatWest – Coutts & Co., HandelsBank NatWest and NatWest International Trust Corporation – have come together to form the new Coutts & Co. Group. This will provide customers with worldwide asset management and private banking from over thirty offices in thirteen areas. The Board of Coutts & Co. Group is entirely composed of directors of Coutts & Co. In the words of the present Chairman, Sir David Money-Coutts, a direct descendant of Thomas Coutts,

We remain utterly committed to maintaining high standards of service ... customers will benefit in that we will now be able to offer a broader range of services. ... In future, the Coutts service you now enjoy will come to be available from our offices around the globe. The vision we have is of Coutts & Co. as a worldwide but select private bank.

I have tried to describe the special quality which distinguishes Coutts & Co. Its particular ethos is unmistakable but elusive. It does not depend on the frock-coats of the managers nor on their beardless chins, nor on their quill pens. For though traditions are jealously guarded, Coutts & Co. was in fact one of the first banks to introduce computers. Neither does it depend on the aura of wealth which its customers provide, though this certainly contributes to the Bank's success.

Although the directors and customers of Coutts & Co. still represent, as they have done in the past, only a narrow section of the community, yet their history digs deep into the nation's history and reveals a human story that transcends class and time.

Part 1

1692–1750

I

At the Sign of the Three Crowns, London 1692

In the early summer of 1692 the Scottish goldsmith, John Campbell, set up his business on the south side of the Strand near the site of the present Charing Cross Station, adopting the 'Three Crowns' as a sign, as was customary in the days before street numbers. We assume that he inherited the sign with the shop, but he was to make it his own, adding his initials interwoven.

When Campbell started his business London was a comparatively small city of 500,000 inhabitants. It was still a pastoral age: the smell and sound of the country was always present, even when fog and smoke darkened the air. There were sheep and cows in Green Park; fields, lanes, farms and woods lay between the Strand and the rural quiet of the villages of Chelsea, Highgate and Hackney. There was a horse ferry crossing the Thames to the meadows south of the river. Along the Strand carts and coaches rattled and rumbled over the cobbles; King William's cavalry jingled by, to and from the royal stables, then on the site of the present Trafalgar Square; and drovers cracked their whips, herding their cattle to market. At the east end of the Strand an immense maypole, permanently in place, dominated the street. Behind the great houses on the south side of the street, gardens stretched down to the Thames. Nearby, the Earl of Northumberland had pleasure grounds below his magnificent mansion, and his orchards bordered the Thames, thronged with sailing ships and laden barges.

In 1692 Britain had come through a period of unprecedented turmoil. In that year men in their sixties could remember the Civil War, when brother fought brother and the streets of many an English city ran with blood. They could have been in the vast crowd that thronged Whitehall on that cold January morning of 1649 to see the execution of Charles I outside the banqueting hall, when, as the head was severed, a boy in the crowd heard such a groan as he had never heard before and hoped never to hear again. They had lived through the rigours of Cromwell's rule, had seen the licence and frivolity of the court of Charles II,

3

and would remember how England was possessed by fear of popery under the stubborn reign of the Catholic King, James II. And it was only four years since, to general relief, James took ship from Whitehall Stairs to seek refuge with Louis XIV in France.

The triple disasters that came like retribution could never be forgotten: the Great Plague, the Great Fire and then the enemy Dutch sailing into the Thames. Like Pepys they had heard the dreaded cry, 'Bring out your dead', and seen the bodies piled in plague pits; perhaps, like Evelyn, they had walked on hot ashes around the blackened streets of the city.

But London was rising from the ashes; Wren was rebuilding St Paul's Cathedral, and wider streets and sturdier houses had replaced the huddled wooden buildings. Merchants had returned to the City and lived above their newly built counting-houses. Many prospered and were making great fortunes.

In 1692 the recent wars with Holland were forgotten: the English and Dutch were allies, united by William of Orange against the common enemy, France. William inspired trust; some might find his manner too 'wondrous grave'[1] after the easy grace of the Stuarts, but he was showing high courage, steady nerves, tact and a generosity to his Jacobite opponents. Mary too, after the initial surprise at the gaiety with which she took over her father's palace, was proving an amiable and competent consort, reigning with charm during William's frequent absences. For his palace at Het Loo in Holland was always to be his real home; in the smoky London air his asthma returned and he hankered after the clear wide skies of his native country. He and Mary preferred to live in the rural freshness of his palace at Kensington or at Hampton Court, while the palace in Whitehall was still the centre for ceremony and for political intrigue.

However, while William was fighting with his army in Flanders, the great Scots nobles grew in power and influence. There were also many followers of the exiled King James who still hoped and plotted for his return from France. They gathered in St James's Park, strolled along what became known as 'Jacobite Walk' and were openly triumphant when French sails were seen in the Channel.

These were dangerous times for the followers of the King over the water: the mouldering heads of Scottish nobles stuck on pikes above Temple Bar were grim reminders of the price of rebellion. In May 1692 the spring breeze that fluttered the ribbons and laces of the gallants along Jacobite Walk struck chill, for it carried the 'Oyez, oyez' of the town crier, calling for the capture of the Earl of Middleton and other rebel lords who were believed to be plotting a French-backed invasion. The Earl was arrested in disguise at a Quaker's house in Goodmans Fields and imprisoned in the Tower. He was released on bail in August and in April 1693 was reported to have taken 'shipping on the coast of Sussex & gone for France'.[2]

The Earl of Middleton's great-nephew, George, was to become John

Campbell's partner at the sign of the Three Crowns in the Strand. And the Jacobite theme, with romantic stories of spies and daring escapes, was to run, an intriguing sub-plot, through the history of Coutts Bank until the beginning of the nineteenth century.

The Earl of Middleton became adviser to King James and friend to his queen in their years of exile at the court of St Germain near Paris. He was to become an acute embarrassment to John Campbell's Whig bank and especially to George Middleton.

John Campbell's origins and his early life in the Strand remain obscure. We assume he was the John Campbell who was apprenticed to John Threepland, goldsmith, on 3 December 1679 in Edinburgh.

We do not know when he first came to London; he does not appear in the rate books until May 1692, when he was established at the sign of the Three Crowns in the Strand. Few records remain of his early years in the Strand: the first letter book is dated 1699 and the first ledgers to survive are for 1712.

Campbell had chosen his site well. Unlike his fellow goldsmiths he settled, not in the City of London, but at the Court end near the palaces of Whitehall and Westminster, the seats of power. This position was important for his business, for here he was out of the jurisdiction of the Goldsmiths' Company in the City of London, which exercised strict control over its members, recording their individual marks and fixing high standards for the quality of work.

In 1696 it was decreed by Act of Parliament that,

on and after 25 March 1697 no plate worker in England should make any article of silver of less fineness than *11oz 10 dwts.* in every pound (Troy), nor offer for sale, exchange etc. any article made after that date but of that standard, nor until it had been marked with the necessary marks to distinguish plate of the new standard.

The worker's mark was to consist of

the first two letters of his surname, marks of the goldsmiths' craft, now to consist of lion's head erased and figure of a woman commonly called Britannia, and a distinct and variable mark to denote the year the article was made.

However, outside the City of London this law was frequently ignored.

This new standard was to deter the turning of coin into plate. It lasted for twenty-three years, but the standard proved to be too soft and in 1719 there was a return to the old 'sterling' (coin) standard.

Campbell was also conveniently situated for political reasons, because his patron and chief of the Campbell clan, Archibald, Earl of Argyll, was one of the most influential peers in England and Scotland. Campbell's own connection with the Earl was distant – his father, Colin Campbell of

Lundie, was a descendant of the second Earl of Argyll* – but he was always proud to acknowledge the Earl and his sons as chiefs of his clan. In return Argyll and his descendants gave to Campbell and his successors at the Bank in the Strand their patronage and protection.

The Argylls had for generations proved their loyalty to the Protestant cause, for which devotion the Earl's father and grandfather had been executed. After the Restoration of Charles II, Argyll had settled in Holland and was one of the powerful Scots who had planned William of Orange's invasion in 1688. As one of the architects of his victory, he remained a close adviser to the new King. So it was fitting that it was he who, on 11 May 1689, as the representative of the Scottish peers, had administered the coronation oath to William as King of Scotland, still a separate kingdom.

On that May morning, Argyll, with Sir John Dalrymple and Sir James Montgomery, led a magnificent procession into the banqueting hall of the palace of Whitehall.† William and Mary appeared, seated under a canopy:

A splendid circle of English nobles and statesmen stood round the throne, but the sword of state was committed to a Scots Lord; and the oath of office was administered after the Scots fashion. Argyll recited the words slowly.[4]

The royal pair held up their hands and repeated the oath. Scotland had graciously accepted William and Mary as her sovereigns.

Many of the 'Scotsmen of note' were to become customers at Campbell's shop, commissioning silver plate and golden jewellery and depositing their treasure with him. So, from the beginning, his business was dominated by Scots, who were mainly dedicated Whigs, loyal to William and Mary and in later years to the Hanoverians. When John Campbell started his goldsmith's shop in the Strand, he was well placed and powerfully backed.

---

* Veronica Stokes has convincingly traced John Campbell's ancestry. It would appear that he was a great-grandson of an illegitimate son of Donald Campbell, Abbot of Cupar. This scandalous priest was the fifth son of Archibald, second Earl of Argyll.
† As Macaulay described, accompanied by 'every Scotsman of note'.[3]

2

Scotland 1692:
Edinburgh, Aberdeen and Montrose

For almost the first hundred years, the men who directed the Bank in the Strand were Scots. Even after that, the Scottish influence was strong, affecting the growth of the business and setting a particular stamp, still visible today. In addition there was a network of Scottish merchants, bankers, officials and diplomats all over the world, often linked by family connections, who acted as agents, informants and spies. This gave the Scots an international influence of a kind which was only rivalled by that of Jewish bankers.

Three men and their families directed the early Bank: John Campbell, backed by the Argylls; George Middleton of Aberdeen; and the Coutts brothers, whose family came from Montrose but who grew up in the City of Edinburgh. Their roots went deep into Scottish history and traditions; their branches spread wide and cast long shadows. It is therefore necessary to understand their background and to set them in time and place.

In 1692 Scotland was, to most Englishmen, a wild, strange and foreign land. It was a separate country with its own currency, its own parliament and its own capital, Edinburgh. When, in 1601, King James VI of Scotland had become King James I of England, the two crowns had been united, but it was not until 1707 that, by the Act of Union, the two countries were to be joined. King James had moved to England in 1603, and many of the powerful Scottish nobles had followed him, thus diminishing the importance of their capital.

Although in 1692 there was no longer a king or court at the ancient palace of Holyrood, Edinburgh was a singularly impressive city. The castle, rising out of great basalt cliffs, dominated the landscape, as it does today. Below, the rocks dropped sheer to the swamps of the North Loch, now drained and transformed into the Valley Gardens. Beyond the loch stretched open country, where the New Town now stands. To the east a long, straight street ran down to Holyrood Palace at the other end of the town.

Daniel Defoe, who lived in Edinburgh some years later, described it as 'the largest, longest and finest street for buildings and number of inhabitants, not in Britain only, but in the world'.[1] The buildings, he wrote,

are surprising both for strength, for beauty and for height; all, or the greatest part, of freestone . . . all is fixed and strong to the top though you have, in that part of the city called Parliament Close, houses, which on the south side appear to be eleven or twelve storeys high and inhabited to the very top.[2]

However, the beauty was somewhat marred by the noxious smells which gave the city its reputation as 'Auld Reekie'. Good Edinburgh housewives were accustomed to tip their domestic rubbish and slops from those high apartments on to the streets beneath. It was a crowded and often riotous city. Between the high blocks, the 'wynds', narrow, winding lanes, ran steeply down on either side of the main street.

Between the castle and Holyrood Palace stood St Giles, the High Kirk of Edinburgh, against whose walls huddled small shops – the 'lackenbooths'; around the square were the goldsmiths' shops, in one of which John Campbell had been apprenticed in 1679. His master goldsmith, John Threepland, was a neighbour of the Dean of Goldsmiths, William Law, whose son John was later to play such an important part in the history of the Bank in the Strand. Here John Campbell worked to pass the strict tests of the guild and to earn his right to use his own goldsmith's mark.

The year he was apprenticed, 1679, was a particularly harrowing time in Edinburgh. If London citizens had looked back in 1692 over decades of turbulence, civil and foreign wars, plague and fire, Edinburgh citizens could remember even more agonising events. The conflict between the Stuart Kings and Parliament had been further complicated in Scotland by clan feuds and sectarian argument. In 1633 Charles I had declared Edinburgh an episcopal see, to be directed by Anglican bishops. This aroused violent opposition in Scotland, and nobles and commoners alike thronged to sign, some of them in their own blood, the National Covenant, which rejected the imposition of Anglican rule on Presbyterian Scotland. There followed decades of struggle between the army of Covenanters and the King's supporters, culminating in the defeat of the Covenanters at the Battle of Bothwell Bridge in 1679.

John Campbell must have seen in 1679 the defeated army of 1,000 men herded into Greyfriars' Churchyard, many to die of starvation and exposure. In that year 100 Covenanters went to the scaffold in the Grass Market, the traditional place for execution. The young apprentice could scarcely have avoided the sight of carts laden with broken bodies and of heads stuck on poles over the toll booth. Certainly he was later to show a fierce hatred of the Jacobites, the followers of James II.

After William III had ousted James and been accepted as King of Scotland, his Scottish followers in their turn took savage revenge. To the fires of religious and political hostility was added the fuel of ancient clan rivalries.

The most powerful and feared of the clans in the Highlands was that of the Campbells under their chief, the Earl of Argyll. Unlike most of the other clans, who were Catholic and therefore followers of James II, the Campbells were, on the whole, passionately, fiercely Protestant and opposed to the Stuarts. However, there were exceptions on both sides. Many a Highland chieftain found it prudent to keep a son on either side, thus ensuring that, whichever side won, their estates would be safe. It has been said that in the Jacobite battles which were fought throughout the next half century, the relevant question was not whether a man was for or against the King, but whether he was for or against Argyll.

During the Restoration when Argyll was in exile, the clan's ancient rivals, the MacDonalds, had gained supremacy, and when, after the accession of William and Mary, the Earl returned, he was given the task of crushing King James's followers in Scotland. He took his revenge for the Mac-Donalds' raids on his territory with a ruthlessness and ferocity that seared the name of Campbell on Scottish memory for ever. The slaughter of Glencoe was to leave a blood feud between Campbells and MacDonalds which burns fiercely even today.

In 1692 a party of Campbells, by order of the Earl of Argyll and his colleague, the Master of Stair, massacred almost the entire MacDonald clan at Glencoe. The Duke's excuse was that the chief had failed to report at the appointed time to swear allegiance to King William. The story of the night of slaughter has often been told: having accepted the hospitality of the MacDonalds, the Campbells, acting on the orders of their chief, the Earl of Argyll, had fallen upon them in the dead of night and killed men, women and children in their beds.

It was many months before the news of Glencoe reached London, confirming the English belief in the barbarism of the Scots. But John Campbell, now established in his shop in the Strand, might well have remembered the grisly fate of the Covenanters in 1679 and felt that they had been avenged.

On the east coast of Scotland, north of Edinburgh in the town of Aberdeen, there were equally bitter memories of a blood-stained past which were to affect the Middleton family for years to come.

The news of the capture and imprisonment of the Earl of Middleton in May 1692 must have come as a great shock in Aberdeen, where his nephew, Dr George Middleton, was Principal of King's College. The Middletons, however, had survived through decades of strife when Aberdeen was the battleground in the bitter struggle between Royalists and Covenanters;

'*Fortis in Arduis*' was their family motto. Like many Scottish families at this time the Middletons had divided loyalties which fluctuated with the changing times. They were not vicars of Bray; they were middle-of-the-road men, too balanced to follow either side when they moved to extremes.

Dr George Middleton had succeeded his father, Alexander, as Principal of the College and, like him, was a 'King and Bishop man'. Cromwell had turned Alexander out because of his Royalist sympathies, but George had so far managed to keep his place. He was a man 'of singular life and conversation, of great learning and qualified to be a principal in any university in the land'.[3] He married an equally remarkable woman, Janet Gordon, who bore him thirteen children and lived until 1753, to the astonishing age of 101, keeping her clear mind and judgment to the end.[4]

In the early summer of 1692 Janet was expecting her twelfth child. George, who was later to become John Campbell's partner at the Bank, was nine at this time; whether he understood his great-uncle's predicament is not known, but even young boys were aware of the grisly fate that awaited traitors: the cruel torture and execution of the Marquess of Montrose and his fellow Royalists were not forgotten in Aberdeen. Nevertheless, George Middleton was to grow up in a stable and affectionate family in an exceptionally stimulating environment. Many of his brothers later took up interesting careers, and he remained close to them and to his sisters and brothers-in-law all his life. One brother became a clergyman, two were goldsmiths, and another went to Poland and became an ambassador there. This Middleton married a Polish lady and their son became a general in the Polish army. Like the Coutts of Montrose, the Middletons of Aberdeen looked across the North Sea to find careers for their sons.

Aberdeen at this time was a fine city, as Defoe was later to describe:

The great market place . . . is very beautiful and spacious; and the streets adjoining are very handsome and well built, the houses lofty and high; but not so as to be inconvenient, as in Edinburgh. . . . The generality of the citizens' houses are built of stone four storeys high, [have] handsome sash windows and are very well furnished within, the citizens here being as gay, as genteel and perhaps as rich as any city in Scotland.[5]

In Aberdeen George Middleton received a sound education, learning Latin and French and having access to a college library exceptionally 'well stocked with books and also with the best and finest mathematical instruments'.[6] From his scholarly father and intelligent mother he inherited the moral values and grit that would see him through difficult times. And though he and his brothers were to become Whigs, loyal to the Hanoverians, his affection for his Jacobite relations made him tolerant of the politics of others.

*   *   *

In 1692, while the Middletons of Aberdeen were worrying over the fate of the Jacobite Earl, another east coast Scot, John Coutts, a wealthy merchant of Montrose, was enjoying a respite from long years of service to the town. He had been Provost three times – in 1677, from 1682 to 1684, and yet again in the years 1686–7 – and would serve once more before his death in 1707. His was a family of high repute: his father William's gravestone carried a fulsome tribute – 'On earth he led a heavenly life. . . . No stains his life or manners could attack. . . .' On his death in 1678 he bequeathed £66 13s 4d to the Old Kirk. John Coutts and his descendants were to bequeath a great deal more, not only to Montrose but to the nation. In the words of a later Provost, 'their business capacity, their reputation for fair dealing and their public spirit secured for them the confidence and esteem of the people among whom they dwelt'.[7]

Provost John and his wife Christian had twelve children. He and his sons showed that 'public spirit' and 'business capacity' to a remarkable degree. In 1692 his eldest son William, at the age of thirty-one, was a town councillor and would become Provost of Montrose in 1694. His brothers, John and Thomas, aged twenty-seven and twenty-six respectively, had been sworn in as 'burgesses and gildbrothers' of Montrose in 1687, paying their '50 marks to ye Treasury and 20 marks to the Gild box'.[8] James, now a boy of sixteen, was to stay in Montrose, make a great fortune and become Provost in his turn, while the youngest son Hercules was also to become a councillor. Thomas was soon to leave home to make his fortune as a merchant in London and plays a part in the history of Coutts & Co. His brother Patrick also left, to become a successful corn merchant in Edinburgh, and it is his descendants who, sixty years later, were to bring the name of Coutts to the Bank in the Strand.

Whether they stayed and prospered at home or moved away, Montrose, its history and traditions, was to mould their lives.

Montrose was – and still is – an exceptionally pleasant, open town with wide streets under great skies. It was built on a spit of land jutting into the sea: on one side was the curving sweep of Montrose basin, on the other links and dunes stretched to the ocean. On either side of the High Street prosperous merchants built their solid, granite houses, fronted by small courtyards and separated by narrow closes. At the bottom of their back gardens, each merchant had a storage barn with easy access to bay or sea. The water was all around, gleaming at the end of the dark closes, carrying the sailing ships that made the fortunes of the merchants of the town.

By May 1678 the Provost had become so prosperous that he was able to buy a house and lands in Fullerton. Provost of Montrose, laird of Fullerton, owning a handsome house in the High Street, John Coutts was one of the most influential citizens in the area. His son James was to buy an even better house opposite the church. It still stands: its oval sitting-room with a fine ceiling reflects the wealth and position the family held in Montrose.

By 1692 Provost John and his family already had long experience in trading overseas, shipping and dealing in foreign currencies, with family connections early established abroad. His uncle, Robert Coutts, had settled in Poland in the early part of the seventeenth century, and his son, Alexander, went to work as a merchant in Danzig. Like many east coast Scots, they had found it easier to sail across the North Sea to the Baltic than to take the rough road to England.

So from early times the Coutts family were outward-looking. One of the Provost's sons, Robert, was to emigrate to Virginia to be the family representative in their highly profitable tobacco business; another member of the family was to be a partner in the Montrose Whaling Company.

Montrose sailors braved the North Sea, taking malt and grain to Norway and the Baltic countries, and bringing back timber. Or they sailed round the north of Scotland, then south to Madeira or the Canary Islands, where they picked up the trade winds which blew them to the American colonies. Some called at Mediterranean and African ports before crossing the Atlantic, exchanging their salt and salmon for wines and brandy. There were some Montrose merchants who also took 'black ivory' from the African coast to the tobacco plantations of Virginia, though the lucrative slave trade was best forgotten. The ships returned home laden with tobacco and brandy, wines, tea and chocolate.

Until the Act of Union in 1707 this overseas trade was illegal, since Scotland, as a foreign country, was forbidden by the English navigation laws to trade with her colonies. However, the merchants of Montrose were laws unto themselves, and the English navy was just one more hazard to be overcome, like pirates or high seas or the excisemen watching on the Montrose shore. In Montrose, smuggling was an accepted way of life: some cargoes might be declared to the Collector of Taxes and the import duty paid, but much more was 'run' ashore to be picked up later and hidden in houses or barns. Provost, bailies and respectable citizens united in the game: foxing the excisemen was a legitimate sport and the sandy dunes, caves and inlets of the long coastline gave them a head start. Often ships were lost at sea, or cargoes to the excisemen, yet Montrose merchants still managed to make sizeable fortunes.

After 1688 and the flight of King James II there was even less reason to pay taxes, for Montrose was not only a smugglers' haven, it was strongly Jacobite – for which the Coutts family and many of the townspeople were to pay dearly in the future. Courageous Montrose matrons wore white gowns and the white Jacobite rose in their hair on Stuart birthdays and their sons sported the white cockade in their caps – and risked their lives.

In the garden of the Coutts's family house at 80 High Street, an old white rose tree still blooms, growing, it is fondly believed, from the stock of the ancient Jacobite rose. John Coutts's granite house stands solid and not without elegance. His sitting-room on the first floor is well proportioned: folding beds were neatly concealed behind the panelled walls. The spaces behind the panels must have been convenient hiding-places when the excisemen rapped on the doors.

From the windows of this sitting-room the Provost could look down to his storage barn and out to the ships at anchor in the basin. In 1692 he would often have scanned the horizon for the sails of the French fleet, which, it was rumoured, was on its way, bringing James Stuart back to Scotland.

3

John Campbell:
Goldsmith Banker

In 1692 England and Scotland were under constant threat of invasion by the French. King Louis had given James shelter in France and pledged to help restore him to the throne of England. One attempt had failed, but there were always rumours of the French fleet in the Channel. So merchants and nobles were glad to leave their gold and treasures in the strongrooms of goldsmiths such as John Campbell.

In 1692 there were already flourishing goldsmiths described in a broadsheet of 1676 as 'new fashioned Goldsmiths or Bankers' and, among these, Francis Child (1642–1713) and Richard Hoare (1648–1718) could rightly describe themselves as bankers. Francis Child and Robert Blanchard had set up their goldsmith's shop 'at the sign of the Marygold' near Temple Bar in 1673 and by 1692 were already beginning to be 'less dependent on its goldsmith's business and increasing devoted to purely banking transactions'. And very profitable they were too: in 1692 Child was able 'to lend the Government £10,000 on the security of the customs revenues and another £50,000 to meet the expense of governing Ireland'. Similarly in 1672 goldsmith Richard Hoare was starting his own business 'at the sign of the golden bottle' in Cheapside, moving to Fleet Street, the site of the present bank, in 1690. Like Child, Hoare prospered and both became Lord Mayors of London.

Goldsmiths at this period were not merely keepers of treasure, craftsmen who wrought in gold and silver, making jewellery and mending silver plate; they also lent money on the security of the treasure deposited with them, dealt with foreign currencies and, as will be seen, had gradually taken on a wide range of responsibilities. They were able to offer banking facilities before banks as we know them today existed in the British Isles.

It was not until 1694 that the Bank of England was founded and the Bank of Scotland was not established until 1695. There were, it is true, banks in Europe in the seventeenth century, in Genoa and in Sweden, and in Holland the Bank of Amsterdam was the most advanced in the world.

Men of many different trades and professions had offered banking facilities ever since the time when the Knights Templar took custody of the Knights' treasure. Merchants had exchanged currencies on benches in mediaeval Italy and, indeed, the name 'bank' originated with the Italian word *'banco'* – a bench. In Florence, for example, in the first half of the fourteenth century there were eighty such *'banchi'* for a population of 90,000.

In England and Scotland men who wished to deposit, to borrow or to exchange money used the facilities offered by merchants and shopkeepers. It was often the local corndealer, draper or grocer who gave credit, discounted bills or arranged the finance for imports and exports. In Scotland, in particular, many banks later developed from such shops, whose owners had to learn to understand complicated accounting in foreign currencies. As the banker Sir William Forbes wrote, banking was in fact 'a graft upon ordinary merchandise'.[1]

Notaries, the lawyers who contracted the sale of land and property, also undertook some of the functions of a modern banker. In Scotland, even the church made loans, receiving deposits on a table in the Kirk, where debtors could be certain of a fiery denunciation from the pulpit.

It was from the goldsmiths' shops that most of the English modern banks have grown. Until 1640 many merchants had kept their bullion and silver in the vaults of the Tower of London, but in that year Charles I seized their treasure in order to enforce a loan; after that they transferred it to the safer strongrooms of the goldsmiths, who issued promissory notes* and notes of receipt, which were exchanged and used as money and were the forerunners of the bank note. However, coin remained for some time the general currency, though some employers paid their workers in tokens or in kind, and barter was still in common use.

There was still a law controlling the lending of money, though it was frequently ignored. For centuries it had been considered morally wrong to demand interest on a loan, but there were money-lenders, who, like Shylock, extracted high interest or demanded outrageous security. In 1552 an Act of Parliament had prohibited all taking of interest as 'a vice most odious and detestable'. However, there were changes during the sixteenth and seventeenth centuries. The Usury Law, passed in 1577, forbade lenders from exacting more than 10 per cent interest. Further changes in the law reduced the permitted rate, and by 1692 it was officially illegal to charge more than 6 per cent interest. The Usury Act was not finally abolished until 1857.

---

* 'A promissory note is an unconditional promise in writing made by one person to another, signed by the maker, engaging to pay, on demand or at a fixed or determinable future time, a sum certain in money, to, or to the order of, a specified person or to bearer.'

According to Defoe many goldsmiths found ways of extorting money at high interest. He quotes the example of a goldsmith he knew in Lombard Street who lent a man £700 to pay the customs duty on 100 pipes of Spanish wine. They were put into a cellar to which only the goldsmith had the key. The merchant was to 'pay him £6 per cent interest on the loan and £10 per cent premium for advancing the money'.[2] He was also charged five shillings a day for the time the goldsmith's man spent in looking after the wine. The loan was for two months, during which time 'by leakage, decay and other accidents the wine begin to lessen'. Then the goldsmith claimed that the wines were not 'worth the money he lent and demanded further security'. In the end the merchant was obliged to sell him the wine at considerable loss in order to pay the customs. So, 'by the extortion of this banker the poor man lost the whole capital, with freight and wine charges, and made but £29 produce of a hundred pipes of wine'.[3]

John Campbell looked after wines for a customer on at least one occasion, but would not have so jeopardised his reputation for honesty, though it would appear that he occasionally took a bottle or two in lieu of interest. Taking care of some wine and brandy for his friend Daniel Campbell, he wrote: 'I have often been trusted with money, but never with good liquor before; how honest I shall be I know not, however, I shall always drink your health.'[4] And so he did with four of his friends at the Globe tavern, demolishing five bottles and finding the wine 'tolerable'. The next day, however, 'I was oblig'd to keep my bead.'[5]

John Campbell, however, was to hold a reputation as a skilled craftsman and a trusted man of business, proud to call himself 'goldsmith–banker', with the emphasis always on 'goldsmith'.

Little is known of his early years at the sign of the Three Crowns. Nor has any picture of his shop yet been found. We can only guess.

In the beginning Campbell certainly lived with his family in apartments above the shop, where there were also bedrooms for clerks and servants. His workshop was probably like those we see in early engravings. A semi-circular bench, near the light of the window, could accommodate four craftsmen working at the same time, from the four fronts of which were suspended two leather bags into which the craftsmen dropped gold and silver clippings as they worked. In the centre of the workbench a glass flask of water reflected the candlelight and enlarged their engravings. The present archivist at Coutts & Co., Barbara Peters, has recreated Campbell's shop in a model displayed at the Strand:

The light falling through the mullioned window shows us the solid goldsmith's workbench with its leather skins and litter of tools; behind lies the long narrow shop, the plaster ceiling and panelled walls darkened in patches by years of candle smoke. On one side the panelling is broken by a cupboard containing samples of the goldsmith's work, a small counter stands in front bearing the scales, such a vital tool of a goldsmith's trade, and close by sits an iron strong box.[6]

We know from his ledgers and letter books that he wrought in gold, made and repaired silver plate, and made handsome jewellery in fine settings.

On 22 May 1704 Queen Anne ordered that John Campbell, Goldsmith, should be paid £316 18s 6d sterling for making the medals of the Brethren of the Most Ancient Noble Order of the Thistle. However, it was difficult to extract payment for these: for many years he appealed in vain for his money, a considerable sum. Not surprisingly he was somewhat cynical about 'our nobility & gentry', who, he considered, 'are not punctual in their payments as we must be'.[7] On 13 June 1704 he wrote to his Scottish correspondents, Alexander Campbell and Robert Bruce:

I allso notice what you wreate about my monny from the Treasury I hope the Chancellor will order itt yow may tell the Lds of the Treasury that its no gift nor pension but a just debt & what I expected ready monny for & if they will not pay itt I most acquaint the Queen of itt. . . .

A month later he complained to the Duke of Argyll of his shortage of money. He was obviously making an onyx pendant for the Duke, probably for an Order of the Thistle:

Onyx allmost finish'd but I have not gott any of Dymds yett for to be free with your Grace I cannot spare the monny. My monny being all out of my hands with one thing and another that I have been verry hard putt to itt to keep my Cd [credit] which is what I value above all the world. . . .[8]

Between November 1707 and December 1709, Campbell supplied ten collars of the Order of the Thistle to Queen Anne. She had particularly asked that they be made by a Scot.

Only one of these gold collars has so far been discovered; it is highly intricate and of exquisite workmanship. The chain is made of seventeen thistle heads, the flowers enamelled in delicate pink, the calices in a tender green, linked by filigree sprigs of rue. A solid gold pendant hangs from the chain on which St Andrew, in dark green enamel, is superimposed.

The labour and expense incurred in making ten such collars was considerable, especially since some of the work, perhaps the basic gold necklace, was obviously wrought by other craftsmen. Certainly Middleton helped Campbell, since it was he who finally asked his brother John to use his influence with the Duke of Argyll to extract payment from the Treasury. Such distinguished debtors made life difficult for Campbell, who was always so short of ready cash.

In December his worries were further increased by the failure of a Scottish bank in which Alexander Campbell was a partner, which putts them all in confusion ... but I would not have the bill protested if possible I am hopeful that AC being a Director of the Bank wold take care of himself I am glad I am in the hands of a man of discretion who will consider to make all things easy to all partys in So Genll a Calamity so I leave itt wholly to doe as you think best.[9]

John Campbell was not only a goldsmith–banker, he was also Army Paymaster. One of his onerous responsibilities in 1708 was dealing with the army accounts of the Duke of Argyll's Regiment of Horse, the Fourth Troop of Horseguards, the Earl of Stair's Dragoons, the Royal Regiment, the Earl of Londonderry's Regiment and the Second Troop of Grenadier Guards. He was also responsible for the accounts of the garrisons of Dumbarton, Stirling and Edinburgh and for the supply of their equipment. He took pride in this work. 'I am verry certain', he wrote to Alexander Campbell in 1708, 'there is none of the forces better p'd yn [paid than] those I am concerned for.'[10] Another of his duties was the provision of army equipment:

a field bed, allso horse & furniture, a tent for my Lord red or blue, bespoke in blue. I have bespoak such a one as my Ld Ilay had, as for a tent he was advised to take none being so late. I did provid a second hand one for him but he did not take itt.[11]

There were many influential Scottish peers among his customers. Apart from the Duke of Argyll, the Earl of Seafield, William III's Secretary of State, the Earls of Buccleuch, Buchan, Dunmore, Glasgow, Leven and Rosebery banked with him. Dealing with these noble customers was no easy task, since he had to pay the bills of their often anxious tradesmen in London as well as arranging their supply of money when they returned to their Scottish estates. This was a constant worry because his noble customers often emptied his coffers of scarce gold and silver coins.

During Campbell's life coins were always in short supply. Gold and silver coins were exported to Holland to pay for the war with France; and the Duke of Argyll and other Scottish nobles expected to be supplied with gold to be transported in iron chests in wagons or ships when they visited their estates in Scotland. Campbell's letters are filled with agonised cries for coin to his Edinburgh correspondents and appeals to them to go easy with payments in specie (coin).

In 1708 he had a more serious worry – the threat of a Jacobite invasion backed by the French, which, as will later be seen, failed dismally. As he wrote to Robert Bruce, 'I was afraide the french would come and take all the [money] out of the mint but I hope by this time the danger is over to the great grief of the Jacobites and the joy of all true brittains. ...'[12] A week later he told a friend, 'so what to doe I know not especially att this juncture there being so great a run upon all Goldsmiths because of an invation threatened by the french'.[13]

From the time he started business in 1692 until his death in 1712 John Campbell relied on the support of the Argylls, firstly of the old Duke, who died in 1703, and then of his two sons. John, the second Duke of Argyll, and his younger brother, Archibald, were an impressive pair. John (1678–1743) was a distinguished soldier, who showed exceptional courage as a brigadier-general with Marlborough at Ramillies in 1706, Oudenarde in 1708 and Malplaquet in 1709, for which services he was made a lieutenant-general in that year. After the death of Queen Anne, George I made him a general and commander-in-chief of the King's forces in Scotland; as such he was responsible for the defeat of the Jacobites in 1715. Though he fought loyally for the Hanoverians, he showed some political independence and incurred the jealousy of Marlborough and the dislike of Swift. But even his enemies admitted that he was 'altogether free of the least share of dissimilation & his word so sacred that one might assuredly depend on it'.[14] 'He had', says a contemporary, Macky, 'all the free spirits and good sense natural to the family. Few of his years have a better understanding, nor a more manly behaviour. He has seen most of the courts of Europe, is very handsome in appearance, fair complexioned.'[15]

His brother Archibald (1682–1761), who was created Earl of Ilay in 1705, became known as the King of Scotland. As one of the sixteen representative peers of Scotland, admitted to sit in the House of Lords under the terms of the Act of 1707, he worked with great shrewdness and dedication to revive Scottish trade and industry. Sir Robert Walpole was to give him full authority to run affairs in Scotland and he had for a long period most of the patronage in Scotland in his gift. He was cultured and sensitive and had one of the finest libraries in Scotland.

Campbell was not only a craftsman and banker to the nobility, he was a trader as well. He dealt mainly with customers in Scotland, but also with merchants in America, the West Indies and even in China. As Forbes later wrote, 'the banker, in consequence of early connections, long continued to supply distant correspondents with articles which would now be ordered from the family grocer and oilman'.[16]

A particular friend with whom Campbell did much business was to play an important role in the history of the Bank. The Edinburgh merchant, Patrick Craufurd, who dealt in many kinds of merchandise, was also a cattle dealer arranging the sale and export to England of one of Scotland's few commodities, black cattle. This was an important part of John Campbell's business, which often took him out of London to country fairs, especially to Norwich. 'Mr. Campbell has gone to the Norwich fair to meet the Scottish drovers,' wrote one of his clerks.[17]

Every autumn, Scottish customers like Patrick Craufurd sent herds of little black Highland cattle down the drove roads to the great October fair at St Fays near Norwich. The cattle thudded down on the hoof, the drovers sleeping in their plaids in the pastures on the way. Fattened on the rich plains of Norfolk, the cattle made particularly tasty beef, much sought after by the London butchers. The drovers set up their table in the inn, counting their masters' earnings into their leather purses and paying the much needed coin to John Campbell. Defoe wrote of the surprising honesty of the Scottish drovers, who were entrusted with large sums of money. According to a modern historian, Professor Roseveare,

The cattle drovers from Scotland and elsewhere had for long acted as slow-moving but very safe carriers of money and valuables. No highwayman would willingly confront these bands of rough . . . men, boys and dogs. So for a small commission, they acted as guards for bills of exchange and money. It was difficult to transfer payments between Scotland and London at any time in the seventeenth or eighteenth centuries. The premium on bills of exchange was quite high. . . .[18]

John Campbell's expeditions to Norwich were part of his work not only as trader but also as banker.

Did the unpretentious John sit beside his countrymen at their seat of custom in the inn? Did he squelch with them over the muddy streets and admire the sleek beasts parading on the Mound? Did he enjoy the frolic and festivities of the country fair? Or did he sit with the local gentry in their carriages and do some quiet business? We do not know; we only know that he looked forward to trips to Colchester, where, after his wife's death, his children lived with his uncle.

For a simple, direct man the many-sided life of a goldsmith–banker was becoming increasingly complex. It was in his family life that he found relief from the stress of business. His wife Elizabeth is a shadow, of whom we know little except that she was frequently ill, had at least five children and died in November 1701. She was buried in St Paul's churchyard, Covent Garden, on 15 November. Fortunately Campbell had a close and affectionate family to console him. Apart from his uncle William Clark at Colchester, who took care of his children, he refers to his aunt, his sister Mary and her children and his cousins, Captain Alexander and George, an army agent and merchant, to whom he was particularly kind. A niece, Mary Brand, cared for him in his last illness and he remembered her in his will.

With so many diverse responsibilities it is no wonder that he frequently sounded harassed and irritated. And John Campbell did not mince his words. For example, to William Sloper, MP and Army Paymaster in Edinburgh, the punch came straight from the shoulder. 'I find you are not a man that regards your word so must not depend more on it. I did not deserve to be thus treated . . . so blame yourself if you meet with what perhaps you will call hard knocks.'[19]

Campbell could not have managed his business alone and he had at least two partners in the early days. We know very little about his first partner, David Lyell (Lyall), who appears to have worked with him in 1694 and 1695 and shared the tenancy of the shop in the Strand. Lyell apparently left London in 1698, for by 1710 Campbell was writing of him as the man 'who was my partner and is now a goldsmith in new yourk'.[20]

In 1703 Campbell was joined by George Middleton, who was nineteen and a qualified goldsmith. No portrait of Middleton has yet been found, but he was said to be like his great-uncle, the Earl, and the family were noted for their strong, dark looks. He brought with him a cultivated mind, self-discipline and moral principles inculcated by his remarkable father, the Principal of King's College, Aberdeen. Under his influence the letter books and ledgers became more orderly and gradually he became indispensable to Campbell, who made him his partner in 1708.

We know little about Campbell's apprentices except that he treated them well. In December 1704 he told a friend,

about yor friend's son so I would have yo wreate about itt to his father you may tell him that my terms are to serve 7 years which is the custom of the place & tho my expectation with a printice is £100 yett on your accot I will take £80 you may also acquaint him that I do not use my printices as they do in Scotland but as Gentlemen's sons ought to be used. . . .[21]

Clerks were at this time often called servants and some were obviously less educated than others, but generally Campbell's letters are copied in clear, firm handwriting which is a pleasure to read and occasionally there are pages decorated by flourishes that suggest some engraver's skilful hand. It says much for Scottish education at this time that when Campbell wanted a gardener, it was to Edinburgh that he sent for one who could 'do everything and could write a good hand'.[22]

Campbell hoped that his eldest son, William, would come into the business, so in June 1708 he sent him to Holland to learn Dutch and bookkeeping, because, as he wrote later, 'I am informed youth is not to be corrupted there as here.'[23] In peacetime the nobility sent their sons on the Grand Tour of France and Italy, but merchants preferred to have their sons 'finished' in Holland. In the late seventeenth century and throughout the eighteenth there were close connections between Scottish merchants and those in Amsterdam, where there was a large and prosperous Scottish community. '. . . I advised Mr Alexr Campbell that you would take care of his son for which he thanks you heartily . . . where he may learn french & Dutch to write and cast acctts . . . it is more for the boys inter'st to stay in Holland. . . .'[24] But Campbell's hope that the meticulous Dutch would instil in William steadiness and a love of business was in vain. He was, his father complained, 'careless and loved to play'.[25] He was apprenticed in

Amsterdam in the merchant house of another Scot, his friend Alexander Carstairs:

I am glead my sone is to come home to your house the end of this month I desire he may know no other but that he is bound prentice & that he may believe it to be so let a writting be drawn up as the usuall way is & lett him putt his name to itt. Lett him never be idle but keep him close at Business & go duely to Church with you. . . .[26]

In 1710 William was brought back to work in the Strand. Two years later his father's death released him from the business to which he was not suited and he became an army captain. He died and was buried with his mother on 22 May 1728. Therefore, it was Campbell's second son, George, who ultimately became a partner in his father's business.

George Middleton, however, was proving more reliable than any son, so Campbell could relax and let him carry the responsibility of the business. In the summer of 1709 Campbell bought 'a little house and garden near Chelsea Bridge'.[27] Chelsea was then a quiet village, surrounded by fields and farms, where he and his family might be together. He sent to a friend in Lisbon for seeds of fruit and flowers; to another friend, the merchant, Patrick Heron, he wrote asking for his 'pretty parrot', which Patrick's cousin had given him. Obviously nagged by his children he asked again for the parrot, 'as for my own part I am very indifferent but my children whose desire is to have it . . . if not I will buy one to please them'.[28]

In September 1711 Campbell and his daughter Mary, his sister, her husband and family went to Bath. A modest man, Campbell chose to lodge with 'a gentlewoman near the cross [in] Bath. She is a very discreet woman . . . my sister you [know] loves to be cheap.'[29] That October he paid his last visit to Norwich fair, because he was now much weakened by consumption.

His last year – 1712 – began tragically with the death of his daughter Barbara. 'Mr Campbell having a daughter to be burid ye evening puts us all in disorder,' wrote Middleton.[30] She was buried beside her mother in Covent Garden. Throughout the year he struggled on, spending much of his time in the country in Epsom, Surrey. But neither the asses' milk treatment there, nor two months' convalescence in Suffolk cured him.

In September he put his affairs in order and made his will, adding a codicil eleven days later. On Wednesday, 22 November 1712, George Middleton wrote to Robert Bruce:

Last night I have ane express from the country with the melancholly news of the death of our dear frind John Campbell who dyed las[t] Wednesday night. I canot say that it was any surprise for have been expecting itt for some tyme past.[31]

John Campbell was buried beside his wife and daughter Barbara on 26 November.

Middleton wrote to a friend:

Las[t] Wednesday it pleased God to remove from world poor Mr Campbell, which is a verry tryering loss to his family, as he lived in ye world with a just & honest character, so he left itt with prudence and conduct having settled all his affairs in verry good order, & that no stopp might hapon in ye Busines he has mead me his executer.[32]

Under the terms of the will, Middleton was also made the children's guardian until William came of age. The four children were to share Campbell's possessions, money, diamonds and personal estate. To his 'faithfull and honest' partner Middleton he bequeathed £200 and to Mary, his daughter, he left an extra £400. Perhaps this was for her dowry, for soon after her father's death she married Middleton. George Middleton was to carry on the business, receiving a quarter of the profits. He was to balance the books within six weeks of Campbell's death and account annually to the trustees, Dugald Campbell, William Sloper and William Elliot.

It was fortunate that Campbell could rely in his failing years on his partner George Middleton, a man of some intellectual sinew and better able to survive the storms of the next decades, when the boundaries of commerce were expanding, exploration was opening up new worlds, and new theories were beginning to disturb the economic world.

In his last years John Campbell had asked a friend to send him from Scotland 'a good, sober gentle horse, not very high not very low'.[33] But the horse had 'too much metal' and was very difficult to mount, so that Campbell, as he said, 'being a bad horseman and having a great care of myself', was forced to part with him.[34] In the coming years he would have found it as difficult to hold the reins of the Bank, for even Middleton, with all his strength, could only just manage to keep control.

As we know so little about John Campbell, we can only imagine him: a solid man, sitting with his friends in the Globe Inn over a bottle of good wine sent to him from Portugal. We see him in his full-bottomed wig, goldsmith's robes and three-cornered hat walking gravely, silver-headed cane in hand, in some procession; or we glimpse him through an open door standing behind his clerks as they copy into ledgers; or he appears in shirt sleeves, glass to eye, meticulously examining his diamonds, or weighing coins; or in leather apron he works at the bench, expertly flicking the gold and silver parings into leather bags. For a moment we see his face in the candlelight reflected in the water glass, but the door shuts and once more he is invisible.

The absence of early records makes it impossible to determine how successful Campbell was as a banker, the earliest extant ledger being 1712. Although he ended his life in comfort, he could not have accumulated great wealth. He had difficulty in extracting payment for his work as a goldsmith; the war with France damaged his trade as a merchant and kept him short of currency; and bad harvests and cattle plague often ruined his farmer customers. He would definitely have recouped himself as paymaster of Argyll's troops, but of that we have no precise knowledge.

Campbell certainly had customers and friends in many countries. His letter books mention dealings with fellow Scots in Spain, Portugal, Italy, Holland, Scandinavia, the West Indies, North America and Africa.

However, although he did not leave a great fortune, he left other valuable legacies to the Bank. The position at the end of the Strand was well chosen and after 300 years the Bank is still there – though across the road – and his seal is still stamped on the cheques of Coutts & Co. He also established enduring relations with correspondents in Lisbon, Holland and Scotland. But most of all he kept the patronage and support of the most influential Scots of the period, especially that of John, second Duke of Argyll, and his brother Archibald, Earl of Ilay, later the third Duke of Argyll. Through the Jacobite and economic disturbances of the next century the Argyll family gave indispensable protection to the Bank. In the words of a later partner, Edward Marjoribanks, 'After the patronage of our sovereign Mr Coutts always looked on the Argyll family as the oldest patrons of his bank.'[35]

4

Early Banking:
Enterprise and Adventure

John Campbell's business as a goldsmith–banker had depended on customers who often did not pay their bills; and his other activities were at constant risk from wars, storms and bad harvests. He had therefore found it difficult to accumulate capital. But at the end of the seventeenth century there were merchants in the City of London who were making considerable fortunes and were looking for profitable ways to invest.

Among them were London Scots, who, while acting as the English correspondents of their Scottish firms, were looking for wider opportunities. One of them, Thomas Coutts, the son of Provost John Coutts of Montrose, acted in London for his brother Patrick, now a thriving corn merchant in Edinburgh.*

The moving spirit among these London Scots was the ingenious William Paterson, who had become obsessed with the idea of the creation of a national bank and who, in 1694, was the chief promoter of the foundation of the Bank of England. King William's wars had left the country deeply in debt and the Government finally accepted Paterson's plan to raise a capital of £1,200,000, which was to be lent to the Government to support the most costly war England had yet fought. In return, the Government pledged future tax revenues to meet the 8 per cent interest owed to the Bank. Thus the Bank of England was born. Paterson became a director for a short time, but he disagreed with his colleagues and resigned.

A year later in 1695 a similar national bank was established in Edinburgh, called the Bank of Scotland and promoted by a group of London Scots, including Thomas Deans, and an Englishman, John Holland. Both the Montrose brothers, Patrick and Thomas Coutts, subscribed large sums to this Bank and were two of the first Proprietors on its ledgers.

On 1 January 1696 Thomas took a shareholding of 20,000 and then on

---

* These Coutts brothers are not to be confused with the grandsons of Patrick, also called Thomas and Patrick.

26 October bought a further 3,000 shares from Phineas Bowlis, paying £6,900 in cash, plus a dividend of £72 on top. On the 26th he sold 17,000 shares to his brother Patrick and on 22 June 1699 he sold the remaining 6,000 to Sir William Baird.

Patrick had also taken a 4,000 shareholding in the Bank on 1 January 1696. On 20 May 1702 he brought 8,000 shares from Walter Stewart and 8,000 from Daniel King; on 10 December 1703 he bought another 2,000 shares and on 3 January 1704 he bought 6,000 shares from David Spence, the Bank's Secretary. His total holding was now 45,000 shares, for which he paid £11,236.* But between 1 October 1696 and 1704 he gradually sold all his shares, until on 21 June he transferred his remaining 16,000 shares to his son, John, who in turn sold them in 1705. After that date the Coutts family ceased to be Proprietors in the Bank of Scotland.[1]

It must be recognised that the Coutts family were not, as has often been assumed, mere merchants, but at this stage were already involved in early banking. They were also involved in the disastrous Darien Expedition.

Scotland in the 1690s was a poor country; bad harvests and cattle plague had played havoc with her economy and she was desperately short of currency. Nor was it easy for the Scots to embark on overseas trade. But in 1693 the Scottish parliament had passed 'an act for the encouragement of Forraigne trade',[2] and two years later King William was persuaded by Scottish peers to give his consent to an Act promoting 'a company of Scotland trading to Africa and the Indies'.[3] English 'adventurers' provided half the £600,000 capital, and Scotland raised the other half. Here was the prospect of rivalling the nabobs of the East India Company.

In 1693 Paterson had his eyes on wider horizons: he was looking to Darien on the Isthmus of Panama. As a young man he had travelled to the West Indies and Panama and had a vision of settling a colony of hardworking, God-fearing Scots in what seemed idyllic country round the Gulf of Darien. Here, at the hub of the New World, they would be able to command the trade of two great oceans – the Atlantic and the Pacific.

Since Tudor times excitement had been fanned by travellers' tales. In candlelight in the slums of Glasgow and the wynds of Edinburgh men read of Eldorados in the Americas, where gold gleamed in clear rivers and rocks of emeralds shone in undiscovered forests. They therefore rushed to subscribe to Paterson's dream.

For Patrick and Thomas Coutts the prospect was particularly exciting. They had known from childhood the thrill of watching the great sailing ships making for the high seas. For months they and their fellow Scots in London had met and plotted in coffee houses and over hearty meals in

---

* This is Scots money. In 1695 1,200,000 Scots pounds equalled £100,000 sterling. Bank of Scotland shares of 1,000 Scots pounds were worth the equivalent of £83 6s 8d.

inns. The bills were carefully preserved so that they could recoup their expenses later; from these we learn that on a hot, August day, Paterson dined with Thomas Coutts at his house in St Dionis Back Church in the City of London. On 7 August 1695, as a reward for services to Scottish trade, Provost Chiesly of Edinburgh made both brothers 'burgesses and gildbrothers – gratis'. They had contributed to the expedition and had earned Edinburgh's accolade.

However, many of the subscribers were never to see their money again. The English contributors got cold feet, fearing that the new company would destroy the old East India Company, and they withdrew their half of the capital, persuading King William to withdraw his support as well. Therefore, the Scots had to make up the deficit, which, for a poor country, was extremely difficult.

In July 1698 1,200 pioneers – men, women and children – sailed from Leith in five small ships with high hopes of bringing back instant fortunes. A second expedition with 1,300 members set out the following year, little guessing that the first had ended in disaster. No travellers' tales had prepared them for the desperate struggle for existence in the fever-haunted swamps; nor had they realised that the Spanish would not readily allow their occupation of such a strategic position in the territories of Spain. Many died, while others fled to New York. The second expedition was finally ousted by the Spanish, who captured their capital, Fort St Andrew. Again and again in the next century dreams of Eldorados beyond the seas were to end in similar nightmares.

For Scotland it was an economic disaster: a quarter of her assets were sunk in this fatal project. The perfidy of the English was not forgotten and the anger of the Scots who lost their money fanned the flames of Jacobite rebellion. The directors of the Bank of Scotland, feeling betrayed by King William, became henceforward associated with the supporters of the Stuarts. On the other hand, the Whig supporters of King William worked with the English Government to save something for Scotland from the wreck.

The ingenious Paterson had made sure that in the last Act of the Scottish Parliament, before the Act of Union was passed, £232,884 5s od was written into the Scottish national debt, which England took over. By the Act of Union in 1707 England agreed to pay Scotland the 'equivalent' of £398,185 10s in compensation for the Darien and other losses, plus a proportion of the increase in tax revenue to be realised in after years: this was confusingly called 'the arising equivalent'. Such was the shortage of currency in both countries that only £150,000 was available in coin. So the Government resorted to the device frequently used in the payment of soldiers' wages: it issued debentures bearing 5 per cent interest. As always the Government was slow in paying interest, and it was not until later that an Act was passed making provision for £10,000 a year to pay this debt. A company was formed of the English debenture holders to collect this interest in a lump sum to create stock for its 'Society of the Subscribed Equivalent Stock'. It was out of this society that a second Scottish bank grew. In 1724 it and a similar Scottish society joined to become, by Act of Parliament, the 'Equivalent Company', which became a bank; on 31 May 1727 it became the Royal Bank of Scotland, which opened for business on 8 December 1727 with a capital of £111,347. Unlike the Bank of Scotland, the Royal Bank became a Whig bank, loyal to the Hanoverians. The first Governor was Lord Ilay, his deputy Sir Hew Dalrymple of the Stair family. It would appear that although the Coutts brothers had subscribed to the Bank of Scotland at the beginning, before the end of the century they had transferred their funds to the bank that became the Royal Bank of Scotland.

5

Middleton and the Jacobites

George Middleton took over the business at a critical time in the history of banking. His goldsmith's business still continued – there are entries in his ledgers for wrought gold and for the repair and engraving of silver; and in 1716 'The Prince of Whales [*sic*]',[1] later George II, bought a magnificent service of gilt. But it was as a banker that he made his mark.

For the next thirty-five years Middleton was to dominate the business in the Strand. John Campbell had expressly wished him to carry on 'The Shop' after his death 'without a stop'[2] until his sons should come of age. In fact his son George was not to become a partner until 1727.

In 1712 Middleton was twenty-nine, experienced as a craftsman, respected as a banker, and with stability of character inherited from wise parents and strengthened by the affection of his numerous brothers and sisters. He was particularly close to his sisters and took a kindly paternal interest in his nephews, David and Robert Bruce, the former becoming his partner and the latter his business colleague and correspondent in Edinburgh.

However, it was his brother, the rumbustious Colonel John, whose close friendship with the Argylls was later to be of great importance to the Bank in the Strand. Totally trusted as a loyal anti-Jacobite, on occasion he amused his Lordship by describing how he had happily drunk the health of the King over the water in order to gull some unsuspecting Jacobite into giving him useful information. He was to earn his spurs fighting beside Argyll against the 1715 Jacobite rebellion; later he became a general and at the end, surprisingly, a Member of Parliament.

George Middleton's letters reveal a man of culture, with some Latin and French remembered from his King's College education. This was particularly useful since he was to have a great deal of correspondence with France. He wrote well, with a vigorous and individual turn of phrase, so in the mirror of his letter books a very distinctive character emerges. Perhaps it is the memory of the grey North Sea in his Aberdeen youth that inspired so much of the sea imagery in his letters. From time to time we hear the voices of two generations of Dominies. 'Do as you would be done by my good friend,' he reproved a colleague. The tone of his letters reflects a man firm and upright in the Scots professional manner, mildly humorous, affectionate with his friends, a man who trusted and who was trusted. There is almost an innocence in his trust of friends and even where he feels betrayed his reproofs are mild. 'I would not have treated you so, my friend,' he writes to Patrick Craufurd, the Edinburgh merchant, who was frequently in debt to him.[3] But it was his tenacity and grit which pulled him through the stormy seas ahead. Without them he would not have survived the wild turbulence of the South Sea and Mississippi adventures. That he was a careful man is shown by his neat ledgers, and his personal accounts are meticulously kept – even the mending of his daughter's watch is noted.

To his secure family background Middleton could add a happy marriage. John Campbell's daughter, Mary, appears to have been a lady of shrewd common sense. He called her 'Honey' and there is an affectionate glow in his references to her.

By 1713 Britain was, in theory, at peace, the Treaty of Utrecht having brought an end to the war of the Spanish Succession. However, the decades ahead were hardly peaceful. The death of Queen Anne in 1714 gave new hope to English and Scottish Jacobites and in the next year a rebellion was mounted which might have changed the face of Britain. Since the Jacobite threat reappears again and again in the history of the Bank, it is necessary to set out the background here.

When King James went into exile in France, he had been welcomed by Louis XIV and given a château at St Germain, near Versailles outside Paris, where he, the Queen and their son, James Francis Edward, lived at Louis's expense. Here, in the château where Louis had been born, ambition was kept alive. Le Nôtre had laid out splendid grounds, terraces and flowery parterres, very long allées, and an immense esplanade with a spectacular view over the River Seine and the forest to Paris on the distant horizon. James II could pace the broad walk, lean on the marble balustrade and look towards the French capital, dreaming once more of conquering his kingdom.

It was a place for plotting: periwigged courtiers could whisper and gossip unheard down the long walks, while Highland warriors rode unseen through the thick forest. Scottish, Irish and English Jacobites came secretly from England even during the war, and with them came spies and counter-spies. For more than a decade St Germain was the hub of Jacobite intrigue.

The Earl of Middleton brought over his Catholic wife from England in 1692 and St Germain became his home for the rest of his life. He raised a daughter and two sons there. Although he remained a Protestant for many years, he became accepted at the Catholic court because of his wife.

James's Queen, Mary of Modena, trusted and relied on them both; and James had proved the Earl's loyalty to the Stuart cause in good times in the past. In exile, James made the Earl his Secretary of State and, as such, the Earl was in a key position during the successive Jacobite attempts to invade Britain. A moderate man, he always hoped that England would in time accept the young James Francis Edward as King after Anne and consequently he kept in touch, through secret agents, with like-minded nobles in England and Scotland.

Meanwhile, after the death of James II in 1701, the Earl acted as a friend and counsellor to the young Prince, preparing him for his future role. When in 1708 a French-backed invasion was planned, he and his two sons accompanied James Francis Edward into action. Every effort was made at St Germain to keep the plans secret, but there is no doubt that the Duke of Argyll was fully informed: the 6,000 French troops assembled at Dunkirk were all too visible to the Duke's many spies.

The expedition was doomed from the start, for the French were unwilling to risk their necks in another foolhardy exploit and Middleton himself was less than enthusiastic. However, in February 1708 he escorted James Francis Edward to Dunkirk, where by 18 March French battalions had assembled with 200 English, Scottish and Irish officers. But storms caused delay and when they finally set sail for Scotland, Middleton and his young master were violently sea-sick. Middleton's sons were on board the *Salisbury*, while the Earl and the wretched James were on the *Mars*.

In London the threat seemed graver than it was: there was panic in the city and a run on the Bank of England. For George Middleton in the Strand it must have been a stressful time. His partner, John Campbell, was fiercely anti-Jacobite, and his brother John was a soldier with Argyll. On the other hand, his great-uncle and his sons were with the Pretender, sailing up the coast towards Edinburgh, where loyal Jacobite gentlemen were waiting to proclaim King James III.

However, the English fleet was ready and waiting and pursued them northwards. The *Salisbury* was captured and Middleton's sons were taken as prisoners to the Tower of London. The French fleet turned tail and by 7 April James Francis Edward and Middleton were back in Dunkirk. The Earl was probably relieved – at fifty-nine he was a reluctant warrior – but he accompanied James Francis Edward when he fought against the English at the Battles of Oudenarde and Malplaquet. In 1710 at the Battle of Douai he enjoyed riding in full view of the English troops across the river, sending over gold and silver medals stamped with his image and shouting greetings. In return, an English officer called across a message to Middleton that he had seen his two sons in London and they were well.

The young men, in fact, had been released on bail on the surety of the Duke of Hamilton and were leading a full social life in London. Again the presence of his Jacobite kin must have caused George Middleton at his Bank extreme embarrassment.

Peace came in 1713 and, by the Treaty of Utrecht, Louis was compelled to recognise the Hanoverian succession and to banish the Stuart court to Lorraine, then outside the boundaries of France. With the death of Louis XIV in 1715 James Francis Edward lost his best ally. The Regent, who assumed power on behalf of the infant Louis XV, was reluctant to involve France in another war, especially since it was becoming clear that James was a born loser. The Duke of Berwick, an inspired general who had escaped to France after the Battle of the Boyne, was now a marshal of France and unwilling to commit himself, although he was a natural son of James II. For the next twenty-five years the Jacobites had little support from the French court.

The Earl of Middleton remained with the old Queen at St Germain and, although he kept in touch with James Francis Edward, he gradually retired. He had little to do with the planning of the next Jacobite attempt.

In September 1715 George Middleton wrote, 'We are alarmed again here.'[4] Once more there was news of a Jacobite invasion. This caused him much difficulty since he was banker to Lord Mar and Lord Nithsdale, who were commanding the Jacobite forces. As he wrote to Lord Leven on 29 November 1716,

I'm so unfortunate to be concerned pritty deeply w'th some persons involv'd in ye late rebellion and thought I had a verry good security for my mony, but by ye act of Enquiry I'm not only like to be depending a long tyme but am in danger of loosing a greate part of itt.[5]

His relations with the Jacobites at this time are obscure, but he certainly visited Lord Nithsdale in the Tower. On 13 December he wrote to Robert Bruce: '. . . the Prisoners in the Tower being confined Close I have not yet got Ld Nithsdale supplyed wt [with] ye sume ye desired, I have been at the Secretarys Office & am told may have a Warrt for going to him in a few days.'[6] Later he wrote to him again: 'I have not yet obtained leave to waite on lord Nithsdale but sent him word by Hen. [Henry] Mills yt [that] had Directions for supplying him wt £100 pr [through] his bill on Lord Traquair he says its very well & will send me word when he wants itt.'[7] We shall probably never know whether Middleton was aware of Nithsdale's plan to escape from the Tower, but he certainly would have been relieved to hear that, on the day before his execution was to take place, his noble customer walked out of the Tower to freedom, in traditional style – dressed as a woman.

The campaign of 1715 was planned as a three-pronged offensive. James Francis Edward was to join with Ormonde in Plymouth and raise the English Jacobites, while the Highland forces were to make for Edinburgh and Glasgow. But Argyll's efficient secret service discovered the West Country plan and the Highland forces were so badly commanded by 'Bobbing John', the Earl of Mar, that they were soundly defeated on 13 November at the Battle of Sherriffmuir. They were no match for Argyll's battle-hardened troops. The English Jacobites who had attacked Preston were also convincingly defeated. James Francis Edward landed in Scotland on 23 December, finding his followers confused and dejected. Once again, typically, he fell ill. Finally Argyll advanced from Stirling, pushing the Jacobite army back to Montrose, from where they set sail for France.

The loyal Jacobites of Montrose sheltered their luckless King that never was. He drank a last dram and sailed from the bay out to the open sea and France – never to return. But in Montrose they kept hope alive. The glass he drank from was lovingly preserved and kept ready for the Stuarts' return. It is still to be seen in the museum of Montrose.

Another rebellion in 1719, this time backed by Spain, was equally dogged by misfortune. Storms and the English navy destroyed the Spanish fleet and all chance of James's success.

After 1719 the Old Pretender lost heart. He was banished from Lorraine and retreated at the Pope's invitation to the castle of Urbino. But neither the magnificent site nor the exquisite marquetry impressed him. Finally the Pope gave him a palace near Rome, as a reward for his fidelity to the Roman Catholic faith. Here he settled, married and had two sons, the elder becoming the 'Bonnie Prince Charlie' of legend, the younger, Henry, serious and devout from childhood, becoming the Cardinal Duke of York: both were to play a part in the Bank's history. The Earl of Middleton remained quietly in retirement at St Germain, where he died in 1719.

The 1719 campaign was the last chance for the Old Pretender. He had never lacked courage, but he was dogged by ill-health and bad luck. In 1708, 1715 and 1719 even the winds and waves were against him. Had he shown the same energy and enterprise that was to distinguish his son, Charles, he might have succeeded in 1708 when many Scots were seething with fury over the 1707 Act of Union. The death of Queen Anne in 1714 might have given him another opportunity but the absence of French support, the incompetence of the Jacobite leaders and his own chronic indecision doomed him.

There were to be no more serious Jacobite attempts for twenty-five years, but the Stuart cause did not die. Secret societies in England and Scotland still observed their mysterious rituals, drinking their loyal toasts to the King over the water, and toasting 'the little gentleman in the velvet coat' – the mole whose molehill had caused William's horse to stumble and brought about his death.

6

The Fiery Trial

George Middleton was certainly disturbed by the Jacobite threats of 1715 and 1719, but the following years were undoubtedly the worst in his life.

The lust for gold blinds men to the lessons of the past. In the early eighteenth century they forgot the disaster of Darien, and those who, like Sir Robert Walpole, tried to remind them, were dismissed as croaking Cassandras. England, France and most of Europe were swept by an unparalleled hurricane of money madness. It was a double whirlwind: France was lured by the dream of untold wealth in the Mississippi, while England fell under the spell of the South Seas. In both countries excitement was whipped up by the brilliant and glamorous Scotsman, John Law, whose magic dazzled even the steady eyes of George Middleton. Middleton was buffeted by both storms, but emerged relatively untouched by the South Sea disaster. It was John Law and the Mississippi adventure that nearly destroyed him.

John Law's extraordinary story must be told briefly here. He was the eldest son of the wealthy Edinburgh goldsmith, William Law, who became Assay Master for Edinburgh in 1670, was called in to assist the Royal Commission on the Mint in 1674 and was Dean of Goldsmiths in Edinburgh from 1675 to 1677. His success enabled him to buy Lauriston Castle in June 1683, but he did not live long to enjoy it: he died in Paris in 1683, leaving his estate to his son, John. William Law's wife, Jean Campbell, survived him until 21 July 1707. Whether she was a relative of the Duke of Argyll is uncertain, but the Campbell name was to help in the future and counted for something. They left five children, but it is John and his younger brother, William, with whom George Middleton was chiefly involved.

William Law Junior was born in October 1675 – his birth was registered on 24 October. He trained as a goldsmith with his father, and his work – his 'assay' – was accepted on 10 September 1703, which admitted him in the next month to the Edinburgh Incorporation of Goldsmiths. The City accepted him in the same month as a burgess and gildbrother. Later he moved to London, where, on 3 July 1716, he married Rebecca. He was to

be overshadowed all his life by his brother John, who was four years older
– he had been born on 21 April 1671 – and infinitely more brilliant. The
children were brought up in their goldsmith's house in Parliament Square,
Edinburgh.

Like many of his distinguished compatriots, John was educated at Edinburgh High School and then at fifteen was sent to a boarding-school,
Englesham in Renfrewshire, where his sister's father-in-law was headmaster. Here the talent for mathematics, for which he had been distinguished even as a child, was encouraged.

After his father's death, John, now master of a fortune and of Lauriston
Castle, neglected his studies for a life of pleasure – and by the time he
moved to London he was already, to quote a friend, 'nicely expert in
all manner of debaucheries'.[1] In London he showed that contradictory
character which marked him all his life, combining a love of pleasure and
idleness with a remarkable power of intensive, creative thinking. At the
green baize tables in gambling establishments, his mind was actively revolv-
ing round the theories of the laws of chance.

He was to become a phenomenally successful gambler and was irresistible to the ladies. Tall, elegant in his flowing curled wig and his brocaded
coat, with scented lace at throat and wrists, he was known as 'Beau Law'
– and to his rivals as 'Jessamy John'. But he was no fop; he was sufficiently
skilled with the sword to kill a rival – Beau Wilson – for the honour of a
lady. The mystery that surrounds this duel may never be unravelled. However he was imprisoned, tried and condemned to death, but subsequently
escaped from prison to exile on the continent.

For the next twenty-six years John Law could not return to England,
although he could safely go to Scotland, since it was still a foreign country.
So he moved from country to country, creating a reputation and making
a fortune. He made gambling a science, and was so successful that he was
usually encouraged by the authorities to move on. But wherever he was,
in Amsterdam, Paris, Geneva or Venice, he observed the money markets
and worked on his theories of credit. In 1700 he slipped back to Scotland,
retired to Lauriston Castle and in 1701 wrote a pamphlet on a plan for
developing the use of paper money, called 'Money and Trade Considered'.
This he presented to the Scottish parliament, which rejected it; but it won
him the interest of the Duke of Argyll, who remained his friend throughout
all the vicissitudes of his extraordinary life.

The Act of Union of 1707 meant that Scotland was no longer a foreign
country where he was safe from English justice. For the next two years he
was once again an exile, moving from city to city all over Europe. He
learned much in Amsterdam and closely studied the Bank there. The city
was the centre of international trade and the Bank had been founded in
the early seventeenth century to regulate the value of the mass of foreign

coins that merchants accumulated there. These coins were valued by their weight rather than their face value and the receipts or bank notes which merchants received in exchange were highly regarded.

It was in Amsterdam that Law worked on his theory of money and credit. He saw no sense in using the scarce supply of gold and silver as currency when paper could do as well. When the elegant Scotsman appeared at the gaming tables he brought with him two bags, one of gold and silver, the other of tokens, which he used to represent coins during play; thus he illustrated his theories. By 1712 he had made a fortune and was able to open an account at the Bank of Amsterdam for £100,000 and to buy a handsome house there.

During his travels it is possible that he also acted as an agent for the Duke of Argyll and Lord Ilay. Certainly the Jacobites and the French authorities suspected that he was a spy. He spent some time at the Stuart court at St Germain, where, in that romantic setting, he fell in love with Lady Catherine Seignieur, wife of a Frenchman and sister of the Earl of Banbury. Catherine eloped with him to Italy and stayed with him for the rest of his life; although they never married, she was always accepted as his wife and bore him a daughter and a son.

By this time various governments had offered him the chance to reform their currencies, but his sights were set on Paris because he longed to reorganise the chaotic French finances. In 1715 he had his opportunity. Louis XIV died and the Duke of Orléans was made Regent in charge of the young King. Philippe d'Orléans had been fascinated by the brilliant Scot and his theories, and allowed him, by an edict of 2 May 1716, to set up his own private bank in Paris with the power – new in France – to issue paper money.* John Law brought over his brother William from London as his partner and together they made the new bank so successful that on 4 December 1718 the Regent made it his Royal Bank. Law was authorised to discount bills of exchange and to issue notes payable to bearer in coin of the weight and denomination of the day. Thus he removed the uncertainty of the value of the specie. Paris was now his home. He had arrived with a reputed fortune of two million livres, which was rapidly increased many times over.

William Law must have known George Middleton in London. The two Scotsmen were certainly close friends and remained so during the most difficult times. Though now a banker, William remained at heart a craftsman, bringing over skilled clockmakers from Britain to teach his French workers. He watched with some awe as his brother became more and more

---

* Law thought 'paper preferable to gold and silver for the requirements of business ... but he understood perfectly well that specie had an intrinsic value which paper money could not have; that coin melted down is still valuable as an ingot....'[2]

powerful until he was virtually master of the French economy. The bank's success was phenomenal: with a capital of six millions 'it would issue 50 or 60 millions of notes without confidence being in the slightest degree shaken'.[3]

John Law was concerned not merely with the creation of capital. He looked to the New World – not this time to the ill-fated Panama, but to the Mississippi basin, which a Frenchman, Robert Cavelier, Sieur de La Salle, had claimed in April 1682 and named Louisiana after Louis XIV. Law now took over La Salle's colony, which had failed, and planned a large French kingdom stretching from Canada down to the Gulf of Mexico, which would unite the fur trade of Canada with the fabled gold and treasure of Louisiana.

The Regent issued an edict in August 1717 giving Law the right to establish a company, which was called the Compagnie d'Occident. Though Law remembered from his time in Scotland the failure of the similar Darien scheme, he was nevertheless absolutely confident that he could succeed where Paterson had failed and that his company would rival the British East India Company. He persuaded the Regent to grant Louisiana all the rights of a sovereign state, except that it was to pay nominal homage to the King of France.

The Compagnie d'Occident had a capital of 100 million livres. Shareholders were authorised to pay one quarter in money and threequarters in state notes: the 4 per cent interest paid by the state on these notes gave the new company the capital for the initial establishment of the colony.

Now John Law skilfully puffed the value of the shares by creating interest and excitement in the potential of the new colony. With a technique that would be familiar today, but was unknown then, he persuaded his noble friends that the shares would be certain to rise in value. He promised to pay 100,000 livres for 200 shares at a fixed future time, and assured his friends that they stood to gain a profit of 40,000 livres on that day's price of 60,000 livres. To create confidence in his scheme he agreed to pay the 40,000 livres in advance – and would lose it if the gamble did not come off. So he brought to high finance the skills he had learned at the gaming tables. By this and other means he succeeded. The shares went up in April and May of 1719, giving the Regent the confidence to grant still wider powers to Law. The West India Company was now merged with the French East India Company with sole trading rights in the Far East. The new company, which was set up in May 1719, was called the Compagnie des Indes. Now Law had acquired the virtual monopoly of most of France's overseas trade. Interest and excitement grew, especially when Law stipulated that no one could buy a new share without having four old shares. Ambition pushed him further, till on 25 August he secured for the new company the right of coining and managing the specie.

By August shares bought originally at 300 livres were worth above 1,000 livres and all Paris became seized by a money mania. A street in Paris called Rue de Quincampoix was the scene of the most extraordinary frenzy. In the days before banks or stock exchanges, this street had traditionally been the place where merchants and their agents came to hear news of the rise and fall of markets and to do business. Every house was taken by buyers, sellers or dealers, who watched every new move Law made. A hunchback offered his hump as a desk – for a price – and made a fortune of 150,000 livres in a few days. Law's coachman became a rich man with a coach of his own. Servants who were sent to buy shares for their masters speculated for themselves. A duchess at the opera found herself next to her cook, who was festooned with diamonds. Those on whom the unexpected golden shower fell were delighted with Law. His tax reforms, the new hospitals he built for the poor, the canals and public works he ordered to be constructed, were all generally welcomed.

On 27 August 1719 the Regent granted Law a new privilege. Until now taxes had been collected and paid to the Treasury by a group of financiers called the Farmers General. This was a highly profitable business and it was now transferred to Law's Compagnie des Indes. When Law offered new shares on 13 September, excitement mounted: shares soared to eight times their original price. A new subscription was opened on 28 September and the scramble became mass hysteria.

Law had moved his residence to the Hôtel de Nevers, where he was mobbed day and night. Shares bought at the Hôtel could be sold on the Rue de Quincampoix at many times their value. Those who had originally bought shares for 500 livres could sell them for from 7,000 to 8,000 livres. Instant fortunes were made. That autumn Law became 'a demigod in whose honour a sort of worship was cultivated'.[4] Mary Stuart Wortley Montagu, passing through Paris, noted with astonishment the extraordinary power that Law now had. Another contemporary recorded that, as he passed, people shouted 'Long live the King and Monseigneur Law'.

Duchesses, desperately seeking shares in Law's golden company, resorted to the most extraordinary devices to catch the eye of the elegant Scot, always richly dressed in gold brocade and velvet. One even faked an accident outside his house in order to gain entry. As the Regent's mother wrote to a friend, 'Law was so beset that he had no repose, night or day. A duchess kissed his hand before a crowd of people. If a duchess will kiss his hand, what will not other women kiss?'[5]

In September 1719 Law became a Catholic and so strengthened his position at court. However, as his power grew so did the envy of his enemies. French ministers had been jealous of the foreign upstart from the beginning and now with alarm watched him dominating the Regent, making him financially independent of them. They plotted his downfall.

But he also alienated old friends like Lord Stair, the British Ambassador, who was reporting back to the British Government that power had gone to Law's head. He had refused to take shares in Law's company and in revenge Law persuaded the Regent that Stair was plotting a run on the Banque Royale and on the Mississippi company. Stair was so incensed that he asked to be recalled and early in the next year did indeed retire to England.

In London George Middleton watched the soaring fortunes of his fellow countryman, and even he, cautious Scot though he was, became dazzled. He felt that he could invest with safety in the French adventures, knowing that his friend William Law would give him sound advice and trusting implicitly in the brilliance of his brother John. The vast sums in which his friends were dealing were far beyond the bounds of his experience, and this world of wild speculation was far removed from the academia of his father with its Scottish values of probity, frugality and caution. He never quite overcame his nervousness in this perilous business of stock-jobbing, and was never quite sure when to sell or how long to hold, so he allowed a compatriot, Major George Skene, to act for him as his broker in Paris. He had an almost innocent faith that Skene would always do for him as he would for himself.

Skene's position in these affairs is not entirely clear, but he certainly had access to John Law, was friendly with William Law and had useful contacts in Paris who kept him informed. He was far subtler than the brokers who flooded into Paris from abroad at this time and

who speculated upon the constant rise but more often still upon the fluctuations which they had the skill to produce. . . . They ranged themselves in a line in the Rue de Quincampoix ready to act at the first signal. At the sound of a bell in the office of a man named Papillon, they offered all at once the shares, sold them, and effected a decline. At a different signal they bought at the lowest and then sold at the highest.[6]

That autumn John Law became more powerful than any French noble. Voltaire marvelled at his meteoric rise

in a short time from a Scotchman to a naturalised Frenchman, from a Protestant to a Catholic, from a needy adventurer to a lord of magnificent estate, from a banker to a minister of state. I have seen him arrive in the salons of the Palais Royal followed by dukes, lords, marquises of France and bishops.[7]

Yet under all this show and dazzle Law had a charm and simplicity which explains why he could always keep the affection of men like Middleton, the Duke of Argyll and Lord Ilay. The latter once called on him at the height of his fame and found him shut away from the thronging courtiers, planning the planting of cabbages in the gardens of his Scottish castle.

But there were few such quiet interludes. As he soared higher and higher, Law was seized by a kind of madness, driven by a manic ambition that would ultimately bring about his downfall. The rumour was spread around by his enemies that he had become insane, that he had been found by his wife dancing wildly in his shirt in his room and that he had had to be restrained.

He certainly was beginning to believe that he was the master of the world. He was heard publicly boasting that he could ruin England and Holland by breaking their banks. With this overweening self-confidence, he now embarked on a mad gamble by which he hoped to break the British East India Company, but which in fact brought disaster to George Middleton and thousands of others. He was afraid that his own trading companies were not succeeding, so he arranged a public parade of sturdy would-be colonists with their picks and spades ready to embark for Louisiana and dig for gold; however, this did not encourage the French to emigrate. He therefore attempted to destroy his British rival by bringing down the value of its stock. In the autumn of 1719 he sold Lord Londonderry £100,000 of British East India stock short for £70,000 for delivery by 25 August 1720 – that is at 11 per cent below its price in autumn 1719. Middleton, who trusted in Law's belief that he could force the price down, was to supply the margin of £30,000. So for nearly a year Middleton had the responsibility of this risky bargain hanging over him.

However, his faith seemed fully justified when, in December 1719, the Regent made Law Comptroller of Finance, crowning his triumphant career. Middleton wrote to William congratulating him on his brother's 'new promotion tho' in effect I conceive he has been the sole Director for a long time past, & am convinced with a deserv'd General applause'.[8] In fact, although Law's success was real, the applause was far from general. But Middleton, at this stage, had no doubts: John Law could do no wrong.

The year 1720 was to be the most disastrous one in the history of the Bank and a crucifying time for George Middleton. But in January, though he was stretched to his limits, he was still full of optimism and conscious of his growing importance: he was the London banker of the most powerful financier in Europe and was also acting as his goldsmith, his estate agent and the shipping contractor for his Mississippi company.

As a goldsmith he was selling diamonds for William and John Law. On 25 January 1720 he wrote to William:

I sent you by Mr Bruce four brilliant Diamonds which I think very good, they belong to a very particular friend of mine & must beg the favour, if you can, to get them dispos'd of to a good advantage; The price they expect is about £3000 Sterling.[9]

Top left: John Campbell's seal, with his initials interwoven

Top right and bottom: The Order of the Thistle, one of ten made at John Campbell's shop at the command of Queen Anne, who specifically asked that they should be designed by a Scottish goldsmith. It is wrought in gold with delicate pink and green enamelling.

Top: The Strand, mid-eighteenth century: one of the many processions which passed by the Bank during its long history

Bottom: An eighteenth-century jewellery workshop illustrated in Diderot's *Encyclopaedia.* Note the bench, with its semi-circular workplaces, and the glass globes filled with water, which concentrated light on the delicate work, and the leather bags for the precious parings.

Top left: The second Duke of Argyll, chief of the Campbell clan

Top right: Lord Ilay, brother of the second Duke of Argyll and later third Duke

Bottom: The south side of Edinburgh castle illustrated in John Slezer's *Theatrum Scotiae,* 1693

Top: Aberdeen in the late seventeenth century, from John Slezer's *Theatrum Scotiae*

Bottom: An advertisement in the London *Gazette* placed by John Campbell in June 1699

Top: George Middleton's receipt to John Law concerning the contract between Law and Lord Londonderry, 15 February 1719

Bottom: A display of eighteenth-century memorabilia including pewter inkwell and sandpot, folding coin scales, a duelling pistol, spectacles, coins and documents

Top: John Law – 'Beau Law' or 'Jessamy John' – the great Scottish financier who, for a brief period in 1719–20, controlled the French economy during the rule of the Regent

Bottom: John Slezer's 'Prospect of Montrose', 1678. Montrose was a smugglers' haven on the east coast of Scotland, where sympathies were strongly pro-Jacobite.

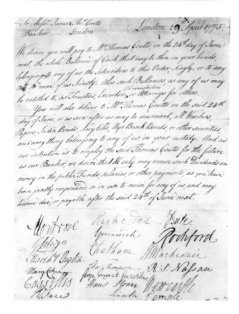

Top left: An engraving of Thomas Coutts after the painting by Sir William Beechey

Top right: A silhouette of Susannah Coutts, Thomas's first wife

Bottom: Document showing the transfer of accounts on the dissolution of the partnership between James and Thomas Coutts, 29 April 1775

Mary Peagrum, granddaughter of John Campbell, and her husband James Coutts. Their marriage in 1755 brought James into the Bank in the Strand.

He also took care of their silver, which was later to be used as security for loans.

His other responsibilities were many and various. He was still acting as paymaster to the Duke of Argyll's Regiment of Horse, to his brother, John Middleton's Regiment of Foot, to the Earl of Stair's Dragoons, to the Royal Regiment and to the Fourth Troop of Horseguards. He also supplied the garrisons of Dumbarton, Stirling and Edinburgh with equipment and acted as their paymaster.[10] He was an estate agent for John and William Law, arranging through Patrick Craufurd the purchase of the estate of Erroll 'on Mr Law's account. . . . I suppose it will be about £10,000 to be paid now.'[11] It is interesting to note that John Law was not only buying estates in France at this time but in Scotland too.

Another of his tasks was to contract for the building, stocking and engaging of the crew for two of the ships which were to take colonists to Louisiana and which John Law wanted to be constructed in England. This caused him constant worry. First of all there was the difficulty of getting the Government's permission for the ships to be built in England; then a captain was ill; and the crew in the ship at Gravesend mutinied, '& would not go except they allowed 40 shillings more than agreed'.[12] Middleton had to send a negotiator to increase their pay, since as he said, it was difficult to get sailors for these ships.

However, Middleton's greatest and most worrying responsibility was as the London banker and stockbroker for John and William Law.

At the beginning of 1720 he was so full of confidence that, infected by the Mississippi fever, he began speculating on his own account. On 4 January he wrote delightedly to Skene of the 'State of our Adventure in Mississippi with which I'm perfectly well pleased, & wish we had some few such Jobbs that would help to make us soon easy'.[13] But new to the game, he was still uncertain:

. . . had you stood in some days longer we should have made something more tho' I'm still of the old mind to secure some thing, & this has answered very well. Now Dr George as you are on the Spott & perhaps may get a hint from our friend, Act in our afair just as you think proper, for am perfectly easy in every thing you do as if it were myself. . . . As for the New regulation of dealing in the French Stock, tho' it makes some of our people here full of apprehensions, I really like it, & think it makes the Stock more secure, and easier dealing.[14]

In fact, ironically, Skene's clever speculation was part of a general movement of the sharper brokers who were beginning to realise their gains, rightly suspecting that John Law was at the height of his fame.

Middleton had followed Law's currency changes at the end of the year without completely understanding them. He had approved of Law's measures to restrict the conversion of gold and silver into bank notes, although, as he told William Law, 'the new method your affairs are put on alarms people here tho' some of the more thinking part do not dislike it. It certainly prevents all roguery of brokers.'[15] On 4 January he wrote to his Edinburgh friend, Peter Campbell, in Paris, 'your new regulation doesn't frighten me',[16] and hoped he would 'make the plumb in Mississippi'.[17] Thanks to Skene's skill he was delighted to inform William Law, 'Our friend the Major advises me of his selling our last adventure in Mississippi by which we clear very handsomely. ... I know I owe this new addition to the many friendly obligations you have laid on.'[18]

But Middleton was treading the speculators' primrose path, unaware of the proximity of the everlasting bonfire, for Skene was not the only one to be selling out. The 'roguery of brokers' intensified throughout January as speculators started cashing in on their gains and hoarding or exporting their gold.

In fact confidence, that magic that can make or break banks, was fast deserting John Law. Now he made a series of desperate bids to save his empire. In February Middleton heard that in a frantic attempt to stabilise the currency Law decided to join the Banque Royale to the Compagnie des Indes. 'It is very probable your Stocks should rise', Middleton wrote to Skene on 15 February, 'if the Bank is join'd to the Company, and if it does you may dispose of 10 Actions for me, which Mr Law will give you.'[19] This union which Law had hoped would crown his triumph was, in fact, to bring his whole empire crumbling down. When the company failed, the bank was dragged down with it.

From February to May Law passed a series of decrees, each of which was exceedingly unpopular: on 27 February purchases of jewellery and plate were made illegal; on 5 March the coinage was further depreciated; on 11 March he decreed that gold was to be withdrawn from the currency after 1 May and silver from August. The final blow came with a disastrous edict on 21 May, which declared that shares in the company were to be gradually reduced in value from 9,000 to 5,000 by 1 December.

For John Law, this was the beginning of the end. There was general consternation, riots in the streets and a run on the bank, which was forced to stop payment. The Regent had no alternative: he dismissed Law as Comptroller of Finance, though secretly he remained his friend and when, in July, Law's life was endangered by the fury of violent mobs, he gave him shelter in the Palais Royal.

Throughout this disastrous spring Middleton watched Law's collapse with increasing anxiety. Yet even then he trusted William's assurances that John would yet triumph over his enemies. In February he had worried about Law's credit, which, as he warned William, with other debts, 'all ... pinches me very much'.[20] He advised William to 'place a certain sum in

Specie both in this place & in Holland for a fund in order to check the fall at any time when 'tis like to come low, for were there 1 or £200,000 always ready on a pinch to supply the market it could not miss to keep it up'.[21] William must have received this piece of advice with a wry smile. In fact gold and silver were flooding out of France, exported by nervous speculators and John Law's enemies.

In February Middleton was caught in a new crisis. It was ironical that, as Law's fortunes in France slowly fell, the directors of the South Sea Company in Britain embarked on a roller-coaster of money madness that would sweep them to dizzy heights, only to crash in less than six months.

For the rest of the year George Middleton was buffeted between two of the greatest financial storms of the century.

Encouraged by the apparent ease with which John Law had conjured up a magic kingdom, unaware that its shining domes were as fragile as the paper of which they were made, the directors of the South Sea Company also hoped to spirit fortunes out of the air.

The South Sea Company and the Mississippi Company had similar origins and ran parallel courses, soaring to astronomical heights and crashing to similar disasters. Both were originally founded to fund the immense national debts England and France had accumulated during the war. The shareholders of both were lured by the dream of trading with a new world, which would bring them treasures of gold and silver. Both in England and France, mainly thanks to the great gambler, John Law, shareholders suddenly realised that there were quicker and greater fortunes to be made in speculation than in the tedious and dangerous business of overseas trading and colonisation. It was faster and easier to manipulate the markets than spades in foreign soil.

Though Middleton caught the French fever from his Scottish friends, he was careful to avoid too close a contact with the South Sea Company. But many of his customers were involved and it was impossible for him to steer completely clear.

The South Sea Company was promoted in 1711 by the Earl of Oxford and the Tory Government to fund the national debt of £10 million, which they had inherited from the Whigs and which had accumulated during the war with France. A group of merchants was to be granted the monopoly of trade with the South Seas in return for a loan to the Government, the interest on which was to come from the taxes raised on the import of tobacco and other goods. So the South Sea Company was formed; its shareholders were encouraged to believe that the King of Spain would grant free trade to four of their ports on the coasts of Peru, Chile and Mexico. In fact, the only concession the Government extracted from Philip of Spain was the right to send one ship a year to these ports, and a thirty-year contract to supply negroes to Spanish colonies.

The Company started slowly; by 1720 only one ship had sailed, but the dream still held that Peru and Mexico would yield their treasures of silver and gold in return for English woollens. On 2 February of that year, the Government, in an Act of Parliament, accepted the South Sea Company's new proposals for the redemption of the national debt, in spite of fierce competition from the Bank of England. At this time Mississippi mania was still at its height and speculators in Britain saw their chance of making quick fortunes on the back of the Company. 'Change Alley' now rivalled the Rue de Quincampoix. A ballad appeared on the streets called 'The Grand Elixir or Philosopher's Stone Discovered':

> Then stars and garters did appear
> Among the meaner rabble;
> To buy and sell, to see and hear
> The Jews and Gentiles squabble.
>
> The greatest ladies thither came
> And plied in chariots daily,
> Or pawned their jewels for a sum
> To venture in the Alley.[22]

The Company's stock rose daily, and other promoters joined, puffing up new bubbles. Some schemes were sensible, others patently fraudulent:

6. For effectively settling the island of Blanco and Sal Tartagus.
28. For insuring of horses. Capital, two millions.
32. For improving the art of making soap.
44. For improving the wrought-iron and steel manufactures of this kingdom. Capital, four millions.[23]

But the prize went to the ingenious promoter who collected a quick fortune in a day and disappeared. His scheme was for 'carrying on an undertaking for great advantage, but nobody to know what it is'.[24]

Alexander Pope described the corruption which,

>   like a general flood,
> Did deluge all; and avarice creeping on,
> Spread, like a low-born mist, and hid the sun.
> Statesmen and patriots plied alike the stocks,
> Peeress and butler shared alike the box;
> And judges jobbed, and bishops bit the town,
> And mighty dukes packed cards for half-a-crown:
> Britain was sunk in lucre's sordid charms.

Middleton had watched the progress of the South Sea Company with mixed feelings; as the shares soared he was tempted to dabble, but lacked courage. In February 1720 he reported to William Law that shares had risen to '175 & folks here talk of £200 how long it will keep I don't know but as I have not ventured winning thank God am clear of losing: it will demolish I doubt some people here'.[25]

Meanwhile, many of his customers were selling their valuables in order to invest. Even the Duke of Argyll and Lord Ilay, reluctant though they were to support the Company, could not resist the temptation to buy. Middleton was now having to act as a broker for his customers, but, unlike George Skene in Paris, he was a nervous speculator.

As the bubbles soared he often regretted his caution. 'I am so unlucky in my opinion of things,' he wrote to Colonel Campbell in Paris; 'Both you and I have been very unfortunate in selling out of the South Sea, it has risen prodigiously, is tonight at 182, all we can say, is to hope Mississippi will make amends.'[26] Middleton had some grounds for this optimism because of the news that John Law was about to join his bank to the Mississippi Company.

But Middleton's confidence was misplaced, for, as has been seen, the Mississippi Company was running into deep trouble and for a while its fortunes affected the South Sea Company. On 3 March Middleton warned Lord Ilay, who had gone secretly to Paris to confer with the Regent, 'the greatest alterations of the Species in France has made a terrible hurle here'.[27]

The roller-coaster dipped, South Sea shares fell from 180½ to 171 and the prestigious Sword Blade Company went under. It did recover and by May was soaring to 510, 'a monstrous price'[28] in Middleton's opinion, but he took advantage and sold Argyll's stock at a profit.

However, 'the madness is so great'[29] and risks 'prodigious'[30] that he was still determined to 'keep my hands clear and not be soon rich, run a chance of being soon reduced'.[31] When even William Law was tempted to buy into South Sea, he was

at a loss what to advise you and am afraid you'l suffer. The Governmt is certainly determined to give them all the assistance possible to raise their Credit but yet I think people mad to give such prices, and am doubtful we shall run it so high that will put it in the Forreigner's power to play on us when they please. . . . What to advise you I really cannot tell, am apt to believe they may run it higher, & yet think it impossible but in some time there must be a great fall.[32]

By June Middleton saw the South Sea Company heading the same way as the Mississippi in a Gadarene rush. 'I think the people running madder every day,' he reported to Argyll; 'they now talk of a new Subscription to be opened at 1200, how long all this will hold God knows, but am doubtfull [i.e. afraid] we shall soon run ourselves into the same difficulties France

45

now labours under.'[33] Yet even now, optimistic as always, he trusted that Law was every day getting the better of his enemies.

In fact, while South Sea shares rose to dizzy heights, John Law was becoming increasingly unpopular. By July even the trusting Middleton was worried by the violent attacks on him. 'We are alarm'd', he wrote anxiously to William, 'here with a report of a Tumult in Paris, & that they attack'd your Brother's coach. I shall be very glad to hear of its being quite over that he is preserved from the fury and rage of the ignorant people who, I doubt, are sett on by the Malicious & Envyous.'[34]

July was an appalling month for Middleton. The deadline of 25 August for Lord Londonderry's bargain was drawing uncomfortably near when he was going to need 'immense sums'. At the same time he was dealing for John Law, who that month bought £20,000 India stock, which Middleton put in William's name, since he thought that 'JL's name would cause alarm'.[35] He was under increasing pressure from all sides, dealing as Law's broker, selling diamonds on his behalf for nearly £5,000, and raising money on the silver which John Law had deposited with him.

At the same time he was being pressed for money by his British customers, who were still madly investing in the South Sea Company. As he wrote to Patrick Craufurd, he was undergoing 'constant hurry and fatigue'.[36] By August Middleton was 'put to all the corners of the saddle'.[37] He was beside himself with worry over the debt he would have to pay Lord Londonderry on Law's behalf, for the disastrous bargain Law had made in the autumn of the previous year. He had warned Law many times that the British Government would not allow the price of British East India stock to fall. On the contrary, as he expected, it was pushed higher. In July the rumour had been spread that there was 'some project to send India stock even higher'.[38] Middleton was assured that Lord Londonderry would not press him, but 'I do not know what hand to turn to if our friend does not fall on some speedy & sure way of supplying me,' he wrote to Skene. He was still confident that John Law 'would rather do anything than I should be ruin'd . . . [but] his own affairs makes him forget the present danger I'm in . . . that in my way of business if I'm not punctual my Credit is undone'.[39]

Desperate for money Middleton proposed to sell John Law's silver which he was holding. 'For', he told William, 'tho' I should sell all the silver in my hands there will still be near £150,000 wanting; that is upon my Engagements to him & the other Accots with your brother and you.'[40]

Once again he warned John Law that the British Government was forcing up the price of East India stock.

Battered between the South Sea and the Mississippi, Middleton wrote in anguish to Skene: 'Were I to get the Mississippi and the whole South

Sea, I would not be obliged to the same vexation and uneasiness of mind I have lain under for some months past.'[41] Yet, even at this stage, he still trusted in John and William Law, though he finished his letter to William in some apprehension:

I shall be uneasy till that affair is over, not but I'm perfectly convinced I'm secure. Please God your brother & you are well but in case of mortality 'tis a prodigious load more than I can bear & am terribly afraid there's still some project afoot to give that stock [i.e. the East India Company stock] a considerable rise.[42]

The rumours of such a project did indeed send up the price of the stock. In spite of Londonderry, who had been 'very serviceable in decrying and suppressing the stock as much as possible',[43] John Law lost his gamble and on 25 August Middleton had to find a huge sum to supply the difference between Law's initial estimate of the future price of East India stock and the high price it actually reached on that date. But by scraping together loans at high interest from money-lenders, Middleton managed to ward off immediate disaster and Lord Londonderry agreed to wait.

Even at this time there were no harsh words. He sent to William Law 'my sincere thanks for the care & concern you shew for me in London Derrys [sic] afair . . .',[44] and thought it 'very kind in you to allow the Major & me the highest Exchange in his Remitting & my drawing & wish it may be in our power to return the friendship & kindness you've always express'd'. Even now he refused to believe that John Law's star had fallen. 'I'm very glad', he told William, 'the reports that were whisper'd here prove groundless but in the manner I learn't that Storey from 2 different hands I assure you it frighted me as much on your & your B[rother's] Account as my own and thought it my Duty to let you be appris'd as soon as possible.'[45] He was generous in his praise of Lord Londonderry's efforts on his behalf in the East India Company affair:

I must own he has taken as much pains as ever I see any Body do for their own Interest, to depress the Price, & there was a confounded Clamour against him to day in the City, insinuating he was an Enemy to the Country by siding with your Brother to sink our Fonds.[46]

On 29 August he was glad to inform William that 'all the India afair is settled . . . shall send you the accot of the whole.'[47] The brothers still owed him a great deal, as he reminded them, when in September he sent his accounts. But the complexity of the Laws' affairs defeated him and for once his statement is distinctly confused:

To Wm Law   8th Sept 1720
Acct of Wm & John Law w.him
(Includes sale of his & John Law's silver)

Dr.	Cr
To Ball of you bro's acct.	By the ball of Particular Acct
£218,232 16 7	£7,259 14 5
	By 438 586 oz of
To Ball of yr Acct Currt	For. silver at
£7,000	5.6 oz £120,611 3 -
To Colebrook Ballance	By the Comp. des
£19,000	Indes £20,000
————————	————————
£244,232 16 7	£147,870 17 5
	Due to G.M.
	£ 96,361 19 2
	————————
	£244,232 16 7
Ball brt forward	
£96,361 19 2	The above silver
Ball due on £50000	is the 73000 ounces of
Ind.	yr brothers &
34,779 3 4	365586 oz remaining of yours
————————	————————
£131,141 2 6	438586
————————	————————

The bills drawn by him [Lord Londonderry] on me amounts to £218,232 16 7 which you'l find I have brot forward to the Accot of the £50,000 India of Gages & the Ballance upon the whole comes to £253,011 19 11.[48]

If it was difficult for Middleton to unravel the Laws' accounts then, it is certainly more so at this distance in time.

Middleton wrote in some confusion to them in September:

Ballance . . . due to me £96,361 and that with the further difference on the £50,000 makes in all £131,146 2 6 owing on this side I told you before all the silver was pledged & the most part for a very considerable time So there will be a large sum of interest to be charg'd on your brother & you when 'tis relieved . . . should think it in your interest to have it sold rather than be paying a running interest for 'tis very probable it may in some months be bought back at as easy a price besides if they make a demand on me for the money I can't avoid selling it.[49]

There was no respite for Middleton that August for, while he was struggling with John Law's affairs, the South Sea Bubble expanded to its impossible limit and burst. That August 'gamesters' throughout Europe were heading for inevitable disaster. Confidence was vanishing, the insubstantial world of the South Sea Company and John Law's empire were both fast disappearing. Stock in the South Sea Company had suddenly soared from 550 to 890 at the beginning of June, and the wiser speculators knew that it was time to get out. In addition, many nobles were about to leave for King George's summer visit to Hanover and decided to take their profits before they left. The result was an immediate fall. However, the directors managed to keep the price up until it reached 1,000 in August; at this stage the public suddenly realised that the chairman and directors had sold out. The bubble burst. As one Member of Parliament wrote, 'thousands of families will be reduced to beggary. The consternation is inexpressible – the rage beyond description.'[50]

As the months went by and South Sea stock crashed still further, 'a terrible press for money'[51] gave Middleton great anxiety. 'For God's sake,' he urged William Law, 'do what you can to put me in some cash for few people's credit is like to draw here.'[52] That September there was 'a terrible cloud in everyone's countenance',[53] but Middleton took comfort that he had not dabbled much in South Sea stock and since 'I had not the good fortune at the beginning I am thank God pretty free of the scrape at the end'.[54] But the fall made 'a terrible havock amongst our people here. So that this day four Goldsmiths of good credit [are] gone off & some more are suspected which makes a runn on all people of our Profession.'[55] Now even Middleton was beginning to panic. 'For God's sake order me some relief,' he begged William Law on 20 September. In London it was 'a melancholy scene ... everybody hurt and complaining'.[56]

'Five goldsmiths gone off I must beg ... you will not order any Body to draw on me,' he wrote in haste to William Law.[57] On 27 September he told the Duke of Argyll to take comfort that he had not lost too much to the South Sea crash:

I now think Your Grace has been very happy to have no concern there and in this miserable juncture 'tis no small comfort to me that since I did not venture at the beginning I'm thank God free of the load and destruction at the end, the beginning of this week five goldsmiths broke in one day & this day also the Sword Blade Company have stopt payment which makes terrible confusion here.[58]

The month ended with a headlong rush to ruin – 'two of the greatest Goldsmiths have stopt payment last night,' he hastily scribbled to Skene; 'South Sea is called at 140 – not a shilling to be borrowed'.[59] He had confidence that 'I have as yet, thank God, escaped very well'.[60] At the beginning of October he began to think the worst was over. He knew Peter Campbell was worried for him: '... may be expecting every post to hear of my being broke with the crowd, indeed I never expected to have had so fiery a trial. ... I believe I shall learn so much experience as always for the future to be in a condition to meet any storm on an hour's warning.'[61] But now he hoped the worst was over: South Sea stock must have reached its bottom at 140 and 'the rise will never be extravagant again'.[62]

Now, as always in a crisis, the cry was for gold. 'Send Gold directly from your place, for God's Sake order some from Holland without loss of time if you intend to save me at this juncture', he begged William Law on 3 October.[63] To Patrick Craufurd's son, Thomas, who was a banker in Paris, he gave instructions: 'Ld Ilay desires the favour you may convert the sum that I remitted, for him, into gold.'[64]

As they waited in England for the King's return from Hanover and the recall of Parliament, 'People of ranks & degree breaking every day,' Middleton wrote.[65] Still, as he wrote to Thomas Craufurd, he hoped that since he had 'as yet stood the Shock it would be very hard to give up at last',[66] and he instructed him to put 'some of those things you have for my Security into several Names that you can safely trust'.[67] Even now he wrote affectionately to William Law, thanking him for the 'kind concern you have always shewn to make me easy'. 'If by your assistance & friendship I can get the better of the storm, it would for ever establish my reputation.'[68] The storm was sweeping all Europe – 'the distress' was as great in Holland as it was in London. No one escaped; Lord Stair was 'much pinched' and all the Dalrymples hurt 'in the scramble'. On 21 November Middleton begged for William Law's help, for in five weeks' time John Law's bill of £15,000 on the money-lender, Joseph Rodrigues, was to come due and 'if I'm not supply'd before that time I can as well raise a million as that sum . . . for God's Sake take some effectual care of me that my Credit may not be ruined.'[69]

But John and William Law could take no care of Middleton; they could not even save themselves.

Throughout the cataclysmic autumn Middleton, beset on all sides, had battled to stay in business, knowing how great his prestige would be if he succeeded where so many of his fellow goldsmiths were failing. But so distressed had he been by the South Sea crash that he failed to notice how perilous John Law's situation was in Paris. In August confidence in Law had been fast disappearing, though the Regent supported him as best he could. An edict of 15 August 1720, by which all notes of 1,000 livres and upwards were to be cancelled by December, was almost the last straw. The disastrous failure of his gamble with Lord Londonderry had weakened his position still further. By September the idol of Paris was now its laughing-stock, a thief and a rogue. Ballad-mongers mocked:

> My shares which on Monday I bought
> Were worth millions on Tuesday I thought
> So on Wednesday I chose my abode
> In my carriage on Thursday I rode,
> To the ballroom on Friday I went
> To the workhouse next day I was sent.[70]

By November shares in Law's company were worth only 200. In December Law's enemies triumphed. The Regent closed the stock market, forbade assemblies, set up a commission to investigate speculators and declared travel without a passport to be illegal. On 13 December Law was exiled to his estate at Guernarche, but three days later his property was sequestrated and he escaped to Brussels with the connivance of the Regent. Katherine and William Law were left to deal with his debts and wind up his affairs.

'I have been obliged to Act, having stopt payment last Tuesday ... has come upon me like a ThunderClap,' Middleton wrote.[71] He now faced disaster: he had lost not only his own extensive investments in France, but he also had to carry the burden of the debts of John and William Law. And all this on top of the load of South Sea debts he was carrying for his customers.

On Christmas Eve 1720 Middleton gave up. His banking business closed and remained so until September 1723. However, he refused to run away, attending daily at his shop where he worked to redeem his honour and to collect the many debts due to him. 'Seeing no relief', he wrote to Lord Londonderry, 'I was seiz'd with a sort of despair. In the mean time I keep my shop open & give close attendance in it.'[72]

It was a black Christmas for Middleton. He was 'in a very melancholly state at present tho' as yet have met with all the friendship and humanity I could expect from my Creditors,'[73] but added, 'nobody has taken any Steps to arrest me as yet'.[74]

Day by day he sat in his office at the sign of the Three Crowns, writing apologetic letters to old customers, explaining that he now had stopped payment. Even his handwriting, usually so neat and controlled, became untidy. He appealed to Patrick Craufurd to pay his debts to him, but even with such a cloud of misfortune upon him he still wished his old friend a Happy New Year. He even wrote kindly to Lady Catherine Law in Paris, who could not have been more loyal if she had been John Law's legitimate wife. He thanked her for her concern and hoped that she would be able to clear Law's debts. 'Both of you have that generosity & justice to preserve me and a poor family from destruction and ruin.'[75] He hoped Lady Catherine would pay Mr Rodrigues, who was then in Paris, the £15,000 that Middleton had accepted for John Law. He had had nothing, he told her, from the Compagnie des Indes, which owed him £3,788 17s 5d.

The next months were spent painstakingly going through his accounts, constantly irritated by the French Commission of Enquiry, which pursued him almost until his death for information about John Law's accounts. These were so confused that Middleton despaired. William Law wanted his accounts separated from his brother's, but 'their accounts are so mixed', he complained, '& their irregular way of advising me that I'm at a loss v.

much how to settle them'.[76] In March he estimated that the Laws owed him £30,000, but the exact amount remains obscure. To Dr James Campbell in Paris, who was dealing with his affairs, he confessed, 'Betwixt you and I there's above £60,000 of this [John Law's balance]. . . . I'm not engaged for any ways but keep that to yourself.'[77] He was, it seems, covering for someone who was deeply involved with Law. Meanwhile, as the months went by, Law moved round Europe, presumably supporting himself in the old way at the gaming tables. Middleton heard rumours of his triumph in Brussels, of his success at the gaming tables in Venice and that, in January 1721, he had become a Roman citizen.

In May 1721 he learnt that Law had great funds at his disposal.* 'It will be very hard', he wrote crossly, 'if his creditors meet not with justice.'[79] He heard with distress that William Law had been imprisoned and Lady Catherine confined to her home, and wrote commiserating with them. The French Government had seized all of Law's papers, but that did not worry him for he was quite confident that he had 'set out Mr Law's account exactly as it stands with me'.[80] Dr Campbell was working on his behalf in Paris, trying to collect the money Law owed him, and, although he had had no success by June 1721, Middleton thanked him in a characteristic letter: 'I have a very great sense of the Service you have done me in so affectionate a manner & if nothing should ever be recovered I shall allways esteem the real friendship you have shewn in it.'[81]

So the summer of 1721 passed. Middleton was hoping to be able to pay his creditors at least 20 per cent. He sold John Law's silver, which had been deposited with him, but by August he claimed that Law still owed him £22,133 19s 11d.

By November he was sufficiently restored to be able to give good advice to Patrick Craufurd, who was allowing his 'spirits to sink with the difficultys you struggle with but . . . that's not the way. I have lately try'd that method & 'till I got the better of that dispiritedness I could never take a Right step.'[82] He was gradually getting clear of his debts and repaying his credi-

---

* It was calculated that Law's income at the time of his highest power was:

From the collection of the national revenue for the interest on 1,600,000,000 of the public debt	48,000,000 francs
Profits on farming the revenue	15,000,000
Profits on the general receipts	1,500,000
Profits on tobacco	2,000,000
Profits on coining the money	4,000,000
Profits from Commerce	10,000,000
Total	80,500,000

This income would have allowed a dividend of 5 per cent at most upon the actual capital of one billion six hundred and seventy-seven millions.[78]

tors: 'whatever money I have recovered of my own I immediately pay it to my Creditors which I must still continue to do 'till I am quite clear'.[83]

In all this trouble he never blamed others. 'Whatever the fate of the French paper may be,' he wrote to Law's agent in Paris, 'I'le no ways repine since it was my own Act, to take what I could have at that time, I have only to blame myself, for at first risquing so considerable a Sum, & for that folly I'm pretty severely punish'd, however there's no recalling whats past.'[84]

William Law was at last released from prison and Middleton hoped 'to see him here after the race we have both run'.[85] He was grateful to Lord Londonderry who was negotiating with the Regent in Paris, but wished 'to God he would take care of [the Jewish banker and money-lender] Mendez bills for that is a Curs'd load on me & neither of us can be easy 'till that weight is removed'.[86]

On one thing he was determined – not to begin again until 'I'm in a Condition of answering any demand that way upon an hour's warning. For I'le never venture another Stock upon any consideration whatsoever once were I fairly free of this.'[87] But he would never hope to get out of the 'labyrinth' until his friends paid their debts to him. So he continued, meticulously arranging his affairs, patient with his friends, but sharp with those who were unjust.

On 20 October 1721 John Law landed back in England, where he was met by the Duke of Argyll, who continued to support him, standing beside him when he pleaded at the Bar of the King's Bench for pardon for the manslaughter of Beau Wilson so many years before. Middleton too was as faithful and trusting a friend to John Law in his years of exile as he had been in his years of triumph.

Middleton was not alone in his distress: the directors of the South Sea Company and even some government ministers were in deep disgrace. On 9 December a Committee of Enquiry had been set up with powers to punish those who had caused a national disaster. Extensive fraud was discovered: the chairman and five directors were imprisoned. Even the Chancellor, Mr Aislabie, was sent to the Tower amid public rejoicing. It was a long time before the nation's confidence was fully restored. Sir Robert Walpole emerged from the disaster as the saviour of the nation. He had warned and been proved right. Parliament accepted his plan to engraft nine millions of South Sea stock into the Bank of England and the same sum into the East India Company. For the next twenty years Walpole guided Britain through an unprecedented period of peace and prosperity.

So, though now Middleton had a hard struggle until he renewed business on 5 September 1723, at least he had the backing and support of influential ministers in power. He was also comforted by the knowledge that because of his reputation for honest dealing, and the affection and trust he inspired, no one pressed him for money. In fact he had foundered, not because of his own fault, but because of the burden of other people's debts. Some of these were never paid and many of them were outstanding for years.

Dunning old friends for the money they owed him gave him acute embarrassment. Patrick Craufurd in particular needed constant prodding. 'I hope you will soon be making me remittances on your account without asking to be longer indulged. ... 'Tis almost three years since that has been the constant request,' he complained.[88] And again in the next month he repeated, 'your promises have been frequent, pray put them in execution'.[89] Sir Alexander Cumming of Aberdeen gave him even more trouble. With his customary kindliness, Middleton asked him to settle a huge debt of £3,396 11s 3d,

by which I should be enabled to get out of my present Labyrinth and established again in my Business. ... I'm therefore to beg dr [dear] Sir Alexr you'l be so kind & good to act with the same humanity, justice & friendship to me at so Critical a juncture as you would expect from me or any honest Man were our Cases the reversed, when you consider Sr your doing me justice at this time will set me again free in the world and enable me to regain my reputation.[90]

But Sir Alexander was deaf to his pleading and Middleton was reluctantly forced to ask his Aberdeen lawyer, Pat Duff, to start legal proceedings. It was 'not in my power to prevent coming to a rupture with him ... will give me greatest pain', for he had always had a great regard for Sir Alexander, but 'in justice to my own family and reputation' he felt bound to do so.[91]

Count Sennecterre needed more diplomatic handling. When French Ambassador in London, he had borrowed 'a pretty large sum'[92] from Middleton. For months he appealed to the Count without effect; finally the Duke of Argyll and Lord Ilay suggested that he should write to the British Ambassador in Madrid, Colonel Stanhope, asking 'if the money could be recovered it would relieve me of a good part of the load I ly under by Mr Law's affairs and by that retrieve in a good measure the Credit and reputation of an unfortunate person, who has nothing so much at heart as to satisfy in full his Creditors.'[93]

It also took the combined efforts of Argyll, Ilay and Stanhope to extricate a debt from the estate of a Mr Cancella, whose possessions had been confiscated by the Inquisition on the grounds that he was a Jew. Middleton had to send a certificate to Madrid to prove that Cancella had died a Roman Catholic.

Of all those who owed him money, none caused him greater or more constant distress than John and William Law. Yet it says much for John Law's charm and Middleton's trusting nature that he continued to believe that Law would be successful; he was still his friend and his banker. He saw Law frequently in London, but lost touch with William when he was in prison in France. But on his release in the spring of 1723 he wrote to say how overjoyed he was to hear from him after two years' silence, 'as nobody was more concerned or touched with the load of hardship put upon you than myself – so nobody was more over-joyed to hear of your being again at full liberty'.[94] However, he had to remind William of the bills drawn by him for William's account:

Two drawn by Your Self for	£ 4,776 10s
Sixteen drawn by Colebrooke for	£19,650
Eleven drawn by Skene	£20,500[95]

In June 1723, prompted by John Law, he wrote to William urging him to make up his differences with his brother. Understandably William had felt aggrieved because he had suffered in prison while John was at liberty. Middleton, ready as always to pour oil on troubled waters, wrote a long letter:

In some conversation I have had lately with your Brother I find him a little disoblig'd with you, which I believe proceeds in some measure from your writing him in a way or manner not altogether agreeable to him, Now I must tell you that ... one of the things he had much at heart was, whenever it should be possible to have the Incumbrance on the Estate of Erroll cleared, so that you might be in full possession & seem'd to have a very great desire to have you made easy. Now as he was by far the most valuable friend you possibly could have, and still express'd himself with much concern for you, 'till of very late, I humbly think you would do well to consider sedately, how far it may be proper for you to disoblige him, as well as how much the World will blame you ... he may yet be the best friend you can depend on. ... You will believe the drift of this is for my own interest ... but do assure you the chief aim is by friendly advice to prevent you going too far in disobliging one you who for your own interest ought to be well with.[96]

The stress of these disastrous years now began to affect Middleton's health and he took a cure at Bath under the guidance of his brother-in-law, Dr Cheyne. After that, as he told a friend, he 'hoped to begin the world again after a long course of penance'.[97]

Although, as he told Thomas Craufurd in Paris, 'I am now as it were beginning the world again',[98] he was still cautious. Two days later he told the Earl of Buchan that he was 'pretty much pinched at this juncture, being now endeavouring to re-establish my self again in my old way of credit by Clearing with every body I am owe money to'.[99] Because of his 'intire regard' for Buchan, he allowed him to draw on him for £150.[100] But to his brother, Colonel John, in Aberdeen on 10 September he confessed, 'all these matters make me half Craz'd'.[101] 'You may draw on me for £100,' Middleton continued, 'but on no pretence whatever exceed that sum.'[102]

He knew only too well the ease with which the jolly Colonel could get into debt. As he had written to Patrick Craufurd,

'till such time as I have discharg'd every Shilling I owe, no motive shall ever induce me to apply any money to any other use than for my Creditors, were it even to save my Brothers or nearest relations from a Goal. Now I must say had I been owing you money and you at same time in difficultys I would make a hundred shifts to have us'd you better than I think you have done me however I am unwilling to complain Any civility or Service I can shew your Wife you may depend on.[103]

He still hoped that John Law would return in triumph to France and would be able to pay all his debts, but any such hope was dashed in November 1723 by the sudden death of the Regent. William now wanted to return to England, but Middleton suggested he should stay on in Paris 'a little longer ... so that you can better battle with these difficulteys'.[104] In any case his 'dear friend' would find that 'another inconveniance I'm afrayd would attend your coming over' as the Laws' creditors would expect them to discharge their debts. John Law was 'very avarss to your leaving France until his & your affairs be settled'.[105] He assured William that John had 'retrench'd very much his Expence he being now in Private Lodgings without any equipage and one footman, and is resolved to continue in that way 'till ... he can satisfie his Creditors'.[106]

At the end of 1724 John was 'so pinched',[107] as he told Middleton, that he could not give William any help, advising him to stay in Paris, give up the house and sell the furniture, keeping 'any pictures or particular furniture you inclined to'.[108] The next year John lived quietly in London, making short expeditions to Aix and Cologne in 1725 and to Augsburg and Munich in 1726. Still befriended by Argyll, he was sent on some obscure diplomatic mission to Venice, where he lived with Catherine and their son until his death on 21 March 1729.

The long-suffering William's patience was eventually rewarded. He lived long enough to see, in 1735, his two sons Jean and Jacques, who were born in France and were therefore French citizens, declared heirs to Law's estates. Jean became a French general and Governor of Pondicherry, while Jacques was to be a marshal and peer of France. Later, as Military Governor of Genoa and Count of Lauriston, he was responsible for tranferring his uncle's remains when the church of San Giovanni was pulled down. The body of the dazzling Scot, whose Midas touch finally deserted him, now lies just inside the door of San Moisé.

George Middleton never recovered all that the Laws owed him, though he continued his patient efforts year after year. It says much for the character of John Law that Middleton never lost his admiration and affection for him and for his brother. After all they had gone through he could still, as he wrote to William, 'keep a lively and grateful resentment [sense] of your friendship . . . there is nothing in my power that I will not do for your service'.[109] Middleton was simple and trusting to the point of innocence, but he was no fool. His judgment of John and William Law must stand as a testament in their favour.

7

Middleton: Quiet Journey's End

The years of fiery trial left Middleton toughened but not embittered. He was cured for ever of the 'fever and itch to venture into Change Alley',[1] having learned the hard way that a banker should not be a stock-jobber. 'No prospect of advantage or saving should make me wade through the sea of difficultys and chagrin', he firmly declared to Patrick Craufurd.[2] Nothing in Middleton's remaining years would so test him. Slowly he began to build up his business again, winning back old customers, but cautious in the choice of new ones, which caused him to be accused of becoming too grand.

The experiences of these years had drawn him closer to the Duke of Argyll and to Lord Ilay, who, after his brother's death in 1743 became the third Duke. Through their influence Middleton had become more and more involved in the development of the Equivalent Company, which, as has been seen, in 1727 became the Royal Bank of Scotland with Lord Ilay as its first Governor.

Middleton was kept informed throughout the negotiations and was shown the first drafts of the Charter which established the Royal Bank.* During this time he frequently wrote to his friend in Edinburgh, Patrick Craufurd, successfully persuading him to become a director to strengthen the Argyll influence. He obviously enjoyed this secret diplomacy: 'take no notice of this', he often wrote to Craufurd. In other words, this is confidential.

Middleton's brother, Colonel John, also brought him into the circle of Lord Milton and other noble Scottish friends. Like Ilay, Milton held great power in Scotland. Andrew Fletcher, Lord Milton, was a lawyer, a Lord of Session and chief confidential adviser to the Duke of Argyll, who was at

---

* The coat of arms of the present Royal Bank of Scotland, granted in 1960, has at its base a blue and silver thistle representing Scotland, and a wavy line representing trading along the Firth of Forth.

The two demi lions also relate to the supporters of the arms of the House of Argyll because the Earl of Ilay was the first Governor. Above the shield there is the motto 'firm' from the armorials of the Earl of Stair, chief of the House of Dalrymple.

this time the effective ruler of Scotland. Milton sponsored schemes for the development of Scottish trade, encouraged the development of the linen industry and was a director of the Royal Bank of Scotland from 1727 to 1736.

An easy man, without pomp or affectation, he was obviously fond of the ebullient Colonel, recording a riotous journey when John rode down from Scotland singing and drinking all the way until his words were lost in a haze of alcohol. On his unexpected arrival at George's peaceful home in Twickenham, he was doubtless received with affection but with some impatience. Colonel John was often in debt; nevertheless, it was he who encouraged an important friendship between Middleton and Milton which would eventually provide a link with the remarkable Provost of Edinburgh, John Coutts.

George's wife 'Honey' enjoyed her visits to Lord Milton in Edinburgh in 1727 and 1737, dancing at the balls with surprising sprightliness for a grandmother, as her husband affectionately remarked. In return the Middletons looked after Milton's sons during their holidays from Eton. George was now able to entertain his noble guests in some style either at his comfortable home and estate at Twickenham, or at Caenwood (Kenwood), the idyllic mansion on Hampstead Heath, which he managed for Ilay and his brother-in-law, Lord Bute.*

Through all the trying years since John Campbell's death in 1712 Middleton had managed the business alone. But in 1727 he took in Campbell's son, George, as his partner; and then looking to his own family for successors he introduced his nephew, David Bruce, as a clerk in January 1734 and made him a partner on 30 September 1740. Neither was to leave much mark on the history of the Bank.

When the lease of Campbell's goldsmith's shop had expired in 1719, Middleton had moved across the Strand to the corner of Lancaster Court and remained there for twenty years. In 1739, as his business was expanding, he moved to larger and grander premises. Now he took the lease of 59 Strand, the central and most impressive unit of a new row of eleven shops and houses. Because of the steep slope to the river there were two basements, the lower one having three vaults and the stairway to Durham Yard. The Bank's address in future years was often 'next to Durham Yard'. The other basement under the Strand pavement had two vaults for coal, with a double-seater 'bog house'[3] next door. Above were the kitchen, pantry, wash-house and scullery, and a panelled back parlour and wine store.

* Lord Bute had bought the house in 1715. He kept it until 1720, when he sold it to William Dale, an upholsterer who had made a fortune in the South Sea Bubble, lost it and mortgaged the house to Lord Ilay, who foreclosed in 1724. Ilay kept Kenwood until 1746, when he sold it to his nephew Lord Bute, who in turn sold it to Lord Mansfield in 1754.

Iron steps led up to the shop door, but the private entrance on the left was grander, with three steps of Portland stone leading to the fanlighted front door, which opened to a panelled hall and central staircase up to the private apartments where Middleton lived with his family. In front a panelled sitting-room looked to the Strand. It was a handsome room lit by three full-length windows with a marble fireplace and carved mirrors. Behind it were two smaller rooms and a water-closet.

On the attic storey above were four bedrooms and a closet; higher still on the garret floor, there were four more bedrooms for servants or for the clerks who lived in.

The banking business had previously been carried on in a goldsmith's shop. The new premises were, for the first time, designed for banking, with a counter separated from the counting-house or offices; behind this were the strongrooms secured by heavy iron doors. However, 59 Strand was still always 'The Shop' and the clients were always 'customers', and so they have remained.

On 10 October 1739 Middleton and his partners dined in the new house, but they were still settling in to their offices on 1 January 1740 when a clerk complained that 'removing to a new house put our books in some disorder'.[4]

Middleton had not long to enjoy his fine, new premises; the many years of stress had left their mark and in his last years he was often in Bath under the care of his brother-in-law, Dr Cheyne, who again and again advised him to give up business. But with his old Aberdeen grit he struggled on, although slowly he was losing his grip on the Bank in the Strand, which was now left mainly in the hands of George Campbell, David Bruce and the clerks, George Innes, George Brassey and Peter Jackson.

For many years Innes had taken increasing responsibility for the running of the Bank, especially when Middleton, battling against ill-health, spent months at Bath taking the waters. 'George Innes will return to you my letters as if wrote by myself,' Middleton wrote from Bath in July 1723. And again, 'George Innes wrote you the 22 past which I approve of, as well as all the other letters he wrote you in my absence.'[5]

George Brassey and John Mudie succeeded Innes, and in January 1748 were living in the rooms over 'The Shop'. We know little of either of them, but we must assume that both were competent and reliable. Brassey, who joined in 1745 with a salary of £30 a year, was by 1760 receiving £150 per annum with board wages. In 1745 Jackson received £20 per year.

In John Campbell's day clerks and apprentices had often been treated as servants, even though they were usually well educated, especially if they came from Scotland. At the end of George Middleton's life, clerks like Innes and Brassey were taking on more responsibility, dealing not only with the business of a goldsmith's shop but also with banking. They acted as witnesses when legal documents were signed and were remembered in the partners' wills. David Bruce left Brassey £10 and George Campbell, more generous, left £20 to his clerk if living with him at the time of his death.

There was much sadness in Middleton's last years, with so many old friends gone. The Laws were dead, but he could not forget them. He never did recover the money they owed him, although he acquired the estate of Errol which John Law had passed to William. In 1743 he heard of the death of the second Duke of Argyll, who had backed him through so many crises, and in July 1746 he was devastated by the death of his much loved daughter, Elizabeth. In the darkening days of September he made his will.

Once again he retired to Bath, where he lingered on, still trying to keep up with the news from the Strand until his doctors wrote that he must not 'be troubled with any sort of business'.[6]

In 1745 news of the new Jacobite rebellion under Bonnie Prince Charlie came muffled to his sick-room. He was worried by the news of the run on London banks and was anxious about Lord Milton and his friends in Edinburgh, but at least now he had no Jacobite kin to cause him distress.

In his last lingering months there was much to remember and much to impress upon his successors. Again and again he emphasised the importance of keeping funds at hand for emergencies. He had learned the hard way that in the new world of finance, bankers should not indulge in risky speculations, nor dissipate their energies in too many different concerns. He had long since ceased to be a goldsmith, stockbroker and merchant. When a relation asked him to arrange the import of a consignment of sugar, he agreed, but only as an exceptional favour.

Over the years he had learned to be selective as he could not afford to take impecunious peers as customers. The Earl of Orkney had been offended that Middleton had not leapt at the chance of getting his custom.

Patrick Craufurd's son, Patrick, had been even more hurt when Middleton had refused to accept him as a son-in-law until the family debts had been cleared. He had had enough trouble with both Patrick and his son Thomas, and he did not intend his beloved daughter, Elizabeth, to start married life with a burden of Craufurd debts. The marriage had eventually taken place in 1731 and Elizabeth bore two sons, John and James, who were later to appear in the history of the Bank. Perhaps because of Lord Milton's influence, the two boys were sent to Eton, where John acquired the nickname 'Fish', by which he was known all his life. So began the long connection between the Bank in the Strand and Eton.

Middleton's second daughter, Margaret (or Peggy), who was obviously at ease with her father's noble friends, was to marry in 1768, after George's death, John Dalrymple, who became the fifth Earl of Stair in 1748. He took a great interest in his father-in-law's Bank, as will be seen later. Margaret, Countess of Stair, like her grandmother, lived long. She died in 1798.

Middleton could reflect with satisfaction that he had redeemed and enhanced the reputation of the Bank in the Strand and had become the counsellor and friend of the most influential men in the kingdom. He could be especially proud that he had helped to establish and sustain the link with the Royal Bank of Scotland. When the directors in Edinburgh were in difficulty during the '45 rebellion, they sent to him for gold. The cashier of the Royal Bank recorded:

Ordered. That the Cashier write to Mr Middleton to give notice when any ship of war is to sail from London to this Frith that the Bank may that way procure a remittance of Gold and Silver: and recommended to Mr Coutts to write to his friends at Newcastle and Berwick to try what specie can be got at either of these places.[7]

But he would never know the value of his latest legacy. One of the most influential directors of the Royal Bank in Edinburgh, from 1742 to 1750, was the ex-Provost John Coutts. Through their mutual friends, Lord Milton and the third Duke of Argyll, a link was forged between the bank founded by John Campbell, London goldsmith, and the family of John Coutts, Edinburgh merchant.

On 28 November 1746 the directors of the Royal Bank recorded:

Ordered. That the Cashier do write to Messrs. Geo Middleton & Co. Bankers in London that he send them specimens of the Twenty shillings Notes of this Bank, and desire of them to employ a skillfull person to engrave four Plates for these Notes: and to transmitt to him specimens of the new Plates to be approven of before the Plates are finished.[8]

The twenty shilling notes of the Royal Bank of Scotland were engraved by the craftsmen engaged by Middleton's bank. The cashier of the Royal Bank in Edinburgh reported:

The Cashier having laid before the Court a Letter from Messrs. Campbell & Bruce, Bankers in London, acquainting him that Mr. Bickham has engraved and prepared four Plates for the Twenty shillings Notes of the Bank; and that they had transmitted specimens of these Notes which were likewise laid before the Directors; whereupon he was Ordered to write to these Gentlemen to send down the Plates by the Carriers; carefully packt up and Sealed.[9]

But when on 27 February 1747 the directors in Edinburgh received the notification that the notes were ready, the letter came not from George Middleton but from Messrs Campbell and Bruce, his successors. For in January, Middleton had ended his last fiery trial.

After her husband's death Mary Middleton, who seems to have won the affection of all, still ran their home at Twickenham, consoling herself with her grandchildren, John and James Craufurd. She lived until December 1764.

Middleton left 'The Shop' to George Campbell and David Bruce, and also bequeathed to them rooms 'necessary for business'. But under their direction the Bank gradually deteriorated. Bruce suffered from an eye disease and was frequently ill. By May 1751 he was 'not able to see to write his name . . . and mends very slowly if at all'. In June he died, leaving 'his half share of the estates bought with his partner George Campbell in Hertford to be sold, first refusal to George Campbell and of that money half to go to George Bruce, his brother, and half to his sisters Anne and Christian.'[10] Apart from these scant details, David Bruce is a shadow.

George Campbell is almost as insubstantial. He was obviously a good fellow, much liked by the customers, but was not a businessman. Few of his personal accounts have survived, and those that have are roughly set out. It would seem that he lived fairly simply at Colehearne House, Earls Court. The height of his extravagance seems to have been playhouse tickets at two guineas in 1752, a weather glass and spectacles at £3 11s od, breeches for William at 15s 9d, one guinea for the peruke maker and modest bills at the wigmaker, hatter and shoemaker, though his bill for wines in 1755 of £51 15s 6d compared with his 'cloathing expenses of £21 10s od'[11] suggests that he had some indulgences. And his fling on lottery tickets brought him £101 10s od.

In the years when George Campbell ran the Bank alone the business greatly suffered, probably as a result of the death of George Middleton, and in 1747 the Bank was even running at a loss.

Middleton's widow, Mary, and her brother, George, now inherited their father, John Campbell's, estate and George invited Mary to invest her share of their father's bequest in the business. The difference between the articulate George Middleton and George Campbell is illustrated by the somewhat confused proposal he sent to Mary:

Proposalls for securing the Buisness [sic] of Mr C-----lls House in the hands of his own and Mrs M-------n's Relations

Mrs M------- to vest her £10,000 in the House with the like Sum of Mr C----- makeing a Capital of £20,000

The Buissness of the House afterwards to be carried on the Name of G C[amp-be]ll and Company. (As the like is now done in the Houses of Child & Backwells, at Temple Barr, and Ironside & Belcher in Lombard Street, to answer the same End that this proposal is Intended). As it is Intended That Mrs M[iddleto]n shall be at no trouble in carrying on the Buisness of the House, nor at any Charge or Expence attending the same, nor her Capital to be anyways liable to any loss that may happen to the house from Bad Debts or otherwise, but the whole Trouble, Expence, & Loss to be bourn by the said G C-----ll & his share made lyable for the same & to Indempnify Mrs M-------n therefrom. Mrs M-------n only to draw out from the house £400 yearly as Interest for her £10,000 at 4 p Cent.

To continue for about 7 years if both live so long.[12]

Mary replied with her customary shrewd common sense:

Jany ye 27 1754

Dear Brother

I have considered on your proposall which is a very kind one, & I thank you much for it, but I am more inclined to take the morgage on Ld Selkirk estate, Mr Middleton chose always to lay out his money on morgageys & I think I cant do better than follow his example, if you live Bro: the business of the house I dout not but will be very secure to whom you please, & if you should dy, you well know how utterly uncappable I am of doing anything towards it.

I should be very glad if you & Mr Craufurd would see Ld Selkirk as soon as you can to let him know of it, I think of going to Bath in three or four day unless you should think my staying in towne necessary, I shall send in to towne a tuesday when I hope you will so good as to let me have a line from you

I am Dear Bro, ever yours
M Middleton[13]

Lord Selkirk was therefore in her debt and in 1762 wrote to her:

Edinburgh the 10th March
1762

Madam

I send you inclosed a bill for four hundred pound drawn by Mr John Gordon on Mr Thomas Fuller Mert. London and indorsed by me to you: it is at six days sight. It was with difficulty I could get it at so short a date & the exchange is at a most extravagant rate.

Be so good as send me the Discharge of Interest for the above sum.

I received yours of the 11th of february & would have answered it directly but that I waited till I could send the Interest due. I am obliged to you for saying you will not desire any thing more formal than my last letter for the additional Interest I am to pay you for the future. I shall therefore look on it as equally binding as if it had been a formal obligation.

I am Madam your most obedt Servt.
Selkirk[14]

It is interesting to see that, at the end of his life, Middleton was putting his faith in mortgages and land, not in stocks and shares.

In his eventful life George Middleton had learned the hard way principles which are as relevant to banking today as they were in his time. He had come to know, as Adolphe Thiers wrote, the danger of 'Credit which anticipates the future, by employing values yet to be produced and using them as already existing. . . .' And that 'it is well founded confidence, based on the real success of labour, slow in its progress, which alone is exempt from these sudden reverses which resemble tempests'.[15]

Part 2

1750–1837

8

Provost John Coutts of Edinburgh

It was not until 1755 that the name Coutts appears in the title of the bank founded by John Campbell. In that year James Coutts, great-grandson of Provost Coutts of Montrose, married John Campbell's granddaughter, Polly Peagrum, and became a partner in the business.

The London bank had survived through a period of unprecedented economic turmoil, but in the last years of Middleton's life, and even more under his successors David Bruce and George Campbell, it was, in the words of a later partner, Edward Marjoribanks, going downhill. The Coutts family was to bring new life, wealth and business expertise to restore its flagging fortune. The credit for the revival and lasting success of the Bank in the Strand has always rightly gone to James and Thomas Coutts, but in fact it was their remarkable father, John Coutts, who inspired them and who played his part in the early history of the bank.

As a director of the Royal Bank of Scotland he had corresponded with Middleton and the Bank in the Strand, and that business relationship led to the union of the families through his son, James. And Thomas Coutts was, throughout his life, driven by the desire to honour and perpetuate his father's name.

John Coutts was the son of Patrick Coutts, who, it will be remembered, left Montrose to become a successful merchant in Edinburgh, while his brother, Thomas, went to make his fortune in London. Patrick had a wide-ranging business, which he conducted with exceptional competence. His records astonished William Forbes, a later apprentice who became a distinguished banker and whose *Memoirs of a Banking House* is a valuable source of information about this period. According to Forbes, Patrick's books were very neatly and distinctly written and 'carried accounts of mercantile adventures to New York, Pennsylvania, to Amsterdam, to France and to the Canaries'.[1]

Patrick married twice: by his first wife he had three children, John, James and a daughter, Christian; by his second wife, Rachel Balfour, he had a daughter, Janet. John's mother was, according to Forbes, 'a daughter of the family of Dunlop of Garnkirk, in the county of Lanark. This relationship gave rise to the intimate correspondence which always subsisted between the Messrs Coutts and the Messrs Dunlop and their connections in Glasgow.'[2] Patrick died in 1704 leaving £2,500 (Scots pounds), a considerable sum in those days, to his three children, and in 1705 the two boys were sent to their uncle, Provost James Coutts, in Montrose to receive an excellent education at the local school. Montrose was famous for producing men of ability, and John was sufficiently grateful to present a collection of books to the school on leaving.

But Montrose gave him more than book learning. His formative years were spent in a family with a long tradition of public service. Listening, as the Provost and his friends talked over their pipes and brandy, he absorbed an understanding of local government. His relations and their fellow councillors dominated the life of the town. They fined wrongdoers, made sure malt supplies were adequate and sent to Holland for advice on the construction of their new windmill for quality corn. At '4 hours in ye morning',[3] they sent out drummers to waken the town and ordered the great bell, 'Big Peter', to ring the curfew at ten o'clock. However, they were not merely parish pump councillors, but looked outwards to the wider world.

Over his uncle's garden wall John could watch the great ships sailing out over the horizon, bound for the Baltic, Africa or America. He must have played in the barns heavy with the smell of tobacco, brandy, grain, chocolate and spices, and among the casks and sacks absorbed the atmosphere of trade with distant lands. He could also not have been brought up in Montrose without learning a great deal of the danger and excitement of Jacobite intrigue. Here, as in the rest of Scotland, religious conflict added tension to political feuds. Government supporters worshipped at the Episcopalian Church, while Catholics prayed elsewhere for the return of the Jacobites.

When he left Montrose in 1723 to settle in Edinburgh, John already had an understanding of local government, so it is not surprising that on 23 September 1730 he was the first merchant to become a town councillor. In the next year he was made a bailie of the City of Edinburgh and on 5 October 1742 he reached the pinnacle of power in the council chamber: he was elected Lord Provost, holding the office with great distinction until 2 October 1744.

John carried on the business at which his father, Patrick, had been so successful, buying and selling goods on commission and presumably using his father's connections overseas. He inherited more than the expertise of a merchant, because his father had been involved in banking in its earliest days: Patrick Coutts appears in the ledger of the new Bank of Scotland as a subscriber of £4,000 (Scots pounds).

John continued in his father's tradition, conducting a dual business as a merchant and as an early banker with wide experience of foreign exchange. According to Forbes, 'There were no country banks and consequently the bills for the exports and imports of Perth, Dundee, Montrose, Aberdeen and other trading towns in Scotland with Holland, France and other countries, were negotiated at Edinburgh.'[4] Much of John's business was in negotiating bills of exchange and in dealing with foreign currencies, and it is rightly said that 'the first house to be firmly identified as private bankers was that of John Coutts and Company of Edinburgh'.[5]

Just as Patrick and Thomas Coutts had corresponding offices in Edinburgh and London, so John's own brother, James, settled in London. It was because the brothers had offices in both Edinburgh and London that 'they gained the right to transmit the proceeds of the Scottish excise to London'.[6] This was a lucrative business, which, combined with his income from his flourishing mercantile concern in London, made James a very wealthy man. When he died in 1740 he left John the considerable fortune of £20,000.

In 1730 John Coutts had married Jean Stuart, sister of Sir John Stuart of Allanbank in Berwickshire. By her he had four sons and a daughter, Patrick, John, James, Thomas and Margaret. His wife died in 1736, a year after Thomas's birth. Years later Thomas was to write that his mother

died in child bed of a son younger (one year) than Thomas who also died, and it was supposed that both mother and child died in consequence of a fall from her horse though there was no apprehension of this sad calamity till it happened.[7]

The stern Scottish code did not allow extravagant mourning. 'Nothing sunor ruins your health than immodest grief,'[8] his great-aunt had written to Provost John on his wife's death. Young Thomas kept the letter and remembered the advice all his life.

The children were cared for by loving aunts, spending holidays in Montrose and at their mother's home at Allanbank. Jean's family brought in a host of powerful relations, Marjoribanks, Trotter, Buchan, Elliot and many others. The day would come when the last of the Stuarts, the Cardinal Duke of York, would claim kinship with the Provost's son, Thomas, through his mother's family. The relationship was unproved, but Thomas certainly believed it.

When John Coutts became Lord Provost he was not only a man of high repute in his own right, but, as a merchant in Edinburgh, he belonged to the most powerful group in the city. Here the social grades were firmly established: the nobility were at the top, below them came the merchants, then the surgeons and then the goldsmiths. John's sons were to carry this sense of 'each man in his station' throughout their lives. It was a peculiarly Scottish attitude, combining a belief in each man's dignity with a firm regard for rank and order. So from childhood, Thomas Coutts and his brothers had a deep sense of pride in their family with its long history of civic responsibility and mercantile success.

When John was elected Lord Provost his family were still young. Thomas was only seven, but he surely would never have forgotten his father's inauguration on 1 November. Did Thomas and his brothers watch their handsome father, splendid in scarlet and ermine, walk in procession led by halberdiers from their council chamber in the old Tolbooth to the High Kirk of St Giles? Were they also rigged out in finery to watch the oath-taking ceremony there? We do not know, but one thing is certain: a large party would have enjoyed the hospitality of the generous and convivial new Lord Provost.

John was certainly famous for his hospitality. According to Forbes, he was the first Lord Provost of Edinburgh to entertain visitors to the city in his own home. At his own expense, he invited his fellow councillors to hold their Tuesday meetings in his sitting-room. The boys were therefore brought up in a sociable household, accustomed to hearing talk of politics, civic affairs and business, and listening to the conversation of some of Edinburgh's most brilliant men.

The Provost also frequently entertained men of political power at his house. Remembering the Jacobite taint that touched his Montrose relations, he was always careful to keep on good terms with George II's ministers in Scotland, of whom the most influential were Lord Ilay and Lord Milton.

Andrew Fletcher, Lord Milton, as Lord Justice Clerk, Keeper of the Signet, had most of the patronage of Scotland in his gift. He was also, it will be remembered, the personal friend of George and John Middleton. It may well have been through Lord Milton that John Coutts established a connection with the Bank in the Strand.

They had much in common: both were passionately concerned to revive trade in Scotland and both were particularly interested in the linen industry. Milton had been inspired by his mother, a remarkable woman, who had secretly gone to Holland, taking weavers with her to learn the Dutch technique of making fine linen and had, on her return, set up mills in her town, Saltoun. Both Milton and John Coutts held stock in the British Linen Company – Milton of £1,500 and John Coutts of £750.[9] This company was later to become Scotland's third public bank.

John Coutts and Milton were also both involved with the affairs of Scotland's second public bank, the Royal Bank of Scotland, which, as has been seen, was dominated by Lord Ilay. In 1742 John was appointed a director and remained one until his death. Thus, he was connected with Scottish banking, industry and politics at the highest level.

From childhood, therefore, Patrick, John, James and Thomas Coutts were accustomed to seeing their father at his ease with the greatest nobles in Scotland.

Thomas was to remember later in life that he and his brothers were 'bred up very expensively by my father, more than any of us ever did since'.[10] The family lived in some style in an apartment on the second floor of a tall building on the President's Stairs, with some of Edinburgh's most distinguished citizens as neighbours. The Dalrymples, of the family of the Earl of Stair, had an apartment above them.

Throughout Thomas's life the memory of his father was engraved in gold on his heart and mind. He later proudly wrote to King George III:

I had the impression of integrity and honesty made on my mind at a very early period by the best of fathers, and I learnt by his powerful example as well as by his precept that Honour and Character were the first acquirements to be desired in the World and that fortune should be considered as the last, or rather as a thing which would follow to the full extent of all that is useful or desirable in the train of common prudence and good conduct. ... If I had fifty sons I would impress the same upon them by every means in my power. My Family, both by my father and my mother, have been remarkable for an uncommon degree of sensibility, overflowing with gratitude and feeling for kindnesses received.[11]

His pride in family and sensitivity of heart were both to be wounded in the coming years. His father was at the height of his fame as Lord Provost when, in May 1743, Thomas's eight-year-old sister, Margaret, died. There were only ten months between them, and the death of 'dear little Peggy' must have shaken him. On his eighty-third birthday, 18 September 1818, he was to write to his daughter:

This is the birthday of one Thomas Coutts a banker in London. He was the youngest son of a very distinguished man, John Coutts formerly Lord Provost of the city of Edinburgh, who was universally and deservedly beloved by all ranks of men in Scotland, but died at Nola near Naples in the fiftieth year of his age having been born in 1700. [According to Forbes, John Coutts was born on 28 July 1699.] He had besides Thomas, three sons and one daughter all now dead. The daughter was a most beautiful and amiable young woman and died in her father's life time, which had almost been his death: he was so fond of her that he always said he would have had all his sons die rather than lose his daughter.[12]

In old age, in his mind the dead girl of his youth had become a woman over the years.

When Thomas was ten the events of 1745 were to shake not only his family, but the whole of Scotland. Bonnie Prince Charlie landed in the Highlands with seven followers, raised his banner, gathered an army and swept across the country. It soon became clear that this was a Jacobite rebellion to be taken seriously, led this time not by the sickly, hesitant James, but by the handsome, brave and enthusiastic Charles Edward, who aroused passionate emotions. Bonnie Prince Charlie was the stuff from which dreams are made.

Already in August 1745 rumours were growing of an imminent French invasion. Archibald Stuart wrote to Lord Minto that 'the noise . . . about a rebellion has frightened everybody from parting with money. As they suspect there may happen to be a run on the banks, which must infallibly distress everybody in this poor country.'[13] These were dangerous days and Jacobite sympathisers learnt to conceal their feelings.

The rumours had been carefully spread by Jacobite agents in order to divert attention from the landing of Prince Charles in western Scotland with his small band of seven. Throughout the glens hundreds of High-landers flocked to his banner. Alarmed, John Coutts and other directors of the Royal Bank met on 10 September and decided to draw £2,000 in gold from the Bank of England to be made payable to John Coutts at Newcastle, within easy reach of Allanbank, home of his wife's relations. This and subsequent transactions were made through George Middleton's bank in London. The Royal Bank directors were clearly expecting a run on London banks.

By September the Highland army, now over one thousand strong, had reached Falkirk and Stirling, and Edinburgh was threatened. Provost John's term of office had ended in 1744, so that it was his kinsman Archibald Stuart who was the chief citizen when, in September, Prince Charles camped outside the city. But, as a director of the Royal Bank of Scotland and a distinguished citizen, John was deeply involved in the events of the following months.

John Coutts was doubly at risk. Archibald Stuart was his wife's kinsman and was suspected of having Jacobite sympathies, and his own relations in Montrose were equally distrusted. During his period as Lord Provost he had been careful to keep good relations with the Whig Government, but during the '45 rebellion he was torn between his Whig masters and his Jacobite relations. As a director of the Royal Bank of Scotland, which had been dominated by Argyll, Ilay and the Whig Government from the beginning, his duty was to protect its treasure from Prince Charles and the rebels. But his sympathy was mostly for the Jacobites. The other public Scottish bank, the Bank of Scotland, or 'the old bank' as it was called, certainly was sympathetic to Prince Charles, and Jacobite clans like the Drummonds were its customers and directors.

On 14 September John Campbell, the chief cashier, met with John Coutts and other directors and recorded that, on information that the Highland army is on their march towards the city, the directors ... judging that in this exigency it is not proper to let the same remain in the office as it is not a place of strength to hold out against an attack, or any insult; and having got notice that the old bank having this evening conveyed their valuable effects to the castle of Edinburgh and lodged them in Major Robertson's house, they passed the following resolution: that the whole gold and silver coin, bank notes struck and unstruck, together with all the old banknotes now on hand, as also the books belonging to and in the several offices, and in general everything that may be of any value or real use be forthwith packed up in boxes and immediately transported to the castle of Edinburgh, and lodged in the place viewed some days ago.[14]

The officers and servants of the Royal Bank, watched by the directors, packed up their coin and notes, marked every box and, 'attended by bank officers, carried them off to the carts upon the street'.[15] An iron chest containing £14,000 in gold and six boxes each holding £1,000 in silver and a parcel of bank notes amounting to £47,600 were taken up to the castle. Various other chests were packed with banknotes and gold and the official papers of the Royal Bank. When they had made a careful inventory, John Coutts and the exhausted directors and clerks returned home to pack up their own valuables. Since John later took his books and papers to his relations at Allanbank, it is most probable that he took his sons there too. Montrose would have been too dangerous, since both French ships, bringing aid to the Jacobites, and government ships with Hanoverian troops were expected to land there.

The chief cashier, John Campbell, was a remarkable man and his diary, *Leaves from the Diary of an Edinburgh Banker*, is an intriguing record of the next month. As a Campbell and an employee of the Whig bank he ought to have been an anti-Jacobite, but in fact during the next weeks he was obviously collaborating with Prince Charles's supporters. Even the loyal Lord Milton, Lord Justice Clerk, kept his head down. Meeting John Campbell in the street on 16 September he asked him for £100 to be left with his lady 'with whom he was to leave a draft on his cash account for the value' and then disappeared.[16] 'The Town in a Consternation all day. ... Deputation of the magistracy sent out to Bellsmiths to capitulate with the Prince as to the surrender of the town; without effect.'[17] It is said that John Coutts was one of the delegation.

On 17 September Prince Charles and 1,000 Highlanders marched into Edinburgh to general consternation. John Campbell, whose sympathy was now clearly with the rebels, watched the government troops scuttle away, with some amusement. The Prince established his court at Holyrood House, while his secretary, John Murray of Broughton, settled at the Abbey. But at the other end of the town, government troops held out in the castle under General Guest and were never dislodged. The Highlanders thronged through the city and triumphant proclamations were read out at Edinburgh Cross. John Coutts and most of the directors of the Royal Bank had left Edinburgh, so it was John Campbell who now took charge. Coutts had gone to Allanbank, leaving his key to the Bank's boxes in the castle with his partner, Archibald Trotter.

On 21 September Prince Charles and his Highlanders soundly defeated the government troops at Prestonpans outside Edinburgh and heartened his supporters in the town. The lads brought out their white cockades, and the Jacobite ladies wore white flowers in their hair and danced at a celebration ball.

Many of the city fathers were prepared to meet with Prince Charles. The Lord Provost, Archibald Stuart, was later to be accused of aiding the rebels, and John Coutts was also suspected. John Campbell accepted the Highlanders' invasion with remarkable equanimity and found time to bespeak a 'frieze coat'[18] and shirts from his tailor – and to write poetry. His duty was to support Argyll and the Government, but it may be that he took heart from a dissident Campbell, the Earl of Breadalbane who hated Argyll and was with John Murray at the Abbey. In his own defence John Campbell claimed that when Murray came to him and demanded £857 sterling in cash, in exchange for notes, he had no choice.

If you don't [Murray threatened] within the space of fortyeight hours from the date make payment to me of the same, for his royal highness' interest at his majesty's palace of Holyrood House, his royal highness will forthwith thereafter, put himself in possession of the estates and effects of the directors and managers of the said bank to the like extent.[19]

The next day the court of directors met and 'after full consideration of the demand made upon the bank resolved "to answer the payment in specie to prevent further trouble and mischief to the company and those concerned therein"'.[20] Then Murray sent another demand for £2,307 with a threat of similar penalties. This time, when John Campbell and three directors, armed with a white flag, made their way past the Highlanders' guard into the castle to collect the coin demanded, they took the opportunity to burn a parcel of notes amounting to £47,600. They were in the castle vaults from 9 a.m. to 3 p.m. and heard the cheering outside as the government troops let down one of their number from the castle walls to attack a shoemaker, who, with his band of Jacobites, was sniping at the guard above. Over the next few days the directors contrived to burn or destroy over £60,000 worth of notes and brought out over £12,000 in gold and silver to satisfy the Prince's secretary. It is not surprising that John Coutts later reported that Lord Milton had 'found fault with almost every part of the directors' conduct'.[21] Prince Charles would seem to have got his gold too easily.

On 19 November the Highland troops left Edinburgh, hoping to march in triumph to London. John Campbell returned to his poetry. 'Tonight', he wrote, 'I finished my composure.'[22] The Royal Bank's books and treasure were brought from the castle on 23 November and every effort was made to re-establish its credit, offering interest 'after the rate of four percent per annum for what money is at present lodged and over above the credit of their customers'.[23] Desperately short of coin, the directors now turned to George Middleton's bank in London for help. They ordered the cashier to ask Mr Middleton to send them a remittance of gold and silver.[24]

On 26 November Campbell told the directors that he had written to Mr Middleton to 'look out for three thousand pounds in gold and the like sum in silver to lie in readiness, because he had been informed that orders were soon to be issued to a man of war to sail hither'.[25] It is probable that Middleton's partners, George Campbell and David Bruce, were dealing with this business since Middleton was ill at the time. But it is clear that there were already close links between John Coutts and Middleton's bank in the Strand, which was obviously acting as the Royal Bank's agent and correspondent in London. Campbell and Bruce in London were themselves under pressure, the advance of Prince Charles into England having caused some panic and a run on the banks.

With the Highlanders away in England, Edinburgh was comparatively quiet and John Coutts could visit his sons and relations at Allanbank. On his return on 4 December he wrote to Lord Minto, who was a Lord of Session:

My lord I thought on my return from Allanbank to have found your Lordship and a great many others in town. Instead of that I find few here but gentlemen of the army, and as all business is at a stand I think of returning back to the country until matters have become more settled.[26]

He reported to Minto that there were 'rebels in arms at ... Montrose, Aberdeen and other parts and that there are French troops landed at Montrose'.[27] At Allanbank he found Archibald Stuart in a distressed state since he was under suspicion of aiding the Jacobites. 'Baldy Stuart left Allanbank on Thursday the twentyfirst of last month,' he wrote.[28] Obviously Stuart had thought it best to go to London to clear his name.

He was civilly received by Marshall Wade and everybody else on the road all the way to London where he arrived Wednesday or Thursday last and by the letter I have received from thence I find he is not destitute of friends.[29]

Stuart was in fact imprisoned and, on his release, established a successful wine business in Buckingham Street near the Strand.

Before long those suspected of aiding Prince Charles were to be in mortal danger, for his rebellion was doomed to failure. The march to London halted at Derby and, against his will, the Prince and his Highlanders returned to Scotland, where they met their final defeat at the bloody battle at Culloden. The Prince escaped to his loyal followers in the Highlands and thence to France and into legend. Meanwhile, his supporters were brutally hunted down by King George II's ebullient son, the Duke of Cumberland. In Scotland he was immortally known as the 'Butcher of Culloden': in London he was received with jubilation as the saviour of the nation, who had given the cursed Scottish traitors their just deserts.

Wherever John Coutts's sons were at this time they could not have escaped the stress and anguish of their family. The news from Edinburgh was unsettling enough, and concern over Stuart's plight was grave, but the news from Montrose was even more terrifying. The boys must have heard with sick hearts of the carnage on the battlefield of Culloden and the torture of the hunted Highlanders. Never in his later life would Thomas Coutts forget the horror of this battle.

In Montrose their own relations were the victims of the Duke of Cumberland's vengeance. King George's spies found enough evidence to accuse James, Provost of Montrose, and his son, James junior, of 'treasonable practices'.[30] The Bailie of Montrose called witnesses and reported to Cumberland that James junior had said 'in an open and Insolent manner that he would not give a Pluck (a third of a penny) who should be King'. He was also heard to say of Prince Charles, 'since he has been at so much pains about it [i.e. getting the crown] I wish he may get it'.[31] Old Provost Coutts of Montrose stoutly denied charges of disloyalty. He had, he said, 'had the Principall direction of the Magistracy & Councill of this town [Montrose] for these 25 years past'.[32] He called the minister to witness that he and his son came to church to hear him preach and pray for His Majesty. His family, he claimed, had always been remarkable 'for Revolution Principles, zealous for the Protestant Succession & well affected to the present Government'.[33] Nevertheless, he was removed from office and later arrested; to his infinite distress he was thrown into a common jail.

In 1746 the city fathers in Montrose were in more trouble for permitting the young to demonstrate on 10 June, Prince Charles's birthday, outside Montrose, where they lit a bonfire and drank the health of their Bonny Prince out of mussel shells. Cumberland ordered that the guilty lads should be severely whipped through the streets of Montrose, 'their parents Assisting'.[34] It was afterwards strongly rumoured that 'Tammy' Coutts was one of those caught drinking the disloyal toast. He may possibly have been there at this time, sent out of Edinburgh to his cousins in Montrose. But whether there or with his mother's family at Allanbank, he must have worried over the fate of his friends among the Montrose boys who secretly wore the white cockade. Certainly the news that the old Provost, James Coutts, had been arrested and thrown into jail with common thieves must have shaken him to the core. Finally, after swearing repeatedly that 'no person in Britain can be better affected than I am & always have been to his Majesty's Person & Government',[35] Provost James and his son were removed from the 'Noisome prison to a convenient place of Security'.[36] But it was not until 8 November 1746 that the order finally came from St James's Palace, London, for their release on bail, with the hope that they were indeed innocent. At this time John Coutts of Edinburgh showed considerable courage by giving his support and his bond to his Montrose relations.

The old Provost may not have been actively involved with the Jacobites, but many of the young of the town were enthusiastic for Prince Charles and many would have echoed James Coutts junior's reported remark that 'he would not give a Snuff though King George was at Jericho'.[37] As a prosperous merchant he might well have agreed with young James that 'he didn't care who should be king for he had friends on both sides'.[38]

There is no doubt that during this dangerous time, John Coutts and his sons owed their safety to the protection of the Duke of Argyll and Lord Milton, for which their descendants kept for many generations a lively sense of gratitude to the Argylls.

Although he rarely referred to these perilous years they left a deep scar on young Thomas Coutts: all his life he retained a secret soft spot for the Stuarts, but like his Montrose cousin he would take care to keep 'friends on both sides'. Like his great-uncle Stuart, he early learnt to hide his feelings and to shut away in the dark of his mind the horrors of this time. But the harrowing stories of the butchery at Culloden, the hunting and destruction of the Highlanders, the hanging, drawing and quartering at Edinburgh Grass Market must have given him nightmares.

In 1749 John Coutts's health failed. Forbes, who only knew him by reputation, reported that, though he was widely loved, he was acknowledged to have indulged in 'excesses of the table'.[39] Perhaps it was the stress of this period, combined with his celebrated good living, that undermined his health. Or it may have been expedient politically for him to leave the country; his Jacobite relations must have been an embarrassment to his government friends. Certainly Lord Milton thought it wise that the former Lord Provost should seek the sunshine of Italy and persuaded him to go abroad.

On 11 August he left Edinburgh for Naples* with his eldest son, Patrick, writing in haste to Lord Milton that he regretted that he could not be at the Royal Bank for the last committee meeting. Perhaps in a reply to a suggestion from Milton that he should stand for Parliament, he firmly

---

* Secret agents in Naples reported to the English Government the arrival of the Jacobite spy, John Coutts.[40]

insisted, 'I have no mind if I should return again to Brittain to dauble in elections.' He was anxious, he said, for news of the success of the British Linen Company, 'because I never knew any project to have so much appearance of saving our poor country as this has'. But he was also anxious for its success for the sake of Lord Milton, who had such 'a strong desire' to serve his country.[41]

The Italian sunshine failed to cure his persistent cough and, on 23 March 1750, he died at his house in Nola near Naples, 'beloved and regretted', Forbes wrote, 'by all his acquaintances, who overlooked the imperfections of his character when they thought of him as the upright citizen and useful magistrate ever zealous in the service of his friends and a most agreeable member of society'.[42]

There was genuine respect and affection expressed in the letters after his death. Archibald Trotter wrote, in his stilted way, to an Aberdeen merchant, William Chalmers:

I am sorry it falls to my share to acquaint you of the melancholy news of the death of one of the best of men, my dear friend and partner John Coutts esquire who it pleased God to take to himself the third current to the unexpressible loss to his young family and all who had the happiness of his acquaintance. I know his memory will be dear to you and that we will have your friendly sympathy, his eldest son my cousin Mr Patrick Coutts and I [are] to continue the business by our present firm and when my cousin returns from abroad you will hear from him. We hope for the sake of our dear departed friend a continuance of your friendship for our house which we shall likewise endeavour to merit by a faithful and punctual execution of your commands.[43]

9

The Coutts Brothers

When Provost Coutts left Edinburgh for Italy, he had taken Patrick with him. He had sent his son John to Holland to be trained as a merchant and entrusted his business and his two younger sons, James and Thomas, to his partner, Archibald Trotter, who rapidly resigned the care of the high-spirited boys. They ragged him unmercifully, as on the day when, to Trotter's alarm, a mouse jumped out of his inkwell. Which of the two boys put it there is not recorded, but their glee and the merriment in the counting-house was long remembered. Their uncle, John Stephen, finally took Trotter's place, until young John was recalled from Holland and Patrick returned from Italy.

The firm was then reorganised: John, James and John Stephen continued to run the Edinburgh house under the name of 'Coutts Brothers and Company', which, under John's direction, flourished with three partners, four clerks and two apprentices. Patrick left Scotland with Thomas to set up a branch in London, and they established themselves in a house in Jeffrey's Square in the City of London. From there they conducted an import and export business, acting as correspondents for their brothers in Edinburgh.

Forbes remembered Provost Coutts's sons: 'the eldest brother Patrick was a man of elegant and agreeable manners, but more inclined to the study of books than to application to business'.[1]

The second son John was the most impressive of the brothers. Forbes served as his apprentice and knew him well; he was, he says,

one of the most aggreeable men I ever knew. Lively and well-bred, and of very engaging manners, he had the happy talent of uniting a love of society and public amusements with a strict attention to business. While resembling his father in his general manners more than did any of his brothers, he was more correct in his conduct; nor do I recollect to have ever seen him but once in the counting-house disguised with liquor and incapable of transacting business. Having received his mercantile education in Holland, he had all the accuracy and all the strictness of a Dutchman; and to his lessons it is that I owe any knowledge I possess of the principles of business, as well as an attachment to *form* which I shall probably carry with me to the grave. Although he was of the most gentle manners in common life, he was easily heated with passion when he thought himself ill-used, and I have seen his eyes, which were black and piercing, flash as with lightning, if any attempt was made to overreach him in a bargain. But his passion was of short continuance and easily appeased.[2]

Forbes's judgment is confirmed by the few of John's letters that exist. He later had the courage to refuse to endorse a candidate for Parliament put forward by the Duke of Argyll, pointing out that, although he was grateful for the protection the Duke had given some members of his family he could not support the Duke's candidate, but would not work against him. It is possible that John had been sent to Holland for safety, since there are many indications that he had Jacobite sympathies. As Forbes records, he was certainly involved with his partners, Strahan and Robertson, in smuggling at Rotterdam.

The third son, James, according to Forbes,

gave as close application to business as his immediate elder brother; but he was by no means of so amiable a character; and, never having been out of Edinburgh, he had not those polished manners which his two elder brothers had acquired by living abroad and mixing in the world. He was nearly as passionate as Mr John Coutts; but he differed from him in retaining a longer resentment.[3]

Since Thomas, the fourth son, was still alive when Forbes wrote his memoirs, he tactfully refrained from describing him. His brothers were fine-looking young men with luxuriant hair, while Thomas was slight, with a head that later in life Hester Stanhope was to describe as the smallest she had seen – a proof, she claimed, that small heads did not indicate lack of sense, since Thomas Coutts was the most sensible of men. Perhaps he was aware that he had none of his brothers' good looks. Certainly he later claimed that he always refused to have his portrait painted, even by his friends Sir Joshua Reynolds and Sir Thomas Lawrence, until in old age the Earl of Buchan persuaded him to sit for Sir William Beechey. But there is an early miniature, set in diamonds, which shows a delicate youth with pale, translucent skin, watchful eyes and a humorous mouth. Even as a young man he was careful of his health to the point of hypochondria and throughout his life was constantly to refer to his 'paper frame'. The shadow of death was always behind him, bringing periods of black depression. Had he been told he would live into his eighty-seventh year, he would have been astonished.

So he was to make up by hard, patient work for his plain appearance and cultivate by a simplicity of dress an invisibility that allowed him to listen and watch in obscurity. But behind the quiet exterior there was a powerful sense of duty and an ambition to be a worthy son of his dead father. Sensitive and affectionate, Thomas Coutts was devastated by his father's death and could scarcely bring himself to write of it to his friend Caleb Whitefoord in London. So few of Thomas's early letters survive that it is worth reproducing this in full:

EDINBURGH, 31 May, 1750

Dear Caleb,

I am favoured with yours, 8 current, – it gives me a reciprocall pleasure to see a letter from you and I hope we shall keep up an everlasting friendship, and if ever it is in my powr to serve you may always depend on it. I am oblidged to you for your kind sympathy on my late great loss and though it is irreparable yet we ought cheerfully to submit to the will of God who rules all things, remembering that all of us must die. It would be needless for me to say much of this disaggreeable subject that but increases my grief which you may easily know is but too great already – my friend Jamie Stuart told me that you thought you woud go to France this summer, if so you must allow me to wish you a good journey and happy return; if not I fancy I may perhaps have the pleasure of seeing you here. I saw your old friend John Bailie yesterday; he gives his service to you and desired me to tell you he fancyd you had forgot your promise of writing him – nothing occurring to me at present worth your notice I shall only at present add that

I am on all occasions, dear Caleb

Yours most affectionately,

THOMAS COUTTS

I beg you woud show my letter to nobody and I have a very good reason for desiring you not to do it which I shall leave to your self to find out from the stile and writ and I am

Yours as above,

T. C.[4]

The postscript reveals that love of secrecy which was to be a lifelong characteristic.

When Thomas and Patrick came to London they might well have called at the Bank in the Strand to pay their respects to George Campbell, who was now in charge. For their father, John Coutts, when he was a director of the Royal Bank of Scotland, had dealt with Middleton and later with George Campbell. And Middleton, as has been seen, was a close friend of John Coutts's patron, Lord Milton.

Shortly after their arrival in London, Thomas and Patrick had opened comparatively small accounts with George Campbell; the ledgers at Coutts & Co. record transactions with 'Coutts, Stephen, Coutts & Co.'[5]* running from May 1752 to 20 June 1755. There is also an account which refers to

* There are also transactions with Messrs Coutts & Co. (London Branch) from 22 February 1753 to 3 April 1753. There are later references to accounts with Coutts Brothers and Stephen from 20 June to 31 December 1760; and with Coutts Bros of Edinburgh from June 1755 to December 1760.

John's old firm in Rotterdam, Robertson, Coutts & Strahan. So obviously James Coutts had brought his brother's Rotterdam firm as a customer to the Bank in the Strand. But there were soon to be closer ties.

Perhaps to escape the drudgery of work under his efficient brother John, who, as Forbes remembered, was a strict master and allowed his apprentices little spare time, James paid his brothers a visit in London in the autumn of 1754.

In the spring of 1755 the Coutts and the Campbell families were finally united when, as the *Newcastle Journal* of 10–17 May 1755 recorded,

Edinburgh, May 8. On Saturday se'nnight was married at St George's Church, Hanover Square, London, Mr James Coutts of Jeffrey's Square, merchant, son to the deceas'd John Coutts Esq, Lord Provost of Edinburgh, to Miss Polly Peagrum of Knightsbridge, niece to Mr Campbell Banker in the Strand, an amiable young lady, with a fortune of £30,000, and that day the new-married couple set out for Bath.[6]

Apart from this glimpse of an 'amiable young lady', and a charming portrait of a pretty young girl, Polly Peagrum's name is 'writ in water'. We know that her father was John Peagrum of Elmstead near Colchester and that she was also called Mary. Her mother, Elizabeth, daughter of old John Campbell, had spent much of her childhood in Colchester, where she presumably met Mr Peagrum. It would seem that she and Polly helped to run George Campbell's bachelor household, since the private ledgers record regular payments to them both.

James Coutts might have met Polly at her uncle's house in the Strand, or at one of the houses of those hospitable Scots who entertained their countrymen in London. There is a suggestion in a later letter that it was Archibald Stuart who had had a hand in promoting the marriage. But wherever they met, that marriage was James Coutts's greatest contribution to the history of the Bank. In 1755 the name Coutts was first brought into the title of the Bank. George Campbell made James Coutts a partner in the firm now called 'Campbell & Coutts'. James withdrew from the Edinburgh house, which was now managed by John and his competent apprentice, William Forbes.

The Coutts's London house was still under the direction of Patrick and Thomas, but it was the younger brother who, for the next five years, was chiefly responsible for the conduct of the business, for Patrick was often away on mysterious visits to the continent. Forbes remembered one such journey which ended in disaster:

Being at Lisle, as he was walking in a careless manner on the ramparts, he was observed to be employed in taking notes in shorthand in his pocket-book, and was immediately arrested as a spy. It was in vain that he urged his having merely been engaged in making a few memoranda for his own amusement, without any criminal intention. He was thrown into prison, where he remained for several months, and it cost his friends considerable trouble to procure his release.[7]

It is still not known whether in fact Patrick was engaged in espionage and, if so, for whom.

In his first years in London Thomas was kept busy in the office in Jeffrey's Square. Few documents have survived of this period, but it was clear that it was Thomas who bore the burden of the business, although he rarely spoke in after life of his ten years there. But he always considered this as a period of invaluable training. He later frequently wrote to friends who asked his advice on their sons' careers, insisting on the importance of having business experience before joining a bank. In a letter to Lord Minto, who wanted him to take his son as a partner, he wrote:

and with respect to Education To Business in general if I had a son I meant for my successor I would not Educate Him in my Shop, for tho' it is an Eligible Place ultimately to fix in, He will be much more fit to Conduct The House by receiving His Education in The Mercantile Line in The City of London or abroad – or even in The Law. Had I not had the Experience of a Considerable deal of General Business – before I had The Government of my House, it never would have risen to what it has in my Hands – or on the Contrary would it have dwindled as it did in the Hands of my Predecessor Mr Campbell – (with many advantages) if He had been educated differently, & had had a more general view of the Conduct of Business.

Patrick and Thomas lived over the office in a house which, as James Boswell later was to describe, was handsome and comfortable. It was probably one of the solid merchants' houses built in the City of London after the Great Fire.

In Jeffrey's Square Thomas and Patrick were the London correspondents of the Edinburgh firm. They were involved in exporting and importing, in foreign exchange and shipping, and Thomas must have learnt there how to keep complicated accounts. Doubtless his brother John had taught him the 'accuracy of a Dutchman', and like Forbes he learned from John 'the principles of business and the attachment to form'.[8] He learned early that efficiency for which he was later famous.

Patrick and Thomas now took in their cousin Thomas Stephen as a partner. Stephen, son of their partner in the Edinburgh house, died within a few years, leaving most of the work to be done by Thomas. For the next eight or nine years Thomas had little time for amusement. His friend, Adam Wood, who was apprenticed to a merchant, regretted that 'he and master Tom were kept busy'.[9] But there were holidays: 'Coutts, Wood, Dewar and your humble servant', wrote Caleb Whitefoord, 'were lately on a short country expedition when you may easily believe we were very jolly.'[10]

Caleb was also a close friend of James Coutts and wrote long letters back to him in Edinburgh about the theatre and art in London. But James was serious, conscientious and ambitious, and deplored Caleb's frivolity. 'Dear Jamie,' Caleb wrote. 'After this I shall be as grave and serious as you please and all my views shall attend to the main point, I mean our mutual improvement in the knowledge of mercantile affairs.'[11] He continued with a solemn survey of Guernsey, its countryside and people, its wealth and particularly the success of the wine and brandy trade there: 'The latter, I believe, they dispose among West Country smugglers.'[12]

London in the mid-eighteenth century was crackling with vitality and the young men from restricting Edinburgh were swept into a world of freedom. There were giants abroad in those days: Dr Johnson held court, and George Frederick Handel, Laurence Sterne, Oliver Goldsmith, David Garrick and Joshua Reynolds were all in London. Their fellow Scot, Boswell, was whirling through London, tasting the excitement of its high and low life. Thomas Coutts was lucky to have Caleb Whitefoord as a guide in this intoxicating world. Even in these early days, Thomas was drawn to exotic and unconventional characters. Caleb, in his unusual wig modelled on Garrick's, and his brilliant waistcoats, dazzled him. Through Caleb he met men like Benjamin Franklin, one of the most brilliant Americans of all time, and many of the most lively intellects of the age.

Caleb was the natural son of Colonel Charles Whitefoord, a brave professional soldier who had fought against the Jacobites at Culloden in the '45 rebellion. He was a year older than Thomas and was educated at the school of the renowned, dedicated teacher, James Mundell. He matriculated at Edinburgh University in March 1748 and, though brilliant in classics, rejected a career in the law for business in London, where he worked in the counting-house of Archibald Stuart MP, son of the old Provost 'Baldy Stuart'. In London he indulged his passion for the arts and the theatre: he watched Garrick strutting on the stage, met writers and painters, and established a reputation as a wit and skilled writer of occasional pieces. He became a connoisseur of painting and later acquired a great collection of Reynolds's pictures. When, after his father's death in 1753, he inherited a small fortune, he went to France for two years and thence to Portugal to learn more of the wine trade. On his return he lived at 8 Craven Street, next door to Benjamin Franklin, a friend who was later to have an immense influence on Caleb's career. Franklin, as will be seen, was to be a most useful contact for Thomas Coutts, especially during the negotiations at the end of the American War of Independence.

As a wit and a writer, his essays, poems and epigrams were much admired by Doctor Johnson. After his death in 1810 Adam Smith wrote of him: 'although the Junto of wits and authors hated one another heartily they had a sincere regard for Mr Whitefoord who by his conciliatory manners and happy adaptation of circumstances, kept his circle together in amity and good humour....'[13] Goldsmith wrote his epitaph:

> Here Whitefoord reclines, and deny it who can,
> Tho' he merrily lived, he is now a grave man!
> Rare compound of oddity, frolic, and fun,
> Who relish'd a joke, and rejoic'd in a pun;
> A Scotsman from pride and from prejudice free,
> A scholar, yet surely no pedant was he.[14]

This was the man who, in 1751, introduced Thomas Coutts to the London world of culture, philosophy and politics and remained a close family friend and confidant to the end of his life. If in the years to come Thomas needed a voice in the press, Caleb spoke for him, and, as will be seen, Caleb kept him in touch with the politics of the period.

The years 1760 and 1761 brought a succession of tragedies. On 28 March 1760 James Coutts's wife died, leaving him with a four-year-old daughter, Frances. In the next month George Campbell also died, bequeathing the Bank and most of his estate to James. Thomas wrote to Lord Minto with regret at their deaths, but with no little pleasure at 'Jamie's' good fortune.

My Lord,

Before this come to hand your Lordship will have [heard] of the great Distress of this family.... First in the death of one of the most amiable of women & now by the Loss of that worthy honest man Mr Campbell.

It is a great Comfort to his & Mrs Coutts friends to see how much & Universally they are both justly Lamented by all who knew them of which Jamie has received the Strongest Proofs – The Great People connected with his Shop seem to vie with each other which shall show him the greatest Friendship & Kindness.

His own Private connections have also been particularly attentive to him on this occasion. Your Son he has reason to think has been of great Service to him of which you may believe that he will always be mindful & our family have always been so much in use of Considering the Interest of one as the Interest of the whole that the obligation is done to everyone of us & I hope there is none [of] us ungrateful.

The settlements Mr Campbell had made are remarkably favourable for Jamie's family & he is in a manner sole Executor as there is only his mother-in-law join'd with him....'[15]

James now had a healthy private fortune, although the income from the Bank during his partnership with George Campbell had been fairly modest. In his first year as partner, the partners' profits had doubled from £2,388 in 1755 to £4,605 in 1756, but in 1759 they had dropped again to £2,537. James was now the sole owner of the Bank in the Strand. Realising that he needed a partner, he turned to Thomas for help. Accordingly, at the end of

1760, Thomas left the office in Jeffrey's Square where he had worked so patiently for the last decade.

The years in Jeffrey's Square had been harrowing. Patrick was beginning to show signs of mental disturbance, and John's smuggling activities in Holland had undoubtedly been an embarrassment. The death of George Campbell had caused him genuine distress for 'Honey' had obviously been kind to the delicate young man. It is not surprising that Thomas chose to wipe from his memory the decade in the counting-house in the City. Perhaps he considered that the story of spies and smugglers and its dark undercurrent of death and madness was better left untold.

All his life Thomas was to battle to suppress the fears that haunted his youth.

10

Early Years in the Strand

On 1 January 1761 Thomas Coutts joined his brother James as a junior partner at the Bank in the Strand. So began the most important chapter in the history of the Bank.

The House was styled 'James & Thomas Coutts': James provided £8,000 of the capital and Thomas contributed the £4,000 he had inherited from his father. Their first duties were to organise the Bank in the Strand and then to reorganise both the businesses in Edinburgh and London. A new contract for a ten-year partnership was made in January 1761 between their other two brothers, Patrick and John, and their uncle, John Stephen. In March the Edinburgh firm was rearranged. William Forbes was made a junior partner under John Coutts and Mr Stephen, with a one-eighth share.

Patrick continued in nominal control of the London business in Jeffrey's Square with the help of a clerk. While Patrick was in Edinburgh arranging the new contract he visited his relations in Montrose. There he commissioned broad steps to be made through the churchyard linking a higher with a lower road. The steps, built in 1761, are still there, a melancholy memorial to a man whose life was to end so sadly.

The new partnerships were not to last long. In the spring of 1761 Patrick suffered a complete mental breakdown and was placed in a house in Hackney under the kindly care of Dr Calder, a friend of the family and an expert on mental ill-health. The stress of his months' imprisonment may have disturbed the balance of his sensitive mind, or he may have inherited mental instability from his mother's family, but certainly from that time until his death, Patrick slips into the shadows. Physically strong and still handsome, Patrick lived in Hackney under the name of Mr Smith and, year after year, the doctor's reports on the condition of 'Mr Smith' came to disturb Thomas. Only two of these letters survive, poignant records of the disintegration of a fine, intelligent man. Patrick's £4,000 share of his father's bequest was invested for him and every care taken for his welfare.

A letter of 4 August 1799 must have been deeply distressing to Thomas. It is unsigned, yet it must refer to Patrick and, since he finished his days at the village in Kensington known as 'Gravel Pits', it is probable that the letter encouraged his brother to remove him from Hackney to a more secluded place:

Philanthropus suggests to Mr Coutts that a much more eligible spot and one as healthy for his unfortunate relation might be found in some retired village where the public ear would not be so shocked by the dreadful cries which he too often utters.

At present by the situation of the house on a public & much frequented Road numbers are constantly attracted to assemble, from the alarm occasioned by noises so shocking to the ear of humanity. Yesterday in particular the writer who was passing by had an instance of the force of this Remark.

Monday 4 Aug. 99[1]*

Thomas was tormented all his life by the fear of the mental instability in his family. It was frequently to rock his own balance, affecting his health and sometimes his judgment. He had reason to fear: again and again members of his family were to be stricken by madness.

The year 1761 was one of tragedy, but the greatest, and most surprising, blow came in August. While on a visit to London, John Coutts was, according to Forbes,

seized ... with a painful disease, which brought him to the gates of death, and so broke his constitution, that, being ordered by his physicians to drink the waters of Bath, he died there in August 1761, deeply lamented by all who knew him, but by none more than by myself [Forbes], who lost in him an able guide and a steady friend.[2]

It says much for John's character that Forbes bore him no resentment for his strict discipline, although he had, he wrote, 'slept but one night out of Edinburgh from the commencement of my apprenticeship in May 1754 till the month of September 1760'.[3]

Now there were only two brothers, James and Thomas, left to run three businesses: Coutts & Co. in Edinburgh, Coutts Brothers in Jeffrey's Square, and James & Thomas Coutts in the Bank in the Strand. Thomas, like James, had withdrawn his capital from the family business and invested it in the Bank in the Strand. From 1761 onwards their involvement in the other businesses was purely as Executors and Trustees for John and Patrick, though they still leased the premises in the City of London and in Edinburgh.

Their uncle, William Cochrane, lived with a clerk in Jeffrey's Square, which for a time remained a counting-house. Cochrane, a retired linen draper from the Lackenbooths in Edinburgh, was married to their mother's sister, who was a great favourite of the Coutts brothers.

John Stephen, too, was allowed to stay in Provost John Coutts's old

---

* When he died in 1808, his only epitaph was a brief note in the Kensington records.

home in President's Stairs, Edinburgh. He was a kindly old man, who had owned a wine shop in Leith, but was no banker. Nevertheless, he remained a partner in the Edinburgh firm. The brothers were loyal to both uncles; their aunts had been kind to them in their motherless childhood and they never forgot their debt to them. The Jeffrey's Square business was soon to collapse, but Coutts & Co. in Edinburgh thrived under the competent direction of William Forbes and his able apprentice, James Hunter.

James and Thomas concentrated their attention – and their capital – on the Bank in the Strand. They cut their connection with the Edinburgh house although it still carried John Coutts's name. And they were still concerned for their uncle, John Stephen, and his debts.

Their immediate task was to bring some order into the business, which had apparently 'gone to seed'. Edward Marjoribanks was to inaccurately record in his memoirs, 'The business had materially declined and indeed had been carried on at a loss in the year of the rebellion in 1745.'[4] Certainly 'As during the fourteen years, that the brothers were in Partnership, the profits about £106,000, in the thirty years from 1725–1755, the Profits scarcely amounted to £50,000.'[5]

George Campbell had been a likeable fellow but had no business experience, unlike his brother William, who had been trained in Holland. James and Thomas Coutts, however, had had the advantage of their brother John's meticulous Dutch training. Marjoribanks, who had access to the early records, noticed the difference 'after the business fell into the hands of Messrs Coutts'.[6] Thereafter,

an improved system of conducting it, [the business] was attained. The books were balanced annually, and balance Books were also signed by the Partners, & the minor details as to Clerks etc were placed upon an improved & more regular method than had been formerly observed ... and it was to the late Mr Coutts that the merit of this improved system of management was due.[7]

It was Thomas, rather than James, who now organised the business.

But Thomas's influence is most evident in the new active pursuit of a wider range of influential customers. There was still a large proportion of Scottish noble names in the ledgers, but, as will be seen, Thomas made an art of attracting and keeping wealthy customers not only from Scotland and England but also from many foreign countries. As Marjoribanks recalled, 'the duty of extending the connections of the house as favourable opportunities offered also devolved on Mr [Thomas] Coutts, which was one of much importance'.[8]

However, the greatest triumph, the capture of the King's account, may well have been due to James's influence, since it would seem that the King placed his account with him from the beginning of his reign in 1760.

*   *   *

Thomas joined his brother at the Bank in the Strand at a turning-point in British history. Both George I and George II had been German to the core, only happy in their native Hanover. However, George III was English-bred and given a solid Scottish education by the Earl of Bute, who was the young King's mentor, confidant and friend. Immediately on his accession the new King appointed Bute his Groom of the Stole and a member of his cabinet. Until his downfall in 1766, Bute was to be the most powerful minister in England and Scotland, where his brother, James Stuart-MacKenzie, held the sinecure office of Lord Privy Seal, which the King promised him for life.

It was fortunate for James and Thomas Coutts that Bute had been a customer at the Bank in the Strand since 1742 and that his family had banked there since 1717, but he and his brother, Stuart-MacKenzie, had also known their father, Provost John, in Scotland. James Coutts may also have known Bute in Edinburgh, since he was involved in politics there. Certainly during the period when he was the King's adviser, Bute, as Thomas was later to write, showed them 'many kindnesses'. The acquisition of the royal account was an honour, but one that was to bring Thomas many a headache. The financial affairs of George III and his sons were to worry him to the end of his life.

Bute's support was of inestimable value. As Prime Minister and the Keeper of the King's Privy Purse, his power was immense. The King relied on his old tutor, his 'dearest friend', for advice in all matters great and small, which roused the intense jealousy of other ministers. It was widely believed, without evidence, that the King's mother, the Princess of Wales, was his mistress. He was also under constant attack from the London mob at a time when Scots were hated and feared. It was because of the influence of Bute and Stuart-MacKenzie that James and Thomas received an allot-ment in the very profitable loan of 1762–3.

The source of the King's income must be explained briefly here. Since 1697 the monarch had been granted a Civil List, which was intended to cover the expenses of government, except those of the armed forces, which were raised by Parliament each year by taxation. Under this system George I had been given £700,000 a year and the Prince of Wales £100,000. If the interest produced a surplus, the excess was to go back to the Government. But in 1727 Walpole, who regulated the financial affairs of George II to his own and his King's advantage, had arranged that he should keep any surplus. The Prince of Wales was to be allowed £50,000 a year, to be raised to £100,000 on his marriage. 'In the last year of the reign of George II the Civil List amounted to £876,000.'[9] Had Bute arranged a similar system for George III, he would have become a wealthy man and the coming troubles would have been avoided.

George II's son, Frederick, Prince of Wales, who was always at loggerheads with his father, in order to gain the support of the Tory opposition, who were angry at the jobbery in high places, promised that when he became King he would 'accept no more ... than £800,000 per annum for his Civil List'.[10] This was accepted by Bute as a promise which King George III must fulfil. So his Civil List for life was £800,000 and, though he was the most economical, even parsimonious, of kings, he was usually in debt. Out of the Civil List he had to provide for the expenses of the Government (except the armed forces), the court, allowances to his family and his own private income, known as the Privy Purse. This last, which at the beginning of his reign was kept by Bute, was supposedly his own private property, details of whose accounts were not published. But the King's private expenses, his charities, the salaries and maintenance of courtiers, and the cost of the librarian for the King's library were all known by the bankers who kept the accounts of the Privy Purse, James and Thomas Coutts.

Unfortunately, at the end of his life Thomas directed that, after his death, all the royal correspondence and accounts with him should be destroyed. Only one of the King's letters to him has survived, a request that his librarian should be paid out of the Privy Purse. Later Thomas attributed their early success partly to the royal favour:

Particular circumstances also were very uncommonly favourable – The known favour of His Majesty & the great Sums of His put into our hands at the accession – The markt kindness of Lord Bute, at the same time that the Heads of opposition were also the firm friends of our Shop – put us in a fortunate light, which did not fail of it's Effect on the Profit.[11]

Like his Montrose ancestors Thomas was always careful to keep 'friends on both sides', and Bute's persistent and finally successful opponent, George Grenville, was also his customer as were the Pitts and Temples and many other members of Grenville's influential family.

11

Public Service and Private Affairs

From the beginning of 1762 James Coutts was quite happy to leave most of the conduct of the business in Thomas's careful hands, for on 27 February he became MP for Edinburgh. Bute's brother, Stuart-MacKenzie, and their agent, Lord Milton, offered the nomination to James. His father, it will be remembered, had declined to 'dauble in politics',[1] although the seat was often given to Lord Provosts of Edinburgh. James was also eternally grateful to the Duke of Argyll, who was, he insisted, 'the great because good and humane Duke of Argyll to whom I owe more obligation than all the world besides'.[2] As MP for Edinburgh James gave his loyal support to the Whigs, and Thomas established an affectionate relationship with Bute, which grew closer over the years. Little did Thomas guess at this time that one day their families would be united.

However, James was not successful as a politician. When asked to go to Edinburgh in August 1763 to influence the results of the local elections, he refused, saying that he had no mandate from Bute and Stuart-MacKenzie. Besides, he argued that his business at the Bank required his 'closest attention till the sitting of Parliament, when the burden must again fall chiefly on my brother'.[3] Nor had he any gift for speaking. Indeed his speeches in the house were 'so strange and incoherent'[4] that his friends sent him an anonymous letter (probably drafted by Caleb Whitefoord) advising him against speaking:

It was with great concern that I saw you rise up to speak several times during the last session, the first time you spoke it was to some degree necessary, would to heaven you had stopped there, for indeed my dear sir you are by no means qualified for speaking. . . . The fair character you bore with everybody and your becoming deportment in business and in every other situation of life made me feel the most sensible concern to see you so unlike yourself.[5]

His candid friend advised him never to speak in Parliament again. James took this advice, though he attended the House and voted.

His strange manner was in fact a sign of the approaching malady which was to afflict him as it had done his brother, Patrick. Historians have dismissed James Coutts, remembering little of him except the mental instability that later destroyed him, but there is something to be said in his favour. He was a hardworking and conscientious Member for Edinburgh. The least intelligent of the brothers, he lacked self-confidence. 'I know my own little consequence in politicks,' he once wrote to William Mure.[6] With a touching self-depreciation he wrote to David Hume:

With all pleasure there are great mixtures of mortification and every instant my limited education stares me more and more in the face. I have hardly looked on any but manuscript folios since I was 14. You'll say from idleness or want of taste. I say no, but from too much business and bad health. My constitution will probably be always unfit for deep study; but pray is there no remedying this great defect a little without much study? ... seriously I wish you would give me some advice on this head, what abridgements to read, etc.[7]

Perhaps it was this lack of confidence that made him so obsessive about his personal appearance. His footman described in his memoirs how particular he was that his hair should be dressed exactly as he wished and took infinite pains to find a valet who pleased him. Nevertheless, in the years 1762 to 1767 he served Edinburgh well. He was much involved in the planning of the New Town and helped to draft the necessary legislation. Although by repute he was easily aroused to anger, he acted as conciliator in a bank war which broke out between the Glasgow and Edinburgh banks.

Nor was he a 'yes man'. When Lord Milton told him to 'lay my *commands* on Mr Stephen to be a Magistrate',[8] he wrote angrily to William Mure:

Lord Milton's behaviour to me with respect to bringing my friends on the Council, I have great reason to complain of, if I cou'd attend myself I shou'd not take it amiss his making me even junior Merchant Counsellor without asking me; but how comes he to imagine I wou'd wish that any of my friend[s] shou'd be so servilely mine, as to come in, in the way he wou'd have them no I pray God I never may chase such friends: if I was a Duke nay a King I shou'd despise such servile dependants.[9]

James admired Bute and was grateful for his patronage, but when Grenville finally ousted him, he refused to beg for the support of his successor. 'Lord B by what my Brother writes me I fancy will give up the Privy Purse, which is a great Loss to us.' If they lost the royal account, he wrote, 'I trust I cou'd say from the Heart – to folks in a cottage contentment is Wealth.'[10] He was genuinely distressed at Bute's fall from grace: 'If it was possible for so good a mind as My Lord B to be thoroughly mortified, what must he suffer. What a sacrifice does he make to his love for the King! who I trust will ever prove deserving of it.'[11]

James was unwilling to court Grenville, but Thomas looked to the interest of the Bank, which, as far as he was concerned, was of greater importance than party politics. So he made every effort to secure the custom not only of Grenville but also of the rest of his wide-branching family. After the resignation of Bute in 1763 there were three prime ministers before the appointment of Lord North in January 1770: Grenville, the Marquess of Rockingham and the Duke of Grafton. Though Thomas's letters to Grenville suggest that he found the minister as tiresome as did the King, he developed a close relationship with William Pitt and his wife, and later with Lady Hester Stanhope, niece of William Pitt the Younger. It was said that Thomas would not be satisfied until he had every member of the Grenville family on his books. Certainly he wrote to Stair on 10 December 1777 asking him to put in a good word with James Grenville: 'his two sons have both accounts at my shop but I have always imagined Mr Grenville had not the same confidence in me as Lord Temple, or the late Mr George Grenville, or his son Mr Nigel Grenville'.

During the early years of their partnership James and Thomas lived in George Middleton's old apartment over the Bank at 59 Strand. In 1769 James commissioned a major refurbishment in the style of their fellow Scots, the Adam brothers, who were at this time rebuilding the area between the Strand and the river on the site of the old Durham House. They gave their names to the streets there and called the classical terrace by the river 'Adelphi', Greek for 'the brothers'. James was at this time much engaged in the building of Edinburgh's New Town and there is no doubt that it was he who planned the improvements to 59 Strand.

When James was preoccupied with politics, it was Thomas who was the willing horse in the Bank. There could have been little time for frivolity, but it was a pleasure to relax among the friendly Scots who kept open house for their visiting countrymen.

It was not an easy time for Scots in London. Memories of the '45 rebellion were still fresh: the rotting heads of Jacobite rebels still gazed eyeless from Temple Bar, peered at by ghoulish citizens through twopenny spyglasses. Boswell, who was in London at this time, recorded in his diary the hounding of Scots officers at the theatre with hysterical shouts of 'No Scots no Scots'.[12] When Dr Johnson ribbed Boswell about his native country, there was a sharp edge to his humour: ridicule was the best weapon against fear.

The Scots in London were a close community and even those like Boswell and the Coutts brothers, who were trying to broaden their horizons and attract English friends, were glad from time to time to take tea and gossip with comfortable Edinburgh matrons and to slip back into their old brogue. Boswell and other Scots took elocution lessons from Thomas Sheridan, father of the dramatist, to rid themselves of their Scots accent. James always retained a broad accent, though it is possible that Thomas did not: always anxious to be inconspicuous he liked to blend in with his background.

In the year 1762–3 Boswell frequently dined with James and Thomas Coutts. He was in London trying to get a commission in the army. Since his father, who wanted him to be a lawyer, would not pay in the usual way, Boswell was hoping to become an officer through influence. So he was an assiduous courtier at the Countess of Northumberland's soirées in her splendid mansion near the Bank in the Strand. On Christmas Day 1762 he 'sat a while at Coutts' before going on to 'play a bold knife and fork' at a dinner, where he met the dramatist Goldsmith for the first time.[13] In January 1763 he 'dined with Coutts in the Strand, my banker, a jolly, plentiful dinner with a Scotch company, and free, easy conversation and went home cool and serene' – and contemplating the seduction of his actress, Louise, the next day.[14]

Strictly speaking James and Thomas Coutts were not bankers to Boswell as he did not have an account with them. But Mr Boswell senior, knowing his son's frailty, had arranged that his allowance should be paid to his good friend, William Cochrane, who still lived in the old house in Jeffrey's Square. He hoped that Cochrane would keep an eye on his lively son. This was an impossible task since Boswell moved with a frenetic energy from duchesses to 'wenches', from literary lions to seductive actresses. His scabrous affairs with light ladies in St James's Park and elsewhere, recounted with engaging frankness in his diary, sent him frequently to his doctor. Cochrane and the Coutts brothers between them did their best to keep him solvent. On one occasion James and Cochrane guided him out of a quarrel with his landlord.

Perhaps, in an effort to steer him into worthier company, James and Thomas took him to dine with

a Mr Trotter who is originally from Scotland, but has been here so long that he is become quite an Englishman. He is a bachelor, an honest, hearty, good humoured fellow. The company were all Scottish, except an American lady, wife to Mr Elliot, a son of Lord Minto's; Mr Stewart, formerly the noted Provost of Edinburgh.[15]

This was 'Baldy Stuart', Provost John Coutts's friend, who also kept a hospitable house for visiting Scots in Buckingham Street. Their host was a son of that Archibald Trotter who acted as the unhappy guardian to the Coutts boys after their father's death. Thomas Trotter, a plain, simple man, had developed a highly successful business as an upholsterer.

On 28 May Boswell 'breakfasted with Mr Coutts, who is a sensible, mild, friendly man. His brother, Mr Thomas, is a very good fellow and has a great deal of little humour and fun.'[16] It is unlikely that Thomas joined in Boswell's wilder frolics, though he always had an eye for a pretty lady.

Unlike his handsome brothers Thomas was small and considered himself plain. Shy and unassuming, he always avoided the limelight. He was often mistaken for a poor man. The legends are many and various, but undoubtedly later in life some benevolent gentleman did slip a secret guinea to the frail old man, so obviously down on his luck, only to discover that the object of his charity was the wealthy London banker. He certainly was delicate, but even as a young man he was obsessive about his health.

He was happiest when invisible: so he could quietly listen and learn – a useful habit for a banker to acquire. In the same way he was the soul of discretion. Nothing reveals this more clearly than the contrast between his private ledgers and those of his predecessors. George Middleton recorded every detail: the purchase of seeds and coals and wine, allowances to his daughters and purchases for them. From Thomas Coutts's pages it is almost impossible to discover how he spent his own money, though the Bank records are meticulously kept. His private ledgers show that he often drew large sums in cash, but give no reason why. But the most startling example of his extraordinary secretiveness is to be found among the papers of his great friend Caleb Whitefoord.

The young Scots in London met frequently and formed clubs and societies, sometimes to discuss profound philosophical questions, sometimes to read each other learned papers, but often to pass jovial evenings in the tavern or coffee house. On 18 December 1763 Caleb, as secretary of their literary society, recorded in his minutes:

Admiral Gordon, Rear Admiral
James Coutts Esq., Banker
Thomas Coutts Esq., Banker
Thomas Brown, Wine Merchant
John Elliot Esq., Captain of the Bellona
Caleb Whitefoord, Secretary of the Society

James Coutts wagers with John Elliot that the said John Elliot shall be married before James Coutts, Thomas Coutts, Caleb Whitefoord or either of them. The amount of the wager is an entertainment of the above six persons & six of their friends. The loser to pay for the entertainment & to make the Winner (a present) of a horse.

The entertainment to be given Wed 21st at St Albans Tavern at St Albans Street.[17]

In fact, although neither his brother nor his friends were aware, Thomas was already married. Seven months earlier, on 18 May, he had wed Susannah Starkie, nursemaid to James's daughter, Frances. We do not know when Thomas confessed, but the truth must have become obvious before long when Susannah became pregnant. Clearly there were those who doubted the marriage, for six years later the minister of St Gregory's made a copy of the 'Certificate of Marriage':

Thomas Coutts of this Parish of St Gregory, London, Batchelor and Susannah Starkie of the Parish of St Martin in the Fields, Middx, Spinster were married in this Church by licence from the Archbp of Cant' this eighteenth day of May in the year one Thousand Seven Hundred and Sixty three by me William Reyner, Minister.

The above is a true copy of the Register of the Parish Church of St Gregory, London. Witness my hand this Twelfth day of May 1769. Benj. Pearce, Minister of St Gregory aforesaid.[18]

Little is known of Susannah's early life except that she was the daughter of a respectable yeoman farmer near Preston in Lancashire and that she had come to James Coutts with excellent testimonials from the Misses Goodwell, three ancient maiden aunts of a Mrs Mary Assheton. Certainly James, who took infinite care over the choice of his footman, would have chosen a nursemaid for his daughter with even greater care. James's private accounts suggest that 'Susan Starkie' was taken on in October 1759 at a wage of £8 1s a year. In May and December of the next year she was paid £5 for mourning clothes for herself and £5 14s 6d for the little girl, Frances. There are no further records of payments until 5 July 1763, when she was given £37 'in full of wages to this day' and £13 17s 4d for Miss Coutts's 'Sundry bills'. On 28 July 1764 she was paid £2 17s 4d 'in full of wages' and £1 7s 9d for Miss Coutts's sundry bills. One can guess, therefore, that the truth was revealed in July and James finally paid Susan the wages owing to her.

Lord Dundonald, a kinsman of James, who often visited him, re-membered her liveliness. He occasionally saw her in the nursery and once, when 'washing of the young lady's clothes . . . his boyish tricks may have aggravated her to throw some of the soapsuds at him'.[19]

She was a blooming, vigorous country girl, strong in character, though not particularly beautiful, with fine, large eyes. A contemporary later described her face as 'irradiated by smiling good humour'.[20] Although she had little formal education she had a natural intelligence and later showed a keen interest in politics and the theatre. Lord Dundonald recalled that 'her good sense, amiable disposition and exemplary conduct endeared her to all her husband's family, and commanded the respect of all who knew her'.[21] Thomas Coutts had doubtless been attracted by her vitality and good humour and, as a delicate young man, would have enjoyed being cossetted by her; and she, a determined young woman, would have insisted on marriage before she succumbed to the young master. When James was away on his parliamentary duties, Susannah must have consoled Thomas in his loneliness.

The secret marriage caused trouble with James and for a time the brothers were estranged. However, there must have been many customers who reflected that a man who could keep his own secrets so well could be trusted with theirs.

Thomas and Susannah took rooms in Dr Garthorne's house on the west side of St Martin's Lane, next door to the famous Old Slaughter's coffee house* – the haunt of writers and artists. Here Susannah bore four sons, all of whom died in early infancy, and three daughters. When a contemporary wrote to a friend in Edinburgh that he had not known of the birth of Thomas's son, he assumed the baby had died, for 'they usually do!'[22]

In spite of these tragedies, Thomas always looked back with nostalgia on his time in St Martin's Lane and his old haunts round the Strand. He could escape to the coffee house next door in the company of some of the most brilliant men of the century.† In 1765 Goldsmith wrote, 'If a man be passionate he may vent his rage among the old orators at Slaughter's Chop House and damn the nation.'[23] The artist, Benjamin Haydon, remembered 'the great happiness' of the days, 'painting all day, then dining at Old Slaughter's Chop House'.[24] In these years Thomas acquired a breadth of vision and a liveliness of mind unusual among bankers.

* A contemporary drawing shows Old Slaughter's coffee house flanked by two handsome houses. In one, a plain Queen Anne building, Thomas presumably lived. The other had been rebuilt in the Italianate style for an actor, James Paine.

† Hogarth's *Marriage à la Mode* (1745) had been set in the house of Dr Misaubin in St Martin's Lane.

12

Banking, 1762-73

Those early days in St Martin's Lane were lively and, although the work at the Bank was demanding, it was a singularly exciting time for a banker. Fourteen years later Thomas Coutts was to explain the reasons for the expansion of banking in general and of Coutts & Co. in particular at this point: 'These 14 years began near the conclusion of a very uncommonly successful war [the Seven Years' War with France] & the Stock rising on the peace the gain upon all the money thus previous invested was very considerable. . . .'[1] As he recalled, 'The great influx of money arising by the success of the War prov'd a source of great gain to the Bankers.'[2] And the brothers thrived in the financial boom. As Thomas wrote, 'The prodigious growth of Credit both real & fictitious serv'd to increase the Banking business to a degree unknown before.'[3]

During this time of expansion, when James was busy in Parliament and Thomas with his work in the Strand – and with his private life – they had the continual worry of the reorganisation of the businesses in the City and in Edinburgh. As Trustees for Patrick and John there were difficult decisions to be taken, which caused great stress to the increasingly neurotic James and even tried Thomas's patience. For the death of John and the disappearance of Patrick left the two merchant concerns in London and Edinburgh without adequate leadership.

In Edinburgh only the efficiency of William Forbes and his apprentice, James Hunter, kept the firm going. For the remaining partner, John Stephen, was, according to Forbes, a man whose 'slender abilities were altogether inadequate to the task'[4] and who was slowly becoming weak in body and mind. 'It was', wrote Forbes, 'the popularity of Provost Coutts and his family in Edinburgh and the established reputation of their firm by which the friends & correspondents of the house were induced to continue their business there as formerly.'[5] For the next ten years, even when Forbes's link with the Coutts family was broken, his bank in Edinburgh still kept the name Coutts & Co.

In the house in Jeffrey's Square in London, William Cochrane was in charge. He was an honourable man with agreeable manners, but was altogether unacquainted with any kind of business beyond that of the retail shop.

To strengthen both houses the brothers decided to bring in Robert Herries, a merchant in Barcelona, as a new partner. He was a sharp, enterprising but ruthless young man, who had built up a considerable wine business in Europe and had worked with their brother John in Rotterdam. On Christmas Day 1762, Herries, Cochrane and Forbes met with James and Thomas at the House in the Strand to sign the agreements. The Edinburgh firm was to be known as 'John Coutts & Co.' and the London firm as 'Herries, Cochrane & Co.' Cochrane continued to live in Jeffrey's Square, and John Stephen and his wife remained in Provost John Coutts's old house on President's Stairs.

On 26 December 1762 James Coutts, Herries and Forbes returned to Scotland to set up the new partnership, leaving Thomas in charge in London. Herries immediately dominated both the Edinburgh and London firms, and was determined to get rid of Cochrane. 'None of us', he later wrote sharply, 'were taken into their houses merely for God's sake.'[6] When, in 1766, the three years' contract of the partnership of Herries, Cochrane & Co. expired, Cochrane was ousted. James and Thomas fought in vain to keep him, but his debts and his incapacity gave Herries a strong case. Finally he was given a settled annuity of £200 with a £100 annuity for the surviving wife or husband; the Cochranes retired from business, but kept the house in Jeffrey's Square. This was the beginning of the end of Herries's partnership with the Coutts brothers; however, they kept on more friendly terms with Forbes, who had, they knew, been a reluctant axe-man.

Herries moved to a new base in Oxford Court, Cannon Street, and brought in his brothers, Charles and William, as partners with a new contract. Now freed from Coutts's supervision, Herries branched out into all kinds of new adventures. He visited France, assiduously courted and bribed the Farmers General, as the French bankers responsible for collecting taxes were called, and won from them the exclusive right to export tobacco to France, which he bought from Glasgow merchants who had purchased their tobacco in North America. Forbes treats him with some generosity in his memoirs, but it is very clear that Herries was an unscrupulous adventurer, capable of bribery, opening the letters of his competitors, and of speculating on his own account on the probable rise in the price of tobacco during the American War of Independence. But he proved too sharp for his own good. At the beginning of the American War of Independence, when he tried to make extra money out of the international situation, the French Farmers General threw him over for his competitor. When France entered the war on America's side against Britain, his lucrative trade failed. Henceforth the French dealt directly with America.

In 1769 Herries came to Thomas Coutts with a clever scheme for intro-

ducing circular notes for foreign travellers, but Thomas refused to partici-
pate. He was later blamed for his excessive caution, but it was probably
Herries he mistrusted, rather than his scheme. In fact it would have been
a timely speculation. For with the end of the Seven Years' War, the Grand
Tour through France and Italy was now an essential part of a young man's
education. Herries, who had travelled extensively in Europe, realised the
inconvenience of deciding in advance where letters of credit should be
changed. So he proposed a universal letter of credit in the form of promissory notes, which could be bought in London at the current rate of
exchange and would be issued without extra charge. Herries was to make
his profit by having use of the money until the notes came round again,
and travellers could change their notes in many capital cities. When Coutts
and other bankers rejected the idea, Herries set up his own firm with the
help of private friends and the banker, Thomas Hope of Amsterdam.

In 1770 Thomas Coutts did at least agree to be the West End bank
where the notes could be picked up. But on 1 January 1772 Herries was
ready to set up his own 'London Exchange and Banking Company' at a
new base in St James's Street with his uncle, Robert Herries, in charge.
His partners were his brother Charles, William Forbes and James Hunter
from Edinburgh, and the private financiers William Pulteney, George
Henderson and Sir William Maxwell. This venture widened the breach
with the Coutts brothers since Herries was now setting up as a banker in
competition with them at the Strand. He vainly protested that he was not
soliciting custom from Coutts's clients, but in fact, by sending out his own
advertising cards, he quite clearly was.

Herries was now anxious to get rid of John Stephen in Edinburgh, who
in his old age was finding it increasingly difficult to keep up with, or
approve, the brash new world of Mr Herries. When, as was the custom,
Edinburgh bankers and lawyers gathered for the regular one o'clock gossip
and exchange of views at Edinburgh Cross, the sight of old John Stephen
tottering up on the arm of his servant did nothing for the prestige of the
firm. In 1771 Forbes and Herries eased him out, with an allowance of
£2,400, half in money and half as £300 per annum during his life. If this
was a more generous settlement than Cochrane had received perhaps it
was because Forbes was becoming impatient with Herries and insisted. Or
perhaps Herries rightly realised that Stephen had not many years to live.
He died in September 1774.

Forbes, who had become increasingly suspicious of Herries's activities,
now broke with him and moved into a house on the President's Stairs, but
not into Provost Coutts's old apartment as he had wished. For James,
resentful and hostile, had refused his permission. Forbes was now firmly
established and no longer needed the shelter of John Coutts's name. In
January 1773 he changed the name of his bank to 'Sir William Forbes,

James Hunter & Co.' and became a distinguished Edinburgh banker, for whom Sir Walter Scott wrote an epitaph: 'Far may we search before we find a heart so manly and so kind.'[7]

Thomas and James no longer had any financial interest in the business in Edinburgh, and the house in Jeffrey's Square was merely a home for Cochrane. The brothers were now solely concerned with the Bank in the Strand.

13

The Separation

Relations between the brothers were increasingly strained in the years following Thomas's marriage. James found it difficult to accept his daughter's nursemaid as his sister-in-law; 'Brothers, however married, ought seldom to be Partners,'[1] he wrote. Quite justly he was annoyed at his brother's deception, particularly as Susannah had continued to work for him after her marriage. But now his strange behaviour, his outbursts of wild temper and incoherence alienated his friends and supporters. In 1767 he failed to be renominated for Edinburgh.

His prickly temper lost him the support of Stuart-MacKenzie and Lord Milton, so that when he stood for the Edinburgh nomination for the parliamentary election of 1767, he lost to the wily Sir Lawrence Dundas. He was then approached by Lord Carlisle to stand for Morpeth, believing that there 'was no other objection to him than his being a Scotsman'. In his favour was his reputation as a great banker, 'known to be worth £100,000'. But he behaved so irresponsibly, failing to appear for a meeting, retracting 'his most solemn promises', that in the end 'Coutts' duplicity, folly and absurdity' so annoyed Carlisle that he withdrew the offer.[2] James made no further attempts to become an MP.

Remembering all he had suffered before with his brother Patrick, Thomas saw that the time had come to end the partnership. He could not afford a partner who was unstable and possibly becoming insane. Reluctantly James agreed, accepting the appointment of Lord Bute and Lord Rochford as arbitrators. In his paranoia James suspected that Bute and his brother, Stuart-MacKenzie, were now hostile to him, and instead would have preferred Messrs Hoare and Child, two fellow bankers he trusted, but he willingly accepted Rochford, who had been Ambassador to Paris and more recently Secretary of State for the Northern Department.

In February 1775 the terms of the dissolution of the partnership were drawn up, which James signed. In March he claimed that he had not been shown a copy of the agreement until too late and, therefore, asked that the dissolution be delayed until 24 June. Thomas, 'really touched with the distress of his mind',[3] agreed, concerned that he should not be thought to take advantage of his brother's illness. Throughout the spring and summer the different claims of the two brothers were presented. On 24 May James sent the judges a confused and querulous letter accusing Thomas of concealing from him the terms of the original agreement and altering them after he, James, had signed. He complained that Thomas had 'my State of Health exposed in the most Cruel manner ... in Circulating so industriously, & I must add so very unfairly, over the Kingdom, copys of the Physicians letter to me given him for perusal'.[4] This, he felt, 'must ever prevent me, in my best Health from havg the confidence of mankind as a man of business'.[5] James's letters at this time show very clearly the state of paranoia that he was now in.

Thomas, on the other hand, presented his case to their Lordships in a careful document:

Mr James Coutts entered into Partnership with Mr Geo. Campbell in the year 1755 & had one half share of the Profit of the Business. By Mr Campbell's death in 1760 he succeeded to the *whole*, free from all burdens or restrictions whatever, & his only child inherited a considerable fortune in her own Power. Mr. James Coutts then made choice of Mr. Thos. Coutts for his partner, who quitted His Fathers House of Business at Edinburgh, & also another House of Business in the City of London, in both which he was a principal partner & in which his successors are supos'd, since his leaving it, to have acquir'd ample fortunes. The share allotted to Mr. Thomas Coutts was one third. There was no sort of stipulation made that Mr. Thomas Coutts shou'd take the Labour of the Business, & accordingly Mr. James Coutts for some time did his part, but afterwards & particularly for these last Ten years it is well known that almost the whole has been done by Mr Thos Coutts.[6]

Thomas claimed that the 'House must have dropt altogether or lost at least much of its consequence had he not dedicated to it His whole time and attention'.[7] Meanwhile, during that time, James had made a fortune. 'Twenty years more of successful Industry (tho' he shoud live so long) cannot sufficiently compensate the labour he has gone thro' on Mr. Jas Coutts's account.'[8] Thomas was prepared to offer James an adequate annuity provided that 'Mr James Coutts shall not after the 24th of June next, carry out or be concern'd in the Business of a Banker in London, or within ten miles thereof'.[9] He expected James to give him the lease of the House in the Strand 'at a fixt price'. In exchange, he was prepared for '*such annual sum as the arbitrators shall think fit.* That the whole debts due to or by the partnership shall be carried & transferr'd on the 24th day of June next into the books of the said Thos. Coutts.'[10] As for James's £8,000 share in the stock of the partnership, he suggested that it 'shall remain in the Hands of Mr. Thos. Coutts till the 24th of June 1776, then to be paid to Mr. James Coutts, together with one years Interest for the same at four p/Ct.'[11] The final clause in his proposal was that on 24 June 1776, and at all times before and after that period, Thomas Coutts should have complete charge of the partnership.

It was suggested that the value of the annuity to be paid to James should depend on the profit of the last fourteen years. Thomas objected, in a detailed document in which he explained that the period 1761 to 1775 had been unusually profitable, because stocks had risen after a very successful war, money had poured into the country and banking business flourished to 'a degree unknown before'.[12]

The Bank had certainly prospered in the last fourteen years. In 1761, the first year of their partnership, their profits had stood at £5,800, more than doubling the figure for 1759. There had been some fluctuations, but by 1765 the profits had risen to £8,807 and by 1775 to a record height of £9,703.

However, in the last years the bank crisis following the collapse of the Ayr bank* had shaken confidence: 'The great Shock Credit has lately receiv'd & the danger still to be apprehended, must considerably diminish the Profit arising to Bankers.' In addition there was now much more competition: 'the numbers of Bankers have greatly increas'd within these few years as may be known by there being only one besides ourselves at this End of the Town Fourteen years ago'.

Therefore, Thomas thought that it would be fairer that, 'If any average of Profit is necessary to form any Calculation upon, it ought not to be taken from a period further back than the last three years. . . .' But he also considered that in the future he was

better entitled to Two thirds share of the Profit for the time to come than Mr. James Coutts was for these fourteen years past, & he cannot expect any partner who will be approv'd by His Friends will take less than a quarter

Suppose therefore _____	48—to be gained
Two thirds of which will be	32
The remainder will be	16
The new partners quarter will be	12
There will remain	4

which four, shou'd seem to be the proper datum upon which the calculation for the partner leaving off a trade (He is unable to carry on) ought to be founded – but take it on the most extravagant Calculation, a tenth of the clear profits without risk, & without Labour, should seem a full compensation for what in the present State is relinquished –. Neither can the situation of the parties be left out of the Question – Mr James Coutts at the age of 42 without any family to provide for has already acquir'd an opulent fortune, a great part of which he owes to Mr. Thos Coutts's Industry – Mr. Thos Coutts at nearly the same age with a very weak

* See page 109.

constitution (much shaken by this unhappy Affair) & growing family, has *such* opulence still to acquire.

He therefore hopes whatever annual sum the arbitrators may give to Mr. James Coutts, will only be to continue while Mr. Thos Coutts shall carry on the business of a Banker – as it wou'd be hard he shou'd be loaded with an Annuity which, with all His Industry perhaps the future Business may not afford, & much more that His Family shou'd be burden'd with such an Annuity after his death. . . .

He also begs to observe that Mr. George Campbell when he took my Brother in partnership (instead of a third) gave him a *half* Share of The Profits, & loaded him at His Death with no Annuities – nor any *restrictions* whatsoever. . . . If I had insisted upon having a half instead of a third share, Mr. Jas Coutts would rather I believe have given it, than taken a Stranger into His House & I was much blam'd by my Brother, since dead, for accepting of any less.[13]

On 3 June Rochford and Bute presented their judgment. Briefly, Thomas was to pay James £50,000, while James was to relinquish all his rights in the Bank and agree not to take any banking business in the future. Thomas should pay £800 per year to James and take over all debts, those which were doubtful to be settled between them. James should give up the lease of the House in the Strand 'as it now stands for £1,600: which sum comes the nearest to the proportion that A [James] originally paid of £2,000'.[14] The House in the Strand had been leased from the Earl of Salisbury by George Middleton for sixty-nine years from 1738. The remainder of the term had been sold to James in 1768 by the Earl of Stair, Middleton's son-in-law, and there were now still seven years of the lease to run.

While the judges considered their verdict, James went abroad under the care of his daughter, Frances. From Boulogne he wrote a more composed letter to Rochford refuting Thomas's claim that he would have to give a new partner a large share of the business, since, as he said,

those Partners who find it worth their while to accept of the smallest shares, generally make the best Drudges. Mr Campbell . . . and I am sure, Mr Bruce, had at first only one eighth share each. Mr Child's partners I have been assured had much less.[15]

Finally and reluctantly James accepted their Lordships' decision. He agreed to give up his partnership and all control over the management of the Bank. A year later, however, he was still refusing to give up the lease of the House. Thomas wrote to a friend:

My bro[the]r has not accepted the annuity & refuses still to assign over his Lease of the House in terms of the award – it would be easy to force him, but *very disagreeable* – I am sure he woud be a happier man if it were done & if he woud . . . frankly & pleasantly view and acknowledge the situation of his Health *as* being what all the world knows it is . . . He might then live pleasantly with all his Friends, not one of whom I am sure ever meant any thing but what was kind and affectionate towards him.[16]

However, James did not have long to enjoy his retirement. His continental tour ended in tragedy. In March 1777 Stuart-MacKenzie, then Ambassador in Florence, wrote to Thomas informing him that his brother had become so deranged in Turin that they were obliged to 'put him in confinement'.[17] Dr Munro, the physician at the Bethlehem Hospital (Bedlam) in London, sent out two of his men to bring him home. They waited at Gibraltar for a ship for England, but there, on 15 February 1778, James died. Once more the black shadow returned to haunt Thomas.

James left a fortune to his daughter, Frances, which, after legacies, amounted to £61,000. Thomas now considered that his niece needed protection. When she had taken her father abroad in 1775, her aunt, Lady Stuart, and her cousin John, had accompanied them. Thomas suspected that Lady Stuart, whom he disliked, was trying to arrange a marriage between Frances and her son, solely for the sake of Frances's fortune. Thomas objected on a number of counts. He was genuinely attached to his niece and concerned for her happiness, which he did not believe would be found with John. He claimed that he was not concerned with her fortune. If Frances died, he wrote, Sir John was welcome to it.[18]

The unusual forcefulness of his letters revealed his deep-seated fear of the insanity in his family. As he wrote, 'I do not like relations marrying and can never approve of it and I am sure her father would never have agreed to it.'[19] More explicitly in a letter to Mrs Peagrum on 18 May 1778, he wrote:

Many unfortunate disagreeable things have happened in my family, as well as in Sir John's, & to join the Children of these two family's together is making a certain accumulation of Misery – I am sorry to revive the memory of disagreeable things, which it is the interest of my own family should be forgot & nothing cou'd make me think of doing it but seeing the whole happiness of Miss Coutts's future life at stake.[20]

These letters deeply offended his niece. She cut short their correspondence and on 16 September 1778 married her cousin John. However, the feud was later patched up, and she and her daughters became welcome guests at Thomas's home.

According to the terms of the settlement, the leasehold of the Bank premises at 59 Strand now belonged to Thomas, but James had refused to leave his apartment there and Thomas was reluctant to disturb him. So it was probably not until after James's death that Thomas, Susannah and their little girls finally moved to the solid comfort of the rooms over the Bank. Here they were to live until the beginning of 1794.

It must have been with some satisfaction that Susannah returned as mistress to the house where she had been a maid. Thomas regretted leaving the stimulating company of the coffee house, but at least now he could keep a closer eye on his work and on the clerks who lived over the Bank. He delighted in the distant views from his windows, over the river to the Surrey hills, for although he enjoyed the bustle of the world, he often longed for the freshness of the country.

Other great bankers bought fine country estates. Mr Child created a magnificent mansion, Osterley Park: 'Oh, the palace of palaces ... such expense ... such taste,' sighed Horace Walpole. Mr Hoare's estate at Stourhead was, and still is, famous for its gardens. But Thomas preferred to keep his cash in hand, ready for emergencies or to help his friends.

Although he never owned a country estate, he greatly expanded his property in the Strand. By the end of his life he had acquired the lease of the buildings between the Strand and the river from John Street to William Street. In April 1775 one of James's last acts before his retirement was to take the lease of 17 John Street, linking it to the bank at 59 Strand by an underground passage. In 1788 Thomas also took over 16 John Street. Ten years later he was granted, by an Act of Parliament, the right to build a bridge across William Street to take the place of the tunnel. Between 1802 and 1817 he also took apartments in the Adelphi at the corner of John Street. There would be other alterations after Thomas's death, but these extensive premises housed Coutts & Co. until the next century, when it moved across the Strand.

14

New Partners

Once James had retired, Thomas needed another partner. Concerned for his brother's welfare he chose a man who would be, he thought, agreeable to him. Adam Drummond, the MP for St Ives, was James's 'old acquaintance and a good humoured man and I hope will continue to live in friendship with him'.[1]

Thomas was, however, a little doubtful about Drummond from the beginning. 'I have been oblig'd to make Choice more hastily than I coud have wisht of a Partner,' he wrote to Lord Stair on 1 September 1775; 'I felt so fearful of the dissipated manners of the young People of the present age that I believe I shall be thought to have gone into the other extreme in taking Mr Adam Drummond the member for St Ives.'[2]

Drummond was, in fact, mourning the death of his beloved wife and, finding the empty house unbearable, needed to occupy his mind with new work. Thomas had also been reluctant to take Drummond because of his association with the Ayr Bank. In the more stable years after the Jacobite rebellion a number of provincial banking companies were established, among them, in the agricultural west of Scotland, the Ayr Bank was launched, a major enterprise based to a large degree upon landed wealth enjoying the support of Scottish noblemen of great possessions. In 1772 it was collapsing, affecting most of the private bankers. It had been badly managed by the directors – important decisions taken without a quorum. At the same time Scotsmen were in the grip of a speculative frenzy, buying estates in the West Indies, building country houses and the New Town in Edinburgh, and borrowing extensively from the Ayr Bank. In June the Scottish bank of Neal, James, Fordyce & Downe failed mainly because of rash gambling by Fordyce. They were closely connected with the Ayr Bank and caused its collapse. The crisis affected not only Scotland but also the international money market. The Ayr Bank's debts were finally liquidated by the Bank of Scotland and the Royal Bank, relying on the security of the great landed estates of Queensberry, Buccleuch and others.

The Bank in the Strand became known as Thomas Coutts & Co. On 7 September Thomas wrote to a customer, the tenth Earl of Huntingdon:

The very great uncertainty of life and health makes it improper for any banker to be long without a partner; I have therefore admitted Adam Drummond Esquire, the member of Parliament for St Ives, to share of my business; but we have fixed the firm or name of the shop (to avoid future changes during my life) to be Thomas Coutts & Co. I trouble your lordship to beg you will be so good to direct your future drafts for money and other commands to Thomas Coutts & Co. and also that Mr. Dawson may appraise any of the country's stewards to remit their bills to me by the same address.[3]

Thomas, it will be noted, usually referred to the Bank as 'the shop' and clients were always 'customers'.

Drummond lived on the premises in the Strand, but did not last long. On 24 June 1780 Thomas wrote to his friend, Colonel John Walkinshaw Crawfurd:

I have thought it expedient on account of Mr. Drummond being a partner in The Ayr Bank that he shoud retire from my House and Partnership which he has accordingly done – it is not proper that any Partner in a Banker's shop shoud in any shape be lyable to Payments w[hi]ch he cannot answer on Demand. My Letters will for sometime at least come as usual under his cover. We are perfectly in good friendship.[4]

Drummond seems to have played little part in the business of the Bank. 'I fear', said Thomas, 'I must still expect to be the slave.'[5]

In fact Thomas was always the master and was so successful that by April 1777 he needed an additional partner. This was made more necessary by the loss of his chief clerk. To Thomas's astonishment Mr Charles Taylor, who had worked in the House for nearly twenty years, had the temerity to demand to be made a partner immediately. If not, he said, he would leave that hour. This seemed such an absurdity to Thomas that he agreed to let him go at once. 'I hardly know any person I think more improper in every respect to be a Partner in a Banker's shop than Mr Taylor.'[6]

In April 1777 he found a new partner in a young stockbroker, Edmund Antrobus, who, he wrote,

will exert himself & will in time give great satisfaction to all my Friends, as well as to his Partners – but I flatter myself I shall always be so much master of my own business as not to depend altogether on any man.[7]

This was an excellent appointment: Antrobus and his family were of the greatest importance in the coming years.

Thomas Coutts, who was to complain of poor health for the rest of his life, recognised that he needed a strong right arm, especially since he could see stormy weather ahead. For the next forty years he was to steer the Bank through rough seas whipped up by the American War of Independence, the French Revolution and the Napoleonic Wars.

*　　　*　　　*

In April 1777 Edmund Antrobus was twenty-seven years old and had established a flourishing stockbroking business in the City. For more than a hundred years the Antrobus family were to bring expertise and stability to the Bank.

How Thomas met Edmund is not known, but they had many opportunities, for Edmund's relations, the Sanxay family, had been customers at the Bank in the Strand for more than twenty-five years. Edmund had come to London from Congleton in Cheshire at the age of fifteen in 1765 and was followed two years later by his brother, Philip. They settled in the Strand under the protection of their uncle, Robert Sanxay, druggist and teaman to George III. In later years his nephews were to claim that uncle Robert had been the foundation of the fortune of all the family. The two families had been closely connected for years and, indeed, had intermarried three times in fifty years.

The Antrobus family had their roots in Congleton and had for generations owned land in that part of Cheshire. Edmund's father, Philip, had a dyer's business, but he usually styled himself 'Gentleman'. His mother, Mary Rowley, brought in more property, particularly around Eaton. Philip's aunt Jane had married the Reverend Daniel Sanxay, who founded the famous Cheam School. Their daughter, Hannah, married Philip's brother, John, and their son Edmund married yet another Antrobus, a cousin, Maria.

Daniel Sanxay had been brought to England as a little boy of five by his father, a Huguenot pastor escaping persecution in his native France. The family had settled in Exeter, where Daniel grew up, and where Daniel's father made his living by teaching the Huguenot émigrés settled around Plymouth and Exeter. A remarkably clever boy, Daniel went to Oxford, where he took his BA in 1700 and his MA in 1703. How he met Jane Antrobus is not known, but they were married in 1711 and with her help they set up a school in Cheam, which became so prosperous that in 1719 they were able to build a new school at the top of the High Street. His son, James, took over and, though he lacked his father's ability, kept the school going.

Daniel had seven children, four sons and three daughters. Edmund became a distinguished surgeon and was famous for his collection of pictures; he was also a friend and neighbour of Caleb Whitefoord. Robert was not only the King's 'druggist and teaman' but was also engaged in banking. Daniel became a 'laceman' with a business 'at the Sign of the Peacock' at the corner of Northumberland and Strand. He was a customer of George Campbell's bank as early as 1759, and ten years later James Coutts bought 'gold & silver lace' from him.

There was yet another relation in the Strand, Philip's brother John, who had married Hannah Sanxay. He was described as a 'teaman', but he was also a banker and stockbroker with a very lucrative business – as his accounts in Coutts & Co.'s ledgers show. His sons, to our confusion, were also called Edmund and John and became bankers and brokers in their turn.

Since the Sanxays had their businesses in or near the Strand there are many ways that Thomas Coutts could have met Edmund. He might have bought his innumerable medical prescriptions from Robert Sanxay. He could, as his friend the Duchess of Gordon did in 1769, have purchased '6lbs of superfine tea at 20/- a lb'[8] from Edmund's uncle John. He could have met the artistic uncle Edmund through his many artist friends, or bought lace from Edmund's uncle Daniel, as James had done.

However, it is most likely that he met Edmund through his bill-broking business, and must have been impressed by the sturdy young man from Cheshire. Edmund had been unusually well-educated at the local grammar school in Congleton by a distinguished headmaster, Mr Mabon, who gave him a lifelong love of classical literature as well as a solid grounding in mathematics. Philip had been sent to a similar school at Burton-on-Trent. Both they and their younger brothers, John and Thomas, were excellent representatives of middle-class, middle England, which provided so much of the solid worth of the eighteenth century.

Edmund was soon to be joined in London by his younger brothers Philip, Thomas and John, who were all under the care of their uncle, Robert Sanxay. It is probable that they made their home with him in his comfortable house in Spring Gardens near Charing Cross, but certainly there was a host of other relations to welcome them; and on their frequent expeditions to Cheam, they were cossetted by aunts and cousins. His Huguenot relations undoubtedly gave Edmund that wider vision which was to become apparent later, especially in his understanding of the importance of contacts with Europe and his insistence on the need to learn foreign languages. His brother Thomas was a shadowy figure; he was to join Lord Macartney's embassy to China and died there.

Edmund and Philip probably first learned the business of broking from their uncle, John Antrobus, and by 1773 they had set up as brokers in the City. Edmund was always the dominant partner, hardworking, sensible and upright. His portrait reveals a strong character: he looks at the world directly with steady eyes under firm brows, but the mouth is kind. Philip was more easy-going, plump and placid and, as Edmund later claimed, inclined to be indolent, but he was a competent and successful broker. When, in 1777, Edmund left their partnership to join Thomas Coutts, Philip stayed on to develop the firm which eventually became the world-famous James Capel & Co.

In 1779 Philip lived in Lancaster House, the Strand, and later in Craven Street, where Caleb Whitefoord was his neighbour. In 1785 he took out his licence as a stockbroker and from then onwards he, and later James Capel & Co., were to be closely allied with the Bank in the Strand. Most of Philip's business came from them; usually around half were credits from Coutts & Co. In 1786, for example, credits from Coutts & Co. were £206,514 out of £413,624.

When in April 1777 Thomas invited Edmund to become a partner, he accepted with pleasure and in 1783 his young brother, John, joined him there. Successful though he had been as a stockbroker, Edmund felt it a privilege to join Thomas Coutts in the Strand. Thus began a partnership which would last for half a century.

15

Friends and Correspondents

Now that James and John were dead, and Patrick was shut away, the honour of the family was in Thomas's sole hands. He felt profoundly his duty to maintain the prestige of his father's name and the responsibility often weighed heavily, bringing stress and illness. Always concerned about his health, from now on he became obsessed.

It must be remembered, however, that he had reason to worry about the fragility of life. His father had died young, he had lost two brothers, his four sons had died in infancy and one of his daughters was showing signs of a nervous illness. Now he felt that his life was drawing to a close and he was beginning to worry about his successor at the Bank. He longed for someone in the family 'to take the oar' from his hands and he sighed for his lost sons. 'Had my first son liv'd,' he wrote sadly to Colonel Crawfurd on 3 January 1786, 'he woud have been now of Age.'[1] At least he hoped one of his daughters would marry what he called 'a man of business'.

At this time he needed his friends. Susannah was occupied in bringing up her three little girls and was hardly a stimulating companion. However, he was fortunate in having so many interesting men and women with whom he could correspond and exchange views on foreign and domestic affairs. His letters, especially during the years 1775–88, reflect the wide extent of his interests and his sound sense. His style is unmistakable, forthright and fluent, frequently laced with Shakespearean allusions. His handwriting, open and generous, often wandering uphill on the page, reflects an unexpected freedom in a banker who prided himself on his exactness.

The talent for friendship was Thomas's greatest gift. His letters to his closest friends range over many years and spanned the globe. In return he received fascinating and illuminating accounts of life in many parts of the world – America, India and Europe. Fellow Scots, constant travellers to distant lands, sent him letters, gifts, and fine wines from France and Portugal. Joseph Farington, whose diaries are the source of much information at this time, noted that there was always a plentiful supply of wine and brandy on Mr Coutts's table. As he followed the travels of his friends on the huge maps on his wall or turned his globe to find their remote stations, he might well have reflected with pride that his was a world bank and that he himself was a citizen of the world. These were the years in which he expressed most freely his ideas on politics and the state of the economy, especially in letters to friends like Caleb Whitefoord, Colonel Crawfurd and the Earl of Stair.

Always conscious of family duty, Thomas kept in touch with his distant relation, the unfortunate Clementina Walkinshaw, mistress of Bonnie Prince Charlie. She had fallen in love with the defeated Prince in 1747 and had later joined him in his wanderings through France and the Low Countries. He treated her so badly that in 1760 she escaped and settled with Charlotte, their daughter, in a convent. She appealed to the Prince's father, the Old Chevalier, who allowed her an income of 10,000 livres and promised that she should always be provided for. After his death in 1766 the Cardinal Duke of York, who took responsibility for her upkeep, reduced her income by half. When Prince Charles Edward separated from his legitimate wife, he sent for his daughter Charlotte and gave her the title of the Duchess of Albany. The Prince died in 1788 and his daughter a year later, bequeathing all her property to the Cardinal Duke of York, asking him to take care of her mother. However, he failed to keep up the payments of the allowance and, in her poverty, Clementina turned to her 'only friend', Thomas Coutts. Until her death in 1802 she received kind letters from him and regular sums of money from his own purse.

Caleb, more than anyone, understood how impossible James Coutts had become. He had been a friend to both brothers, and remained kindly and sympathetic to James in his distressed last years. Indeed, before James had left for the continent, he had given Caleb the delicate task of paying off his mistress in Soho. Apparently she had become a nuisance, appearing at the Bank to ask after him. James wanted her to be allowed an annuity provided that she stayed away from London.[2] So Thomas kept no secrets from Caleb and could write to him in perfect confidence. Susannah was also at ease with him, inviting herself to supper and telling him of the death of her favourite dog. But she did not trust her pen even to him: her letters are in Thomas's handwriting.

John Walkinshaw Crawfurd was Thomas's cousin and a distant relative of Clementina Walkinshaw. He was unmarried and the owner of a ruined castle and run-down estate, Crawfurdland in Ayrshire, which Thomas always referred to as his 'watery acres'. A brave soldier who had served at Dettingen and Fontenoy, he was never to be promoted because of his loyalty to his friend, the Jacobite Lord Kilmarnock. After the '45 rebellion, when Kilmarnock was condemned to death and went shaking to the scaffold, the Colonel had stood beside him to the last to give him courage. He was partially pardoned when George III came to the throne and in 1761 was appointed Falconer to the King in Scotland. He gave Thomas the same loyal friendship and, indeed, planned to make him his heir. Thomas and Susannah always kept a room and a welcome ready for him in their home.

Many of Thomas's closest friends were his kin, for though a lowland Scot he had as strong a sense of family as any Highland clansman. Through his mother's family he was connected with the Stuarts; with the Earl of Buchan and his relations the Erskines; and above all with Gilbert Elliot, who became Baron Minto in 1797 and the first Earl in 1813. Thomas's mother's aunt married Elliot's grandfather and the two families were on particularly friendly terms. Thomas wrote to Elliot with an especial confidence and freedom until his death in 1814.

Elliot's career may be briefly outlined here. He studied as a boy in Paris under their fellow Scot, David Hume, who was then a secretary at the British Embassy. In 1771, after Oxford University, he was called to the Bar and two years later became a Whig Member of Parliament. He was appointed Governor of Corsica in 1794. As will be seen he became very useful to Thomas when, in 1800, he was the government envoy to Vienna, and even more so when he became Governor-General of India in 1807. In return for the help he gave to Thomas's friends and relations, the banker used his influence to persuade the Government to pay his overdue salary.

No one was more affectionately regarded or more in Thomas's confidence than William Adam. William, who became a distinguished lawyer, was the son of John Adam, one of the famous brothers who were at this time building in London with classical grace and elegance. Educated in Edinburgh he was called to the Scottish Bar in 1773 and nine years later to the English Bar. His friendship with Thomas really began in 1791, when Thomas asked him to be a Trustee for his will. He was immensely useful as a lawyer to Thomas, especially when, in 1805, he became Attorney General to the Prince of Wales. He became a Baron of the Exchequer of Scotland in 1814, but his career was crowned when, two years later, he was appointed Lord Chief Commissioner of the Jury Court of Scotland. In politics he was a Whig and an enthusiastic supporter of Charles James Fox, and he represented Scottish seats in Parliament from 1780 to 1812.

It was perhaps through Adam's influence that Thomas began his surprising relationship with that most brilliant and most dissolute of politicians. Fox had been encouraged from childhood in his extravagant habits by his amoral father, Henry Fox, later first Baron Holland. In spite of a wild youth, womanising and gambling, he absorbed a deep knowledge of the classics at Eton and Oxford and became one of the outstanding politicians of the age. A Member of Parliament from 1768 he became a junior Lord of the Treasury in 1772, but was dismissed by the King two years later. George III's dislike was increased by Fox's violent opposition to the war against the American Revolution and to Lord North and his Tory Government. When the Whigs returned to power in 1782 he became Foreign Secretary, but resigned soon after. The controversial Fox–North coalition of 1783 damaged his prospects. In the election of 1784 his campaign in Westminster became famous when the lovely Duchess of Devonshire canvassed for him. Thanks to her enthusiastic support he won Westminster though the Whigs lost the election. They did not return to power until 1806, when Fox became Foreign Secretary for the brief time until his death in that year.

Throughout his tempestuous parliamentary career he managed to make brilliant extempore speeches after all-night gambling sessions. His great black eyebrows and careless dress were the delight of the caricaturists. In 1782 he took as his mistress a beautiful and intelligent courtesan, Elizabeth Armistead, who, according to contemporary reports, could already 'claim the conquest of two ducal coronets, a marquis, four earls and a viscount'[3] – to say nothing of the Prince of Wales. But she and Fox fell deeply and lastingly in love and were faithful to each other until Fox's death. At the end of his life Fox told her that he loved her more than life itself. She managed to wean him from gambling and they lived openly together at Fox's pleasant house, St Anne's Hill, near Chertsey in Surrey. Later in 1795 he married her, but they chose to keep the marriage secret until they went abroad together in 1802.

This then was the man whose charm and brilliance dazzled even Thomas. They first became acquainted either through Fox's friend, 'Fish' Craufurd, or through William Adam or Lord Macartney in 1787, when Fox's debts were so horrendous that his friends combined to bail him out. Fox was encouraged to appeal to Thomas for a loan, which he did in August 1787. In a typically frank letter he explained his debts, his inability to pay the £3,000 of annuities he owed to creditors, the £3,500 to tradesmen and the £1,500 to people in Paris. He frankly confessed to Thomas that he would probably not be able to repay him and offered no security; even after his death his Executors would not be able to settle his debts.

This honesty appealed to Thomas, who, on 20 September 1787, lent him £5,000; in June the following year, when Fox was still in debt, he gave him a further £5,000. These were in fact gifts, which he later acknowledged in his personal record. Against the Fox debts he wrote, 'not to be press'd or any interest ever ask'd for', and 'NB never to be demanded'.[4] This generosity was not without some self-interest. Fox was a bosom friend of the Prince of Wales and at this time Thomas was desperately trying to retain his custom. Nevertheless, Fox was, as will be seen, always welcomed as a guest by Thomas and his family.

However, the friend to whom Thomas wrote most freely on the state of the nation and its finances was John Dalrymple, the fifth Earl of Stair, who must have known the Coutts family in Edinburgh, for the Dalrymples had an apartment above them in their house on President's Stairs. There was also a common connection with the Bank since, as will be remembered, he had married George Middleton's daughter, Margaret, in 1748.

He was a lawyer who became a representative peer for Scotland in 1771. He fiercely opposed the war against the American colonies and so lost his seat in the House. In his retirement he wrote unpopular pamphlets recommending the increase of the land tax and the cession of Gibraltar and North Canada as expensive luxuries. Thomas Coutts had much sympathy with the 'Cassandra of the State' and enjoyed a correspondence in which he could write with frankness on the follies of the Government. They both had foreseen trouble in America, even before 14 April 1775, when the first shots at Lexington had signalled the beginning of the American War of Independence.

On 1 September 1775 Thomas wrote to him that

the prospect upon a rebellion & a foreign war is gloomy enough. . . . I am assur'd there has been considerable aid in different ways sent from Bristol to The Americans & that there is great suspicion of insurrections in that neighbourhood which have alarm'd administration – when once it comes to that & the danger is at hand the pannic will be great. Meanwhile violent coercive measures appear to be seriously determin'd. . . . I should think great sums of money will be wanted.[5]

In 1775 Thomas shared the Earl's impatience with the Government's handling of the economy. The Prime Minister, Lord North, was complacently resting on a period of unprecedented prosperity after the end of the Seven Years' War, unwilling or unable to see the dangers of rebellion brewing in the American colonies, and blind to the threat of renewed war with France. In the summer of 1775 the Earl had asked Thomas to find out the exact state of the 'funded debt', since he believed that the Prime Minister had overestimated the nation's reserves. Thomas, who had eyes and ears everywhere, knew that government resources would be seriously drained by a war in America, and he was alarmed by the 'wonderful ignorance & disrelish' about the state of the nation 'among men of rank'.[6] He shared the Earl's concern about the economy and was depressed that there were only one or two ministers capable of understanding the document the Earl was preparing.

Like most businessmen, Thomas was aware that a war against the American colonies would be disastrous. No one knew better than he how much depended on trade with America. After all, his Montrose relations had been engaged in the tobacco trade to Virginia for generations, and he had many customers who traded with the colonies and who would be bankrupted by a war. On the surface, as he told the Earl on 17 October 1775,

Every thing here continues to wear the face of Public prosperity. . . . The stocks rise and The dependants of administration give out that no money will be wanted.

... These things will serve perhaps to furnish expedients for Lord North to continue the deception, on people who are incapable of understanding the Subject, & who are besides very willing to be deceiv'd. ...

However, he added, 'I cannot after all see how these American operations are to go on without borrowing – & largely too.'[7]

As the War of Independence blundered on, Thomas became more and more depressed. He wrote to the Earl on 10 June 1776:

If no termination of American disputes comes this year, God knows what will be the consequence, or whether it will be in the Power of the best abilities to relieve us. Meanwhile the sum funded this year I suppose is hardly sufficient to make good the deficiencys on the last instead of being equal to the expense of the present.[8]

In the summer of 1777, both Thomas and the Earl realised how hopeless was the war against the American colonies. Thomas, who was also aware of the growing threat of a war with France, almost welcomed such a war since it would at least, as he supposed, mean that the army would have to leave America. 'In the desperate situation we are brought into by this American affair', he wrote to Stair, 'I know not whether an immediate war with France is most to be dreaded or wisht for ... neither shou'd I all together dispair of success if I cou'd see there was one person fit to conduct the ship in such a storm.'[9] There was only William Pitt the elder, now the Earl of Chatham, but he was old and ailing. 'At any rate in case of a war [we] must I suppose withdraw the Army from America – how happy wou'd it have been had it never been sent there.'[10]

Even good news from America depressed him because 'I fear ... it will only give Administration Spirits for another ruinous Campaign – ruin seems certain if they go on & near the same if they do not.'[11]

There was still no hope of peace at the end of 1777, which, as Thomas told Stair, 'makes Business very ticklish ... 'tho' Business seems rather to grow upon me, & I have the good luck to be I believe as much in the confidence of those who deal with me as any body cou'd wish'.[12] As the war continued, Thomas became more and more openly critical. Trade was affected and many of his customers were ruined. The ships which had sailed laden with furs, cotton and hogsheads of tobacco from the colonies and with sugar from the West Indies, and which had returned across the Atlantic with manufactured goods, now stood idle.

Thomas became increasingly depressed by the inefficiency of the military in America and by the financial disaster which he anticipated at home. At the end of 1777 he was so alarmed that he even took it upon himself to get politically involved – a most unusual step for one who had always tried to keep out of politics. By January 1778 the situation was desperate, because North was hopelessly inadequate and knew it: 'Your Majesty's service requires a man of great abilities,' North told the King. 'I am certainly not such a man.'[13] Thomas believed that such a man was the great Earl of Chatham, now retired. On 13 January 1778 he wrote to the Countess of Chatham,

thoroughly convinced if conciliatory measures be practicable with America, that they can only be brought about by his Lordship; nor is his aid less necessary in any other view of public affairs, which grow every day more desperate and alarming, without another hand in either house of Parliament that any man in the kingdom thinks capable of guiding us through the storm – I mean of taking the lead.[14]

The Earl of Chatham, who had been the architect of victory in the Seven Years' War, had been for some years crippled by gout, had withdrawn as Chief Minister in October 1768 and was now, in his retirement, communicating with the world mainly through his wife. In 1777 and 1778 Thomas had been trying to extract Chatham's overdue pension from the Treasury at the Countess's request, since she did not want the Earl to be worried with money matters. Therefore, she was grateful for Thomas's intervention on their behalf, his kind concern and the money he lent her. Chatham had undoubtedly been extravagant, building a great estate and living in grand style, and the Countess was weighed down by their debts. She knew her Lord 'means to give a settlement to his affairs, but would wish at present to preserve himself free from any business, in this sad crisis for the public. How humiliating, how ruinous!'[15] It was the Countess who had to suffer the humiliation of going begging to his banker. Certainly Thomas was touched by the Countess's distress and, in spite of Chatham's financial troubles, Thomas had great admiration for him as a statesman.

On 21 January 1778 Thomas wrote again to the Countess, attempting to persuade Chatham to return to power:

As no peace with America can ever be made by the present administration, I apprehend the King would be very glad, at the present moment, to receive a proposal from the only person who it is possible should *now* succeed in a point so essential, not only to the welfare, but even to the existence of Great Britain as a powerful nation; providing it was accompanied with an offer to allow of one nobleman being in the cabinet who may be called in the language of politics his friend: Lord Rochford, I apprehend, would be satisfactory to his Majesty, and less objectionable and more popular than any other.[16]

This, he claimed, was a view he had heard and written down, and with which he completely agreed, since he saw 'so plainly the danger to every man of any property'[17] Only 'Lord Chatham's abilities, being still and only able to save us'.[18]

His Lordship replied through the Countess on 22 January that, 'To rescue a falling country from the last consequences of their own fatal errors

... is a work too dangerous. ... Nothing short of command can be a motive to act in desperate cases; zeal, duty and obedience may outlive hope.'[19] To which Thomas replied that '*commands*' – that is, from the King – must inevitably come 'now when there is no hope left but in his Lordship's abilities and magnanimity, to make, peace, or war, with credit or success'.[20]

Meanwhile, Thomas reported to the Earl of Stair that he had information that France was preparing for war – though the City did not seem to believe it. During February stocks went down and up with the news from America: North was now offering peace, free pardons and to treat with Congress on any terms short of independence.

In March Thomas wrote to the Countess again. He was surprised that the King had not yet publicly called on Chatham, but he knew that, if his Lordship took power again, Lord Rochford would be willing to help. Meanwhile, as he wrote to Stair, 'the merchants are breaking in The City every day & every thing wearing a face of ruin & bankruptcy'.[21] However, in April all hope of Chatham's return was dashed: after speaking in the House of Lords, he suddenly died. Thus ended one of the few attempts made by Thomas to influence the course of political history.

In June 1778 Thomas retired to Bath, depressed and ill, though he still wrote kindly to the widowed Countess, who was weighed down by her late husband's debts. As he said to Stair, 'Every thing in Public matters appears as gloomy as possible.'[22]

By July, he was writing to Stair that all were anxious: 'the ruin hanging over us is dreadful, & the imbecility of government unequal even to the conduct of quiet times'.[23] In the autumn he took his family on an agreeable jaunt to Scotland to improve his health, calling in at Liverpool on the way, where he talked to merchants and where he found that, in spite of the war now in progress with France, in September there was a temporary lift in spirits. There had been 'rich prizes' from the sea battles and the 'safe arrival of West India and other Fleets'. And, much to Thomas's surprise, stocks rose.

The war dragged on. In August 1781 he wrote to Colonel Crawfurd:

I see little hope of National Peace this year – in America we still are going the wrong way to work. These expeditions into the Country however brilliantly executed by Lord Cornwallis end in nothing but distress on our side & encouragement to The Rebels – The Rancour and Hatred of all America to the very name of Briton gains ground every year ... we must fall by the slower hands of consuming Expence & it's certain consequence National Bankruptcy.[24]

He believed that the Government would have to borrow another £15 million to pay for the war and raise taxes of about £1 million to pay the interest on the loan.

Once again, in the autumn of 1781, he took a long 'ramble' to Scotland and returned still despairing of peace, and still fearing national bankruptcy, although he saw no appearance of a country at war. He travelled by way of Lancaster, where he found 'nothing but symptoms of apparent prosperity. The War fills their pockets.' On 23 November 1781 his gloomy forecast that the prospect in America was 'melancholy' was proved true. Two days later the news reached London that the British army had suffered a catastrophic defeat at Yorktown and that Cornwallis had surrendered his whole army on 19 October.

In February 1782 Thomas saw no hope of peace and at last, in March, the King reluctantly allowed Lord North to resign. Yet in April stocks had risen to above 14 per cent premium. Thomas had, as he wrote, 'never been of an adventurous Temper' and had long since sold out his share, but others profited by the war.

In July 1782 he was still writing glumly to the Earl of Stair, 'what may be in the Power of chance to do for the Salvation of the Country, I know not, but I am sure with regard to myself I see no means of shelter from the coming storm'.[25]

At last it became clear that Britain had no hope of holding her colonies in America. On 20 January 1783 preliminary peace treaties were signed with France and Spain. The King was forced to accept the inevitable.

In the new administration Lord Shelburne, whom Thomas knew well, became Secretary of State for the Colonies and was therefore in charge of the peace negotiations. It may be that it was Thomas who suggested that Caleb Whitefoord would be an excellent intermediary with the American Ambassador to Paris, Benjamin Franklin. Certainly, as Franklin reported, 'an old friend and near neighbour of mine many years in London appeared in Passy and introduced a Mr Oswald who gave me letters from Lord Shelburne'.[26] These made it clear that the new administration wanted peace. Oswald became an informal negotiator with plenipotentiary powers and Caleb gave up his work in London to become the sole secretary to the commission set up to draft the peace treaty. He remained in Paris for thirteen months and undoubtedly kept Thomas in touch with the progress of the negotiations. In his usual discreet way, Thomas left few letters from this period. Excellent though Caleb's work was, as Franklin testified, he had great difficulty in persuading the Government to compensate him and it was not until 1793 that he extracted from them a paltry pension of £200 a year.

The end of the American War of Independence brought little comfort to Thomas. 'I tremble to think', he wrote to Colonel Crawfurd on 8 May 1783, 'of the load of Debts & decline of Trade & Empire which must follow the late ruinous Wars.' In June he agreed with the Earl of Stair that there was 'just reason for apprehension as to The Stocks'. Now at last he wished he had invested in land and property and confessed that,

Were I free of Business I wou'd not hesitate a minute – but my Situation is peculiar at the head of a considerable Business, which is founded in the power of obliging my customers with Loans of money (or at least it has from custom become necessary), which I durst not do without a considerable fund for I shou'd not choose like my predecessors to do it trusting to The Shop – as you know it is all payable on Demand – besides I do not see how a Banker can be safe from the crash of Public Credit for even Bank notes must *go* in the general ruin.

Another objection or two weigh also with me against buying land.

1st. The trouble attending it superadded upon me who have already more Business than I can do.

2nd. Having no son – & only Three Daughters who probably will divide what I leave, in a few years, for my Life is by no means a good one.

I have not however made up my mind entirely on the Subject & sometimes have thought of looking for an Estate – nearer the Capital wou'd give me less trouble, & is therefore preferable if the terms were as good.[27]

In December 1783 the situation looked even blacker:

Nobody more than a Banker feels the impending ruin – what he can do or how conduct himself (continuing in Business) so as to avoid falling under it, I cannot see. He is a Trustee – accountable to His Friends – for sums far beyond His private fortune. He must keep (principally) Bank notes to answer their demands – if he were to lay out His private fortune in Land – it is tied up in the meanwhile (& *may incommode him*) & is answerable to His Friends in the long run for more than it is worth.[28]

16

Thomas Coutts, Banker, 1777–88

In many ways the years 1777 to 1788 were the most creative period of Thomas Coutts's career. For the next decade he was not only to set the direction the business would take for more than a century, but he was to create that special ethos which distinguishes Coutts & Co. even today.

During that period the Bank had achieved spectacular growth. In 1774, the year before the partnership with James was dissolved, the ledgers show the partners' profits to be £5,350. In the year of the dissolution there had been a sharp rise to £9,703 and, although after that there had been some fluctuations, in 1779 profits had increased to £12,279 and rose further, reaching £27,946 in 1782. Though they fell again to £17,980 in 1788, this was still a healthy advance on the Bank's position over the last fourteen years. For this Thomas could take the credit.

He was now fifty-two, with thirty-five years of solid business experience behind him. His overriding aim was to develop a bank which would honour the name of Coutts as his father had done, a bank in which his family would always have 'the ascendancy'. This he repeatedly insisted when he came to draft the terms of partnership. As he later wrote to Edmund Antrobus, on 4 May 1791, 'I hope the house will forever go by the name of Coutts & Co., vanity may perhaps have its share but I hope reason had a greater share in the wish for I am sure it is essential for a banking house to keep always the same name.'[1]

The customers he sought were not only men and women of rank, power and influence, but people of distinction in the wider world of the theatre and the arts. In their pursuit he was quick to seize opportunities and persistent in following them up. Though cautious, he rightly trusted his judgment of human nature and was prepared to take risks with a needy man for whom he saw a future. He took infinite pains to keep his customers' accounts, even sometimes at a loss to himself. Thus he kept their loyalty through difficult times.

By far the greatest profit of his business came from lending money, but his rules were strict: no loan unless the security was firm. However, there were many times when his kind heart overruled his wiser head. When his friend Colonel Charles Stuart, fourth son of the third Earl of Bute, wanted a loan of £4,000 for the purchase of property at Highcliff, near Christchurch, Hampshire, he had to refuse as a banker what he could grant as a friend. As a banker he wrote to Stuart: 'In the latter capacity it is impossible to advance 4000£ on a Security – the Purchase money of which is only that sum, & the whole property bringing in no income to pay the Interest.'[2] But as a friend he was 'willing & ready to give my aid & advance the 4000£'.[3] As he explained:

I did not mean that my House was not safe in lending you 4000£ secured by The Purchase you was going to make and the Domain of High Cliff: but money lent on Mortgage should never exceed one Half or Two Thirds of the value of The Land – and unless this is the case, & also that there is the same proportion of Rent payable by Tenants for The Premises to secure a Fund for Payment of Interest – any Mortgage will be thought ineligible to a lender.[4]

This caused him embarrassment and some offence to his friend, so that he had to explain:

I must further beg you to observe further that Bankers in general do not practice much lending money on mortgages – even the most eligible – and that for myself I never lent any in that way but to oblige & serve my Customers or my Friends.

I am always better pleased with the lowest rate of interest and to have my money within my command.[5]

At this time lending money was a very risky business. For though great fortunes were quickly made in India and in the West Indies, they were lost even more swiftly at the gaming tables, when men threw away great estates in a single evening. So compulsive did the gambling mania become that some of the greatest families, from the royal family downwards, were in deep financial trouble.

During the years of peace young men and women travelled through Europe on the Grand Tour and came back with extravagant dreams of Palladian mansions, embellished with magnificent pictures and statues. They commissioned the great gardeners of the period to lay out the grounds of their estates, creating lakes and eminences and planting great avenues of trees – to our present delight but to their financial ruin. As Thomas toured the country, staying sometimes for weeks at the great houses of his noble customers, he not only enjoyed himself, but was quietly assessing the value of their estates should their owners need to mortgage them, or borrow on their security. The royal dukes in particular were smitten by this *folie de grandeur*: the Prince of Wales, the Duke of Kent and the Duke of York all spent immense sums creating dream palaces.

However, there was another important reason why great men needed large loans at this time. The Government frequently failed to pay their pensions or salaries for years at a time. In the past, George Middleton had tried in vain for months to get the Earl of Stair's allowances paid when he was the British Ambassador in Paris. Time and again Thomas Coutts used all his influence to persuade the Government to pay its debts and prided himself that no other banker had such a pull at the Treasury as he did. Even so, when he tried to get Gilbert Elliot's allowance paid, he had to use near blackmail – threatening to expose the Government's inefficiency.

The failure to pay salaries was the cause of much of the corruption in high places of this period. If the Government would not provide, diplomats, civil servants and even ministers helped themselves. Securing a place in the Civil Service or promotion in the army depended on the use of both influence and affluence. This is well illustrated by a frank letter of 13 May 1800 to Thomas Coutts by Mr Thomas Barry, a director of the East India Company, offering to find places for Mr Coutts's protégés, but obviously expecting him to pay for the service. Since he received so little salary as a director, his

principal recompense must therefore flow from the patronage usually allotted to him as a Director. That patronage it has been my practice to confer on those I respect as my friends in which description I have the honour to consider Mr Coutts. If any number of cadets should be appointed the ensueing season you may rest assured I shall bear in mind your request.[6]

With so many of his customers in such dire straits, it is not surprising that Thomas complained that he was overwhelmed by demands for money – so much so that he was forced to refuse even old friends, though for some – like the Countess of Chatham – he would always make an exception.

Most of the Bank's profit during Thomas's lifetime came from the interest on money borrowed. There were few opportunities for other investments. For example, in 1761 in Thomas's first year, the credits in the Profit and Loss Account read:

By sundry credits	£1089	12	3
Exchequer Tallies	255	6	
" Bills	811	10	2
India Bonds & Stock	67	5	9
Navy & Victualling Bills	543	2	1
Long & Bank Anns	116	4	
Commission	642	8	8
Interest (i.e. on loans)	3018	14	1[7]

In June 1766 there was additional income of £40 from the York building share. The interest on loans remained around that figure until June 1768, when it reached £4,725 7s; it then leapt to £6,474 os 9d in June 1769 and dropped slightly to £6,154 1s 6d in June 1770.

In June 1772 interest on loans soared again to £7,337 15s 5d, falling back in the next year to £3,780 os 5d. Navy and Victualling bills are shown again in the Profit and Loss Credits in 1765. In 1770 a profit of £28 13s 7d comes from Royal Bank stocks, which now make an occasional appearance on the credit side. In the following years interest on loans still makes the largest contribution to the credits.

Another source of profit appears with the interest on the subscription of 1778–9, in that year amounting to £5,229 18s 2d and in 1780 to £865 7s 9d.

In 1781 the profit on the subscription was £6,316 17s 6d. In that year interest on loans was a record £8,822 4s 3d. Profit from the Navy and Victualling bills rose to £1,801 18s 8d and to a record £4,000 in 1782.

The years 1781 and 1782 were particularly profitable, the subscription of 1782 producing £9,987 2s 7d. But generally, until the last years of Thomas's life, the profits come from as few sources as at the beginning of his career:

1812 By Sundry Credits	512	3	2
" India Bonds	65	13	7
" Exchequer Bills	2978	5	9
" Consols/Anns	8196	13	9
" Interest	9375	12	5
" Taxed Interest	25615	1	2
" Commission	6002	4	10
	52745	14	8[8]

In business Thomas was a cautious man. As has been seen he had been unwilling to take the plunge with circular notes, though he might have foreseen that travellers on the Grand Tour would find them immensely useful. As for stock-jobbing, the South Sea Bubble was still remembered in Coutts & Co., and his firm rule was that partners should not engage in broking. He looked back with some pride to his success in the Bank during the last years and especially since it had been achieved, he said, by 'the straight way of business without jobbing'.[9]

He was also unwilling to risk investment in the new search for minerals, though he was interested to know when his customers found coal or tin on their lands. But, as he wrote to Colonel Crawfurd, 'I am sorry to see you engaged in coal and lime. I never knew a gentleman make anything of either, nor of farming.' However, he did have some enthusiasm for new discoveries in weaponry. On 27 February 1787 he took Sir Thomas Miller's book on new artillery to show King George III, although one suspects that this was a move to oblige Sir Thomas rather than to promote the industry.

The investment that gave him most pleasure and excitement was in shipping. He firmly believed that England's safety depended on her ships – her 'wooden walls'. But he also took a romantic pleasure in the thought of the great East Indiamen sailing to the exotic coasts of India and the Far East. So he and James owned one ship in their early days at the Bank and Thomas took shares in many more. In the Profit and Loss ledgers of 1762–5 there are reference to the ships *True Briton, Hunter Privateer, Piggott, Earl of Bute East Indiaman* and the *Duke of Albany*. In 1765–9 the ship *Dawkins* was added to the list. The *Duke of Albany* produced a profit of £198 15s 5d in 1775, and *Piggott* £717 3s 0d. More than one of them in the coming years was to sail the high seas to India and China with the Thomas Coutts crest on the prow and his name on her side.

This mixture of romance and caution, love of the exotic and yet of simplicity gave him his special quality. He was distinguished as a banker for a unique combination of what he called 'exactness' and generous kindness, strict standards yet a ready acceptance of human frailty, so that he was not merely banker but also trusted friend. Lady Hester Stanhope wrote that he was not like other bankers. 'You are my father,' the Duchess of Devonshire insisted, and so did many other ladies – especially when in distress. He treated the sons of his customers as though they were his own, invariably friendly even when his advice was unpalatable. Many times when his rules of business conflicted with his wish to be kind to friends, friendship won.

What drove him, frail as he was, through years of stress as a banker? It was not lust for gold, because he had little desire for wealth for its own sake nor for its trappings. Simple and frugal in dress and habits, he would have been happy to remain all his life in his rooms over the Bank in the Strand. Certainly he was not ambitious. He did not ask for honours for himself. Nor did he, as many bankers did, aspire to Parliament, although at least three seats were offered him, without strings and at no expense to himself. What he did desire was prestige and the power to secure patronage for his friends. Above all he wanted his father's name to be honoured.

The friendship with customers, his visits to their country houses, his understanding of their family problems, and his discretion in dealing with mistresses and their 'children of the mist', all resulted in customers whose children, grandchildren and great-grandchildren remained loyal to the Bank long after his death. This was particularly true of the royal family. John Campbell had been goldsmith to Queen Anne, George Prince of Wales had bought plate from Middleton's shop, but Thomas Coutts could count himself the friend of kings and princes.

17

Of Princes, Painters
and a Lovely Duchess

For some years Thomas had been on easy and friendly terms with George III, and the King had learned to trust his banker. In March 1785 he had given the King a horse which the King of Spain had sent him as a mark of his satisfaction by his friend Sir Alex Munro, then Consul General in Spain. Thomas could thereby please the King and subtly inform His Majesty of the prestige of Coutts & Co. in the world. He hoped that the King would 'have the condescension to accept it as a small & humble testimony of his sincere attachment'.[1] He had also procured 'some curious Asiatic botanical seeds for the Prince of Asturias'[2] and had given 'credit to some Mercantile Companys trading to the Manillas, & recommending them to those gentlemen at the English settlements in India, who it is believed can be mutually of use to each other'.[3]

In November 1787 the King gave him an unusual honour, admitting him 'in to the Place and Quality of Gentleman of His Majesty's Privy Chamber'.[4] As a Gentleman of the Privy Chamber he now had access to the King and could give him private advice on his financial affairs. Thomas was too discreet to keep any record of his personal talks with the King, but it is clear from his later letters that the two men chatted frankly about their family problems, the King showing concern for Thomas's daughter, Fanny, who, from childhood, had a strange nervous disorder, and Thomas listening to his worries about the Prince of Wales and the company he kept.

'The damndest set of millstones round the government's neck,' so the Duke of Wellington is said to have called the King's sons. Certainly their affairs were a constant burden to Thomas. When they came of age each had his allowance paid into Coutts & Co., and from that time onwards each brought not only his load of debt but his personal problems. Royal mistresses and morganatic wives were to turn to Thomas for support and sympathy – and he dealt with them with kindly tolerance, which won him their genuine affection.

The Prince of Wales was the most difficult of his royal customers, not only because he was self-indulgent, undisciplined and wildly extravagant, but also because he always opposed his father. He and his Whig friends were a constant irritation to the Tory King. Although politically Thomas Coutts had more sympathy with the Whigs, he was genuinely fond of the King; moreover, the royal patronage was vital to his Bank's success and, as he frequently said, to his honour. So he had followed the antics of the heir to the throne in the last years with distaste.

After a series of wildly passionate love affairs the Prince had fallen violently in love with the apparently unattainable Mrs Fitzherbert. She was a lady of impeccable virtue, a Roman Catholic and twice widowed. Only after he had staged a melodramatic suicide attempt did she finally agree to go through a secret marriage ceremony with him. She was chaperoned by the Duchess of Devonshire, and the couple were married by a bribed clergyman released from a debtors' prison. The union was doubly illegal. The Act of Settlement forbade the marriage of the heir to the throne to a Catholic. King George III had also in 1772 passed the Royal Marriage Act, which declared any royal marriage contracted without the King's permission null and void. So the marriage remained secret and was even denied in the House of Commons by Charles James Fox. Thomas may not have been aware of the details, but he certainly knew of the marriage since he dealt with Mrs Fitzherbert's financial settlement.

According to her later letters to the Prince of Wales, 'when the memorable event of our Union took place in the year '85 . . . you were at that period pleased to settle on me £10,000 per ann'.[5] Unfortunately, his 'difficulties in money matters' prevented this generous offer and Mrs Fitzherbert had to manage for years on £3,000 a year, out of which she paid their joint expenses. Consequently she was frequently in debt and had little help from the Prince, since he himself was submerged in debts of more than £100,000.

On his twenty-first birthday in 1783 the Prince had hoped for a government grant from the Civil List of £100,000 a year, which the economical King had vetoed. He was finally settled with £50,000 a year, which, with the income from the revenues of the Duchy of Cornwall, was considered an adequate income even for the Prince. But he spent a vast sum refurbishing Carlton House in Pall Mall, which had been given to him as part of his settlement. He employed the architect, Henry Holland, and the gardener, Capability Brown, and created a magnificent mansion regardless of cost. Furniture was imported from China, statues from Italy. The Prince of Wales indulged to the full his mania for building, which was to culminate later in the Brighton Pavilion, and which was one of the causes of his colossal debts. To pay these he borrowed huge sums from bankers and money-lenders in Britain and even from Philippe d'Orléans in France. It was to conceal this that he moved his account from Coutts & Co., where his father's eye was upon him, to Hammersley.

The Prince had banked with Thomas on coming of age, but took his account away in 1787 and transferred it to Hammersley because Thomas had refused to increase his overdraft. Colonel Hotham, who had been in charge of the Prince's Privy Purse, honourably resigned rather than arrange such a transaction. He personally disliked Hammersley, the banker, and felt a sense of duty to, and affection for, Thomas Coutts.

But in May 1787 Thomas was aware that the King's health was deteriorating and that he needed to draw the heir to the throne back to the Bank in the Strand. He wrote to the Prince on 24 May 1787:

I hope there is not any impropriety on the present occasion in my once more submitting my case to yr R H's goodness & justice. As to the emolument of being Banker to any appointment I am perfectly indifferent – but I suffer severely in the point of honour, having been for so many years Banker to three Royal generations. To be deprived of such a distinguished situation without a fault being imputed, I think must be considered as very hard – & I flatter myself your RH in your great goodness will at the proper time, & in your own way, remove from me the disgrace that at present so cruelly covers & afflicts me.[6]

Although he had not met Mrs Fitzherbert, Thomas wrote to her in 1787, appealing to her to use her influence with the Prince to persuade him to return. She replied that she was 'flattered' by his 'very obliging expressions'[7] and explained in what high estimation the Prince had always held Thomas's character and how reluctantly he 'felt himself *Driven* into taking any step that could throw the slightest stigma upon you, but which he considered as absolutely necessary to preserve a proper authority in his own family'.[8] She was not able to change the Prince's mind, but wrote soothingly again on 11 June 1788. So began a friendship which was to have repercussions which would echo on into this century. Perhaps it was because of her influence that the Prince partly renewed his account with Coutts & Co. in 1791. But he did not return completely until 1793.

The Prince's debts continued to mount and Parliament finally and reluctantly came to his rescue. He was to receive another £10,000 from the King from the Civil List, £161,000 from Parliament to pay his debts and £60,000 towards the completion of Carlton House.

Thus he felt free to engage in even greater expenditure. He retired with Mrs Fitzherbert to Brighton, where he employed Henry Holland to rebuild the Pavilion, which he eventually bought for £22,000. In October 1803, Thomas's lawyer and friend, William Adam, informed him that 'the total expense of works at Brighton to last Midsummer was £18,350, which was an increase of £5,000 since the prior estimate of Michaelmas 1803'.[9]

The most dazzling example of the Prince of Wales's extravagance was the Brighton Pavilion. All the exotic dreams of the period were realised in Chinese fantasy, Indian magnificence and oriental splendour. The Duke of Kent was similarly obsessed. When he was stationed in Canada and Nova Scotia, he created a splendid mansion with gardens laid out with the lakes and grottoes beloved by the 'improvers' of the period. Even when he was deeply in debt in England he indulged his passion to the limit. At his house at Castle Hill near Ealing even the closets were spectacular – one was a grotto with a running stream and fountain. The Duke of York also caught the fever and, though he owed an immense sum to Thomas, began building a palace at the edge of Green Park, which would be fit for the king he hoped to be. He never saw it finished, but Lancaster House stands today, the marble halls a monument to the Duke's grand dream.

For the rest of his life Thomas was to be plagued by the royal princes and their finances, so it is necessary briefly to outline the careers of the troublesome princes. All the sons of George III were customers of Coutts & Co., though some accounts were more active than others and later the Duke of Cumberland was to withdraw his custom.

After the Prince of Wales, the three princes who were to cause Thomas most concern were Frederick, Duke of York, William, Duke of Clarence (later William IV), and Edward, Duke of Kent (father of Queen Victoria). Prince Ernest, who became Duke of Cumberland and later King of Hanover, was more notorious for his sexual than his financial affairs. Prince Augustus, who became Duke of Sussex, was delicate and spent most of his life abroad. It was his morganatic marriage to Lady Augusta Murray in 1793 that would later involve his banker. Prince Adolphus, who became Duke of Cambridge in 1801, was the most respected and least troublesome of the royal princes. His daughter, who became Duchess of Teck, and his granddaughter, who became Queen Mary, were to become close friends of Thomas's granddaughter, Angela. But in 1787 the three youngest princes, aged eighteen, fifteen and thirteen respectively, were at the University of Göttingen about one hundred miles south of Hanover, where Adolphus was, according to George III, 'the favourite of all'.[10]

In this year Prince Frederick returned to London after seven years' military training in Hanover, to be greeted ecstatically by the Prince of Wales. The brothers had been inseparable as boys and were devoted to each other. To the King's distress Frederick, his favourite, was captured and led off to a riotous life at Carlton House, now 'Prinny's' centre of opposition to the King.

Frederick was a womaniser and a hard drinker and had his brother's total incapacity to deal with money, but he was not totally amoral. He was a brave soldier with a strong sense of duty, which he was to prove as commander of the British forces in Holland in the war against France in 1793. His failure there was due to a lack not of will but of military ability.

In 1787 he was tall and good-looking and not yet the immensely stout figure of later cartoons. He deserted the King and became as dissipated as his brother. The head of his household, Major-General Richard Grenville, complained that the Prince led Frederick 'into all the extravagance and debaucheries'.[11] In return the Duke taught the Prince 'to lose his money at all sorts of play – quinze hazard etc to the amount we are told, of very large sums'.[12] The King had every reason to keep his younger sons abroad, away from the Prince's influence. Nevertheless, Thomas had a certain affection for the Duke of York, even though, as the years went by, as will be seen, he was to sink deeper and deeper into a morass of debt. Even his critics found it difficult to hate the easy, good-humoured Frederick and the King never ceased to love him in spite of everything.

Like Frederick, Prince William was to become not only a customer but a lifelong friend of Thomas Coutts. He forgave them their sins not just because they brought prestige to the Bank but because he had a fatherly interest in them, and they were fond of him.

The King had sent William to sea as a boy of fourteen, accompanied by a tutor who made him study Latin and history while serving as a midshipman. He was a better sailor than student, saw action at Gibraltar and became captain of the frigate *Pegasus* in 1786 when he was only twenty, by which time he was deeply in debt. In 1790 he left the sea and, after numerous amorous affairs, settled down for more than twenty years to an unconventional but stable and happy life with his mistress, the enchanting actress, Mrs Dorothea Jordan – of whom more will be heard later. William was straightforward, bluff and kindly, with a tendency to eccentricity, which became more pronounced as he grew older.

Prince Edward, like his brothers, was sent to Germany for military training and in 1786 was made a colonel in the Hanoverian army. He too was deeply in debt and for that and other misdemeanours the King sent him to Geneva in the charge of a fierce military governor. For seventeen months, as he complained, he had not a line from the King and only one letter from the Queen. At last, in desperation, he escaped and returned home without leave. The King, who had no patience with Edward, paid his debts but packed him off to Gibraltar. Here he showed those contradictory traits which were to mark the rest of his career – an excessive extravagance combined with a rigid observance of military rules and discipline.

Like many of the King's sons he made up for absence of home life in childhood by embarking on twenty-eight years of domestic though unconventional stability. A friend, sent to find him a suitable companion for life, brought him the charming French lady, Julie de St Laurent, whose origins remain obscure but whose intelligence and beauty were universally admired. She followed him throughout his years of service in Canada and the West Indies and lived openly with him in his years of retirement in England. As Madame de Montgenet, she was generally accepted.

Edward has gone down in history as a brutal disciplinarian, notorious for flogging delinquents unmercifully. His father and the Duke of York disliked him, his brothers regarded him and his 'old French lady' with amusement, and to his sisters he was hypocritical and pompous. Though these judgments are caricatures, they are based in fact. However, it must be said in his favour that Thomas was patient with him and planned schemes for 'retrenchment' when his debts swamped him. His exasperation with Edward must often have been tinged with amusement as he went through accounts in which Edward carefully noted his debts to the last half penny, knowing that the whole lot would disappear in the wildly extravagant 'improvements' to every house he lived in.

These then were the King's three sons who, with the Prince of Wales, were to reappear again and again with problems right to the end of Thomas's life. But it was the Prince of Wales who was his greatest concern. He was determined to keep the royal custom and, during the years when the King's health frequently failed, this meant wooing his successor. This he did with unaccustomed humility.

Thomas was assiduous in his pursuit of customers among the great and powerful, but he also accepted and even supported penniless characters from the world of the arts. For though he had left school early, Thomas became a man of wide-ranging culture with a well-stocked library and a good collection of pictures, as the inventory of his possessions made after his death shows. His daughter Fanny proudly claimed that he always carried a volume of Shakespeare in his pocket. And Farington noted in his diary that if one began a Shakespeare quotation, Mr Coutts could always finish it. He loved the theatre and was lucky as a young man to have seen Garrick strutting the boards; he admired and helped him. Nearly a hundred years later, his granddaughter, Angela Burdett-Coutts, presented a ring, said to be Garrick's, to Henry Irving after his triumphant performance in 1877 as Richard III.

Thomas took ninety-nine-year leases on boxes at Drury Lane and Covent Garden and gave generously to the rebuilding of both when fires destroyed them. He was considered to have the best box at Drury Lane, one which the Prince of Wales coveted. Leasing the box was not only a means of supporting the theatre, but was also good business. Many of his distinguished customers were delighted to have seats for a play or opera.

Thomas was a complex character – an exact man of business, punctilious in his work – yet he enjoyed the company of the exotic and unconventional. He had a discerning eye for real talent, as with painters like Reynolds, Lawrence, Haydon and the sculptor, Joseph Nollekens, but, as he ruefully wrote, he also backed losers, and even the successful lost him more than he gained. However, as with his other customers, he was prepared to lend the Bank's money on adequate security although, if a risk was involved, he used his own. And no one will ever know the extent of his private charity.

He was naturally kind-hearted, but also had an unusual understanding of the artistic temperament and sympathy for sensitive souls in a rough world. He knew the fine line drawn between madness and genius. Had he not watched his brother Patrick slip across the boundary? So he accepted the odd looks and voices of men like Nollekens, Goldsmith and Fuseli. Time and again he rescued Haydon, an artist tortured by a demoniac drive to create his enormous canvasses, yet obsessed by a sense of failure. Haydon asked for Thomas's help in 1817, encouraged by Fuseli, who told him how generously the banker had supported him when he was painting *The Lazar*. Thomas replied in a letter which Haydon considered 'did honour to his House heart and head'.[13] Thomas began by confessing that he ought not to consent to his request since he had so many requests of this kind from people who 'have superior claims'. Nevertheless, he

felt an inclination to put ... £400 in your power and to indulge the flattery of seeing by that means your picture finished ... on the other hand experience almost blasts all hopes, as I have assisted several in your line in the course of a long life & have never succeeded.[14]

After Thomas's death his partners continued to support Haydon. Nevertheless, he became so overwhelmed by debt that he committed suicide. Had Thomas still been alive perhaps he might have been saved.

Thomas knew and respected Reynolds and had guided the artist through a difficult financial affair. Reynolds had trusted a friend to place his money in the Bank in the secure government long annuities, but Thomas, on investigation, discovered that the funds had in fact been used in speculation. Reynolds's money was refunded to him and properly invested.

The most remarkable of Thomas's artist friends, however, was the brilliant and eccentric Swiss, Johann Heinrich Fuseli (who was later known as Henry). He had come to London in 1763, drawn by the fame of the London literary clubs, with a mission to develop an international literary association. Although in the beginning he was mainly concerned with the world of letters, his great passion was for painting. His father had tried to frustrate his desire to be an artist, but had merely driven the urge underground: as a boy he had painted with his left hand under the desk, while his right hand was openly engaged in legitimate work.

Thomas later claimed that he first knew Fuseli in the early days as a friend of Dr Armstrong, the poet physician. Certainly it was as a poet and a man of letters that Thomas befriended him. Then, seeing his artistic talent, he urged him to visit Italy. Dazzled by Florence and encouraged by Reynolds, Fuseli took up a career in painting that led him finally to become Professor of Painting at the Royal Academy. His love of literature fused with his art, and Thomas backed him in his great Shakespeare and Milton exhibitions and bought his paintings, many of them considered bizarre and even obscene at the time. Tactfully Thomas was to give him in advance the tax on a sum of money he intended to bequeath to him, writing to him on 21 December 1813:

The heavy tax on Wills & on succession under them is an inducement to a man to save money to His Friend by paying it to him in His Life Time: on a sum I meant to leave to you I find you would have to pay the tax of Fifty pounds to get at it and as I can anticipate without inconveniencing I have sent it inclosd & I hope you will not disaprove. Besides the tax there is a chance for tho' improbable who can be sure that you will die before me so my intention towards you be frustrated.

I am very sincerely yours
T. Coutts[15]

Fuseli regularly took his Sunday tea with the Coutts family and Thomas accepted the oddities of the artist who would hide in a corner of the room when people he disliked appeared. Farington reported that Thomas told him that this was 'a sort of madness' in Fuseli and that 'with all his talent he still had a sort of distortion in his mind something similar to what is seen more or less in all his pictures'.[16] No one could understand this better than Thomas. In later years Fuseli taught Thomas's daughters to paint, and they and their daughters were sometimes his models. With one of his grandchildren, Sophia Burdett, Fuseli developed an odd, semi-flirtatious relationship in old age, writing strange letters in Greek characters to the young girl. After Thomas's death his daughter Susan, Lady Guilford, continued to support and protect Fuseli, who died at her house in Putney. Thomas supported Fuseli because he loved him and saw his genius, but Mr Coutts, the banker, would also have been pleased if he could have known what a sound investment Fuseli's pictures proved to be.

Lawrence was a totally different character, but Thomas was equally supportive over many years. A man of great charm, Lawrence, from childhood, had an uncanny gift of catching a likeness. He rapidly became the darling of the fashionable world with more commissions than he could undertake. Because he, like many other artists, was hopeless with money, he found it easier to collect the advance on a portrait, start it and then put it aside while he took on another, ending up with a studio full of half-finished portraits. Some great ladies were flattered to receive in middle age portraits he had begun in their youth! Thomas tried over many years to guide him into solvency, but Lawrence was always in debt. From the time when he borrowed £500 in 1799, he caused his banker many a headache. In November 1802 Thomas tried to take him in hand. He lent him £2,000 on conditions which were carefully set out in a long memorandum. All his professional earnings were to be deposited in a separate account with Coutts & Co. From this £800 a year would be paid into his other account. For his part Lawrence vowed never to exceed the £800 nor to incur new debts. His bankers hoped gradually to pay off his old debts from the quite substantial income he was receiving from his pictures. Lawrence, in signing the memorandum, added a final paragraph:

As I am very sensible that I owe my release from impending Ruin to the Friendship of Messrs Coutts & Co ... and have disinterestedly lent me a large sum without common security to assist me as a Friend ... I do hereby promise and engage in the most solemn manner that ... I will adhere to every article in this paper.[17]

Andrew Dickie, Thomas's confidential – and diplomatic – clerk, was sent to Lawrence's studio to value his unfinished portraits and to urge him to complete them. But by 1807 Lawrence was again in debt. This time his friend Farington acted as intermediary. He visited Thomas and once more a plan of 'retrenchment' was formulated – soon to be discarded yet again. In the end Thomas had reluctantly to recommend that Lawrence declare himself a bankrupt. This he could not bring himself to do and took himself to another banker, though it would seem he still remained Thomas's friend.

Thomas not only made friends of the King and the most influential men of his time, but he also had an outstanding talent for dealing with their ladies – old and young, from his simple aunts to the great Countess of Chatham. Wives, daughters and mothers found in him a sympathetic listener, a shoulder to weep on and even a gallant to flirt with. With an eighteenth-century tolerance for unconventional relationships he dealt kindly with the mistresses of his distinguished customers, discreetly setting up trusts for them and for their illegitimate children. So, as will be seen, he was to befriend Mrs Fitzherbert, morganatic wife of the Prince of Wales; the actress Dorothea Jordan, mistress of the Duke of Clarence, and their ten children; and Madame de Montgenet, companion of the Duke of Kent. He was also a benefactor to the countless ladies who led difficult lives in the shadows of great men.

Thomas was rarely shocked by eccentric characters: none of his customers was more so than Lady Hester Stanhope, granddaughter of the Earl of Chatham and niece of the Prime Minister, William Pitt the Younger. Thomas had known her from her childhood and had pitied her harsh upbringing by a brilliant but eccentric father. She and her sister spent some time with the Coutts family at Tunbridge Wells in November 1797, where Hester and Fanny became great friends. Thomas was concerned enough about Hester to write to her grandmother regretting that she and her sister were 'so much sequestered as their spirit cannot be repressed and might be better directed'.[18] That spirit drove Hester to leave home and escape to her grandmother's house. Afterwards she became the hostess for her uncle, William Pitt. The rest of her life is well known – how she travelled to the Middle East and lived a strange life in a disused convent on a remote mountainside.

She took as her lover a young man, Michael Bruce, who agreed to make her an allowance of £400 a year. This was to be paid by his father to her 'old friend' Mr Coutts. Hester, like so many of Thomas's unconventional friends, was often in debt. She had a government pension which her uncle had given her and which Thomas sent out to her. She also had 'expectations', which never materialised. When she and Bruce separated his allowance ceased. From her mountain fastness she sent long letters on philosophy and world affairs to the banker she called her father and her friend. They are still in the archives as he received them, their envelopes slashed by the authorities so that they could be disinfected against the plague that was then rife along the coast.

However, the lady who most disturbed him was Georgiana, the lovely Duchess of Devonshire. The involvement of the banker with the Duchess is an extraordinary story, the triumph of heart over a shrewd Scot's head. She had known Thomas some time before 1786, when she opened an account at Coutts & Co. In her first surviving letter to him she writes of 'the goodness you have always shewn me'.[19] Certainly Thomas would have known the dazzling Georgiana by reputation. He would have heard of her wild electioneering in 1784, canvassing for Charles James Fox when she and other great Whig ladies, adorned with foxes' tails, swept into the slums of Westminster and, as her opponents claimed, sold kisses for the butchers' votes. He must have heard the gossip of her friendship with the Prince of Wales, but above all he knew that she was a compulsive gambler and in debt to money-lenders and almost every banker in London and some in Paris.

He must also have known that her letter of 1786 was a sprat to catch a whale. She sent him £100 as an instalment on a sum of £900, which she said she had to invest for a friend, and she asked him to undertake it for her 'since I am ignorant of business of any kind'.[20] Since she also asked him not to tell 'Fish' Craufurd, George Middleton's grandson, he would have been right to be suspicious, because her friend Craufurd had already lent her money, as Thomas would have been well aware.

When in 1787 the Duchess asked Thomas for a loan of £3,300, he agreed, moved by her 'horror and misery'.[21] Once more she insisted that he should not tell her husband or Craufurd, since the latter had already helped her and the Duke thought that he had settled all her debts. But, in fact, neither now or at any time could Georgiana bring herself to confess, even to herself, the full extent of her gambling debts. Thomas was appalled at the thought of the destruction of a young woman of such beauty and intelligence and wrote her a long, fatherly letter:

Strand 23d May 1787

Your Grace very kindly desir'd I would write freely what at any time occurred to me. I find it impossible to express all I feel, but I think Your Grace believes that my good wishes are sincere, and my motives of the purest kind; which encourages me, and I *will venture* and *endeavour* to give a faint Idea of how much it shocks me to think what your Grace puts into hazard by indulging a Passion for Play. There is nothing yr Grace can acquire; you have already Titles, Character, Friends, Fortune, Power, Beauty, *everything* superiour to the rest of the world. Permit me also to add *Conjugal Happiness* to the list, and to say that all these, the first article only excepted, you *risk* to gratify this destructive passion.[22]

All his experience had taught him how destructive a passion for gambling was among men, making them 'dead to every feeling of Honour'. It was even worse for women.

I should be happy beyond expression if I could think I had even the smallest share in saving Your Grace from the dreadful Consequences I forsee. . . . I can only take Shelter in the purity of my *intentions*, and your Grace's goodness to see them in the true light. I do not wish to Preach, or tire your Grace with a long letter, but I must add, *Pecuniary Obligations* even among the best Friends shou'd be avoided. I hope your Grace will confine Them to me. And I should wish you to order The Duke's Agents to pay in your Grace's Annual allowances of Pin money &c &c to my House to be drawn for by your Grace as you have occasion. I will confess a Selfish View, 'tho' I disclaim any interested one, in desiring this viz. that it will give me the opportunity perhaps of more frequently having occasion to see or correspond with your Grace, but my Principal Object is that by having Accounts brought before you in this Way upon Paper, Your Grace may be led habitually to grow more attentive to, and better acquainted with the true value and proper use of money and thereby be better able to indulge the generosity of Temper which is evidently so natural to you, and, if possible, adds a grace to every thing you do. I am, Madam, with the utmost humility and most sincere Respect and Regard Your Grace's Faithful and devoted Hand Servant.[23]

It was true that Georgiana had everything a young woman could desire. The daughter of Earl Spencer and the granddaughter of the formidable Duchess of Marlborough, she had been brought up by loving parents at her father's country house at Althorp in security and freedom. At seventeen she had been married to the catch of the year, the handsome and immensely rich William, Duke of Devonshire, and was now mistress of the great houses of Chatsworth in Derbyshire and Devonshire House in Piccadilly. She took London by storm. Although she was not a great beauty it was said that the word 'charm' might have been coined to describe her. Her radiant smile, shining eyes and the ease and grace of her manner enchanted all who met her, from the Irish workman who said he could light his pipe from her bright eyes, to the sharp-tongued Horace Walpole.

But the hectic life she began to lead in London, her gambling and her extravagant headdresses crowned with three immense feathers soon became the talk of London. The truth was that she had been thrown, while still an immature girl, into a world for which she was unprepared. Married too young, she easily discovered that her ebullient and affectionate nature was chilled in her husband's presence. It could not have been easy for an innocent girl to discover that her husband kept a mistress, a milliner, by whom he had a daughter. But with characteristic generosity she accepted the child and later drew her into the family circle. Even more shattering must have been the later discovery that her beloved friend, Lady Elizabeth Foster, had become her husband's mistress. She accepted that too and the natural children, Caroline St Jules and Augustus Clifford, were eventually also to find a home with her.

The Devonshire story cannot be told fully here, but these events helped to explain the frenetic energy with which Georgiana threw herself into gambling and the whirl of society life.

When she came to Thomas, she had finally, after barren years, produced two daughters, but she desperately needed an heir, for, unless she had a son, the Duke's estates and fortune would go to his brother, and, in the event of the Duke's death, her creditors would ruin her. Thomas was therefore glad that she had decided to take a cure at Spa with her husband in the hope of becoming pregnant.

Before she left the Duke had promised to pay her debts and give her an allowance, which she proposed to place with Thomas, rather coyly asking him, 'if you please you shall give me my book . . . and teach me how to use it'.[24] Full of good intentions she wrote to her mother: 'In a few days I shall be 30, a great period of my life over, and God Knows, over in folly'; now she hoped to surmount her past follies: 'love of dissipation, admiration, dress'.[25]

It is not surprising that Thomas was dazzled and for once forgot all his own rules about lending on adequate security; the Duke of Devonshire was not even his own customer, though Georgiana was. But there was some method in his apparent madness. He hoped for a return for his kindness. Firstly, the Duchess was a close friend of the Prince of Wales. Should the King die, as it seemed at this time possible, she could use her influence to persuade the Prince to bring back his custom to the Bank.

Secondly, the Duchess was planning to break her journey in Paris. Since Thomas was proposing to send his three daughters there, he hoped she would introduce them to French society.

18

The Grand Tour

For the last twenty-seven years the Bank had been the core of Thomas Coutts's life. Now the education and welfare of his three daughters were to take precedence. For the next decade he was to be out of London and even, in the years between 1788 and 1791, out of the country most of the time.

In 1787 he decided to send the girls to Paris to study French, to be finished and to learn to take their place in society. Susan at this time was sixteen, Fanny fourteen and Sophia thirteen years old. The three girls had been educated first at Mrs Stephens's school in Queen's Square; little is known of this chapter in their life except that Fanny, the most intelligent, delicate and spoiled of the three, was very unhappy there. Fanny was her father's favourite and had been totally spoiled all her young life. Her response to discipline was hysterical fainting fits, which were to worry her family for the rest of her adolescence. She was so delicate that when it was decided that the girls should continue their education in Paris, Fanny stayed behind with her parents.

Thomas's friend, General Ross, took Susan and Sophia to France and settled them with a chaperone, Madame Daubenton. However, the General soon realised how unsuitable Madame was; what the 'shocking improprieties' were we shall never know, but remembering the loose morals of pre-revolutionary France it is easy to guess why Ross suggested to Thomas that his daughters should be sent back to England.

Susan and Sophia, however, loved Paris; even the outrageous behaviour at the theatre when the audience forced the actors to get down on their knees to beg pardon amused them tremendously. There was 'roaring and squealing' night after night because a favourite actor had disappeared. Susan wrote home in delicious excitement over the Paris fashions, and no doubt the two pretty girls in their orange bonnets turned many heads:

Orange is no longer the Tip Top Fashion. *Pink* & *Black* is the great rage. . . . Black ribbons tip'd with a little pink fringe is the most newest Fashion, then black, pink or white feathers . . . orange is not quite *ridiculous*. . . . Our bonnets . . . [are]

orange all except the Lining which is white & the ribbons are those black with orange spots that you sent us.[1]

Susan laughed at the General's fears and insisted that they should stay in Paris. With relish she wrote home, quoting a favourite remark of Fanny's: 'Since life is no more than a pleasure at last, let's strew the way over with flowers.'[2]

So they did until 18 July 1788, when their parents and Fanny came over to take them to Switzerland. Thomas and his family left Paris on 30 July for a tour of the Swiss lakes, stayed at Geneva and Lake Constance, marvelled at the glaciers at Grindelwald and returned through the grape harvest of Champagne to Paris, where on 10 October they settled at a hotel in the Rue de l'Université. Thomas had intended to stay for one week only, just long enough to see the girls established in the convent of Penthémont, which his friend, the Duchess of Devonshire, had recommended. The convent was very exclusive, very expensive and the girls there were indulged in every luxury, wore excessively fashionable clothes and held balls once a week. Such an education would prepare them for the most exalted positions in society.

Rather surprisingly, Thomas found Paris most agreeable and it was increasingly difficult for him to tear himself away. Life there was 'so organised for comfort and I feel it to be cutting myself in four to leave my three daughters'.[3] So his visit was extended and extended. There were other reasons for staying. As a friend of the Duke of Dorset, the British Ambassador in Paris, he had an entrée to the best society and, though there were fewer English visitors to Paris that year, there were enough of his customers to make him feel that his continued presence was worthwhile. They dined frequently at the British Embassy and Susannah could entertain her distinguished guests at the hotel with little inconvenience. Lady Auckland maliciously reported: 'Mrs Coutts never says or does anything now without consulting a peer.'[4] Indeed it was the banker and his wife who started the round of balls in Paris that winter with a brilliant evening at their hotel. Thomas wrote an account of the ball to Caleb Whitefoord in London, which he wished him to publish in the journals. King George III was seriously ill at this time and even, it was rumoured, at death's door. Thomas was anxious that it should not appear that he was revelling while the King was dying, so Caleb's report made it clear that the ball came after the news of the King's recovery:

Last week, on the account arriving of his Majesty being so much better . . . Mrs Coutts gave a ball to all the ladies of fashion . . . at the hotel de l'Université, Prince Henry of Prussia honoured them with this company; and at midnight Mr Fox joined them from Italy. . . . The news received since of the King's continued ill-health has plunged us all again in melancholy and everyone talks of going home.[5]

The illness of the King cast a shadow on their Paris gaiety. If the King had died, Thomas, as he wrote to the Duchess of Devonshire, would 'lose a good Friend'. He would certainly have rushed back to London to ensure his position as the royal banker with the new King. For, he told the Duchess,

I was His *First* Banker, and he has always approved my conduct. I should wish much Your Grace would speak to The Prince in case the mellancholy Event proves true. My Honour is so much interested in being continued banker to The King's Privy Purse, . . . I was Banker to His Father and to His Grand Father and to lose *him* without any cause is very hard.[6]

He begged the Duchess to use her influence with the Duke of York, whom he counted as a friend, and with Sheridan, who had the Prince of Wales's ear. 'I was told', he added, 'Mrs Fitzherbert, though I do not know her, has expressed herself favourably towards me.'[7]

Tenacious as always in pursuit of a royal customer, he sent a letter under cover to the Duke of York, which would immediately be handed to the Prince of Wales should the King die. Thus he hoped to beat Hammersley at the post. But the King recovered and the Prince of Wales still kept his account with Coutts's rival.

With the King's return to health, Paris was again gay, and the Coutts family enjoyed the social round. It was reported that the balls begun by Mr Coutts 'have been followed by every person of distinction'. The family dined at the British Embassy, where Susan was much admired and Sophia was said to be 'very clever'.

It is strange that they seem to have seen little sign of the bloodbath ahead, no hint of the guillotine which would remove so many of their new French friends. Indeed Thomas urged the Duchess of Devonshire to 'carry' his daughters to Madame de Polignac and the Duchess of Orléans at Versailles, and was quite offended when the Duchess explained that the riots made it difficult.

Thomas took advantage of his presence in Paris to do much business with his correspondents there and with other financiers like Charles de Calonne and Jean-Benjamin Laborde, who, he wrote afterwards, had been kind to his daughters 'beyond measure'. None of his influential friends could, however, help him to override the rules of the convent. He wanted an old abbé, Beaurieu, who had taught the girls history, to continue their lessons in the convent. But permission was refused because no men were allowed. Thomas nevertheless persisted. He was even bold enough to ask the Duc de Polignac to approach the King on his daughters' behalf. However, in June 1789 Louis XVI had other things on his mind than the education of the Misses Coutts. On 14 July the Bastille fell.

Beneath the elegant surface Paris was seething. One young English visitor, Francis Burdett, saw the contrast between rich and poor. On 19 April 1789 he had written from Paris to his aunt, Lady Jones,

Such a mixture of Pomp & Beggars, filth & magnificence, as may be truely said to beggar all description. Suffice it to say, that it is the most ill-contrived, ill-built, dirty, stinking Town that can possibly be imagined; as for the inhabitants they are ten times more nasty than the inhabitants of Edinburgh. At the same time there are many Publick buildings & many parts of the Town which are extremely magnificent.[8]

It is most probable that Burdett met the Coutts family in Paris at this time since he was a frequent visitor at the British Embassy. A year later Coutts recommended him to the Duke of York at Berlin as 'my young friend', and some time during his continental tour he met the family and paid special attention to Fanny, who seems to have encouraged him. Sophia was an impressionable girl of fourteen and did not forget the dashing young man who cut such an elegant figure and who, in the words of the poetess Anna Seward, was 'the handsomest young man she had ever seen'.[9]

Burdett was of an old family, owning immense estates in Derbyshire and Leicestershire, and would not have been dazzled by the banker's wealth; he was however enchanted by the simplicity and beauty of the three girls. At the beginning of May, Thomas finally tore himself away, leaving his daughters in the convent. By the 12th of the month he was back in the Bank and remained in London until October. On his return he had two audiences with King George III, one of an hour's length during which he undoubtedly reported on the situation in Paris. But he may also have received the King's commission to visit Rome and to make the acquaintance of the last of the Stuarts, the Cardinal Duke of York, brother of Prince Charles Edward.

At this distance in time it seems incredible that Thomas should have allowed his daughters to stay in a city that was on the verge of a bloody revolution. But even after the fall of the Bastille, Charles James Fox could reply to the banker's anxious enquiries that his daughters were as safe in Paris as they would be in London. It was not until early October that Thomas decided to take them out of Paris. Even then he was not so disturbed by the state of Europe, for he chose to spend the next eighteen months doing a Grand Tour. In November 1789 they left Boulogne; some time before the end of the year they had reached Rome, where Susannah appears to have caused some amusement among the English there: she is said to have remarked that the amphitheatre in Rome would make a fine building if only it were done up.

While in Rome Thomas paid a visit to Henry Cardinal Duke of York in his palace at Frascati. It was, without doubt, one of the most significant and moving experiences of his tour. Henry Benedict Stuart was, in Jacobite eyes, King Henry IX. His brother had died the previous year, no longer the 'Bonnie' prince but coarsened by drink and debauchery. The Cardinal was a totally different man: calm, gentle, studious and deeply religious. He was also at this time immensely wealthy and lived in great state at Frascati.

It is unlikely that Thomas would have called on the Cardinal without the express approval of the King; indeed it is probable that he was encouraged to do so. Now that Prince Charles was dead, the King would have been concerned to know whether he might expect trouble from his younger brother, the Cardinal, and the Jacobites, since he was aware that there were still Stuart followers in England and Scotland. Thomas, for his part, welcomed the chance of being the messenger from 'the best of kings' to the last of the House of Stuart.

The family left Rome for Naples, where they stayed in February 1790 and where Thomas would certainly have looked for his father's grave at Nola. Here Fanny fell in love with the scented bay where she would spend so much of her later life.

In June Thomas thought that they were coming to the end of 'a pleasing and successful journey' and would be home in fourteen days. They travelled quickly through Verona and the Tyrol, but at the beginning of July Sophia was taken seriously ill with a violent inflammation and fever and they were forced to rest for almost a month at Augsburg. Here the Electress of Bavaria sent her personal physician from Munich to treat the girls, until Sophia was well enough to travel to Aix La Chapelle. Now it was 'poor Fanny' who was quite unable to move. 'Her looks are as good as when quite well and her life in no hazard,' he wrote to a friend in Scotland, 'though she eats nothing, literally nothing but fruit.'[10] Though they were ill at Augsburg, the girls had their admirers. Prince Ferdinand de Rohan and other distinguished gentlemen were most attentive. Clearly the ladies were very reluctant to move, so Thomas returned to London alone and came back after Christmas to bring them home.

He escorted Susannah and the girls to Paris, but Fanny was still ill and once again they stayed longer there than they had intended. It was not until 29 March 1791 that the family reached Calais, to be held up yet again, this time by bad weather.

From July 1788 until the end of March 1791 the great banker had spent very little time at his office in the Bank in the Strand. Nevertheless, absence had not meant abdication. Thomas had learned much from his European tour and his residence in Paris. He had been received by the men in power in every country from cardinals in Rome to princes in Germany and the French royal family in Paris. He had been able to check on his correspondents throughout Europe and make useful contacts with experts like de Calonne. Friendships were forged which would be of great importance in the coming years. When he took such a kindly interest in the young Louis

Philippe in the years before the Revolution, he could not have foreseen that he would later become his customer and that, when King of France, he would keep his account at Coutts & Co. Nor that the close links between Coutts & Co. and the Orléans family would continue for generations.

The long absence abroad had unsettled Thomas and the closing years of the century were to bring a multitude of troubles. As he complained to Edmund Antrobus on 31 January 1793, 'I have for the last 12 months been much disturbed by various causes and many things have fretted my mind.'[11]

His return had started well enough. The King had greeted him warmly. He told the Colonel, 'I have seen the King twice since my return . . . I was with him above an hour.' When Thomas left England in July 1788 the King had just celebrated his fiftieth birthday, and he and the nation were comfortably settled under the premiership of William Pitt. The son of the great Earl of Chatham had come into power in 1783 at the age of twenty-four, but had immediately taken control with an astonishing assurance. Britain's prestige stood high abroad and at home prosperity had followed the end of the American war.

During his absence the King had suffered what his doctors described as 'an entire alienation of mind'. By December 1788 the Duke of York considered him now 'a complete lunatic', and the poor King was subjected to the most brutal of treatments by his doctors, in spite of which by February 1789 he had recovered. His illness is now believed to have been caused by a disease called porphyria, but whatever the cause the effect was to unbalance the King's mind completely for three months. Eleven years later the illness returned finally to overcome him.

We do not know whether or not the King spoke of his illness to his banker, but no one would have understood better than Thomas the King's fear of madness. He has left no detailed account of this meeting with His Majesty, but he must have described his visit to the Cardinal Duke of York, and reported on the state of the politics and finance of the countries he had passed through. He had met bankers, politicians and many of the leading European aristocrats during his tour and was now singularly well informed.

Later he wrote to the Cardinal that, on his return, he had given an account of what he had seen abroad to His Majesty King George III. 'I did not omit a particular detail of the honours I had received at Frascati, and of the uncommon politeness'[12] the Cardinal had shown them. He presented the Cardinal's silver medal to the King and discussed the likeness. George III was glad to be able to talk frankly to Thomas about the Stuarts. 'Few', he told Thomas, 'would have mentioned the subject but they were very much mistaken who imagined he did not very sincerely regard the family of Stuart, was it only for their misfortunes.'[13]

The King's welcome was not matched by his Prime Minister. Although Thomas had been a kind friend to his father, the Earl of Chatham, and was at this time helping him in his own difficult financial situation, the younger Pitt, now in power, was not only cool but positively snubbed him. Thomas complained to the Countess:

I only thought [that] after so long & uncommon an absence, it was particular that he should hardly even on seeing me by accident take any notice or make a single enquiry about me, or my family: and it struck me the more forcibly that really from His Majesty to my humble neighbours in the Strand, I met with nothing but the most flattering congratulations.[14]

He was anxious to assure Lady Chatham that he had not wished to plague Mr Pitt with requests for patronage for his friends, though, he added, he had wanted to bring Mr Walpole to Mr Pitt's attention. He was glad to report to Lady Chatham that 'I have had occasion in my Tour to see many courts, and to hear a good deal of the world's opinion of Mr Pitt ... nothing can stand higher in men's minds than his character does everywhere.'[15]

This made his coolness to his banker even more hurtful. Thomas feared that his influence was waning and that his private door to patronage was now closing. Nothing was more wounding than this, for his greatest pleasure had been to serve his friends through his influence. But Thomas did not suffer rudeness, even in a Prime Minister. When he was kept cooling his heels in Pitt's waiting-room, he went home in high dudgeon and sent a sharp note of rebuke.

He had been particularly offended when, in July 1789, Pitt failed to respond to his appeal on behalf of the Royal Bank of Scotland, which, he believed, should be given the privilege of transmitting Scottish taxes to the Government. This had been a right granted to his family ever since his grandfather Patrick's day. But now that he had no connection with the Edinburgh business run by William Forbes, he felt that preference should be given to the Royal Bank of which his father had been a director.

As he explained to Pitt on 7 July 1789,

The produce of the excise in Scotland was for a long period, nearly half a century, remitted by my father, my brothers and myself: having survived all my race I did not choose to continue any further concern in business than my shop here, and Sir William Forbes and Mr James Hunter Blair having been my apprentices, and successors to my House at Edinburgh, continued to make the remittance, which for various reason and Mr Hunter Blair being member for the town and connected with government, I did not choose to oppose. Mr Blair is now dead, and Sir Wm. Forbes being a Nonjuror, can support no political interest in the town; but I would not have opposed his remitting the public money had they not erected themselves into a Bank lately and used every exertion to circulate their notes as cash over the country (in opposition to the National Banks) and become rivals to the Royal Bank of Scotland which was established under, and has always enjoyed the patronage of Government.

Private banks are certainly very dangerous things to any country – a difficulty that occurred last year on the failure of the distillery, *is a recent proof of this proposition*, and I am sure if you will see this matter with *your own eyes*, you must be convinced it is much more for the public safety and advantage to have this money remitted by the Royal National Bank, than by any individual or private House of Business – and if on account of long usage it should be thought proper to give a partial preference to any individual – that preference in this case, is due and certainly belongs to *me above all others*. But private interest must yield to the public good, and the Royal Bank no doubt should remit the money. It is true, indeed, they will probably do it by bills on my House; and, perhaps, it may be thought very proper considering the circumstances that it should come through *me, the King's Banker*, rather than in any other channel; and I am very sure His Majesty if it were worth while to trouble him on matters of such a nature would not disapprove of what I have desired.

A letter of direction from the Treasury to the Excise would settle this business; and though Mr Dundas or Mr Rose may have private motives, unknown to me, for objecting to the alteration, I am very sure they cannot offer any sufficient reason against it.

I flatter myself, therefore, you will attend to my letter, and I am very sure you will find it, *in the end*, a very *salutary* as well as generally *well approved* and *popular measure*.

I am Sir [etc. etc.]
THOMAS COUTTS

It is probable I may be a bad politician, but it appears to me that the measure I have proposed might even be the best for securing the political interest of Government in the Election; and Mr Ramsay, who is the principal Director of the Royal Bank – a man of the highest character in Scotland, and one of the richest men of business in Great Britain, I dare say would give every aid in his power, which must be very considerable indeed, if exerted – much greater than any other person, or than the late Mr Hunter Blair.

Understandably the directors of the National Bank were furious, especially since Coutts was their London agent, and wrote an irate letter to Pitt, which convinced him of the justice of their case. Finally, in 1796 the argument was settled: the Bank of Scotland, the Royal Bank, the British Linen Company and Sir William Forbes each received a quarter share of the produce of the excise.

There were other shadows on his homecoming: his daughters were acknowledged to be charming and accomplished and were known as 'The Three Graces', but no eligible suitor had yet asked for their hands.

In May 1791 the girls were presented at court by the Duchess of Buccleuch; their fond parents watched them set off in their carriage, dazzled by the beauty of their daughters in their court dresses. Their grace and elegance owed much to their training at the convent and in French society, but they had a naturalness which was all their own.

The social round began and Thomas complained that they had been hurried about from morning to night. They stayed at Cowdray Park with Lord Montagu, where his Lordship began to take an interest in Susan. The Earl of Bute's son, Lord Mountstuart, pressed them to visit him on his Isle of Bute. In the summer they spent two days on board the fleet at Portsmouth, where Thomas had many old acquaintances among admirals and captains, while the young officers made much of 'The Three Graces'.

In the summer of 1791 Thomas planned to take a long-desired tour of Scotland, but was delayed by the Earl of Bute, who, now retired from politics and sick, wanted to visit him in London; Thomas also wished to say his last farewell to the old man. He was 'deeply affected'; as he wrote to the Countess of Chatham,

it is so much like a last farewell ... the adieu of a worthy character who has through life been always doing me kindnesses, is too affecting and makes me almost wish to be divested of these quick sensibilities which are sometimes trouble-some both to ourselves and our friends.[16]

Since his return from Europe Thomas had become increasingly restless. He made long journeys partly, it is true, for the sake of his daughters, but there were deeper reasons for his itch to travel and to be away from the Strand. Edmund Antrobus was running the Bank almost too well and he was beginning to feel like an outsider.

In August Thomas set off once again, leaving the Bank in the care of the efficient, though restive, Antrobus, who had expected to take a holiday now that Thomas had returned. This time Thomas and the family made for Scotland and had a difficult journey to Novar, the seat of Sir Hector Munro on Cromarty Firth. They travelled up the west road to Carlisle, Glasgow and Crieff, where Munro's 'ten long-tailed English bays' met them and they 'cut a dash through the Highlands, and got all safe and well to Novar. Never was such fine warm weather'.[17] Munro, who often accompanied the Coutts family on their holiday expeditions, was a particular friend. He was a gallant soldier who had won fame in India, capturing Pondicherry from the French and Negapatam from the Dutch. The family always felt safe when he travelled with them.

In his native country Thomas expanded, riding every morning and watching the girls dancing every evening. They stayed with the formidable Duchess of Gordon in Gordon Castle, where they were so popular that the Duchess persuaded them to stay until the beginning of November. By the 4th they were back in Thomas's home town of Edinburgh. There he was held up for longer than he had planned, since so many of his old acquaintances wanted to see him. At last he headed for London, staying on the way with his cousin, Sir Gilbert Elliot, and the Duke of Newcastle.

It was not until the beginning of December that he was at long last back at his desk in the Strand. Even then the ladies were unwilling to return to London and stayed at Luxborough House, near Chigwell in Essex, with his old friend, Admiral Sir Edward Hughes. Here they were all so happy and comfortable that they refused to move. 'The graces', Thomas wrote, 'were never so happy or so well as when they were in the country.'[18] He worked in the week at the Bank and joined them on Sundays. Finally Susannah had to return to London to get the house into shape since it had been neglected in their long absence.

The year 1791 had been a rackety, restless one for the old banker, and by December both he and Susannah were thoroughly worn out. He was ill and depressed; and, despite the social whirl, none of the girls had yet found a husband. But above all he was desperately worried by disturbing news from France. That dawn, in which Wordsworth and so many others found it 'bliss' to be alive, had ushered in black days that would bring misery and death to many of his friends.

19

1792: A Black Year

Thomas Coutts does not seem to have been aware that 1792 marked the first centenary of the Bank under the sign of the Three Crowns in the Strand. But looking back at the end of 1793, he would hardly have thought it a time for rejoicing. For these two years were probably the worst in his life, when troubles and disasters beset him on all sides. In public affairs these were years of revolution and wars, death and destruction. In his business world it was a time of change, and there was distress and disaster in his private life. By December 1793 he felt that the world he knew was coming to an end and that he was ready now, as he said, to 'drop the curtain' on life itself.

It was indeed a turning-point in his life and in that of the Bank. It was not, however, the end: new life and new ideas grew out of the flames and he himself had thirty more years to live.

Edmund Antrobus and the partners had managed the Bank well during Thomas's frequent absences. The partners' profits, which had been £19,525 in 1790, rose to £22,561 in 1791 and in 1792 were to reach £26,922, of which Thomas's individual share was £21,874 4s od. Thomas, who for so long had been depressed by the state of the nation, was surprised by the unexpected general prosperity.

At least the year began with the hope of growing prosperity. As he wrote to Lady Chatham,

The produce of the Taxes, the increase of Arts and Manufactures, the high price of Stocks, and the prospect of even redeeming the expense of the American War, exceed the expectation of the most sanguine, while it astonishes men of more desponding tempers.[1]

In the spring of the year he could count himself among the most 'desponding'. As he walked on 3 March as a pall-bearer in the funeral procession of Sir Joshua Reynolds at St Paul's Cathedral, he felt the chill of the tomb. Aching with rheumatism, he longed for the blue skies of Italy and wished that he could winter there, but both partners, Edmund and

John Antrobus, were now ill and he could not get away. Thomas had hoped for a great future for Edmund's brilliant young brother John, who had been made a partner at the tender age of eighteen, but who was now showing early signs of a strange illness.

Instead Thomas spent some weeks at Easter at Cowdray Park, the home of Lord Montagu, where he hoped to regain strength and maybe gain a son-in-law. When he returned to London, the match seemed possible.

In June he wrote sadly to the Duchess of Devonshire:

As to myself, I am quite broken down, and am sure I am ten years older than when I last saw your Grace. ... I am at a loss what to do with my business. I laboured with pleasure at it for many years, always hoping my daughters would find me young men fit to take the oar from my hand; but they seem to me very unlikely to marry at all.[2]

He complained that he had experienced 'disappointments & ill treatment ... though indeed I have always had too much sensibility to bear the rubs and natural ills that flesh is heir to, and wonder much how I have ever arrived at threescore'.[3]

In a cold wet summer, crippled with rheumatism, Thomas took the family once more to try the waters at Cheltenham, but now they all fell ill and even the servants caught violent colds, so they retreated back to London. He had intended to go again to Buxton to take the treatment there and then on a northern tour to Scotland. He had promised the Earl of Bute before he died that he would visit him on the Isle of Bute, and the new Earl wanted him to keep his promise. But once again Susannah was very ill and they spent some weeks at Cowdray with Lord Montagu, getting up their strength for what promised to be a strenuous northern tour. However, they were delayed further because Thomas and Susannah were badly bruised when Lord Montagu's post-chaise was overturned, so the Scottish tour was abandoned. Instead they proposed to winter in Italy.

It seems surprising to us that, though Paris had been devastated in the September massacres, Thomas should have still thought it possible to travel to Italy via France. 'Fish' Craufurd, who was to travel with them, left before them to try out a route via Lyons and Marseilles. If that were not possible, they were to try the long sea route. But the Italian tour had to be abandoned, because both Fanny and Sophia were again dangerously ill, and John Antrobus was suffering from a mysterious, debilitating illness. Thomas needed to give time to the concerns of the Bank.

During 1792 Thomas was, for the first time, worried about his own bank balance. He was risking his reputation as a prudent banker by lending vast sums of money, sometimes without adequate security. As he wrote to the Duchess of Devonshire, 'As late as last summer [I have] given away

£10,000. ... It is really romance what I have done with money already, and how to reconcile to any bounds of discretion I do not know.' Edmund Antrobus, who must have known the state of Thomas's private account as well as that of the Bank, was rightly concerned. He had suggested that it would be wise for the Bank to keep a sinking fund of £100,000, but Thomas replied that he personally always kept such a sum ready. In fact during this period his personal loans must have drained his reserve. He had lent £30,000 to the Prince of Wales alone. And if he hoped to get his three daughters married, he would need a total of £75,000 for their dowries. He had told Antrobus that any risky loans were always made out of his private account, but the exact extent of these loans we shall never know, since his ledgers are discreet to the point of blankness.

One debtor in particular caused him great distress and concern at this time. In November 1791 Georgiana, Duchess of Devonshire, had suddenly gone abroad and did not return until September 1793. By early 1792 rumours were reaching him that she and the Duke were to be separated. If this were true, he would probably never recoup the vast debt she owed him. When in 1790 she had made an attempt to face her debts, Thomas headed the list of her creditors at £16,000; but when she left in November 1791, she owed him £20,000. Some of her other debts were to the French financier, de Calonne, £8,000; her husband's banker, Denne, £8,000; Hammersley, £14,448; and, to her shame, her maid's brother, £2,638.

In January 1792 she wrote apologising that she was 'obliged to leave England with your immense debt unsettled either as to interest or to principal. ... I feel more than usual solicitous about the payment of £4,500 of your debt.'[4] She offered to insure her life for that amount. In his reply Thomas made it clear that he would feel safe with the Duke's bond as security.

The Duchess had given her sister's dangerous illness as the reason for her sudden departure. But if Thomas knew the truth about Georgiana's absence he must have been even more worried. For, in the manner of the great ladies of the day, Georgiana, having at last in May 1790 produced a son and heir for the Duke, now felt free to engage in her own love affair and had finally succumbed to the cold charm of Charles Grey (later the Prime Minister, Earl Grey). She had retreated to Bath with her sister Harriet, when in November 1791 the Duke had thundered down and forced her to confess not only to the extent of her debts but also that she was pregnant with Grey's child. The fact that he himself already had two natural children by Lady Elizabeth Foster did nothing to calm his righteous wrath. He had insisted that Georgiana immediately go into exile abroad and she had obediently left for the South of France with her sister and Lady Elizabeth. At Aix-en-Provence on 20 February 1792 her baby was born and given the name of Eliza Courtney. The little girl was later brought up in the Grey household, leaving Georgiana doubly desolate, having lost both Grey, who abandoned her, and her child.

So it is not surprising that she failed to write to Thomas for a long time and, when she did, her letters were often frantic and unjust to him. He wrote on 19 February 1792:

I confess I have been hurt by your never writing to me. As you would see by my letter, which I find by yours of 26th January had come to hand, I had the same feeling of your silence when I was abroad in Italy. . . . You ask me would I take payment, if you can engage the Duke to do it at 2000£ a year till all is paid and 4 pct interest in the mean while? You may rest assured I will never stand in the way of any arrangement the Duke may agree to make. If he will give me his bond for the money, I will take it at any distant time he pleases, or at 2000£ as above, or even 1000£ a year and interest (of all) by half yearly payments. In short I have run this risk of an immense sum from no motive but that of serving your Grace. I am ashamed of it, because I see now that I judg'd ill and have done you no manner of good, nay perhaps I have aided you to pay debts you ought not to have paid, and which never could have been made legally or honestly clear against you. Yet still I am desirous to go on and let the mode of payment be suited to the Duke's convenience, as that of lending was to yours. All I wish with respect to myself is that it may be soon settled and fixed one way or the other, for if I must lose the money I would rather at once know I am to suffer. Certainly it will make a very material difference in my system of life, but I will arrange myself to it, and endeavour by working hard, while I have any remaining ability, to make my children some amends for my imprudence. . . .[5]

The Duke made no attempt to pay his wife's debts and for months ignored Thomas. When they were fellow guests at dinner at 'Fish' Craufurd's house, the Duke took no notice of him. 'Surely', Thomas complained to the Duchess on 25 May 1792, 'He might have somehow noticed me as one he had seen before. God knows I am so tired of the World that I care little for any distinction.'[6] His pride was hurt, but what made the Duke's attitude even more galling was that he was not one of Thomas's own customers – and his wealth was immense. In September Thomas's patience snapped and he wrote a stiff letter to the Duke:

Strand. London. Fourth of September 1792

Above eighteen months have passed since I had the honour of some conversation with Your Grace on the subject of the Duchess's debts, and tho' it [is] unwillingly that I now write, yet I am induced to it, from my anxiety to know whether Your Grace had *yet* come to any final determination upon what concerns me. It makes a very considerable object in my affairs, but if I have no hopes from Your Grace I had better see the worst at once, and by economy and dilligence endeavour to make up to my family what my imprudence has lost them. The nature of that part of the debt which arose a little time before the birth of the young marquis I believe Your Grace knows. . . .[7]

The Duke could give his bond, he wrote,

payable at any distant period by instalments, without interest, or with interest at the lowest rate of the best secured mortgage. *Anyway* Your Grace pleases will satisfy me perfectly. I stated before the whole sum due to me in December 1790 is 20,000£ including the bond of 4400£ on the back of which Your Grace wrote and subscribed a promise to pay it and to consider it as your own debt. . . .[8]

This at least, a month later, produced the Duke's bond for £5,610, 'in payment of the £4400 I lent the Duchess the 13th of March 1787, with Five and a half years interest'. Thomas would remain patient, 'tho' in suspence', for the rest. The postscript was brief: 'The sum now remaining due to me by the Duchess is 15,800£.'[9]

By now Thomas must have picked up the rumours that the Duke and Duchess were separating. If that were so, he knew it would be hopeless to expect Georgiana to be able to pay her debts. Her continued absence worried him. After a long silence, on 2 November 1792 Georgiana wrote from Milan that 'the reports of separation are groundless', but that the Duke could not fetch her until the spring and 'Oh, my dear, dear Sir, my heart is sick for my children and for England.'[10]

Thomas was infuriated that the Duke had chosen to pay his wife's debt to her jeweller before settling with him, and even more deeply hurt by the angry letter she sent when Antrobus had refused her an overdraft. To Antrobus the whole affair must have seemed incomprehensible. But this time Thomas too was out of patience:

Strand, Fourteenth December 1792

Your Grace cannot have been more *hurt* at the time of writing me the angry letter from Florence the 20th of November than I am this day at receiving it. I have gone on for years never refusing anything. Your letter says I have been in the punctual receipt of 500£ a quarter, yet *I would not have a little patience.* I absolutely know nothing of this regular 500£ a quarter, any more than I do of my want of patience, for I think I have shown patience beyond example. . . . The truth too is that, notwithstanding, we have paid £132.13.9. of overdrafts, but which goes for nothing as others have been refused. I had no reason to expect overdrafts, for you have always told me that you was determin'd against ever running into debt again, and that you have never done it since December 1790. . . . I will pay no more for the future and hope nothing will be expected from me, which will at least save me the mortification of receiving angry letters.[11]

Georgiana had the grace to apologise. Nevertheless, she still did not clear her debts. Throughout 1793 Thomas worried over the Duchess's debts, and, though she finally returned to a forgiving Duke on 18 September 1793, her debts to Thomas were still unpaid. But, as will be seen, he never gave up.

*　　*　　*

Perhaps it was a contrite Duchess of Devonshire who interceded with her friend, the Prince of Wales, on behalf of Thomas Coutts and persuaded him to bring his account back to the Bank in the Strand.

The Prince, who liked to divide his favours among his creditors, had run an account at Coutts & Co. again in March 1791, but his main custom stayed with Hammersley. Thomas had been anxious to persuade the Prince to make him his sole banker, especially since the King had not fully recovered. At the end of 1792 the Prince wanted a large loan, but this time Thomas was determined that if the Prince came back to him he must do so under his conditions. He prepared a long, stern memorandum, which he solemnly read out to His Royal Highness. The memorandum starts with third person formality, then Thomas slips more comfortably into his usual role of father confessor:

Mr Coutts feels a very earnest desire of proving to the Prince of Wales his sincere attachment to himself and his Majesty's family as well as of resuming the very honourable distinction of being his Royal Highness's Banker.

On these motives, which he can with great truth affirm far exceed any of interest that could be offered to him, it is that he means to depart entirely from every rule of business – and to ask his partners to consent to a breach of an article of long standing in his House never to permit jewels or personal ornaments to be taken as a security for money – and to lend out of his private fortune the sum *unsecured* except by the personal bond and life income of his Royal Highness – not choosing that his House should deviate from their practice or engage in anything dangerous or in any loan not specifically secured.[12]

In fact, Hammersley had been quite prepared to receive jewellery as a security for the loan to the Prince of Wales. Thomas could not afford to be outdone by his rival. He continued:

After thus straining every exertion to the utmost, so as to preclude all *power of going further*, I hope his Royal Highness will rigidly adhere to the system of never asking me for any further advances of money, as there is nothing would hurt me so much as refusing – which therefore I beg may be made a condition – that I never shall be put to that necessity.

And unless what I am now about to do is sufficient to extricate the Prince so as to enable those employ'd by him to carry into execution the settlement with the *creditors* to *their* satisfaction & for the Prince's final relief from demands for payment of money – I *hope* and *entreat* it may not go forward, as it will be putting me under a very considerable embarrassment, follow'd by disappointment and vexation, without producing any lasting or essential good to his Royal Highness.

I beg leave also most humbly to suggest that unless his Royal Highness goes *heartily firmly* and *decidedly* into the plan of reform, and will *obstinately persevere in it for years to come*, he will do himself an injury instead of any good.

The confidence and good opinion of the people of so much *mutual* consequence to the Prince and to themselves, will be entirely shaken. They will think themselves deceived, and will never again believe or trust to any professions – or any future plans however *specious* – or *even sincere* – that may hereafter be proposed.[13]

Thomas was well advised to be firm. As he reminded the Prince, he had 'already lent the Prince of Wales £10,000 on Lord Rawdon's security'.[14] A vast new loan would severely stretch the banker's resources. Not surprisingly, the Prince of Wales resented this fatherly advice and complained to his friend Sheridan. So when Thomas sent the Prince a copy of the memorandum, he accompanied it with a letter of explanation:

I have felt myself very unhappy since Mr. Sheridan inform'd me your Royal Highness had been displeased with the freedom I made use of in the papers I had the honour of reading to your Royal Highness. I can only say in my defence that the opinions I took the liberty of offering proceeded from zeal and respectful duty, and I am confident will not be disapproved by any of your Royal Highness's real friends. The exertion I was in the act of making for your Royal Highness's accommodation (a very large and important object in the affairs of any individual) I am bold to assert in the face of received opinions either general – or of individuals (be their knowledge or abilities what they may) proceeded much more from my sincere love and respect for your Royal Highness and His Majesty's Family, and the flattering hope of contributing to the dignity and comfort of your situation, than from any motive of my own interest present or to come. The consiousness of this truth induced me to express sentiments which perhaps may have been thought my situation rendered improper, tho' among those who know me I flatter myself nothing is more the reverse of my character than improper presumption or forwardness in any respect.[15]

However offended the Prince might be, he had complete confidence in Thomas's discretion. And though Thomas was always reluctant to grant mortgages without security, he made an exception for the Prince, who had bought a house for Mrs Fitzherbert with a loan from Thomas. He always had sympathy for the Prince's morganatic wife and was her trusted and affectionate friend.

Your Royal Highness mentioned to me something of your delicacy in regard to making any new burdens on Mrs. Fitzherbert's house – and on hearing from Mr. Sheridan yesterday that you still felt a difficulty in giving the security proposed upon it – I not only immediately gave it up but desired not even to have the £5000 mortgage continued.

No man can feel more sincerely the propriety of your Royal Highness's desire to fulfill your intentions of giving Mrs. Fitzherbert the house totally unincumberd – or of every attention that can be shown her; and it was on that account, as soon as I heard of her allowance of £3000 a year, that I desired it might be placed first in the list for payment, and take place even of the interest money of the sum I was about to advance.

Tho I have written a tedious letter about myself I cannot end it without saying I have found it impossible to resist the impulse of stating myself to your Royal

Highness *as* (I think) *I really am* – a person acting towards you on the purest and best motives – extremely sorry if want of art or ability should have made what I have said or written appear disrespectful or over-presuming – most humbly declaring it to be directly contrary to my intention, & begging on that ground your Royal Highness will have the goodness to pardon any impropriety there may have been in my proceeding.

I should most chearfully embrace the opportunity of clearing myself – on the present – or future occasions from every sort of imputation of blame that can be laid to my charge – and shall never doubt of doing it completely if your Royal Highness will be my judge yourself and have the goodness to give me your attention & hearing.[16]

So the Prince was granted his loan. At the beginning of 1793, as Thomas wrote to Colonel Crawfurd:

The Prince ... has lately changed many things for *the better* and I hope among others the change of His Banker is one – He came back to me this winter & has appointed me Receiver General of all his Revenue – with the full approbation of His Majesty.[17]

20

1793: A Year of Tragedy

If 1792 had been a difficult year, 1793 was to bring a succession of tragedies.

It has been necessary to describe separately each wave in the 'sea of troubles' that engulfed Thomas Coutts in the years 1792 and 1793. But it must be remembered that much of the buffeting happened at the same time, and that there were strong undercurrents running throughout the years which threatened to drag him down. While he was struggling through a bank crisis, the American War of Independence, the French Revolution and domestic tragedies, he was consumed by a secret, gnawing fear of madness. Fanny's strange malady revived memories of Patrick and James, and he himself suffered periods of black melancholy and giddiness. 'I was not so giddy when I was young,' he wrote wryly to Caleb Whitefoord.[1] There were times when he deeply offended Caleb and Colonel Crawfurd by his withdrawal into gloomy silence. The Colonel was once so angry that he wrote in fury that, had they been younger men, he would have called him out. As Thomas wrote to Edmund Antrobus, 'an alarming disorder is threatening me with the crisis of decayed powers, and . . . I feel quite unfit for further exertions in the arduous task of guiding & attending so large a concern'.[2]

His constant worry during these terrible years was that he might at any moment be left without partners at a time when, tired and ill, he most needed them. Edmund Antrobus was often ill and it was obvious to him that John Antrobus would never be strong enough in mind or body to take the stress. The clerks were well organised, but he needed a new partner and had already, as he confided to Lord Minto, thought of 'Mr Coutts Trotter, whose father had some share in my education'.[3]

Thomas watched John Antrobus throughout the months with some anxiety, recognising symptoms that reminded him of his brothers. He wrote to Colonel Crawfurd on 13 February 1793:

I fear for some time I must be tied by the Leg, for Mr John Antrobus continues incapable of Business & Mr Ed Antrobus in so uncertain a State of Health that I

160

must take another Partner. I think of Mr Coutts Trotter who I believe you know. He is a very deserving Young man & clever.[4]

Coutts Trotter was the son of Archibald, whom the young Coutts brothers had so mercilessly teased in Edinburgh after their father's death. Trotter had much in his favour: he was a Scot, he was a member of the Coutts family and he had been named after his beloved father. His mother had also been kind to Thomas in his youth.

Thomas was comfortable with the tall, slightly gauche, young Scot, who worked hard and was anxious to please. He had been trained in the Paymaster General's Office and was quick with figures. Thomas took pains to point out to his new partner his rules for the partnership in the Bank:

One half of it in that case to belong to my Family (according to my appointment by will or otherwise) and the other half to the acting partners according to a proportion pointed out and depending on their seniority and standing. They all perfectly understand my intention as to retaining in my family the supremacy (if I may so express it) of the house as well as the half share, and if after myself, my Wife and Daughters shall be extinct without heirs that it should belong to Lady Stuart and her children. And it is on their honour quite as much as on any legal tie that I depend on their performance towards my Family of these conditions – Sensible as I am that this is a much more pleasant as well as a more secure tenure.

By the Supremacy of the House is meant the disposal which is to rest with me while I live and with my family at my death on the share or shares of my partners who may die or retire. And that everything on any partner quitting business shall be left in the hands of the person holding the supremacy.

Mr. Trotter's share is compared with Mr. Antrobus's as one is to three.[5]

At least the partnership was now soundly based.

In February 1793 he lost one of his closest friends, Colonel Crawfurd. The Colonel, who was unmarried, had planned to leave Thomas his estate in Ayrshire, which he hoped to pass on to his daughter, Fanny. When Thomas heard that the Colonel was dangerously ill, he wrote urging him to make his will. This the Colonel did, four days before his death. But his relations contested the will since, by Scottish law, a period of sixty days between the signing and the decease was necessary. The case dragged on for many years until in 1806 the Crawfurd relations won and succeeded to the estate. This was a double blow for Thomas: he had lost a dear friend and the chance of at last owning some land. The Colonel's death depressed him deeply. The loss of the estate he wryly accepted, though he was beginning to regret that he had never invested in property. In those uncertain times he would have felt more secure if he had owned land.

Events in France, however, overshadowed personal disappointment. On 21 January Louis XVI had been guillotined and on 1 February war had been declared between England and France. Not only were many of

Thomas's French friends in danger, but there was also a collapse in business confidence. The outbreak of war caused panic in the City, reaching its climax in March. The Scottish banker, James Dunlop, went bankrupt and in April other banks in Edinburgh and Newcastle collapsed; there was even a run on the Royal Bank of Scotland. There was the additional concern that the run on the banks was caused not just by French affairs, but by deliberate action of those in England who were inspired by the French Revolution. It was not until 16 June that the financial world returned to normal. Fortunately Coutts & Co. was not affected.

In February 1793 the war with France, as Thomas wrote, had now 'fairly begun, God grant us a good ending and if England to herself do be true, there can be no doubt of it'.[6] But he hoped that England would not, as Russia had done, declare 'Monsieur Regent of France, . . . for our war with France is on different ground as we do not want to meddle with their internal Government more than we desire they should meddle with ours'.[7]

Thomas shared the general fear that Britain might become infected by French revolutionary fever. His personal experience of France in the early stages of the Revolution made him anxious, and he disapproved of the new reactionary 'Associations of the People' that were springing up.

There ought to be force in Government to suppress seditious meetings. If there is not, that Government cannot stand. But we shall become like France, if we are to be governed by Clubs, and the Counter-reformist Clubs are as illegal as the other.[8]

Revolution, he believed, could be avoided by forethought. He had once written to Colonel Crawfurd:

As to reform of Parliament or of laws they should always be reforming and repairing. The Constitution with all its excellencies is not perfect, and is subject to dilapidations. But let such things be gone into temperately and at proper time. The truth is a good wise Minister should look before and do things before they are asked by the people.[9]

William Pitt had his own ways of defeating revolution: he was to keep a close watch on rebels at home and develop a more efficient system of espionage abroad.

Thomas's hope for a quiet, orderly progress was to be rudely dashed. In the coming years the clamour of revolution was to be brought to his very home by a turbulent young man who, in 1793, became his son-in-law.

21

Thomas Coutts
and the French Revolution

The full story of Thomas Coutts and the French Revolution will never be known, since the discreet banker has left few records of his activities at this time, but it is certain that both personally and as a banker he was deeply concerned. Of the friends he had made during his long stay in Paris, some were in mortal danger, some were guillotined and many had escaped to Britain. Throughout these years the rattle of the tumbrels was never far away.

During the Revolution and after, Thomas kept closely in touch with affairs in France. He had many contacts: there were English friends like John Hare, who stayed in Paris during the Revolution and sent him reports. 'Fish' Craufurd was in and out of France on various curious missions; as George Middleton's grandson, he had a long connection with France. Thomas himself personally knew many of the French bankers who were in exile or under threat of death. Émigrés like the financier Charles de Calonne brought him news of French financial affairs. It is very probable that he had first-hand accounts of the flight of the French King and Queen and their capture at Varennes, since he knew Quentin Craufurd,* who had paid secret visits to Marie Antoinette and who, with Count Fersen, helped to plan the attempted escape. It was in the courtyard of Craufurd's house that the coach was waiting which took the royal family on their fateful journey. When the escape failed, Craufurd came to London to try to raise funds for the counter-revolution. It is unlikely he would have passed by the bank of a fellow Scot in the Strand.

So Thomas was constantly reminded of the blood and horror on the other side of the Channel. His friend, the painter Masquerier, often told how the head of the Princesse de Lamballes, stuck on a pole, had been pushed up to his studio window. Every day such stories were brought by

---

* Quentin Craufurd was not the same family as 'Fish' Craufurd, but was of another Scots family which settled in Holland and made its fortune there.

the refugees who flooded into London, and many came to the Bank in the Strand, bringing their jewels to be kept in its strongrooms as security for loans, or to be sold when Madame Guillotine had done her work. Thomas must have been reminded of his early days in Edinburgh, when the 'Iron Maiden', the predecessor of the guillotine, was at work in the Grass Market. Like many who generously gave help, he often lost patience. There were the usual problems of an émigré community, squabbles between factions, between followers of the Orléans branch of the royal family and the senior branches. Many of the aristocrats could not adjust to their new lives, living miserably in borrowed houses in remote places without their carriages, cadging meals and overstaying their welcome at country houses. Even Stuart-MacKenzie's wife, Lady Betty, the daughter of the Duke of Argyll, who had entertained many émigrés, finally exclaimed, 'enough is enough'.[1] Sometimes Thomas turned a deaf ear when grand French ladies swept into the Strand expecting loans without security.

The discreet banker never revealed the full extent of his generosity to his French friends, but two stories can be pieced together from various records. Perhaps the most touching is that of the lovely Duchesse de Biron, whose tale can only be told briefly here.

Two years earlier, in July 1791, Thomas had received a visit from the Reverend Louis Dutens, one of the most intriguing characters of the time. Officially he was secretary to Stuart-MacKenzie, but he was in fact a secret agent, philosopher, antiquary and friend and confidant of many great men and women. On this occasion he came to Thomas as the escort of the Duchesse de Biron, a French émigrée of great beauty and quiet elegance.

Amélie de Boufflers (1751–94), Duchesse de Biron, was the granddaughter and heiress of the Maréchal de Luxembourg and the stepdaughter of the Comtesse de Boufflers. Before the Revolution her salon, in her exquisite house overlooking the Seine, attracted many of the philosophers and literary men of the age. Her library of rare books contained important manuscripts, including that of Rousseau's *Nouvelle Héloïse*. To her contemporaries 'she was without fault', 'an angel'.[2] These virtues did not appeal to her husband, the Duc de Lauzun, better remembered as the Duc de Biron. A dashing philanderer, he left her, literally, to her harp, which she played excellently, and continued his life of amorous adventures. A reckless but brave soldier, he was at that time 'Citizen General of the Army'.

Amélie, however, was in danger and had come to England to bring her jewels and arrange her affairs. She now laid her treasures before Thomas – a casket of pearls and diamonds. Mr Dickie made a careful inventory, which still remains in Coutts & Co.'s *Oubliette*.

On her return to Paris Amélie was imprisoned as an émigrée, but released on the appeal of her husband. Though he had been parted from her for fifteen years, he wrote that he felt for the first time painful remorse.

Amélie was released and lived quietly for some time with her stepmother at Auteuil. From this retreat in 1792 she had written sad letters to Dutens, asking him to arrange her affairs with Coutts – and giving instructions for the disposal of her jewels in case of her death. She entrusted her will to 'Fish' Craufurd. To Dutens she sent a second box of jewels, with a message to Thomas that he should sell them if necessary; she enclosed the valuation for all of them except a diamond necklace her grandmother had left her, which she did not want to sell unless it was absolutely essential.

Amélie needed courage too, for she was again imprisoned with her stepmother, the Comtesse de Boufflers. In the dank prison she wanted to write a codicil to her will and, having no paper, tore a piece off her petticoat on which she wrote her instructions; this was sent to 'Fish' Craufurd by a fellow prisoner, an Englishwoman later released. Amélie was condemned to death and called to the scaffold, it is said, by mistake: it was her 'man of business' whose name should have been called. It is said that she walked out of the prison with great composure on the arm of an old marshal. She bent her beautiful head to the blade with quiet resignation and, perhaps at last, with relief.

Thomas had treated her with great kindness, but her stepmother the Comtesse had received a chilly reception. She had written on 21 July 1791 in some indignation to Dutens that Thomas, who had previously been so '*généreux et si délicat*',[3] now refused her a loan. 'I explained my situation to him and asked him if he could advance what was necessary until my funds arrived.'[4] But Thomas assured her that it was never the custom among bankers to lend without security and he could not agree to one if he refused another. 'I don't deny', she wrote, 'that I was piqued by the cold manner of Mr Coutts and that his refusal was not accompanied by any manner of regret.'[5] She was particularly annoyed because she had been kind to Thomas's daughters in Paris. Thomas, however, did not warm to imperious great ladies.

The French émigrés were, in fact, becoming a nuisance at a time when Thomas had other demands on his resources.

But perhaps Thomas's most important connection with French émigrés was with the family of the Duke of Orléans and with Madame de Genlis, governess to his daughter. Philippe d'Orléans, who was known as 'Égalité' when feudal titles were abolished, trod an uneasy path between revolution and royalty and was trusted by neither. In 1791 his son, Louis Philippe, was in favour with the Revolutionary Government and was fighting bravely with the French army against the Austrian invaders. Madame de Genlis had been his tutor and also, if Louis Philippe's memoirs are rightly understood, introduced him to the joys of manhood. She certainly had been his father's mistress. Madame de Genlis had a foot in both camps: her brother was a royalist and an émigré and her son was fighting with Louis Philippe.

In 1791 she believed that she was in danger and was desperately scared. She was now the governess of Louis Philippe's fourteen-year-old sister, Mademoiselle Adelaïde de Chartres, or Adèle as she was then called, and used Adèle's ill-health as an excuse to escape to England. The Duke had been very reluctant to let them go and insisted that they came back in a month. However, Madame de Genlis, with her niece, Henrietta de Sercey, and Adèle, stayed for three months in Bath and then took a little house in the middle of Bury St Edmunds. It was, as Louis Philippe wrote, 'a bizarre choice',[6] but doubtless the clever lady had her reasons. Here she stayed until the autumn, making trips to London and at least one mysterious visit to the Isle of Wight.

Thomas had met the Duke in London and in Paris, and his son, Louis Philippe, had shown his daughters some kindness. So he agreed to look after the financial affairs of Adèle and her governess while in England.

Madame de Genlis certainly did not shirk her duty as tutor for Adèle; in later life Madame Adelaïde was said to be the éminence grise behind Louis Philippe and was noted for her intelligence. Mrs Coutts warmly welcomed Adèle, inviting her to their house in the Strand. Adèle replied that, though she 'made it a point never to go into society, she made an exception for Mrs Coutts',[7] apologising that she could not call before 1 p.m. because of her studies. She had, she said, 'so little time here that she spends all her time seeing curious and instructive things and therefore cannot take up the offer of the "tribune", Susan, Fanny and Sophia, to see the fête of the Duchess of York, but would sometimes be delighted to see the play.' She was going again to the *Cabinets du tableaux*'. She sent her dear love to Mrs Coutts's three daughters, promising eternal friendship. In July Henrietta de Sercey wrote: 'Time nor absence can diminish our friendship with the three dear & charming friends, Suzu, Fanny and Sophie.'[8]

So Madame de Genlis, Henrietta and Adèle took tea in the apartment over the Bank in the Strand and watched the splendid 'Mme Sydons' (Mrs Siddons) from Thomas's box at the theatre. Thomas arranged a visit to Parliament and to Carlton House. In return, Madame de Genlis made his daughters crystal earrings and threaded *cailloux* (beads) to make collars; she also sent a prescription for cough mixture to Thomas. 'Her syrup of aromatic gum',[9] however, failed to cure his chronic cough.

In spite of the Duke's angry appeals, Madame de Genlis refused to return to France. Finally in November 1792 he sent a messenger, M. Hugues Maret (later Duc de Bassano), armed with an order to bring back his daughter. On their arrival in Paris they were arrested and imprisoned, for, as the Duke had warned Madame, their long stay abroad condemned them as émigrées. Only through his influence did they manage to escape. On Wednesday, 4 December 1792, Adèle tearfully wished her father goodbye. She never saw him again.

Adèle and Madame de Genlis now settled at Tournai to be near Louis Philippe, who was with the army there. His younger brother, Montpensier, who had acted as his aide-de-camp, returned to Paris to be with the Duke, his father, and his place was taken by Madame de Genlis's nephew. But the net was closing in around even those who, like Louis Philippe, had shown some sympathy with the Revolution. After the execution of the King, Madame de Genlis and Adèle escaped again, under false names, this time to Switzerland. Louis Philippe left the army and escaped on foot to join them in Switzerland.

By the decree of 5 April 1793 all the Bourbons were arrested. The Duke, now Citizen Égalité, was interned at Marseilles with Montpensier. His wife, from whom he had long been separated, was also arrested. But because her father, the Duke of Penthièvre, was universally popular, she was allowed to join him. On 12 September 1797 she was expelled to Spain with her court.

Meanwhile, Égalité was tried and found guilty, although he had actually voted for the execution of the King. Before his execution he sent a sad letter to Thomas Coutts asking him to send him two Wedgwood medallions – one of Hope and one of Justice. But he received neither. On 7 November 1795 Égalité was guillotined.

Louis Philippe – now Duke of Orléans – made his way across Europe in disguise. Under the name of Corby he worked as a secretary and lecturer, until in March 1795 he arrived at Hamburg. Then began a long odyssey which took him, often on foot, through Germany, Denmark, Sweden and Norway. When later he became King, he sent a corvette laden with marble busts in gratitude to those who had sheltered him in his exile. (One still stands at the North Cape, gazing out towards the North Pole over the icy sea – covered with graffiti – a hammer and sickle on his breast.) Throughout his journeys he kept in touch with Thomas, sending letters, often unsigned or with a false name. Thomas had many such friends, who, with his own intelligence agents, kept him well informed.

'We do not want to meddle with the form of government' of other countries, Thomas wrote, yet he must have been aware of the network of agents and spies set up by Pitt at home and abroad. He had a personal knowledge of the secret world of espionage: his brother Patrick had been imprisoned as a spy and his brother John had been involved with secret agents in Holland. Among his friends there were many who almost certainly worked in that mysterious world. 'Fish' Craufurd, his friend Fawkener and his brother James were involved at various times in undercover activities. Thomas, who had his own sources of information all over the world, was well aware of the government office known as the 'Foreign Letter Office', where mail to and from suspected persons was opened, read and resealed. Under Pitt the government system was taken further: some agents not only reported, but also took an active part in plotting abroad and at home.

In June 1792 and January 1793 the Westminster Police Bill had led to a new system of surveillance in order to counter the threatened revolution in England. Seven police officers with three stipendiary magistrates were set up with the power to commit to prison without trial anyone who declared revolutionary intentions.

In August 1793 the Foreign Secretary, Lord Grenville, appointed a certain William Wickham as one of these three magistrates, to report on the activities of the London Correspondence Society. Spies and *agents provocateurs* were infiltrated into the meetings of such clubs, and Wickham compiled a list of suspect aliens for the Home Secretary, Lord Portland. He was later sent to Switzerland and 'meddled' to some effect in the affairs of France, helping to organise counter-revolution, fostering anti-Jacobin groups in Paris. With the connivance of the Alien Office – the British secret service – he encouraged the abortive rising in the Vendée, which was so brutally suppressed.

Thomas certainly knew Wickham well enough to entrust to him in 1795 a particularly delicate mission. Charles Edward Stuart's discarded mistress was a relation of Thomas's through his mother's family and he had been generous to her in her exile. She now called herself the Comtesse d'Alberstorff and lived in Paris. Thomas advised her that if she visited Switzerland and needed help she should call upon Wickham, writing to the secret agent asking that he should 'do me the greatest kindness possible by showing her any attention in your power'.

Agents like Wickham were paid by the Government through the Foreign Office from a secret service account. Their wages were paid through banks like Perregaux in Paris, which were assumed to be loyal to the monarchy. At home Thomas had shared with Hammersley and other bankers the privilege of dealing with the secret service account, but on 24 May 1795 he was appointed the sole banker to be entrusted with this prestigious account. On that day 'Lord Grenville's Separate Account' was opened, which was in fact the official Foreign Office secret service account. Thomas regarded the payment of secret service accounts as a great honour, confirming the trust that the King and the Government placed in Coutts & Co.

Miniature of Thomas Coutts as a young man by J. Meyer

Top left: Caleb Whitefoord in his distinctive Garrick wig

Top right: Sir Thomas Lawrence by Landseer – a highly successful artist who was nevertheless for years in debt to Thomas Coutts

Bottom: Henry Fuseli – a self-portrait, c.1779. He was a protégé of Thomas Coutts from his earliest days in London.

Top left: George III by Sir Thomas Lawrence, one of the royal portraits commissioned by the King

Top right: Georgiana, Duchess of Devonshire – lovely, but certainly no angel

Bottom: Cartoon of the secret marriage of the Prince of Wales and Mrs Fitzherbert, 'designed by Carlo Khan', i.e. Charles James Fox

Top: Portrait of Sir Edmund Antrobus, Thomas Coutts's partner from 1777 to 1826, by Sir Thomas Lawrence

Bottom: HEICS *Thomas Coutts* from a painting by W. J. Huggins

Sir Francis Burdett by Sir Thomas Lawrence, 1793

Top left: 'The Three Graces': Susan, Fanny and Sophia, the three daughters of Thomas and Susannah Coutts, by their friend Angelica Kauffman

Top right: A draft letter from Thomas Coutts to Lord Minto, 24 November 1800, showing his wandering handwriting

Bottom: Thomas Coutts's house at 1 Stratton Street, decorated at the end of the nineteenth century to celebrate a royal wedding

Top left: Portrait of Edmund and Gibbs Antrobus, nephews of Sir Edmund Antrobus, by Sir Thomas Lawrence. Edmund junior became a partner in the Bank from 1816 to 1870.

Top right: Sir Coutts Trotter, partner from 1793 to 1837

Bottom left: Edward Marjoribanks junior, partner from 1838 to 1877

Bottom right: Andrew Dickie, the first clerk to become a partner in 1827

Harriot Mellon as Volante, her most successful role

22

Francis Burdett

In 1793 a young man reappeared in Thomas's life whose revolutionary activities were to interest Pitt's spies and who was to cause the banker infinite distress throughout the rest of his life. In early spring Francis Burdett visited 1 Stratton Street to pay his respects to 'The Three Graces'.

They had met the young man in France when Fanny had been the object of his attentions. After his return from France he had retired to his grandfather's house, Foremark, near Repton in Derbyshire, but he came to London from time to time during the autumn and winter to escort his aunt, Lady Jones, on the social round. Fanny was ill at the time and in the absence of the sun he took notice of the gentle moon, Sophia. Certainly at this time Sophia was bewitching. She was eighteen, tiny and delicate, with long fair hair, and, although childish for her years, she had been thought 'very clever' in Paris. She was somewhat in awe of the strong-minded, handsome Susan and was well aware that Fanny was not only her father's favourite but also the most generally admired of the sisters, who had found Burdett an uncomfortable man and had rejected him. At some time early in the next year he was writing passionate love poetry to Sophia and in April Burdett asked for her hand in marriage.

Burdett was, even at this time, an unusual young man, powerfully driven by a desire to know and to serve mankind. He had returned from France deeply moved by the sight of squalor in the midst of extravagant wealth and, possessed by a hunger for knowledge, had set himself to study philosophy and politics under the guidance of his tutor, the Reverend William Bagshaw Stevens, whose journal is the source of much information about the Coutts family in the following years.

Stevens was chaplain to Burdett's grandfather at Foremark and Master of Repton School. He was a scholar and poet and later became a visiting lecturer at Magdalen College, Oxford, obliged to give 'lectures in a dead language to a compelled audience'.[1] He wrote prefatory verses to the works of Erasmus Darwin, the grandfather of Charles Darwin, the great scientist and poet, who was the Burdetts' family physician at Foremark. Stevens encouraged Burdett's passion for learning and doubtless also his humanitarianism and political sympathies.

Burdett had spent most of his youth at Foremark, riding and hunting over the Derbyshire hills. Throughout his long and tumultuous life, he remained a country squire at heart and, though he became a silver-tongued orator, he was always happier on a horse than on a platform.

The dominant character at Foremark was his grandfather, old Sir Robert, who appears in Stevens's journal as 'the old Bart', selfish and autocratic. In his great Palladian house he ruled his court – his daughter Miss Burdett; his relative Mr Pyott, who managed his estates; and his steward, Mr Greaves.

Francis Burdett's mother had died when he was seven. His father was, according to Stevens, 'a silly giggling man', who played little part in his children's lives. In contrast, Francis was 'serious and manly'. After his mother's death Francis was sent with his brothers to board at Westminster School in London, where, as Stevens later said, they 'learned nothing, absolutely nothing'.[2]

Sedley, the second son, an attractive but wild young man, never regretted his ignorance, but Francis (who had been called Frank in his early days) did and, at the Bart's request, Stevens coached him in Latin. The third son, Jones, who, in 1793, was about to go up to Oxford, adored his brother and modelled himself on him; through all Francis's turbulent life, Jones was his loyal friend and supporter. The sisters, Eleanor and Eliza, were mostly brought up at their aunt's beautiful home, Ramsbury Manor in Wiltshire. Lady Jones was their mother's sister and co-heiress of great Wiltshire estates. Eleanor was a beautiful and good young woman, much admired in Ramsbury and deeply mourned when she died young. Stevens helped Francis to write her moving epitaph, which can still be seen in Ramsbury Church.

Stevens watched Francis's development with growing admiration, though he was never blind to his faults. 'Who has got Mrs Pyott's maid with child?' he asked, and was relieved to find that it was Sedley, not Francis.[3]

The engagement between Sophia and Francis did not run smoothly. The old Bart, hearing rumours that there was insanity in the Coutts family, sent his spies down to London and was not convinced by their reports that Thomas's brother was not insane, but 'ruined by early debauchery'.[4] Had he known that two brothers were insane, that a third had mysteriously died young, and that there was almost certainly insanity in Thomas's mother's family, he would have roared his disapproval and stopped the marriage. As it was he gave in, persuaded by the report of a Dr Calder in London that there was no family history of mental instability. Since Dr Calder was a friend of Thomas's, his evidence was somewhat suspect.

On 5 August 1793 Sophia was married so quietly at St Martin's-in-the-Fields that even the maids were unaware until it was over. Years later King William IV, then Duke of Clarence, would recall in his kindly, bumbling way that he had been present at their wedding. It is possible that he was there, since he was a frequent visitor at the Coutts's house at that time.

Burdett and his bride set off on a honeymoon tour of Wales, escorted by Thomas, Susannah and their two other daughters. Not surprisingly Burdett frequently retreated with his books. Thomas took the opportunity to combine business with pleasure and paid a visit to Lord Newborough at his seat, Glynllifon Park, near Caernarvon. There 'on the King's coronation day we had such a jubilee', he wrote delightedly to Caleb and enclosed a description of the scene which he wanted him to 'put in the newspapers'.[5] He was particularly anxious that Newborough, who had just returned from a long residence abroad, should be seen to be loyal to the House of Hanover. So he described the flags, the artillery hired from a fort, and the country games ending in a ball and masquerade.

They were intending to spend some time at Buxton before proceeding to stay with Sir Robert Burdett at Foremark, but on the way they received news of an appalling tragedy, which had occurred on 9 October. Lord Montagu and Sedley Burdett had gone together on a continental tour and at Schaffhausen, in Germany, deciding to shoot the falls in a canoe, were drowned. Stevens wrote in his journal:

Never did two men so fool away their Lives. They had been to see a fall of Water on the Rhine between Lucern and Lauffenberg – by way of experiment they let an empty Boat down the Stream which most unfortunately for them floated safe down the Cataract. These rash Young Men were determined from an idle bravado to float down this fall which the Natives thought impassable. And some days after they put their foolhardy project into execution. Four Servants rowed them from Lucern till they came nearly within the reach of the influence of the Fall, and then prudently refused to proceed. Their Masters persisted. The Servants, Cowards or Fools, as these unhappy Young Men called them, were landed on the Bank, and the two adventurers gave themselves to the force of the Stream, their attendants with tears in vain dissuading them. In the space of a moment, in the twinkling of an eye, ere they reached half the Fall, the Boat was dashed to pieces against a projecting rock and these unfortunate Youths were seen no more. . . . It is remarkable that these Young Men before they committed themselves to this merciless Cataract gave their money and watches to the care of their attendants – An express with this melancholy news was immediately sent off from Foremark to Mr. Burdett at Ramsbury and another to Frank who is his Brother's Heir at Buxton. It was judged prudent not to communicate the event to the old Man till tomorrow.[6]

Susan, who had become engaged to Lord Montagu, lost a fiancé, Burdett lost a brother, and Fanny lost a lover. For, before Sedley had left on his journey, Fanny, unknown to her parents, had fallen in love with him and promised to marry him. The grief of the others was understandable; Fanny's grief was hysterical because the reason was initially concealed. Deeply conscious of a sense of guilt, she confessed and once more succumbed to her strange fits and faintings.

They proceeded to Buxton, where they sank in distress and awaited the invitation to Foremark. While the tearful ladies kept to their rooms, distracted by grief, Thomas wrote a long letter to the King, which clearly illustrates the easy, friendly relations between the King and his banker:

16 November 1793 at Buxton

Sire,

[though he was] Sensible how trifling the concerns of so humble a person as I am may appear, I am emboldened by repeated instances of humanity and condescension and feeling a certain consolation in complaining *there* – where my deepest respect is *due* and *fix'd*, to *state* that after the marriage of my Youngest daughter to Mr Burdett . . . and finding my health impaired by too close application and attendance in the Strand for nine months, I accepted of an invitation from some friends in North Wales to view that beautifuly romantic country, my whole family including Mr and Mrs Burdett, accompanying me in the tour.

Mr Charles Sedley Burdett, next brother to Mr Burdett, a most amiable youth, had engaged the affections of my second daughter . . . his family, confiding in the friendship between the elder Mr Burdett and the Viscount Montague consented to the younger joining His Lordship in Switzerland without any person attending him –

My eldest daughter having been equally engaged to Lord Montague, the two young gentlemen seem'd the more happy together, and we received every week the most agreeable letters from them –

. . . we were altogether on our journey to Foremark, and I had almost forgot my own infirmities in seeing the happiness of all those most dear to me – when an express overtook Mr Burdett, giving him the mellancholy news of his dear brother and Lord Montague having perished together by a useless and infatuated exploit of descending a cataract on the Rhine near Lucern. The numberless cruelly aggravating circumstances attending this mellancholy event, and the sad effects of it upon my family are not to be described – but it may easily be conceived the shock must be terribly severe to young minds unaccustomed to disappointments, endowed with too great a share of sensibility. . . .

My second daughter immediately relapsed into these singular swoonings and nervous affections – (so difficult to describe or understand). Concerning which I have formerly been honoured and much comforted by Your Majesty's remarks and enquirys – and the eldest suffers equally – tho' in a different way Reason and the kindness of friends – cannot be supposed to do much at first against such heart-rending affliction – but there is no fault on their parts – and as they have innocent minds and good natural understanding – and are strongly impress'd with religion and their duty to submit with resignation to the will of God who works all things for the best and knows what is for our good much better than we do ourselves, I hope in time they may recover from the blow –

This may detain me some time in this country, and unsettles all our future plans. If there was peace perhaps I might carry them for a year abroad – if not, I would wish to hire some gentleman's house near town for a year 'till we can see further – for I fear London society will not be bearable by them this winter –

The goodness and humanity so universally known and acknowledged – and by me so uncommonly experienced can alone give me the hope of pardon for this intrusive interruption. I will not make it longer, than to add my sincere and ardent prayer for the long preservation of Your Majesty's health and most precious and valuable life – and the happiness & prosperity of all your royal family –

> I am Sir,
> Your Majesty's
> Most Dutiful subject
> And
> Devoted Servant
> Thomas Coutts[7]

While the ladies were prostrated with grief, Thomas trudged around the bleak Derbyshire countryside, sometimes in black despair, sometimes wrestling with the problems of his Bank and with the new political ideas that were shaking his world, for on the long journey with Burdett he had been forced to look at the world through fresh, young eyes. Burdett and his radical principles, expressed with passionate sincerity, made him reassess his own attitudes.

It was a relief to unburden himself in a long letter to Caleb. He began by complaining of the inaccuracy of newspaper accounts of the war with France, for the disaster of the Duke of Brunswick's campaign had been reported as a victory: 'Exactness is a very uncommon thing, I think, in the World, and truth not every day to be met with neither.'[8] And, 'we are ridiculing the French Sans-culottes & Carmagnoles – while they are actually beating the first armies of Europe'. He thought the campaign at sea was conducted stupidly, and as for the argument that the war against France had been started to prevent the growth of revolutionary opinion, it was exactly the way to encourage them:

There is no instance of opposition by force of Arms subduing opinions! which by such measures have always grown stronger and more inveterate.

God grant we may experience no revolution *even here* – for *here* it would be more dreadful than anywhere. Men are too much enlightened nowadays to be driven or deluded, and reason must be reverted to. You see where they are most enlightened, viz in Scotland, they are most violent. It should be the business of a great Minister to foresee the storm, and the turn of the times and by wise and *gradual* measures, prevent the mischief and make such reforms by degrees as may suit best – retrenching useless sinecures, simplifying the customs, so as to make them as productive as the Excise, regulating the Clergy – above all getting the people at large easy access to law and right – for though no man can injure another rightfully and legally, be he ever so great or rich, yet it is too clear that a poor man can hardly get at his right at all, if a rich or litigious man disputes it with him. If we have no Minister to prevent such evils, they will accumulate till the people begin to cry out, and then comes the rascally part of the community with a few clever villains at their head under pretence of good, throwing everything into anarchy, confusion, blood, and ruin – which crisis may Heaven avert! Such are my ideas walking about here solitary among wild mountains and a dismal country, oppressed with many ailments myself, and my family depressed, and ill with vexations and disappointments. . . .[9]

To Burdett's chagrin and Thomas's deep hurt, the invitation to Foremark did not come. The Bart was in a bad mood. Mr Burdett, Francis's father, was ill and he thought that they should not come until he had recovered. Then he invited Sophia to come with Francis, but ignored the rest of the family. Thomas, the King's banker, friend of princes and prelates, who had been kindly received by the crowned heads of Europe, was now snubbed by a country squire. It was only when Mr Mundy, Burdett's relative and one of the great landowners in the county, asked them to call on their way home that the old Bart jealously and grudgingly invited them.

They were coldly received: Sir Robert did not appear to welcome them. Francis's aunt, Miss Burdett, who never approved of the match, fanned the flame of the Bart's disapproval. To her the great banker was a kind of Shylock, gloating over his daughters and his ducats. Thomas and his family were always to be the 'abominable Coutts'. But the Reverend William Stevens was ravished by his first glimpse of Francis's bride and her sisters.

Poor Stevens was stifled at Foremark, bullied and patronised by the irascible Sir Robert and nagged by Miss Burdett. Night after night, as he played cards with the old Bart, he longed to escape but searched in vain for another living. He was stout, ungainly and plain, and an unhappy love affair had blighted his youth, but he still looked longingly at plump bosoms and immediately fell hopelessly in love with Fanny.

Stevens was glad to meet Thomas, because it was possible that such an influential banker could help him to get a new living. And the arrival of Francis, his bride and her sisters made a welcome diversion in the bleak Derbyshire winter. 'Mrs B low of stature, very young and very girlish, the sisters were perfectly simple unspoilt by art.'[10]

On Sunday the Coutts family caused a stir in the gloomy Foremark chapel. Thomas was, according to Stevens, 'a meagre withered man of about sixty, plain in dress, mind and simple in manners, modest of speech, but what he says to the point and sensible'.[11] Susannah was 'a strange outré figure. Her face does not resemble one of flesh and blood it is as a plaster model of ugliness',[12] but it was 'irradiated by a smiling good nature'.[13] In contrast the girls shone in the dark chapel. 'The young ladies', sighed Stevens, 'blooming brunettes, the youngest Miss Coutts is fair. Fancifully dressed, without caps, their long tresses flowing nymph-like down their shoulders and bosoms.'[14]

The Foremark visit was a disaster throughout. The Burdett women were openly hostile, the old Bart scarcely spoke to them, and Francis kept to his room, studying and mourning his brother. To crown all, Francis's father became desperately ill and died on 3 February. Thomas did not wait for the funeral on 11 February, but set off for London on the 7th. The family travelled slowly via Oxford, where they set down Jones Burdett at Magdalen College.

Francis inherited £9,000 and was now an extremely rich man, since he had already received from his father on his marriage an additional income of £2,000 a year. 'Frank has now', wrote Stevens, 'a neat £3,500 per annum without deductions. On his Grandfather's death he will have £5,000, on his father's £9,000, on his Aunt's £13,000 in all and it is very probable that his Father-in-law will not give him less than £100,000.'[15] With characteristic generosity, Burdett increased his father's legacy to his agent and took over the responsibility of Sedley's illegitimate child. He also offered to free Stevens from his 'beastly servitude' at Foremark by granting him a pension of £150 a year. Wisely Stevens refused, believing that to be Burdett's pensioner would destroy his self-respect. For the rest of his life poor Stevens was to seek his freedom. And Thomas, with infinite patience, was in vain to badger his influential friends on Stevens's behalf.

While in Derbyshire, Thomas had written to Caleb asking him to find them a house in Piccadilly large enough to take the family and the Burdetts, for 'the bustle of the world is what I wish'.[16] As for his daughters, their grief must take its course, but they might recover more quickly in town. '*"Dissipez vous"*', he told Caleb, '*"et le temps vous consolera"* says some gay Frenchman.'[17]

23

The Rift

During all the troubles that beset Thomas in these years nothing distressed him more than the fact that he nearly lost the friendship of his loyal partner, Edmund Antrobus. The letters they exchanged,[1] especially during the years 1792 and 1793, are an illuminating and sometimes moving record of the overcoming by two wise men of personal differences which might well have wrecked their partnership and the future of the Bank. In order to understand them it is necessary to remember the many and great pressures on both of them at this time.

Edmund, like Thomas, was under great strain. His health had not been good for some years and, during Thomas's frequent absences, he and his young brother John had worked 'not two days out of the business'; often Edmund bore the burden alone. In January 1786, as Thomas had written to Colonel Crawfurd,

Mr. Antrobus is in bad Health. . . . He is going to a Warmer Climate for The Winter which is likely to keep me in Hot Water at Home. I have reason to be thankful I am so well, & with my Paper Frame & delicate Health able to shove on when others much stronger are tottering. If Mr Antrobus does not get well I shall become a Prisoner as much as ever. I have great confidence in His Younger Brother but he is only one.

However, John was often ill, not only physically but with a worrying nervous disturbance. Neither treatment in Bath nor the prescriptions of his doctor seemed to help.

When Thomas returned from the continent, Edmund hoped that they could be relieved of some of the pressure. But it soon became clear that Thomas was wanting to retire, at least partly, and was even proposing to take another Italian tour. 'Certainly,' he wrote to Edmund, 'whether I go there or not I would not wish to lie [ally] myself to the fatigue of Business which is not suitable to my age & infirmities, but whenever I am on the spot & well, it is my greatest pleasure to do my part.'

In August 1786 Edmund, who had taken an unaccustomed holiday in Boulogne, had suggested that they employ a 'corresponding clerk' to deal with the increasing number of letters. Thomas had replied that he did not consider this necessary. 'Mr Dickie', he thought, 'has somewhat of a mercantile stile but does pretty well, I think for many of the common course letters. . . .' Thomas insisted that important letters should always be answered by a partner. This remained a firm rule at Coutts & Co. almost to the present day.

His confidential clerk, Andrew Dickie, patient, competent and hard-working, was to be his trusted right hand until Thomas's death, and the keystone of the Bank right up until his own death.

At the beginning of 1793 Thomas was considering taking in Coutts Trotter as a partner, but was reluctant to do so until he saw whether his daughters would marry, since he wanted to keep a place in the partnership for a son-in-law.

Edmund was overworked and, though they had a mutual trust and respect, the suppressed irritation grew. Undoubtedly Thomas felt a little piqued that the Bank had been so well run in his absence and began to feel excluded. Their relationship had not been improved when, in June 1791, John Antrobus had become engaged to Anna Crawford, the daughter of Gibbs Crawford MP,* one of Thomas's oldest friends. Neither John nor Edmund had told him and he had only heard of it 'in the street'. Thomas had been deeply wounded, and though he claimed that he did not blame Edmund, he clearly did. He never quite forgave Gibbs Crawford and was later to bring up the grievance again.

In January 1793 Edmund's patience finally snapped and for a whole year letters were exchanged, sometimes conciliatory, sometimes aggrieved. Often they chose to write to each other rather than to speak, even when they were at work together, so that they could give each point their quiet consideration. As the year progressed old grievances emerged which had been long suppressed; sometimes they were trivial but indicative of a deeper malaise.

In Edmund's first letter he complained of Thomas's 'apparent . . . want of confidence, arising from the distance & reserve you are pleased to observe towards me'. He had never mentioned his hurt because he hoped 'time or accident would have removed cause of them, & then I should spare myself the pain of giving you uneasiness'. He wondered 'to what end' he was spending his time and his health. His health had been 'so much impaired by the close attention I have paid for so many years' that he hoped he would be allowed 'more relaxation' if another partner was taken on, though he hoped John would be able to 'attend Business as usual'.

---

* Gibbs became an MP for Queensboro' and Clerk of the Ordnance; he was also a valued customer of the Bank.

Thomas was thunderstruck. He had been so absorbed in his own worries that he had failed to notice Edmund's growing exasperation. He was astonished that Edmund should think he had showed

any want of confidence in you, real or apparent! ... Did my leaving the Kingdom & going to a distant part of Europe for a year together, show want of confidence real or apparent? Have I not, on every occasion of Loans, consulted & almost decided by your opinion, & where sums were lent to old connections – the safety of which was not clear, taken them on myself?

He assured Edmund that he had always had the greatest confidence in him: 'The only transaction I ever decided without your previous concurrence was this of the Prince. ... However the security I think is very good for £30,000 ... though you may blame me. ... I am sure Drummonds would have done it at once.' Thomas was obviously afraid that Edmund might think he had bought the Prince's renewed favour at too high a price.

Thomas claimed that he had always spoken of Edmund 'in the language of sincerest regard', but he did not want to give Edmund a greater share in the partnership until he saw his daughters' futures.

As to your share of the Profits of my House ... I refer you to the Books to show you who received most from His Share in the First Fifteen years of being a Partner. ... Look further back ... to my brother's share under Mr Campbell, & to Mr Campbell's and Mr Bruce's under Mr Middleton.

He was anxious to stress to Edmund that he had not made excessive profits for himself.

He had, he claimed, given 'up my Father's House & Business to come into this – in which my successors have acquired Fortunes much superior to mine'. He fully realised that Edmund needed more help and would have taken another partner, but, aware of John's growing weakness, he had not wished to hurt his feelings. In a postscript he underlined what was his overriding aim, his determination

of preserving my House in my Family, and of admitting my three daughters' husbands to shares upon Marriage – and that on my death half of the House should go among the Efficient Partners (not my sons-in-law) and the other half to my Family. The sovereignty to remain in my Family.

Before waiting for a reply, Thomas wrote again on 31 January 1793 to confess that perhaps his manner had been distant, though he himself had been unconscious of it, explaining that he had 'for the last twelve month been much disturbed by various causes'. If there were any way he could prove his true feelings, he would be ready to do it, for he had never intended anything but of the most friendly kind. He was continuing to think about Edmund's share in the business and the possibility of taking another partner since Edmund's health was not so good. As a postscript

he added that it was 'dangerous and wrong ground to be offended by
MANNER I have many times been hurt by yours ... and have said often to
myself "make allowance. I am convinced his meaning in the main is
right."'

On 11 February Thomas wrote to tell Edmund of his decision to take
Coutts Trotter as a partner, 'his being connected with me by blood has
been some inducement with me though it is not the principal one'. He
had hesitated to do so before out of delicacy, thinking John, whose health
was deteriorating, might be hurt at the suggestion that he was not up to
the job. Edmund approved since he had 'a sincere regard for Mr Coutts
Trotter'.

If Edmund's first letter had shaken Thomas, the next came as a thunder-
bolt. Edmund hoped that John would soon be well enough to resume
business, but he himself wanted to retire; he was conscious that he had
done everything he could for Thomas and his family, and the 'extraordinary
increase of the Business is a proof that my exertions in that field ... have
not been unsuccessful'. His small fortune would provide him with an
annuity enabling him to live in a decent and independent manner. He
hoped that, since for sixteen years it had been his 'constant study ... to
anticipate ... your wishes and the wishes of those most dear to you',
Thomas would continue his friendship to his 'unfortunate brother'.

In reply Thomas wrote a long memorandum on 18 or 19 February 1793.
He was accustomed, he explained, to write down his opinions so that he
could view them rationally, 'endeavouring to put myself in another man's
place'. He advised Edmund as a friend not to resign – his health could not
be considered sufficient reason – adding with something approaching moral
blackmail, 'By retiring ... you will do your character no good.' He hoped
that John would recover and that with Coutts Trotter and Edmund the
partnership would thrive. He was astonished that Edmund wanted to retire.
If Edmund had been upset by his manner he was sorry, but he could not
expect it to improve at his time of life.

Thomas repeated that he had no intention of changing Edmund's share
in the House: 'I find Mr Antrobus' share producing a sum equal with mine
... on an average £2,500 a year & his brother's about £1,300.'

Then an old grievance which had obviously rankled surfaced: Edmund
was living in too grand a style.

I have had many speak to me saying that the Banking Business must be an excellent
one, for that Mr Antrobus showed away in Entertainments, Carriages with laced
liveries, Horses, etc. ... I know indeed my predecessors & even my brothers &
myself were many years without a Carriage & never had any laced liveries –
though we were bred up very expensively by my father, who lived much better in
proportion for HIS time than any of us ever did since.

He had often denied himself 'many gratifications & actually laid aside my carriage one year after Mrs Coutts had been accustomed to use it'.

Edmund replied with dignity on 19 February 1793 that he was sorry to have caused him distress, but he found Thomas's distance and reserve very mortifying. As for his style of living, he quite rightly defended his right to please himself. How he entertained his friends and dressed his servants was his own affair; when he had friends to dine, he liked to entertain them well: 'A single man may occasionally exceed ... without deviating from economy.' He felt that he had been snubbed. Thomas used to dine with him in the old days, but had not done so for 'many years past'.

Edmund certainly liked to see his servants properly turned out. Their dress liveries were of light blue cloth edged with black, with black velveteen breeches and plated buttons. As for carriages, it was true that he kept two four-wheeled ones, a two-wheeled gig and later six riding horses for himself and his nephews. These were necessary since he spent any spare time he had in the country air at Cheam, where his brother, Philip, had a house.

Then the argument became sharper. Edmund had been deeply hurt that, though he had worked ceaselessly for sixteen years, his share in the Bank had not increased. When he first came the business was worth £8,000, now it had tripled. When Thomas began, he had had a one-third share as junior partner and after sixteen years he, Edmund, had only an eighth share and 'no prospect of advancement'. He accepted that all previous partners had been taken in for family considerations, but the business had grown 'in an uncommon degree' and, therefore, he believed his share should be increased.

It was true that the stockbroking business he had left had turned out very 'lucratively', but he could 'assure you with great truth, I would much rather hold the respectable situation of a Partner in your House, and the power of serving my Friends, with half the money I possess, than to have continued in the City with three times the sum'. He was sure that there should now be another partner and he agreed with the appointment of Coutts Trotter.

Finally, he had to clear himself of the charges of extravagance and ingratitude and would 'cheerfully acquiesce in any arrangement ... as to the pecuniary part of the Business'. And he would try to 'get the better' of his impression that Thomas Coutts meant to slight him.

Thomas replied with some impatience on 27 February 1793 that, though he had been hurt exceedingly, he would consider Edmund's complaints 'as though they had never been'. In a memorandum he explained that he regretted giving Adam Drummond a quarter share in the business, or taking him into it at all, but 'I cannot see why ... my having got rid of so useless incumbrance should make Mr A expect that his share should be made greater'. His partnership with his brother was quite different: 'my brother came in with half a share, when he married Mr C's niece. It was her fortune, for she had no other, & unless he had been fond of the Lady he would not have left a better situation at Edinburgh.' But he was at a loss to understand Edmund's argument that 'a share producing 3 times more than was expected should be an argument for that share being increased'. In fact he thought it should mean the contrary. Above all he made it clear that the success of the business had depended mainly on the confidence of the world in Thomas Coutts himself: 'The long period of my holding the House (under many trying circumstances) . . . that from conviction . . . in men's minds in my prudence & discretion . . . has been . . . the principal cause of the increase of the Business.'

In the spring of 1793 Thomas was occupied with the plans for the proposed marriage of Sophia and Francis Burdett. So for the moment they left the argument, Thomas pointing out the dangers of writing: 'It seems always ten to one in matters of delicacy, that in removing one error you create another.' He hoped that, after his death, his partners 'would *find* and *think* one half of an established House as valuable as the whole of most others'.

Then, in the summer of 1793, Edmund was shattered by news of his brother, John, to whom he was deeply attached. John had been ill throughout the spring of 1793, but neither the waters of Bath nor his doctor's treatment had cured him. He had no relief from 'A blister to the neck every 5 or 6 days . . . 20 grains of mustard seed & 10 grains of Gum Guiacum . . . washed down . . . with a drachm of powdered Valerian in a glass of brandy and water . . . 3 times a day'. His recovery was slow and, while he was convalescing at home near East Grinstead, he had an accident which cut short the brilliant career that Thomas had hoped for.

On 17 June John was thrown from his horse and, according to Mary Egidia Antrobus, the family biographer, 'he was carried senseless to the house . . . the shock was too great for his poor little wife – the next day she gave birth to a second boy, and died'. John regained consciousness but not his reason, and remained a helpless imbecile for the rest of his life. The boys, Edmund and Gibbs, were brought up at their grandmother's house near East Grinstead; and their uncle, Edmund, became their legal guardian. He made generous arrangements for the boys, who were to be his heirs, proposing in June 1794 to give a bond of £2,500 to each child at the age of twenty-one.

In August Edmund took John to Brighton, where he hoped he could find a cure, but here the strain of watching his beloved brother's helplessness reduced him to 'a very melancholy state'. In September Edmund gave up hope and suggested to Thomas that John's partnership should be ended. No one knew better than Thomas what a strain it was to watch a brother become an imbecile. He wrote to Edmund with understanding:

I know what it is to love one Brother [Patrick] who was in the prime of youth and the hope & adoration of all his connections – and the effect upon me on account of the unfortunate circumstances, that happened respecting another [James], had almost brought me to the grave at the time you first came into the House.

Sophia's marriage to Burdett gave Edmund renewed concern. To his horror Thomas suggested that his young son-in-law might be brought into the business. Burdett, who consorted with political extremists? Edmund could imagine the City's reaction. He need not have worried: the last thing in the world that Burdett wanted to be was a banker. He had no interest in the making of money; even thinking about money bored him, he once said. It was a surprising lack of judgment on Thomas's part ever to consider it and, aware of this, he was sufficiently sensitive on the subject to be annoyed with Edmund. He had not consulted Burdett, 'Neither do I know certainly that he will like it. However . . . I am rather inclined (if he likes the concern) to take him into it.' It was clear that he felt he must assert himself as master of the House.

Once more, now that John was obviously not going to recover, Edmund wanted to retire. Again old grievances were brought up. He wrote from Brighton in August:

I have only one eighth share of the Business and am told at the expiration of sixteen years' close and successful attendance, that it is unreasonable in me to expect an addition, nor have I a day through the year on which I can call myself at liberty, without asking for it like a School Boy – there is another circumstance too which has hurt me a good deal because *in my situation as a Partner*, it seemed to carry with it some imputation upon my character, but which I have, never mentioned, in hopes time would either do it away, or something would occur to lead me to know the cause of it.

Edmund had apparently long nursed a wounded pride:

When I first came into the Strand, I was in some degree of intimacy in your Family, that however has ceased for a long time, and it is seven or eight years since I have been invited to dine in the House; I have been desirous to learn whether anything in my conduct has occasioned this change, that if it had I might endeavour to remedy it. . . .

This astonished Thomas, who now realised how deeply John's condition was affecting not only Edmund's health, but also his judgment.

Again Thomas reiterated his plans for the business:

One half of my House on my demise would have fallen to your Brother and you – which and my preference to your Brother, in taking him in, I think showed no small mark of regard to you. My hope was to leave you this half to you and your Brother, and to have seen three Son-in-Laws in the House with you. But if you had stated to me that you wanted more liberty, I would not have delayed, but readily and long since have taken a third Partner, which I very often thought of proposing, and indeed I did once mention it in my letter to Boulogne, and I would have taken a fourth even, if you had ever showed the least desire that way. But Two or Three or Four must all have been provided for from the half at my Death for *I did not*, nor do I think it too much to reserve the other half to my Family when I am gone.

As for not asking Edmund to dinner, 'it may be impolite', he explained, 'but I strongly deny to have been unkind. I never was political in my Dinners.' In fact, though he was always concerned for his honour and reputation as a banker, Thomas never cared a toss for social niceties. As far as he was concerned the least fuss the better, and that went for dinners, weddings and funerals.

Since my children were abroad in 1787, I have been quite out of the way of asking anybody in the way I used to do to dinner, and since the Family's return home, I have had little pleasure in dining at home myself, as unless when the Ladies were ill, they were always going out. I believe many of my old Friends and some relations have taken it ill my never asking them, and I have and confess been all my life rather indolent in that way – but the truth is I have hardly ever asked anybody since we came from abroad, but I left it to the Ladies, and they hence not asked any but those young folks, that came in their way, without form or previous invitation.

Then, in what Edmund must have considered hardly an enthusiastic invitation, 'I have not the smallest unwillingness to see you whenever you please at my House to Dinner, or to dine at yours when desired.' Edmund's hurt feelings were justified. Hester Stanhope's friend, Michael Bruce, once wrote to his father that it was well known that 'Coutts treats his partners as if they were his footmen'.[2]

What Thomas failed to understand was that Edmund did not have his Scottish self-esteem and needed to establish his status with the clerks at the Bank and with the world. This Edmund tried to explain to him:

... that sort of opinion which arises from not seeing a man treated as a friend, by those with whom he is connected, is not easily got over, and must for a time at least, have diminished very much that influence, which in such a case it would have been the interest of your Family and of the Business, that I should have possessed with the Friends of the House.

Thomas was later to write with dignity to the Duke of Devonshire, claiming that he came from as good a family as he. Edmund, the boy from Congleton, needed reassurance in society.

He must have been wounded again at Thomas's final remarks: 'If you think you should be on the same footing as with *myself*, I confess I differ from you.' Edmund replied firmly: 'I am too sensible of our respective situations originally, to think of comparing them at this time upon any footing of equality.' This sudden flash of the old Edinburgh pride in his

superior status and, indeed, the whole correspondence show Thomas's least
attractive side.

Thomas had hoped to go quietly with the Burdetts on their honeymoon
tour of Wales, showing his confidence in Edmund by leaving him in charge.
In fact Edmund, having started the argument, could not let it go and
doggedly pursued his partner with letters of explanation throughout September. At the end of September he was still worrying: how could Thomas
write that he was 'sorry, mortified and astonished' by his letters? Every
change in the partnership had been to Thomas's advantage:

Whatever may have been the previous situation of any Business, I believe it is the
groundwork of all Partnerships, that any subsequent [change] not provided for in
the articles, should be for the mutual advantage of all parties – if, therefore, it
appears that every subsequent change, since I have been in the Strand, has been
in your favour, and that so far from being exclusively benefitted by either, some
of them have taken from me advantages, which I once possessed, I appeal to your
own candour and experiences, to the usual practice of merchants and bankers in
similar cases, and to the general rules established by common consent in every
department of life, whether *such a circumstance* added to *sixteen years' service* might
not give me room to state to you, the justice and reasonableness of my claim to
your favour, without the imputation of acting improperly. When I first became a
Partner in 1777, you had $^3/_4$ of the Business, Mr. Drummond $^1/_8$ and myself $^1/_8$.

Upon Mr. Drummond retiring in 1780 you had his $^1/_8$ and continued with $^7/_8$
till 1783, when you took in another Partner to whom you gave $^1/_{16}$ (this preference
you gave to my Brother, whose conduct has I hope justified the device you made)
from 1783 till this year, the Business has continued in the same manner viz.
yourself $^{13}/_{16}$, myself $^2/_{16}$, my brother $^1/_{16}$. I believe it will appear from this statement
that you possess a larger share of an increasing Business, in the management of
which the other Partners have had so active a part, than usually falls to the lot of
a Senior Partner for so long a period, and, what is of still more consequence, the
articles which in 1777 gave your Family a reversion after your death to $^1/_3$ of the
Business were altered, and those in 1783 gave them not only a larger share, but,
also the reversion of the whole as the other Partners died – this was certainly a
change, which benefitted essentially your Family, and though in this respect it put
me materially in a less advantageous situation. . . . An additional share of $^1/_{16}$ in
the Business, and some indulgence with regard to time would have made me
perfectly content, and in having preferred this request, I hope upon second
thoughts it will appear to you, that I have not been unreasonable, *surely not too
ungrateful.*

He was anxious that he should not think there was 'anything of ingratitude,
still less of contempt or irony in the manner in which I proposed to
retire from business'. The charge of ingratitude rankled, so much so that,
although he had intended to look to his future ease and comfort in the
latter end of his life, he could not do so now because of the

imputation upon my character and my gratitude, which you are pleased to suggest, in case I retire at this time . . . to indulge myself with the plan I had formed, nor shall you or your Family ever want my assistance under such circumstances, whilst I have the power to give it, as nothing would afford me more satisfaction than to convince you I am incapable of acting towards you with ingratitude.

Edmund, anxious to clear himself, raised once again in his letter of 12 October the fact that they had not told Thomas of his brother's intended marriage and that this 'want of attention' must have so offended him. After all 'your being abroad at the commencement might plead some little excuse'. Now another partnership was proposed,

with new partners unacquainted with Business, without one single article exclusively in my favour, more than I possessed when I begun, as differing so much from the usual practice in every situation of life, where length of service and experience are entitled to some preferment. . . .

He was sure that his friends would understand his retirement, which he took 'without pique or resentment'. Finally he excused his persistence in writing while Thomas was away, but he could not 'drop the subject . . . without feeling a mortification, which would make me constantly unhappy'.

His letter reached Thomas, who was then at Lord Newborough's Glynllifon Park, at an unfortunate moment. He had, he replied, been 'much distressed with giddiness'; Burdett was ill and 'an alarm too about a gentleman being drowned near the house' was affecting him at that moment. He dismissed Edmund's new complaint that he had been offended by John's marriage. Plaintively he continued: 'The old friends are gone that supported me in former severe trials, and I little thought to have lost him [Antrobus] too or at my time of day to have new partnerships to form.'

Even the patient Edmund at times lost patience with Thomas's obsession with his health and his occasional lapses into self-pity. Thomas reiterated that any change in his 'behaviour or friendship' to Edmund was imaginary, though in an illuminating sentence he did concede that

Many various vexations, which I have kept all to myself, may have altered my manner (which would principally appear to those most intimate or near, and who, I was dearly in the habit of seeing), . . . but most powerfully I felt that, if I forgot the dues and rights of attention to other men, it could only be because I was at war with myself.

Now he appealed to Edmund with something approaching moral blackmail, adding to the list of the year's troubles a confession of the suppressed fear that he himself would be seized by his brother's malady:

You have now informed me you decide to quit business and I think it is scarce possible to form a more disagreeable or uncommon situation than I am thereby now to be placed in; deprived of your brother's aid which I considered as a great blow, I am to be deserted by you at the same time that an alarming disorder is threatening me with the crisis of decayed powers, and that I feel myself quite unfit for further exertions in the arduous tasks of guiding and attending to so large a concern – at the beginning too of a dangerous War when all money concerns are in hazard, when perhaps I have launched further in Loans to the House's friends, than I ought to have done, and when I am likely to be called upon for daughters' fortunes – of course I am to be deprived of the aid of the fortune you have acquired, which would always be something in such a case, though nothing when compared with the reliance on an experienced and active partner, who I have established, with great pains, firmly in the confidence of all my friends, and who is better acquainted than myself with what belongs to the ways and means of commanding money from the resources in your power. . . .

In spite of his confidence in Edmund's business ability, he was oddly reluctant to increase his share though, he claimed,

that it was always my fixed purpose so soon as your Brother should become out of the question, to have given to you the addition of the share he held.

I wished however to do it of my own accord or not at all and I endeavoured all I could to prevent you asking it. . . .

Finally, he made a shrewd appeal to Edmund's pride, the reason for Edmund's retirement which will be given to

all who desire to know it, viz. That five years before the expiration of the existing partnership upon some alterations becoming necessary from your Brother's unhappy illness – you insisted on your share of the profits being augmented, which I declined to consent to.

Even as Thomas was writing this a messenger was on the way with news of the tragic deaths of Lord Montagu and Sedley Burdett, in the face of which both men put aside their grievances. Edmund sent a letter of deep sympathy and told Thomas:

I am only anxious now to assure you that it will not only afford me very sincere satisfaction to relieve you, as much as it is in my power at this time from every anxiety respecting the Business, but I shall consider you allowing me to do so as a mark of your regard, whilst you have uneasiness of so serious a nature pressing upon your mind.

At the end of the year Edmund wrote regretting that

this correspondence had taken place at a time when you have had so many other causes of uneasiness, but it appeared to me unavoidable – it commenced not a great while after Mr. Trotter had entered into the Business, and on the eve, as I thought, of Mr. Burdett becoming a Partner, and when I considered my brother's situation as perfectly hopeless. It is my sincere wish, however, that a similar correspondence may never occur again, and I shall endeavour for the future to make you forget what has past that has been disagreeable.

On Christmas Day, a day of 'goodwill to all, forgiving all offences', Thomas set his seal on the ending of the rift. Edmund was not resigning, and he only wished to 'forget all that is past that is disagreeable & cannot be recalled. . . . You will never find that what is past will make any alteration in my constant sentiments and future conduct towards you.'

So Edmund loyally took up the burden once more and remained a faithful partner until his death in 1826. He kept Thomas informed of John's desperate condition, and Thomas sent him a New Year message – that 1794 'may prove happy and unobscured by the unfortunate circumstances that have rendered 1793 so unfavourable to us all'. On 27 April 1794 John died and Edmund's health improved, helped by Thomas's new consideration.

24

Private and Public Affairs,
1794–1800

For Thomas Coutts the last blow after the year of many troubles was the uprooting from his home in the Strand. On the family's return to London in 1794, he had taken Lord Yarmouth's house on the corner of Stratton Street, Piccadilly, renting the great mansion for £750 a year. It adjoined 78 Piccadilly, where Burdett and Sophia and their children were later to live with a connecting door between the two houses. The easy comfort of the apartments over 'The Shop' was exchanged for the echoing grandeur of the mansion at the corner of Stratton Street and Piccadilly. No. 1 Stratton Street was a house which was to see much exciting history over the next century, but Thomas never felt at home in it. However, he organised the domestic staff as he had regulated the clerks at the Bank, establishing not only rules but also principles of behaviour. Everything was covered, from the use of dusters to behaviour in the servants' hall. His instructions to his major-domo on 26 January 1795 were probably dictated by Susannah, but the organisation bears his stamp:

As there are Two Kitchen maids employ'd Mr B is to see They do Their Duty & are fit for Their Situations. New ones to be provided in case of bad behaviour neglect or incapacity. Mr B is not to allow any Servant to intrude or come into the Kitchen – but such as are employ'd in it.

The Housekeeper to give to the Butler, to the Cook, – and to the Maids, weekly, proper Cloaths Dusters etc – and on every Saturday to get them back that is to say such as are dirty, and to give clean ones in their stead.

To keep Coffee Tea Sugar Spices, Soap Candles etc – and Bread & Butter – & give out the same & other materials – The Bread must be lock'd up – but Pieces & sufficient quantity also kepd in Her room in a Pan open to be come at at all Times even when she happens to be out of the way.

The Cook's duty is to attend to the orders for Dinner in proper time and to see that the Servants are properly and suitable Served as well as the Masters –

To use economy and management in the provisions laid in, and in Coals Charcoal – Candles etc; to prevent waste – which can do no good to any body – or tend even to the immediate comfort of any of the Family . . . .[1]

In the coming years, Thomas was often glad to be away from the great house and out of London. In April 1794 he took a palatial house at Kingsgate near Margate, where he and the family stayed until the end of December. Here Susannah entertained grandly and gave a great ball; Mrs Fitzherbert came to dinner and the royal dukes called. When they finally returned to London they expected to stay for two days only and then go to Bristol, but the whole family were so ill that they were imprisoned in Stratton Street. Even the stalwart Susan had a sore throat and Susannah remained seriously ill until July 1795, when they left for Cheltenham. They had hoped to stay for two weeks and then spend the summer touring Wales. In fact the appearance of Lord Guilford as a suitor for Susan kept them in Cheltenham until 16 September. Their autumn tour took them to Abergavenny and Swansea and then by sea to Bristol and Bath.

During the next years Thomas was to take his family on many such holidays – long coach journeys through beautiful countryside, staying, often incognito, in simple inns. Frequently he was out of touch with the Bank for days at a time, but there was usually a messenger at the end of each week – and he himself wrote many letters to his customers.

So now he spent little time at the Bank in the Strand, leaving the running of the business in the competent hands of Antrobus and Coutts Trotter. For the most part Thomas was deeply preoccupied with his three daughters and their problems, but he still followed national and international affairs with informed interest and the major decisions of the Bank were made by him, though usually he consulted Antrobus.

It was as well that Antrobus was back in charge at the Bank, for during the closing years of the century Thomas was almost completely immersed in family troubles. Fortunately there is a witness for this period with an observant eye, a keen ear and a sharp pen: Reverend William Stevens was a frequent guest at the Burdetts' home, travelled with them and was their friend and confidant.[2] Thomas, too, invited him to stay with the family in London and on his visits to Cheltenham, Bath and Bristol.

Stevens was to be triply involved with the Coutts family. As we have seen, from the beginning he thought of Thomas as a saviour, who, through his influence with his powerful customers, would release him from his slavery at the school and from old Burdett. He hoped that Thomas could find him a warm living in a gentler climate, where he could live in peace with his books and his poetry. Indeed, for six years Thomas was doggedly to pursue his friends on behalf of this obscure country parson. The Chancellor, Mr Pitt, Lord Lansdowne, Lord Moira and even the Duchess of Devonshire were all badgered, but without success. It was not until just before Stevens died that the Chancellor found him a small living, with a poor house. But it says much for Thomas's respect for the undoubted merits of Stevens that he never gave up. 'What unwearied kindness this good man shows,' Stevens gratefully recorded. The trouble was that he never took Thomas's advice – 'Pray be quick on the lookout'. Thomas knew from long experience that preferment in any field only came from prompt appeal. His customary technique was to have a letter ready to send the moment the chance came. He wrote a letter for Stevens which he left with Coutts Trotter at the Bank. The moment Stevens should hear of a vacancy or a cleric should 'drop' he should let Trotter know and the letter would promptly be sent. But, though Stevens kept a constant lookout for ailing clerics, he was never lucky. So he was left playing interminable card games with the domineering old Bart, preaching dull sermons, enduring the back-biting of a small society, but relishing the gossip.

He was fascinated by the world of fashion and power to which the Coutts family introduced him, and had been most impressed at Foremark by the sheaf of letters Thomas had received from London. He was allowed to read the letter the Duke of Clarence wrote about the dangers of a French invasion, and was amazed that great men and women like Lord Lansdowne and Lady Chatham wrote to him not as their banker, but as their friend.

However, he had another powerful reason for his interest in the Coutts family: he was besotted by Fanny. From the moment he saw her with her long flowing hair shining in his dark chapel at Foremark, he was totally captivated. There was 'only one Fanny Coutts' – such was her simplicity, intelligence, charm, he could 'lay down his life for her'. And Fanny, still raw from the loss of Sedley, found his devotion soothing, confided in him and drew him on, finally giving him a lock of her hair – and hope. But as he wryly wrote of himself, 'Cupid's team of Doves find a fat fellow turned of forty very heavy drawing.' But he never quite gave up hope and Fanny could not bring herself to let him go completely.

He was attached to Thomas not only because of his personal interest and love of Fanny. After Burdett's marriage he was always to be a welcome guest in the Burdett houses they took first at Canterbury, then at The Vale, and spent many vacations with them. He was therefore involved in the family during a critical period.

Thomas invited him to London in July 1794, where he stayed at Stratton Street, which he thought 'a palace'. He was so delighted to take part in the brilliant conversation at a dinner given by Thomas that he recorded it in detail in his journal. Charles James Fox was a guest and dazzled the country clergyman with his charm and brilliance, lounging after dinner on a sofa and talking in 'an easy unaffected chit-chat way till near 12'. Stevens noted the table-talk: Fox said of Pitt that 'he had less general reading than perhaps any man who did read. . . . He believed that the war would last another two years.' Fox thought that 'in the subscription business Pitt had been disappointed. The money it would raise was a bauble. . . . Its sole object was to excite an enthusiastic spirit among the People.' Fox's manner of speech, Stevens remarked, was 'very quick with a broken sharpness of tone. . . . He smiles delightfully. He is above the petty vanity of playing the Great man at table and running away with all the conversation. He has almost constantly the forefinger of his left hand on his eye, an odd habit.' The brilliant Fox was always a welcome guest at the banker's house although, like the Duchess of Devonshire, he was a hopeless gambler.

Stevens reported:

At Dinner a Monsieur Laborde, the Great Banker's son from Paris, and his Brother-in-Law, Count de Noailles, Son of the Prince de Poix. Laborde's Father and Mother now under arrest, as are the Grandfather and Grandmother of the Count, and his Wife, Laborde's Sister, who had very reluctantly at her Father's earnest request returned to Paris and had been compelled to take another Husband.

After dinner, while Thomas's French guests were 'caroling their grief à la mode de Français, about 11 o'clock I stept down to the House of Commons'. Stevens's sympathies were not with decadent aristocrats, but Thomas felt their tragedies deeply. These were the friends who had been kind to him and his daughters when they were in Paris.

Stevens was slightly shocked at the way the Coutts family spent Sunday: a visit to the Duke of Devonshire's Chiswick villa, a musical entertainment at the Duke of Queensberry's – 'that said Duke is but a beast. . . . Such a London Sunday! The Coutts never go to any place of worship.'

He was taken to dinner with Lord Lansdowne, whom Thomas had known since the days when, as Lord Shelburne, he had been Colonial Secretary. His London house was a 'princely palace of a man of letters, his library 110 feet by 38'. Later, at Bath, Thomas introduced him again to his Lordship, and Stevens confided to his crony, the Reverend Thomas Bosvile, in Derbyshire that he had 'an hour's conversation with that once great minister . . . he talks volubly & graciously and wreathes his whiskered smiles from side to side'. He kept Bosvile amused with facetious letters about his new, grand acquaintances – the Duchess of Devonshire at Chatsworth was now 'his friend and neighbour'.

He spent months with the Burdett family in the crucial year of 1795, when the Burdetts were in Bath for Sophia's health and the rest of the family were at Cheltenham. So no one was better placed to observe the growing rift between Francis and Sophia and Thomas's increasing irritation with his difficult son-in-law. Burdett, conscious of his lack of knowledge and desperately anxious to study, shut himself up for long periods with his tutor, the clever Frenchman, Chevalier. 'He is', wrote Stevens, 'the most fagging student I ever knew.' He totally neglected Sophia: 'He has no idea of those sweetening attentions, Birthdays, marriage days & all fond memories he tramples upon.' And again, 'he is too much a Philosopher to be happy or to make happy'. As for Mrs Burdett, she was 'a spoiled child ... expecting her husband to be her slave, her doll'. As Burdett himself confided to him, 'she had no resources of amusement in herself'.

Burdett insisted that his children be brought up according to the theories of Rousseau, who was, in Thomas's opinion, 'a madman'. He remarked drily to Stevens:

Mrs Coutts I know took a great deal of pains with her Children, much more than Most Mothers – and having succeeded tolerably I am inclined to prefer her Practice to Rousseau's Theory, who for ought I know perhaps never saw a newborn infant in his Life. . . .

Then Chevalier complained of their spartan life: 'no wine set on the table. . . . His [Burdett's] democratic spirit tears the livery from his servants. He would regulate the whole world.' Stevens agreed with Chevalier that Burdett was 'always right, always positive, intolerant of contradiction ... with excellent intentions & correspondent generosity ... yet making Everybody around him uncomfortable'. His appetite for books was the 'strongest of his passions'.

In fact Burdett was becoming increasingly restless and even proposed to leave England and live in Switzerland. As the marriage neared breakdown, Stevens was sent with a desperate letter from Burdett to Thomas at the house the Coutts family had taken at Cheltenham. Burdett wanted a separation, but Thomas replied in a fatherly manner, rousing Stevens to admiring apostrophe:

What good sense! . . . What affecting appeal to his Honour and Humanity! What a simple touching display of the mournful Consequences! The misery of thy House O Coutts I have not prophesied in vain! I saw the little cloud at a distance that was to spread till it darkened the Horizon and burst in thunder over thy astonished Head!

Stevens was the peacemaker and, at least for the time being, Burdett's marriage was saved. When Sophia's daughter was born, Stevens was delighted 'to make her a Christian as Coutts asked'.

'Coutts motto', Stevens declared, '[was] that of a Proud modest man. *Esse quam videri* [To be rather than to seem].'

Thomas's dislike and distrust of Burdett grew during the coming years, but Lord Guilford was received with favour. In the summer of 1795, while Thomas was trying to prevent the break-up of Sophia's marriage, he was also encouraging Guilford in his pursuit of his eldest daughter, Susan.

George Augustus, third Earl of Guilford, was the eldest son of Lord North, the Prime Minister whose incompetence during the American War of Independence had so provoked Thomas. By his first marriage, George had three sons, who had died in infancy, and a daughter, Maria. At this time he was thirty-eight and an active supporter of the Whig opposition in the House of Lords, attacking with some courage the war against France. Lord Holland thought him 'indolent . . . averse to any exertion of mind',[3] yet he praised his 'high honour, great frankness . . . sound understanding, considerable talents for public speaking, and a temper more conciliatory than any man, Mr Fox excepted, among the leaders of the opposition'.[4] Thomas was genuinely fond of Guilford, finding him a soothing companion after the uncomfortable Burdett, and went out of his way to encourage him. Guilford had every reason to welcome Thomas's attentions, since the banker was helping him to sort out the tangle of debts his father had left him. So while the Burdett affair was crackling on, Guilford was nightly visiting Susan at Cheltenham.

But great as was Thomas's concern for Sophia's happiness, and his determination to secure Guilford as a husband for Susan, his deepest anguish in the winter of 1795 was for Fanny, who at the turn of the year was at death's door. Stevens, who had been invited to spend Christmas with them, was as distraught as Thomas, whose love for Fanny was the other side of idolatry. She seemed to her father 'like a being dropped down from Heaven who had no business here'.

The ever-watchful Stevens noticed how lovingly they looked at each other. There was no doubt that Fanny, as a friend remarked, 'directs that household'. Her charm was extraordinary, as such formidable ladies as Hester Stanhope and Lady Holland confirmed, and she certainly knew how to make use of it.

However, as we have seen, Fanny, since childhood, had a mysterious disorder which was partly mental and partly physical. She had occasional fainting fits of an epileptic kind and went through a period of self-starvation, which today would probably be called anorexia. Her present illness was, as Stevens reported, 'A violent Rheumatic inflammatory Fever' with intense pain accompanied by constant fainting fits – not surprising since she was 'blooded' nine times in three weeks. She frequently alarmed the family with her fits of hysterical screaming.

Her condition was made worse by an overpowering sense of guilt. She had only recently, at their insistence, shown her parents Sedley's letters. Thomas was furious. They were, he complained, 'in the Style & Taste of a valet-de-chambre'. But he suppressed his rage since Fanny was so ill. However, Stevens heard through an open door an uncharacteristic outburst when Thomas raged hysterically to Susan against Burdett, whom he believed had encouraged the affair. 'I detest the very sound of his voice – I cannot bear to see him with Patience or Peace.' Burdett and all his friends and connections were the cause of his unhappiness: 'He would always think of him as her murderer. He had destroyed the happiness of one of his daughters, murdered another & would even kill Mrs Coutts.' The unaccustomed extravagance of his anger was roused by his deep-seated fear of the family curse of madness, which seemed about to destroy Fanny as it had done his brothers.

Stevens was now the universal father-confessor to the family. Thomas walked with him in the long alleys at Cheltenham and told him of his dislike of Burdett; 'he had never known misery till he knew him'. In his library at Bath, Burdett talked to Stevens of Fanny, with whom he had been 'violently' in love on the continent. Unlike Sophia, she had 'exquisite judgement' and had 'overcome in defiance of her mother's Examples & Precepts the most seductive prejudices unmoved by the common vanities of her sex – above the influence of wealth or title'.

Back at Cheltenham Susannah refused to let Stevens see Fanny. Susannah now became, in his eyes, 'the old Ape woman' who would hug her daughter to death. He was amazed at 'the vulgar cunning of the mother & the father's good sense perpetually stooping to adopt the opinions, likings & aversions of his mate'. Sophia came from Bath to see Fanny and talked to Stevens of her own unhappiness and her suspicion that Fanny's trouble was 'more in the mind than in the body'. He even pumped the maid, who told him of Fanny's extraordinary fainting fits. At the beginning of January no one expected her to live, and the despairing Stevens had to return to Foremark without seeing her, the sound of her wild screams ringing in his ears.

By 22 January 1796 he read with relief in the *Morning Chronicle* that 'Miss F. Coutts' illness was yielding to the skill of Dr. Fraser', and that 'Lord Guilford would shortly be married to her sister'. In February Thomas could assure him cheerfully that Fanny was now completely recovered: 'Her whole Frame having undergone a thorough Revolution if we may be allowed nowadays to use that word'. His concern now was for his wife, who,

indisposed as she was before the Fatigue, Distress and Anxiety of six weeks past almost night & day at Fanny's bedside cannot fail to have put her in much danger and it seems astonishing to me how she has supported herself even as she has done.

Susannah, in fact, was now slowly degenerating into a chronic invalid.

Fanny at this time was mesmerised by the wild charm of Charles James Fox and even, it would seem, set her cap at him. She may or may not have known of his liaison with Mrs Armistead, but Thomas certainly knew of her existence since Fox had frankly explained in 1787 that he accepted her debts as his own, and he had met them together at Cheltenham.

In spite of this he seems to have encouraged Fox as a suitor for Fanny. At her request he wrote asking for a lock of his hair and, in an oblique letter to him, explained that his unmarried daughter 'distressed' him by her ill-health but that he hoped she would improve. 'I would wish', he wrote, 'they had more good connexions in case I die.'[5] As to fortune, his daughters would have enough. His own 'principal ambition is to acquire the friendship and acquaintance of men eminent for benevolent minds, great talents and respectable characters'.[6]

Why he tried to promote this extraordinary affair we shall never know. Perhaps he imagined that Fox would improve Fanny's health, or that she would improve his morals. Mrs Armistead tearfully offered to release Fox so that he could acquire a fortune and Miss Coutts. But Fox, who was astonished at Thomas's offer, protested that he could not endure belonging to any other woman: 'Neither by word or look did I ever give the least reason to Miss C even to think that I thought her pretty not till Mr C asked me for the hair had I the least suspicion. . . .'[7] To convince her, Fox insisted that they get married, which they did on 25 September 1795, although for some time the marriage was kept secret. That, at least, Thomas could understand.

In the spring of 1796, Susannah was cheered by the marriage of Susan to Guilford. There had been anxious months and delays. Guilford had fallen from his horse while presenting a basket of fruit to Susan and was seriously injured, but he was at last sufficiently recovered and they were quietly married at Speen near Newbury. Susannah would have liked a grand wedding in London, but Thomas felt a delay might be dangerous and as usual wanted no fuss. Stevens had hoped to officiate at Susan's wedding, but he was outranked by the bridegroom's relation, the Bishop of Winchester.

Meanwhile, Thomas continued to worry about Sophia's unhappiness, which was deepened by Burdett's growing enthusiasm for radical politics.

Burdett's voracious appetite for learning had been sharpened when he was drawn into the circle round the Reverend Horne Tooke, a brilliant radical lawyer. At Tooke's famous Sunday dinners at Wimbledon, where intelligent men of all classes gathered, the young Burdett was given the place of honour at Tooke's right hand. When he was painted in old age he took care that the bust of Tooke dominated the background as he did his life.

These were dangerous times for radicals. After the euphoria of the early days of the French Revolution, they now had to come to terms with the French massacres of September 1792 and the executions of Louis XVI in February 1793 and of Marie Antoinette in the same year. However, the principles of liberty, equality and fraternity were still their inspiration.

Clubs and associations pledged to these principles and to the reform of Parliament sprang up, supported by men like Tooke, who had been involved with the Society for Constitutional Information since 1780. In 1792 Charles Grey and progressive Whigs established 'Friends of the People' and in the same year Thomas Hardy, a shoemaker, founded a workshop association, The Corresponding Society. On the other side, counter-revolutionary clubs were formed, which increased tension. Burdett had thrown himself with passion into this heady world, risking jail and even his life.

Fear of bloody revolution pushed the Government to repression. In May 1793 Parliament had thrown out Gay's bill for parliamentary reform and, with no constitutional means available, anger led to riots. Pitt, afraid that sparks from the French fire might set alight this dry tinder, introduced harsh repressive measures. In 1794 the Habeas Corpus Act was suspended, and suspected revolutionaries were imprisoned without trial. The Treasonable Practices Bill made it a capital offence to write or speak against the constitution or the monarchy. The definition of treason was so stretched that to demand reform or attack the Government could lead to prison and even the gallows. The declaration of war with France in February 1793 gave Pitt the excuse to round up suspects.

Pitt had reorganised the secret service and his spies were infiltrated into The Corresponding Society. In October 1794 Hardy and Tooke were imprisoned; Tooke was only acquitted by the skill of his advocate, Erskine, and his own witty defence. Hardy was released because Whigs like Grey, fearing for their own safety, put pressure on the Government. When Burdett wrote, as he frequently did, in letters in the following years that he was risking prison and execution, he was not being melodramatic. His campaigns were to take real courage.

A bad harvest in the autumn of 1795 increased the fear of revolution and, after a huge demonstration took place in Copenhagen Fields organised by The Corresponding Society, the Government introduced even more repressive measures.

In 1795, Burdett, despairing of reform in Great Britain, even proposed taking his family and settling in France. Thomas, believing that responsibility would encourage him to settle down, secured a seat in Parliament for him, without his knowledge. He first wrote unsuccessfully to the Duke of Devonshire, but finally bought for £4,000 the constituency of Boroughbridge, which was in the gift of the Duke of Newcastle. This was just the kind of corrupt practice that Burdett and his friends were attacking. However, hoping that through Parliament he could bring change, in May 1796 Burdett accepted. Ironically, therefore, the man who was to do so much to bring about the reform of Parliament came in as a member for a 'rotten borough'.

It might have been as well for Thomas's peace of mind if he had allowed his son-in-law to emigrate. For, during the rest of the banker's life, Burdett was to cause him personal distress and positive damage to the Bank. At this time Thomas hoped that Burdett would mellow with age and he had some sympathy with his passionate hatred of war and cruelty of all kinds.

He was even sympathetic when Burdett confessed that he thought that 'marriage is the grave of love'. But when he heard that in the autumn of 1796 Burdett, in the company of the Irish firebrand, Roger O'Connor, was making a secret visit to Ireland and that he was planning to sell his Leicestershire estates, his anxiety increased. Stevens was equally alarmed: 'I cannot but say that I tremble at the connexion of a warm enthusiastic character with Rash Ruined Irish Politicians.' In fact Burdett was passionately attracted to the Irish and was to be involved for many years in their dangerous politics.

There is no doubt that from 1796 onwards Thomas was keeping an eye on Burdett's political activities. There are long letters from a Mr Barry reporting on the situation in Ireland and on Burdett himself. As a banker, with customers in Ireland, he was concerned at the rumours of Irish collaboration with the enemy French and was afraid that an invasion was imminent.

In December 1796 a Dublin banker, Sir William Newcomen, had written to inform Thomas that the 'wind & waves' had defeated a French attempt on the south coast of Ireland.[8] Thomas replied that the situation was of 'so interesting and alarming a nature', but he hoped that the whole of Ireland would show 'the unanimity and spirit demonstrated in the Southern part of the Island', which would secure

a very early & complete defeat of any attempt of Invasion, and I sincerely hope if the Winds and Waves shoud not have done the Business that the distinguished Military Character of your Country, and the Exertions you mentioned, will keep the Enemy's force in Play 'till succour can arrive.[9]

Then with great tact and courtesy Thomas pointed out that 'the continuation of this unfortunate War has brought all money matters into a situation so new & so alarming that we have been under the necessity of restraining our Disposition to oblige and accommodate our Friends'.[10] At that moment there was a debit on Newcomen's account of nearly £7,000 and, if 'the troubles in Ireland were to grow serious', it might be thought 'prudent' on his account to 'pause on answering demands in this way'.

I took the liberty of Suggesting it as a very wise and eligible Plan for any Bank in Ireland to keep at all times a considerable sum in England in the Government Securities least lyable to Fluctuation and most readily saleable and transferable. The present Calamitous times show particularly the good if not the necessity of such a measure when we are forced tho' very unwillingly to restrain our Disposition to oblige and to beg you will not over draw or push us in advance.[11]

Thomas must have known how active the Alien Office was in Ireland at this time. In 1797 it had agents planted to inform on rebels like Wolfe Tone, whose sympathies were with the French and who were plotting a French invasion on the Irish coast. Thomas's friend, James Craufurd, brother of 'Fish', who was then chargé d'affaires at The Hague, was certainly supplying names of rebels to the Government arch-spy Wickham.

On 25 February 1797 even the level-headed Thomas was so concerned that he wrote to the Treasurer of the Bank of Scotland:

The situation of the Country with regard to money concerns has become within these days very alarming and tho' we are inclined to believe the real state to be much more favorable than it was a few months ago it is difficult to say what may be the consequences if men's minds are not quieted and confidence restored, the present alarm does not appear founded upon suspicion of any Individual House, or any public Body, but merely to arise from an apprehension of an Invasion or some public Calamity which induces people to go to the Bank to get specie that may be prepared for any Event that may Happen – this however cannot be consider'd to have gone so far as to occasion the smallest inconveniency to the Bank, & we understand Mr Pitt intends to enter fully into the resources of the Nation on Monday & of the means of defence in case of Invasion which we hope will have the effect of preventing the mischiefs from going further.[12]

So serious was the fear of invasion that Thomas was prepared to take his friend Sir John Sinclair's advice to send gold to the Bank of Scotland. He wrote to Mr Alexander, his contact there:

[He] prevailed upon Mr Campbell Marjoribanks & Mr Home who intended to have set out for Scotland this morning to postpone their Journey that we might pack up any Sum which Sir John should think it might be right to send & as these Gentlemen were so good as to undertake the Charge of it we got a Box made to go into their Chaise seat to carry £6000 but Sir John upon calling this morning & finding your letter did not say any thing upon the Subject, said he thought the Money might not be wanted in such haste as to justify him taking the responsibility of ordering it to be sent – We sincerely hope the delay will not be attended with any inconveniency to the Bank but the opportunity was so favourable that we shall not perhaps be able to meet with such another if however it should be necessary the Bank will probably do as the Royal Bank we understand have done, send two of their Clerks to London for that purpose. We shall send £4000 by the Waggon on Friday next or if it should appear by your letter on Monday to be wanted sooner we will send it on Tuesday – The Carriers wish to have the Box early in the day to put in a secure part of the Waggon & your letter did not arrive time enough yesterday to pack up the £4000 or we should then have forwarded that sum.[13]

At the beginning of 1797 the outlook was bleak indeed, as Thomas wrote in a depressed letter to the Duke of Kent:

I am very sorry on every account that the hope of Peace seems now to be removed to a greater distance than it appeared some time ago – and that it is not likely to be immediately revived – but must depend on the Events of another Campaign – That they may prove favourable & be the means of permanent tranquility in England & the World, must be the sincere wish of all Lovers of order, & every friend of Humanity. Meanwhile we must endeavour by perseverance in patience & moderation to do what is in our Power to lessen those evils it is not in our Power entirely to cure.[14]

The last years of the century were certainly difficult for a banker. The greater part of Thomas's income came from lending money, but at this time many of his customers were so deeply in debt that he himself came under the greatest pressure. In addition, the Government itself needed money.

In 1796 when England was at war with France and there was a real danger of invasion, Pitt decided, by appealing to the loyalty of citizens, to make good the large budget deficit by raising a loan of £18 million at $5^5/8$ interest. On 2 December the major London bankers met to decide their reaction to the appeal for this 'loyalty loan', and Thomas reported in a private letter to George III, 'His Majesty might like to hear the result of the meeting of bankers.' He had himself urged

as much as he was able the plan of paying at once the whole sum to be subscrib'd – but Mr Drummond had alter'd his mind since yesterday upon it, and of the whole number present, as he was only able to carry Mr Dent's opinion on his side the question, he was obliged to give it up and subscribe in the common way each for £50,000. [At] The meeting were Mr Dent for Child & Co, Mr Snow, Mr Hoare, Mr Gosling, Mr Drummond & Mr Coutts.[15]

Thomas's relationship with his fellow-bankers was, on the whole, friendly. Both he and James had considerable admiration for the House of Child & Co. and frequently quoted it as an authority on banking practice. But there was often an edge to his references to Drummond, whose clan, it will be remembered, had been in the past supporters of the Jacobites. Now, however, they were Coutts's rivals for the King's favour. So the reference in this letter was a subtle suggestion that Drummond's 'loyalty' was not always to be trusted.

One perpetual cause of worry was that the Government itself often failed to pay the salaries and pensions of its diplomats, servicemen and politicians. It is not surprising that corruption was rife when an ambassador was kept waiting for months, even years, for his salary and allowances. In March 1799, for example, Thomas wrote to the British Ambassador in America, Robert Liston, asking him to 'moderate his demands as much as possible'.[16]

I intended, by writing a sort of Circular letter in the same stile to all my Diplomatique Friends, to induce them to remonstrate to The Secretary of State, & by that means to prove to Mr Pitt the necessity of paying up their appointments, which were running on Seven Quarters in Arrear, & no disposition intimated of relieving them –

I am confident the measures I took at that time of letting all the numerous list of Persons connected with me, in that predicament, feel the difficulty of being supplied with Money, produced the improvement there has since been made – which I hope will be continued, & even still further improved upon, – for though they are only four Quarters in Arrear, yet it is hard on those who are to live on their Salarys that they should not receive them regularly as they become due.[17]

He claimed that by refusing to lend any more to the 'numerous list of Persons' connected with him, he had forced the Government to mend its ways. He encouraged Liston to instruct the Government to assign his salary to Coutts & Co. He explained that when some years previously Lord Bute had been the Ambassador in Spain, he

did not choose to give his Power to any Person but me to receive his Salary etc – Mr Grenville, now abroad, & many others have acted in a similar manner, & we have never declined to act for our friends in this way. It is at least of this small advantage to them, that we never make any charge of Agency – or otherwise for the trouble – and in general their Money comes sooner into our hands, as the the [sic] Office Clerks seldom pay it to the respective Bankers immediately on receiving it –[18]

Grateful diplomats in return were glad to give advice to Thomas on the prospects for investment in their countries. Generally speaking, Thomas was a very cautious investor, preferring to keep his money in government securities or elsewhere equally accessible. But in 1795 he had invested considerable sums in American funds on behalf of Philip Antrobus, Susannah and Fanny. In 1797 he was tempted to lay out more money in America. He asked Liston's advice:

I should be very much obliged to you to give me your Opinion on this subject, you can contrive to send it to me unobserv'd – and you may depend I will never notice what you write to any one – Would you recommend a Purchase of Land, or rather prefer the Public Funds of the United States?[19]

His experience with the Bank of Philadelphia had not been encouraging – they had not answered the letters he had sent on behalf of Lord Stair, who had bought

some American stock & we sent the certificates to the Bank of Philadelphia but finding them very unpunctual lately we wrote . . . to Messrs Willings & Francis requesting they would be so good to apply to the Bank Directors & to see to get the business done.[20]

In spite of all the troubles that beset him at the end of the century Thomas could at least look at his Profit and Loss ledgers with some satisfaction. The partners' profits for 1799 had risen to £35,776, more than a triple increase on the £10,212 of two decades earlier. His own share in that year was £22,869 2s 4d compared with his individual profit in his first year, 1761–2, of £1,312 17s od.

25

'A Banker's life is not a bed of roses'

In these difficult times, with a banking business that was expanding rapidly, Thomas needed more help. He felt ill and jaded and that the best part of his working life was over. 'My cold is better', he wrote to his old friend Edward Marjoribanks, 'but I find these ailments shake me more, the old frame becoming less able to bear it.'[1] So he turned to Marjoribanks's son, Edward, as a new partner. As he explained to Lord Minto, he had first taken in 'Mr Coutts Trotter, whose father had some share in my education,' and in 1798 'Edward Marjoribanks, who's Grand Father, our great uncle Archd Stewart,* was the means in some measure of my family coming into my present house. They are both very amiable ... intelligent and it often happens that old kindnesses are thus repaid to the Heirs of those who never expected it.'[2]

Edward was young and, as Thomas told his father, might have made his fortune more quickly in the 'India line'. But Edward never regretted the decision and served the Bank loyally for almost seventy years, beginning a connection between the Marjoribanks family and Coutts & Co. which lasted into the twentieth century.

So anxious was Thomas to acquire the talented young man that he generously offered to advance the £1,750 as his proportion of the partnership stock. But he offered no illusions. He told Edward Marjoribanks senior:

Your son begins business when a Banker's life is not a bed of roses & when the whole world is in a very alarming state of confusion & England beset with domestic & foreign enemies. No business stands more forward to be affected by such calamities than ours. ... However we have some fellow sufferers so we must take our chance & hope for the best. The young people may see it out but I have little chance for Peace seems a thing now hardly thought of or even spoken of.[3]

*   *   *

* This is 'Baldy' Stuart, Provost of Edinburgh in 1745, whose son was now a wine merchant in Buckingham Street.

As Thomas had written, 'the whole world was in a very alarming state of confusion'. The French had advanced into Italy and had occupied Rome, forcing the Pope and his cardinals into exile and confiscating their property.

Thomas's old acquaintance, the Cardinal Duke of York, had made his way to Venice, where he was living in great poverty. In 1799 a fellow cardinal, Stefano Borgia, appealed to the King and the British Government on his behalf and, through the good offices of Sir John Coxe-Hippisley, finally succeeded in gaining a pension of £4,000 a year for the old Cardinal. Almost all the players in this little drama were connected in some way with Thomas Coutts. Sir John had married his cousin, Miss Stuart, and, although Thomas had despised him as a young man, he was now a diplomat employed on a confidential mission in Italy. The British Ambassador in Venice, Lord Minto, was Thomas's kinsman and close friend and Lord Loughborough, the Lord Chancellor, was his school fellow. All this Thomas carefully pointed out in a letter to the Cardinal of 20 January 1800. He was anxious that the Cardinal's pension, which he had certainly had a hand in arranging, should be paid through his Bank.

So he reminded the Cardinal of the visit to Frascati in 1790. This letter is reproduced here verbatim since it gives a rare account of his interview with George III, and also because an earlier biographer omitted one vital sentence which proves the Jacobite sympathies of Thomas Coutts in his boyhood:

London, 20th January 1800

Sir,

Your Highness will remember to have seen at Frescati in 1790 a Mr. Coutts a Scots Gentleman (by his Mother of the Family of The Baronets Stuart of Allanbank) with his Lady and three Daughters – Your Highness received us with uncommon kindness and attention, and at the same time with the dignity and Majesty natural to your Birth and Station.

The Eldest of my Daughters is now Countess, being married to the Earl of Guilford son of the ci-devant Lord North the minister of England. Another is married to Sir Francis Burdett of Foremark in Derbyshire a family (so late as to 1745 and since) very much attached to The House of Stuart. The Third is unmarried and living with her Mother and me and remembers the distinguished honour she receiv'd at Frescati when you put on her Finger with your own Royal hand a Ring which King Charles wore at his Coronation: on my return to England giving an account of what I had seen abroad to His Majesty King George the Third – I did not ommit a particular detail of the honours I had received at Frescati – and the uncommon politeness as well as the Elegant and Princely manner in which they were conferr'd neither did I fail to notice the very handsome and most liberal terms in which your sentiments of his Character were express'd. I had also the honour of showing at that time to his Majesty the silver medal given to me with so much condescension at Frescati.

He questioned me of the likeness said he was much pleased to have seen it imply'd that he supposed few would have mentioned the subject to him, but that they were much mistaken who imagined he did not very sincerley regard The Family of Stuart who were worthy of all good men's attention were it alone for their misfortunes.

He was so good to receive and to accept from me with His *own hand* the medal I had the honour to receive from *Yours* and I have no doubt has (as much as any Briton could) always valued and carefully preserved it; Neither am I altogether without the pleasing hope that my Communications on that occasion left in his Breast a permanent impression that never has been eradicated; and I learnt with the most sincere and Heart felt pleasure that some marks thereof have been apparent in a respectful remembrance he has lately shown of your Highness's situation that must recommend Him to all good men – Even those who never had the happiness to know him – to those who have been more fortunate or have known him as I have known him, there required no Proof of his being the most generous most amiable, and best of men – I have been long acknowledged to be his Banker and I have also transacted the Business of all his Royal Sons – and have from them all received the most flattering marks of approbation. I have more Pride in such testimonies and value them more than I wou'd do all the riches of the East – But in this and in every respect their goodness has left me nothing to desire or wish for – and at the close of my Life no object for Ambition. One thing *alone* my Heart aspires to which is in your Highness's Power alone to Confer. I can with the more ease sollicit for it as it is impossible it ever should be attended with any pecuniary advantage – Nay I am even in hopes it may eventually have been productive of some advantage to your Highness – My Profession too puts it naturally in my line, and sincerely attach'd as I have been for Threescore Years to the Illustrious Royal House of Stuart (who's Blood I believe ran in the veins of my mother) – My remaining and only ambition is to be *the Hand* by which the Benevolence of Britain from the *best of men* shall be convey'd to the last of that Illustrious Royal Line – The rightful former Sovereigns of Scotland, England and Ireland. The Person receiving money in all Cases appoints the Hands to be employ'd in that respect – The Payer never can – Two Words from Your Highness to my near relation Lord Minto, (who is also of the Family of my Grandfather Sir John Stuart Baronet of Allanbank) – to Mr. Pitt or to Lord Grenville who are both my Friends – or to Mr. Dundas or the Lord Chancellor my Countrymen – will settle the matter and be highly gratifying to me especially if your Highness is so good to notify the same by a letter to myself directed as follows. Viz.

To Thomas Coutts Esqr.
Banker in the Strand
Private   London
I am Sir

with the most dutiful respect and most sincere and devoted attachment your most faithful most obedient and most Humble Servant

THOMAS COUTTS[4]

This letter is particularly interesting for the confession of Thomas's long-held, long-concealed Jacobite sympathies and for his belief in his royal blood.

Thomas's request was granted and the allowance from George III to the last of the Stuarts was paid by Coutts & Co. The Cardinal's devoted secretary, Monsignor Cesarini, Bishop of Milevi, later asked in vain for an increase. Nevertheless, the Cardinal, in gratitude, bequeathed 'a gold snuffbox, an étui de voyage, two china vases & a gold medal of James II to Mr Thomas Coutts'.[5] And Thomas had the deepest satisfaction in drawing together the two dynasties that had so shaped his life.

It was significant that it was Fanny Coutts who caught the old Cardinal's eye and that it was she who received the gift of the royal ring. In the last years of the century she was to entrance another mature gentleman.

John Stuart, Marquess of Bute, was the son of King George III's friend and minister, the Earl of Bute, who had died on 10 March 1792. The old Earl had called on Thomas in London just before his death and insisted that he should bring his family to the Isle of Bute. Though Thomas saw in the old man's eyes the shadow of death, he gave his promise to the friend who had helped him at the beginning of his career.

Lord John succeeded his father and was created Marquess in 1796. He had been glad of Thomas's assistance in his diplomatic days. He had married an heiress, Miss Windsor, who had brought him great estates in South Wales, including most of Cardiff, and he owned the Isle of Bute and estates in the North of England. Because these were all badly managed and brought him little income, he was deeply in debt while abroad. His wife wrote a desperate letter to Thomas urging him to persuade Bute to regulate his affairs and to stay abroad, where living was cheaper. More recently their marriage had foundered and he began paying marked attention to Thomas's daughter, Fanny, who, as usual, could not resist the delights of flirtation. Stevens had jealously noticed Bute's admiration in 1795, and that he had left his little dog with her. He also recorded Fanny's comment that 'there was much to be said for Susan's marriage to an older man'.[6]

In May 1796 her father had watched Fanny, now recovered, as she soared up the Malvern Hills attended by his Lordship. Never, he said, had the nightingales sung so sweetly. As for the Marquess, he was enchanted: Fanny and the nightingales restored his youth.

But in the summer Fanny's strange hysterical fits developed once more, and her parents, deeply worried, decided to consult Burdett's family doctor, Erasmus Darwin. Thomas wrote a long letter describing Fanny's medical history from childhood. Only one detail was missing, and that the most important: the family history of insanity. Thomas, haunted by the memory of his brother James's violent end, and of Patrick still confined in an asylum in Hackney, desperately tried to dissociate Fanny's illness from that of his brothers. Darwin replied with a detailed analysis of the case and his prescription.

In August Stevens had heard that Fanny 'has been electrified by Darwin's advice and on their return Beddoes is to try his experiments on her'.[7] The new electric treatment did not succeed. Still worried, in November Thomas and his wife took Fanny on what he hoped was a secret visit to Darwin. Fanny's identity was concealed as 'Miss G.' – and no one was to be told, not even Burdett. But as Stevens reported in his December journal:

The Coutts's could not muffle in secrecy their Derby journey. Coutts was known at Matlock. They took Darwin with them from Derby to Matlock. He [Darwin] described his unknown patient as a very fine young woman with whom he was much pleased. She conversed freely and he said he was quite astonished at her understanding. She looked in perfect health – she had two fits while he was with her but neither Features nor Pulse were at all altered. He had never seen such fits.[8]

Whether it was Darwin's treatment or not, by 1797 Fanny was in full beauty again. Thomas kept his promise to the old Earl's ghost and took his wife and daughters to visit the Marquess on the Isle of Bute.

Fanny was enchanted by the romantic island and flattered by Bute's attention. In 1800 Bute's wife died, freeing him to propose to Fanny, who, to everyone's surprise, accepted him. Thomas was not enthusiastic and hastened to tell his friends that it was entirely her own decision. He himself found his new son-in-law somewhat chilling – unlike his father, the old Earl, for whom he had genuine affection. Bute certainly had an overbearing pride; he was, wrote Fuseli, 'a satrap, he never visits them'. And to Thomas he was often unbearably patronising. But Bute adored Fanny and spoiled her as her father had done. They were married in September 1800, quietly as was Thomas's custom. William Bagshaw Stevens did not live to see Fanny become a Marchioness. He died on 28 May 1800. Fanny and the Marquess now moved to their country house, Luton Hoo, and her life passed in splendid comfort in country houses in Kent and South Wales and at Mount Stuart on the Isle of Bute. She made frequent journeys to Italy for her health, where she travelled like a queen incognito. She bore the Marquess two handsome children, Fanny and Dudley Coutts Stuart, and after Bute's death in 1814 retreated with them to Italy. She refused to accept a pension from the new young marquess because, she said, her father would provide for her – as indeed he did.

Fanny's marriage left an aching void in Thomas's life, in spite of the fact that she wrote constantly to him and he visited her. Although Susannah could reflect on her daughters' success – the Countess of Guilford, the Marchioness of Bute and Lady Burdett had brought her distinction beyond her wildest dreams – Thomas was less than enthusiastic. It was something to have captured the sons of two former great ministers, and his daughters had the country estates he had always wanted for them. But Bute was far too grand, Guilford was hardly likely to drudge it in a Bank, and for Sir Francis he felt a growing and uncharacteristic hatred. And none of them could conceivably be imagined as the bankers he needed to take the oar from his hand.

26

New Century – New Problems

At the end of 1800 Thomas Coutts could reflect that at last he had now seen his three daughters well placed. But he was obsessed by the determination to keep 'the ascendancy' in his own family and desperately wanted to hand over the reins at the Bank to a younger member of the family.

The tragic memory of Thomas's own dead sons was sharply revived when, in 1802, Susan's baby son died. He and Susannah were with the Guilfords at the time and Susannah struggled frantically to save the child, staying up night after night and so further destroying her own health. Thomas had seen in this little boy the standard-bearer of the future. Never 'did any infant appear in every respect so promising'.[1] Heartbroken, he asked the Guilford family for permission to be buried with Susannah beside his grandson in the family vault at Wroxton Abbey. For the Earl of Guilford the death of his son was the last straw. His first wife had borne him four sons, all of whom died young. He was, he wrote, doomed to bring tragedy to all around him. Within three months he too was dead and buried beside his little son. Susan now came to live with her parents at Stratton Street. Sir Francis Burdett and Sophia had taken the house next door at 78 Piccadilly.

The death of their little grandson had rocked Susannah's already unbalanced mind and now, frequently ill, she was no longer an easy companion for Thomas. He had always needed the affection of women and now that his daughters were married he felt increasingly lonely.

Sadly he watched the slow decline of the once lovely Duchess of Devonshire. In 1796 she had had an operation on an eye which had left her half blind and, though she wore her black patch with some panache, the old gaiety had gone. She wrote to Thomas from Chatsworth, where she was 'retrenching': 'We sit down 23 besides the children & we consume 15 sheep and 2 oxen in a week.'[2] In 1798 the Duke paid most of her debts – or at least as many as she would bring herself to confess – and in April 1799 he arranged to pay her debts to Thomas by instalments.

Another 'full confession of her debts' took place in 1804, when they were assessed at £40,000 and were probably much more. For example, she mentioned that she had secretly borrowed £5,000 from Sir Richard Arkwright in a letter to Thomas about her debts on 16 September 1801. There were many others like him. In her last years she was increasingly worried about her sister, Lady Bessborough's debts, and she herself was still borrowing. Thomas resisted her demands, but Susannah did not and, in June 1804, lent her £200 when she was at her 'wit's end'. Three months later she sent again 'a second petition to Mrs Coutts for another two hundred pounds'.[3] She was still in need on 15 March 1806, writing sad appeals to her mother for £100; but this was her last one. On 20 March she died after three days of acute agony.

It was a distressing end to one of the most charming women of the period and Thomas, who had been more than a little in love with her, was depressed by her death. But now, unhampered by sentiment, he could pursue the Duke for the rest of his debt, which was not wholly cleared until long after her death. With dogged persistence he wrote to the Duke:

Strand London 13 January 1809

I hope I may without impropriety recall to yr. Grace's memory that no interest has been paid on four thousand pounds still due to me on your bond dated December 17th 1804. ... I hope I need not repeat the readiness I feel ... to receive it in the way most convenient to yr other arrangements. . .[4]

On 21 May 1811 Hartington, Georgiana's son, became twenty-one and Thomas sent to him a copy of the letter his mother had left with him to be delivered on his coming of age. This letter begged Hartington to pay her debt to Thomas and the interest on it. His covering letter explained his motives in helping the Duchess – 'his inexpressible regard', his 'fervent desire to extricate her from pecuniary difficulties and to recover her (to reclaim her I was vain enough to hope) from habits of gaming which I saw (with unfeigning grief) could only end in misery and distress'.[5] When Hartington succeeded as Duke of Devonshire on 29 July 1811, Thomas pursued him once again. He wanted £4,000 due from the late Duke on his bond of 1804, together with seven years' interest. The new Duke jibbed at paying interest since his mother had thought that the loans were to be without it, but Thomas did not give up. His last letters to the Duke were masterpieces of near blackmail. He had many letters from the Duchess, which, he was sure, the Duke would not wish to be published. He returned these letters when Hartington had paid almost the whole debt, but kept back some until the final clearance. His shrewd Scots head had finally conquered his heart.

Thomas's hope of finding an immediate successor in his own family was now fading fast. But he could at least take comfort that the Bank was running smoothly under the loyal Edmund Antrobus, who, as he said, 'lived in great harmony' with the other partners, Coutts Trotter and Edward Marjoribanks. For although the daily running of the Bank was now left to the partners, Thomas still made himself responsible for attracting new customers and continued to pursue the great and powerful. In 1801, Thomas had persuaded Henry Addington, then Chancellor of the Exchequer, and Lord Radnor to move their accounts to him. But in the case of Addington and Radnor he was poaching from Edmund's cousins, John and Edmund Antrobus, sons of the John Antrobus of Odrode who had married Hannah Sanxay. They were running Robert Sanxay's tea business at 480 Strand,* but were also engaged in banking and broking.

Furious with Thomas, the cousins threatened to remove their account from the Bank – a serious threat since they had brought a great deal of custom. John Antrobus's account in Coutts & Co.'s ledger shows that immense sums passed through his hands. Edmund, in a firm letter, tried to dissuade them. He must have been annoyed, however, that once again Thomas had conducted business with the mighty without consulting him. Since Addington does not appear as a customer on the books of Coutts & Co., perhaps Edmund's family secured a quiet victory.

One more incident in 1802 might have revived the old irritation. Thomas had increased the share of the other two partners and Edmund rightly felt hurt that he had not had a similar increase. Thomas immediately repaired the oversight by increasing Edmund's share by another $1/16$. This Edmund felt was too much. If he had, like the others, an additional $1/32$, he would be satisfied. He wished to be

on the same footing as the other partners; a larger share might be considered as placing me above them, which I should be equally desirous to avoid, as I have a sincere regard and esteem for them, and we live together in the most perfect harmony & friendship which I hope will always continue uninterrupted.[6]

The settlement of 1802 left Thomas with his half share in the Bank – and his 'supremacy'. Edmund had a quarter, Coutts Trotter $5/32$ and Marjoribanks $3/32$. According to the Profit and Loss Accounts, 'it would seem that Edmund's $1/4$ share in the profits of Coutts & Co., 1802–3, amounted to close on £7,234 a year'.[7]

For the rest of his life Thomas could be confident that, even in his frequent absences, 'The Shop' in the Strand would run smoothly under the harmonious triumvirate, Edmund Antrobus, Edward Marjoribanks and Coutts Trotter. He left the day-to-day business to them, but they referred all major decisions to him and he always took a close interest in the appointment of the clerks, as one of them remembered at the end of his life.

At the beginning of the nineteenth century the work at the Bank had greatly increased. There were now twenty-two clerks, whose combined

---

* In 1807 the firm was named 'Antrobus, Seaman & Antrobus' and in 1810 'Antrobus & Green', and there is an unconfirmed tradition that it became merged in the well-known firm of Twinings.

annual salaries amounted to £4,110, and it seems that discipline had become somewhat lax. So in January 1801 Thomas set out clearly in a long and detailed memorandum the system he wished to establish at the Bank.*

Jany 1801

Notwithstanding the great increase which has of late been made to the number of Clerks in the House, and the arrangements which have been formd for their attendance great inconvenience is daily experienced in consequence of the absence of some during the Busiest part of the day; and the New Buildings besides making it necessary to form a New distribution of the Business, Mr Coutts had made the following Arrangements which as He has consulted individual convenience as far as Regard for the Business would admit, He will in return expect to be rigidly & punctually attended to – He desires however to be understood (where it is not expressd otherways) as applying the Regulations only to the Clerks junior to Mr Price those of a longer standing not requiring any alteration as to their Business or Mode of conducting it.

The Fourteen Junior Clerks by Rotation to take the Balances above £2000 every night, and to attend on Sundays from the Usual Hour in the Morning till the Clerks who sleep in the bank come Home at Night –

The Common Hours of Attendance are to be from Nine in the Morning till Six in the Evening – or from Nine in the Morning till Seven in the Evening allowing an Hour (at such part of the day as may be fixed upon for Dinner – the Duty allotted to each Clerk will determine which of the above modes of Attendance will be expected –

During the absence of any Clerk from Indisposition or upon Leave – His Duty must be performed by those to whom it is allotted in the following statement – but as the absence of any one must be attended with much inconveniency it will be considered as a necessary mark of attention not only due to those on whom the greatest part of the inconveniency will fall but also to the general Arrangement of the House that the Medical Person who attends him should call on the first instance for communicating to one of the Partners the nature of his complaint & afterwards from time to time the progress of it & the expectation of being able to return to Business –

Mr Charlton the Senior Clerk in the Front Office is particularly enjoined to attend to these regulations being so far as they relate to the Pay Room being strictly complied with and to mention to one of the Partners any deviation from them – more particularly if any Clerk comes too late to Business or is absent too long at Dinner.

It is to be understood that the regular attendance & the Current Business herein before & after expressed is meant to apply to ordinary Juniors – & that it is exclusive of the general assistance which every one must contribute on Balancing at Midsummer & Christmas on [receiving] the Dividends Quarterly – and on any

* The memorandum drawn up by Thomas Coutts in January 1801, for the regulation of his business, was discovered during the move across the Strand in 1904. The whole of this long document is in Thomas's own handwriting.

other extraordinary or pressing occasion – these cannot be particularly innumer-
ated but they will often arise & it will be obvious that nothing will recommend a
Clerk so much to consideration & attention as a general readiness to forward
Business.[8]

In the 'Front Office' in the Strand eight clerks sat at their allotted desks
– three cashiers, two Fair Cash Book writers, the Shop Ledger writer, the
Keeper of the Bill Book and the Keeper of the Shop Cash Book. The Fair
Cash Book writer was expected to:

Write Fair Cash Book A to F.
Shop Cash Book. Bank of Scotland. Commrs of P of W, etc.
Go to the Stamp Office and the Navy Office.
Take in & Deliver Plate Chests and attend Carriages at the Door in the Absence
of the Second Fair Cash Book writer.[9]

For this he received £120 per annum.

In the 'Back Office' across the street the rooms were smaller; the 'Great
Room' held six clerks and each of the other rooms accommodated two
men. There were also three Outdoor Clerks, who went about London on
the Bank's business. The West Walk Clerk took the area which included
all places west of the House in the Strand and of Tottenham Court Road.
The North and South Walk Clerks shared all London east of 'The Shop',
with their respective spheres divided by the line of the Strand and Bishops-
gate Street. In the 'Debenture Office', with one assistant, sat Thomas's
chief and very confidential clerk, Andrew Dickie.[10]

For the rest of his life, Thomas was often ill and frequently out of London
for long periods, but he could be confident that the Bank was meticulously
organised. Above all he knew that he could rely utterly on Dickie, a man
who for three decades was as invaluable to him and to the Bank as any
other single individual. His gentle benevolence shines through his portrait
and attracts, even today, the greatest affection of the staff, for whom he
is a living presence in the Bank.

Unassuming, he chose to live with his sister in a modest little house,
because it was near the Bank, rather than have the comfort he deserved
and in later years could afford. His letters, dated not merely with the day
but with the hour, and his clear, neat handwriting all reveal his careful
competence. In the beginning Thomas had been a little dismissive of his
'somewhat mercantile stile', but, as the years went by, his letters show a
delicacy of touch and skilful diplomacy.

That he held an extremely responsible position is clear from the description of his duties:

Mr Dickie
   To take charge of Exchequer Bills
                  India Bonds
                  American Stock
                  Lottery Tickets
  To Superintend & write
                  India Correspondence
       any particular part of Continental Do [ditto]
              and of American   Do

To attend at the Treasury & Exchequer & other Public offices – pay & receive
Money there – apply for the appointments of Royal Family members etc & make
transfers depending thereon
To accept Bills with the Partners
At Midsr – make out the Balance[12]

Attending at the Treasury Office was no light duty. It often meant hours
of waiting in outer offices, sometimes after his work at the Bank was
finished.

Dickie's assistant clerk's duties were equally onerous:

Foreign office.
Assistant Clerk
  To have Charge of West India & American Correspondence
  – except as below
  To have charge of Continental Do with the exception of such part as Mr Dickie
  may take
  To enter the Substance of every Letter received containing an order in foreign
  order Book – on the day the Letter is received
  To post the Lists of Pensions Salaries Tontines Renters shares etc = and to
  make out new ones with 2d. Clerk at Midsr.
  To take charge of consignments of Goods & wine & Sales at the India House
  Assist at the Treasury Exchequer & other offices in obtaining warrants – notary
  powers – assignments &c
  Charge Interest on Money Lent Monthly
  Keep Lists of   Exchequer Notes
                India Bonds
                Lottery Tickets
                American Stock[13]

'Mr Dickie received £350 "Shop" Salary and £300 "private" salary, or £650
in all.'[14]*

It was 'good Mr Dickie' who dealt with the allowances to the King's
sons. Dickie wrote from his home, 8 Southampton Street, on 31 March
1806 to Thomas's friend, the lawyer William Adam:

* The 'private' salary for the chief clerk remained as a special bonus until the twentieth
century.

As it may be agreeable to you to know in what state of forwardness your exertions on behalf of the Royal Dukes have placed the promised issues of money for their respective benefits, I beg leave to acquaint you, that I saw this Day at the Treasury a list of Warrants preparing with the utmost expedition to be sent to His Majesty for signature consisting of

> £20,000 for HRH the Duke of Clarence
> £10,000 for   the Duke of Kent
> £5,000 for   the Duke of Cumberland
> £20,000 for   the Duke of Sussex
> £20,000 for   the Duke of Cambridge

and made out to *your good self* and William Dalrymple Esq. They will all be payable by the King's Proctor at Doctors Commons – and, as in the late instances of similar Warrants to the Dukes of Kent and Cumberland, I conclude free of all deductions.

There will, however, be the stamps on the Warrants to be paid at the Treasury when they are taken from hence – It is probable some few days may elapse before they can be returned from His Majesty and signed by the Lords and if I can be of any use in expediting their delivery from the Treasury I can only say that I shall be happy to obey your commands.[15]

Dickie was frequently sent on confidential missions to the King and to foreign royal and distinguished customers, and in gratitude they gave him handsome presents: royal dukes asked permission to give him silver plate, and Louis Philippe sent him a gold snuffbox.

In dealing with royal and distinguished customers, Dickie was always deferential but never servile; indeed, if necessary he could be disconcertingly direct. His tact was legendary. Whenever a customer needed a quiet reminder of the state of his overdraft, it was often Dickie who dealt with him – or her. As we have seen, when the painter Sir Thomas Lawrence was hopelessly in debt, it was Dickie who was sent to his studio to list the stacks of unfinished portraits and encourage him to complete these frozen assets. His kindness and his quiet competence won him the affection and trust of men and women in all walks of life. He was infinitely patient with Thomas's daughters, especially Fanny, who frequently sent requests from Italy for purchases to be made, awkward shapes to be wrapped and shipped, knowing that 'dear Mr Dickie' would always oblige.

As the years went by he took more and more of the burden from Thomas, reminding him of bank business of many years ago. 'You will recollect . . .' he would tactfully write, well aware that Thomas was now past remembering. Perhaps the supreme example of his skilful diplomacy was to come in later years, but it may be mentioned here. In 1820, after the death of King George III, the difficult Princess Caroline returned to England, hoping to take her place as Queen beside her estranged husband, George IV. Her government allowance was paid to her through Coutts & Co. and her bankers were often acutely embarrassed by the cheering mobs who surrounded her. She had the support of many prominent Whigs and radicals, including Sir Francis Burdett, who were furious with the King for deserting his old allies. Though her supporters might concede that her morals were somewhat doubtful, the King had hardly led an exemplary life. Dickie's letter to Thomas is self-explanatory and deserves to be quoted in full:

STRAND, 7th June 1820
Wednesday, 5 o'clock.

Dear Sir,

I have now to acquaint you of an Interview, which unexpectedly fell to my Lot today, to have with Her Majesty Queen Caroline. This morning I rece'd a Note from Mr Vansittart desiring to see me in Downing Street at 11 o'clock, where I was punctually to the time, and found Lord Liverpool, Mr Vansittart, Mr Huskisson and Mr Harrison together. Lord Liverpool informed me that it was desirable that a Communication should be made as speedily as possible to the Queen, and, being of a Pecuniary nature, his Lordship had considered the best mode of making it would be through the medium of her Majesty's Bankers, and therefore had sent to me, as being confidentially employed in your House, to request I would deliver the Communication alluded to (contained in a written Paper, which he would give me) to the Queen in Person. His Lordship then read to me the Paper, a Copy of which I send annexed, and desired I would lose no time in delivering it as requested. Previous, however, to taking charge of it, I beg'd leave to ask his Lordship what was to be understood by the words '*any reasonable temporary Advance*', as it would be material for your House to know to what extent they might honour The Queen's Dfts. [Drafts] under a Guarrantee from the Treasury. To this his Lordship observed it would be impossible to give a conclusive answer, as it would depend on Circumstances, but that in addition to the Treasury Guarrantee already given for £1000, another would be given for £3000 making together £4000. This point being so far settled, I requested permission to go to the Strand to inform the House of the Business I was to be sent upon, and that I should immediately return to Downing Street. I did so, and proceeded direct to Alderman Wood's House in South Audley Street, where about 2000 People were about his Dwelling, and on my sending up my Name, as coming from your House, I was immediately ordered up Stairs, into Her Majesty's Presence, who rece'd me very kindly and with much good nature. After acquainting her Majesty with my instructions, I delivered into her hands Lord Liverpool's Memorandum which She read over, and desired me to thank his Lordship for the Communication. Her Majesty then made many Enquiries concerning your own health & that of your family and expressed her regret at not having fallen in with Lady Bute in her Journey, etc., etc. I asked the Queen if She was then in want of money to which She immediately replyed in the affirmative and wished to have £1000 sent to her in various Notes, and She signed a Dft. for the amount, which Mr Marjoribanks delivered to Her Majesty this afternoon. The Queen expressed a great desire that you would allow Her & her few Servants to occupy a few Rooms in your house (not in front) in the most retired part, as She could not stay longer than a day or two more at Alderman Wood's, who had very politely gone with his family to a Hotel 'till She could find apartments else where, and as you were out of Town, She hoped you would accomodate Her for a few days, only with Lodgings, for She had Her own Cook & would purchase all the Necessaries She should want. As I could not help thinking that both You & Mrs Coutts would wish to be excused from such an honor, I took leave to tell Her Majesty, that, however much disposed I was sure you would be to do any thing agreeable to Her, I very much feared it would be impossible for you to comply with Her Wishes in this respect, as the House was repairing, painting etc., and could not afford suitable accomodation – in short I said all I could to prevent an Application to you; but Her Majesty would have Lady Anne Hamilton, who was present, write a note to you in Her Name on the Subject, which She requested me to transmit to you this afternoon, tho' I told Her Majesty you were forbid by your Medical attendants to receive, or answer any Letters. This Note was not sealed (as I was desired to seal it before sending it) and is in the hands of Sir Edmund. I have, however, the pleasure to add that Mr Marjoribanks in seeing the Queen this afternoon has said as much to Her Majesty on this Subject as I hope will set it at rest – of which he will I believe inform you. – I have seen Lord Liverpool since my Interview with the Queen, and his Lordship approved, with thanks, what I had done. I have also got the Treasury Guarrantee for the additl. £3000 – and, to a Question I took leave to put to Lord Liverpool what was to be done when the whole £4000 should be nearly exhausted, his Lordship desired he might be informed. I did not think myself entitled to say so much to Lord Liverpool, but I could not help saying to Mr Harrison that it is a pity Government has not taken care of the *House* part, as well as the *money* part – it might have been prevented the remarks of ill disposed People, and even of those who are well disposed. – Mr H. seemed to be of the same opinion. I have to apologise for troubling you with so long a letter, but could not well make it shorter.

Your most faithful
humble servant
A. DICKIE
Pray turn over.

Copy.

The Earl of Liverpool has received His Majesty's Commands to state that under the present circumstances, and until Parliament shall have come to some Decision on the Business now depending, an allowance will be continued to The Queen conformably to the Provision made by Parliament in 1814, which has now expired by His late Majesty's demise. And if the Queen should require any reasonable temporary advance with a view to providing Herself with a Residence, any application to this effect will be submitted by the Earl of Liverpool to His Majesty.

FIFE HOUSE

7 June, 1820[16]

His Majesty obviously had taken heed of Dickie's hint and provided Caroline with an allowance for a residence. Nothing better illustrates Dickie's important position in the Bank at this time. He was totally trusted by Thomas, his partners and the royal customers.

The number of clerks continued to increase. In August 1807, Joseph Farington RA had occasion to visit the Bank on behalf of his friend and fellow painter, Lawrence, and he jotted down in his diary some notes on the partners and staff at that time:

Coutts Trotter I went to and waited some time. The old Porter told me that Mr Coutts has now 26 Clerks including 3 Cashiers – & 4 Clerks who go out daily, – one to Somerset House – two to the City, & one to the West End of the Town. – Formerly there was only one Cashier.

Mr. Coutts has now 3 partners: viz. Mr. Antrobus, who is a native of Congleton in Cheshire & was formerly a stockbroker & resided in Bank Buildings. He has been with Mr. Coutts 27 years. – Coutts Trotter, on his coming from Scotland, was first a Clerk in the Navy Pay Office under his Brother Alexander Trotter, Deputy Paymaster under Lord Melville. Coutts Trotter has been a partner with Mr. Coutts about 10 years. – The third partner is Mr. Marjoribanks, brother to Captn. Marjoribanks the India Director. He has been with Mr. Coutts about a year and a half and is about 28 or 30 years old. . . .[17]

With such partners, Dickie and his well-organised clerks, Thomas could withdraw from the day-to-day supervision of the Bank. But he still dealt personally with his royal customers, whose financial affairs needed his full attention.

Thomas now had an impressive list of customers, ranging from the King and the royal family to a poor widow with nine daughters to support. He had developed a relationship with his customers that was peculiarly his own. He could talk to dukes and earls like a brother, and to their sons and daughters like a firm but friendly father. Even his letters to the King, though they began formally enough, soon slipped into a more familiar style. He could bend a humble knee if he thought it necessary, but servility, even to the greatest, was out of his character.

Though from time to time his heart overcame his strict business principles, he did not usually stray long from the path of the 'exact man', as he was proud to call himself. This combination of friendliness, directness and competence, allied to his reputation for total discretion, was the foundation of his unusual success as a banker.

27

Sir Francis Burdett
– The 'Frantic Disturber'

The new century brought Thomas fresh problems, but none of them caused him so much trouble as his son-in-law, Sir Francis Burdett. Again and again during the next decades he was the cause of Thomas's personal distress and was the greatest embarrassment to the Bank in the Strand. His career can only be described briefly here.

There was much in the young man that Thomas could admire, much that could be excused as springing from a warm heart. They shared a love of books and a passion for Shakespeare. Although, over the years, the old banker would explode with irritation and intense anger, Burdett throughout rarely showed anything but admiration for the judgment of his father-in-law. But Burdett's political beliefs threatened to destroy the banker's world.

For the first years in Parliament his old Tory grandfather had to be considered and Burdett was quiet enough. He lived in London with the Coutts family at 1 Stratton Street from March 1794, where his first child Sophia was born in June, until Thomas bought the house next door, 78 Piccadilly. But much of the time he spent in rented houses in Kent or on his family estates, Ramsbury Manor in Wiltshire and Foremark in Derbyshire. When his grandfather died in 1797, he inherited Foremark, the Derbyshire estates and the title. In 1800 his aunt left him Ramsbury Manor and most of her fortune. So Burdett began the new century an extremely rich man, who could now afford that independence which was to distinguish his parliamentary career. He took his own line, tied neither to Whig nor Tory parties. Nor did he allow himself to become the catspaw of extremists.

Handsome, with a fine patrician head, he appears in the caricatures of the day, his long thin legs and hands exaggerated, with captions like 'Burdett and no Bastille' and 'Burdett England's Glory'. He is pictured in his triumphant chariot, drawn by his adoring constituents, elegantly reclining like a Roman emperor. Such adoration, when even hardened observers like Princess Lieven were moved to tears at the sight, certainly fed his vanity. William Cobbett, who veered between excessive love and hatred, described his impact on his period. Byron, who was his friend, praised his oratory and silver voice. Benjamin Disraeli, who knew him well in old age, praised him as an unequalled orator,

all grace and music ... the range of his subjects was limited ... [to] the constitution, the rights and grievances of the people ... but of those he was master. His declamation was very fiery and thrilling – but always natural. ... In politics he was a Jacobite. He was sprung from a Jacobite family and entered life with the hereditary opinions of his class.[1]

Disraeli saw him as more Jacobite than Jacobin and, while admiring his simplicity, described him as 'the greatest gentleman I ever knew'.

Almost all the causes to which Burdett dedicated his life were honourable and are accepted as such today. He campaigned for prison reform, having seen for himself the appalling conditions in which some of his friends were held. He attacked flogging in the armed services, and demanded better pay and conditions in the navy. He passionately fought against all forms of cruelty to man and beast and was a founder member of the RSPCA. His political demands were not extreme by modern standards: he wanted Parliament to be more representative, but did not go so far as to demand universal suffrage, and he battled ceaselessly against the bribery and corruption that was a commonplace of the time. This often brought him into conflict with many of Thomas's influential friends by whom these practices were anathema, and he earned the anagram of his name, 'Frantic Disturber'. Nor is it surprising that Pitt and the King, whose spies were everywhere, were increasingly cold to Thomas.

Thomas had no sympathy with Burdett's extremist friends, but he understood his humanitarian concern. He agreed that the war with France could have been avoided and, as a banker, he was deeply worried at the increase in the National Debt. He realised the need for some reform of Parliament, but believed that a wise government would anticipate trouble by removing grievances. Above all he wanted to maintain that calm and equilibrium which he believed essential to the stability of the nation.

It was not only in politics that Burdett was a 'Frantic Disturber'. Thomas's anger with him during Fanny's serious illness at Bath, and his fears for Sophia's happiness, were both increased when Burdett added infidelity to his other failings. From 1798 onwards the cartoonists and gossip writers had had sport with the Baronet's affair with Lady Oxford. He found her charm and golden-haired beauty irresistible, and he enjoyed her warm affection for many years. Whether or not Burdett made his contribution to the Harleian Miscellany, as her children were called, would be later much debated. Certainly until his death he helped to support one of Lady Oxford's illegitimate daughters.

Burdett was one of her early lovers; Byron was her last in 1813 and wrote with genuine love of her 'autumnal beauty'. On 28 January 1798 Burdett wrote to Thomas: 'marriage is ill calculated to realise the fleeting dream of happiness. . . . Indeed (you will think me wild) I am convinced all the present ties of society are calculated to obstruct human happiness.' He maintained that 'there is a certain something in our characters which does not assimilate'. He recognised that Sophia was 'endowed with the purest & greatest virtues' but that 'virtue neither creates love nor procures happiness'.[2]

It says much for Thomas that his son-in-law could write to him so frankly of his marriage. Thomas was not censorious – many of his friends had mistresses, and he himself was susceptible to feminine charms – but Sophia's misery and the unpleasant publicity caused him constant concern over a long period. After the initial unhappiness Sophia 'anaesthetised herself', as Stevens said, and her patience was rewarded. The Oxfords left England in 1813 and, after some lapses and extravagant promises of reform, Burdett could write with genuine affection to his 'dearest love'.

Sophia had to endure more gossip and other scandals. It was said, for example, that Burdett was one of the Princess of Wales's lovers, and even after 1813, his enemies would renew again and again the old gossip.

For the rest of his life Thomas was often away from London, not only because of ill-health. Again and again Burdett's politics conflicted with the interests of his Bank, causing him mental anguish and making him physically ill. As always, he chose to avoid the scene of conflict.

Burdett had by now established a reputation in Parliament as a fiery radical. His maiden speech on Ireland, his mysterious trip there in 1798, his friendship with Roger O'Connor, Horne Tooke, Francis Place and other disturbing characters, were constant sources of worry to the responsible banker. Thomas accepted Burdett's sincerity, but his speech in the House of Commons on 12 April 1802 had been too violent. At a time when Thomas was trying to gain favour with Pitt, it was hardly helpful that Burdett should speak of 'the blood and treason so wantonly lavished during the late war'[3] which he considered was 'against the liberties, proprieties, laws, constitution, manners, customs, habits and character of the English nation'.[4]

The behaviour of his followers in the Middlesex election in July 1802 was the final straw. Burdett had left his 'rotten borough' and contested the Middlesex seat in opposition to a banker, Mainwaring. It was the first of many riotous occasions when the street outside Thomas's house in Piccadilly was thronged with Burdett's cheering supporters, many of them wearing the red caps of the French revolutionaries. But the worst moment came when the band leading Burdett's triumphant victory procession played the dreaded '*Ça Ira*' at the very gates of the King's palace in Kensington. The King was furious and the Queen saw the guillotine's sharp edge descending.

Thomas had made a tactical retreat in July to Guilford's house at Petersham, where he remained, desperately ill, until September. News was brought to him on his sick-bed of the procession from Covent Garden to his house in Piccadilly, led, as was the custom, by the butchers with their cleavers and aprons; he also heard that Burdett's carriage had been lifted on sturdy shoulders and that his turbulent son-in-law basked in the adoration of the riotous mob. 'He was our idol,' one of them later wrote.[5] But to Thomas he was the devil and, like the devil in the street ballad, who found the Middlesex election 'so hot, I'll return to the place whence I came', he must have echoed, 'what's Hell compared with your Brentford election?'

The King and his ministers were well aware of the activities of Burdett's friends. Lord Pelham sent the King letters from an informer on Burdett's committee, a man who was known as 'Notary' and who was a well-known *agent provocateur*. He was one of the many spies employed by the Government at this time.

Lord Pelham takes the liberty of sending to your Majesty two letters from Notary (whose correspondence your Majesty has occasionally seen); he is one of Sir Francis Burdett's committee sitting at Mr. Coutts's in Piccadilly.

Lord Pelham flatters himself that the precautions which have been taken for preserving the peace in London will prevent any bad consequences from the very mischievous handbills which have been circulated.[6]

The King replied from Weymouth:

Lord Pelham acted very properly in having taken steps to prevent the peace of London being disturbed at the close of the Middlesex Election, as the contest can have been made for no other object but to try whether mischief could not be effected.[7]

Polling at that time occurred over a period of days and, having begun on 13 July, it was still taking place on the 19th; the longer the Brentford poll continued, the longer the danger of riots. The King wished 'that the poll at Brentford should be closed, but as Sir Francis Burdett is not guided by any rules of propriety it must be difficult to ascertain when that will take place'.[8]

The poll finally closed on 29 July – a fortnight of great worry for Thomas. He himself was now accused of supporting Burdett. In great distress he wrote to exonerate himself to Addington, confessing that he had encouraged Sir Francis to stand for Parliament so that he would not leave the country and settle abroad with his family as he had threatened. But he claimed he had taken almost no part in canvassing, since he had never voted himself, and he certainly had every reason to want peace in London.

In July 1802 a double blow fell. Lord Hawkesbury, who was Foreign Minister at that time, withdrew the secret service accounts from Coutts & Co. without Pitt's authority, with the excuse that Thomas had given support to his son-in-law; and King George III now transferred his account to Thomas's rival, Drummonds. This was a twist of the knife. Drummonds had been the Jacobite bank and had only in later years proved its loyalty to the Hanoverians. In great distress Coutts wrote to the King of the pride he had felt in being the royal banker.

... Lord Cardigan having said abroad that Your Majesty had withdrawn Your money from my House – and many who had often flatter'd me with the appellation of Your Majesty's Banker having express'd both Surprise and regret in showing me Drafts in The Royal Signature on another House – cannot fail to operate strongly against my character and Interest – but The mortification to which it has subjected me is inexpressible – and tho' Certainly I can make no claim – and tho' in the face of Heaven my Mind is clear of every inward reproach – yet it has been almost more than I have been able to bear – The blow comes heavily from such an Elevation – and my Family and Friends have express'd with much concern the appearance of wasting and decay visible in my Countenance – The true cause of which remains a Secret in my own Breast, having never mention'd it even to those nearest to my Heart; and there it will remain for the little Time remaining of my Life – without murmur or complaint. My only wish is that I may *appear as I am* in Your Majestys Eyes – and if I have been accused that I may not be condemn'd unheard – as face to face I am convinced there is no man would dare to injure me so falsely.[9]

On 12 July 1802 Thomas sent a long letter to Pitt, explaining that he took no responsibility for his son-in-law, that he had given him no financial help and that he had only done the minimum in the election – merely because of his daughter. He sent the letter by the hand of his friend Thomas Grenville, who wrote to Pitt that

neither of us are likely to attribute bad principles to him [Coutts] because he got ten or twelve votes for his daughter's husband. ... Coutts is no Jacobin, but if the Government announce him as such, they do all that in them is to make him so; he is not young, and he is sick, and he is very susceptible upon these subjects....[10]

Pitt's reply was curt and cold; he said that he had not known of Hawkesbury's action, but he made no move to counteract it. So the King, who was to become hopelessly mad, never returned to Coutts & Co. The Duke of Cumberland followed his father. As a high Tory, he hated Burdett and all his friends, but the other Princes remained and wrote Thomas soothing letters. The Princesses, however, also kept their modest fortunes with Drummonds.

In fact the fear of Thomas's revolutionary son-in-law was not the only cause of the King's desertion. George III had long ago found it politically convenient to have another banker as a second string to his bow. In 1780, anxious that the Prime Minister, Lord North, should succeed in the election of that year, he had promised him £1,000 a month for his election expenses. So North borrowed £30,000 from Drummond, using the King's name as his security. His Majesty would not have wished to use Coutts & Co., since he would have known of Thomas's contempt for North and his hatred of the American War of Independence.

Four years later, on 22 March 1784, the King wrote privately to Henry Drummond asking for a loan, 'being under the necessity of raising a Sum of twenty-four thousand Pounds, and chusing to deal with a Gentleman rather than . . . the Common sort of moneyed Men'.[11] He still owed North £6,000, but assumed that his Prime Minister had paid off the remaining debt to Drummond. When Drummond tactfully pointed out that North still owed him £17,000, the King was furious with his former friend. Drummond's tact, however, won him the King's favour, and in that year he opened a private account with a deposit of £22,000 in the name of an official at the Hanoverian Chancery in London, appropriately called George Best.

The alarm caused by Burdett and his followers gave the King the excuse to confirm his desertion and his account at Drummonds was now opened in the royal name. It is very probable that in 1802 Thomas was fully aware of this background. After all North's son, the late Earl of Guilford, was his son-in-law, and at this period he was spending much time in sorting out the family's precarious finances.

In spite of this Mr Coutts and Mr Drummond were friendly, at least on the surface. Drummonds became its landlord when Coutts & Co. acquired part of the Adelphi building as an extension to its Strand premises. Coutts & Co. remained their tenant until 1904, when its lease expired and it moved across the Strand.

Thomas Coutts lost his royal friend, for George III slowly slipped into his long night of darkness which only ended with his death in 1820. In his last rational year he insisted that the office of Keeper of the Privy Purse be discontinued and the funds placed with Drummonds.

But at least Thomas's friend, Charles James Fox, ensured that the secret service money of the Foreign Office was once more kept at Coutts & Co. In the brief 'Ministry of all the Talents' in 1806, Fox was Minister for Foreign Affairs and could now repay his banker's kindness. But Fox's term of office was cut short: he died on 13 September 1806. To make sure the account stayed at the Strand under William Windham, Secretary for War and the Colonies in the new Government, Thomas wrote to Viscount Howick on 18 September 1806, reminding him of the 'unhandsome & unjust manner in which the official money of the Foreign Secretary and the War Department were ordered to be removed from my house on account of Sir Francis Burdett's election'. He now wished it to 'be con-

tinued by whoever is destined to that office'. He hoped Howick's recommendation 'will no doubt be attended to and will do me much
honour'.[12] Thomas's request was granted and the secret service account
remained with Coutts & Co.

In addition to his other worries, in these years he was pestered by Lady
Augusta Murray, the morganatic wife of Augustus Frederick, Duke of
Sussex. She had married the Duke in Rome in April 1793, but in accordance
with the Royal Marriage Act, the King declared the union void. Lady
Augusta was allowed an annual pension of £4,000 to be taken from the
Duke's government allowance of £12,000. When they separated and her
allowance stopped, she filed a bill against the Duke and Mr Coutts,
demanding that the banker should be restrained from paying her £4,000
to the Duke. The argument was not settled until the spring of 1806, when
the Duke agreed to give her an allowance, but took charge of their son.
Lady Augusta assumed by Royal Licence the name d'Ameland: her children
took the surname of d'Este. She was to try Thomas's patience in the
coming years, but he treated her kindly and was rewarded by letters of
extravagant gratitude, and the loan in 1819 of her house in Ramsgate.[13]

Thomas's customers were often a nuisance, but he was always reluctant
to let them go. He sought assiduously men and women of distinction, of
widely differing politics and professions. The great rivals Charles James
Fox and William Pitt both had accounts with him. His successors maintained this tradition: Earl Grey, Sir Robert Peel, Lord Liverpool, George
Canning and William Huskisson all banked at Coutts & Co. So did army
and navy officers, among them soldiers like Napier of Magdala; George,
Lord Lucan, of Crimean War fame; and Sir Thomas Picton; and sailors
like Sir William Sidney Smith, hero of Acre; William Bligh, villain of the
mutiny on the *Bounty*; Thomas Cochrane, tenth Earl of Dundonald; and
Sir Samuel Hood.

The withdrawal of the King's account had touched Thomas to the quick
for it had been his proudest boast that he had His Majesty's confidence.
But, before long, there was another severe blow to his honour. Once again
Burdett and his friends were on the other side. His friend and customer,
Henry Dundas, Lord Melville, was impeached for 'High Crimes & Misdemeanours' during the years 1786–1800 when he was the Treasurer of
the Navy. With him was charged his Paymaster, Alexander Trotter, elder
brother of Coutts Trotter and also a customer.

In 1802 a commission of enquiry showed that large sums of navy money
had been misappropriated in the years when Melville was Treasurer. The
case dragged on until 11 June 1805, when Samuel Whitbread moved Melville's impeachment. He lost, but the trial was renewed in the House of
Lords in April 1806, when once again Melville and Trotter were acquitted.

The affair, popularly known as 'The Tenth Amendment', caused considerable public excitement, and the proceedings in Westminster Hall were followed closely by all fashionable London.

Briefly, the case was that Melville, then Henry Dundas, allowed his Paymaster to transfer navy funds from the Bank of England to Alexander Trotter's account at Coutts & Co., where Trotter invested it on his own behalf. For Melville the irony was that he himself had introduced an Act in 1785 intended to prevent corruption in the payment of government funds. Trotter's defence was that he regarded himself 'as banker rather than accountant to the State' and, as such, he was justified in using its money wisely. He claimed that the nation had lost nothing and that he had paid all bills regularly. Indeed, he himself had instituted reforms in the Pay Office to ensure prompt payment of accounts; thousands of servicemen owed him gratitude. But there is no doubt that Melville and Trotter enriched themselves.

Thomas, deeply embarrassed, was required to send his ledgers to the commission of enquiry. He resisted this demand for some time – pleading illness and that he needed to take advice from Antrobus. He wrote on 3 August 1804 somewhat plaintively:

Gentlemen,

The indisposition you might observe I laboured under when I had the Honour of attending you yesterday obliged me after I left you to go to Bed, and prevented my calling on a very respectable Friend who I wish to consult on a matter of so much delicacy, and as I find He is unfortunately gone out of Town & will not return till Sunday, I hope it will make no difference my delaying till Monday Morning giving my answer which you desired to have to day. This will also give me the opportunity of having Mr Antrobus's opinion which I feel very desirable on the occasion as he may judge better perhaps than I can do, which mode will prove the least exceptionable in our situation as Bankers –
I am,
   Gentlemen
     Your most obedient Humble Servant[14]

Again he delayed, explaining how difficult and unprofessional it would be to send his ledgers to court. Finally he agreed, but set down firmly his own conditions:

Gentlemen,

I find the manner of complying with your request by sending you our Books will be less laborious than furnishing an entire Copy of Mr Trotter's Accounts – and also avoid the reproach of inaccuracy we might be liable to in a Work so tedious and unpleasant.

Our Books are made new Annually at Midsummer therefore every year is a Volume – and supposing you to go through a year's Transactions each day it will be a Work of about three weeks. Each Volume contains many Accounts besides Mr Trotter's, therefore the necessity will no doubt be obvious to you of our Clerk who brings the Book remaining present *all the time* during your inspection of it – and to bring it back with him every day.

I have the honour to be

PS Mr Trotter's own Account began in my House some years previous to 1791 – but the first Entry of any money arising from his Draft on the Bank is dated 13 July 1791. I therefore presume it to be your Wish to see the same in our Books from that period only.

Mr Trotter's Paymaster Account – Separate Account – and Trust Account for Mr Jellicoe will be sent from their respective commencement.[15]

He himself was examined and spoke warmly in defence of Alexander Trotter. How could he do otherwise when his own partner's brother was concerned? But there was no doubt that immense sums were involved. During Melville's time as Treasurer of the Navy, £15 million had been deposited at Coutts & Co. out of £130 million allotted to him.

Both men were finally acquitted, though it was clear that Melville had shown negligence and Trotter incompetence. Melville declined to answer difficult questions, blaming Trotter 'for the manner in which Mr Trotter kept my accounts'.[16] He blocked all difficult questions with 'it is impossible for me to answer that question', or by simply stone-walling, claiming as authority 'the 5th clause of the Act 43 Geo III cap. 16'.[17] Melville was removed from the Privy Council, though he won his place back in 1807. Trotter was reprimanded, but not prosecuted. He had already quitted the Pay Office in 1805 and retired to his estate at Dreghorn. The reputations of both men, however, were tarnished and Alexander Trotter of Dreghorn and his descendants were later to feel the chill wind of Thomas's disapproval.

The impeachment widened the breach between Thomas and Burdett. The Melville Affair, with its scent of corruption, was just the kind of case that roused the wrath of Burdett and his friends.

As Burdett's fame – or notoriety – grew, Thomas retreated more and more into the quiet of Cheltenham, or Bath, or Bristol, or Tunbridge Wells, or to his daughters' country houses. Plagued with rheumatism, bronchitis and other ailments he would have been happy to retire, but even though so often absent he still had the worry of the Bank. And these were difficult times. There seemed no end to the war with France, Napoleon was a growing menace, and there was a constant threat of invasion. Arthur Wellesley was not yet the hero who, as the Duke of Wellington, would defeat the Corsican monster.

At home the political scene was chaotic. Fox and Pitt had both died in 1806 and the 'Ministry of all the Talents' had been short-lived. George III, increasingly obstinate as his mind weakened, had refused to accept the bill giving concessions to Catholics and had dismissed his ministers in April 1807.

Thomas's world was disintegrating. He was an eighteenth-century man and belonged to the age of realism, when each man knew his station; when patronage was accepted and even, when used for family and friends, considered honourable; when bribery and corruption were excused as inevitable; and when harsh discipline was expected. All this was giving way to a world of mobs shouting slogans, waving the banners of liberty, equality and fraternity. And it was his own son-in-law, the 'Frantic Disturber', who was in the vanguard.

The turmoil in 1802, 1804 and 1806, when Burdett had been elected as MP for Middlesex, had been bad enough, but his election for Westminster in May 1807 passed all bounds. While ecstatic crowds were cheering Burdett, Thomas escaped, as will be seen, and found his own way to comfort and consolation. Burdett had also wanted to escape, deciding that 'in this desperate situation I cannot become a candidate for any seat'.[18] But he was finally persuaded by the Westminster election committee to stand as candidate for their constituency, which had a long and strong radical tradition.

He accepted on the same terms as he had fought the last Middlesex election. He believed that 'electors ought to seek representatives not candidates solicit electors'.[19] He would therefore neither 'canvass, nor bribe nor treat'.[20] If they wanted to elect him without his interference, he would 'do the duty of a faithful steward'.[21] So, independent of party 'without spending a guinea',[22] he was elected as MP for Westminster and remained so for the next thirty years. Even had he wanted to he could not have taken part in the electioneering, for on Saturday 2 May he fought a duel with James Paull, one of the candidates for his old seat of Middlesex. Paull, without Burdett's consent, had claimed that Burdett would actively campaign on his behalf, which Burdett had hotly denied. Finally Paull, a quarrelsome character, challenged him to a duel. Both men were wounded and Burdett was carried to his house in Piccadilly to recuperate, so he could take no part in the election.

His platform was a simple one: he was for the freedom of elections, the re-enactment of the Act of Settlement clause excluding government pensioners and placemen from the House of Commons, and the disenfranchisement of rotten boroughs. In his election address of 30 May he pledged himself to the 'abolition of the whole present system of corruption' and promised to 'restore to my countrymen the undisturbed enjoyment of the fair fruits of their industry'.[23]

Cobbett described in the *Political Register* the reaction to Burdett at this time:

'Everyone I meet,' said a person to me the other day in Oxford Street; 'every one I meet reprobates the Address of Sir Francis Burdett.' 'Which way did you come?' said I. 'Why,' replied he, 'from Whitehall, across the Parade, through St. James's Palace, and up St. James's and Bond Street.' 'Well, then,' added I, 'now go to Somerset Place, the 'Change, the India House, Lloyd's, the Custom House and the Excise Office, and you will meet with exactly the same cry. But when you have heard the hundreds at these places, then go and hear the thousands and hundreds of thousands in the manufactories, in the shops, in the work-shops, upon the river and in the gardens. Go and hear those, whose labour, whose ingenuity, and whose industry in every way are taxed to support the clamorous whom you have heard; go hear the laborious father whose means of provision for his children is taken away by the income tax; go hear the merchant, who is compelled to make an exposure of all his most private concerns, and who by the taxers is frequently not believed upon his oath; go hear the numerous annuitants from whose scanty means of subsistence one-tenth is annually taken in a direct tax; go hear in short all those, who have nothing but their labour, of one sort or another, to subsist on, and who have no share in the taxes; go hear these, and then come and tell me, on which side you find the majority.'

On 29 June 1807 enormous crowds flocked to Burdett's victory procession. It started from Covent Garden about noon, headed by the butchers with their marrow bones and cleavers. There was the usual display of flags and banners inscribed with 'Burdett and our Country', 'Burdett the Choice of the People'. There were bugle-boys, trumpeters and bands. Electors, marshalled under the flags of the different parishes of Westminster, marched four abreast. There followed the triumphal car of Sir Francis, and the procession was closed by horsemen and carriages.

Did Edmund Antrobus, Edward Marjoribanks and Coutts Trotter watch from the Bank as the cavalcade made its noisy way up the Strand or did they, like Thomas, beat a strategic retreat? Certainly Edmund must have raised a silent prayer of thanks that Burdett had never been made a partner of Coutts & Co.

The cavalcade reached 78 Piccadilly, where a monstrous chariot awaited. Burdett, unable to walk, was carried to the car. Two gentlemen lifted him on to his pedestal, where he reclined like a Roman emperor, his wounded limb resting on a purple cushion, the other on 'a sort of imperial footstool, under which the monster, Corruption, was seen in an agonising attitude'.[24] Adorned with wreaths of oak and laurel, draped in crimson and gold, and drawn by four white horses, richly caparisoned and decorated with purple ribbons, the chariot trundled through cheering crowds to the election. Burdett's colours streamed, flowers and laurels were scattered on the car from the crowds at the windows, on scaffolding and even on rooftops. It was said that there were half a million people in the procession, yet there was no disorder.

Henry Hunt wrote:

Sir Francis Burdett was that day in sober earnest and in the honest sincerity of their hearts the pride of the people. It was not fiction, no joke, but in fact and in truth Sir F. Burdett was on that day 'Westminster's Pride and England's Glory'. All was peace and good order, every face beamed with good humour, and upon every brow sat a sort of conscious pride, as if each person felt that he had performed a duty by offering a tribute of devotion to the Baronet.[25]

Burdett might be Westminster's Pride and England's Glory, but, as Cobbett pointed out, to Thomas's friends in Whitehall and the City he was a threat to England's security.

Again and again Burdett was to charge full tilt at Thomas's most valued customers. Burdett, in fact, was himself always stoutly loyal to the monarchy, but to many of his followers the King was an expensive anachronism and Burdett suffered guilt by association. In the quarrels between the King and his sons, Thomas had always trodden delicately, but Burdett gave offence to both sides. One after another he attacked Thomas's royal customers. He took the Princess of Wales's side against the Prince of Wales – not because he believed her unspotted, but because he detested the Prince of Wales's hypocrisy. He conducted a long and passionate campaign against flogging in the army, knowing that the Duke of Kent had ordered the most merciless floggings both at Gibraltar and when he was in charge in Canada. The Duke of Clarence was affronted by Burdett's support of rioting seamen – near treason, in the Duke's view.

As for the Duke of York, Burdett helped to bring about his resignation as Commander-in-Chief. He seconded the motion in the House of Commons, brought in by a dubious radical MP, Colonel Wardle, who, on 27 January 1809, accused the Duke of York of actively conniving with his mistress, Mary Ann Clarke, who, by her own admission, had accepted bribes to secure army promotions. The trial on 11 December 1809 was the sensation of the season, and it was not only Thomas's royal customer who was under attack; his Bank received unwelcome publicity when it was claimed that Mrs Clarke forged one of the Duke's cheques on Coutts & Co. Luckily the discreet banker, who was terrified that he would be called to testify, escaped without much publicity.

But by now his anger against Burdett was intense. Fortunately, though the King deserted Thomas, only the Duke of Cumberland followed his example. The other brothers stayed with him and remained his friends, and he was consoled by their sympathy and understanding at this difficult time.

However, the worst was still to come. In 1810 Thomas's house in Piccadilly was the setting for one of the most sensational sieges in parliamentary history, when Parliament condemned Burdett to imprisonment in the Tower for breach of privilege.

The fact was that Burdett had made too many enemies who hoped to see him silenced. In January 1810 he fiercely attacked the Government for the failure of the Walcheren expedition,* and in February he opposed the annuity of £2,000 to Wellington as he had opposed all sinecures. In the same month he supported a bill for the reform of Parliament and in strong language accused Castlereagh and Spencer Perceval, the Prime Minister, of corruption. Burdett was now becoming dangerous and his enemies waited for an opportunity. It came when Burdett protested at the exclusion of the press during the debate on the Walcheren débâcle. On 19 February 1810 an apothecary called Gale Jones, the secretary of a debating society, attacked the Government's 'insidious & ill timed attack on the liberty of the Press'. Charles Yorke MP claimed that this was a breach of privilege and Gale Jones was imprisoned.

On 12 March Burdett made an impassioned and learned speech in the House on Jones's behalf, claiming that the Speaker's warrant was illegal. When his motion was rejected, he published an open letter to the people of Westminster in which he claimed that the House of Commons had no right to 'imprison the people of England'.[26] Perceval, who loathed Burdett, encouraged the MP for Somerset, Mr Lethbridge, to accuse him of having written a 'Scandalous and libellous' paper. On 5 April the House debated Burdett's alleged breach of privilege and in the early morning of the 6th condemned him to be committed to the Tower. Burdett's constituents exploded with fury. The MP who moved his committal was hounded out of London, and even his bank in Wales was threatened with ruin.

There was an element of farce on the succeeding day. On Friday 6 April Burdett received a courteous letter from the Sergeant-at-Arms offering to wait on him to convey him to the Tower 'at his convenience'. There followed four days of extraordinary scenes. The whole of London from the Tower to Piccadilly seethed with the fury of Burdett's supporters. Passers-by were forced to shout 'Burdett for ever' and wave their hats or be stoned. Piccadilly was barricaded by a ladder from a nearby building site, and an angry crowd threw bricks at the soldiers. Men talked of a barrel of gun-powder brought in to defend Burdett. There was a real danger of civil war. The Foot Guards and Life Guards were called in and terrified the crowds by 'prancing on the pavements'.

It was not until 10 a.m. on Sunday morning that, after days of riot, the Sergeant-at-Arms, with an army of constables, forced a way into the basement of the house and up into the drawing-room where the Burdetts were at the breakfast table. There was a touch of melodrama in the scene at 78 Piccadilly. Breakfast was just finished, but most of the family were still there – Lady Burdett and their son, Robert; Lady Guilford and her

---

* During the war against France in 1809, after capturing Flushing, the British expedition under the second Earl of Chatham came to a disastrous end and was withdrawn.

three daughters; Sir Francis's loyal brother, Jones; and the Irish radical, Roger O'Connor. Robert was seen to be piously studying the Magna Carta. Old Susannah had stayed to support her son-in-law, but Thomas had prudently withdrawn. The agony of mind that the most discreet of bankers suffered can be imagined.

Finally Burdett was forced to submit. He was seized, taken to a waiting coach and, surrounded by four squadrons of the 15th Light Dragoons and the Life Guards, two battalions of Foot Guards and another troop of the 15th Light Dragoons, was swept off to the Tower.

That day there were serious riots; many were wounded and some killed. Burdett spent weeks in the Tower, where he was not uncomfortable: he was visited by Lady Oxford and the Duke of Sussex, and wined and dined his visitors well. But during his weeks of imprisonment Burdett had time to consider. Blood had been shed on the day of his capture and, though he was no coward, he could not bring himself to lead his followers into a battle in which there would be more loss of life.

On 21 June Parliament was prorogued and, therefore, Burdett was released. A demonstration was planned such as had never been seen before, and Burdett was to be brought home to Piccadilly by an adoring throng. The streets from the Tower to Stratton Street seethed with an excited multitude: Burdett's blue cockades were everywhere; an immense procession formed up and, once again, bands played and banners waved. Their hero was to be taken home in triumph. Alas it was to be *Hamlet* without the Prince. Burdett had quietly slipped across the Thames to his house in Wimbledon. The disappointment was intense as his empty carriage rattled through the waiting crowds to his house in Piccadilly. From that moment something of his magic disappeared, though until his death he remained for many 'Westminster's Pride and England's Glory'.

Those days became legendary in the family history. Burdett's eldest daughter, Sophia, loyally celebrated in verse her heroic father:

> Let all the ends thou aim'st at be thy Country's
> Thy Gods, and Truths, then, if thou fall'st
> Thou fall'st a blessed martyr.[27]

28

Enter Miss Harriot Mellon

During the years 1804–10, while his turbulent son-in-law was stirring up trouble in London, Thomas retreated for long periods to the country, taking the waters in Tunbridge Wells, Bristol or Buxton. In the summer of 1805 he had gone to Cheltenham. He was ill and depressed. The impeachment of Melville hung like a dark cloud over him. He was worried about his business and the world and shadowed by the thought of his approaching seventieth birthday. King George had recommended the waters of Cheltenham, and the little town suited him. As yet it was still a comparatively unspoilt watering-place and here he could saunter by the stepping-stones over the clear stream that ran through the town, and wander under the great lime trees down the Long Walk till the pressure lifted. It was here, on a June morning, that he encountered the delectable young actress who was to change his life. He had met Harriot Mellon before in the Green Room at the Drury Lane Theatre, when she was at the height of her popularity.

Her success, particularly as Volante in *The Honeymoon*, had brought her to the notice of Colonel MacMahon, equerry to the Prince of Wales, and through his influence she had secured the office of postmaster at Cheltenham for her stepfather, Mr Entwisle, who, with her mother, had been running a music shop in the town. Shrewdly, Harriot was investing her savings in building a house for renting in Cambray, an increasingly popular area.

That summer she was playing at the Cheltenham Theatre and, as was customary, solicited patronage for her benefit night. Her mother, learning that a wealthy banker, 'a moping thin old creature',[1] was taking the waters at the Pump Room, sent him an invitation to take a box at the theatre. So, when the shabby old gentleman bowed to her on the Long Walk and reminded her of their earlier acquaintance, she dazzled him with her brightest smile. He apologised that, pressed by business, he had only just sent her his subscription. She treasured the five golden guineas he sent to the end of her life; they were her 'luck money', never to be spent. And they certainly brought her a golden future. When he returned to London,

Thomas renewed their friendship and rapidly established himself as her protector.

Thomas was no fool. He would not have taken Harriot under his wing if he had not observed her closely. She had a good reputation in Cheltenham and was admired not only as an actress but also for her generosity to difficult parents. Her stepfather was too fond of the bottle, and her mother's incandescent rages were legendary. Thomas had also heard of her cheerful good humour in the Green Room at Drury Lane, where she was known as a hardworking, unpretentious trouper, equally ready to play the countess or the maid. She was not a great actress, but was an excellent mimic and had good examples. A fellow-actor compared her with the great actresses of the day:

Miss Mellon was a remarkably handsome brunette, but did not look a bit like an actress. She was more like one of the genuine beauties of a quiet village two hundred miles from town. Miss Farren was then, despite the smallpox, the reigning toast; she was an elegant woman. Mrs Jordan was in her bloom; she was a fascinating one; to say nothing of the majestic Siddons, to whom none dare express admiration. These ladies had each a style ... but Miss Mellon was merely a countryfied girl, blooming in complexion, with a very tall, fine figure, raven locks, ivory teeth, a cheek like a peach, and coral lips. All she put you in mind of was a country road and a pillion.[2]

To Thomas she was irresistible and very soon she filled the place that his daughter Fanny had left empty in his heart. If he had any doubts about Harriot's character, there were many actors and actresses who could vouch for her good reputation. He would certainly have talked to Mrs Jordan, one of his customers, who was the acknowledged mistress of the Duke of Clarence. This remarkable lady managed to combine a highly successful career as an actress with a singularly fruitful, if unconventional, domestic life. She had four children by a previous lover and now lived openly with the Duke at Bushey Park. She gave him ten children, all of whom he acknowledged and honoured when he became King. As a highly paid star it was she who helped to keep the Duke for many years.

She would have had a good word for Harriot, who had admired her ever since, as a young actress, she had walked all the way from Otley to see her play at the Harrogate Theatre. Henceforward she had modelled herself on Mrs Jordan, played Maria to her Viola and Celia to her Rosalind, and stood in for her many times when yet another young Fitz-Clarence made its appearance.

There was another impressive Green Room testimonial to Harriot's character. Thomas, a frequent visitor to the theatre, had heard how Mrs Siddons had introduced Harriot to the Green Room reserved for the stars – a great honour for a minor actress. She had been impressed by Harriot when they had both been playing at the Liverpool theatre in 1796, according to a contemporary actor who introduced them. He had told Mrs Siddons how properly Miss Mellon had conducted herself in the provinces, and Mrs Siddons had replied, 'She seems a nice pretty young woman, and I pity her situation in that hot-bed of iniquity, Drury Lane.'[3] She had never 'heard of anything in the least degree wrong in her conduct since being in London'.[4] On their return to Drury Lane, in her magisterial way, Mrs Siddons took her by the hand and announced to the company in the Green Room that, since she had heard that Miss Mellon had always conducted herself with the utmost propriety, she wished to introduce her 'young friend' to them all. Though these and other stories, told by Harriot's admiring biographer, Mrs Barron-Wilson, may not have been exactly correct, it is certain that then and ever afterwards Thomas was completely convinced that, in the mire of Drury Lane, Harriot had remained pure and unspoiled.

He must have been amused and impressed by Harriot's own account of her life, which she always told in her inimitable way, never concealing that, like Mrs Jordan and Miss Farren, she was of lowly Irish origin. Her mother, a handsome girl, had been apprenticed as a milliner, then became stage-struck and joined a troupe of strolling players. Not good enough to be an actress, she became their wardrobe mistress and 'money taker'. Later she had gone to London with a mysterious Lieutenant Mellon of the Madras Infantry and claimed that he married her there before disappearing for ever. When Harriot was born or where remains a mystery – it might have been in London in 1777 or later in Lancashire. Her mother was often heard to claim that she came from distinguished stock, but Harriot always made fun of her pretension that Mr Mellon was a lord in disguise. Mrs Mellon later married Mr Entwisle, a Lancashire musician, and together they toured the North of England, she as wardrobe mistress and he as leading violinist in Thomas Bibby's Players. They were based in Ulverston, where the theatre was in a large barn owned by the White Hart Hotel. Here, as 'Little Pickle' in the farce of *The Spoiled Child* on 16 October 1787, Harriot, aged ten, had made her first appearance. She was later remembered for her lively performance in a dashing 'laurel green tunic, with her sparkling eyes, blooming cheeks and profuse black ringlets under a fancy riding cap'.[5] According to her biographer, Harriot was long remembered in Ulverston not only as a competent little actress but also as a mischievous but popular pupil at Miss Calvert's school. She certainly never forgot the love of poetry she first learned there.

Undoubtedly she horrified the old banker with accounts of her mother's wild rages: how, ambitious for the child and genuinely fond of her, Mrs Entwisle had frequently shown her love by beating her, leaving her locked in dark cellars and generally maltreating her.

It was when they moved to a better theatrical company, and settled in Stafford, that Harriot's acting career had really begun. She played not only in the undistinguished popular comedies of the day, but also in Shakespeare, where her first role was Phoebe in *As You Like It*. Her charm and sparkling personality won her acceptance in the homes of the leading Stafford citizens, especially that of Mr Wright, a respected banker. His daughters took Harriot up, invited her to stay at their home, and lent her their dresses and jewels. Thomas possibly knew Wright – he certainly did later on – but, in any case, the admiration of a fellow-banker would have been a striking testimonial.

When Sheridan, who was then MP for Stafford, came up for the annual races, Wright introduced Harriot to him as a promising young actress, who had been brilliant as Lydia Languish. He persuaded Sheridan to invite her to act at Drury Lane, where the many-talented dramatist was manager. But, unreliable as always, Sheridan forgot, and though Harriot and her mother moved to London to take up her new career, it was not until September that he finally offered her the part of Lydia Languish in the recently reopened Drury Lane Theatre. Thomas had experienced difficulties in dealing with Sheridan and sympathised.

Harriot, settled with a companion in Henrietta Street, gradually established herself as a good, minor actress at Drury Lane. Once again she won the affection of respected citizens like Mr Graham, a Bow Street magistrate, who, as her biographer reports, 'felt so much pleased with her artless manner and unassuming cheerfulness ... that he took a great interest in her welfare'.[6] He certainly could have given no surer token of his respect than that he entrusted his wife's orphan niece to her care. Miss Eleanor (Nell) Goddard became her constant companion and, after 1812, lived with her until 1831, when ill-health forced her to retire.

At the Grahams' house Harriot met Sir Henry and Lady Tempest, cousins of Mrs Graham, who invited her to stay at the delightful Highgate villa they were just building. Holly Lodge, an unpretentious rambling house, set high on Highgate Hill with a spectacular view of London over the sloping green lawns, was a welcome retreat from the smoke and fogs of London, and Harriot loved it from the beginning and set her heart on owning it.

When she met Thomas, Harriot already had a comfortable bank balance with Thomas Wright, a banker in Russell Street, Covent Garden, who was connected with her patron, Mr Wright. Wrights of Covent Garden was a long-established firm which had been founded at the end of the seventeenth century by a goldsmith. Thomas knew and trusted Wright, and had there been any skeleton in Harriot's past, his fellow-banker would certainly have warned him. Even after Harriot opened an account with Coutts & Co., she still kept her account with Mr Wright. It was with a cheque on him that she bought an estate in Essex – and she did the same when she later bought Holly Lodge.

Thomas, who gave her an allowance, encouraged her to keep it with her own money with her original banker, and to invest it wisely. So the details of his financial arrangements with Harriot were hidden from his partners and clerks in the Strand. Her allowance and presents of money were given to her in cash, though his partners certainly were aware of Thomas's patronage of the actress.

Artists, actors, magistrates and bankers all testified to Harriot's good character. But Thomas trusted his own judgment and, when kind friends like William Adam worried about his reputation, he assured him that she was all that was good. As for Harriot, who had recently been deceived by a suitor who claimed to have a fortune that did not exist, she had had enough of disappointed love and was happy to rest on the security of an old man's affection. She could not have envied Mrs Jordan her life of perpetual pregnancy; Miss Farren was a more attractive role model. This exquisite actress had been the companion of the Earl of Derby and, carefully chaperoned by her mother, had kept an unsullied reputation. It was generally acknowledged that, when his old, sick wife died, the Earl would marry her, as indeed he did. As the new Countess of Derby, she played the role impeccably. Since Thomas too had an old and ailing wife, and since Harriot was also always discreetly chaperoned, first by her mother and then by a young friend, theirs seemed a perfectly acceptable relationship.

So his visits to Henrietta Street were more and more open. For the first time in many years the old banker was given the comfort and affection he so needed. Harriot knitted him woollen scarves and Mrs Entwisle took care of his shabby old clothes. It was reported that he was so neglected at home that his much darned socks crippled him and his shrunken vests stifled him. Skilled with her needle, Harriot's mother set him up with new socks and a dozen flannel vests.

Susannah was frequently ill during this period. Whether she knew of her husband's new interest, and whether it hastened her physical and mental deteroriation, will never be known. But before long his daughters became worried. Susan, Lady Guilford, who with her stepdaughter and daughters had the care of the increasingly difficult Susannah and was the toughest and most outspoken of the sisters, became impatient with her father's folly. Fanny, who was living mostly in Italy, wrote in her usual tactful way. She knew her darling papa believed in the spotless character of Miss Mellon, but she had heard that Drury Lane Theatre was notorious; and she pressed home the gentle reminder of what her darling mamma always had to say about actresses.

There is no doubt that Thomas retained a great affection for and a sense of duty to Susannah. 'He loves his old wife,' Fuseli once remarked.[7] Certainly he presented her with a diamond crescent on their wedding anniversary on 18 May 1807 with this fond verse:

We have been married this day full years Fourty Four
& are nearly approaching the Age of Fourscore
Accept then this present which justly is owing
as an Emblem that true love will always be growing[8]

But alas for Susannah, her crescent was already waning. For by 1807 Thomas's paternal affection for Harriot had become an infatuation that was to hold him for the rest of his life.

Nothing shows more clearly the banker's genuine love, nor his unshakeable faith in her purity and virtue, than the letters he sent her, sometimes written when they were parted, sometimes when she had gone into the next room. Harriot kept them to her dying day in a special box, which travelled with her wherever she went. The first two letters of September and November 1805 are affectionate but paternal in tone, suggesting that he was proposing the kind of relationship that she had had with Mr Wright and his family.

He hoped that her health had recovered and declared that he would 'ever retain for you the sincerest sentiments of affectionate regard'. He teased her with a rumour that 'a lady belonging to the Theatre was about to have a Coronet added to Her name: it may be you! None deserve any pre-eminence so well . . . .'[9]

The letter he sent on 11 November, her birthday, settling an annuity on her, reflects a deeper commitment, but still he merely wanted to protect a virtuous lady by making her financially secure. As any banker would, he gave her financial advice. She had already saved a tidy sum, which brought her in £210 10s a year clear. To this he added enough to give her £235 a year in the Long Annuities. He advised her to manage her money in this way: 'as to the £105 in the Reduced leave the interest to be accumulated & laid out as it comes due in more of the same stock and I wish you should understand & practice management in this way till you add £105 to your income in order that you may have a clear Five Hundred pounds a year'.[10]

Then, again as her banker, he suggested that she should make her will and that the money he had given her might be left to Lady Guilford's children, Lady Susan and Lady Georgina North. These girls had always had an easy affection for the grandfather they addressed as 'Dear Tom'. 'I also recommend,' he continued, 'in case you shoud ever incline to make any man the happiest of his Race, that previous to such a connection you shoud make over your Fortune to Trustees, & by your marriage contract secure it to be your own. . . .'[11]

Then, in words which he was to repeat over and over again in the coming years, he praised

the Philosophic Eye with which you can look on the Honours & Riches of this World; & I consider it & your preserving so pure a mind with so much natural gaiety & vivacity of Temper in the midst of Temptations and in a Profession which exposes a young & beautiful woman to more danger than any other, as almost a miracle. But you have come like gold from the crucible more bright than ever you entered it . . . .[12]

At this time he was perfectly prepared to accept that she might marry someone else.

Mr Wright was obviously in their confidence, aware that Thomas was making a handsome allowance to Harriot, and her new protector encouraged her to trust Wright as her banker. Thomas himself not only gave her shrewd financial advice, but also encouraged her to invest in property – perhaps wishing that he had done so himself. And he certainly was a sharp negotiator. In August 1807 he sent her details of two estates, one at Otham and the other, '494 acres for £1300 near Tunbridge',[13] which seemed 'so very cheap for so much land, there must be some objection to it'.[14] So he proposed to hook the bargain at Otham by telling the owner, Mr Collins, that he had a friend with ready money who wanted it. 'This may retard the sale & whenever you are ready to go to see it, I will send a letter to Mr Collins to say my friend has otherwise disposed of his money. Disappointed of that purchaser he will be the more ready to treat with you.'[15]

We do not know whether Wright advised her to buy Holly Lodge, nor whether Thomas actually paid for it, but she bought the house in 1808. She continued to invest in property; buying an estate in Essex in 1813, Thomas wrote, 'I dare say Mr Wright would advance it [the deposit]; you can tell him you shall have the whole before the rest is wanted.'[16]

Thomas wrote more than sixty letters to Harriot and after 1807 he was clearly deeply in love; but passionate though these letters are, and though they were obviously exchanging kisses, there ran through them the constant affirmation of her virtue and purity. Certainly he would not have introduced her to his daughters had her reputation been doubtful, nor would they have called on her. It is likely that they believed, as Harriot's biographer claims, that she was their father's natural daughter and, in the way of their world, accepted her as such, or they saw it as a passing infatuation which gave him so much obvious happiness that they were willing to receive her. So Lady Burdett in 1810 found time to take her father's letters to his 'sweet young friend'. Fanny herself, always the great commissioner of favours, made frequent use of her. 'Fanny wants Kelly's song', Thomas wrote on 13 December 1811, 'to be sent to Cowley House near Exeter', where the Butes were living.[17] The willing Harriot would pack up and send a 'magic lantern', or the 'music for Macbeth', or fancy-dress costumes for her children.

During the years when Burdett was rousing London to riot, Thomas retreated further and further into his private life, where, with Harriot, he could shut away his worries. By 1810 he was deeply concerned about his wife's health. Although Susannah had been present at the famous breakfast during the siege of Piccadilly, she was becoming increasingly mentally disturbed.

As Thomas wrote to Harriot, he could 'not judge of this disorder. All I know is my distress is great and quite wears me out.'[18] Only the 'thought of your pure mind, your sincere affection' consoled him. 'Heaven bless and reward you! my dearest Love, will ever be my sincere wish, and prayer to The Almighty to whom your truth and honour is known, and who must delight in your virtuous mind.'

With his birthday gift on 10 November 1810 he sent her an even more extravagant letter, wishing with 'the kindest kisses' for 'every blessing to attend you till the good Angels who delight in honour & virtue, generosity and benevolence, like yours, shall waft you to their realms of everlasting happiness prepared for you in Heaven'.[19] Now his letters were often signed with an imprint of a kiss in a cupid's bow – asking her to kiss his letter in that place.

The world, however, was more cynical. When Harriot won £1,000 in a lottery, it was assumed that it had been a gift from her old banker. When she bought herself a paste necklace of brilliants, it was thought that she was flaunting his gift of real diamonds. Though he shrugged off the gossip, she could not; in his view, 'tho' sensibility is the foundation of all goodness, yet there is the tax on it of being too easily injured ... one is almost tempted to wish you were without it, forgetting that *then* you would not be the charming creature you are'.[20]

He wrote to her of the affairs of the theatre; he owned a box at Drury Lane and at Covent Garden, and when Drury Lane burned down he took a box at the Lyceum. He asked Harriot to tell Sheridan to cancel it when the new Drury Lane was built, since he did not need three boxes. The message was not delivered. Harriot probably forgot or Sheridan mislaid it, and Thomas was charged for a year's rent of a box he had not used. His Scottish blood up, he fought a long battle with Sheridan, even calling in his legal friend William Adam. Generous though he was, nobody – and certainly not the unreliable Sheridan – was going to cheat him.

It was now generally accepted at Drury Lane that Harriot would soon be leaving the stage to follow Miss Farren's example. James Grant Raymond, the theatre manager at both the Lyceum and Drury Lane, was particularly fond of Harriot and allowed her more freedom than other actresses. Thomas encouraged him to allow her time off to take a holiday in Brighton – and suitably rewarded him. Raymond, more than anyone else in the theatre, understood and encouraged their relationship, and Thomas trusted and confided in him.

Imprisoned with his old, mad wife, he dreamed of Harriot bathing in the Brighton sea: 'Dearest and best, the blessing of Heaven be upon you!

I think I see you dashing among the waves so fresh and so beautiful.'[21]

Preoccupied as he was with his domestic affairs, he no longer wrote long letters on the political situation, or if he did, few have survived. Many of his old correspondents were dead: Caleb Whitefoord, the Earl of Stair and Colonel Walkinshaw Crawfurd were gone and the Earl of Minto was to follow them in 1814. So Napoleon's retreat from Moscow and Wellington's rise to fame were all distant thunder. Thomas's battles were for sanity and for life itself.

29

The Second Secret Marriage

Ever since the King's decline Thomas had been deeply distressed, recalling the black shadows that had haunted him all his life. His brothers, his wife and the King were all to be lost in the nightmare world of madness, and he felt himself in danger of joining them.

The King had recovered from his illness of 1789, but, after other attacks in 1801, 1803 and 1804, his condition was a constant source of worry. By 1806 he was going blind, suffering 'with patience, resignation and unutterable good humour', wrote his secretary, Herbert Taylor; '... it is impossible to be with our good King without finding fresh cause to love and admire him.'[1] Thomas shared the general affection and sympathy for the old King and must have heard with horror of the brutal restraints put upon him by his 'mad doctors'. The final blow to the King came in October 1810 with the death of his beloved daughter, Amelia. He was now seventy-four, had been blind for some years and from 1812 onwards retreated into a world of his own from which he was only released by his death in 1820. In 1811 the Prince of Wales became Regent and the prospect of the reins of government in his wilful hands increased Thomas's gloom in the dark years of his wife's illness.

In the old days he would have followed the stirring events in Europe with the greatest interest, and even in the midst of his gloom he must have heard with pleasure of the victories of one of his most distinguished customers, the Duke of Wellington. It was Antrobus who dealt with his financial affairs, when, in 1812, he asked Coutts & Co. to advise him on the purchase of an estate:

Having by fortunate circumstances acquired a great situation in the World which will devolve upon my children, it is my duty to secure to them as far as it [is] in my power the means of supporting the Dignity which the favour of the Crown has conferred upon me; and I [conceive?] that I can effect this object solely by a purchase of land.

Such was the Duke's confidence in the judgment of his bankers that he left it to them to find a suitable estate.

Provided the purchase is made in Gt Britain, preferably in England, it is a matter of indifference to me in what county; nor do I wish to have a House upon the lands as I think it more than probable that I shall never be allowed to live in it, nor do I care whether the features of the country in which the land should be purchased are beautiful to look at or otherwise. On every ground therefore the cheapest purchase will be the most desirable.[2]

He instructed them to invest in this way all his stock in the Funds and the money due to him by the East India Company; leaving only £3,000 of stock to 'answer any demands which may suddenly come upon me'.

This was the kind of commission which Antrobus enjoyed, having bought much property for himself. When Stratfield Saye was chosen, he bought one of the other possibilities, the Amesbury estate in Wiltshire, which included Stonehenge. Thomas was glad to leave this and so much else to Antrobus, but he himself wrote to advise the Duke.

Depressed though he was, on 24 June 1814 he stirred himself to come to the assistance of Louis Philippe, who, after the defeat of Napoleon, was returning to France. He gave him a letter of credit for £10,000 and recommended him to the French banker, Perregaux, as a man of excellent character whom he had known intimately for twenty-five years, when Louis Philippe was a young man in the Palais Royal, before the French Revolution.[3]

Walled up in his private misery, he became so ill that his daughters begged him to take a rest but he insisted on watching over poor Susannah. He was persuaded to spend some days with the Earl of Bristol at his magnificent country house at Ickworth, but he was blind to the beauty of the landscaped grounds and, almost suicidal in his despair, begged his host to let him return home.

Once again the memory of Patrick and James deepened his anguish and he refused to allow his wife to be put away. Only the thought of Harriot consoled him. On 15 June 1814 he wrote to her that he had 'truly thought the awful moment was near', but Susannah recovered her senses and speech, and the agony went on. 'I have quite given up all the world. My Beard is grown long & I am I am sure a deplorable looking wretch.'[4]

Finally, however, he gave in, since he was persuaded that his presence made his wife worse. He moved to his old rooms over the Bank in the Strand and left Susan and her daughters to care for his wife. This they did with exceptional tenderness, though it cannot have been easy. There were times when even the sight of the maids was enough to send her into fits of wild raving. But they took her for rides in the country, soothed her to sleep and wrote comforting notes to Thomas. There can be no better testimonial to the love Susannah had inspired in her daughters than their devotion to her in her madness. The burden fell entirely on Susan since Sophia was expecting her last child and was under the care of a resident doctor. On 12 April 1814 she gave birth to Angela Georgina, but Thomas was so upset that he scarcely noticed the arrival of the baby who was to become his heiress.

Susannah became increasingly unmanageable and, according to Harriot's biographer, some time before Christmas she upset a saucepan of boiling water, scalding herself severely, and died after weeks of agony. The date of her death is not known, but it was said that on Twelfth Night, 6 January 1815, Thomas rushed distraught to Harriot, crying, 'Harriot, she is dead.'[5]

On 14 January Susannah was buried in style in Lord Guilford's family vault in the Parish Church of All Saints at Wroxton beside her son-in-law and her little grandson. Nothing was spared – the coffin was handsome and satin-lined and even the nails were solid silver. Her careful soul would, however, undoubtedly have approved her husband's practical sense: he asked for, and got, a rebate on the funeral director's bill for ready cash.

It was not until a hundred years later that Francis Money-Coutts – her great-grandson – placed a tablet to her memory on the chancel wall. Even then '*Quod habuit haec fecit*', 'She did what she could', is a somewhat patronising dismissal. In fact, although for her last fifteen years she had been physically and mentally broken, in earlier days she had been an excellent wife and mother. She was no mere servant – Reverend William Bagshaw Stevens was amazed at the deference with which Thomas treated his wife's judgment. She was deeply interested in politics and even Francis Burdett could write to her daughter that he loved her mother. She became passionately involved in the trial of Warren Hastings,* attending Westminster Hall every day when she could. She shared her husband's love of the theatre and was at ease with his intellectual friends like Caleb Whitefoord, and even, in her later years, with princes and dukes.

Her husband's noble friends might smile at her, but it was usually with affection rather than malice. In fact, though she sometimes appeared eccentric, she was no stranger than some of her husband's great lady customers. The unconventional Duchess of Gordon did not mind when, her guests being late, Susannah bustled to help, explaining how to keep fish warm without spoiling. Thomas admired her practical good sense and so did Caleb, to whom she gave instructions, when building his new house at Hastings, not to use sea sand in the mortar as it never dried out.

* As the first Governor-General of Bengal he held office for thirteen years, 1772–85. After his retirement he was impeached for his conduct of affairs in the province. His trial before the House of Lords, which lasted from 1788 to 1795, when he was acquitted, became a major social occasion.

But perhaps the best testimonial to Susannah was that to her daughters, even after their grand marriages, she was always their 'dearest Mamma'.

In 1815 Thomas was eighty, overcome by the strain of the last years, plagued by an attack of erysipelas, and convinced that he was about to die. He was also worried by the thought of Harriot's future, since he did not want her to suffer the same fate as Mrs Fitzherbert and Mrs Jordan.

Mrs Fitzherbert had been discarded by the Prince Regent in 1811, and Thomas had felt sympathy for her. On 11 September she had written a sad letter to the banker she loved and trusted. She apologised for the delay in answering him, thanking him for his

very kind letter and anxiety about me ... but I was so oppressed and miserable that I had not courage or resolution to take up my pen or indeed attend to anything. I will not enter more fully on this melancholy subject for it only tears afresh the wounds which nothing but time can heal. ... I am sorry Mrs Coutts continues so indifferent.[6]

Undoubtedly it was Thomas who advised her to write as she did in 1813 with unaccustomed firmness to the Prince Regent. She reminded him that 'when the memorable event of our Union took place in '85 ... you were ... pleased to settle on me £10,000 per ann. ... your difficulties in money matters put it out of your power ... to give me more than £3000 per ann',[7] which was in 1810 increased to £6,000. Now she asked to receive the allowance he had promised her twenty-five years earlier. A year later in August 1814 she was still appealing to the Prince, reminding him that the allowance she was asking for was to pay debts incurred when they had been living together.

Thomas, though submerged in his own troubles, gave Mrs Fitzherbert what help and comfort he could. However, it is possible that it was Mr Dickie who actually arranged her affairs at this time.

There was another reminder of the delicacy of Harriot's position. In the summer of 1811, Mrs Jordan was at the theatre in Cheltenham playing the part of Nell in *The Devil to Pay*, when, instead of the expected ripple of her famous laugh, she suddenly burst into tears. It appeared that she had received a message from the Duke of Clarence asking her to meet him at Maidenhead to discuss their separation.

The news must have shocked Harriot deeply and concerned Thomas. The Duke had been so obviously happy with Mrs Jordan for many years, had enjoyed his home and family, and was constantly grateful to her for her love and often for her financial support. Loyally, Mrs Jordan insisted it was only because of his need of money that he had deserted her: the Duke had to find a rich wife. He made her an allowance with the condition that she should not return to the stage. But, like Mrs Fitzherbert, she became reduced to near bankruptcy and returned to her acting, thus provoking an uncharacteristic letter from Thomas to Harriot. He found the reports of an ageing actress back on the boards thoroughly distasteful, blaming her for her greed. Once again he was made too uncomfortably aware that ladies who lived outside the rules had 'The Devil to Pay'.

The knowledge of Mrs Jordan's and Mrs Fitzherbert's misery made Thomas acutely aware of Harriot's vulnerability should he die. There was only one solution: he must marry her immediately.

The real story of the next months will never be fully known: legend, gossip and scandal cloud the truth. But some facts are firm. On 17 January 1815, three days after Susannah's funeral, Harriot attended the Vicar General's office to 'pray a licence' to solemnise an 'intended marriage' in the Church of St Pancras, swearing that she had lived for four weeks in the parish of St Pancras, that is at Holly Lodge, Highgate. On the next day both Harriot and Thomas signed a marriage contract, which was witnessed by the curate, the Reverend W. B. Champneys, and by J. G. Raymond, the theatre manager of Drury Lane.

By this contract Thomas made sure that all Harriot's estates and personal property in Essex, Middlesex and Gloucestershire, her jewels, silver plate and securities, her stocks and money in the bank, should be always and entirely at her own disposal and command, the same as if she was still unmarried; and that she could sell or dispose of her money without her husband's consent. Finally, if she outlived him, he left her '£1000 as a clear annuity free from all taxations'.[8] Harriot for her part agreed to accept the annuity 'in Bar of Dower or claim on the estate of Thomas Coutts'.[9]

The wedding took place at old St Pancras Church on 18 January 1815.

If the contract bears the banker's stamp, the curious arrangements to conceal the wedding suggest the hand of the theatre manager. Raymond's part in the business is obscure. It was said by his biographer that Thomas gave him £1,000 as a bribe to secure Harriot's consent, but it is more likely that, since he was ill at the time, he paid Raymond to deal with the marriage arrangements. So that the names Coutts and Mellon should not be obvious in the register, two fictitious entries were added below on the same page, both signed by Mr Champneys, the curate who married them, and both witnessed by James Raymond and a mysterious Wm Houghton.

Once again Thomas took refuge in obscurity, his second marriage being as secret as his first.

After the wedding, Harriot returned to Holly Lodge and Thomas to Stratton Street, where he collapsed. For weeks he was near death and Harriot was beside herself with worry. It was said that a month after their marriage Harriot drove to Stratton Street to ask how he was; on being told that he was worse, she cried out, 'Good Heavens, tell me all, I am his wife!'[10] Such a melodramatic outburst was in character, but whether the story is true or not, it was certainly not until the end of February that Thomas confessed to his daughters. Even then it was with obvious reluctance that he sent what he called 'a paper' to Susan, asking her to pass it on to Fanny and Sophia.

At the end of February he told Harriot that he had

given Her my paper ... (that lay with my will) ... if I hear nothing from her by next Monday I will ask it from her again & send it to Lady Bute and acquaint Lady G with 'the happy Wednesday at St Pancras' & a week after my paper goes I will acquaint Lady Bute of the same. Lady G will probaby tell Lady Burdett & I think I will desire her to do so.[11]

Secretive and unwilling to face argument as always, he put off the evil day of confession, urging Harriot to 'be more composed & bear things with more patience', and 'to be happy and think of your own Tom'.[12]

Susan, who must have taken care of her father during his illness, was shocked and incensed:

... I should not speak the truth were I to say I considered that day as happy when you first met her at Cheltenham, or that if I could recall that day I would *not*. But no doubt all this IS permitted is to be considered *as desirable* spite of all appearances and wishes – still there is something attached to this connexion which strikes at my heart. *I cannot, cannot help it*, and you must forgive me! – but I will certainly fulfill to the utmost your request as long as the Almighty in his infinite goodness is pleased to grant me life and capacity and with happiness too will I fulfill it in the full confidence that my dear Mama who is looking upon me must approve – as *I do* because *it is YOUR wish*, and from this moment forward to the end of my existence I am perfectly willing to do whatever you may express. God Almighty bless, preserve and guard you, for of such *I am sure* is the Kingdom of Heaven.[13]

Next Thomas informed the editor of *The Times*, who announced on Friday 2 March that 'On Wednesday the marriage took place of Thomas Coutts and Harriot Mellon'. Readers were meant to assume that the wedding had taken place two days earlier. The affronted vicar, the Reverend J. Moore, of St Pancras, who was quite unaware that the famous banker had been married in his church, investigated and declared the marriage null and void, writing the words 'this marriage was illegally solemnised' against the entry in the register. Burdett was said to have rushed up to St Pancras, determined to prove that Thomas had acted illegally in inventing witnesses.

But Thomas was determined. On 12 April 1815 he married Harriot again at St Pancras Church. This time a different curate, the Reverend W. Fallofield, officiated. Champneys had been disgraced and presumably the vicar did not want to get involved. Once again Raymond was a witness, supported by the sexton, G. Hamp. However, Thomas and Harriot always celebrated as their true anniversary their first wedding day of 18 January.

Sophia was as shocked by her father's marriage as Susan but accepted it, with extravagant expressions of undying love:

Never can I be *sufficiently* grateful to the Almighty God, who has permitted and granted me the heart felt delight of shewing you *during your most precious and invaluable* life, how religiously I should abide by *all* your dear, dear wishes should it be my destiny to survive you.[14]

Fanny, from the distant comfort of her Italian villa, could afford to be philosophical and, during all the subsequent rows, became the peacemaker. Thomas had expected his daughters to accept their new stepmother as mistress of 1 Stratton Street, but Susan had been running her father's house for years and resented Harriot, and her black eyes could flash with a temper as fierce as Harriot's own.

There were such unforgettable scenes, such spectacular rows that Thomas, as he wrote to Fanny, now realised 'that to live together must be hell upon earth if people are not cordial & easy with each other'.[15] He withdrew with Harriot and lived for some months in a small house in Southampton Street, Covent Garden. Here they could have been happy, were it not that Harriot worried that he might be considered 'degraded in society'[16] by living there. For his own part he was glad to be out of Stratton Street. 'I never was attached to the residence,' he told Fanny; 'on the contrary I have almost always wished to get rid of it.'[17]

Finally a solution was found. Harriot bought both houses, 1 Stratton Street and 78 Piccadilly, from Thomas for £30,000 'out of the stocks', 'which money', he wrote to Fanny, 'will go into the mass of my fortune & you all three of you will share it'.[18] Thomas explained to Fanny that Harriot had always begged him to take her money, but he had, in the past, insisted that she remain independent. But now he said he was really glad of her money. He had 'lent an enormous sum to the Duke of York and indeed nearly the same to several old friends of my house in the Strand'.[19] He felt no guilt about Susan, having already 'bought & paid for two country homes' for her.[20]

Sophia might have been prepared to accept Harriot, but Burdett was passionate in his wife's defence. Undoubtedly he saw himself as the champion of daughters deprived of their rights, and his hasty reaction to Harriot was patrician rather than democratic. In 1816 Thomas was so incensed by Burdett's attitude that he gave him orders to quit the house next door in Piccadilly. He regretted Sophia's distress but, as he told her, 'I must ever express the contempt I think his conduct & letters to me deserve. They were such as, was I a man of his age, I do not believe he durst have shewn.'[21] Burdett had written that he considered himself degraded by remaining in the Piccadilly house, and they moved across Green Park to a house in St James's Place, which remained their London home for the rest of their lives. Disraeli remembered it: 'Everything stately and old fashioned but agreeable. The house charming: the dining room looking into delightful gardens, with much old timber, beyond it St James's Park.'[22]

Susan was offered the Piccadilly house which they had vacated and there was temporary peace, at least on the surface. But the daughters still showed their bitter resentment and Harriot, wounded, responded with spectacular rages.

Thomas was often offended that Susan and Sophia made no effort to introduce Harriot to their friends, but he was consoled by the continued friendship of the Prince of Wales and the Dukes of Kent, York and Clarence, who dined with them at Holly Lodge and Stratton Street. The daughters must have read with chagrin in *The Times* of 17 May 1815, 'Yesterday the Prince Regent dined with Mr & Mrs Coutts at their rural villa of Holly Lodge where there was a select party of distinguished guests to meet His Royal Highness.'

However, the unkindest cut came in July 1817, when Thomas heard from Colonel MacMahon that Susan had offered to present Harriot at court, knowing that Queen Charlotte would refuse to receive her. On 15 July Thomas wrote a sizzling letter to his daughter: 'So you was carrying my wife to the Queen when you knew she was to be rejected & affronted: not to do her honor, but to witness, and, I must suppose, to enjoy her disgrace. What could be so wicked so malicious or so spiteful?'[23]

On 5 January 1818, in a letter to Fanny in Italy, he complained of the cruel way

Lady Guilford ... has treated us since the day of our marriage, now three years. I have not a fault to find with my wife ... and to the tranquil way in which we now live I feel assured I owe the life I have – without her I do not wish to live ... but all has gone (astonishingly) for nothing, and wicked abuse has been her return even in the hearing of my own & her servants; and my eyes & ears have seen & heard such things that human nature could support no longer and all intercourse must be at an end.[24]

Susan's disgrace was complete when, in 1818, she refused to invite Harriot to the wedding of her stepdaughter, Maria North, to the young Marquess of Bute, the son of the first Marquess by his first marriage. Enraged, Thomas tried in vain to persuade the Duke of York to cancel his offer to give the bride away. Understandably, the Duke refused, though he would like to have obliged his banker. Susan moved to her house in Putney and was never forgiven: Harriot's wrath pursued the Guilfords for generations, even beyond the grave.

Harriot had at least the consolation of her husband's adoring letters, some of which were written on the spur of the moment, as it delights me to express the comfort I feel & the pleasure I know any repetition of my love & affection always gives you. Thomas Coutts. PS Oh, my dearest. You are a most extraordinarily good intelligent person; intuitive knowledge from Heaven & perfect goodness graces every action of your life. The gift of Heaven! ... Actions can never repay all your noble & unceasing & most affectionate consideration & love to your own Dearest Coutts.[25]

There was one step he could take to repay her. In 1818 he made a will giving 'all I might possess, or that hereafter I might acquire or be entitled to at my death, wholly & solely to my dear wife, irrevocably'.

On 18 September 1818, his eighty-second birthday, he wrote a solemn summary of his life, in King Lear vein, to his daughter Fanny:

Thomas Coutts after he had settled as a Banker in the Strand, married an amiable good woman by whom he had four sons, who all died in infancy & three Daughters. ... [They] lived always with their Father who was devotedly kind to them, & they were always dutiful & kind to him till he thought fit to marry in old age a young woman of most admirable character in every particular ... from her cradle universally beloved ... but his three daughters incited all nearly connected with them to abuse & ill treat her, which Thomas Coutts could not suffer with patience & at last was forced to cut off all intercourse with them.[26]

Two years later, concerned that his will was not adequate, he wrote to his solicitor, John Parkinson, reaffirming his decision and asking him to draw up a formal will to that effect. He hoped no one would accuse him of injustice to his children since he had given each '£25,000 on their marriage and also settled on each £25,000 besides many gifts of various kinds'.[27] He hoped that his wife would reward his daughters 'according to their deserts, but not by any means beyond the same'.[28]

In 1818 Thomas was not only concerned about the succession to his own kingdom, the Bank in the Strand, he was also deeply involved in the affairs of the royal princes, who were now belatedly realising that the succession to the British throne was threatened.

Of George III's children, twelve remained: five childless princesses and seven ageing princes, only three of whom were legitimately married. The death in childbirth of the Prince of Wales's daughter, Charlotte, wife of Prince Leopold of Saxe-Coburg, had shocked the nation and roused the royal dukes to the danger. Unless an heir could be produced, George III's line would become extinct.

The Prince and Caroline were separated and would have no further children. The Dukes of York and Cumberland were both childless, and the Duke of Sussex ruled himself out. He had separated from Lady Augusta Murray in 1801 and was now living with Lady Cecilia Underwood. The other three princes therefore began a comic race to produce an heir.

For Edward and his 'old French lady' it was no comedy. The Duke had already secretly considered deserting her, not to breed an heir, but to acquire an extra allowance from Parliament. Now it was doubly important to win a legitimate bride. On 11 July 1818, to the infinite distress of Madame de Montgenet, he married Leopold's sister, Victoria. Edward secured an allowance from Parliament of £25,000 a year, and gained a daughter, born on 24 May 1819. Madame de Montgenet was granted an allowance and with quiet dignity retreated broken-hearted to a convent in Paris and thence to an obscure end.

William, Duke of Clarence, who had long ago discarded loyal Mrs Jordan, now joined with Edward on 11 July in a double wedding. His bride was another German princess, Adelaide of Saxe-Meiningen. Though he had fathered ten lusty children before, Adelaide's babies did not survive. The Duke of Cumberland's son, George, was born on 27 May, a sad child who was to become the blind King of Hanover.

The Duke of Kent did not live long to enjoy his triumph in the royal matrimonial stakes. Eight months after the birth of his daughter, Victoria, he caught a chill while on holiday at Sidmouth and suddenly died. Thomas's impecunious customer had left many debts, but had at least bequeathed to the nation a child who was to become a most remarkable queen.

30

The Antrobus Family

In the years after his marriage, while Thomas wrestled with his ill-health and domestic problems, it was Edmund Antrobus who directed the Bank during the difficult post-war years. The economy had boomed during the war, but now disbanded soldiers returned to find no work, nowhere to live in the overcrowded industrial cities and nothing to eat in a half-starved Britain. Inevitably there were riots in the cities and rick-burning in the countryside. Castlereagh wrote despairingly to Wellington of the 'sour, discontented temper among our friends, considerable distress throughout the country and endless debates on the economy'.[1] His proposal to keep income tax was defeated in the Commons to the relief of the City, but the problems remained: how to pay the £30 million for the army of occupation, the massive sums needed to pay the pensions of disbanded soldiers, and the rest of the cost of the long wars against France?

Wellington, commander-in-chief of the army of occupation, negotiated three loans to France raised by the bankers Baring & Hope, which enabled France to pay reparations, and came back to England with a dazzling reputation as soldier, diplomat and financier. On his return he was appointed Master General of the Ordnance and made his home at Apsley House, a few minutes' walk from Stratton Street. It is unlikely that he had much to do with his neighbours in Piccadilly, though in the last years of his life Thomas must often have seen the slight, upright figure riding by on his way to Whitehall. Certainly the partners in the Strand viewed their famous customer with some apprehension. In 1823 he was to introduce his Spanish friend and old ally at Waterloo, General Alava. 'This is my friend', he told them, 'and as long as I have any money at your house, let him have it to any amount that he thinks proper to draw for.'[2]

Though Thomas no longer followed public affairs as closely as of old, he could not completely shut out the problems of poverty and unrest in post-Waterloo Britain, especially since once again Burdett emerged as the champion of the oppressed.

In 1819 Burdett had read the account of the massacre at Peterloo, when a peaceful demonstration had been brutally attacked by soldiers, killing some and wounding many. Ever since the anticlimax of his return from the Tower of London in 1810, he had been quiescent – still admired by his followers but no longer their idol. Now he charged once again into the ring: he immediately wrote a passionate attack on the Government, which was alleged to be seditious. The case against him took months to complete, but finally he was let off with a comparatively small fine and a short spell in prison.

Edmund Antrobus has, for too long, been overshadowed by the greater fame of Thomas Coutts, but it must never be forgotten that for the last twenty years of Thomas's life it was he, with the help of Coutts Trotter and Edward Marjoribanks, who held the Bank steady through the perilous years of war with France, when there was a constant fear of invasion, and through the distress and turmoil that followed Waterloo.

After their disagreements of 1793 there was now harmony between them, though Thomas must often have watched Edmund's acquisition of more and more property with some envy, for the older he got, the more he regretted that he had not invested in estates. Edmund and Philip bought back land in Cheshire which had originally belonged to their family. When Philip died in 1816 all his property in Cheam and in Cheshire* went to Edmund, who, as we have seen, also bought the Palladian mansion and estate of Amesbury in Wiltshire. He also bought land in Roxburghshire, which gave him the right to vote in the post-war election – a right he exercised with great enthusiasm on behalf of Gilbert Elliot, rushing up to Scotland to give his support.

When 'Fish' Craufurd died in 1814 Edmund took over his house at Hyde Park Corner, which he had bought some time before Craufurd's death. Now he reflected with some satisfaction that his drawing-rooms were as large as Thomas's at 1 Stratton Street. So, as he drove along Piccadilly in his new chariot (which cost him £384 0s 6d), or dined on his handsome silver plates (£1,366 0s 0d) under the bronze candelabras (at £153 6s 0d), Edmund could feel secure. In 1816 through Thomas's influence he was made a baronet. Sir Edmund was now a man of property, and his air of solid success was good for the image of Coutts & Co. He brought his nephew, Edmund, into the Bank and the young man sat beside him to learn the business. He could now occasionally take time off, travelling abroad for his health, but he rarely visited his Scottish property or his estate at Amesbury. Congleton in Cheshire remained his real home, where he could relax completely. He was particularly close to his sister Jane, who

* Between 1791 and 1804 Edmund bought Horton and Rushton on the borders of Staffordshire and Philip bought about 2,000 acres of land near Rushton. Their cousin, Thomas Rowley (died 1819), acted as their rent collector and Edmund proved a great help to his son when he was deported to Australia.

was greatly loved in her home town. He paid for her street to be paved and, at the end of her life, bought the house next to hers because she was worried that a silk weaver might take it over and dreaded the noise. Nor did Edmund forget his Sanxay relatives at Cheam. He secretly made an allowance to three cousins, elderly ladies, not wishing to embarrass them by his charity.

Above all he looked after his nephews: his brother John could not have taken better care of young Edmund and Gibbs or given them more affection. Thomas thought sadly of his four dead sons as he watched Edmund and Gibbs growing into two handsome young men. For Sir Edmund was looking to the future of the Bank and ensuring that young Edmund and Gibbs were fitted by their education for a changing world. One of them he hoped would be his successor in the Bank in the Strand. In fact Gibbs became a diplomat, leaving Edmund to follow in his uncle's footsteps.

Sir Edmund had himself been thoroughly grounded in the classics by the formidable headmaster of his Cheshire school. He was a man of wide culture with an interest in and a knowledge of art, which had been encouraged by his uncle, a connoisseur and collector of pictures. He knew the importance of learning foreign languages and one of his enduring contributions to the Bank was his insistence that his nephews should be fluent in French and German. Likewise he encouraged the clerks to learn other languages. So he strengthened and increased the contacts in Europe that Thomas had made at the end of the eighteenth century. His Huguenot relations perhaps could take some credit for this outward-looking banker.

Soon after the deaths of their mother and father in 1793 and 1794, Sir Edmund had been appointed the boys' guardian by the Court of Chancery, promising an allowance for each boy of £75 per annum. He also, 'wishing to have the bringing up of two young people who might probably inherit his fortune',[3] proposed a bond of £2,500 to each on attaining the age of twenty-one. In fact, thanks to Sir Edmund's financial skill, the boys inherited much more than this and Edmund showed them unfailing kindness and generosity throughout their young lives.

So the boys had a secure and happy childhood with no financial worries. Sir Edmund had explained to their grandmother that the boys had inherited £24,000, which he invested for them and which brought them an annual income of £1,130. Twenty years later their stock had quadrupled in value.

At first the boys had lived with their mother's family at Saint Hill near East Grinstead, where they were happy and loved and ran free in the Sussex meadows. When Mrs Crawford died on 7 September 1797, their maternal uncle, Charles Payne Crawford, took over their care for a short time. But Sir Edmund never much liked him – he was a fussy man and 'too generous to ladies not necessarily of his own family'. Young Edmund was sent to a private school at the age of five and a tutor was found for little Gibbs. The Reverend Richard Littlehales was to be for the next decade closer than a parent, their devoted counsellor and friend. Sir Edmund decided to give the boys 'a liberal education' before sending them to Eton. He settled them with Littlehales at the home of a French émigrée, Madame de la Bourdonnaye, where they remained for four years and became fluent in French.

Charles Payne Crawford, who felt shut out and jealous, now wrote a pompous letter to Sir Edmund complaining of the lady's morals and suggesting that she was Littlehales's mistress. Sir Edmund replied coolly that it was no business of theirs even if it was true, and that the boys' own uncles had mistresses too. It is perhaps surprising that in an age of licence, no echo of scandal has survived about either Edmund or Philip, neither of whom ever married.

Once the boys were fluent in French, he sent them with their tutor for two years to Hanover and Dresden to learn German. On their return Edmund entered Eton, to be followed later by Gibbs. Thus began a long connection between Coutts & Co. and a school that was to provide many of its directors until the present day. The obliging Littlehales took a small house nearby with their uncle's housekeeper, Mrs Fellows, in charge. After a short period in Dr Vicabe's House, it was finally agreed that the boys should live out with their tutor. They remained at Eton until 1809, where they both made excellent progress.

They spent their holidays at Cheam with Uncle Philip or at Brighton or in London with Uncle Edmund. Sir Edmund watched their progress with pride. Usually a tolerant man, only once did he deal sternly with young Edmund, whose passion for hunting led him to 'subscribe for the keeping of hounds at Eton'. Even then he promised that he would not tell Uncle Philip – who was more severe – nor 'to show his displeasure in public', because he did not want young Edmund's 'very high character to be diminished'. But he punished him by cutting his holiday riding.

The boys left Eton with glowing praise from the headmaster. It was customary at that time for the pupils to give the head a leaving present – and Edmund, as Littlehales reported, 'gave the Doctor his present, which was a very handsome one & came home with a very happy countenance'. Dr Goodall had asked for his portrait, 'as a mark of his favour', and was fortunate to receive an excellent painting by Sir Thomas Lawrence, which hung for years in the Provost's Lodge.* The grateful Doctor wrote enthusiastically to Sir Edmund that there were 'no boys in the school from whose parents he had received such kind attention'.

* Lawrence was paid £36 5s 0d on both 10 and 29 November 1809, and £15 0s 0d for the frame.

Before Edmund went on to St John's College, Cambridge, both boys spent six months at a house at Mudeford near Christchurch, where Littlehales coached the older boy. But their faithful tutor now 'wished to be relieved of his care', because he felt that he was 'advanced in life' – he was fifty-four – and he had for years past neglected his living. However, he was persuaded to stay with Edmund through his Cambridge career since his uncle felt slightly concerned at Edmund's 'natural volatility'.

The boys were now separated. Gibbs was sent to be tutored by a Dr Middleton, rector of Tansor near Oundle, but he visited Edmund at St John's and spent the Christmas of 1810 in college, where they were joined by Uncle Edmund. Gibbs found Middleton a sterner master than his devoted Littlehales, but he earned high praise for his 'goodness of heart and rectitude of principle'. Edmund, Middleton thought, had 'talents probably in soundness and solidity not inferior to Gibbs, but he was less popular'. Edmund was to take these talents with him when he became a partner at Coutts & Co.

Since 1810 Philip Antrobus had lived in contented retirement at his home in Cheam. In June of that year he had written to Spencer Perceval 'relinquishing the sale of Exchequer Bills for Government' and recommending his partners Wood & Brown as his successors. They had in fact been conducting the stockbroking business for many years and continued the close co-operation with Coutts & Co. The link remained after the firm became James Capel & Co. and continues to the present day.

In 1814 Thomas had been occupied with Susannah's illness and, anxious that Sir Edmund should not be overworked, had gladly agreed to take in his nephew, young Edmund, as a partner. He left it to Sir Edmund to fix the 'plan of his share of the profit, as well as the arrangement of your attendance'. As was his custom he insisted that the new partner should read the articles of partnership, but his word of honour was enough: he never asked for a legal contract to be drawn up. He was sure that everyone would now give 'every indulgence to Sir Edmund with respect to attendance', to which he was well entitled after being so many years in the House.

Sir Edmund proposed

not only to give my nephew, if you should be pleased to admit him, a 1/32nd share out of my proportion, but also to give a similar share in equal moieties between Mr. Trotter and Mr. Marjoribanks, or to make any other arrangement you may think proper or liberal on my part ... as I have now been nearly forty years a Partner, I hope it will not be thought unreasonable that I should be desirous to have some time that I may more particularly call my own. I would therefore beg to submit to your kind consideration that my attendance on Monday and Saturday should be optional on my part.

Thomas was saddened by the death of Philip Antrobus in 1816. He wrote to Sir Edmund:

May heaven prepare us all for the great change he has now experienced, but few appear to possess the same placidity and equality of mind he did, which indeed fits us better than any other quality for the vicissitudes our lives are more or less subject to – as well as for the happy close his has come to. The loss of so near a tie and so constant and steady a friend, cannot fail to be severely felt however expected or unavoidably looked for, and I have continued ever through life to feel the effect occasionally recurring deeply to my mind – like what I have often heard say of bodily wounds and hurts.

No one could have been more delighted than Thomas and Harriot when, in 1817, young Edmund married Anne Lindsay. Harriot arranged a splendid wedding feast. Her lively aunt, Lady Ann Barnard, described the celebration:

Were I to repeat the number of Tureens of Turtle the Turbots – Haunches of Venison – Wines of all sorts with every man and every woman their own bottle I should not finish till to-morrow – the whole was crowned with Pap Hugh's carving up the last 4 pineapples after the Chinese fashion which was applauded by all, and he looked not a little proud – I sat by Sir Edmund as did Jane and I never saw him in such spirits. . . .

Sir Edmund had reason to be proud. He had cared for his nephews as kindly as any father, and now could hope that his name would be carried on in the Bank to further generations. Thomas might well have felt a shadow of regret and envy over the merriment of the feast.

31

Thomas Coutts, Finale

For the last years of Thomas's life his partners worked together in harmony. They were an impressive team, inspiring confidence. The direction of the Bank was in the firm and steady hands of Edmund Antrobus. Coutts Trotter was more than competent, and they were supported by diligent, painstaking Edward Marjoribanks.

The organisation of the Bank ran smoothly under Andrew Dickie, who was becoming in practice, if not in name, a fourth partner. When Thomas was away or ill, as he often was, Dickie wrote daily: his letters show how much responsibility he was now shouldering. The partners wrote too, always careful to ask Thomas's advice, though increasingly he would reply, 'do as you think best'.

However, in 1818 there were decisions to be made that only Thomas could take. The Duke of York's debts were now horrendous, and Thomas agreed to come to his rescue. His partners in the operation were his old friend, William Adam, financial adviser to the Prince Regent, and his lawyer James Farrer. Together they raised a huge loan on the security of the Duke's Oatlands estate. Once again Dickie was invaluable in dealing with the details of the loan. No one, not even Thomas, knew more about the royal affairs since he had dealt with them for so many years. But also increasingly in the last years Thomas had relied on the advice of William Adam, delegating much of his private business to him.

In Thomas's last years Fanny lived mostly in Italy, and Susan had moved to her house in Putney and had her home at Waldershare. When in London Sophia and Burdett lived at St James's Place, but they were often away at their house in Wimbledon, or at their country houses in Ramsbury in Wiltshire or at Foremark in Derbyshire. So Harriot reigned in Stratton Street. The absence of Thomas's daughters and the new sense of security mellowed her and gradually, thanks to her, harmony was restored in the family. And though for the rest of her life there would be spectacular outbursts, particularly with the hot-headed Burdett, there would always be generous apologies on both sides: but she never forgot or forgave Susan's abusive language and insulting behaviour.

On the surface at least it was a happy and united family that surrounded Thomas. For this, as for everything else, he was deeply grateful to Harriot. With her he found peace and comfort, especially in the simplicity of their villa at Highgate. Holly Lodge was the place Harriot loved best in all the world. From the top of their hill they could look down on the city wreathed in fog and be content to let the world go by. The grandchildren remembered them wandering arm-in-arm through the lawns and groves of Holly Lodge – Thomas carrying a nosegay of the gillyflowers she loved.

He always claimed that Harriot prolonged his life and certainly she gave him the comfort, warmth and affection that, as a motherless boy, he had never known. She knitted him shawls for his rheumatic shoulders and made him nourishing soups.

It was Harriot who persuaded him to be immortalised in marble and paint, something he had always resisted. She took him to the sculptor, Joseph Nollekens, whose biographer, J. T. Smith, vividly recorded the scene in the studio as Mrs Nollekens remembered it. Mrs Nollekens found the 'savoury soup' scene 'comically curious'. She herself watched from her high chair, crippled, wry-necked and with swollen legs:

Mr. Coutts was blowing his broth, attended by Mrs. Coutts, a lively woman, most fashionably dressed; whilst Nollekens, to use the commonest of all similes, nearly as deaf as a post, was prosecuting his bust, and at the same time, repeating his loud interrogations as to the price of stocks to his sitter; who had twice most good-temperedly stayed the spoon, and turned his head to answer him.[1]

Thomas also, thanks to Harriot, agreed at last to be painted for the Earl of Buchan and commissioned Beechey to paint Harriot's portrait as well. At the same time the artist painted his niece Frances's two daughters, Lilian and Sophia.

The best study of Thomas, it is generally agreed, is Sir Francis Chantrey's full-size statue, which was done posthumously in 1827. The sculptor told the Duke of St Albans that it was the 'finest thing he ever did' and that he was 'very proud of it'. He himself chose the best place for it in 1 Stratton Street, 'on a marble slab in the green drawing room opposite the glass at one end of the room'.[2] It now dominates the garden court of the banking hall at Coutts & Co. in the Strand.

At least in his last years Thomas could look once again on a united family, and on a young grandson, who, it was generally accepted, could succeed him as head of the Bank.

Fanny's son, Dudley Coutts Stuart, was born on 11 November 1803. His birth had been a rare ray of sunlight in the gloom of that year and from earliest childhood he radiated an uncommon charm. There are glimpses of the 'handsome stout boy' sailing at Sidmouth in 1811; or in his

Harlequin's dress at a party at Petersham; or shining in a play that he and his cousins performed for their grandfather on his birthday in September 1813. Encouraged by Fanny, Dudley never forgot to send Thomas a charming birthday note on what Fanny called 'that blessed day'. Dudley and his lovely sister, Frances, gave their grandfather hope for the future.

He was educated at home by a gifted tutor, the Reverend E. Mortlake, who may perhaps have been responsible for Dudley's later humanitarian sympathies. He and Frances were brought up in the grandest style, living in great country houses – Mount Stuart on the Isle of Bute and Petersham in Hampshire. Bute also owned most of Cardiff, including the castle, and other Welsh properties which he had inherited from his first wife. The children spent some of their early years happily in Wales, though it is doubtful whether they ever lived in Cardiff Castle. A large part of their youth, however, was spent abroad. Fanny took them on the Grand Tour to Rome, Florence and Naples, where they climbed Vesuvius and sailed on a halcyon sea.

Adored by his mother, Dudley might well have become a gilded youth, spoilt and extravagant. Even their father, the domineering Marquess of Bute, seems to have softened to his last children. In contrast he had bullied his other sons by his first wife, taken custody of his grandchildren and insisted on their rigorous education. When the Marquess died suddenly in Rome in 1814, Dudley and his sister were heartbroken. Fanny was touched but not a little surprised at their grief. After their father's death the two children lived with Fanny in comfortable Italian villas near Naples.

With such a background it seems surprising that Fanny ever thought of Dudley as a banker. Yet she wrote constantly to her father emphasising his suitability. 'His right headedness in him which is I often tell him quite Coutts,' she wrote in 1817.[3] And again, 'my delight would be to have him the instrument of continuing your name & business when you & I shall have disappeared from this busy scene'.[4] She delighted to think of 'Dudley *Coutts* going down to the Strand with you in the morning'.[5] She hoped that 'altho' he is a Lord that you will in his particular instance wave this impediment . . . he is even very anxious to begin already keeping accounts . . . & seems really quite alive to it'.[6] If anyone could have persuaded Thomas to break his firm rules it was Fanny. Sons of nobles, he had always insisted, did not make good clerks, and partners ought to have outside previous experience.

It had been Bute's wish that Dudley should go to Cambridge and, in 1821, he was admitted to his tutor's old college, Christ's. Here, according to Lady Holland, who was no flatterer, he was 'universally beloved'.[7] His uncle, Sir Francis, joined the chorus of praise: 'I have but one fault to find in him. He is too handsome.'[8]

As for Thomas, he had watched Dudley with increasing pleasure during a three-month visit in 1818, when, as he wrote to Hester Stanhope, 'he is really a most uncommon character, full of good sence and information and elegant in his appearance'.[9] Now he could die happy, with his beloved Fanny's son to carry on his name and his business. But was there the slightest hint of doubt that 'uncommon' and 'elegant' Dudley might not want to be a banker?

In the last two years of his life Thomas found it increasingly difficult to attend to the affairs of the Bank. His memory – once exceptional – was now fading, his handwriting on his last letter of September 1821 to Fanny was written in an agony of effort and was almost indecipherable. Burdett remembered that on his last visit he appeared to have become quite senile, yet there were periods when the strong mind triumphed, and he attempted to keep in touch with the Strand until the end.

In his final year he fell and broke his ribs, and a resident doctor was now necessary. Harriot herself was often ill and so demanding that their doctors did not stay. There was the additional distress caused by a doctor who left them and committed suicide. Though Harriot was cleared by his family, it was assumed that her temper was to blame.

On Sunday, 24 February 1822, Thomas died, with his daughters, Sophia and Susan, and their children around him. He was eighty-six years and six months. Fanny was in Italy, but Dudley represented her. Robert, Burdett's only son, was now estranged from his family, so it was Dudley, the only other male grandchild, who was the chief mourner and the heir apparent.

Harriot made sure that the funeral was worthy of her 'dear Tom'. The procession left Stratton Street on Monday 4 March for the five-day journey to the Guilfords' family tomb at Wroxton.

The hearse was drawn by six black horses, bearing on the palls the armorial escutcheons of the family. There were supporters with scarves, three mourning coaches with six horses, the carriage of the deceased drawn by four black horses followed by above forty noblemen and gentlemen's carriages among which were those of Their Royal Highnesses the Dukes of York, Clarence and Sussex. . . . The principal mourners were Lord Dudley Stuart and Mr Coutts Trotter.[10]

Thomas was buried beside his wife and grandson as he had wished. It was a splendid funeral for so plain a man. Of all the obituaries that now flooded in, perhaps the simplest was that of his lifelong friend and relation, Lord Buchan:

His life was one of great & useful exertion – he possessed a singularly clear judgement with a warm and affectionate heart. Few men ever enjoyed to the degree Mr Coutts did the confidence & esteem of his friends, or obtained unaided by rank or political power, so much consideration and influence in Society. The large fortune which he acquired was the consequence & not the object of his active life, which at every period was devoted to the aid and advancement of those he loved.[11]

The widowed Duchess of Kent wrote a touching letter of sympathy to the partners at Coutts & Co.:

Gentlemen,

I assure you, I heard of the death of Mr Coutts with emotions of sincere regret, I had been taught by my dear husband to entertain a very high opinion of him. All those sentiments were realised by the generous & feeling letter he spontaneously addressed to me, at a moment, when I felt myself relieved by knowing, that if necessary, I could rely on his aid. And the recollection of that act, will never be effaced from my memory

In my intercourse with the late Mr Coutts's Partners, I have received proofs of Their kind attention; and I owe it to him and the sentiments I shall always associate with his name as head of the House, to continue the same confidence and regard to it, Very sincerely trusting that the members of the house, will reap all the advantages, They are so well entitled to

I remain
Gentlemen
Yours, hn
[signed] Victoria[12]

Thomas's will was short and simple. He left everything to Harriot, including his 50 per cent share in the Bank. He could have given no better testimonial of his deep love and respect.

Not everyone wrote enthusiastically after his death. Cobbett exploded in his *Register* on 30 March 1822: 'A million or more of money got together during a marriage with one wife has been made to pass to a second to the total exclusion of the children by the first wife.' He protested that the will should be set aside by Act of Parliament.

Thomas's confidence was justified. Harriot gave each daughter £10,000 a year. She estimated in her own will that she had given Lady Burdett a total sum of £118,602 and bequeathed her an additional £20,000; and the other daughters received similar sums.

Thomas left a legacy of more than gold. Although he had slipped into the background for more than a decade past, his partners worked in his tradition and maintained the trust of his customers. His share in the stock of £100,000 remained, so his death caused no crisis and, when the great bank panic came in December 1825, although Sir Edmund Antrobus was ill at the time, Coutts & Co. weathered the storm. 'While all the other banking houses were in a state of trepidation,' *The Times* reported, 'the Courier remarks that Messrs. Coutts & Co. had not a single cheque drawn

upon them more than was warranted by the ordinary demand of business.'
Only one other bank could claim as much.

Marjoribanks attributed their success to 'the advantage of general good
management in banking affairs', and recalled that in 'the years 1825 &
1826 ... in the short space ... of the four or five months ending in
February 1826 there were nearly sixty Banking establishments in London
& the country, that were insolvent....'[13]

This was a black period to be remembered by bankers with horror
through the century. Nathan Rothschild had seen the crisis coming and
told the Financial Secretary to the Treasury, John Charles Herries, on 30
April 1825 that

the result of admitting foreign goods without corresponding liberality on the other
side of the water was that all the gold was going out of the country. He had himself
sent 2 millions within the last two weeks ... the funds fall rapidly.[14]

On 17 December 1825 there was a run on the Bank of England. Herries
told Mrs Arbuthnot, Wellington's friend, that 'the country bankers had
started a run on gold' and that to meet them 'the Bank of England was
completely drained of its specie and was reduced to £100,000 sovereigns'.[15]
Rothschild saved them by bringing over enormous sums in sovereigns
from Paris, and the accidental discovery at the Bank of England of a box
containing notes to the value of one and a half million sterling completed
the recovery. The Bank of England did not have to suspend cash payments
after all, but many smaller banks suffered.

Undoubtedly the other reason for the survival of Coutts & Co. was the
healthy state of its reserves. Again, Marjoribanks gave the credit for their
establishment to Thomas, though, as has been seen, Antrobus was also
responsible:

Mr Coutts also reserved to himself a larger portion of the shares than the other
Partners had which enabled him to have at all times a large floating Balance of
from £80 to £100,000 on his account besides keeping a very considerable sum
under his own immediate control to assist the friends of the house with pecuniary
aid when it seemed expedient to do so – and from his well known abilities in
matters of business, and his correct and liberal way of transacting it, aided by the
long and efficient assistance he received from his Partners ... he happily lived to
see his House established in a high state of credit and respectability.[16]

Marjoribanks attributed this success to Thomas's competence and foresight. Above all it was Thomas who had, from the beginning, created that
confidence without which any bank fails. The quiet old banker had exerted
an extraordinarily powerful influence which continues to pervade the philosophy of his successors even today. Antrobus had once written to Thomas
that, during his absences abroad or at home, he had always tried to think
'what would Mr Coutts have done,' and acted accordingly.

Thomas's partners, however, found it easier to harden their hearts and, after his death, the 'money lent' ledgers show a comfortable inflow of funds, as debt after debt was marked 'paid up'. Nevertheless, they remained generous in the Coutts tradition. In 1823, as *The Times* reported,

A gentleman who had amassed an immense fortune in India, at his death bequeathed the sum of one hundred and fifty thousand pounds to Messrs. Thomas Coutts & Co. the celebrated Bankers, with whom he had transacted business for many years, but from some unknown motive he left his widow only £500 per annum.[17]

This seemed unjust and therefore the partners, 'to their lasting honour be it told, they most generously acting on the impulse of the moment, agreed to allow her for her lifetime the interest on the original legacy, so that the lady, who is now in her forty-fifth year, possesses an income of £7,500'.[18]

Letters to customers were written with the same care and courtesy that Thomas had always demanded. Many years earlier he had resisted Antrobus's suggestion that they should employ a 'corresponding clerk' since he believed that important letters should always be written by partners: each customer was different and needed different treatment. Until comparatively recently Thomas's rule was observed: important letters were always answered by partners. Long after Thomas's death, customers who withdrew their accounts in a huff received letters written after his model. Courteous and friendly, he would wish them well, would praise the bank to which they were going and gently suggest that his door was still open. Many came back.

It is a tribute to the unique and strong personality of Thomas Coutts that customer relations and the style and tone of the Bank remained as he had set them, not only during his years of illness and absence but even after his death.

At the end of 1825 Sir Edmund, knowing that his death was imminent, arranged his affairs with the same care and competence that had marked his career. He had already made sure that his devoted sister, Jane, was comfortably settled at Congleton, having bequeathed a life interest in the house and estates there to her in his will; they were to revert to the family trust on her death.

He appointed as his Trustees his partners, Edward Marjoribanks and Coutts Trotter, and Sir John Marjoribanks, the head of the family. The other Trustee was his fellow-pupil from Cheam School, Henry Addington, now Viscount Sidmouth. To them he left his estates in Chester, Staffordshire, Warwickshire and Wiltshire and his estate of Rutherford in Roxburghshire, in trust for his nephew, Edmund, and his heirs. The Trustees were each left £500 for their pains. To his nephew Edmund he left his 'part share and interest in capital stock in the Banking House of Coutts & Co.' and also the rest of his 'personal estate & chattels'.[19] Gibbs received £20,000 'bonds for money' and an annuity of £500. He also left them sound advice: 'they should never enter money transactions with relations or connections as trouble arises out of this'.[20] According to family records he transferred the Cheshire estates to Gibbs 'on his deathbed', shrewdly suspecting that Edmund would be tempted to spend his time hunting there instead of minding his duties at the Bank.

He did not forget his Sanxay relations at Cheam, leaving the old ladies Katherine and Caroline Sanxay an annuity and the four daughters of Henrietta Anne Cholmely at Ewell £9,333 6s 8d in 3 per cent consols. The bachelor banker had reason to be grateful to the wives of his relations and partners. Anne, the much loved wife of his nephew, Edmund, received £1,000 and his partners' wives 100 guineas each. Mr Dickie was remembered with a bequest of £200 and the other clerks at Coutts & Co. were each given £20 for mourning. He remembered everything – even to leave an annuity for the care of his parents' grave in Congleton.

To Harriot he left 100 guineas for a mourning ring, which she undoubtedly bought in fond remembrance. She had never forgotten how, in old age, he had willingly journeyed to Cheltenham to settle her affairs with her difficult stepfather. She had frequently visited him in London and in Cheshire and in his last illness wrote to him with great affection.

As Sir Edmund lay dying in the quiet comfort of the house at Cheam that Philip had left him, he could well reflect with satisfaction on a successful life. He had founded a stockbroking firm that, as James Capel & Co., would thrive through the centuries, and he had forged permanent links between them and Coutts & Co. He had, by his own efforts, made a great fortune and was able to buy a handsome house in Piccadilly and great estates in England and Scotland. But he had also been generous with his wealth, caring for his nephews and sisters and family with tact and uncommon kindness. He had earned the trust, respect and affection of his family, his friends, his customers and all those with whom he worked. Much of the credit for the lasting success of Coutts & Co. rightly belongs to Thomas Coutts. But he in turn had for half a century greatly depended on the wisdom and loyal support of Edmund Antrobus.

32

The Partners,
1826–37

With the death of Sir Edmund in 1826 something was lost which would never quite be regained. His nephew, Edmund, succeeded him, inheriting his title, but he had neither the experience nor the temperament of his uncle. As Sir Edmund had suspected, his nephew was always to be happier on his horse than on his partner's stool at the Bank. A certain abruptness comes through in his letters, but his early training was not wasted. Fluent in French and German, he was competent to deal with foreign customers, and the self-confidence acquired at Eton gave him an ease of manner when dealing with diplomats and foreign and British royalty.

Sir Edmund's other nephew, Gibbs, had taken up a diplomatic career and served at the British Embassy in Vienna during the peace negotiations of 1814. His experience of foreign affairs and his diplomatic contacts were useful to his uncle, and later to his brother when he became a partner in the Bank. But relations between the partners after Sir Edmund's death were never as harmonious as they had been in the old days.

Coutts Trotter was now the senior partner and Thomas Coutts, in the last year of his life, had written to the new King, George IV, to secure a baronetcy for him. Even so he felt his position in the Bank was now threatened. As senior partner Trotter thought that he had the right to bring in a member of his family who would eventually succeed him, and, as he had no sons, he wanted to nominate his nephew, Alexander Trotter, son of that Alexander Trotter of Dreghorn who had caused Thomas so much distress in the Melville Affair. The nomination was refused by Harriot and, in spite of long and plaintive letters from Trotter, she was implacable.

Why Harriot should have been so adamant is not clear. Thomas might have nursed a long grievance against the man who had brought some dishonour to his Bank and he may have given Harriot instructions. It is possible that Harriot had never forgotten that, when she had first known him, her 'dear Tom' had been deeply pained by the affair. It may also be that the Trotters had slighted her at some time. Certainly it was remembered in the Antrobus family that 'Sir Coutts Trotter lacked tact & courtesy' during the months of acrimonious correspondence with his partners. But Coutts Trotter felt deeply hurt, for he claimed that he and his wife had always been kind and hospitable to Harriot, especially during the difficult years after Thomas's death. Whatever the reason, the Trotters of Dreghorn were to feel the frost of her disapproval for years to come.

Coutts Trotter was especially aggrieved since his nephew, like young Edmund Antrobus, had been bred to banking and trained abroad in business, just as Thomas had considered desirable. In fact young Alexander Trotter, the cause of all the argument, seems to have found some relief that he was barred from the Bank where his uncle reigned, and where his father's name was remembered with some distaste. A solution was found: Alexander was placed in the broking firm of Capels; his son, William, followed him and his grandson, Charles William, was a partner until 1925.

In the 1820s Alexander was involved in a scandal in which Coutts and Capels were implicated. The broker's office manager, Richard White,

held powers of attorney to enable him to transfer clients' Government stock in the books at the Bank of England, and he is said to have used these powers in the 1820s to transfer stock belonging to Coutts' clients into his own name. Some £20,000 stock is said to have been misappropriated in this way before White was discovered. It was agreed that the matter would be settled by Coutts & Co. retaining a proportion of the brokerage due to the stockbroking firm for their transactions over a period, until the sum misappropriated was repaid. The practice therefore developed of Coutts withholding commission, and accounting for it to Capels quarterly: this arrangement continued even after the debt was paid off, and was not finally terminated until the early 1960s.[1]

One senses a certain satisfaction in the letters of Alexander Trotter junior at being able to find Coutts & Co. guilty of carelessness, even though the crime was that of White of Capels.

After Sir Edmund's death it was clear that it was necessary to find new partners, and William Matthew Coulthurst was introduced as a working partner with a salary. A quiet, competent man, he was welcomed by the other partners, who admired his capacity for hard work and his benevolence. William was the son of John Coulthurst of Gargrave in Yorkshire and the grandson of Nicholas, who had come to London as a solicitor and became a colleague of Oliver Farrer, a fellow Yorkshireman. Since Farrer and his descendants were Coutts & Co.'s lawyers, it was because of this connection that William became a salaried partner at the Bank in the Strand on 14 June 1827.

Harriot's choice was typically unconventional. She requested that Andrew Dickie be made a partner, the first clerk at Coutts ever to be so distinguished. The other partners willingly agreed, knowing that Dickie was indispensable. Harriot loved Dickie. Discreet, loyal and helpful, he explained bank business to her and advised her as he had done Thomas. When the Bank's profits dropped in 1826, it was Dickie who explained the critical economic situation to her.

In fact, Dickie knew the business of the house better than anyone and had acted as a partner in all but name for years before Thomas's death. He took the honour with his usual modest serenity, though he wrote somewhat sadly to Fanny, Lady Bute, in reply to her letter of congratulation, that he was now old and frail and felt less excitement at the honour than he would have done had it come earlier. However, Dickie had had his moments of triumph.

Harriot's companion, Nell Goddard, wrote to her from Brighton, reporting with wicked satisfaction a visit of Dickie to Lady Guilford. Her Ladyship apologised to Dickie because she could not invite him to dine. He replied with his usual quiet modesty that he quite understood, but that he was in any case engaged to dine with the King at the Pavilion. Dickie continued to deal with the affairs of the royal family, as he had done for years.

Nothing better illustrates the trust which Dickie inspired than that Mrs Fitzherbert asked that her most treasured documents should be sent to Coutts & Co. and placed in the hands of Mr Dickie. On 16 August, after the death in 1830 of George IV, she gave up to the late King's Executors 'all the personal estate and effects of every description belonging to his . . . late Majesty'.[2] She had unbounded trust in the Duke of Wellington, who was one of the two Executors, but the other, Sir William Knighton, had always been her enemy. So it was with great reluctance that she agreed to give up her letters and private papers, appealing to William IV for permission to keep some of her documents, particularly those which proved the validity of her marriage to the late King.

On 24 August 1833 Wellington, Mrs Fitzherbert and her representative, Lord Albemarle, spent the day burning all the rest of her papers in the grate of her house in Tilney Street, nearly setting fire to the chimney in the process. 'All the letters on either side', Albemarle reported the next day, were burned, 'with the exception of those which Mrs Fitz Herbert chose to keep.'[3]

Wellington apparently acted with great courtesy and friendliness and Mrs Fitzherbert was perfectly satisfied. 'After our great work of burning was over', Albemarle wrote to Lord Stourton, Mrs Fitzherbert's other representative, 'I went to Messrs Coutts and delivered into Mr Dickie's hands (by Mrs Fitz Herbert's desire) the parcel containing the documents and letters reserved, signed and sealed by the Duke of Wellington and myself'.[4] Later Stourton added his seal.

It was remarkable that she specifically entrusted her precious papers not to the chief partner of Coutts & Co., then Sir Coutts Trotter, but to Dickie. On 28 August 1833, in his neat precise hand, he recorded:

Mr Dickie of the house of Messrs Coutts & Co. acknowledges the receipt of a Sealed Packet to remain with Messrs Coutts and Co. at the disposal of his Lordship and Lord Stourton and it is deposited in Messrs Coutts strong room accordingly.

Here follows a list of the papers and documents retained by Mrs Fitzherbert:

1. The Mortgage on the Palace at Brighton.
2. The Certificate of the Marriage dated Dec 21st [15th], 1785.
3. Letter from the late King, relating to the Marriage signed.
4. Will written by the late King.
5. Memorandum written by Mrs Fitzherbert, attached to a letter written by the clergyman who performed the Marriage Ceremony.

Correct Copy, STOURTON.[5]

Other valuable letters and possessions which had been deposited at Coutts & Co. were given up to her Executors on her death in March 1837. But the packet of documents in its brown paper wrapping was kept unopened in the vaults of Coutts & Co., in spite of persistent demands by Stourton's descendants. Wellington rejected all such demands in his most trenchant manner:

Mrs Fitzherbert expressed a strong desire to retain undestroyed particular papers in which she felt a strong interest. I considered it my duty to consent to these papers remaining undestroyed if means could be devised of keeping them as secret and confidential papers as they had been up to that moment.

Mrs Fitzherbert expressed an anxiety at least equal to that which I felt, that those papers, although preserved, should not be made public.

It was agreed, therefore, that they should be deposited in a packet, and be sealed up under the seals of the Earl of Albemarle, your Lordship, and myself, and lodged at Messrs. Coutts, the bankers.[6]

Messrs Coutts kept Mrs Fitzherbert's trust and only relinquished the parcel by royal command in 1905.

Dickie acted as Harriot's confidential agent, but there is little in the letters of the period to suggest the other partners' attitude to Harriot. They were professional and conventional businessmen, unlike Thomas, who had belonged to an age when eccentricity was accepted. But it would seem that they took her seriously, for, in spite of her theatrical extravagance, Harriot had a hard business head and an eye made sharp by experience at the players' box office. She had been brought up in a world where every penny counted. She was not the only woman banker at that time: Lady Jersey was at the head of the House of Childs for many years. The partners knew that Thomas had valued her judgment of people, but they were also more than a little scared of her: Harriot, when roused, could put on a spectacular performance.

Harriot took her position in the Bank very seriously, watching the profits and losses with an eagle eye, noting on one occasion a discrepancy of £10 in her account. She also played a major role in the appointment of junior partners and used her power of veto to some effect, as has been seen. What the discreet old bankers thought of Harriot's lavish lifestyle is not known. Young Sir Edmund Antrobus seems to have taken it in his stride, and old Sir Edmund had, at the end of his life, been genuinely fond of her, and had invited her to visit him in Cheshire.

For a bank that prided itself on its quiet discretion, Harriot had an embarrassingly high profile. Almost immediately after Thomas's death, the newspapers began a campaign of libellous vilification which pursued her with increasing vindictiveness to the grave. In an age of brutal satire, the actress who had become a partner in a great bank was not allowed to escape. Pamphleteers brought her their scurrilous sheets in the vain hope that she would buy them off, but Harriot was reared in a tough school: players in her young days were bombarded with objects more objectionable than words. In Yorkshire 'lakers', as actors were called, were often thrown in the river. So although the pamphlets and caricatures were hurtful, she never allowed them to change her style of living and giving.

The title page of one of the pamphlets was typical: 'Secret Memoirs of Harriot Pumpkin ... and her extraordinary marriage to old Croesus. ... The Art of making an ostentatious Shew-off under the Color of CHARITY. The whole pourtraying HER NEVER-FORGIVING AND MALICIOUS DISPOSITION.' Another called itself 'Strictures on an OLD ACTRESS, Bet the Pot Girl, Alias the Bankers sham widow'. Since her persecutors claimed her marriage was illegal, she was 'a strolling troll', 'a vile, wicked lying She-Pharisee', a 'wanton Harlot' and 'a fat, greasy voluptuous Mother Pumpkin Croesus'.[7]

Even the partners came under attack for their support of Harriot. Sir Coutts Trotter, in particular, was castigated as an upstart and contrasted with his brother, who, they claimed, had been an honest carpenter and was now the respected owner of the Bazaar in Soho Square.

The virulence of the attacks was perhaps caused by Harriot's refusal to fade genteelly into the background as Miss Farren had done when she became the Countess of Derby. Harriot's generous charitable donations, so it was said, were given only for self-advertisement. It is true that she was often wildly indiscriminate. While Thomas was alive she attracted all the beggars in London to her charity table at the gates of Holly Lodge until he put his foot down. She sent gifts and money to Ireland, her mother's home, which never reached the needy. But she never forgot the hunger and cold of her early life and sent blankets and coals to the poor of the East End in the bitter winter. Although her uncertain temper often lost her friends, she was generous to her former Green Room cronies and gave an annual allowance to her old dresser at Drury Lane.

It was true that she enjoyed displaying her wealth, but it was not so much a love of showing off as a delight in putting on a show. The theatre was in her blood; her balls, receptions and dinners were magnificent productions. As for her fêtes, they were masquerades in true theatrical style. Once she came across a poor child in a hovel on a Brighton beach and, in a trice, transformed the hut into a comfortable cottage with a hot meal to greet the astonished mother on her return. She was, in fact, performing stage magic, but she genuinely felt that child's cold and hunger.

If, however, the cartoonists and pamphleteers were offensive to the banker's widow, they were to have even greater sport with Harriot, Duchess of St Albans.

33

Harriot, Duchess of St Albans

In 1825 the journals had become even more libellous and obscene when it was observed that the young Duke of St Albans had come a-wooing. William Aubrey de Vere, ninth Duke and the descendant of Charles II and Nell Gwynne, was twenty-six, and Harriot must have been nearly fifty. The Duke was, however, genuinely attracted to her. He was passionately fond of Shakespeare and dazzled by the glamour of the stage that still shone around Harriot – even if her luxuriant beauty was now somewhat over-blown. Harriot did not leap at the Duke's proposal and asked the advice of Sir Walter Scott, a distant relation of Thomas's.

In September 1824 she had taken a pilgrimage to Scotland to follow in the steps of Thomas's 'sweet youth'. Sir Walter had invited her to stay with him at Abbotsford, with her suite. The newspapers made much of Harriot's progress. She travelled in magnificent style with liveried outriders beside the long procession of coaches carrying servants and doctors and companions. In her own silk-lined carriage she took the precious casket containing a packet of 'Tom's' love letters, which she read and re-read. And woe betide anyone who mislaid it. These letters were the proof of his deep love for her and his unbounded trust.

Sir Walter had visited Mr and Mrs Coutts often in London and always regarded Harriot with amused affection. His other guests, a group of high-born Scottish ladies, were irritated by Harriot's late arrival and the ostentation of her procession, and snubbed her. Sir Walter, hurt for her, took the youngest of the ladies aside and reproved her. After that they went out of their way to flatter her, calling for her to sing for them.

Harriot never forgot the 'horrid ladies', but she was eternally grateful for Sir Walter's kindness. She copied the inscription from a tombstone in Melrose Churchyard and signed it:

> The earth goeth on the earth glistening like gold
> The earth goeth to the earth, sooner than it wolde
> The earth builds on the earth castles and towers
> The earth says to the earth 'All shall be ours'.

Harriot Coutts – written with Sir Walter Scott's *own pen*, sitting in his own Chair. How I shall be envyed.[1]

The next year she returned, bringing with her the Duke of St Albans and his sisters, and in November Sir Walter noted in his journal:

If the Duke marries her, he ensures an immense fortune; if she marries him, she has the first rank. If he marries a woman older than himself by 20 years, she marries a man younger in wit by twenty degrees. I do not think he will dilapidate her fortune – he seems quiet and gentle. I do not think she will abuse his softness – of disposition shall we say, or of heart? The disparity of ages concerns no-one but themselves, so they have my consent to marry if they can get each others.*

On 13 June 1827 Harriot sent 'dear Mr Dickie' with a letter to King George IV asking his permission to marry the Duke of St Albans, which, after teasing Dickie for his role as 'mercury galant', he gladly gave. The style of Harriot's letter suggests Dickie's careful pen: 'Permit me, Sire, humbly & dutifully to acquaint Your Majesty that arrangements have been finally made for my marriage with the Duke of St Albans on Saturday next. . . .'[3] She signed it 'with every sentiment of duty & grateful acknowledgement of Your Majesty's untiring kindness'.[4] The King replied, 'My dear Madam. Everything that can contribute to your happiness will always give me sincere Pleasure and I beg to offer my congratulations to you and the Duke on the occasion. Your very sincere friend.'[5]

So Harriot became Duchess of St Albans and played her last role with relish. Her balls and soirées at Stratton Street were legendary. Disraeli, who portrayed her as Mrs Millions in *Vivian Grey*, accepted her invitations with delight, though he, like other guests, smiled behind her back.

She celebrated their wedding anniversary each June with a fantastic fête at Holly Lodge. Guests feasted in silk-lined pavilions on the green lawns, listened to yodelling Swiss maidens, and ate syllabub and drank fresh milk from garlanded white cows. The Duke, splendid in his green and gold uniform as Hereditary Grand Falconer, was greeted by fanfares of trumpets.

While Harriot's guests danced through the groves under the lanterns, the real world was in turmoil. And Sir Francis Burdett frequently exploded with fury at her extravagance. At home, in the years leading up to the passing of the Reform Bill, riots threatened to become revolution.

---

* There is a postscript to this story. At the end of his life, when Sir Walter was desperately in debt, an anonymous offer of a large sum of money came to him, which he proudly refused, as he did all such offers. It came in fact from Harriot, though this was one act of charity which she wanted to go unsung. After her death, Lockhart, wishing to record this in his memoirs, asked permission of Miss Angela Burdett-Coutts. She refused: the Duchess had not wished it to be known and so it has always remained.[2]

Abroad, 1830 ushered in a time of tumult. In Paris in July the reactionary Charles X was ousted and Thomas's old friend, Louis Philippe, became King, with his sister, Madame Adelaïde, a power behind the throne. Lady Burdett wrote affectionately to congratulate the Adèle of the old days and renewed their friendship. Sir Francis toasted 'Louis Philippe and the French nation' at a public dinner. A French friend wrote of 'the astonishing revolution which has changed in three days all our destinies . . . we are awakened as if from a dream'.[6] Harriot, in Burdett's eyes, still lived in the land of dreams.

The times were difficult, but Coutts & Co. gave every impression of prosperity. In June 1830 the Austrian Ambassador, Philipp von Neumann, dined in some style with Sir Edmund Antrobus, who had inherited a handsome fortune from his uncle. In addition, according to the Ambassador, he was now drawing £20,000 a year as his share of the profits of the Bank, 'the Duchess of St Albans . . . having for her part an income of £80,000; Sir Coutts Trotter £25,000: and Mr Marjoribanks about the same which makes a profit in a single banking house of £180,000 a year'.[7]

The four partners were vividly remembered by an old clergyman, the Reverend E. C. Wilshere in 1880, who wrote:

In 1834 Sir Coutts Trotter was there, a shapely, elegant figure over six feet, dressed in black, elderly with a fine aristocratic countenance, slightly reserved. Sir Edmund Antrobus was shorter than Sir Coutts, handsome, with a slight colour, partial to buff coloured cloth, physically strong, in the prime of life. Mr Edward Marjoribanks was above six feet in height, colossal in strength with a slight stoop, absent and rather anxious expression; not firm seemingly in gait . . . a person who could not be expected to live to the remarkable age of ninety-six. Mr Coulthurst was of average height, fresh coloured in complexion, with a pleasant open countenance, with quiet and collected manners and of an enduring constitution.[8]

In 1834 Coutts & Co. lost its most valued partner, Andrew Dickie. For months he had suffered a painful illness but still managed to struggle to his desk. On 22 April 1834 he wrote to the Duke of Cambridge, who had wished to secure a place for the son of his steward as a clerk in Coutts & Co., that he had been ill:

a destructive & serious Malady (called a Tumour in the Stomach) has confined me to my Bed for these five months past with much severe suffering, and which seems likely to continue, with little intermediate ease, so long as it may please the Will of the Almighty . . . but how long this may continue, God alone knows.[9]

On 1 May he was still doggedly persevering. He had obviously interviewed the young man, but he was under age and could only be employed as a supernumerary. Thereafter, wrote Dickie firmly, 'it must be solely on his own merits & attention on which his future prospects must have their dependance'.[10] Those are exactly the words that his master, Thomas Coutts, would have used.

Not long afterwards good, patient Andrew Dickie was at last released from pain. There are not many clerks or partners in the history of the Bank who have left so heartwarming a glow.

No one knew better than Harriot how important the succession to his Bank had been to Thomas. He had always insisted that the name 'Coutts & Co.' should be kept, but even more that his successor should be worthy of the great wealth he would bestow. So in the years after his death, as she considered her will, she looked among his grandchildren for her successor.

Susan's daughters were firmly ruled out because their mother's slanderous attacks had never been forgiven. Fanny's son, Dudley, who had seemed the obvious choice, had ruined his chances by his marriage to Lucien Bonaparte's daughter. Dudley had been at Cambridge when his grandfather died and returned for the funeral, taking on all the responsibility of an heir apparent, comforting Harriot and writing to friends. He took his MA at Cambridge in 1823 and left to a chorus of praise. As Lady Holland wrote to her son on 6 December 1826, 'all concur in praising Lord Dudley Stuart . . . he is universally beloved at Cambridge'.[11] No one, it would seem, could be better fitted to inherit Thomas's mantle.

However, when he returned to Italy, Dudley fell in love with Christina Alexandrina Egypta Bonaparte, daughter of Napoleon's brother, Lucien. She was five years older than he and was married to a Swedish Count, Aarvid de Posse, whom she believed to be dead. Dudley married her in 1824 in a Catholic church near Rome, and their only child, Paul Amadeus Francis, was born in 1825. Fanny was horrified, but wrote to Harriot asking her to accept the marriage and appealing to her 'kind regard . . . to aid in remedying what it is now too late to prevent'.[12] This Harriot did, since she was genuinely fond of Dudley, and warmly received the couple at Holly Lodge and Brighton. But Fanny's hope that she would give him the situation which she had originally proposed for him was immediately dashed. As Agar Ellis wrote to the Duke of Devonshire, 'Mrs Coutts won't make him a partner.' 'Christina', he wrote, was 'old, humpbacked, of a bad character, a Frenchwoman, a Catholic and a Bonaparte'.[13] That catalogue of crimes ruled Dudley out of the succession. In 1827 a new scandal broke which confirmed Harriot's judgment. The Swedish Count turned up, alive and well. Throughout the winter Dudley negotiated in Sweden and Rome to prove that Christina's first marriage had not been cosummated, paying the Count £5,000 to undergo a medical examination proving impotence. Finally on 12 May 1828 Dudley wrote to Harriot from Genoa that the Count's marriage had been proved null and that he had no doubt of his marriage, 'tho a clandestine one being approved and recognised at Rome'.[14] Accordingly they passed a delightful winter at Genoa and busied themselves buying statues for Harriot and the Duke. Harriot remained friendly and generous, but Dudley now had no hope of following his grandfather in the Bank in the Strand.*

One by one Harriot ruled out Thomas's other grandchildren. Dudley's sister, Frances, does not seem to have been considered as Thomas's heir. Frances had made no effort to please Harriot and, indeed, had snubbed her on occasions. Thomas's other grandson, Robert Burdett, was a difficult man, who had long ago offended Thomas and had cut himself off from his family. The boy who had been seen studying the Magna Carta during the siege of Piccadilly had become estranged from the family; too much money and too much liberty had spoiled him and at Oxford he drank heavily and ran into debt. Thomas helped him at first, buying him a commission in the army through his influence with the Duke of York, then Commander-in-Chief. Sir Francis, for whom this kind of patronage was anathema, was not consulted and was justifiably furious. But Robert soon forfeited his grandfather's affection and now led his own life, though Sir Francis continued to send him an allowance. He was in no way a worthy successor.

Of the Burdett girls, the eldest, Sophia, had been in some scrape over a lover, and none of the other daughters was remarkable, except the youngest, Angela, who from childhood had been Harriot's favourite. With the shrewd eye of one who had learned from the stage to understand character, Harriot saw in young Angela the hope of the future.

Harriot also considered all the other young people, kin to dear Thomas. When she went on holiday to Portsmouth she took with her the two sons of Edward Marjoribanks and, watching them closely, decided that, if she needed to look beyond the family, Dudley Marjoribanks would be her choice, rather than his older brother, Edward. Once again her judgment would in time be proved sound.

---

* The marriage did not last. Dudley became the MP for Arundel in 1830 and, following in the tradition of his uncle, Sir Francis, made his maiden speech in favour of the Reform Bill. But Christina disliked England and they separated. In January 1840 Dudley stopped her allowance and refused to be responsible for her debts. She died in Italy in 1847. Their son, Paul, became a captain in the 48th Regiment, but became brain-damaged after a riding accident and died 'a lunatic', according to the records. Dudley never became a banker, but his excellent qualities were not wasted. He became a national hero in Poland for his tireless work in the cause of Polish freedom, sacrificing his political career for his Polish friends. Some, like Prince Czartoryski, became customers of the Bank, and Dudley introduced Chopin to Coutts & Co. when he came to play at a concert for Polish refugees in 1848. In 1854 Dudley travelled to Sweden to appeal to the King for help in Poland, but he died there on 17 November. His epitaph in an obituary would have pleased Sir Francis Burdett: 'His constituents were the oppressed of all nations.'[15]

But for the last years of her life her attention would centre on Angela, the youngest child of 'dear Tom's' youngest daughter.

Later Angela was to remember an 'ideal childhood' in security and freedom. She was the child of her parents' reconciliation and only saw them mellowed and affectionate in middle age. Sir Francis, inspired by Rousseau, allowed his children unusual freedom. Lady Burdett, who was as perpetually concerned with her health as her father had been with his, was glad to leave her daughters in the charge of Sophia, the elder sister whom Angela remembered as a second mother. Later a governess was appointed, who was to be closer than mother or sisters. Little Hannah Meredith, clever, vivacious and possessive, was to be at Angela's side all her life.

Angela apparently was unaware of the existence of Angela's brother Robert during her early years. It was said that she only saw him once, when, as a young ADC, he was sent with an official message to Sir Francis. Henceforth she was to look for a substitute for the missing brother in her life.

Although she was brought up in a predominantly feminine world, her life was not without excitement and adventure. The family was constantly on the move, travelling in lumbering carriages along dusty roads from one great country house to another. At Foremark she rode with her father over the Derbyshire hills and at Ramsbury in Wiltshire she ran free with her sisters in the green meadows by the River Kennet. Occasionally Lady Burdett would complain that the little girls took no pains with their appearance and would send them to Harriot to be dressed up in flowery bonnets and pretty dresses.

Harriot, who loved children, spoiled them, romped with them at Holly Lodge in the 'Rumpus' Room, and gave Angela the warm affection she needed. Lady Burdett had always made good use of her father's box at Covent Garden and at Drury Lane, but it was Harriot who opened the door of the magic world of the stage. Angela, like her grandfather, was always to be fascinated by actors and the theatre. At the end of her life she could recall Harriot's tales of the eighteenth-century stage and talk of Garrick and Sheridan to Sir Henry Irving. Like Thomas, Angela was to become a patron of artists and a collector of paintings. Her interest in art was stimulated in her earliest years by their neighbour in St James's Place, old Sam Rogers, the acid-tongued banker poet. Often after her morning walk in the Park she would call on him and he would show her the famous collection of pictures in his exquisite house, many of which she would later buy in the sale after his death. His sharp claws were always sheathed when he entertained his young neighbour; and she was always to be a patient listener, more at her ease with the elderly than with her contemporaries.

Much of her childhood was spent with her mother at watering-places in England and abroad. Some years Lady Burdett took a house in the Royal Crescent in Bath, where one year the young James Brooke was a dashing neighbour. In later years he confessed that he did not remember the little girl, trotting by on her Shetland pony, but she never forgot the handsome young man who was to play such an important part in her life.

Sir Francis was often absent, but when he rode down from Westminster with his political friends her world came alight. When she was only seven, his colleague, John Cam Hobhouse, the radical MP, sent charming messages to Angela. 'We have a little ball here tonight', he wrote on 9 January 1821; 'I wish she was here that I might have the honour of asking her to dance.'[16]

Sir Francis did not believe in banishing children to the nursery, so from her earliest years Angela listened to some of the most brilliant men of the day talk of politics and literature: Lord Brougham often held the floor, sparkling and voluble; Tom Moore gossiped about their mutual friend, Lord Byron. The serious little girl, who listened while Moore played and sang his sweet Irish melodies, would catch something of his romantic enthusiasm and her father's passion for all things Irish. Ireland and its problems were to be a prominent theme in her life.

She could have had only the shadowiest memories of her grandfather since she was barely eight when he died; but a child who attracted the attention of so many elderly men would not have gone unnoticed by Thomas and, if he showed particular affection, Harriot would have remembered.

Lady Burdett, Angela and her sisters were abroad when Harriot was transformed into a duchess. From 1826 to 1829 they were on a prolonged tour of Europe. Lady Burdett, normally so plaintive an invalid, planned their route with relish, following the road that Thomas had taken her on so many years before. She was, her husband wrote, 'a summer bird that loves the sun'.[17] Sir Francis joined them whenever he could get away from his parliamentary duties. So Lady Burdett's great procession of carriages and baggage wagons lumbered through France to Italy and back through Germany, staying for weeks at a time at Nice, Montpellier, Genoa, Pau, Baden and Spa.

At Paris Lady Burdett presented her daughters to Louis Philippe and his sister Madame Adelaïde, who remembered with pleasure the eternal friendship she had long ago sworn to 'Sophie' and showed particular interest in her youngest daughter, Angela, who in later life was noted for the grace of her formal curtsey and for her excellent French; both were acquired during her stay in Paris. Tutors travelled with them, or were engaged from time to time, teaching them German, French and Italian. Dancing, music and art masters finished their education. And clever Miss Meredith supervised.

The Grand Tour had been a liberal education, transforming the lanky little girl into a young woman, whose quiet composure and dry humour reminded the Duchess of Thomas: Angela had the same affectionate heart combined with his cool, clear judgment. In 1832 Sir Francis wrote gratefully to Harriot thanking her for 'dressing Angie so beautifully'.[18] Nothing delighted her more than transforming the young woman with the long sad face, whose severe hairstyle and poor complexion made her look plainer than she was.

Sir Francis increasingly relied on 'Angie', especially after the marriage of his elder daughters, Sophia and Susan. Susan married in 1830 an impecunious Cornishman, John Trevanion, and Sophia, after an unhappy love affair, finally married an MP, Hon. Robert Otway Cave. During these years, when Sir Francis suffered from gout, Angela wrote his letters in her illegible handwriting and absorbed many of his ideals, especially his hatred of cruelty to man and beast.

In her last years Harriot often took Angela as her companion on her journeys; and, as her cavalcade of coaches, wagons and liveried outriders swept through the countryside, read to her again and again dear Tom's love letters. Angela was to remember that an old man could make a young woman happy, and that Harriot's second marriage to a young man half her age could also bring its comfort. The double pattern would be repeated in her own life. She would also remember Harriot's indiscriminate charity, the cheating beggars and wasted gifts. She would be more watchful in her philanthropy, more mistrustful of sycophants.

In the last months of her life Harriot often retreated to her beloved Holly Lodge, where, drawn in her pony carriage round the grounds, she felt that she could breathe more easily. Looking down over the long lawns to the murky city, she wrote to Angela one of her rare letters, full of warm affection:

My dear Angela,

I knew you would all be famished when I left therefore I have ordered a *Pie* for you which with *Mulligatawny* what a long word and some Grapes . . . all of which I hope will arrive good *Carriage Paid* . . . . Mind you all behave properly till I return, Mama and all, she really is too frolicksome. I beg you consider my writing to you as a great favour; what a beautiful day we had yesterday Arrived at half past two [at Holly Lodge] and ah such primroses and daffodils

Love to all
Yours affectionate
Harriot St Albans[19]

As death approached she returned to Stratton Street, determined to end her days in the room where Thomas had died. There, at ten o'clock on

Sunday morning, 6 August 1837, Harriot, Duchess of St Albans, made her last exit.

She was to be buried, not with Thomas and Susannah in the Guilfords' church at Wroxton, but in the St Albans's family vault at Redbourne Hall in Lincolnshire. Crowds flocked to Mr Banting's funeral parlour in Pall Mall to see her coffin before the coaches of the Guilfords, the Butes and the Burdetts set off on their long journey to Lincolnshire. There, in the great drawing-room of Redbourne Hall, she lay in state until Saturday, when it was announced that 'obsequies conducted with the greatest splendour will commence at an early hour'.[20] The shadow of Nell Gwynne, mother of the first Duke of St Albans, would surely have dropped a sympathetic tear as Harriot was lowered into the ducal vault.

'You should write my life,' Harriot had told Sir Walter Scott in July 1827, and gave him a pen and inkstand that he might tell her story.

What a strange eventful life has mine been, from a poor little player child, with just food and clothes to cover me, dependent on a precarious profession, without talent or a friend in the world! 'to have seen what I have seen, seeing what I see.' Is it not wonderful? Is it true? Can I believe it? first the wife of the best, the most perfect being that ever breathed, his love and unbounded confidence in me, his immense fortune so honourably acquired by his own industry, all at my command – and now the wife of a Duke.[21]

Harriot's inkstand remains at Abbotsford, but Sir Walter never did write the life of his 'Dame of Diamonds', the most extraordinary partner that Coutts & Co. would ever know.

Old John Campbell's pastoral world was disappearing, though remembered with nostalgia in Harriot's fantasias at Holly Lodge. The Duchess of St Albans, in formal court dress, often sighed for the freedom and merriment of the old days.

It was the end of an era. Thomas and Harriot belonged to a more leisured age, when a great banker could wander round the continent for two years, or take long summer holidays in Wales or Scotland, spending months at great country houses. There, in the calm of their libraries, ministers could hold long conferences with their colleagues and their bankers. News of the outside world came slowly in the days before railways and the electric telegraph brought bustle to business. Power and wealth were in the hands of a few families who knew each other well, intermarried and had their own code of morality. Their natural children were often openly acknowledged, just as the Duke of Clarence honoured Mrs Jordan's ten children when he became king.

Harriot was already dying when in June news was brought of the death of her old friend King William IV, the last survivor of her tinselled past.

Princes and royal dukes were all gone and their mistresses long discarded. Mrs Jordan had died in 1815 in obscurity and poverty in Paris, where the Duke of Kent's 'old French lady' also quietly finished her days. Mrs Fitzherbert, the Prince Regent's injured morganatic wife, had ended her days in March in recognised respectability. Both Sir Coutts Trotter and Lady Guilford were near their end; they would not long survive the Duchess.

Even Burdett had changed: the 'Frantic Disturber' of the old days had turned a Tory. Once the Reform Bill was passed, his life's mission realised, he now longed to leave the political battlefield. He was crippled by gout and wanted, as he said, 'now that the enemy was destroyed, a little respite, a breathing time'.[22] He was eagerly welcomed by Tories like young Disraeli, but old colleagues like Hobhouse, who still loved him, listened to his speeches in the House and buried their heads in their hands in embarrassed shame.

When Burdett's constituents in Westminster demanded an explanation of his change, he told them that he now totally disapproved of the Whig Government's foreign and domestic policies. Honourably, he offered his resignation and in May 1837 fought the seat again – as a Tory. His constituents, grateful for a lifetime's work on their behalf, re-elected him. As one wrote, 'Sir F. Burdett ought to be treated with at least as much indulgence and liberality as the Duke's horse.'[23] So Burdett, like Wellington's Copenhagen, after so many battles was given the run of the paddock.

Burdett had not expected to stand in the election called after the death of William IV on 20 June 1837, hoping to retire to his beloved Derbyshire and finish his days as the country squire he had always been at heart. But when he was invited to stand as the Tory candidate for North Wiltshire he could not resist the call and accepted. So at the age of sixty-seven he began, as he said, 'a new epoch in my life'.[24]

In the darkened rooms of 1 Stratton Street, Burdett's youngest daughter, touched by Harriot's magic wand, also stepped out into a 'new epoch'.

Part 3

1837–92

34

The Heiress

The news of Harriot's death came to Sir Francis Burdett in the middle of the election which was to return him to Parliament as the Tory MP for Wiltshire. 'What she has done', he wrote to Susan, Lady Guilford, 'Heaven alone knows ... she always talk'd of herself as being left as Trustee for you all.'[1]

It was not until Harriot's will was read at 2 p.m. on 10 August that the closely guarded secret was out. Burdett's daughter, Angela, Thomas's youngest grandchild, was, as he later wrote, 'the richest woman in all England'. At the age of twenty-three she inherited Harriot's 'houses in Piccadilly, her watches, jewels, trinkets and ornaments of the person'.[2] That was not all. Harriot left to her Trustees all her 'moneys stocks funds and securities for money, and all my parts shares and interest of & in the Banking House and Business in the Strand ... and the Capital employed therein, & all the gains, profits and produce, benefit and advantage from time to time to arise or accrue therefrom'.[3] All this was on trust 'to pay the annual rents, issues, dividends, interests and gains and profit thereof to Angela Georgina Burdett'[4] and thereafter to her son. Her Trustees were Sir Coutts Trotter, Sir Edmund Antrobus junior and William Matthew Coulthurst – the partners of the Bank; Thomas's old friend William Adam, Accountant General of the High Court of Chancery; and Harriot's lawyer, John Parkinson of Farrers, the Bank's solicitors. Should she have no son, Angela's sister Joanna or her son should succeed; and, after her, her other sister, Clara Maria, and her son. If there were no sons of any of these three sisters, then Dudley Coutts Marjoribanks, Harriot's godson and son of Edward Marjoribanks, was next in line. Should he have no son, the succession was to light on another godson, Coutts Lindsay, grandson of Coutts Trotter and son of Colonel James Lindsay.

So the succession to Thomas's kingdom was clearly marked – merit taking precedence over age: Angela came before her elder sisters, and Dudley Marjoribanks before his elder brother, Edward.

The other members of the family did not share the Burdetts' astonished delight. There was nothing for Lady Guilford or her daughters. Fanny,

Lady Bute, had died four years earlier, but there was no mention in the will of her son, Dudley Coutts Stuart, or his sister, Frances. Margaret Trotter, daughter of Coutts Trotter, and her godchildren, Dudley Coutts Marjoribanks and Harriot Marjoribanks, received £500 each. Lady Burdett received £20,000, 'such sum being over and above the sums that I have already given to her amounting to £118,602 15s 0d'. The late Lady Bute's £20,000 was to be invested for her children 'in such stocks as the Trustees shall think fit'.[5]

Harriot, though warm-hearted and generous, never forgot or forgave Susan's violent attacks on her good name. She might have wished to reward Fanny's daughter, Frances, now the wife of Lord Sandon, later to be the Earl of Harrowby, since she knew how her 'dear Tom' had worshipped Fanny, but Frances had made no effort to conceal her disdain and disapproval and discouraged her visits. On Harriot's marriage to the Duke of St Albans, at her mother's request Frances had done an 'odious duty . . . composing letters of congratulation to Mrs Coutts on her approaching marriage'.[6] She considered Harriot's fête on her wedding anniversary in 1829 vulgar and 'disagreeable', and wrote scornfully to her mother of the 'haymakers in costume'.[7] She accepted Harriot's invitation to take the place of honour at her side, but 'only gave myself as much trouble as civility required'.[8] Harriot was too shrewd an observer not to notice and be hurt. As for Dudley, for whom she had genuine affection, she could never be sure that his wife would not squander Thomas's fortune, or that he would not bestow it all on Polish refugees. So neither Frances nor Dudley received a penny in her will, though she had previously been generous to them both.

To make sure that Dudley's mistake would not be repeated, she inserted a clause in the will by which the prospective heiress or future heir would forfeit their inheritance if they married an alien. Half a century later this clause was to cause infinite trouble.

In another clause she insisted that the heir should take the name of Coutts within six months. This may well have been on Thomas's advice, since he had always emphasised the importance to the Bank of keeping the name in perpetuity. She hoped that the heiress would make 1 Stratton Street her home – perhaps to ensure her independence from her family.

The Duke of St Albans was bequeathed £10,000 a year; given a life interest in Holly Lodge, with all its contents, and in 80 Piccadilly, with its silver gilt service of plate plus £10,000 to furnish it for his lifetime. He was also allowed to use the room over the Bank in the Strand rent-free, and to choose plate to the value of £2,000. But Harriot kept a hand on him from beyond the tomb: neither his brothers, Lord Frederick and Lord Charles Beauclerk, nor their families were to reside with him for as much as a week in any year. If they did, all her bequests to him would cease 'as if the said Duke were actually dead'.[9]

One family was barred, in a melodramatic sentence which was to ring down the years, successfully keeping it out of the direction of the Bank: 'I expressly direct that no son or descendant of Alexander Trotter of Dreghorn, near Edinburgh, Esquire, be admitted as partner in the said Banking Business.'[10]

Angela's role was clearly defined: unlike Harriot, she was not to be a partner, nor to interfere in the running of the business, nor could she touch her capital or anticipate the interest. Nevertheless, she always considered herself the head of the House of Coutts & Co.; and so did the world. Just as Thomas had been the public face of the Bank for more than sixty years, even when he was absent or ill, so his granddaughter would be, for the rest of the nineteenth century, the public representative of the Bank in the Strand, even though she was in fact neither as rich nor as influential as the world imagined.

Her fortune was believed to be £1,800,000. The *Morning Herald* estimated that 'the weight in gold is 13 tons, 7cwt, 3qrs, 13lbs and would require 107 men to carry it, supposing that each of them carried 289lbs'. In fact it was probably half this sum; even so, in modern terms she was a multi-millionaire.

Harriot had made a shrewd choice. Angela Burdett was to become, in the opinion of Edward VII, after his mother 'the most remarkable woman in the Kingdom'. Victoria and Angela had much in common: both were serious, intelligent and strong-willed young women taking up heavy responsibilities in a man's world. Both were determined to be independent: Queen Victoria broke away from her mother's dominance, and Angela soon left her father's house and set up her own establishment at 1 Stratton Street – a courageous step at that time.

Victoria and Angela each had an influential governess: the Queen relied on Louise Lehzen and Angela was devoted to Hannah Meredith, who was to be her close companion until her death in 1878. Above all, both young women were determined to understand the business each had inherited. Victoria, with no particular liking for politics, laboured doggedly to master the business of government, and Angela, with no knowledge of banking, was obstinately determined to understand the working of the Bank. If Victoria found the father she had missed from childhood in Lord Melbourne, Angela would, after her father's death, turn to the Duke of Wellington.

On 14 September Angela Burdett, by royal licence, assumed the surname Coutts; for a while she was known as Miss Burdett-Coutts, later simply as Miss Coutts. In the isolation of her great wealth there were few who would call her by her Christian name.

Harriot's choice was surprising, but she had thought long and hard before entrusting Thomas's fortune to a girl of twenty-three. The old actress understood human nature: she had watched Angela from earliest childhood and saw that she was well equipped by background, education and character to bear the golden burden.

The young woman who took up her inheritance in the great house in Stratton Street brought to her lonely new life a determination, a lively and cultured mind, and a wider experience of life than most women of her age. With surprising assurance, she appointed her household, major-domo, cook and coachman. And she was not alone. Hannah Meredith, no longer a governess but a devoted friend and counsellor, was always at her side. Although she was engaged to be married to Dr William Brown, her love for Angela always came first, and the kindly, patient Brown had to wait until December 1844 for his bride.

Angela's wealth did not bring immediate happiness; indeed, late in life she claimed that it never made her happy. She was inundated by begging letters, the most embarrassing of which came from her own family. Her sister Susan's husband, John Trevanion, who was, according to Sir Francis, a 'sad man', who had twice ruined himself, pestered her for a whole year with 'unfair and improper applications',[11] which her father advised her to reject. But she settled an annunity of £2,000 on each of her sisters and gave her mother £8,000 a year. Though she loved her father dearly, she was determined to make her own decisions.

It was not easy to have an independent life as a wealthy young heiress at that time. Sir Francis was concerned that she was 'without a protector', for there were many young men who suddenly discovered the charms of Miss Burdett-Coutts. She was, in fact, no beauty – the portrait by Masquerier shows a thin, tense young face. The stress of the unexpected inheritance had brought out a rash and she had become excessively thin under the strain, but she had her father's silvery voice and a grace and quiet composure that made her a restful companion. Lord Houghton thought she 'had a pleasing face, her figure though not full is good, her voice melodious, her expression sweet & engaging'.[12] He later recalled how all young men of 'good family' considered it to be their duty to propose. *Punch* reported that

the world set to work, match-making, determined to unite the splendid heiress to somebody. Now, she was to marry her physician; and now, she was to become a Scotch countess. The last husband up in the papers is Louis Napoleon. How Miss Coutts escaped Ibrahim Pacha when he was here is somewhat extraordinary. For if the Emperor of China were to vouchsafe to let fall his shadow upon the British Court, in the shape of an Ambassador, it would very soon appear in the papers that 'His Excellency Ching-Chow-Cherry-Chow – having cut his pigtail and conformed to the Christian religion – was about to lead Miss Burdett Coutts to the Hymenal altar'.[13]

Angela and Hannah developed a technique for dealing with these suitors. Hannah would wait in the next room while they proposed; then Angela would cough, which was the signal that she had refused and that Hannah could make her entrance.

Even Disraeli, it would seem, considered trying his luck. He was, at this time, an admirer of Sir Francis, canvassing for him in the election of 1837. Certainly he made his hero in *Endymion* consider marrying Adriana, 'the greatest heiress in England', the 'angelic being' so closely modelled on Angela. She too had 'a melodious voice', 'choice accomplishments and agreeable conversation and the sweetest temper in the world'. Unfortunately she 'wanted a little self-conceit' and was remarkable for a 'doleful look and an air of pensive resignation . . . alas this favoured maiden wished for nothing. Her books interested her . . . but she liked to be alone, or with her mother.' Disraeli, at his most perfumed and exotic at this time, had dazzled Harriot, but in his gorgeous gilded waistcoats he had little charm for the modest Angela.

However, there was one suitor who was not so easily dismissed. For nearly eighteen years Angela was pursued by a mad Irish barrister, Richard Dunn, who was to cause infinite distress to her, and some embarrassment to the Bank in the Strand. The persecution began in the summer of 1838, when, overwhelmed by her new responsibilities, Angela retreated to Harrogate with Hannah to take the sulphurous waters. Dunn, a good-looking, middle-aged man, took a room opposite hers at the Queen's Hotel and pestered her with his attentions. Finally she sent for Mr Marjoribanks, who rushed to Harrogate to protect her, bringing a policeman, William Ballard, who remained as her bodyguard. Sir Francis was hurt that she had turned to the banker for help rather than to him. But in his last years he was crippled by gout and she was reluctant to worry him. Dunn was arrested and imprisoned, but on his release pursued her to London, where he continued to harass her. Two years later the *Spectator* described her 'martyrdom' at the hands of this terrible Irishman:

Dunn had blockaded Miss Coutts for two mortal years. If she went to Harrogate he followed her; if she returned to Stratton Street he entrenched himself in the Gloucester Hotel; if she walked in the Parks, he was at her heels; if she took a walk in a private garden, he was waving handkerchiefs over the wall, or creeping through below the hedge. With his own hands he deposited his card in her sitting-room; he drove her from church, and intruded himself into the private chapel in which she took refuge. In vain her precaution to have policemen constantly in her hall, and a bodyguard of servants when she moved abroad. Denied the use of his tongue, he *bombarded* her with letters, smuggling them into her hands under all sorts of disguises. He is unparalleled in history.

In the spring of 1840 he followed her to Norwood, where she was staying with her parents. In June he pursued her so insanely that she was forced to take refuge in a friend's house. He was arrested again and imprisoned, but he was sufficiently sane and skilled as a barrister to issue a writ against her friend claiming wrongful imprisonment on insufficient evidence. In November he actually won his case and was discharged. Encouraged by his success, he now sued Angela's friend, Mr Alexander, for wrongful arrest and had the effrontery to call her as a witness. This time he was sent to the Fleet prison, where he remained until he got himself released.

The years in prison must have further deranged him, for now he began the most bizarre campaign against her. In 1846 he wrote to Marjoribanks claiming compensation from Coutts & Co. for injuries caused by wrongful imprisonment. He claimed that Angela had encouraged him, by sending him amorous verses, promising to pay him £100,000. Accordingly he presented himself at the Bank demanding his payment, which Marjoribanks naturally refused. In February 1847 he was tried at the Guildhall on the charge of perjury before Lord Denman. Angela was obliged to appear in court and hear the preposterous evidence he offered. A packed court listened as the ridiculous verses she was supposed to have written were read out:

> When to Harrogate sweet papa beats a retreat,
> To take spa waters supersulphurious,
> I could hear your heart thump as we stood near the pump,
> While you bolted that stuff so injurious.
>
> But at last I'm relenting, my jewel, repenting
> Of all that you've suffered for me;
> Why, I'm even grown tender, disposed to turn lender
> Of cash, your sweet person to free.
>
> Send to Coutts's your bill – there are lots in the till –
> I'll give the clerk orders to do it;
> Then get your discharge, your dear body enlarge,
> And in Stratton-street do let me view it.
>
> And, by-the bye, love, my affection to prove,
> For your long cruel incarceration,
> Fill a good round sum in (as I've plenty of tin)
> To make you a fair compensation.[14]

This time Dunn had gone too far; he was convicted of perjury and once again imprisoned until he was released in 1851. Even then the harassment continued.

The ridiculous case against a modest young woman, who by this time was famous for her charitable works, inspired Charles Dickens to describe her persecution in *Household Words* in an article, 'Things that cannot be done' on 8 October 1853 and in another on 24 March 1855. Finally in 1856 the agony ended when Dunn transferred his affection to Princess Mary, later Duchess of Teck. This time he was shut up in an asylum and remained there until his death. 'Remarkable', Dickens wrote to Angela, 'how brisk people are to perceive his madness the moment he begins to trouble the blood royal.'[15]

Dunn's story is the more remarkable because, throughout the eighteen years of his persecution, Angela had the advice of the experienced bankers in the Strand, the friendship of Henry Brougham and some of the most distinguished lawyers of the period, and, in the early years, the protection of a father who was the famous champion of those in distress.

35

The Marjoribanks Years

The madman Dunn was not only a plague to Angela, he was an embarrassment to the partners at Coutts & Co. Indeed, the whole procession of suitors concerned them. Although Harriot's capital was protected by the terms of the will, a difficult or impoverished husband would be a danger to the reputation of the Bank. They need not have worried. Angela assured them that she had no intention of marrying at this time.

The partners must have expected that the quiet young woman would be a relief after the temperamental Duchess. They regarded her with affection and were touched by her gentle kindness, but if they expected a docile, sleeping partner, they were soon to be disappointed. As they were to discover, Angela's gentle hand had a firm grip.

The strain of the new responsibility had made her ill for months and, after her return from convalescence in Harrogate, she went to take the cure at German spas. Invigorated and renewed, she took up her duties with surprising energy.

The partners were soon alarmed to realise that the young heiress was actually interested in the working of the Bank, and wanted to understand the ledgers and the Profit and Loss Accounts. Worse, as time went by, she began to have ideas for the improvement of the clerks' working conditions and even for the role of the Bank, urging them to support the Irish Famine Relief Fund. She had been specifically excluded by the terms of the Duchess's will from interfering in the conduct of the Bank's business, but she was convinced that, since her income came from the Bank, it was her duty to understand its working. Such intervention was not welcome at 59 Strand, for the partners at the Bank were an impressive and experienced team under the firm guidance of Edward Marjoribanks.

In 1837 Sir Coutts Trotter, the senior partner, died, thus ending the rivalry with Marjoribanks, who in 1838 brought in his son, Edward, as a junior partner and who, for the rest of his long life, dominated Coutts & Co., becoming increasingly autocratic as the years went by. The period until his death in 1868 may well be called the Marjoribanks years: he gave the stability and continuity on which rested the confidence so essential to a bank's survival.

In 1838 Marjoribanks, now senior partner, was sixty-two with forty years' experience at Coutts & Co. Devoted to Thomas's memory, he maintained his traditions and principles and was prepared to serve his granddaughter with the same dedication. This he did, giving her paternal guidance and affection to such a degree that his own daughters became jealous. However, he was not prepared to allow any interference in the running of the Bank, so there was sometimes friction.

Over six feet tall, immensely dignified and grave, he set his own mark on the Bank in the Strand. Like Thomas, he was an 'exact' man, careful and punctilious. In old age he wrote his memoirs in a clear, neat hand, and his accounts were meticulously presented. He was, however, made of sterner stuff and was less generous than his master. Although, remembering Thomas's example, he also occasionally risked a loan to a needy artist. Haydon recalled him with gratitude and in 1846, with a painter's pen, brought him vividly to life.

I fear nothing on earth but my Banker, when I have not 5/- on acct & have a bill coming due and want help! The awful & steady look of his searching eyes; the quiet & investigating point of his simple questions: the 'hums' as he holds down his head, as if he had Atlas on his shoulders and the solemn tone when he declares it is against the rules of the House; the reprieve one feels as the tones of his voice begin to melt & give symptoms of an opening to let in light to the heart, are not to be described, & can only be understood by those who have been in such predicaments. Marjoribanks is always kind at last. The Clerks seem to be wonderstruck at the charm I seem to possess among the Partners.

The fact is, Coutts have had a great deal to do always with men of Genius, & they have a feeling for them, & seem to think it is a credit to the House to have one or two to scold, assist, blow up, and then forgive. This is the way I have gone on with them 29 years.[1]

Marjoribanks's second in command was Sir Edmund Antrobus, who had now been at Coutts & Co. for more than twenty years. The nephew of the first Sir Edmund, he had fluent French and German, and an understanding of Europe, which enabled him to deal with distinguished foreign customers with ease and confidence.

When Haydon saw him to ask for another loan, he noted that Antrobus

was looking much older than I. His head trembled a little and his hand shook. He said, 'I am fifty to-morrow.' 'Why, sir, I am sixty.' 'Sixty?' says he; 'no!' 'It is twenty-nine years ago since I opened my account. Mr. Harman paid me £300, and I came to your house.' 'Time passes,' said he. Sir Edward [*sic*] Antrobus was looking old and wrinkled. I declare I feel as young as ever. These rich men always look older than we struggling men of talent.[2]

The third partner, steady William Matthew Coulthurst, had quietly undertaken much of the drudgery of the work during his ten years at the Bank.

Marjoribanks's son, Edward, was at this time very much in the shadow of his father. Gentle and conscientious, he adopted his father's grave manner.

There was not always the harmony between the partners that there had been in the days of the first Sir Edmund. Marjoribanks senior was determined to establish his family ascendancy, and there was an undercurrent of jealousy between Sir Edmund Antrobus and Marjoribanks which surfaced when Antrobus wanted to bring in his son, Hugh Lindsay, as a partner.

At first Marjoribanks was prepared to give Hugh Lindsay a trial; indeed, on 29 June 1843 he wrote to Angela recommending the 'early admission of a new partner into your House, and none of us can now feel more strongly than I do that Mr Lindsay Antrobus (after such trial as you and Sir Edmund may think right) is the party to whom a preference ought to be given'.[3] But for some reason, after Hugh Lindsay had worked for two years in the Bank, Marjoribanks changed his mind. Sir Edmund wrote to him on 19 June 1845, saying that he had called 'this morning on Miss Coutts to speak to her about my son and ask her permission to admit him as a partner on the 24th. She has very kindly assented to my request. . . .'[4] Edmund's hope that Marjoribanks would agree was dashed. The old man refused; it was, he said, too short a notice and too near the end of the Bank's financial year. Was Marjoribanks worried that the wealthy Antrobus family would become too dominant? Was he annoyed that Edmund had gone over his head to Angela? It is puzzling, since Hugh Lindsay was charming and hardworking and Marjoribanks himself claimed that he had not diminished his 'very good opinion of your son'.[5] But, in spite of Edmund's continued appeals, he refused to admit Hugh Lindsay as a full partner, though he was allowed to remain on a salary. Finally he closed the subject by referring Edmund to his lawyer for an explanation. Angela must have at last overcome his objections, since Hugh Lindsay became a partner in 1857 and was ever grateful to 'our lady', as he affectionately called her.

Partners and clerks alike carried on the Bank in the tradition of Thomas Coutts, and because they represented continuity they gave confidence. Customers could come to Coutts & Co. and find familiar faces who knew them and their families. Visible and accessible at their desks in the Bank, the partners were symbols of stability in a changing world.

When Marjoribanks wrote his memoirs in 1862, he could look back on this period with some pleasure:

It is satisfactory to the present Partners to be enabled to state that since 1837 when the Business was placed under their charges it has not only maintained its former character of respectability but also added materially to the annual returns of profit – This has been done too without any addition to the same joint Stock Capital that was employed 40 years ago – The difference being now (on an average percentage of years) nearly 30 per cent in favor of the present time.[6]

This was much to their credit, since this was a difficult time for private banks when there was keen competition from joint stock banks. Coutts & Co. survived for a variety of reasons: because the Bank was directed by competent partners and clerks with long experience and honourable traditions; because it kept well-filled coffers and a Reserve Fund; and because royal patronage and an impressive list of aristocratic customers inspired confidence. So it was able to withstand the competition, which, as Marjoribanks wrote,

was to be expected from the formation during the last thirty years of Joint Stock Banks with their many Branches spread over London giving interest on the deposits placed therein – the Rate of interest on which, has amounted on several occasions from 8 to 10 per cent varying with the fluctuations of demands in the Money Market. . . .[7]

The rivalry between private banks and joint stock banks at this time needs some explanation. The boom years of 1822–4 had been followed by the 'panic' of 1825, when even the Bank of England's gold was nearly exhausted. This caused major changes in financial legislation.

Before the Act of 1826 private banks were not allowed by law to have more than six partners unless permission was granted by Royal Charter. When they failed, other private banks were affected and a 'panic' followed. In 1820, when a financial crisis of this nature happened in Ireland, the London Government, in an attempt to widen the source of capital, allowed banks of more than six partners to be formed, provided that they were fifty Irish miles outside Dublin. This provided a model for the Act of 1826, which similarly lifted restrictions in England. In May 1826 the Banking Co-Partnership Act allowed the formation of banks with an unlimited number of partners, provided that they operated outside a radius of sixty-five miles from London. But it retained the obligation of unlimited liability on those partners for the debts of the banks. It was hoped that larger partnerships would provide wider access to greater capital, greater confidence and fewer 'panics'.

The result was the growth of a large number of joint stock banks which flourished, often replacing small private banks. They had an additional advantage: they paid their customers interest on deposits – a practice which, in the past, Thomas Coutts had regarded with horror.

The question of paying interest on deposits was a particularly vexed one for Coutts & Co., since the Scottish and Irish banks with whom they were allied had always been accustomed to do so. It was not until the 1850s that it became clear that the Bank in the Strand would also have to give way. At first it made an exception for the Royal Bank of Scotland, but it was some time before the Bank of Ireland was similarly accommodated. Even then it was a privilege only accorded to special customers with large deposits.

The competition from the rapidly growing joint stock banks put considerable pressure on private banks, many of which collapsed. Others, like Hammersleys, had to lose their identity through amalgamation.

Thomas Hammersley had been a clerk in the banking house of Thomas's old rival, Robert Herries, and had in 1780 started his own bank in Pall Mall. After his death, his successor, Hugh Hammersley, found it increasingly difficult to carry on and, in 1838, approached Coutts & Co. with a view to amalgamation. On his death two years later, his Executors stopped payment and Coutts & Co. took it over. They pensioned off the old clerks but kept on four younger ones. There was a certain irony in this transaction. Apart from the earlier rivalry, Thomas had been considerably annoyed when the Prince of Wales had transferred his account to Hammersley in 1787. Although the Prince had returned to Coutts & Co. as his chief bankers, he had still kept some funds with Hammersley.

Marjoribanks claimed that Coutts & Co. survived partly because he had had the foresight to put down a reserve fund. The 'panic' of 1825 had shaken the Government and caused a series of investigations and reviews in which bankers and economists emphasised the need for reserve funds, which, as Marjoribanks realised, were doubly necessary for private banks. In Thomas's day, Sir Edmund Antrobus had suggested such a fund, but Thomas had always insisted that it was not necessary since he himself always kept a reserve of at least £100,000.

Just as important was the efficient organisation which Marjoribanks and the partners inherited from Thomas. In 1873 the economist Walter Bagehot wrote:

The great private banks will have, I believe, to appoint in some form or other, some species of general manager who will watch, contrive and arrange the detail for them. . . . The want of a good organisation may cause the failure of one or more of these banks (i.e. private banks); and such failure of such banks may intensify a panic, even if it should not cause one.[8]

Coutts & Co. had always had just such a man in charge of the organisation. Andrew Dickie and, after him, George Robinson were called chief clerks, but in fact they dealt as general managers with the detail of day-to-day business and had great responsibility and influence. Thomas had set high standards: he was not only, as he always said, an 'exact man', he was also an 'exacting man'. Dickie handed on the traditions to his successors, and when later, Robinson became Chief Clerk, he kept the principles Thomas had taught him when he arrived as a young clerk in 1815. So there was continuity which lasted throughout the century. Robinson was to remember, in old age, how careful Thomas had been in choosing competent clerks who could stand the inevitable drudgery of the job. The same care was exercised in the appointment of clerks as there had always been. Even their distinguished customers could not plant their sons or protégés as clerks in Coutts & Co. unless they met Thomas's exacting standards. The work was hard and the hours were long, but clerks often remained with Coutts & Co. all their lives. Their pay was good by contemporary standards and they received an annual supplement from the Clerks' Fund.*

Undoubtedly one of the main reasons for the survival of Coutts & Co. in the changing and competitive world of nineteenth-century banking was that it was Queen Victoria's bank. The Duchess of Kent had impressed upon her daughter how much the Duke had owed to Thomas Coutts, who had not only been his banker but also his friend. As will be seen, Angela Burdett-Coutts was to play an important part in maintaining the same relationship with Queen Victoria, so making a personal contribution to the stability of the Bank. When Lord Melbourne wanted to discuss the debts of the Duchess of Kent, he came to the young heiress. Queen Victoria noted in her diary:

Lord Melbourne said she was clever, for that she had behaved very well about the money for Ma's debts; when they came to her (as she is the principal person in the House). She made no difficulty about it; they told her she must not speak of it; she said she never told her father these things as he was engaged in politics but that she would not mention this even to her mother.[9]

Since Angela was as discreet as her grandfather it is difficult to assess exactly how much the Queen and her family were indebted to her personal generosity.

The partners too came to the rescue of Victoria's mother, for which she was duly grateful. She wrote to the 'Gentlemen', from Buckingham Palace on 7 March 1838:

Lord Duncannon has just informed me, of your having so Kindly assisted me, in raising money, to pay off Debts, I had incurred previous to the Queen's accession, for Her maintenance.

His Lordship tells me the sum is larger than what your House is in the habit of advancing; but that you do so, to evince your respect for me.

---

* In 1833, for example, the Fund, which was made up of donations from customers and partners, totalled £1,479 3s 6d. This was divided into eighty-two shares and allotted according to seniority to thirty-nine clerks. Salaries ranged in scale from that of the chief clerk, which was increased between 1827 and 1880 from £1,010 to £1,591 13s 4d, down to the most junior, who received £100 per annum in 1827 and £317 7s 0d in 1880.

Permit me to say, that I gratefully acknowledge your feeling – it corresponds with that of the late Mr Coutts, who, on the great and sad calamity which befell me in 1820, and which was accompanied by pecuniary embarrassment, generously placed any sum at my command.

> I remain Gentlemen
> Your obliged and sincere friend,
>   Victoria[10]

Not only the royal family but also a great number of noble lords and ladies continued to bank at Coutts. Such customers were sometimes more bother than they were worth, but nevertheless they brought prestige and that most valuable of commodities – confidence. There were old Scottish friends among the new customers like the publisher, John Murray, and there was also a new kind of customer appearing in the ledgers: Arthur Guinness, brewer, and Samuel Ries of the Cigar Divan in the Strand, which later became Simpsons.

Portrait of Harriot Coutts by Sir William Beechey

Top left: Part of a love letter from Thomas to Harriot, with the mark of his lips on it

Top right: Bust of Thomas Coutts by Nollekens

Bottom: The garden of Holly Lodge, Harriot's villa in Highgate

	1778	1799	1816	1823	1829	1838	1839
Number of Accounts exclusive of Private Ledger	566	2004	3988	4721	5324	6192	6174
Amount of deposits by Customers	£491582 · 1 · 0 £117790 · 6 · 9 £1799771 · 14 · 6	£1432822 · 15 · 3 £807376 · 7 · 8 £624447 · 7 · 10	£1153347 · 7 · 10 £43828 · 4 · 2 £1157510 · 3 · 8	£2140708 · 12 · 9 £76385 · 17 · 1 £2067302 · 15 · 8	£3070539 · 9 · 4 £64748 · 11 · 8 £3005790 · 12 · 8	£2775735 · 16 · 4 £52329 · 4 · 5 £2523406 · 11 · 5	£2503697 · 8 · 1 £22887 · 11 · 3 £2526809 · 16 · 6
Profits of Business expenses being deducted	£12278 · 12 · -	£33764 · 3 · 6	£75029 · 6 · 8	£72393 · 5 · 9	£77122 · 19 · 11	£84663 · 10 · 2	£89152 · 8 · 7
Amount of Expenses	£533 · 8 · 11	£2163 · 5 · 10	£5525 · 12 · 6	£5471 · 6 · -	£7461 · 2 · 1	£8481 · 8 · 8	£8682 · 2 · 3
D° · Wages	340 · - · -	2637 · - · 2	6939 · 15 · -	7453 · 14 · -	8402 · 5 · 10	8966 · 17 · -	8725 · - · -
	£873 · 8 · 11	£4800 · 6 · -	£12465 · 7 · -	£12925 · - · -	£16003 · 7 · 11	£17448 · 5 · 8	£17407 · 2 · 3
Amount of Capital Stock	£24000 · -	£58000 · -	£172,000	£200,000	£200,000	£200,000	£200,000
Accounts with Balances of £2000 & upwards	20	75	141	214	266	271	227
Number of Clerks	5	19	34	38	40	42	42

	1849	1850	1851	1852	1853	1854	
Reserve Fund	£10,000	£20,000	£20,000	£20,000	£15,000	£15,000	£130,000

Top left: Watercolour portrait of Sir Francis Burdett by William Ross with the bust of his mentor, the radical lawyer John Horne Tooke, in the background

Top right: William Matthew Coulthurst, partner in the Bank from 1827 to 1877

Bottom: A page of neatly written Bank accounts from Edward Marjoribanks's memoirs

Top: 59 Strand – the old 'Shop', 1885

Bottom: The banking hall, 59 Strand, around 1900

Angela Burdett as a young girl, by her old friend Masquerier

Top: The Duke of Wellington with his grandchildren, one of whom was to become the wife of William Rolle Malcolm. This painting by Thorburn was commissioned by Angela Burdett-Coutts.

Bottom left: Sir James Brooke, Rajah of Sarawak, supported by loans from Miss Coutts and from the Bank

Bottom right: Charles Dickens, valued customer and close friend of Miss Coutts

Top left: Queen Victoria on horseback, 1849

Top right: Engraving of Louis Philippe, one of the Bank's French royal customers

Bottom left: Princess Victoria Mary of Teck, later Queen Mary, the daughter of one of Angela Burdett-Coutts's particular friends

Bottom right: Letter from David Livingstone from the Zambezi, 20 February 1862, instructing that his salary as Consul should be paid to Coutts & Co.

Top left: George Robinson by W. W. Ouless. Robinson, a clerk at the Bank from 1815, became a partner in 1869, only the second clerk in the Bank's history to be so honoured.

Top right: Frederick Augustus Shannon, the Bank's confidential agent who handled its affairs in France

Bottom: A vividly illustrated South American share bond, 1878

36

A World of Change

Angela Burdett-Coutts took up her inheritance in 1837 in the middle of two decades of unprecedented, convulsive change, not only in domestic and international politics, but also in finance and industry, in religion and in social life, which profoundly affected how men and women lived, worked and thought. Old patterns of life, beliefs and systems were shattered and remodelled. New inventions and discoveries brought growth, but so turbulent a time also brought much pain and distress.

In that period the new railways spanned the country, the new steamships spanned the seas. It was a restless time with thousands of people on the move, some fleeing the revolutions that rocked Europe between 1830 and 1848, some emigrating to America to escape the great Irish famine of 1846. Many in 1849 were driven by gold fever to the mines of California. A correspondent wrote a vivid account to Coutts & Co. of the sudden increase in the value of property in Melbourne after gold was discovered.

At the same time there was a great and hitherto unexplained population explosion, which drove people from the countryside to the cities, where they starved and lived in squalor. Bad harvests increased the price of bread and the Corn Laws prevented the import of cheap corn from abroad. These laws, fiercely attacked from all sides, provoked violent demonstrations until Sir Robert Peel was forced to repeal them in 1846. His action split the Tory party, but diminished the danger of the revolution that many believed was imminent. The situation in Europe reinforced their fears.

Events in Europe over that period were of particular importance both to the partners in the Bank and to Angela. In the seesaw of that time they saw their friend and customer, Louis Philippe, raised to the throne of France in 1830 and dashed down by revolution in 1848. And they saw Angela's supposed suitor, Louis Napoleon, rise from exile to become Emperor of the French in 1851.

From 1830 onwards Europe had been disrupted by revolutions and by movements for national liberation. In that year the French King, Charles X, was overthrown and Louis Philippe became King of France. In that quick coup, his sister, Madame Adelaïde, and Lady Burdett's 'chère amie' of earlier days, had played a decisive role. It was she, the *'forte tête'* of the family, as Thiers called her, who encouraged her brother to stay in France rather than follow Charles X once more into exile. Louis Philippe's other close adviser, the banker, Lafitte, was another old acquaintance of Thomas Coutts and the partners in the Strand.

Marjoribanks and Trotter remembered Louis Philippe from his days in England and now placed his account in their ledgers under 'K' for King of the French. He too did not forget old friends. The partners at the Bank received valuable mementos in gratitude for their kindness in his days of exile. But the bourgeois King, who tried so hard to remain a plain, simple man, and who accepted with easy humour the caricatures of his pear-shaped head, had inherited a shaky throne.

In Paris and throughout Europe, rebels were on the march waving the old banners of liberty, equality and fraternity and new banners proclaiming their desire for national identity. The new movements 'Young England', 'Young Germany' and 'Young Italy' aroused wild enthusiasms, overturning kings and governments. In attics and salons, at banquets and in cafés, men and women of widely differing backgrounds and professions, lawyers and poets, artists and musicians, came together with workers to plot and plan for the new dawn.

Some rebellions were quickly crushed. In 1830 Russia invaded Poland, forcing hundreds into emigration. Thomas's grandson, Dudley Coutts Stuart, as has been seen, took up the Polish cause with enthusiasm; and his cousin Angela was to continue his work. But the disturbances lasted throughout the decade, reaching their climax in 1848, the year of revolutions.

In fact, although every European country was affected by the turmoil, all the revolutionary forces were defeated within the year. In 1848, however, the movements had grown in strength and the old world seemed about to be swept away. In smoke-filled rooms in Brussels, Karl Marx and Friedrich Engels drew up their Communist Manifesto, calling on the workers of the world to unite – they 'had nothing to lose but their chains'. This was the first shot in the year of revolutions in which the first throne to fall was that of Louis Philippe. A libertarian at heart, had he been a younger man he might have accommodated himself to the new world. But his sister Adelaïde, his strong right hand, had just died and his spirit was broken. As Proudhon, his devoted supporter, wrote, *'On craint pour l'année qui vient.'* His fears were justified. In vain King Louis Philippe sacrificed his unpopular minister Guizot and introduced reforms. His troops fired on insurgents, killing some. Roused to fury they sacked his Palais Royal, and Karl Marx could report with glee how his friends were now camped in the Tuileries in Louis Philippe's splendid rooms.

On 24 February 1848 Louis Philippe abdicated his throne in favour of his grandson, the Comte de Paris. He and his old wife, Marie Amélie, walked on foot through the Tuileries gardens to the Place de la Concorde, to await the carriages that would take them first to his childhood home, the Château de St Cloud, and then to the coast to take ship for England. According to Victor Hugo, as he sank into his carriage, Louis Philippe took off his toupee, so beloved by caricaturists, and covered his head with a black scarf. His wife turned to him and said, 'You look a hundred years old.'

When he landed in Newhaven, one of his first acts was to send a message to the partners at Coutts & Co. announcing his arrival under the name of Le Comte de Neuilly – in France he had travelled with his wife as M. et Madame Le Brun. Angela herself came immediately to their assistance. Leopold, King of the Belgians, who had married the daughter of Louis Philippe as his second wife, lent them his house at Claremont in Surrey, which had been given to him and his first wife, Princess Charlotte, by her father George IV. Here they lived for the rest of their days and here Louis Philippe died at the age of seventy-seven on 26 August 1850 – he was buried at Weybridge. Marie Amélie lived on for another sixteen years, becoming increasingly religious and slightly eccentric, obsessive about the arrangements for laying out her body after her death and her funeral. She outlived five of their ten children, from whom some of the present customers of Coutts & Co. are descended.

Angela visited Claremont and entertained the Orléans family at Stratton Street, keeping alive, until the end of the nineteenth century, a friendship which her grandfather had begun before the French Revolution. How much financial support she gave them we shall never know, but in the years when the Orléans possessions were sequestrated by the French Government, it is certain that they were often glad of her help. Members of the French royal family later wrote remembering these days with great gratitude.

The partners at the Bank took care of their financial affairs. But the French connection with Coutts & Co. endured not only because of the competence of the partners, but also because of the genuine personal friendship that Thomas Coutts, his daughter Lady Burdett and his grand-daughter Angela developed over more than a century.

This was a period not only of political revolution, but also of great industrial and social change, and all these elements affected the banking world. Perhaps the most important development at this time was the growth of the railways and steam navigation. Steel and coal industries were stimulated; labourers were imported – mainly from Ireland – to dig the cuttings; cities were disrupted, houses demolished and water supplies cut, exacerbating the already grave problems of homelessness and poverty. The march of progress often left desolation and destruction behind. It was to rescue the wounded on this battlefield that Angela was to direct her energies.

The march of progress also brought prosperity to the banking world and that prosperity made Angela's generosity possible. In Thomas's day, the Bank had made few investments, because he himself was extremely cautious. Now there was spare capital and a new home for it in the expanding industries. The spread of railways at home and abroad attracted speculators. Fortunes could be made and lost on the railroads and Coutts's customers were among the many who took the gamble.

One of the interesting results of the boom in railway expansion which was to involve Coutts & Co. closely was the development of the town of Surbiton. It is a good example of the drive and energy in Victorian England. The new railways made it possible for commuters to live outside an over-crowded London. The population explosion stimulated the building boom, encouraging new ideas in housing for the growing class of skilled workers. Increasing prosperity put capital in the hands of men who were often not trained to deal with their ambitious schemes. Such a man was the extraordinary entrepreneur, Thomas Pooley, who saw the potential of land near the new railway station at Surbiton.

In 1838 the new London and Southampton Railway opened a station at Surbiton, then an isolated village on a hill near Kingston in Surrey. Pooley, a wealthy maltster, bought a tract of land nearby, previously owned by a rich merchant, Christopher Terry, who had died in January 1838 leaving instructions that his estate be sold in order to pay the beneficiaries of his will. Pooley realised the value of land near a station with easy access to London, and he bought most of the estate at what *The Times* considered the surprisingly low price of £105 per acre. He could have made an instant profit by accepting the offer of a London consortium of £120,000 for the estate, but instead decided to realise a dream and build a new town centred on the railway. It was to be, he said, 'beautifully designed, and a great number of houses of various descriptions and sizes suitable for the occupation of persons of various means and circumstances'.[1] Who knows what had inspired this vision at a time long before the fashion for garden suburbs and new towns?

Pooley was a man of extraordinary energy – part rogue, part visionary. He was a Cornishman, who had moved to London at the turn of the century and made enough money to be able to establish a thriving business as a maltster in Kingston; he also owned three cargo ships, the *Agnes*, the *Elizabeth* and the *King Mahon Castle*. His son, Alexander, married the daughter of another successful maltster, George Wadbrook, who, according to the Kingston Bailiff minutes, was fined for 'cursing and swearing ten times during time of divine service'.[2] Wadbrook built a handsome house, The Elms, on the Surbiton road, which he subsequently left to his son, William, who was an equally rough diamond. According to the *Surrey Comet*, Wadbrook 'went about in corduroy knee breeches and maltsters' cap'.³ He was considered a man of great wealth, having five stars to his name as a holder of shares in the East India Company – each star denoting the sum of £20,000.

The Wadbrooks were not the only new rich to invest in Pooley's town. A brickmaker, John Selfe, who had married William Wadbrook's daughter, bought prime sites on Surbiton Hill to the annoyance of the more distinguished residents. With such family backing, Pooley began building crescents and streets, and moved into one of his newly built houses in Claremont Crescent (now The Crescent); his twenty-eight-year-old son, Alexander, took the first house in Victoria Street.

From the beginning he met with fierce opposition from the old established residents of nearby Kingston. The Town Council rejected his application for the erection of a corn market and, according to *The Times*, he had to encounter 'prejudice, both of communities and individuals and to contend single-handed against a host of selfish feeling and interested opposition'.⁴

The speed with which fields and farmlands were transformed into building sites horrified the residents of Kingston. Contemporary writers dismissed the new houses as of 'a somewhat capricious style of architecture'. But Pooley had employed a distinguished architect, Harvey Elmes, who was later awarded a gold medal by the Prince Consort. *The Times* was more generous:

Nothing in the history of railway improvements has been more extraordinary than the creation of this singular new town. On the spot where, last harvest two years, a large crop of oats was reaped, now stand rows of handsome houses, terraces, villas, Swiss and other ornamental cottages, a splendid hotel and tavern, with assembly, billiard and coffee rooms, and other useful and ornamental buildings; while gasworks, waterworks and other necessary adjuncts to the health and comfort of a town are about to be commenced, as also an episcopalian church, and a Wesleyan meeting house. . . . In addition to any detached houses which are dotted about the parklike scenery of the new town a large crescent named after her Majesty's Palace at Claremont, is laid out for villas in pairs and detached, some of which are already inhabited, and foundations for others are being daily excavated. The wide and handsome roads that meander through the town are hourly frequented by the fashionable equestrians and characters of the neighbourhood.⁵

The value of the land, again according to *The Times*, had

increased to an incalculable extent, in some cases to an extent almost beyond belief, and the land is becoming more valuable every day . . . on some situations the prospects are magnificent, embracing the parks of Hampton, Bushy, Claremont and other places, the Castle of Windsor and the spire of Harrow. . . . Great credit is due to the good taste of Mr Pooley, the founder of the place, as well as to his enterprise and unceasing exertions to carry out his design . . . when it is taken into account that all the works at this place have been planned and directed by one individual, and that the whole expense of the operation has been defrayed by one purse, the rapidity with which the whole has proceeded, and the judgement by which it has been conducted, are surprising.[6]

However, by December 1840 Pooley was beginning to get into financial difficulties and in that month borrowed £2,000 from Coutts & Co.[7] But his debts still mounted. He had taken on a project far too great for his resources and had not the intellectual ability to deal with it. His letters show him as an almost illiterate man, but one of great imagination. On 4 October 1841 he was taken to court for non-payment of debt and judgment passed against him.

In January 1842 Coutts & Co. refused to lend him any more and he turned to the bankers, Drummonds, for help. Now he was assailed on all sides: unpaid seamen from his ships *Agnes* and *Elizabeth* threatened to kill him; banks, solicitors and more than twenty claimants harassed him over the next two years. Even his solicitors wrote despairingly to Coutts & Co. that there was 'bad feeling existing between himself and certain parties living at Kingston who will always endeavour to injure the property as long as Mr Pooley is connected therewith'.[8]

In 1842 his unfinished houses were vandalised; it was clear that Pooley would never be allowed to succeed and, therefore, although the value of his estate was more than adequate as security for his debts, Coutts & Co. decided to break with him. If they allowed him to become bankrupt, they would never recover their loan. Some say that Coutts & Co. treated Pooley shabbily, and certainly it is difficult to understand why, when Pooley offered to sell all his holdings to Coutts & Co. in exchange for a life annuity of £1,000, they refused.[9] But it was clear to the partners that Surbiton would never prosper while Pooley was in charge.

In June 1842 Pooley, now at the end of his tether, agreed to hand over his holdings to Trustees appointed by his principal creditors in exchange for £5 per week. Harassed by his creditors, he fled to Boulogne, but came back in 1843 when his son Alexander was dangerously ill. In January 1844 he met his solicitor at his house in the Old Kent Road, who advised him not to return to Surbiton and persuaded him to sign away all claim to his Surbiton property. Pooley later said that he had been plied with drink and forced to sign and for two years fought his case in the Court of Chancery. Who knows where or when he died, but Alexander continued the battle for his father's cause until the 1850s, when he too disappeared and died – presumably abroad.

The estate was sold piecemeal until in 1898 there was an auction of freehold ground rents.[10]

Meanwhile, in 1844 Coutts & Co. took charge of the development of Surbiton, taking possession of most of the new town. They employed John

Stevens as an architect and surveyor. He had been Pooley's confidant throughout and now, according to contemporaries, 'each day on Coutts' behalf [he] drove from London in his four-in-hand and toured his newly acquired domain in lordly style'.[11] Coutts & Co.'s records show a payment of £300 on 4 July 1844 to Stevens. He was later paid off and replaced by Mr Hardwicke, the architect used by Angela in London.

William Coulthurst had watched over the development of Surbiton from the beginning; with Marjoribanks he had helped to guide Coutts & Co. through the traumatic affair of Thomas Pooley. Coulthurst never married, but was devoted to his brothers Nicholas and Henry and especially to his sister, Hannah Mabella. In 1851 they all lived with him at Streatham Lodge, Croydon, cared for by twelve servants. Henry died on 13 May 1870 and Nicholas emigrated to Canada in 1871. But although only his sister and his nephew, Edmund, were still with him, he kept a considerable establishment at Streatham Lodge, with seven servants: butler, footman, groom, housekeeper, lady's maid, housemaid and kitchen maid.[12] The outdoor staff lived in six adjoining cottages which he also owned.

He had brought Edmund in to the Bank as a junior partner in 1857, but his nephew was no banker. He and his brother seem to have enjoyed their uncle's wealth, buying themselves a handsome yacht, but Edmund remains a shadowy figure in the history of the Bank. It was a sign of the changing times that Coutts & Co. should now help to build a garden suburb. Thomas Coutts had lent money to create fantastic palaces for princes.

37

Miss Coutts – Loving and Giving

No one could have faced the challenges of the new world with more zest than Angela Burdett-Coutts. Once she had conquered her initial shyness and regained her health, she looked for ways in which she could use her great wealth.

If Queen Victoria began her reign determined to be good, Angela decided that her role was to do good. Of all the philanthropists of the Victorian age there was no one who supported such a variety of worthy causes and was so actively involved in bringing about change.

Her first aim was to spend her wealth in the service of the Church and, under the influence of her clerical friends, she contributed to the church building campaign of the Bishop of London. She built St Stephen's Church in Westminster at a cost of £100,000, as a memorial to her father. Sir Francis would have been touched, but in fact neither he nor Sophia had been particularly religious. But he would have approved her addition of a school and rooms for society and guild meetings, and later a technical institute, making the Church the centre of the community. The foundation-stone of St Stephen's was laid on 20 July 1847 and the Church was consecrated on 24 June 1850. The Duke of Wellington presented the altar cloth and a sixteenth-century silk curtain, taken from Tippoo Sahib's tent at the storming of Seringapatam.

Angela built a second St Stephen's in Carlisle, with a fine peal of eight bells. In 1847 she extended her work for the Church overseas, paying for the establishment of bishoprics in Adelaide, South Australia, and Cape Town, South Africa; and in 1857 she founded the bishopric of British Columbia in Canada – each at a cost of £50,000.

However, she managed to combine her deep religious conviction with a fascination with the new world of science. Even as a girl she had shared her mother's interest in fossils, and like her aunt, Lady Bute, had enjoyed lectures on astronomy. In her new position she encouraged and supported almost every branch of science.

It says much for Angela's foresight and intelligence that she had seen, as early as 1839, the genius in Charles Babbage, the man whose 'calculating engine' was the forerunner of the computer. The directors and staff, who, in the twentieth century, unveiled the first computer at Coutts & Co., were perhaps unaware that, so long ago, Angela had been taken by the inventor to see his huge analytical engine in his backyard. When the Government refused to renew their grant so that he could produce an improved model, she encouraged him, and though there is no record of her financial support, it is likely that she would have opened her purse to a man she so admired. When later he wrote a book called *The Views of the Industry, the Science and the Government of England – the Diatribe of a Disappointed Man*, he proposed to dedicate it to her in gratitude for her support, but decided that so sour a book was not worthy of her.

Michael Faraday became her close friend and invited her to see his experiments in his attic. She was a regular visitor to his Friday lectures at the Royal Institution and he encouraged her to apply for membership of the Royal Society, since, as he wrote to her, 'I earnestly desire to see lady members received among us'.[1] In February 1847 she became a full member and Faraday remained her friend – making her an exception to his firm rule not to accept social engagements. He even watched the fireworks at the end of the Crimean War from the roof of her house, where the Reverend Julian Young remembered him as 'he halloaed out with a wonderful vivacity . . . there goes magnesium, there's potassium'.[2] Faraday later helped Angela to conduct some experiments with an ozonometer, with which she tested the air of Torquay.

Charles Wheatstone, who invented the stereoscope and the concertina and made an important contribution to the electric telegraph, was another frequent guest at Stratton Street. Charles Dickens once accompanied Angela to a Friday lecture at the Royal Institution, hoping that 'Wheatstone in the exposition of those marvels will not be too shrill'.[3]

She was fascinated by the early experiments in photography, and spent many an evening with the Astronomer Royal watching the stars through his new telescope. Later she was to take a bright young Cornish geologist, William Pengelly, under her wing and founded a geological scholarship at Oxford in his honour. Her interest in geology stimulated a passionate enthusiasm for archaeology, which led her to an important friendship with Austin Henry Layard, the explorer, archaeologist and diplomat.

Angela was fortunate that at the beginning of her career she had the advice and friendship of two of the most remarkable men of the time. The Duke of Wellington encouraged her to understand and take care of money; Charles Dickens taught her how best to spend it.

Nothing better illustrates the quality of the young heiress than that she gained the respect and affection of two such men. Angela became Dickens's 'dearest friend' and, in his eyes, 'the noblest spirit we can ever know'.[4]

After two decades of friendship he could write, 'How I love and honour you, you know in part though you can never fully know.'[5] Two years older than her, his love for her was that of a brother: she was Agnes to his David Copperfield. From 1838 until the collapse of his marriage in 1857, he wrote her hundreds of letters – more than 500 of which she carefully preserved. Unfortunately only a handful of her letters to him have survived; the rest were presumably burnt when Dickens made a great bonfire of his friends' letters in his garden at Gad's Hill.

The Duke of Wellington, too, loved and respected her. 'You have', he wrote on 12 January 1847, 'a clear correct judgment: which with an excellent heart will always keep you right.'[6] These are words that might well have been written about her grandfather, Thomas Coutts.

She kept Wellington's letters, carefully bundled together, tied with strips of paper and sealed with her ring, and left instructions that, after her death, they should be returned to the Duke's descendants. There are 842 in all, the first dating from 18 May 1839. Little remains of her letters to him, so that she emerges in all this double correspondence as only a reflection, mirrored in their eyes.

These letters, so different, often arrived at 1 Stratton Street on the same day – Wellington's addressed to 'Miss Angela' in his illegible, but gallant, eighteenth-century style; Dickens's were headed 'My dear Miss Coutts' and, later, 'Dearest friend', and written in clear, neat handwriting. The two men were poles apart in personality and in their attitude to life. Dickens was an idealist whose faith in people was, as he once said, 'illimitable'. Wellington was generous and, as he told Angela, endeavoured to 'do good effectually'.[7] But he was profoundly sceptical with a limited understanding of ordinary men and women. When their advice differed, it was Dickens who usually won, for though the great Duke touched her heart, Dickens opened her eyes, her mind and her imagination. It was with him that she began a vast and varied programme of philanthropy, in a partnership that lasted until the breakdown of his marriage.

'I have never begun a book . . . or done anything of importance to me but it was a Friday,' Dickens later wrote to Angela; '. . . it must have been on a Friday that I first dined with you at Mr Marjoribanks.'[8] The date of that dinner party is not known, but it may have been some time in 1838 that the grave old banker first introduced his brilliant young customer to Angela.

Dickens had opened an account with Coutts & Co. in November 1837 with his first substantial earnings from the *Pickwick Papers*. It was a book that immensely amused not only the Burdett family, but also Marjoribanks, who, in the tradition set by Thomas Coutts, made a point of encouraging men of promise in the world of the arts.

Dickens, glowing in the full flush of his first success, made an immediate impact on the quiet young heiress. For some time afterwards she pursued him with 'cards of invitations', which, as he told her, 'reached him in Scotland, in Yorkshire and Kent'.[9] But there were more 'regrets' than acceptances among his early letters to her. One of her few letters to be preserved described how, 'Notes and cards having failed, a body of cavalry, headed by Mr Marjoribanks and myself made an attempt on your house'.[10]

Dickens, the radical, regarded Sir Francis as a political renegade. He had not known him in the days when he was 'England's Glory' and saw him now as an old man in his dotage, but he was flattered that he had referred to *Oliver Twist* in a speech at Birmingham. Sir Francis had been disturbed by the book: 'Whether anything like it exists or not', he wrote to Angela on 27 November 1838, 'I mean to make enquiry, for it is quite dreadful and to society in this country most disgraceful.'[11] In fact the 'bow of burning gold' had already slipped from his hands; it was left to Angela to take it up and build, if not Jerusalem, at least adequate homes for the poor, in place of the East End slums that had spawned the likes of Fagin and his boys.

In August 1840 Angela invited Dickens to Stratton Street and he asked Marjoribanks's advice. He was nervous at

the solemn mention of a Royal Duke and Duchess – are gentlemen expected to wear court dresses in consequence? I have already appeared in that very extraordinary costume ... but I have no confidence in my legs, and should be glad to hear that the Etiquette went in favour of Trousers.[12]

In April 1841 Dickens dined at Burdett's house in St James's Square and that evening he 'greatly enjoyed a quiet setting down of [Thomas] Moore by [Sam] Rogers, for talking exaggerated Toryism'.[13]

Angela recognised in Dickens something of her father's idealism and immediately responded to him. But it was not until the beginning of 1841 that Dickens began to get her measure and to realise that she was no ordinary wealthy lion-hunter. He sent her advance copies of the next instalments of *The Old Curiosity Shop* with the account of the death of Little Nell, which set her and Hannah and later the whole country weeping. When he returned in July 1842 after a seven months' visit to America, their friendship grew.

Marjoribanks had given him a list of the Bank's correspondents in America from whom, as he wrote to the banker, he received the 'greatest attention' – except from 'the poor gentleman in Washington who had been dead six years'. The mere enquiry about him upset 'a very old clerk who staggered to a stool and fell into a cold perspiration',[14] as if he had seen a spectre.

While he was abroad, his father, John Dickens, deeply in debt, wrote to Coutts & Co. asking in pure Micawber language for an advance of £25:

'Contemporaneous events of this nature place me in a difficulty from which without some anticipatory pecuniary effort I cannot extricate myself, and my good or evil genius as the case may be has prompted me to state my case to Miss Coutts & Co.'[15] The reply from Coutts & Co. was brief, but almost as florid:

As you seem to have anticipated, no directions were left with us by Mr Charles Dickens for any payment to you on his account, and for the reasons to which you allude towards the conclusion of your letter we regret that in our capacity as Bankers we feel precluded from complying with the request you have made us.[16]

His father's behaviour made Charles acutely embarrassed. When he wanted to find work for his brother, Alfred, he applied to Marjoribanks rather than to Angela, but it was she who used her influence on his behalf. Edward Marjoribanks remained on friendly terms with Dickens, later attending as one of the specially invited audience at Dickens's private theatricals. He and his son, Edward, continued to deal with Dickens's account, advising him through the years of success when his balances grew, and afterwards when dependent parents and ten children diminished his savings.

Until the summer of 1843 Angela had dealt with her immense correspondence with the help of Hannah Meredith, but increasingly she felt the need for someone to investigate the many appeals for money which she received daily. On 27 July 1843 she wrote asking Dickens to administer her large donation to an actor's orphaned children. He replied:

I will not attempt to tell you what I felt when I received your noble letter last night. Trust me that I will be a faithful steward of your bounty; and that there is no charge in the wide world I would accept with so much pride and happiness as any such from you.[17]

For more than ten years Dickens was to be her almoner and unpaid secretary.

Two years later, in return for his help, she undertook to pay for his six-year-old son's education. Charley's years at a preparatory school, Eton and afterwards his training in Germany were all at her expense. She later obtained for him a post at Baring's Bank and supported him in later life when he was in financial difficulties.

She opened a separate account for Dickens at Coutts & Co., which he drew upon for expenses connected with their work together. This was the method she employed with other men who worked on her behalf. The Reverend John Sinclair, for example, had a similar fund at his disposal. But it is impossible to estimate exactly how much she spent with Dickens. Often she would puzzle him with an odd packet of money. 'I cannot divine what this sum is for,' he wrote when she sent him a '£10 note, a sovereign, a half sovereign, three shillings and sixpence'.[18]

Dickens was amazed at the confidence with which she would send her steward through the streets of London carrying large sums of money. He, who was himself almost excessively orderly, kept careful accounts and desperately tried to persuade her to organise her immense correspondence.

Such was his phenomenal energy that his work for Angela was carried on while he was immersed in the creation of his greatest novels. *The Old Curiosity Shop*, *Barnaby Rudge* and *Martin Chuzzlewit* were written in the early stages of their friendship. Sairey Gamp in *Martin Chuzzlewit* was modelled on the nurse who attended Hannah in her frequent illnesses. *Dombey & Son*, *David Copperfield* and *Bleak House* grew during the height of their friendship. No one who reads his letters to Angela at this time can fail to see something of her shadow in Agnes in *David Copperfield* and Esther Summerfield in *Bleak House*. His energy was matched and fired by the extraordinary drive that impelled the gentle Miss Coutts.

At the beginning of 1844 Angela experienced a double tragedy. Sir Francis had suffered for many years from rheumatism and gout and had experimented with many treatments. In 1843 he had undergone the rigorous hydrotherapy practised at Malvern by Dr Gully, which, as Angela later complained in a letter to *The Times*, destroyed the finest constitution known to man. On 12 January 1844 Lady Burdett died after a long illness; eleven days later Sir Francis followed her, broken-hearted. They were buried together at Ramsbury, their funeral cortège followed by hundreds of mourners. 'They were lovely in their lives and in their deaths they were not divided,' Angela wrote to a friend.[19]

So they had been for the last twenty-five years, and Angela had only known her father as an affectionate and devoted husband. After his death, however, she suddenly learned, to her deep distress, of his affair with Lady Oxford.

In the days after the funeral, her brother Robert, who made a brief appearance in her life at this time, received an appeal on behalf of Lady Charlotte Bacon, a natural daughter of Lady Oxford, asking that the annual allowance Sir Francis had always paid her be continued. Sir Francis could not be sure that she was in fact his daughter, though his friends accepted that she was and thought her very like him. But, as became a gentleman of that period, he did not quibble. As he had supported his grandfather's and his brother's natural children without complaint, so he accepted responsibility for Lady Oxford's daughter.

Robert rejected the appeal and Angela was approached. Unable to believe that her father could have committed adultery, she was horrified and refused to continue the allowance, in spite of her cousin Dudley Coutts Stuart's continued entreaties. Not even a sharp attack from Lord Brougham moved her. 'I would not for ten times her large fortune be the possessor of her conscience,' he wrote to Dudley.[20] Angela's stubborn determination and self-will had always been part of her character, but as she grew in experience and confidence she frequently refused to listen to advice, and once she had made up her mind it was almost impossible to move her. Deeply shaken by the discovery of her father's possible infidelity, she retreated to the continent, ignoring a long and wise letter from Dudley. Her father was above reproach and that, as far as she was concerned, was the end of the matter.

But now she became painfully aware of the prostitutes who congregated on the steps of her Piccadilly house – after all were not they and Lady Oxford sisters under the skin?

The death of her parents left a void in her life; she had not been particularly close to her sisters, especially since her accession to her inheritance had caused some jealousy. For her cousins – Dudley Coutts Stuart and Frances, the children of Fanny Bute – she had a great deal of affection. Frances – or Fan – and her husband, who became the second Earl of Harrowby, were her particular friends, who supported her during the most difficult period of her life. Harrowby was, she wrote later in life, her 'best and truest friend'. But it was Hannah Meredith who gave her more than family affection. On 19 December 1844 Hannah at last married the patient Dr Brown. However, Hannah did not leave her; it was Brown who left his practice and lived at Stratton Street as the family doctor. But Hannah was not now so constant a companion and Angela was, indeed, as Dickens later wrote, 'so isolated in the midst of her goodness and wealth'.[21]

Dickens undoubtedly saw the sharp edge beneath the sweet, sometimes gushing, affection of the little lady.* He understood the difficulty of Hannah's position in the household – was she governess, secretary or lady's companion? As Angela's fame developed, so did Hannah's strange illnesses. Indeed, Dickens's children thought that she spent all her time in bed. In fact, retired to her own room, or at her own side table at Angela's dinners, Mrs Brown, as she must now be called, established a unique position.

Unlike ladies of fashion, who put on pretty aprons to run bazaars for their pet charities, Angela, as Dickens discovered, was 'very, very far removed, from all the Givers in all the Court guides between this and China'.[22] He encouraged her to face reality – the prostitutes in Piccadilly, the sewers of Westminster, the great dust heap of Bethnal Green, and the children of the Ragged School 'with not the elements of a whole suit of clothes among them all'.[23] His practical approach became the hallmark of her particular kind of philanthropy.

Angela's father had advised her not to dribble away her great fortune in little charities but to undertake some great project. So in 1846 with the

---

* Dickens's biographer, John Forster, claimed that Rosa Dartle in *David Copperfield* was modelled on Hannah.

help of Dickens she began the most remarkable of her philanthropic works.

The revelations of her father's early life had opened her eyes. Now she looked at young prostitutes with compassion and determined to give them a chance of a new life in a pleasant home. Early in May 1846 she consulted Dickens, who at first was doubtful, but on consideration took up her idea with enthusiasm.

There had been other refuges for prostitutes before, but in many ways the home that she and Dickens set up was a pioneer. The aim of Urania Cottage, in Shepherd's Bush, was to give the girls back pride in themselves, to train them and then to encourage them to emigrate so that in a new environment they could start a fresh life. The emphasis was to be on encouragement not punishment, and Urania Cottage was to be not an institution, but a home with flower gardens, books and music. The inmates were to be recommended by Chesterton, the governor of the Middlesex House of Correction. Dickens drafted 'An Appeal to Fallen Women', which Chesterton read to them in their cells. It offered them a chance of a new life.

Dickens urged Angela to go with him to Chesterton's prison to see the girls in their cells and praised her 'moral bravery'; indeed, it took some courage for a sheltered young woman at this time to visit prisons, even more to tackle the unmentionable subject of prostitution.

For a decade from 1847, Angela and Dickens planned and worked for their home. Dickens, with the aid of the Reverend William Tennant, supervised – attending monthly meetings, interviewing the difficult girls and appointing the matrons. It was hard to find the right women to run the home: some were 'mincing dowagers' easily provoked, and Miss Cunliffe was 'a woman of an atrocious temper' who looked 'like a stage maniac in a domestic drama'.[24]

Some of the girls were beyond hope. Sesina was, Dickens wrote, 'the pertest, vainest and most deceitful little minx in this town – I never saw such a draggled piece of fringe upon the skirts of all that is bad'.[25] But there were some successes. In November 1856 one of the girls, Louisa Cooper, returned from South Africa 'nicely dressed', Dickens reported to Angela, 'and looking very well to do. . . . She brought me for a present the most hideous ostrich egg ever laid – wrought over with frightful devices, the most tasteful of which represents Queen Victoria (with crown on) standing on top of a Church receiving professions of affection from a British seaman.'[26]

Nothing better illustrates the wide range of Angela's benevolence than the fact that while she was receiving grateful letters from South Africa from émigrée ex-prostitutes, she also heard from Lady Smith, the wife of the Governor of Cape Colony, thanking her 'from the bottom of my Spanish heart'.[27] Angela had lent Sir Harry Smith the means to equip himself for his new post and his Spanish wife wrote fulsomely in gratitude.

38

'Miss Angela' and the Duke

Dickens was the brotherly friend Angela needed at this time, but no one replaced her father until the Duke of Wellington entered her life. He was living nearby at Apsley House, Piccadilly, had known Thomas Coutts at the end of his life and been an acquaintance of Sir Francis in his last Tory years.

In June 1846 the Tory Government was defeated; Wellington was out of power and, at seventy-seven, unlikely to be called on again. He missed his old friend and confidant, Mrs Arbuthnot, and was touched by his young neighbour's gentle affection. She made him feel youthful and wanted again. Upright and gallant he escorted her during the London season, and she called on him for advice.

In September, he invited her to stay at Walmer Castle. He would have preferred her to come alone – his daughter would be her chaperone – but, since she insisted, grudgingly he invited Mrs Brown. Angela was thirty-two and the Duke was more than twice her age, but she knew what happiness Harriot had brought her grandfather in similar circumstances, and she saw no reason why they should not repeat the pattern.

The Duke encouraged her determination to understand and play a part in the business of the Bank, and supported her when she was at loggerheads with Marjoribanks. Dickens, who had been a clerk himself, had opened her eyes to the condition of the employees at the Bank, so now she wanted to raise their salaries. Marjoribanks refused and the Duke drafted a letter for her:

You must recollect that there are points connected with the management of my House upon which I cannot alter my opinions, founded as they are upon the invariable practice of my grandfather and of the Duchess of St Albans. I am anxious to know whether you will consent to have prepared by next week our arrangement for a general rise in public salaries of the clerks of the House; which contrary to the practice of my grandfather and of the late Duchess has not taken place for some years.'

Understandably, Marjoribanks was somewhat affronted. He did not consider that she could call it 'my House', and she was explicitly denied the right to interfere in the running of the Bank by the terms of the will.

The Duke, whose sympathies were more with the banker than with the clerks, counselled patience, but he was prepared 'to converse with Mr Marjoribanks if such conversation were likely to conciliate him'. He 'was fully sensible of your ... understanding of your justice, rectitude and moderation', and hoped that her patience would solve the problem. He was, he felt, 'not sufficiently informed of the characters and reputations of the men belonging to your House'.[2]

Wellington had, in fact, been a customer at the Bank for years, but he had rarely dealt with the partners personally.

Later he intervened on Angela's behalf in a cause for which he had little sympathy. When, in 1848, the partners suggested shortening the opening hours of the Bank, in line with the practice of other banks, he wrote a testy letter to Angela:

But there never was anything so absurd: not one Clerk will seek Instruction at that Hour of the afternoon. He will go [to] the Publick House, the Coffee House, the Play House or other place of resort of vice or Idleness, and the Hour lost to himself, His employers and the Publick Interests will be passed in Dissipation and only lead to renewed Idleness and Mischief. This concession is like many others advocated and applauded by the Newspapers, such as Feasts and Shews for the people which occasion only idleness and vice, loss of time, increase of Want.[3]

It was, however, her right to have a say in the management of the Bank that he wished to have established. So he encouraged her to 'go through the stationery accounts. It will have a good effect to show your partners that you can and will go thoroughly, and what is more it is your duty to attend as head of the House.'[4] It was her assumption that she was indeed the head that Marjoribanks was challenging. But, encouraged by the Duke, she continued to consider herself as such and did so to the end of her life.

Dearly though she loved Wellington, and though she listened to his counsel, it was Dickens whose advice she took. When she proposed opening her home for fallen women, the Duke disapproved:

There are certainly no such objects for Commiseration as those to whom you have referred. Whenever I can hear of the Means of saving one, I make the endeavour. But, alas, I am much afraid that experience, as well as the Information to be derived from Statistical Works, have taught us that there is but little if any hope of saving in this World that particular Class of Unfortunates to whom you have referred: such as those very young whom you saw on the Steps. I am afraid that it has been found that there are irreclaimables of that particular class who earn their Bread by the commission of the Offence. Others misled by bad example, deceived, influenced by their feelings, may be reclaimed; but the others never! The only chance for them is that which it is your object if possible to attain: the removal of them to another scene in which they may be placed each in a situation in [which] she will not know want, and will not be exposed and tempted by its feelings to Her former Practices for Relief.[5]

Doubtless the Duke remembered only too well how he had been black-mailed by one such 'object', Harriet Wilson.

As for her proposed famine relief for Ireland the Duke was again sceptical: he had no faith in the people of his native land. When in 1846 the potato crop failed and Ireland was devastated by famine, Coutts & Co. had been invited to subscribe to an Irish relief fund. 'Best to wait', the Duke cautioned, 'to see what the Bank of England does and what the great and ancient houses do.'[6] He himself had no doubt that, if large sums were subscribed, 'not an Irishman would work anywhere! All would flock to the spot at which he could receive His share of the Elemosynary Gift without working for it! So much is not known of the Highlands of Scotland, as is of Ireland.'[7]

Angela, however, remembered her father's passion for Ireland, listened – and went her own way, as will be seen. But she had something in common with the Duke. He told her:

You, as well as I, like and endeavour to do good effectually. I cannot bear to be called upon and to be used [as a] stop Gap to provide the Means for going on in the same vicious course, and there to leave the matter. You appear to have the same feeling, and you are quite right.[8]

Gradually their friendship grew and by the end of 1846 she was deeply in love. In spite of the disparity of their attitudes and their ages, with a disregard for convention reminiscent of her grandfather, at the beginning of February 1847 Angela made up her mind. When the Duke called on her on 7 February she proposed marriage. The Duke did not reject her out of hand; he considered the idea gravely. The next day he wrote kindly but firmly:

My dearest Angela, I have passed every Moment of the Evening and Night since I quitted you in reflecting upon our conversation of yesterday, Every Word of which I have considered repeatedly. My first Duty towards you is that of Friend, Guardian, Protector. You are Young, My Dearest! You have before you the prospect of at least twenty years of enjoyment of Happiness in Life. I entreat you again in this way, not to throw yourself away upon a Man old enough to be your Grandfather, who, however strong, Hearty and Healthy at present, must and will certainly in time feel the consequences and Infirmities of Age. You cannot know, but I do, the dismal consequences to you of this certainty. Hopeless for years! during which you will still be in the prime of your Life!

I cannot too often and too urgently entreat you to consider this well. I urge it as your friend, Guardian, Protector. But I must add, as I have frequently, that my own happiness depends upon it. My last days would be embittered by the reflection that your Life was uncomfortable and hopeless. God Bless you My Dearest! Believe me Ever Yours Wn.[9]

It may be that they decided on a secret engagement. Angela carefully preserved with the Duke's letters a little packet of plaited silver and brown hair dated in June of that year. In Queen Victoria's day this would have been a symbol of engagement; and certainly he wrote to her on the next day, 'You was so happy yesterday.'[10] Rumours of a secret marriage have persisted even until today. This has never been confirmed and probably never can be, but it would not have been out of character – she was so like her grandfather and, as she once wrote of herself, 'I am, and always have been peculiar [i.e. unusual].'[11]

Throughout the season of 1847 the Duke was her constant escort. According to the diarist Greville, the Duke was 'astonishing the world . . . by a strange intimacy he has struck up with Miss Coutts with whom he passes his life and all sorts of reports have been rife of his intention to marry her'.[12] When, in October, she and Mrs Brown set off for a holiday in Europe, he wrote day after day the most loving letters. She wrote from the Loire valley and he replied:

. . . but don't imagine that I doubt for a moment where your Mind, your Heart and Soul are during all these amusements. As mine are from morning till night and during the whole night. We have both much to occupy our attention! But I believe we both of us give as much of our thoughts to the other as is possible.[13]

He wrote of her tender skin and advised her to improve the circulation of the blood:

Above all keep your feet dry and warm. If mine are very cold I rub them against each other at night as I have entreated you to do! I think of you when I am in the act of doing so and whether you have adopted that practice and it succeeds in making you as comfortable as it does me and that immediately. . . . Then you might think again of your companion who has given you this advice! Do this My dearest and tell me how you feel. Let me know and feel that you have enjoyed it. God Bless you ever yours with sincere affection. Wn.[14]

He advised her to take care of their letters since, were they to be discovered, they would cause a sensation.

However, on her return, Angela felt that he was growing preoccupied and distant. In fact the Duke was becoming increasingly deaf and was feeling his age, but he reassured her, 'I know and feel, God Bless You! that I have only to say the word and that I shall have you at my side at all Times! Is that reflection very presumptuous? No. It is the truth, you delight in it as I do.'[15]

In 1848, the year of revolution in Europe, Dickens and Wellington were on opposite sides of the barricades. Dickens, aware of the rising tide of revolutionary fervour, became increasingly radical, convinced that unless the Government listened to the shouts for reform there would be bloody revolution in England. The Duke, on the other hand, had a typically brisk solution – to call out the troops.

A monster Chartist demonstration, planned for 10 April 1848, had caused the Government some concern. But Wellington, placed in charge of the defence of London, was well prepared. He concealed troops in strategic places – some in Angela's cellars – and called out special constables, among them Louis Napoleon. The organisers lost heart and after a meeting on Kennington Common, they ordered the disappointed crowds to go home. Wellington wrote to 'Dear Miss Angela': 'The Mobs have dispersed. There are but two or three hundred people about Palace Yard ... not a shot has been fired or an individual injured – nor has a single soldier been seen.'[16] Louis Napoleon called to tell Angela that it was all over. There was some irony in the situation: Wellington aided by a Napoleon assuring Burdett's daughter that the people's revolution had failed.

In France too the heady days of revolution ended in anticlimax, but there in the 'June days' there was much bloodshed on the barricades. Out of the ashes emerged not a phoenix, nor even a Corsican eagle, but Angela's old friend, Louis Napoleon, nephew of the great Bonaparte. At last he fulfilled the destiny that only he had seen and, in a remarkably short time, took over as head of state. Angela happened to be in Paris with Mrs Brown in the autumn of 1851 at the time of the coup d'état. She wrote in great excitement to Wellington, who replied stiffly:

I should have thought the Ambulances quite sufficient to shock any Person not even a Young Lady, who should have to see them. The dead, the wounded, the dying of loss of Limbs or other sever mortal[?] Wounds, Men killed in the streets all [round] you! Surely this is too much for even any Tour of Pleasure![17]

In fact Angela kept her friendship with Louis Napoleon until the end of his life. When he became Emperor she called on him and the Empress on her frequent visits to France. She was invited to at least one of their famous house parties in the Forêt de Compiègne, where the Empress Eugénie and the ladies rode and drove down the long avenues, gossiped and changed their clothes at least three times a day. In that brilliant assembly Angela, one of the first customers of the couturier Worth, could hold her own. Her grace and elegance and fluent French made up for her lack of beauty.

Although during the last years of his life the gossips linked the Duke's name with other young women, and though he was often irritable and moody with 'Dear Miss Angela', there is no doubt that theirs was a very special relationship. In January 1851 he wrote with unmistakable affection: 'To be sure! it does amuse me mightily at times to find a veteran eighty-two years old, deaf with all, turned into a lover!'[18]

In September 1852 she proposed to visit him at Walmer Castle, but Mrs Brown was ill and the visit was postponed. Mrs Brown, who was always uneasy with the Duke, must have viewed a possible marriage with alarm. In the Duke's household she would undoubtedly dwindle into a humble governess. It was a convenient time to be ill. The Duke wrote recommending for Mrs Brown that which he wanted so much for himself – tranquillity above all things. On 16 September he found quiet at last. Ironically, on that same afternoon, Dickens was walking near Walmer Castle and heard of the death of the great man who had shared his love and respect for Angela Burdett-Coutts.

After his death the Duke's family treated her as though she were his widow. Lord Douro escorted her to the lying-in-state at Chelsea, which he considered appallingly ostentatious, devoid of taste and feeling. On the day of the funeral she went with the family to St Paul's and returned on the next day to the empty cathedral quietly to mourn not the nation's hero, but the simple, kind old man she loved.

Six days after the death of the Duke of Wellington, in the midst of her grief, came new bright hope – the birth of a son to her sister. In 1850 Clara had married an elderly clergyman, the Reverend James Money, and the baby, the only legitimate grandchild of Sir Francis, brought promise of new life for the family. Although called Francis Burdett Thomas – a weighty inheritance – he was always known as Frank.

Angela lavished all her affection on the baby and would have adopted him if Clara had permitted. Instead she supported him and Clara generously for many years. Dickens, whose tenth child, Edward, had been born in March, replied with amusement to her enthusiastic letters. Neither of the two miraculous babies was quite to fulfil the bright promise, but Edward, nicknamed Plorn, or 'Plornish', did become a Member of Parliament in Australia and Frank Money, as will be seen, began a line which was to include the present Chairman of the Bank, David Money-Coutts.

After Wellington's death Angela threw herself with renewed energy into her philanthropic work with Dickens. One of their oddest joint projects was inspired by her wish to help the Duke's soldiers in the Crimean War. Her friend Florence Nightingale had told her of their misery on the sodden battlefield. Another friend, Layard, a Member of Parliament, had shocked her by his eye-witness account of the conditions in the Crimea. With their usual practical good sense, she and Dickens arranged for a washing-machine and spin-dryer to be sent out to Scutari. Dr Sutherland reported to Dickens that 'the machine does great credit to Miss Coutts' philanthropy & also to your engineering'.[19]

In their charitable work together, Dickens, who was efficient, thorough and businesslike, was often irritated by Angela's worthy but ineffectual clerical friends. When, in December 1852, Angela, with his advice, was trying to improve the sanitation in a block of houses between Willow Street and Coburg Row in Westminster, the vicar of St Stephen's handled the owners of the houses so badly that they refused to accept her offer of one-third of the cost of the new installation. He described the vicar as a pigeon taking the chair at a meeting of bulldogs.

Some of her architect friends were not much better. In the early stages of her plan for building workers' flats in Bethnal Green, she employed the Duke of Wellington's architect, Philip Hardwicke, who, to Dickens's intense anger, arrived at their meeting without plans. He was later replaced by Henry Darbishire, who finally finished the buildings after a long delay, caused by the refusal of the owner of a giant dust heap to remove it. The flats were opened in 1862 and praised by Dickens in an article, 'Hail Columbia Square', in *All the Year Round*. The four blocks each contained forty-five apartments, with gas and water laid on, a laundry and a huge spin-dryer on the top floor. There was even a reading room, the symbol of Angela's passion for educational reform.

In this field she had first been inspired by Henry Brougham, Lord Chancellor of England in her father's day and the champion of popular education. But her present guide was Sir James Kaye-Shuttleworth, who, as Dr Kaye, had been a tireless campaigner in the battle against cholera. Now having married an heiress and taken her name, he was building his reputation as the founding father of education for the people. Dickens found her educational friends and their theories inexpressibly deadening. 'I am so dreadfully jaded this morning', he wrote to Angela on 1 April 1853, 'by the supernatural dreariness of Kaye-Shuttleworth, that I feel as if I had just come out of the great Desert of Sahara where my camel died a fortnight ago.'[20]

The 'Shuttleworry' system of education received a hammer blow in *Hard Times*, but Angela continued to consult Kaye-Shuttleworth. To the end of her life she spent much time and money in the cause of education. In addition to her school at St Stephen's in Westminster and the technical institute nearby, and a similar school attached to her church in Carlisle, she insituted a scheme for peripatetic schoolteachers in rural areas, which she called 'The Ambulatory Schoolmaster'.

Angela devoted time and a great deal of money to the problems of London's poor, but it would not have occurred to her to put on a sympathetic sackcloth, unlike her father, who, during his revolutionary days, made something of a parade of his spartan life. Angela lived in style at 1 Stratton Street. Porters and flunkeys ushered guests up to the great drawing-room on the first floor, which was dominated by Chantrey's marble statue of her grandfather. The gilt mirrors reflected the statue, the silk and damask curtains and drapes, the priceless pictures and objets d'art.

For a long time the room remained as Harriot had left it until Angela called on Dickens to be her interior decorator. Nothing gave him greater pleasure than redesigning the room for her, replacing carpets and moving the tables and mirrors. Like many of Angela's guests, he was somewhat intimidated by the grandeur of Stratton Street. Everything about her, he said, was on so grand a scale. When in 1857 Hans Andersen came to stay, he was so terrified of her haughty footmen that, when he wanted his bed remade in the Danish fashion, he dared not ask them but crept down to Angela for help.

It was said that there were too many bishops at Angela's soirées, and certainly there were always grave old men in serious conclave. But she delighted in mixing interesting people. She had even on one occasion to be discouraged from inviting Louis Philippe and Louis Napoleon at the same time.

The drawing-room at Stratton Street over the next half century was to be the setting for innumerable dramas and encounters. Queen Victoria herself came to visit and liked to sit at the window overlooking Piccadilly and watch the passing show. Unlike her grandfather, Angela loved 1 Stratton Street – here she could be in the midst of what she called the 'bustle of life'.

Angela, like Thomas Coutts, never bought a great country estate; when she wished to escape from London, she stayed in hotels in Harrogate or Edinburgh, Brighton or Bath. But in 1849, on the death of the Duke of St Albans, she at last acquired Holly Lodge, Harriot's delightful villa on Highgate Hill.

The Duke had neglected the house and the grounds. The lawns were overgrown and Dickens wrote facetiously of her bumper hay harvest. He had bought a plot in the newly opened Highgate Cemetery, which sloped down the hill just over Angela's garden wall. Here his little baby Dora, his father and his wife Catherine were all to be buried and here, he expected, he too would end his days.

From 1849 until 1858 Dickens was a frequent visitor. In the evenings he would read his latest work in the cosy, unpretentious sitting-room, or by the firelight tell ghost stories to make her flesh creep. Together, he and Angela walked through the glades and flowery gardens, up the rhododendron drive to the highest point of her grounds. There they could look down to where distant London stretched from Bethnal Green to Westminster, Piccadilly and Shepherd's Bush, and there they planned its transformation.

Angela grew to love Holly Lodge, though at first it seemed neglected and remote, and too near the wilderness of Hampstead Heath. She held great garden parties there – not as fantastic as Harriot's, but impressive just the same. In 1867 she gave a spectacular reception for 2,000 Belgian volunteers as a favour to the Queen and to Lord Granville, but also as a gesture to an old customer of the Bank – Leopold, King of the Belgians. Holly Lodge was then described in the journal of the Belgian, M. Bertram, as 'a modest villa. A Belgian banker', he considered, 'would have painted the shutters and the walls.'[21] However, the feast was a triumph – worthy of Harriot herself. 'Oh the beef and the lamb, the salmon and the lobsters, the baskets of fruits, the creams and the jellies ... six hundred waiters ... and then the cider, the ale and the wine!' sighed Bertram.[22]

The invitation card to this splendid reception shows two surprised llamas on the lawns – a reminder that the practical Angela used her rural retreat for research. She hoped to persuade the llamas to breed and so make possible an alpaca industry in Britain. At her model farm on her Highgate estate she bred goats and encouraged research into the causes of cattle plague. She even introduced nightingales into her gardens until they were stolen by the bird fanciers of Camden Town. She was a particularly active President of the Society for the Protection of Birds, and encouraged the Highgate Horticultural Association, which held its annual meetings in the grounds of Holly Lodge.

At the bottom of Highgate Hill she built a school for St Anne's Church and, in 1865, an extraordinary mock-Gothic model village set in quiet lawns. Statues of Angela and Mrs Brown and their pets stood over the entrance gates. Dickens had persuaded her to build flats in Columbia Square, but Angela, with her usual foresight, wanted to bring a country village to the expanding city. Both Surbiton and Holly Village were, in fact, forerunners of new towns and garden suburbs.

In the last years Angela had come to rely on the medical advice of patient, kindly Dr Brown. But in October 1855 he was suddenly taken ill and died at Montpellier, where he was recuperating with Hannah and Angela.

Dickens, who was at this time busy in Paris and immersed in *Little Dorrit*, immediately returned to London and took charge of the transportation of the body and the funeral arrangements. In spite of a cold and a painful eye, and plagued by ineffectual curates, he arranged the burial in a vault in St Stephen's, the church Angela had built in honour of her father.

Three years later another blow fell: Angela was to be deprived of the help of her 'dearest friend', Dickens. In May 1858 the world was shocked to learn that Dickens's marriage had broken down and that his wife Catherine was now living apart from him. Months of scandal followed. Angela tried in vain to intercede on Catherine's behalf, but Dickens was adamant: 'Nothing on earth – no not even you – no consideration human or Divine, can move me from the resolution I have taken.'[23] As the world buzzed with the scandal, it was obvious that their work at Urania Cottage could not continue. Gradually the inmates were dispersed and the home was closed. Thus ended a project begun with such high hopes; it finished in gloom, yet it had been remarkably successful.

Angela's work with Dickens ceased and, since Mrs Brown was now a widow, both ladies needed to get away from London and its sad memories.

In the spring of 1857 Angela had rented a house in Hesketh Crescent on the cliffs above Torquay and for the next twenty years she spent many months of every year in the bright, clean air of the little town. In 1861 she leased Ehrenberg Hall, a cool, white-painted house with terraced gardens stretching down to the sea, which now became her second home. Here a new phase in her life began, away from the stench and squalor of London. She renewed her interest in science, in archaeological exploration in the area, in the study of seaweeds and grasses. And in this calm anchorage she planned new projects and found new friends. The geologist Pengelly partly filled the gap in her life left by the loss of Dickens.

Instead of the Friday evenings at the Royal Institution, she and Mrs Brown took their places in the front row at the little Torquay Museum and listened to lectures on caves and fossils, flowers and grasses. There is no record of her meeting Charles Darwin, but they were both in Torquay at the same time, and she was interested in the scientist, the grandson of Erasmus Darwin, her father's family physician. Certainly she later sent flowers to his funeral at Westminster Abbey.

After 1858 Angela and Dickens went their separate ways, but they wrote occasionally with the old affection. In June 1865 Dickens, returning from Boulogne, was involved in a terrible rail crash and afterwards replied with 'an unsteady hand' to Angela's 'kind kind letters'.[24] By this time Ellen Ternan had, finally, become his mistress; she and her mother were, in fact, with him in the carriage of the wrecked train. Angela probably never learned the truth of his last driven years. And neither shall we, but if she saw him in the last years of his life, she must have grieved to see the lined and haggard face – so different from that of the shining young author with the lustrous eyes she had first known.

The partners at the Bank, like his lawyer, must have known of Dickens's relationship with the actress, Ellen Ternan, for regular payments to 'E.T.' appear in his accounts. Old Marjoribanks, who had dealt with Dickens's account, was still active, though now living mostly in retirement. George Robinson, the chief clerk, who enjoyed a gossip, might have studied Dickens's account with interest and remembered Thomas and Harriot and the old scandals of long ago, when he had first joined the Bank. In their long history, Coutts & Co. had handled with discretion more sensational stories than that of Charles Dickens and Ellen Ternan; as always their lips were sealed.

While Dickens broke with other friends who took Catherine's part, Angela held his affection until the end of his life. 'I think you know how I love you –', he wrote in one of his last letters to her, 'how I could do anything in your name and honour, but thank you.'[25]

Dickens died in June 1870; his 'dearest friend' had thirty-six more years of useful life.

39

Miss Coutts
and the Wider World

The phenomenal energy which Dickens had tried to channel and direct was, in the 1860s, to drive Angela into even greater activity. He had always discouraged her overseas adventures; now, without his hand on her shoulder, she turned her eyes to the wider world. In 1858 Angela embarked on what was to be the most remarkable of all her overseas adventures. For the next ten years the gap left in her life by Dickens was to be filled by James Brooke, the White Rajah of Sarawak.

Brooke had inherited a modest fortune and travelled to the Far East, where he developed a lifelong passion for Borneo and more especially for Sarawak, the small state on the north-western frontier. His courage in helping the ruler to put down a rebellion was rewarded when, in 1841, he was made Rajah under the sovereignty of the Sultan of Brunei. He proceeded to defeat the rebelling Dyaks, clear the seas of pirates, and restore peace and order. Moreover, he reduced the onerous taxes, only keeping the monopoly of the antimony sales for himself.

Though his rule was firm, he was tolerant and just and, because he respected the traditions of the people, he won their respect and affection. His aim was to create a harmonious and economically viable state, but for this he needed British protection to maintain order on land and sea. There was internal strife and constant conflict between the dominant Malay ruling class, the Chinese immigrant workers and the native Dyak tribes, headhunters on land and pirates at sea. For the rest of his life he strove to persuade unwilling British governments to take responsibility for the state.

In October 1847 when he returned to England to a triumphant welcome, Angela met him and was impressed. He became a customer of Coutts & Co. in 1851 and, during the coming years, the partners backed him with occasional loans. But it was Angela who was his greatest benefactor, and since, like her grandfather, she often concealed her private loans, it is impossible to know the true extent of his debt to her.

The Rajah and Angela exchanged over a thousand letters during their ten years of friendship, many dealing with the continuing negotiations over the future of Borneo. Sometimes he sent gentle verses. He wrote of religion, poetry and riddles to Mrs Brown, whom he appeared to regard with much affection. Angela Coutts was 'The Missus' – 'the whirlwind'; Mrs Brown the 'lightning in the midst'.[1]

In 1857 he survived a surprise attack by Chinese rebels, restored peace and order, and came home to recuperate, leaving his nephew, Captain Brooke, in charge. He bought a cottage, Burrator, on the edge of Dartmoor, an easy ride from Angela's house in Torquay, where she and Mrs Brown spent much of their time. He was now exhausted and wanted to retire, but Angela was determined that the little kingdom he had established with such pain should not relapse into chaos after his death.

Angela was no longer the shy, reluctant heiress, the self-effacing girl. In 1858 she was forty-four, strong-minded and practical, with powerful friends. Though she still was, in Dickens's words, 'most considerate and kind',[2] she could now be fierce and trenchant and found it difficult to forgive those who offended her friends. The Rajah more than once received a touch of her 'arctic manner'. As he once said after one of their disagreements, 'Your expressions often wound when you do not mean it.'[3]

With great determination she backed him in his efforts to persuade the Government to accept Sarawak for the crown, using all her influence with her friends in the Government. Palmerston was sympathetic, but when he and his party were defeated, the new Prime Minister, Lord Derby, was reluctant to take on such a distant and unrewarding commitment.

The merchants of Manchester, however, gave the Rajah some support and he now tried to raise a memorial fund which would provide financial backing for Sarawak, though Angela felt that this was somewhat demeaning. When he asked her for a loan in January 1859, she lent him £5,000, free of interest, with the antimony mines of Sarawak as security. Her lawyer, William Farrer, cautioned her: 'What is the value of the antimony royalties? In a new and unsettled country such as Borneo, the security must of necessity be of a doubtful character.'[4] But Angela trusted her judgment and, during the following years, became the chief creditor of Sarawak. Farrer advised that she should charge interest on the loan when it was repaid in 1864. He also suggested that she kept her name 'as a lender off the face of the transaction'.[5]

As her grandfather had done, Angela often lent money from her private account, especially when the security was doubtful. But in the case of Sarawak, she also persuaded the partners at Coutts & Co. to grant a loan.

Since the British Government was unwilling to back Sarawak, the Rajah now turned to France and began, with Angela's help, negotiations with her friend, Louis Napoleon. However, Captain Brooke refused French support and the annoyed Rajah decided to return to Sarawak.

Meanwhile, the memorial fund managed to raise only £8,800 so Angela offered to buy a screw steamer for Sarawak, which could also act as a gunboat in time of war. This would give temporary protection and would be a link with Singapore. She and Mrs Brown chose its name, *The Rainbow*. The total cost when the ship was fitted out was over £5,000. Angela must have been unwilling that the partners in the Strand should know of her rash investment, for she paid the money into Brooke's account at Baring's Bank.

In November 1860 the Rajah left to spend a year in his troubled country. He returned to England on 30 November 1861, having settled the country, expanded Sarawak and improved her trade. Angela's *Rainbow* now bridged the seas to Singapore and put Sarawak within thirty-seven days from England.

Encouraged by Angela, he engaged again in secret negotiations, this time with Belgium, for the transfer of Sarawak, though they still hoped to persuade Lord John Russell and the British Government to accept responsibility. Once again she could use her influence with her old acquaintance King Leopold.

Captain Brooke again refused to consider the transfer of power to a foreign country. He even objected to the 'sale' to England. His rebellious attitude sent the Rajah speeding out to Sarawak – once again backed by a loan of £5,000 from Angela, which this time was paid into his account at Coutts & Co. Furious with his nephew, the Rajah took an extraordinary decision before he left. He made a new will leaving the sovereignty of Sarawak to Angela. He did so 'as a Public Trust in implicit confidence that she will arrange the future Government of Sarawak for the welfare of the people and for the security and permanence of the liberties they now enjoy'.[6] He also left her all his personal property and rights in the state of Sarawak. There could be no greater proof of the confidence he had in her ability and judgment.

He wrote long letters to the 'dear friends of my solitude' and Angela sent him flowers from Holly Lodge. A white cockatoo brought by a sailor from him for many years swung on its perch in her window. 'Cocky' became the signal that she was at home; when he died she replaced him with a white china replica.

During the months in Sarawak the Rajah reorganised the state's finances and paid his nephew's debts, including the overdue instalment of £400 on the loan from Coutts & Co. Angela reported that the partners at Coutts & Co. were delighted, and no doubt relieved; they had always been uneasy about the security for the £3,000 loan.

The Rajah now wanted a new gunboat and asked her for another loan of

£3,000. How could she refuse when the Rajah promised to call it *Heartsease*, because, as he wrote, 'I remember you wore one in your hair'?[7] It was a touching if inappropriate name for a gunboat, but, since it eased the Rajah's heart, Angela, after some hesitation, agreed. The new boat was built in Singapore and was in action in 1865.

While the Rajah dealt with gunboats and rebels in the sweaty heat of Sarawak and dreamed of the flowers and birdsong of Holly Lodge, 'the Missus' was not idle. With the help of John Abel Smith MP she badgered Gladstone and her friends in government on his behalf. At last they secured Great Britain's recognition of Sarawak as an independent state under the rule of Rajah Brooke, and a British consul was appointed. Angela sent a triumphant telegram, which, for the moment, relieved the Rajah's mind, but she and her friends never ceased to work for something better.

The Rajah returned to England in November 1863, exhausted after his work in Sarawak and determined to retire at last and live in peace with his family – much to the annoyance of Angela, who felt that she would look ridiculous in the eyes of the powerful friends she had badgered on his behalf. She decided to stake a more permanent claim in Sarawak. She bought a tract of land near Kuching on which she proposed to grow sugar, tea and coffee. This time it was the Rajah who was slightly annoyed: Angela lacked his long experience of conditions in Sarawak.

In the following years, their friendship cooled. The Rajah was concerned about her proposal to establish a Moravian Mission on her Quop estate. She in turn must have regretted the Rajah's decision in June to make a new will, leaving his state to his nephew, Charles, although she had always recognised that her inheritance of Sarawak had been a temporary measure.

The future of Sarawak was still uncertain. Nevertheless, she continued to give him financial support. The new steamer *Heartsease* was now in use, but he wanted to replace *The Rainbow*; once again she lent him the money to negotiate for a new gunboat until *The Rainbow* should be sold. It was bought by the Government of Singapore for more than its purchase price, but the money was retained to pay for Sarawak's debts. So once again the Rajah was in debt to Coutts & Co. for £18,000, which he hoped to pay off in a month.

Angela still continued to press the Government to take over Sarawak, and in September 1866 the Rajah offered to hand over the state to the British Government provided that he was compensated for the £30,000 he had invested in the country, and provided that the religion, laws and customs of the people were respected. In spite of all their efforts, however, the Cabinet refused the Rajah's offer to cede Sarawak to the crown.

Persistent as ever, Angela tried in vain to interest the Italian Government. Decisions were now more urgent, since in December 1866 the Rajah had a stroke which nearly killed him. In May 1868 he was approaching the end. His last letter to 'My dear Miss Coutts', written on the 20th, ended with 'I must recommend a change to Holly Lodge for you. It is the spot on earth which suits you best. I say farewell with kind regards to Mrs Brown and yourself until better inclined to write. Yours very sincerely.'[8] He died on 11 June.

In his will the Rajah left Sarawak to his nephew, Charles, and his heirs, and failing them to the Queen and her heirs. The sovereignty of the state was to be protected by Angela Burdett-Coutts and two other Executors. Although she never forgot Sarawak, Angela ceased to play an active part, selling her farm and estate in 1872 and relinquishing her role as Executor at the end of the century.*

Angela's interest in the wider world was not confined to Sarawak: she set her mark in country after country across the globe.

But no one, certainly not Dickens, could accuse her of being a Mrs Jellaby, the earnest lady in *Bleak House* whose eyes were so fixed on the distant Borioboola-Gha that she failed to see the problems under her nose. In the 1860s her energy was phenomenal. At the same time that she was planning an experimental farm in Sarawak, she was trying to breed llamas at her farm in Highgate. While she was building workers' flats in the East End, she was founding schools for aborigines in Australia. Only the briefest account of her worldwide activity can be given here, but she could be rightly called a citizen of the world. She used to claim that she had gypsy blood in her veins, inherited from the Coutts family in ancient times. In fact she inherited the wanderlust of the merchant sailors – the Coutts brothers of Montrose.

She kept in touch with explorers and missionaries, and they wrote to her from all parts of the globe. Her knowledge of the world overseas was remarkably extensive. On the huge map at Holly Lodge, she could follow the travels of her protégés, or spin her grandfather's great globe at Stratton Street and trace her influence across continents.

Her father had given her a special interest in Ireland and for many years after the potato famine of 1846 she gave practical and lasting help. She sent agents to study the situation, especially in the area around Baltimore and Skibbereen in southern Ireland. Their reports horrified her, but though she sent them to the Government, she failed to move them to action. So

---

* In old age she received the widow of Charles Brooke, the Ranee Margaret of Sarawak, who recalled how, when she was quite young on the eve of her departure for Sarawak, she had called 'on the two ladies as I knew them and loved them, to say goodbye. The Baroness looked at me and said, 'Are you a real Ranee to the people? Do you see them and love them – or do you call yourself Ranee and do nothing?' 'I see them as much as I can,' I answered, 'and I love them very much. They are so good to me.' 'That is right and as it should be,' she said, patted my hand, kissed me and I went away.'[9]

she provided immediate supplies of food and blankets, but she did not want 'the hard-working willing islanders to be treated as mendicants'.[10] Her aim as always was 'not to make dependents on my bounty but to bring them comforts which can be secured by their own industry hereafter'.[11] Therefore, she lent money to fishermen who wished to buy their own boats, and she founded a fishing school so that the Irish could learn to make use of their most plentiful natural product, fish. She introduced a flock of sheep on Clear Island for the same purpose – to provide an alternative to the rotting potato. Her offer to W. H. Smith, then First Lord of the Admiralty, of £250,000 to buy seed potatoes, and her encouragement of research into the cause of potato blight, were typical of what was called the 'reproductive' nature of her charity. One result of her work was that the harbour at Baltimore, formerly deserted, became the centre of a flourishing mackerel industry.

When prospects in Britain were hopeless, she paid for whole communities to emigrate from villages in Ireland and Girvan in Scotland to Canada. Her interests in that country ranged from the bishopric she had founded in 1857 to investment in railways. Two villages, originally stations on the railway, on the Canadian borders still bear the name of Burdett and Coutts. And in Victoria, British Columbia, streets were named after her in gratitude for her work for the church there. The iron church she sent out in sections from England is still remembered there.

Africa fascinated her, but when she began her missionary work there, Dickens had tried to discourage her: 'The history of all African effort, hitherto, is a history of wasted European life, squandered European money, and blighted European hope.'[12] Her interest in South Africa stretched from 1847, when she established a bishopric there, and continued with her financial support of Sir Harry Smith when he was setting up as Governor at the Cape. Later in the century she chaired a committee to aid sick and wounded soldiers in the Zulu Wars of 1879. And, as will be seen, she was deeply concerned with the conditions in prisoner-of-war camps in the Boer War.

She also gave assistance to one of the Bank's most remarkable customers. She had read Livingstone's *Missionary Travels* with great interest, not only because she responded to his Christian work, but also because she saw the practical value of finding in Africa an alternative source of cotton. Inspired by him she gave her backing and blessing to his Zambezi expedition of 1862. It was typical that her farewell present to him was the finest microscope she could buy – to help him in his battle against disease in Africa.* She had been generous to his wife, Mary, in her years of loneliness with

---

* In fact Livingstone did not take it with him and it is now, still unused, in the Livingstone Memorial in Blantyre, Scotland.

the children in England and Scotland while Livingstone trudged across Africa from coast to coast. After his triumphant return she encouraged his secret desire that, while exploring the River Zambezi on behalf of the Government, he should found stations in the healthy highlands, where a chain of missions could be established to bring Christianity and commerce and wipe out the scourge of slavery. But, practical as always, she saw the industrial potential of the Highlands in minerals and cotton, especially at this time when, because of the Civil War, the supply of American cotton was blocked.

Livingstone wrote long letters to her from the Zambezi and gave her the first news of his discovery of Lake Shirwa. The expedition failed, but Angela did not lose faith in Livingstone's purpose and later, when Stanley returned from his famous encounter with the old missionary, backed him when others were sceptical and unwelcoming. When, after his death in 1873, Livingstone's body was brought back to England and buried in Westminster Abbey, the coffin was covered with her flowers. Under Livingstone's influence she founded a college for the education of the sons of native chiefs.

The work she did for Africa, spanning decades and stretching from coast to coast, was only a part of her life, but it was an important part with lasting results. 'We are sowing seeds', wrote Livingstone, 'that will bud and blossom when our heads are low.' Unfortunately in her lifetime she was only too often to taste the bitter fruit – failed missions and brave missionaries killed by war and disease. But she lived long enough to see Livingstone's belief in the mineral wealth of Africa more than justified. There was indeed gold, copper and diamonds under his wagon wheels.

In order to show the extent of her work throughout the world it has been necessary to move ahead in time. But it must be remembered, when we return to the 1860s, that all these various activities were taking place at the same time as her social work in England.

40

The Bank in the Strand

The partners in the Strand followed Angela's whirlwind progress across the globe with a mixture of affection and amusement. To the younger partners she was 'our lady' who should be humoured. Old Mr Marjoribanks had transferred to her the respect and admiration he had felt for her grandfather, and he was well aware that her friendship with the royal family, foreign princes and noble families at home and abroad gave prestige to the business.

Now the partners wanted her to turn her attention to their working conditions. Marjoribanks had been wanting to extend 59 Strand for some time. When it came to spending money on rebuilding he was quite prepared to acknowledge that Angela was the head of the House and therefore responsible for the cost of the improvements. She had already spent more than £21,000 on alterations to the premises in the Strand; £8,523 6s 11d in 1840 for moving the counter, etc., £8,499 2s 11d for alterations to the chapel they had acquired, and £4,554 13s 7d to repair the ceiling of the large room. Now Marjoribanks wanted further improvements. In 1852 he had written to her:

Our foreign office is now so much better than it was before you allowed the Adelphi Chapel to be bought – that we have always felt very thankful for the change – but it could be still further enlarged by throwing the two small rooms into it (even tho' the room would be of an irregular form) it would unquestionably be a great improvement, and so far from the two small rooms being a loss, I think we should be better without them, feeling that, the more also that is going on can be seen by every one, the more desirable it is –

The addition of the house in John Street would be a most valuable acquisition & so far back as Mr Coutts time he & his partners had that feeling about it – but it was occupied by Messrs Brown and Whitefoord (whom Lady Burdett had she been alive would have remembered as two of Mr Coutts's oldest friends). . . .[1]

His appeal on health grounds was well directed. In 1861 Marjoribanks was still complaining that the cramped office 'had led to much illness',[2] an argument that carried weight. No one was more aware than Angela was at this time of the dangers of cholera in London. In fact in the early 1860s working in the Strand was particularly unpleasant. Overcrowded, dusty and noisy as buildings were demolished and rebuilt, the street was also redolent with the stench from the Thames. So offensive was it that Members of Parliament hung gauze soaked in disinfectant at their windows to ward off 'King Cholera'. Nevertheless, it claimed many victims.

During the 1850s Angela, encouraged by Dickens, had been battling against the causes of disease: tainted water and an outdated, inadequate sewage system. So she had been unwilling to take on the extra expense of enlarging the premises in the Strand. But now she was persuaded to do so at her own expense at a total cost of £18,167 12s 2d.

Abstract of Bills for Alterations[3]

Messrs J & G Rigby	Builders	£13324. 14. 6
Baily & Sons	Smiths	502. 7. –
do	do	96. 18. –
W. Strode & Son	Gas Fitters	90. 6. 5
J. Clemence	Carpenters etc	3289. 12. 3
		£17303. 18. 2

P. C. Hardwicke Esq		
Commission	£687. 4. –	
Clerk of the Works	176. 10. –	
		863. 14. –
		£18167. 12. 2

The architect, Mr P. C. Hardwicke, excused this astronomical expense in a letter to the partners on 21 July 1859:

The Cost of this work was much increased by the difficulties in the construction as it had to be carried on without stopping the business of the Bank for one hour, and to effect this object it was necessary to use every precaution, not only to prevent the clerks being disturbed by the building operations but to protect them from the possibility of danger, which made unusual precautions necessary as well as obliged me to have a large portion of the works executed at night.[4]

Coulthurst wrote to Angela regretting the size of the bill and explaining that

a great deal was found to be necessary that was not anticipated when the estimate was first made. The whole has certainly been most successfully & well done and No. 59 Strand may now be reckoned as the most commodious Banking House in London and worthy of the splendid business transacted within its walls.[5]

Not only were the offices expanded but, characteristically, Angela insisted on including a dining-room and a library for the clerks in the new building. By 21 August 1863 the extension was ready and Coulthurst was able to report to Edward Marjoribanks junior that Angela had come that morning to go over the new offices, had minutely inspected every part and 'declared herself *perfectly delighted*'.[6] She was particularly pleased with the arrangements for 'dining and lunching of the clerks without going out of the House for their convenience'.[7] This gave her

the greatest satisfaction as it was a subject she had long had at heart. The carrying out of the arrangement she wished to leave to us as we thought best and she would like to be informed from time [to time] and would assist in anything she could.[8]

Marjoribanks replied that

Miss C, as she says herself, has her peculiarities, but the readiness she has shown to convert my old chambers to so good a purpose I am confident would never have been done by those who went before her and it is well it has not been left to those likely to succeed her.[9]

In fact between 1840 and 1873 Angela spent a total of £53,156 16s 6d on improvements to the premises. During the work she ordered one curious – and typical – device. As a later member of the staff remembered:

Mr W. E. Benbow, himself one of the kindest men to ever serve Messrs Coutts & Co., loved to tell how, upon the outer wall of Fifty Nine, was fixed a bird table. Behind it there was a hole in the wall sealed with an interior plug. The first daily duty of the resident messenger was to remove the plug, insert a funnel in the hole and trickle bird-seed onto the table. This was by order of the Baroness, whose charity to mankind, as well as to birds, was endless.[10]

During the 1850s Britain had enjoyed a period of great prosperity, in spite of the Crimean War and troubles in India. The Great Exhibition of 1851 had been a sign of the nation's industrial growth and a stimulus for men of ideas and invention. Coutts & Co. shared in this success. The partners were now making money not only through safe investments in government bonds and on the interest on loans as in Thomas Coutts's day, but through investments in building, mining and railways at home and abroad.

As a result profits had greatly increased, as Marjoribanks's careful accounts show. Profits including the reserve fund had ranged around £83,385 15s 7d in 1834 to £84,645 15s 8d in 1846, with a drop in 1841 to £74,307 13s 4d. 1847 and 1848 – the years of general economic and political crisis – had been bad years, with a drop to £69,576 6s 0d in 1847 and £72,934 17s 7d in 1848. But after that there was steady growth from £115,336 11s 2d in 1849 to £121,678 4s 1d in 1861.

Increasing success brought problems. In 1778 there had been five clerks, but in the 1850s that number had grown tenfold. In the hot summers the clerks stifled in the overcrowded little rooms. Coutts & Co. needed to expand, so an adjoining brewery was bought and converted into offices.

The improved premises and the new facilities made life a little more pleasant. But the life of a bank clerk in the 1860s was still one of long hours and 'close confinement', and at Coutts & Co. there was not even the hope of rising to become a partner one day.

When in 1868 the partners politely rejected the son of the Bishop of Ripon as a clerk, they explained: 'There is no prospect of any promotion here as in some Houses of business where young men if duly qualified rise to high and lucrative positions.'[11] Andrew Dickie had been the sole exception to this rule. Yet the clerks were expected to be well educated and, as the partners later wrote,

to know some foreign language German or French, to write a very good hand and to pass an examination in arithmetic and other subjects. . . . All clerks enter at the bottom of the list and have necessity to undergo the drudgery of juniors.[12]

Robinson also remembered what long hours and how few holidays the clerks had. A letter to Angela by an irate guardian of a clerk in later years might well have been written at any time during the century. The labour, he wrote, almost amounted to slavery. 'The usual attendance of a Clerk in the Bank of England and general of a Banker's Clerk averages from seven to eight hours daily i.e. from 9 o'ck in the morning to 4 or 5 o'ck in the afternoon. . . .'[13] But, as he complained, the junior clerks at Coutts & Co. are almost

constantly kept many hours beyond this. My Ward seldom or ever gets home before eight or nine o'clock during the whole of last winter it was ten, eleven and even twelve o'clock at night and at the present time his hours of leaving are one and two in the morning. With some of the Clerks it is even worse than this for he tells me, a Clerk was lately kept at work till seven o'clock in the morning i.e. for 22 hours consecutively and was even then expected to be at his post at 9 o'ck, that is two hours after. Of course he came but was found utterly exhausted and useless. . . .[14]

Life at Coutts & Co. was not usually as harsh as this, but this letter was written on 26 June, the busiest time in the Bank when the year's accounts were made up and when the clerks often worked all night – fortified later on by beer and sandwiches provided by Angela. It was still customary for some of the clerks to live 'over the shop', above 59 Strand. This was an advantage financially, but meant that the ever watchful porters could keep an eye on their comings and goings.

There was never a lack of applicants for a clerkship with Coutts & Co. – even though promotion was slow and the seniors seemed to live for ever – for the prestige was undoubted. The salaries compared well with clerks in other banks and there were bonuses from distinguished customers, as well as the Christmas box received by all the clerks.

The Clerks' Fund first appears in the records in 1817, though there were donations at Christmas paid as early as 1781: 'To the Bank Clerks their Christmas Box £5 5s od'. But from 1817 it was properly arranged under 'Donations from Customers', divided into shares and distributed among the thirty-five clerks. In 1817, for example, Dickie received £63 13s 4d, Messrs Charlton, Lamb and Thomas £53 1s 1d, and the rest £21 4s 6d. This gradually increased by about £2 a year, until 1821, the year before Thomas Coutts's death, when Dickie received £82 4s od, the other senior clerks £68 10s od and so on down the grades until the thirteen juniors were given £13 14s od. After Thomas's death the contributions were reduced by £6. In the following years the Clerks' Fund was paid out of the estates of Thomas Coutts and the Duchess of St Albans. Generally the clerks were required to have been with the Bank for a year before receiving a share of the Fund, which after 1864 became the 'New Clerks' Fund' from which each clerk received £2 once every three years. In that year there were thirty-nine clerks.

The Chief Clerk was well paid by the standards of the day. In 1818 Dickie received a salary of £870, rising to £1,010 in 1827. The most junior clerk had to make do with £110 in 1818, whereas his equal in 1880 earned £139 14s 6d, by which time there were ninety-seven clerks.

Robinson, who came into the Bank in November 1815 at the age of twenty-two, began with a salary of £105 per annum; after thirty-five years' service he was earning £841 4s 3d, which rose to £1,017 13s 6d in 1860 when he became Chief Clerk. In 1868, the year before he became a partner, his total salary was £2,171 13s 4d. Thereafter, as a salaried partner he received £3,000 per annum.

There were lighter moments. In 1859 Robinson received a letter supposedly from Messrs Walker & Co.:

Messrs Walker & Co, Tailors, Hosiers, Clothiers, Hatters, Perruquiers and general milliners having been informed that it is the intention of Messrs Coutts & Co to introduce an uniform into their establishment, on the first of April next, beg most respectfully to submit the enclosed design to their consideration, hoping that they (Messrs W) might be favoured with the contract which they would undertake on the lowest terms compatible with excellence, elegance and gentility.

The Suit will comprise a Coat of the purest buff; Waistcoat and Breeches of the very best red plush: white cotton Stockings for the gentlemen behind the Counter; silk for those who enjoy the honorable distinction of having to dance attendance upon their numerous aristocratic and titled carriage customers. The gilt buttons and gold lace used, warranted of the purest water. Hat with black cockade; neat necktie of the finest white cambric; collars of the orthodox Coutts pattern, not less than 4½ inches from tip to neckband; warranted to keep the head erect on pain of mutilating the ears; shoes with the largest and most recherchée silver buckles, and a gold headed cane 6½ ft long, which, in order to distinguish their gentlemen from others of the Plush, will be ingeniously contrived to represent a quill pen.

W & Co likewise beg to suggest that the gentlemen should be requested, or if necessary compelled, to visit their extensive Haircutting and shaving department, at least three times a week, where every vestige of objectionable and treasonable whisker, beard, moustache imperial or other hair will be carefully obliterated. It will also be absolutely necessary in order to complete the above unique and elegant costume, that every gentleman attend their haircutting rooms each morning between the hours of 8 and 9 to have their hair arranged and properly powdered.

Convinced that this most reasonable and gentlemanly suggestion will meet Messrs Coutts' entire and unqualified approbation, Messrs W & Co will do themselves the inestimable honor of calling in person on the fifth of next month (guys day) to arrange with the hon. Principals as to terms and other details connected with the contemplated guise.

Snooks House 22 Oct 1859[15]

This *jeu d'esprit* was sent to Robinson, presumably in the knowledge that he would find it amusing. For as George Robinson's letters show, although he was a strict disciplinarian, he was a man who enjoyed a joke. He had been appointed by Thomas in 1815 and so brought long experience and habits of work inculcated by Thomas himself. Edward Marjoribanks junior would have liked to promote Robinson to a partnership, but his father stubbornly refused to accept the idea. Mr Coutts would not have approved. 'Do not bring the matter before me again,' he tetchily insisted.[16]

In the last years of his life old Marjoribanks spent little time at the Bank, but, sitting at his desk in his country home, he was still absorbed in the Bank's affairs. He wrote his memoirs and included detailed bank accounts going right back to the beginning. He could look with some satisfaction at the increase in business after Thomas's lifetime, as he made clear in his memorandum of 1859. His handwriting was now shaky, but his mind was as orderly as of old.

During the last six years of Mr Coutts's life the profits of the business amounted to	£431,200
out of the above sum the joint stock Capital was increased by	£ 36,000
& the sum divided among the partners was diminished accordingly	
During the last six years of the Duchess of St Albans' life the profits of the business amounted to	£478,600
& an addition was made to the Joint Stock Capital – the whole £478,600 being divided among the partners.	

During the last six years the profits
of the business have amounted to   £693,500
out of which £150,000 has been added to a
reserve fund which has been established
(being in fact an additional joint stock
Capital) and which now amounts to   £254,000[17]

His accounts for the period since the 'panic' of 1825 show how little Coutts & Co. was affected by the successive bank crises. The year 1837–8 shows a drop in profits, excluding expenses, to £64,643 10s 2d from £77,122 19s 11d in the previous year; but by 1839 they were up again to £89,157 8s 0d. Similarly the crisis of 1847 is reflected in the drop from £84,645 15s 8d in 1846 to £69,576 6s 0d in 1847. But by 1849 profits were up again to £106,196. In 1861 he calculated that the average profits made in the last twenty-three years were £100,001 3s 9d. The year 1864 was a disappointing one as his clerk, Lewis J. Engelbach, reported on 7 July:

The Reserve Fund does not come out so flourishing as I could wish, but with the exchange in Reserves at 238, you will be prepared for any falling off in all the American Securities & looking at the wretched exchange I could not take the Ohio & Mississippi above 50 all round.

Most of the other securities are also flatter but if we should happily get rid of Rumours of War in Europe, we should share a very different result.[18]

Nevertheless, in the last year of his life Marjoribanks had the satisfaction of seeing profits up to £190,449 14s 11d.

Marjoribanks was becoming increasingly autocratic, sometimes clashing with Sir Edmund Antrobus and even with Angela, whose obstinacy and strong will developed as she grew older. She had the right of veto in the selection of new partners and used it to the great annoyance of Marjoribanks's second son, Dudley Coutts Marjoribanks. She refused to accept him as a partner, giving as her reason that he lacked 'the habits of business' required by Thomas Coutts. Not only that, but she steadfastly refused to allow Dudley's sons to come in as partners.

Her opposition to Dudley, which she maintained over the years with characteristic obstinacy, is difficult to understand. Perhaps she considered that there was a danger that the Marjoribanks family would gain the 'supremacy' which her grandfather had always insisted should remain in his family. Perhaps she was jealous that Dudley had secured the old Duchess's favour. He was, after all, Harriot's godchild and was fifth in the succession to inherit the family share of the Bank. But for whatever reason, she and Dudley were, as his sisters were to say, 'at scissors'.

In 1865 the partners agreed to take in as a partner Henry Ryder, son of the Earl of Harrowby. He was the grandson of Fanny, Marchioness of

Bute, and great-grandson of Thomas Coutts. At last Angela had a member of her own family as a working partner in Coutts & Co., and he became her eyes and ears at the Bank in the Strand. Dudley, whose temper was always on a short fuse, exploded and wrote scathingly of Ryder's non-existent 'business habits'.

When Ryder became a partner in 1865, the solicitor at Farrers, Mr Ouvry, wrote to him to explain the situation at Coutts & Co. The present partners were, in order, 'Mr Edward Marjoribanks, Sir Edmund Antrobus, Mr William M. Coulthurst, Mr Edward Marjoribanks'.[19] These four senior partners 'alone have shares in different proportions'. The junior partner, Hugh Lindsay Antrobus, received a fixed sum, as did Coulthurst's nephew, Edmund, who had been taken in to assist his uncle in 1857. Ryder would not be able to receive a share of the profits until three of the existing partners had died.* Ryder could only be a senior partner if he survived the six persons above named, but as each died he would be entitled to an addition to the fixed yearly income. This would be at present £2,000 per annum. 'You will not be called upon to contribute to the capital of the House until you become one of four senior partners.'[20]†

He was expected to give punctual attendance from 9 to 6, except one day a week, and he would have six weeks' vacation a year. His duties were to sign letters; to read over and examine the vouchers of the previous day; to go into the City to receive dividends and make transfers at the Bank of England; and to collect dividends from companies. The work, Ouvry solemnly warned him, would 'demand close attention and much labor'.[21]

Angela wrote a delighted letter to Ryder from Brighton. It was a plan she had had at heart for many years and she was 'quite satisfied that in my recommending you to the Acting Partners I have rendered them a service as well as a gratification to myself'.[22] Ryder certainly gave the Bank devoted service until his death in 1900. To Angela he was invaluable: when she was in London his carriage was regularly seen in Stratton Street, where twice a week he came to take tea and report. He was a gentle, conscientious man, with a great sense of responsibility to his great-grandfather's bank.

Although during the 1860s Angela spent much of her time in Torquay, she was nevertheless concerned about the affairs of the Bank. In December she was asking advice 'on the delicate mode of making some addition to the Income of Mr H. L. A. [Hugh Lindsay Antrobus] and my nephew at Midsummer'.[23] She was anxious that they should earn enough to enable them to save and become, as bankers should be, 'men of substance'.

*   *   *

* 50 per cent of the shares were, of course, owned by the Trustees of the Duchess of St Albans.
† It was not until midsummer 1870 that Ryder's salary was increased from £2,000 to £3,000. Hugh Lindsay Antrobus, whose salary had been £4,000 per annum in that year, became a partner with a share of the profits. His salary was then reduced to £3,500 a year.

In the past three decades Angela had undoubtedly brought fame and prestige to the Bank, but, as she herself acknowledged, she had been able to do good because of her grandfather's 'great means', or rather the interest she acquired from his half-share in the Bank. She could not have been so generous had the Bank not flourished. While old Marjoribanks was alive, caution and steady progress had been the watchwords as they had been in Thomas's day. As has been seen, he and his partners had brought the Bank through the economic crises of 1825, 1836, 1847 and 1857; they had survived competition from the joint stock banks; and neither the revolutionary 1840s nor the Crimean War had damaged them. Coutts & Co. shared the growing prosperity of the 1850s and 1860s.

But there were financial problems in the 1860s. Some of the customers of Coutts & Co. undoubtedly lost money in the American Civil War, because they invested in Confederate Bonds,* which became worthless when the southern states lost. The Civil War damaged the Manchester cotton trade, and the cotton crisis caused a great drain of silver from Europe to India to pay for the import of Indian cotton. Angela, as has been seen, encouraged Livingstone's quest to find new cotton fields in Africa. Bagehot, writing in 1873, claimed that, had it not been for the right principles of the Bank of England, there would have been a 'panic to rival the earlier ones. . . . But because they had in their till an exceedingly good reserve',[24] they were saved.

These 'right principles' had certainly been those of Thomas Coutts and old Marjoribanks, who had again and again insisted on keeping healthy reserves at Coutts & Co. The importance of the backing of a strong reserve was proved in the crisis of 1866.

In that year the distinguished private bankers Overend & Gurney went bankrupt. The failure of a firm that had been so much respected caused widespread panic. Once again Coutts & Co. survived; the confidence created by Angela, the caution and experience of the partners, especially of Coulthurst and Marjoribanks senior, were elements in their survival. Once again Bagehot's wisdom was demonstrated:

During the period of reaction and adversity just even at the last instant of our prosperity, the whole structure is delicate. The peculiar essence of our banking system is an unprecedented trust between man and man; and when that trust is much weakened by hidden causes, a small accident may greatly hurt it and a great accident for a moment may almost destroy it.[25]

---

* Confederate Bonds had been issued to raise money for the war effort at an attractive interest rate of 6–8 per cent. A large number of the bonds were left in the vaults of Coutts & Co. and were recently sold. They were decorated with vignettes and are now of some value.

The collapse of Overend & Gurney was a triple warning to the partners and to Angela. Not only was it necessary to keep a sound balance, but, to quote Bagehot again, 'an hereditary business of great magnitude is dangerous. The management of such a business needs more than common industry and more than common ability.'[26] The founders of Overend & Gurney were exceptionally clever, but 'the rule in it passed to a generation whose folly surpassed the usual limit of imaginable prosperity. In a short time they substituted ruin for prosperity and changed opulence into insolvency.'[27] His conclusion was that, 'A great private bank might easily become very rotten by a change from discretion to foolishness in those who conduct it.'[28]

The Overend & Gurney affair taught another lesson which had been learned long ago by Thomas Coutts and his successors. The Gurney family had sold their estates to pay for the firm's losses: it was this 'visible ruin' which destroyed their credit. 'If', as Bagehot said, 'the great losses had slept a quiet sleep in a hidden ledger – no one would have been alarmed ... and the business of "Overends" might have continued until today.'[29] In the coming years the bank was to undergo severe trials on all these counts: the 'deterioration of old blood', the difficulty of finding new blood, of maintaining good management by inheritance, and of keeping 'essential secrecy'. Throughout, Coutts & Co. survived all these difficulties partly because the partners were, as they always had been, masters of the art of discretion.

Bagehot's remarks written in 1873 are particularly relevant and describe so clearly the problems that faced Coutts & Co. in the next decade. These were problems of a bank that relied on family supremacy, of management in an increasingly complex banking world, and of surviving through 'panics'. It is very likely that Angela, who kept closely in touch with current theories, read his work. Certainly she was to advise, as he would have approved, the maintenance of a healthy reserve fund and kept a close eye on the appointment of new partners.

As old Marjoribanks became increasingly frail she felt responsible for the future of the Bank, and she was now well qualified. In 1868 she had thirty years of experience in many kinds of business and had acquired an exceptional knowledge of world affairs.

Seeing that his father was near to death Dudley, who by this time had accepted exclusion for himself, but still had hope for his son, rushed up to Harrogate where Angela was staying, trying to get a letter from her approving the admission of his son as a partner. This he could show to his father and get his blessing. Angela sent an affectionate message to the dying old man, but made no mention of Dudley, who, infuriated, sent an angry reply to what he called her wicked letter, on the corner of which he scribbled 'destroyed'. He kept it, however, among his papers.

Worse was to come. When Marjoribanks died in 1868 and his will was read, it was discovered that the bulk of his fortune went to Dudley. The old man had obviously had misgivings about Edward, who had already had the advantage of a partnership in the Bank, and had also married a rich wife. Marjoribanks's efforts to redress the balance angered Angela, who felt that the elder son, 'her excellent friend' Edward, had been wronged. The partners were equally indignant. Edward, they said, had given forty years' devoted service and had been snubbed. Angela was so incensed on Edward's account that she felt unable to accept the £2,000 Marjoribanks had left her. The explosion in the family echoed round and round for months. Dudley's sisters were fierce in his support, their letters circulated, fanning the flames. 'Couttsy' was intolerable – their father had worshipped her for thirty years and now she dishonoured his memory. The suppressed jealousy of many years surfaced.

Angela withdrew in a dignified silence. It was her practice either to speak out frankly or to ignore argument. Ten years later she was to discover that the old man had probably recognised that, charming and hardworking though Edward was, he had some grave defects.

Dudley was deeply wounded, but gradually the dust settled and Edward Marjoribanks, Hugh Lindsay Antrobus and Henry Ryder worked at the Bank in the Strand in a friendship and harmony which is reflected in the relaxed and humorous tone of their letters. They were joined by George Robinson, who, following the death of Marjoribanks, was made a partner.

He enjoyed his new status, and Antrobus and Ryder were amused to watch his way with debtors: he would solemnly take them into a private room to emphasise the magnitude of their offence – a technique he no doubt learned from Thomas Coutts himself. But he also certainly remembered how Thomas had always taken an interest in the clerks and he himself never forgot his old colleagues. Though now a partner he still acted as a general manager, dealing with the training of clerks and even of new partners.

The death of Marjoribanks was succeeded by more than two decades of troubles in political affairs, in banking in general and in the private concerns of Coutts & Co.

The Franco-Prussian War of 1870 affected the Bank, and Angela in particular. In that year Angela's old friend, Napoleon III, Emperor of France, rashly took up arms against Prussia and was finally defeated at the Battle of Sedan. Sick and dejected, he and Empress Eugénie fled to England and settled in comparative obscurity in Chislehurst. When he became seriously ill, Angela took him fruit and flowers from Holly Lodge. After his death she remained on friendly terms with the Empress, repaying the hospitality of those grand days long ago at Compiègne. She remained fascinated by the Bonaparte family, no doubt relishing the curious fact that she was related to them by her cousin's marriage.

Coutts & Co. had come to Louis Napoleon's rescue and similarly, in the aftermath of revolution and uncertainty that followed the French defeat, were able to help many of their French customers and banking colleagues. They had had a close connection with the French House of Lafitte since 1788, when it was known as Perregaux. On 13 November 1868 old Ferrere Lafitte had given them advance warning that he intended to liquidate his bank in January 1869 when he would be seventy-four. He recommended to them his relation, Prosper Ferrere, who was trained in his House and had now established a 'solid house' – Prosper Ferrere & Co. – and wished to continue the connection with Coutts & Co.

Other French banks had closed during 1870, the year of war and revolution. Messrs Mallet Frères hoped to reopen at the end of 1870, but, as Charles Mallet wrote from the security of the Grand Hotel, Cannes, 'How is all this to end & when? God alone knows, and when the end comes, what will follow? ... Houses of standing are now clogged with a great quantity of paper which is in a state of legal abeyance.'[30] There was no communication between Paris and the country. He was afraid that when Paris reopened customers would flock in; therefore, he asked Coutts & Co. for a credit of £80,000 against their securities which Coutts & Co. were holding for them. Engelbach, the confidential clerk who dealt with the French customers and colleagues on behalf of the Bank, offered the loan for six months: they would 'only desire moderate terms'.[31]

Many distinguished French customers, like the Orléans family, sent their silver and treasures to Coutts & Co. for safe-keeping during the disturbances. The partners were proud of their strongrooms: as they told a correspondent from the Bank of Ireland, they were immensely strong and doubly locked.

A new flood of refugees flocked to London, many of them bringing their treasure to the Bank in the Strand. The daughter of Dudley Coutts Stuart's Polish friend, Princess Czartoryska, came over from Paris to deposit her papers and jewels at Coutts & Co.

In March 1872 the King of Hanover asked Coutts & Co. to take care of 'a great quantity of silver and gold plate, including massive ornaments of great worth and historical value'.[32] The quantity was so large that it could not be moved in a sudden emergency without creating much notice. There were '70 till 80 boxes'. On 22 March the partners agreed to take in the King's boxes, but, they added sternly, 'they must be delivered here between 10 and 3'.[33]

In 1871 other overseas colleagues were in trouble. The bankers Wright and Tyrell, their correspondents in Chicago, wrote in great distress of the 'terrible calamity' of 8 and 9 October, when 'a terrible fire swept over our city destroying in about eighteen hours nearly two hundred millions of dollars of property'. There had been an appalling loss of life.

Their bank vaults, however, withstood the intense heat and their correspondent assured them that businessmen were 'buoyant', in spite of the destruction of 3,000 acres, and already

the debris is largely cleared away and foundations and walls are rising on every side, we hope in five years to have Chicago more beautiful & prosperous than before; Eastern capitalists have offered our firm and others large sums to loan out on real estate security to enable those owning lots to rebuild, we shall have to repay a little more interest but we can afford to do that to get back where we were a month since.[34]

With new-world energy and resilience Chicago was rebuilt and the 'city in a garden' rose from the flames. Twenty-two years later at the great Chicago World Exhibition, the work of Angela Burdett-Coutts was honoured with a special display, and her brief biography, written at the request of the Duchess of Teck, was given pride of place.

41

Years of Honour

For the past decade it had been Angela Burdett-Coutts who was the public face of the Bank: her fabled immense wealth, the respect she had won from all classes from kings and queens to costermongers, had brought an aura to the quiet reserve of the partners at Coutts & Co. At the age of fifty-four she was a figure of some consequence at home and abroad: in her own eyes and in the eyes of the world she was the head of the House of Coutts & Co. In the 1870s she was to be crowned with honours and the Bank would catch the glow of her reflected glory.

No longer the drooping girl of 1837, Angela could now look kings, queens and prime ministers in the eye and call them friends. Queen Victoria took tea with her at the window overlooking Piccadilly and brought her children to admire the gardens at Holly Lodge.

Princess Mary Adelaide of Cambridge, later Duchess of Teck, was particularly close; indeed, her 'dearest Miss Coutts' was Godmother to her son, appropriately called Francis. As for her daughter, Princess May, later Queen Mary, there was from her earliest days a rapport with Angela, the generous friend who so often came to their rescue when 'retrenchment' became necessary and they came to stay at Holly Lodge.* It was Angela who encouraged Mary Adelaide and her daughter to take an active interest in the East End and the lasting popularity of the royal family there owes much to her influence. Affectionately known to the Cockneys as 'Fat Mary', the Duchess was a popular figure who was accepted as genuinely interested in their welfare.

Angela had many personal friends among the European royal families. King Louis Philippe of France and his wife and family, Emperor Louis Napoleon, and King Leopold of the Belgians and his wife, had all been particularly close for many years. At her house in Torquay she entertained

---

* The author was told that during the Second World War Queen Mary was seen at the top of Holly Lodge Gardens with the Duke of Windsor. Doubtless she was remembering her visits as a girl and perhaps, as the old gardener recalled, the day he slapped her hand when she raided the strawberry bed.

Queen Sophia of Holland on her visits in 1868 and 1870, and took her to hear Pengelly lecture on fossils in the little lecture hall.

Now even prime ministers regarded her with respect – and with some awe. She had known Disraeli since she was a young girl, and Gladstone and his wife and daughters became her friends, although she was frequently to battle with him. She was capable of using MPs in support of her causes almost as ruthlessly as Florence Nightingale used Sidney Herbert. She was the close friend of many of the greatest men of the age.

Other philanthropists might boast similarly important friends, but none had such a wide-ranging circle. After three decades of work she herself was now acknowledged as 'Queen of the Poor'. She might have been Queen of Sarawak and in Ireland she would be hailed as 'Queen of Baltimore'. She was considered almost as royal as Queen Victoria and certainly more visible than the widowed Queen.

In 1866 she was cheered as 25,000 working men passed her house on their way to the Reform demonstration. She had earned their praise. No other man or woman at that time did more in such a variety of ways to improve living conditions at home and abroad. Her memorial was all around in schools and housing and churches. She was regarded almost as the patron saint of the costermongers of the East End. She had provided stables for their donkeys on her Columbia estate. In return she was presented by the Columbia Costermongers' Club with an address and a silver model of a donkey.

Her most ambitious project for the East End was, however, a failure. Fond though she was of the pearly kings and colourful and lively street markets, she was very aware that the foodstalls on pavements, 'green with refuse leaves',[1] were breeding-grounds for disease. The police tried to drive the costers off the streets; Angela built Columbia Market at a cost of £200,000. *The Times* described it as 'a market the like of which for lavish decoration and almost extravagant adornment does not exist in the world. The Halles of Paris and the Central Market of Brussels are nothing when compared with the beauty of this almost cathedral pile.'[2]

The building began in 1864 and the market was opened on 28 April 1869. Angela, who never did anything by halves, had excelled herself. *The Times*'s correspondent was breathless: 'From the carved doorway by which you enter, to the topmost finials of the beautiful clock tower, all is finished with the careful minuteness of a painting or ... with the conscientious labour of the Gothic sculptors of old.'[3]

The main hall was part of a larger complex including a huge market yard for the unloading of carts. 'The buildings included fourteen apartments for city clerks,' who, as Angela knew, often found it difficult to find accommodation.

Angela had brought beauty and magnificence to the poorest part of

London. But as a market it was a failure. Within six months the buildings closed. The project was defeated partly by what was called the 'Ring', 'the vested interests who were alarmed by the serious invasion of their monopoly'.[4] But it also failed because it attempted to draw East Enders into a pattern of life which was totally alien to them – no swearing was allowed and, worse still, no Sunday trading.

Angela refused to accept defeat. In February 1870 she reopened the Columbia as a fish market, but the machinations of the Billingsgate traders again doomed the project. In 1871 she handed the market over to the City Corporation. In December 1874 the Council threw in its hand and gave Columbia back to Angela; with characteristic stubbornness she tried again. In 1879 a Columbia Meat Company was an experiment that failed. In 1881 she tried another London fish market and National Fishery Company, but this too went into liquidation in 1884. The next year even Angela acknowledged defeat: in 1885 Columbia Market was closed for the last time.

The marble halls became the haunt of pigeons; gradually the whole complex became derelict and was finally demolished in 1958. It was a shameful example of civic neglect and vandalism. But the concept of the covered shopping centre, so ahead of its time, lived on.

Her exceptional contribution to public life was now universally recognised.

In the coming decade Angela was to receive many honours unique for women, but none caused her more surprise and pleasure than the one she received in 1869 from the Freemasons of Victoria Park, Hackney.

On 22 June 1869 a committee met at the Approach Tavern, Victoria Park, to found a new Lodge, which they asked Angela to allow them to name the 'Burdett-Coutts Lodge'. In a brief history of the Lodge compiled on their hundredth anniversary the author, A. S. Gay, explained that they had honoured Angela because 'she personified those characteristics which Freemasons strive to maintain and uphold'. She was known 'throughout the land and indeed throughout the world' because she had 'devoted herself to the task of lessening the aggregate of human misery and vice'.[5]

She replied from her house in Torquay that it was difficult to express how much she valued their 'mark of regard'. She commended the work of the RSPCA and she took the opportunity to hope that 'their lodge would especially take up this great branch of charity'.[6]

At their meeting on 23 September, the Lodge was duly given her name and the Freemasons were presented with a very handsomely bound Bible. Her cousin, Colonel Francis Burdett, was made an honorary member and acted as her representative. She kept an interest in 'her' Lodge and in 1883 laid the memorial stone of the Royal Masonic Institution for Boys.

In 1871 it was the Government's turn to honour Angela. In May, Gladstone, now Prime Minister, consulted his colleagues. Among his papers a scribbled note to Lord Granville has survived, perhaps passed in a meeting: 'Miss B. Coutts has handed over in trust to the Corporation of London, Columbia Market. . . . Is there any way in wh. the remarkable services of Miss B. C. to the public cd be acknd?'[7]

Granville considered the question and returned the paper with his answer: 'I like the notion of peerage.'[8] Queen Victoria, who had watched Angela's progress over many years and who had herself been indebted to her, was delighted to honour a friend, who 'had made such generous and admirable use of her money'.[9]

It took Angela two days to think about the offer, perhaps remembering how her father had twice refused such an honour. But Mrs Brown wrote an effusive letter of thanks to Gladstone, and no doubt exerted her influence, and Angela became Baroness Burdett-Coutts of Highgate and Brookfield, the two parishes in which Holly Lodge was situated. From now on, though the Queen always called her 'Lady Burdett-Coutts', she was known to most people quite simply as 'The Baroness'.

She had given much thought to her title. She wrote to Gladstone:

The *Coutts* are of the gypsy families of the lowlands of Scotland, and I suppose the wandering instincts of my tribe have prevented my attaching myself to the soil and I have only pitched a tent here and there. So you have caged the wild bird. I will do my best to give it a local habitation and a name. . . . The other place to which I could connect myself was Ancoat in which the first Burdett founded a priory. He was that excellent and wise soldier to whom I am under such infinite obligations who came from Normandy with the Conqueror.[10]

The Baroness made it clear that Mrs Brown was included in the honour – her New Year card for 1871–2 was sent in both their names, with Mrs Brown's portrait beside hers.

This was the first of many honours and it was unique: Angela was the first woman to be made a baroness in her own right. London Guilds now added their tribute: on 10 July 1872 the Turners made her a Freeman of their Company; eight days later the City of London, in a splendid ceremony, made her their first woman Freeman. In the following year she became an Honorary Freeman of the Clothworkers' Guild and in 1888 the Haberdashers followed suit. No woman better deserved the honour. Thirty years earlier, she had been among the first to encourage the teaching of needlework, handicrafts and technical subjects.

However, no ceremony moved her more than that on 15 January 1874, when the City of Edinburgh made her their first woman Freeman. Here, in the flower-filled music hall, she understood perhaps for the first time the depth of her Scottish roots. Wearing her Turner's badge, with Mrs

Brown beside her, she stood in front of her great-grandfather's portrait and spoke with simple eloquence. Provost John Coutts's and Thomas Coutts's names still had resonance in Edinburgh and her audience was deeply moved. As the Lord Provost spoke of her predecessors, old memories stirred: Dickens and Disraeli, Sir Walter Scott and her grandfather Thomas Coutts had all been honoured here. When he spoke of the Baroness's work for the RSPCA, she was touched that he remembered that it was her father who had brought in the Martin Act in 1824, which had made cruelty to animals an offence.

In her reply she said that, because it was an honour for women, she was proud to be enrolled among Edinburgh's burgesses. She acknowledged her debt to her grandfather from whom, as she said, 'I derived that position which has placed me under such gracious and kindly notice today and has placed in my hands the ample means which alone have enabled me to further those public objects to which you have referred so kindly.'[11] Was she aware that 180 years earlier her great-great-grandfather Patrick, and his brother, had also been made burgesses and guildbrothers of the City of Edinburgh?

She took her new position in Edinburgh seriously. Proud of her new honour, and anxious that the Bank's influence should be developed in Scotland, she suggested that Henry Ryder and his wife, Maria, should come up and have a holiday with her in Edinburgh. 'Urge it as a desirable business move. The House has so many Scotch connections and there are not banking influences in the North so that I think it would be a good thing if you came among them.'[12]

She took up arms against the maltreatment of the horses that pulled the trams up Edinburgh's steep hills and left at least one permanent monument behind. She erected a memorial to Greyfriars Bobby – the faithful dog who had watched for years over his master's grave. The imposing, seven-foot drinking fountain designed by the sculptor, William Brodie, and embellished with a Latin inscription, still stands on the George IV bridge.

She often sat with Mrs Brown at the window of her hotel: and so she was painted, looking over Princes Street and up to the castle and old town where her grandfather had been born. Nothing gave her greater pleasure than that Mrs Brown should have been beside her during the years of honour: for now her companion for so many years was old and frail. Of all the worries that beset her in the coming years, Hannah's failing health was the greatest.

42

Years of Stress

The years of public honour had also been years of private stress. The Baroness was concerned about the future of the Bank and about Mrs Brown, who was losing her sight. Both the Bank and Mrs Brown had for long years given her the stability she so needed in her isolation, and had both taken the place of family. In 1873 her main worry was about the succession to the partnership.

After the death of Marjoribanks, William Coulthurst had become the senior partner, supported by Hugh Lindsay Antrobus, Hugh Ryder and the newly promoted George Robinson. But Coulthurst and Robinson were getting old and the Bank needed new men with capital, and the Baroness considered that they should also be men of social standing. For the unique prestige of the Bank depended, she believed, not merely on wealth; indeed she mistrusted 'new money'. 'Gentlefolk all', she once wrote approvingly of her candidates for partnership. This was not snobbery: it was a longing for the stability of deep roots.

Her visits to Edinburgh had reminded her of the Scottish past of her family and the part the Duke of Argyll had played in its foundation. So she put forward Archibald Campbell, son of the eighth Duke of Argyll. She had heard from Mr Marjoribanks that her grandfather had always acknowledged his family's debt to the Argylls and welcomed this opportunity to repay an old debt. Dudley Marjoribanks must have ground his teeth once more, for though Archie had great charm, he certainly had no 'business habits'! An artist and poet, a romantic with a passion for all things Scottish, he could not have felt at ease in the confined world of banking. He was not a good manager of his own money and undoubtedly would have been quietly dispensed with, had it not been for the backing of the Baroness and the financial support of his brother, the Marquess of Lorne, and his father, the Duke of Argyll.

The other partners and the clerks seem to have regarded him with amused affection. Antrobus and Ryder tolerantly wrote of Archie's poor health and frequent absence, and the clerks collected his blotting pad after meetings for the amusing portraits and caricatures doodled upon them.

However, Archie did have some success in other fields: he pleaded for the retention of the kilt by Highland regiments and preserved grey horses for the Scots' Greys.

In 1873 the Baroness's nephew, Frank Money, would have seemed the obvious choice as a new partner, but neither she nor the partners were ever to consider him suitable. The 'Suffolk baby', whom Charles Dickens had refused to consider as superior to his own Edward, was then twenty-one and studying law at Cambridge. Frank, as he was beginning to realise, was not cut out to be a lawyer and wanted to leave Oxford without taking his degree. Nor was he the stuff that bankers are made of, though he fancied himself as a partner in the Strand. His real interest was in the arts. He eventually became a competent poet and the Spanish court composer, Isaac Albéniz, wrote the music for some of Frank's librettos. In fact, for ten years Frank supported Albéniz. But at this time he was a rather weak young man without direction – and, unknown to his family, he had a mistress to support. He was also on the brink of becoming engaged to Edith Churchill, the daughter of a successful timber merchant. Just before his twenty-first birthday, Frank made a special journey to visit the Baroness in Edinburgh, anxious to improve his relations with the aunt he had always found so formidable.

In the beginning his mother, Clara, had been unwilling to allow her sister to adopt Frank as she would have wished, and for that and other reasons there had been some coolness between the Baroness and her sister over the years, although Angela had always been exceedingly generous to mother and son, making an annual allowance to them both.

Now the Baroness, who was good with young men, invited his confidence. He explained that he was not really in love with Edith. This pleased her since she considered he was too young to marry and should finish his degree. But she also disliked the Churchills; they were, she believed, scheming people, as she later said, 'of a rather second rate flashy mercantile kind'[1] and most unsuitable to be connected with Coutts & Co.

Frank returned to London assured of her friendship and affection. A month later, however, she was infuriated to hear that her advice had been ignored and that Frank had become engaged to Edith. In these years she had come to rely on the advice of her cousin Frances's husband, Lord Harrowby, to whom she could speak freely as to no one else. Now, as she wrote to Harrowby, she was concerned for the Bank. 'Naturally it is founded too securely to be shaken by any one act of circumstance, but its prestige may be impaired, and there are not wanting those not sorry to see or promote this and certainly not unwilling to lower my own position.'[2] Her campaign for cheap food and Columbia Market had made her some enemies.

However, she failed to stop the marriage, which took place in 1875, so she not only refused to attend the wedding but persuaded Henry Ryder not to be a Trustee for the marriage settlement. Henry, a gentle peacemaker by nature, explained apologetically to Frank, 'I am nearly related to Lady Burdett-Coutts and have always been on the most cordial terms with her. I am also under obligation to her for placing me here.'[3] She had, he said, been offended because he had attended the wedding and now he was afraid that his relationship with her would suffer further if he acted as Trustee for him. The Baroness could be as rigidly unforgiving as the Duchess of St Albans. Hurt that her advice had been ignored, she was also genuinely fond of Frank and believed that this marriage was bound to fail. As indeed it did – although Edith bore him five children before they separated in 1887.

Thanks to the traditions of the House, so clearly laid down by Thomas Coutts and maintained over at least seven decades, first by Andrew Dickie and then by George Robinson, Coutts & Co. was well organised, but it needed new partners and above all, as the Baroness realised, it needed a substantial reserve fund.

She was well informed and undoubtedly followed the current economic arguments which Bagehot had so clearly expressed in 1873; and, remembering the Overend & Gurney affair, she was alarmed.

On 3 July 1877 Henry Ryder wrote to Antrobus that she had gone over the midsummer accounts and was concerned that, after redistribution, only the capital of £200,000 was left. She knew that Marjoribanks senior had always been attached to the idea of a healthy reserve fund and his arguments were even more forceful now. So she wrote to Edward Marjoribanks:

Your attention and that of the other friends of the Bank ought to be directed at once to a subject you may all feel a natural delicacy in opening to me. I therefore think it right to state that we ought each of us in our proportion contribute what may be necessary to the reestablishment of the Reserve Fund. I should propose to replace the £76,000 just allotted to me from the Reserve Fund just distributed and that you and Mr A[ntrobus] Mr C[oulthurst] and Mr R[yder] should between you contribute the like amount in your respective proportions.[4]

She wrote a similar letter to Hugh Lindsay Antrobus.

Marjoribanks was appalled at the idea and replied defensively that they had themselves already considered this, but, he claimed, at the moment Mr Robinson was in great distress. In fact it was Edward himself who was in distress, shuddering under the burden of an immense debt.

Courteously the Baroness wrote again, repeating her concern: 'it looks as though the only Reserve Fund is £50,000 which is to be increased by £24,000 – still not enough for business now'.[5] But she would not press the case since Edward was going abroad for his health and Robinson was 'distressed'.

Nevertheless, as she wrote to her lawyer, Mr Ouvry, she continued to feel 'a vague disquiet about banking affairs'.[6] She had to accept the partners' explanation of the reserve fund, but she was still not happy. 'I feel more directly responsible than heretofore,' she wrote. She had so much regard for all her friends, but 'the growing feeling of mystification was quite painful. . . . It would be a grave mistake on the part of the partners of the bank if anything affecting the business was withheld from *me*.'[7]

Deeply concerned, she wrote to Ouvry that she was sure he would explain clearly. And so he did in a brief statement:

When Mr M[arjoribanks]'s interest in the reserve Fund ceased his Executors received from that Fund £86414. If the new partners had to make up that amount the respective sums would have been

Sir E. A.	£24690
Mr Coulthurst	£24690
Mr Marjoribanks	£24690
Mr L. Antrobus	£12344
	£86414

Instead of this there was set
apart for sundry debtors £18000
Profit & Loss Separate Acct't   17000

£35000[8]

The Baroness's unease about the Bank was justified, but it was not merely the weakness of the reserve fund that was causing concern.

The partners were deeply worried about Edward Marjoribanks, whose financial situation in the summer of 1877 had become desperate. For some years he had lived beyond his means, for, as a friend later wrote, he lived in such style in his enormous house that he wondered that Coutts & Co. had allowed it. Marjoribanks, who had inherited his father's house at Bushey, was rebuilding it and, as he claimed, improving it so that it could be sold.

It was not only the expense of the house at Bushey which was crippling him. He had, like many of his contemporaries, made a number of rash investments. Indeed, old Marjoribanks himself must have realised that Edward was not reliable when he made his controversial will in 1868, leaving the bulk of his estate to his younger son, Dudley. The collapse of Overend & Gurney must have reminded him that banking skills are not necessarily inherited, and he must have seen that what Bagehot called 'the diminution of the blood'[9] had diminished the Marjoribanks ability.

In 1872 William Coulthurst had quietly warned Marjoribanks, who wanted a loan from the Bank on the security of the house at Bushey. Coulthurst had reminded him that this was difficult since the house was entailed and recommended that he should 'take immediate steps to order this Estate in yourself absolutely'.[10] Marjoribanks replied that he wanted to sell the 'horrible house', but he needed to 'enhance its value' first. He was 'very low, dispirited about myself' and had 'depression of nervous power and could not walk across the room'.[11]

As senior partner, Coulthurst had kindly and patiently urged him. 'It is of the utmost importance', he wrote to Marjoribanks, '[that] each partner should be free from any suspicion of pecuniary difficulty . . . in the interest of the House, in your own interest and for the sake of those who are dependent on you to tell me without reserve your real position'.[12]

'Perfect unreserved communication', Coulthurst asserted, was the only foundation for partnership. A partner had no right to claim

my private affairs do not concern you . . . the Credit of a House, a banking House especially, rests mainly on the opinion entertained of the character and position of the individual partners . . . your pecuniary position is to a certain extent known outside the House, your style of living I know has been commented upon.[13]

Marjoribanks, however, could not bring himself to do so and his debts mounted. He continued to make risky investments and still spent too much on the rebuilding of his house. Although Coulthurst believed that credit was not yet affected, he was sure that it would be if Marjoribanks succeeded as senior partner.

In June 1875 Marjoribanks was still a problem. The partners offered him a loan to extricate him from the difficulties he was in because of an investment he had made in the Colne Valley Water Company. But he refused, saying that 'since you all concur that I am a distress rather than an advantage to the House',[14] he wished to leave at midsummer. With great kindness and patience, Robinson and Coulthurst persuaded him to stay, although he was clearly becoming increasingly neurotic. During the following two years he sank further and further into debt, but became more and more unable to face his desperate situation.

In July 1877, when the partners heard of Angela's 'mystification', Marjoribanks chose to take it as a charge that he had deliberately mystified accounts in the banking business. He was obviously physically and mentally ill at this time. In a letter of almost paranoiac anger, which was written for him by his wife in her fierce, strange handwriting, he complained of the Baroness's direct attack on him: 'After 40 years of faithfull and uninterrupted service in the Strand . . . (it would have been) the merest ordinary courtesy . . . if she had communicated to me in the first place instead of appointing the firm's solicitors to watch and report.'[15]

He was furious that she had discussed his private affairs with the partners: 'she had no more right to ask him about Bushey than he would have to enquire about Columbia Market or some other scheme you might be engaged in'[16] – a shrewd thrust delivered perhaps by his wife. It was she who also added that Marjoribanks was prepared to have his books professionally examined in the Baroness's or Ouvry's presence, for Marjoribanks must have known that his debts would then be revealed.

Ryder recorded the painful sequel. After a sleepless night worrying about 'our unfortunate friend', old George Robinson decided that he must go to Marjoribanks, get a clear statement of his affairs and take him an offer from the Baroness to relieve him of his liabilities on conditions. When this failed he decided to explain the situation to Mrs Marjoribanks, who had 'no previous knowledge and was much shocked and alarmed'.[17] The fact was that Marjoribanks was now quite unable to face the truth. However Robinson, who was genuinely fond of his partner, kindly but firmly persisted, finally extracting the fact that Marjoribanks's liabilities exceeded £420,000, of which there was an immediate claim due of £40,000.

By 4 September it was agreed by the remaining partners, with the entire concurrence of the Baroness, that the partnership must be dissolved. For now, according to Ryder, there were sinister rumours in the City. Ouvry was abroad at this time, but as soon as he returned it was decided that the dissolution must definitely take place. In order to pay his most pressing debts it was necessary that Marjoribanks should sign an order for a loan from the Bank, but this he was too ill to do. The Baroness, concerned for the reputation of the Bank and anxious to prevent any feeling of panic, wrote to Coutts & Co. on 8 September suggesting that they repay the loans to Marjoribanks amounting to £83,000 'and charge the same to my account'.[18]

Meanwhile, in a flurry of activity, the partners sought to prevent a collapse of confidence in the Bank. Hugh Lindsay Antrobus explained to the Governor of the Bank of England, and Ryder went to the City and transferred all the stock out of Marjoribanks's name into Antrobus's and Coulthurst's accounts. James Capel & Co., their stockbrokers, were informed, as were the Scottish, Irish and Oxford banks. The Baroness herself wrote to the Queen and her personal friends. Engelbach went over to France to assure the French royal family and finally it was made known to all the clerks.

The problem was whether to act boldly by dissolving the partnership because of Marjoribanks's insolvency, or to let him retire on the grounds of health. It was decided that it was best for the credit of the House to face a possible nine days' scandal and dissolve the partnership. It would need £200,000 to clear Marjoribanks's debts and finally the Bank advanced £30,000 out of his capital, which he withdrew on retirement, in order to pay the Bank of Scotland. The Baroness had given £83,000 towards his debt to Coutts & Co. and Dudley took out a loan to cover the rest. The partnership was dissolved and reformed without Edward Marjoribanks.

The affair had been conducted with the greatest discretion, but it did indeed cause a scandal. One newspaper reported that 'an active partner has been "Bearing" Russian stocks expecting great military disasters and consequent depression in value – the operation was undertaken with an adventurous Scotch broker in Capel Court . . . the liabilities were said to be ½ million'. There was some other unpleasant newspaper comment. One writer asked, 'In a private bank, guarantee consists in the total private fortunes of the partners. If the Baroness were to die, where would be the cover for investors?'

In September, Mr Sinclair, an old friend of the Baroness, with the best of intentions, foolishly took it upon himself to send a note to *The Times* by which he hoped to prevent a loss of confidence in the Bank: 'In reference to the fact that the senior partner in Coutts is no longer a member it should be that neither he nor any partners hold any ownership in the bank which belongs solely to the Baroness, the heiress of the immense fortune of Thomas Coutts.' This was indeed the situation as he and the general public saw it, but it was entirely wrong. The Baroness was horrified. The partners had to act swiftly to put the record straight. In the light of the events which followed four years later it was as well that the partners clearly established the truth.

On 22 October Antrobus sent a letter to the press explaining that the partners in the Bank owned half the capital and adding that 'all the partners from the Baroness to junior partners are liable to the full extent of their private fortunes'.[19] In fact the Baroness was not actually a partner and, therefore, her private fortune was not liable.

Meanwhile Marjoribanks's son, George, who had made such a good start in the Bank, had been advised to stay at home during the crisis. On 20 September Antrobus, in a typically kindly letter, hoped he would now come back. George's early promise was to be fulfilled: he eventually became Chairman of Coutts & Co.

The Baroness, who was now the most experienced among her 'friends in the Strand', as she called them, became even more concerned. With the deaths of old Edward Marjoribanks and Edmund Antrobus junior their several fortunes had been withdrawn and the reserve fund had been liquidated on the dissolution of the old partnership. As the Baroness noted, this temporarily had left the Bank with only the original £200,000 share capital. Then in 1877 a further blow fell.

Patient, hardworking William Coulthurst died of acute bronchitis at his home, Streatham Lodge, Croydon, where he had lived in great comfort for more than twenty years. He was greatly missed: the Bank lost a partner whose kindness and tact had smoothed many a rough patch; the Baroness mourned a friend, whose philanthropy and deep religious convictions matched her own; and Surbiton lost a benefactor.

Coulthurst had become a wealthy man in his last years. Undoubtedly he had profited by investment in Surbiton – certainly he and Marjoribanks owned houses in Elmers Avenue – but he more than repaid the town by his charitable gifts. He contributed to the building of the Churches of St Andrew's and St Martin's, and built the Church of St Matthew's entirely at his own cost, giving £24,000 for the building and paying for the bells and the vicarage. Coulthurst had laid the foundation-stone in 1871, but did not live to see the Church finished. His sister Hannah's portrait, coins and a parchment stating that the Church had been given by Mr Coulthurst were placed in a cavity in the stone.

St Matthew's held a congregation of 800 and was, in fact, much larger than the parish needed at that time, but Coulthurst had confidence that the area would be developed. At the consecration, after the High Sheriff of Surrey had toasted Coulthurst's memory, a later speaker remarked facetiously that they had been 'obliged to build a series of villas in order to find a congregation for St Matthew's'.[20]

Even after his generous gifts to Surbiton, Coulthurst was able to leave £500,000 – most of which went to his nephew, Edmund. And he left 200 guineas to the Baroness in 'token memory'. Nor did he forget the Bank in his will: he left £10,000 for a trust fund to be set up for the widows and orphans of the staff of Coutts & Co.[21]

To Angela the death of Coulthurst came as a grievous blow, since he had been her quiet ally in philanthropy. *The Times* recorded that at the time of his death she cancelled a reception she had planned to give at Stratton Street. She had watched the development of Surbiton with great interest, especially as, during the years between 1850 and 1870, she was actively engaged in building the flats in Columbia Square and afterwards the model village at the foot of Highgate Hill. She would also have known the area well, since she was a frequent visitor to the royal residence at nearby Claremont. Certainly she gave £2,000 to St Martin's Church in Surbiton, and laid the foundation-stone of St Andrew's in 1871.

She must have been well known in the new town because in 1867 the residents of George Street asked the Surbiton Improvement Committee for permission to change the name to Burdett-Coutts Street. Unfortunately the Committee decided that cottages, built for workers, did not deserve so distinguished a name and refused. If she heard of the request and the refusal Angela would have been appalled at such snobbery.

43

New Hands at the Helm

The loss of Edward Marjoribanks, the death of William Coulthurst and the illness of George Robinson left the Bank in a difficult position. But throughout the autumn of 1877 the partners wrote to each other with remarkable kindness and good humour. Antrobus and Ryder treated Robinson with every consideration. In November he was 'recruiting his strength' at home at Ayot Bury, Welwyn, but the other partners kept him closely in touch with Bank affairs.

They valued his long experience and trusted his judgment of people, understanding that nothing kept him so active and alive as his belief that he was essential to the Bank. 'We must be careful about taking G.R.'s desk without first writing to him about it,' Antrobus wrote to Ryder on 24 November; 'if we did not do so he might think we had made up our minds that he was not coming back.'[1]

'I am sure', Robinson had once written to Ryder, 'that nothing can disturb the harmony between us four.' There had been 'harmony' for years until the defection of Edward Marjoribanks: it is a word that recurs again and again in the correspondence. It was the word that the first Sir Edmund Antrobus liked to use about the relationship between the partners at the end of the eighteenth century. And for long periods in the history of Coutts & Co. this harmony between the partners helped to ensure its survival.

When Ryder, who, as the intermediary with the Baroness, had borne a great deal of the stress, also fell ill, Antrobus wrote to reassure him:

[He] was not to worry about them in the Strand. The figure [i.e. a loan of £50,000] for Sir Dudley is a large one but can easily be provided for. Enjoy your shooting and lay in a good stock of the rudest health. I worried myself a good deal some time back and took in the early morning to writing letters (in my sleep) ... and making abstruse calculations. But I have given all this up and am now quite easy in my mind and in my slumbers – go thou and do likewise.[2]

And to cheer him: 'There is an increase in our profits this year (to Oct 31) over last of £3,800. Not so bad I think you will say.'[3]

Ryder worried that the scandal over Marjoribanks had caused a recent 'falling of balances'. Antrobus, however, attributed this not to scandal but 'to the insane desire on the part of our customers to push into good investments'.[4] This was not good sense since 'brokerage is higher than it has ever been'.[5] Marjoribanks had, in fact, been one of the many speculators at this period who had been seduced by the promise of quick profits in overseas investment.

Throughout November Dudley was still trying to raise £120,000 to save Edward from bankruptcy, but the partners and the Baroness refused to give him the loan without adequate security. However, by selling property he was able finally to settle his brother's affairs.

In December 1877 the Bank lost yet another partner when Edmund Coulthurst, William's nephew, retired. Robinson had been doubtful about him from the beginning, as he later wrote to Ryder: 'when he came first he was put to fill up books ... but he made such a mess that it could not do and he had accounts given to him to copy'.[6]

The Baroness reported to Antrobus that Edmund had 'for good or bad or indifferent reasons ... decided to leave the Bank'.[7] Briskly she advised them to 'waste no time in regretting it';[8] she was firmly convinced that his retirement would 'cause no damage and you and Mr Robinson and the excellent working staff will be quite sufficient'.[9] They should 'say as little as possible. Health must be given as the reason.'[10] So Edmund's departure was as little noticed as his work at the Bank had been.

But now Coutts & Co. was in danger; there was no strong hand at the helm. For once Lord Harrowby intervened. With his usual gentleness he wrote to 'Dear Angela' that he felt he must say that since Coulthurst was leaving on Monday, 'The House cannot be left with no-one at its head but Antrobus, Henry [Ryder] and young George Marjoribanks.'[11] Robinson was 'out' because of his age and health. There must be a new partner of 'weight and character'.[12] He would have liked the nephew of Coutts Trotter, but the clause in the Duchess's will concerning 'the notoriety of seventy years ago'[13] made that difficult. The Baroness felt that she could not go against the Duchess's wish, but in any case Trotter's 'being a grandson of Sir Coutts Trotter is not a recommendation to me myself – I have not very pleasant recollections and my side of the family traditions about him are not agreeable'.[14]

Robinson too felt anxious. He wrote to the Baroness:

I have been in the Strand upwards of sixty years and ought to be a fair judge of the working of Messrs Coutts & Co. I ought to know the business of the clerks and partners. ... The House has been placed in a most painful and peculiar position by the loss of three efficient partners, the death of one, the delinquency of another and the most unaccountable withdrawal of the third. ... [This] leaves only two efficient partners to carry on this important and extensive business.[15]

He himself had had a 'full collapse of the lungs' and doubted whether he would be able 'regularly to attend to business again'.[16] Ryder's health was 'indifferent if he had only one day off a week, but his health was good if he could have two days'.[17] He too suggested Trotter, but as the Baroness told Antrobus, her 'sense of what is right goes strongly against it'.[18] Knowing her 'dear Duchess' as she did, she was sure that she had introduced the clause barring the Trotter family because she knew it was Thomas's wish.

Seriously concerned, Lord Harrowby discussed the problem with his son-in-law, W. H. Smith. He had always been anxious not to interfere in the Bank's affairs, trusting his son, Henry Ryder's judgment. However, he felt that Coutts & Co. was seriously at risk and that a new partner must be appointed. He suggested that the new man should be 'no banking theorist, no adventurer . . . but a solid man not too old . . . with a sufficient private fortune'.[19] Perhaps it was Smith who suggested a promising civil servant at the Colonial Office, William Rolle Malcolm. Their judgment proved sound. He was to be the mainstay of the Bank right up until his death on 23 February 1923 at the age of eighty-three. It was a suggestion that the Baroness took up with pleasure.

The Baroness had known him for some years. The Malcolm family had been close friends of the first Duke of Wellington and William had married Georgina, daughter of Charles, the second Duke of Wellington. The Baroness had been fond of Wellington's grandchildren and William's daughter, Angela, was her godchild. His marriage was to end in tragedy in 1880: one night, while dressing, a candle set Georgina's hair alight and she died in agony.

When the Baroness approached Malcolm he was thirty-seven. A Scot from an old family, the Malcolms of Poltalloch in Argyllshire, he had been educated at Eton and gained a double first as a Scholar at Balliol College, Oxford. A man of considerable academic distinction, he was elected a Fellow of All Souls, Oxford, in 1864 and was called to the Bar in the following year. In 1870, although he was a Tory, he had attracted the attention of the Liberal minister, John Bright, who appointed him Railway Secretary to the Board of Trade. Four years later Lord Carnarvon made him Assistant Under-Secretary of State for the Colonies.

Thomas Coutts himself could not have chosen a more suitable partner. And Robinson, whose standards were as high as those of his first master, enthusiastically approved.

Ayot Bury, Welwyn
13 July 1878

My dear Ryder

Antrobus and you will expect me to make a report of my impression respecting 'Mr Malcolm'.

It is decidedly favourable. In giving any account of his antecedents I may be telling you what you already know. He was of Balliol College and afterward I know of All Souls both feathers in his cap: I asked him about his employments. When in the Board of Trade he had a good deal to do with the Railway Departments and I suppose must have been thought well of from being removed to the Colonial Office when it seems he drafted the Despatches for Lord Carnarvon to see.

I think his manner and voice are both agreeable and when he has got accustomed to our business I cannot help thinking he will be found a very valuable man –

I hope you are not so pressed with business as you have been.

Yours sinc'ly, George Robinson[20]

Robinson was not so sure about the other new recruit, Robert Ruthven Pym, who was, as he wrote to Ryder, 'too tall and too stout but one cannot have everything'.[21] He was 'a pleasant mannered man – not quite what one could wish but still agreeable . . . a man of business. I should think there is no man in London better known. He could be useful in the front office where discipline is necessary.'[22] Antrobus was amused at 'G.R.'s idea that Pym was too tall and stout, he might be told that he will make up for all those undersized boys that he has taken as clerks for years past'.[23] He thought Pym would do, he told Ryder. He himself was recruiting his health after the stress and was now 'as hungry as an ogre'.[24]

There was one solution to the problem of the weakened partnership – amalgamation with a City bank. In February 1878 the Baroness took up a suggestion that had obviously been discussed. She wrote to Ryder of a 'city offer' which had been declined. She 'inclined to it'.[25] She was sure that he and Antrobus could carry on, but 'the city offer would give an enlarged area for the founding of a yet larger House and a *backbone* which the taking in of isolated partners *would not* does not afford'.[26] It might place the 'firm on a more solid footing and unite it to more permanent interests'.[27] Once again Angela showed judgment and prescience. This particular offer came from the National Provincial Bank, and though it was refused at the time, forty-two years later the two banks did indeed come together.

In April the Bank suffered yet another loss. Engelbach, their confidential clerk who dealt with the affairs of the French royal family and other distinguished foreign customers, suddenly died whilst dressing. The partners decided to appoint Frederick Augustus Shannon in his place, a man who had an intimate knowledge of French and spoke the language with unusual elegance.

Accordingly the French dukes were informed. A slightly surprised letter from Coutts & Co. was sent on 26 April 1878 to the Comte de Paris thanking him for his letter and 'for his offer to continue the allowance paid to Mr Engelbach'. They had, they wrote, 'no record of any such payment'.[28] 'Poor Engelbach', remarked Ryder, 'with all his good qualities was often very injudicious.'[29]

Ryder wrote a glowing testimonial to the Duc d'Aumale. Shannon had already been with Coutts & Co. for twenty-six years and was

thoroughly imbued in its most valuable tradition. He had passed some fifteen years of his life in France, and has acquired a most complete knowledge of the language. Further he is in every sense of the word a gentleman both in feeling and education with a happy combination of business capacity and discretion. Hitherto he has occupied the post of Chief of our Stock Department and has hence obtained a thorough familiarity with all investments. I am sure that your Royal Highness would agree with me in thinking that Mr Shannon has peculiar qualities which would render him of great value in any private business you might entrust him.[30]

Shannon's portrait shows a man of gentleness and distinction, whose subsequent long service to Coutts & Co. justified Antrobus's enthusiasm.

So by July 1878 the new partnership was considerably strengthened. Antrobus was now the senior partner, supported by Ryder, and the two new partners, Malcolm and Pym, added considerable weight and prestige to the Bank.

Robinson explained their financial arrangement to the Bank's lawyer, Mr Ouvry:

Our midsummer practice has been for years past to give the Baroness about the same sum she has been accustomed to. This done and the other partners getting their shares the remaining sum has been appropriated ... what was necessary for bad debts and the remainder as a Reserve Fund.[31]

Pym would get a $1/_{32}$ share, for which he would have to put down £4,250; he would receive, according to the previous year's dividend, about £7,000. On the death of a senior partner he would have to put down £12,500 more and would then be entitled to $3/_{32}$.

Malcolm was an immediate success, but Pym was still not quite accepted at the Bank in the Strand. Old Robinson, sitting at home at Ayot, picked up all the gossip and was still uneasy about Pym. Ryder too was not quite happy. Robinson wrote to Ryder:

He is as you said a considerable talker, but ... I should not think he will in business waste time in talking when he gets used to our ways. He seems judicious in not attempting to do much. .... He has very frank manners but he rather wants the polish of a gentleman tho' he is a well bred man and his associations have been good. He is connected by marriage with the Smiths.[32]

Pym had other problems which Malcolm attributed to his being 'under anxiety about a relative'. Robinson hastened to enlighten Ryder. Pym's wife's 'habit of drinking was well known and sometimes when engaged to dinner they could not go in consequence of the state she was in'.[33]

Once again Robinson's instinctive unease was proved sound, just as was his disapproval of young Robert Antrobus, a nephew of Hugh Lindsay's who had been introduced in the summer and who, according to Shannon, was 'a sadly unlicked cub'. Robert came to a sad end. He shot himself – by accident his relations insisted, but there was the suspicion of suicide.

Shannon met with Robinson's full approval. 'He is a pleasant well informed and well mannered man,' he wrote.[34] Robinson was right: both Malcolm and Shannon were to give long and exceptional service to the Bank. Nevertheless, Robinson insisted that even the most brilliant newcomer had to be trained in the impeccable standards of Coutts & Co. Young Antrobus, he considered, should have 'a year or two probation'.[35] Young George Marjoribanks was given the duty of writing up cashbooks 'for the Royal Bank or the Bank of Scotland. But he may soon become very useful for he certainly shows great ability.'[36] Even Malcolm, the Fellow of All Souls, Robinson decided, should begin with some drudgery. He wrote to Ryder that he thought he might after a time 'let him do a pass book. I was afraid there would be grumbles but it has always been the case and he must not mind it.'[37] It gave him some grim satisfaction to hear that Pym had complained to Shannon that 'there was so much to learn'.[38] 'Shannon says', he told Ryder, 'he will probably find more than he thinks.'[39] In the summer of 1878 Robinson lived in the country at Welwyn, supervising the haymaking and desperately trying to defeat illness and old age. But Ryder and Antrobus always consulted him and kept him informed of the state of the balances. In June 1878, at the end of the Bank year, he wrote with satisfaction to Ryder: 'the annual balance is a very handsome sum and will astonish Pym, as a great many other figures will, when he comes to know all'.[40]

Robinson was in fact invaluable to the other partners. His understanding of human nature was profound, he had a canny ear for the cracked vessel, but above all he knew the organisation of the Bank inside out and had absorbed over the years the meticulous standards of Thomas Coutts and Andrew Dickie, which he handed on to Shannon. These three men, Dickie, Robinson and Shannon, were the pillars on which Coutts & Co. rested for over a hundred and fifty years.

So by the end of 1878 the Baroness could rest assured that Coutts & Co. was once again efficiently directed and soundly based. But there were troubles ahead that would rock her and deeply trouble the partners at the Bank.

44

'The Mad Marriage'

'These great successes are charming', Mrs Brown had written to Henry Wagner in September 1875, 'and I am thankful, but *these publicities are trying.*'[1] In fact for the next three years Mrs Brown's health was the Baroness's greatest worry. Since childhood Hannah was at her side as governess, companion and friend, and the sharp little governess had become a lady to whom the great Duke, an empress and two queens had sent their 'compts'. Now it was the Baroness who cared for her old governess, who, approaching eighty, was growing blind.

In her last years Mrs Brown found a hero to replace Rajah Brooke, with whom she had been more than a little in love. One of the Bank's most distinguished customers, Henry Irving, then in his early thirties, had created a Hamlet that made his reputation. Mrs Brown became his greatest fan, seeing the play thirty times, even though she was often ill at this time. She developed an odd friendship with 'her brave boy', who called her his 'shadow mother'.[2] She wrote increasingly illegible letters to him, and he was unusually gentle with her. The Baroness invited him frequently to Stratton Street and after the first night of *Richard III* in 1877 presented him with Garrick's ring. Undoubtedly Harriot long ago would have told her of her grandfather's friendship with Garrick.

In April 1877 the Baroness called in the best eye surgeon of the day who operated on both eyes, but by September Mrs Brown was 'never free from the oppressive sense of darkness, although she was at times 'as cheerful and argumentative as ever'.[3] The Baroness was, as she wrote, 'in constant attendance on my poor sorely afflicted friend'.[4]

Even so she found time in the summer of 1877 to undertake a campaign on behalf of Turkish refugees fleeing from the Russians during the Russo-Turkish War. In 1876 Turkish forces had slaughtered 12,000 Bulgarians, and the avenging Russians were now savagely exterminating Turkish men, women and children.

The Baroness organised the Turkish Compassionate Fund, writing an appeal to the *Daily Telegraph*, commissioning a yacht – the *Constance* – and stocking it with medicines, bandages and food. She appointed as commissioner to the fund a young protégé, Ashmead Bartlett, whom she had known since he was a schoolboy in Torquay, where his mother had brought him on her arrival from America. Impressed by his charm, she had paid for his education at Highgate School in London and later at Oxford, where he read for the Bar. She and Mrs Brown had kept him at his studies when his interest flagged and he was now one of the young men the Baroness collected round her who acted as her secretariat. Now she sent him with an introduction to the British Ambassador at Constantinople, Sir Henry Layard. It was because of her long friendship with the latter that she had become so passionately involved in the Turkish relief campaign. Perhaps she hoped she could turn Bartlett into a hero like the Rajah, but he caught typhus and the Baroness, beside herself with anxiety, had him sent home. Bartlett was too precious to be exposed to danger for, of all her young friends, he was the favourite.

In recognition of her work for the Turkish Compassionate Fund, Abdul Hamid, Sultan of Turkey, offered the Baroness the First Class and Star of the Order of the Medjidiyeh. It was an honour given to no other English women except Queen Victoria and Lady Layard.

This was the last triumph of her beloved Baroness for Mrs Brown. On 21 December 1878 she died at the house in Stratton Street to which she had come in such excitement forty-one years before.

After Mrs Brown's death not even her closest friends were prepared for the depth and intensity of the Baroness's grief. As Bartlett wrote to the Layards,

it has been an even greater blow to her than those who knew the relations between them could have expected and though the state of Mrs Brown's health for the past year must have prepared her friend in some way it does not seem to have lightened her grief or to have relieved her of the sharpness which suddenness always adds to death.[5]

Mrs Brown was buried on 27 December beside her husband under the altar of St Stephen's Church. The Baroness could not face her friends on the morning of the funeral, but sent a printed message, which was read to them by the Reverend Richard Barnes:

My dearest kindest Friends

I am deeply grateful for your loving kindness to *us* in being here today, and to all who have whether from afar or near ministered to my poor Darling in her darkness and affliction. ... Could any wish of my dearest earthly Friend – the companion and sunshine of my life for fifty-two years – be known, it would be that you should all be here in our Home to support and comfort me, in the midst of our Household.[6]

Bartlett, in a poignant letter to the Layards, described the funeral:

Lady Burdett-Coutts was in one way quite overcome and yet her great strength of character and self-control pulled her through the first part of the ordeal. The funeral was to all who had known the two together most impressive and painful, and when, having stood close behind it all the time, she knelt down and placed both hands on the coffin as it was lowered into the grave, there could have been few in the church who did not feel deeply for her.[7]

Blinded by grief, she remembered little of the ceremony and for weeks afterwards remained in a state of shock. Even The Queen's letter of sympathy, which, as she wrote, came 'in the first hours of my grief',[8] remained unanswered until 27 January. She was overwhelmed by letters of condolence, among them letters from the Empress Eugénie, widow of Louis Napoleon, and King Leopold of the Belgians. Their sympathy was undoubtedly for the Baroness, yet few Victorian governesses would have been so mourned or could have found so special a place in the affection of the famous.

To Ryder and the partners who had made all the arrangements for the funeral, the Baroness wrote gratefully:

Dear Henry,

I know my kind friends at 59 will be glad to hear I am well – and I know how they will agree with me that every arrangement was made and carried out by those to whom all was entrusted with most loving care.

Give my affectionate regards to Lindsay and . . .

With thanks to all

Your affectionate Burdett-Coutts.

It took the Baroness months before she could face the world again, but gradually she took up her old interests. The loss of Mrs Brown, however, had left a permanent wound that would never really heal. Her work was duty without joy; as she wrote, 'all was dark and burdensome' now her 'poor Darling was gone'. She had many friends anxious to console her – clergymen like the Reverend Henry Baker, chaplain at Whitelands; the vicar of her own church, St Stephen's; and bishops like the Bishop of London – but it was only to Lord Harrowby that she could open her heart.

The partners at the Bank watched her distress with double anxiety. Ryder and Antrobus were genuinely fond of her and conscious of their debt to her in the past. They were sensitive enough to see the vulnerable undeveloped girl beneath the great lady. 'It is sad', Antrobus had written to Ryder in 1875, 'to think the House takes with her the place of family ties, as when poor Mrs B is gathered to her fathers, as she must be at some probably not very distant day, it will be a lonely existence to have no family.'⁹ She had never been close to her other sisters, though Susan Trevanion, who was now frail and ill, was to stand by her in the difficult days ahead.

The partners had another worry. The Baroness was now sixty-four and, if she died, the Bank would be in great difficulty: her sister Clara was next in line, but it would be her nephew Frank who would succeed to the interest on the half-share in the Bank and they were all aware of his inadequacy.

In the black days after Mrs Brown's death, the Baroness became increasingly dependent on young men like Henry Wagner,* whom she employed as secretaries and assistants and who regarded her with genuine affection. Indeed it was said that Wagner was more than a little in love with her. But it was Bartlett who took the place of a son at this time. She had watched over his career with more than motherly love and now she was deeply grateful for the support of his strong right arm.

In the summer of 1879 the Baroness decided to take a cruise for the sake of her health. She chartered a yacht, the *Walrus*, and set sail for the Mediterranean, taking with her old friends, Admiral and Mrs Gordon and Edwin Long, the artist, who was to paint a full-length portrait of Mrs Brown. Henry Irving and Bartlett joined the ship off the Isle of Wight.

Irving was planning a production of *The Merchant of Venice* and the Baroness was anxious that he should consider a new interpretation of Shylock. She had many friends and acquaintances in the Jewish community, including the banker Nathan Rothschild and the great philanthropist, Moses Montefiore, and she knew how offended they were by the caricatured Jew in the play. During the cruise, in some Mediterranean port, Irving saw an old Jew in a fearsome rage yet maintaining immense dignity. This was the inspiration for a new and subtle Shylock. Somewhere in the Mediterranean, perhaps in the opalescent light of Venice itself, the Baroness found more than inspiration: she found love.

Who knows how it came about? Perhaps Bartlett, moved by her aching grief, consoled her with the promise of undying affection – and sealed it with a kiss. As far as the Baroness was concerned, that was an engagement. For Bartlett it was not an unattractive proposition: marriage to the Baroness would give him security and position, and she could help him achieve his ambition to become a Member of Parliament.

Photographs taken on the yacht at this time show Bartlett protectively standing at her elbow, or in his cabin, lying indolently on his sofa, his tennis racket above his head. Tall, broad-shouldered and handsome, he

---

* Henry and Arthur Wagner were the sons of the wealthy and eccentric Henry Michell Wagner, vicar of a church in Brighton, who had been tutor to the sons of the Duke of Wellington.

turned many young women's heads. To the elderly Baroness he was incomparable, and she became totally captivated.

By the time the yacht reached Guernsey, however, Bartlett had second thoughts. An attractive young lady, Miss Shirley, and her friend joined the cruise. 'Nice girls rather of *the* period', the Baroness wrote to Irving on 18 September, 'who would be pretty if they would only leave their poor hair to grow as Nature meant. Life on board you know does not admit of much vanity.'[10] Miss Shirley and her curls conquered Bartlett and the young lady obviously considered that she had received an offer of marriage.

Irving, who had left the ship at Marseilles to hurry back to London, opened at the Lyceum as Shylock with Ellen Terry as Portia on 11 November to a resounding triumph.

The Baroness and her party survived a storm off Jersey and travelled overland to St Malo, where she was due to inspect a lifeboat she had presented to the town. All the sights and sounds of France poignantly brought back the past: 'the horses neighing as the diligence enters the old French courtyard . . . the bells jangling, links that long ago with the bells of today in a curious union'. But every 'homely sight unfolded pictures of that life of mine which, until now, has never been without one dear little figure'.[11]

On her return to England, unable to face loneliness, she determined to secure the constant companionship of Bartlett, and for that marriage was the only sure hoop of gold. She may have asked help from the Reverend Richard Barnes; certainly it was at this time that he broke off his long friendship with her, perhaps shocked at the suggestion that he should conduct the ceremony.

Her isolation was increased by the death of her brother Robert on 5 June 1880 in Paris. Since there was no will, his sisters, the Baroness, Susan and Clara, were the co-heirs. Once again came the painful aftermath of death; his papers and possessions had to be dealt with and, since Susan was ill and Clara unaccustomed to business affairs, it was the Baroness who took the decisions. She would certainly have destroyed anything which could have caused gossip. Nothing remains of Robert's private life, although from time to time there are repeated rumours of descendants in New Zealand or Australia.

One more blow struck in June. She visited her old friend W. H. Wills, who had succeeded Charles Dickens as her almoner, and found him 'sick of death'. He was to die on 1 September. 'If I have struggled through,' she was later to write to Lord Harrowby, 'it has been mainly if not solely through Mr Bartlett's being constantly there.'[12] By July 1880 she had determined that Bartlett should never leave her.

The partners must have watched her growing dependence on Bartlett with alarm, but the truth took their breath away. On 4 July, as Ryder recorded,

Malcolm told me he had casually met W. T. Farrer at the New Life Office who had asked him if Ouvry had said anything in particular in the Strand. The Baroness had an idea in her head from which he had vainly tried to turn her and which was very foolish. His lips were sealed, he could say no more.[13]

Finally Ryder extracted the truth from Arnold White, Clara's solicitor. 'Come', he said, 'it is no use concealing it. Is it matrimony? Is it Ashmead Bartlett?'[14] White nodded his head, saying the matter was most secret.

From that moment the partners at the Bank, bishops, the Establishment, The Queen herself intervened to try to prevent what The Queen called, 'the mad marriage'. 'Lady Burdett really must be crazy, since poor Mrs Brown's death she seems to have lost her balance.'[15]

Unwilling to interfere personally, The Queen acted through Lord Harrowby. She wrote:

The Queen is anxious to learn from Lord Harrowby privately whether a report that has reached her as to Lady Burdett-Coutts marriage is true, as The Queen has been told there are circumstances which make the marriage an unusual one. She trusts that Lady Burdett-Coutts has given the fullest consideration to this step before making her final decision. The Queen knows too little respecting the subject to offer an opinion on it but it would grieve her much if Lady Burdett-Coutts were to sacrifice her high reputation and her happiness by an unsuitable marriage.[16]

Lord Harrowby forwarded the letter to the Baroness with a note: 'You may suppose that I have been much startled by the receipt of the enclosed letter – what answer am I to give?'[17] The Baroness replied briefly: 'I think you had better say (what is true) in reply to the enclosed rather singular letter, that you have no information on the subject alluded to. . . .'[18]

The partners at the Bank were appalled; they had no doubt that Bartlett was an adventurer, interested only in her money. Antrobus wrote to Ryder: 'I wish our lady would come back to her senses and would wait until after her death to bestow £10,000 a year on Mr A.B. – I should not object to that – far more respectable than bestowing it with her hand.'[19] Ryder was even more worried when he heard that his father had replied to The Queen 'that he had no information on the subject'.[20] 'It looks', he wrote, 'like a snub to her majesty; this is a pretty kettle of fish.'[21]

The Baroness, in her innocence, had imagined that she could marry Bartlett quietly in London out of season, and that it would be a nine days' wonder and forgotten. She had good precedents. Both her grandfather's marriages had been secret and he had been blissfully happy with Harriot, who was half his age. Harriot in her turn had been content with her Duke of St Albans, who was half her age. She was sorry, the Baroness told Lord Harrowby, that she had not informed him, but 'the will of my poor duchess had made it extremely desirable that for the moment nothing should be said or known beyond the few absolutely necessary'.[22] For Harriot's will forbidding marriage to an alien was proving a stumbling-block because Bartlett was an American and as such would cause the Baroness to be disinherited; Clara, the next in line, would then succeed. So she persuaded Clara to waive her right. Frank was not so amenable; he consulted his lawyer, Arnold White, who was determined to prevent the marriage. It was he who, without breaking his vow of silence, had indicated the situation to the partners.

Throughout the following months every pressure was exerted to stop the marriage. The partners persuaded Clara and Frank that they should insist on their rights, convinced that Bartlett only wanted her money. Antrobus, like Dickens so many years before, felt sympathy for her, so isolated and vulnerable in the midst of her wealth. 'I should be really grieved', he wrote to Ryder, 'to do anything to hurt B.C.'s feelings as in former years she stood my firm friend against old E. M. [Edward Marjoribanks] which I can never forget and since then she has always been most friendly and kind.'[23]

Lord Harrowby too was protective, and wrote to her on 16 July:

Dear Angela [it is a measure of her loneliness that he was almost the only one left to call her Angela], I do not like to let this crisis of your future pass without seeing whether I can be of any use to you. You have had recourse to me at different times, and it has been a pleasure to me to comply with your requests. Now that you have lost your faithful friend of childhood almost, I looked round in vain for an adviser for you. Can I be of any use to you? At least I do not think you should be without the offer. Your position is not one which you can think so unimportant to yourself or others as to make the advice of a friend indifferent or superfluous. I will not knock at your door or go further in the matter without your leave. I am, dear Angela your affectionate cousin, Harrowby.[24]

To such a moving letter she replied gratefully and frankly. Bartlett, she told him, offered her the only chance of comfort now that she 'could never be a first object to anyone except a husband'. Without him she was left with 'a future from which I not only recoil but which I feel I cannot face'.[25]

Bartlett buckled under the weight of opposition and offered to release the Baroness from any engagement to him. The partners were delighted. Malcolm rushed to Kensington to tell the Duchess of Teck the good news, 'for which intelligence', he wrote, 'I thought she was going to embrace me'.[26] They had all reckoned, however, without that iron streak of stubbornness which had always been part of the Baroness's character. She refused to release him. The Archbishop of Canterbury suggested that she should adopt him, but nothing could move her.

An old friend, Mrs Gascoigne, tried another tack. Miss Shirley, she wrote to Ryder, claimed that Bartlett had made 'violent love' to her on board the yacht, though he told her he could not marry her, being 'obliged to marry a lamppost of a woman (his very words, repeated again and again). And that her money would help on his ambition!'[27] But the Baroness refused to listen and Bartlett renounced Miss Shirley. The Baroness, Mrs Gascoigne wrote, was 'like a girl of 15. She does not *know* the storm of censure, indignation, grief, amazement that is going on everywhere.'[28]

In a letter to Mr Hassard, her secretary at the time, the Baroness however insisted that no marriage, 'however singular or if you like eccentric, was a matter of scandal'. Her friends 'in low life' knew her husband to be a 'good liver' and understood. Her position, she wrote, was always peculiar. She believed that the alien clause did not apply to Bartlett, who was only half-American, and that she could keep her inheritance and marry him. Impulsively she now turned to Dudley Coutts Marjoribanks whom she had rebuffed so much in the past. 'Instinctive feelings', she decided, 'were a more reliable guide than the sense of duty.'[29] To his credit Dudley put aside all his old hurt and, although she had, as he said, 'ruined his life', wrote her a friendly letter advising her to 'marry first and argue the alien clause afterwards'.[30]

In September the Baroness wrote to Gladstone, the Prime Minister. She had crossed swords with him in the past over Rajah Brooke and over her wish to keep the colonial churches she had established under the control of the Crown, and they had been on opposing sides in the Turko–Russian War. But now, though she hesitated 'to bother him in a heavy session', she felt that 'the situation is marked by such peculiar circumstances and may pass quite soon openly into public question I feel a great wish to see you and speak to you upon it. . . .'[31] But Gladstone characteristically did not wish to get involved:

If I were thought to understand and concur, my concurrence would have little value. If it happened on the other hand that I was not able to declare a similarity of judgement, the issue of the conversation might give us both unnecessary pain, without any prospect of compensating advantage.[32]

He suggested that she should see Mrs Gladstone.

Deeply hurt, the Baroness retreated to St Leonards, where her sister Joanna had died eighteen years earlier. By her grave on the hillside at Fairlight, looking down to the distant sea, she felt her isolation most cruelly. The verse she wrote, or had written for her, is now scarcely visible on the mossy headstone:

> Memory repaints each group around the stone
> Where now one woman stands and stands alone.

There was one final shock. Her lawyer, Farrer, told her that a young woman claimed that Bartlett was the father of the baby she was expecting.

Even this she rejected, shutting her mind to all argument as she had done in the past over her father's affair with Lady Oxford.

Her friends watched helplessly as, upright and obdurate, she made arrangements for the wedding. In February 1881, Prince Arthur of Connaught saw her with Bartlett at the Albert Hall and was astonished that such a handsome young man could marry an old woman. Her friend, W. H. Smith, remained constant but deeply concerned. As for Disraeli, he could not have invented a more improbable ending for the story of Adriana. He wrote to The Queen:

Next to Afghanistan I think the greatest scrape is Lady Burdett's marriage. I thought Angela would have become classical and historical history, and would have been an inspiring figure in your Majesty's illustrious reign. The element of the ridiculous has now so deeply entered into her career that even her best friends can hardly avoid a smile by a sigh![33]

On 17 January The Queen wrote to a member of her household: 'Lady Burdett's mad marriage which we had hoped was off – is a most lamentable act of self-abasement.'[34] Lamentable it may have been, but for Angela there was no 'self-abasement'; she kept her dignity throughout, though, as she wrote to Lord Harrowby, she was 'deeply pained . . . and stunned . . . by the conduct of her friends'.[35]

On Saturday morning, 12 February 1881, she stood beside Bartlett at the altar of Christ Church, Down Street, Piccadilly. She wore an elegant dress of white velvet and brocade, her sad, strained face half-hidden by a long lace veil. She was accompanied by her cousin Sir Francis Burdett and attended by her bridesmaids, his two daughters, and Miss Maria Keppel.

The wedding breakfast was at her sister Susan's house in Chester Square. Afterwards the bridal pair were greeted at Charing Cross Station by Sir Edwin Watkin, Chairman of the S.E. Railway Company, and led across a red carpet to the royal saloon in a special train to Ashford, Kent. Here, at the home of her old friends, Admiral and Mrs Gordon, who had watched the story from the beginning, they began their extraordinary marriage.

One man in the congregation had observed the ceremony with concern and remembered the scandal of another marriage so long ago. George Robinson had begun his career in the Strand as a clerk in 1815, appointed by Thomas Coutts in the year of his marriage to Harriot. The grandfather's unconventional behaviour had caused no diminution in the prestige of the Bank in the Strand, but the granddaughter was in a different position. A Victorian husband might take control of his wife's money, even though in this case it was legally out of his power to do so. Robinson, who had picked up the gossip about Bartlett's illegitimate child, thought the whole affair 'disgusting'.

The partners immediately took steps to prevent a collapse of confidence in the Bank. Discreet announcements in the press made it clear that the Baroness was not a partner in the Bank; that she could not touch the family half-share of capital; and that over the years her charities had been financed out of the interest on the capital. It had been useful that the Baroness should be seen as the head of the House, but now that must be changed. She must be persuaded to resign her inheritance in favour of her sister. However, the Baroness was determined to fight and after her marriage was ready to contest the 'alien' clause. The family argument raged throughout the spring. Clara and Frank prepared for victory by taking the surname Coutts and now rejoiced in the appropriate name, 'Money-Coutts'. Clara, who is a shadowy figure, was a reluctant fighter, but Arnold White, her lawyer, urged Frank onwards.

In July the partners were in despair – a legal battle would be disastrous for the Bank. 'Could you not get Mrs M.C. to come some day when B.C. was there and lock them in together?' Antrobus suggested to Ryder; 'if on opening the door nothing but their two tails was found it would save us all much worry and vexation'.[36] Realising the danger to the Bank the Baroness in November finally agreed to 'avoid a law suit prejudicial to the Bank of Coutts & Co. and fatal to my sister's character'.[37] She agreed to a compromise: she would remain in possession of Holly Lodge and 1 Stratton Street and receive two-fifths of the income from her grandfather's estate. The other three-fifths went to Clara. She immediately received £21,500, which, with the two-fifths interest, still gave her a comfortable income, though she was no longer able to embark on great philanthropic ventures.

If the Baroness could no longer consider herself head of the House in the Strand, she was still the dominant partner in her own home. Bartlett took her name by royal licence and became William Lehman Ashmead Burdett-Coutts-Bartlett, although he was always to be known as Mr Burdett-Coutts. He had gained everything he hoped for – wealth and position – and even became the Member of Parliament for Sir Francis Burdett's old seat, Westminster. As for happiness, who can tell? Friends reported that he always treated the Baroness with kindly affection and with a charming old-world courtesy.

Against the advice of Ryder, who, on his occasion, was uncharacteristically outspoken, the Baroness gradually transferred most of her stocks and shares to Bartlett and bought Holly Lodge for him from her co-heirs out of the Duchess's estate. Her money enabled him to indulge his passion for breeding horses in the Brookfield stud at Highgate. In 1885 she made over to him the freehold of 1 Stratton Street and the house in Piccadilly. The Baroness had secured a handsome escort, a secretary, a companion and, according to many witnesses, many years of happiness. It was more than most spinsters of sixty-seven could expect to find.

It was not until November 1881 that the terms of the settlement were finally agreed. 'You will I know be rejoiced to hear that the Agreement between Angela, Clara and Frank Money-Coutts is now very fait accompli, all parties having signed it,' Ryder wrote to his father, Lord Harrowby.[38] Her relationship with her sister Clara had for years been cool; now it was distinctly frosty. She took some grim satisfaction in transferring to her and Frank some of the Bank expenses that in the past she had so willingly borne. Either Clara and Frank or the partners, she now determined, must pay for the luncheons.

She had no hesitation in removing from the apartments over the Strand any furniture she considered hers. Mr Banting, the furniture remover who was also a funeral director and general factotum, was sent by the Baroness to remove the chandeliers from Thomas's old drawing-room. Her sister and her solicitor were furious to learn that, while there, Banting had investigated the possibility of removing the Macartney wallpaper. The Baroness had given no such instructions, she insisted, adding frostily, 'I should think the gentlemen in the Strand would next expect me to send for the roof of the House.'[39]

The 'gentlemen in the Strand' were getting more than a touch of what Rajah Brooke had called her 'arctic manners'. Even her favourite, Ryder, was dismissed with a cold handshake. The fact was that she was deeply hurt. Since her accession she had spent her whole life and a great deal of her money in the service of others. She had given generously to the Bank, paid for the extension of the Bank premises and provided comforts for the clerks. And in her lonely old age they were punishing her for seeking some support and consolation for herself. Convinced that Bartlett was a gentleman and a good man, she completely failed to understand their attitude. Wounded, she withdrew her friendship – at least for a time.

Since her income was reduced she needed to make other savings. She had in recent years given an extra £3,000 a year for the expenses of the vicar at her church, St Stephen's, at Rochester Row. She could no longer afford so considerable a sum and in 1890 discontinued the grant. This won for her husband the implacable hostility of the vicar's wife, Mrs Twining. In her unpublished memoirs she wrote of Bartlett with venom. His expenditure on his stables at Highgate was, she considered, the reason for the Baroness's unaccustomed meanness. There were dark hints, unsubstantiated, of an affair with an actress. This may or may not have been true, but certainly in November 1892 the Baroness drove to St Stephen's vicarage, as Mrs Twining recorded, in a state of unusual agitation, bringing three large oak boxes. These were her personal archives that she wanted no one to see, not even the Reverend William Twining, until after her death.

In 1923, after the deaths of both the Baroness and Bartlett, the Vicar took the boxes to Lambeth Palace for safekeeping. Some of her papers remain there, others were inherited by Bartlett's family. The Duke of Wellington's letters were returned – as she had instructed – to his family. Dickens's letters were sold to America in 1922 and were acquired by the Pierpont Morgan Library in New York. The Brooke correspondence was deposited by Bartlett's heir in the British Museum. A few of her own letters to Dickens escaped his bonfire and are in the Huntington Library in California. But undoubtedly some of her immense, and mostly illegible, correspondence remains undiscovered.

If society expected the Baroness to retire into oblivion after her singular marriage, it was disappointed. On 4 May 1881 she was, as The Queen recorded, 'presented on her marriage with Mr Bartlett 40 years younger than herself. She looked like his grandmother and was all decked out with jewels – not edifying.'[40] The Queen might have looked with some envy at the tiara which once belonged to Marie Antoinette! In 1845 Angela had quietly shown it to Thomas Moore after a royal ball and had then, as he reported, supposed it to be worth 'a hundred thousand pounds'.[41]

Nor did the Baroness keep a silent pen. She took up the cause of Gordon of Khartoum, organised a campaign for his relief and wrote a passionate letter to *The Times*. According to the Duchess of Teck,

She joined with a few other private friends in engaging an English merchant resident in Morocco to undertake the perilous enterprise of finding his way into Khartoum, in disguise, with a packet of letters and English newspapers which were the last words Gordon ever had from England and which told him how deeply the national heart was stirred on his behalf.[42]

Gordon died with her lettercase in his pocket – the one she had given him on his last visit before leaving for Khartoum.

There were still triumphs. In 1887 she visited Ireland to open the Baltimore Fishing School. She sailed into Baltimore harbour on the yacht *Pandora*, lent to her by W. H. Smith, and was greeted with wild enthusiasm as 'Queen of Baltimore', 'a hundred small fires twinkling far in the air on the wild hillsides, signalled a welcome that was repeated in the booming of a salute from the shore'.[43]

In 1893 she received a royal accolade from the Duchess of Teck. The organisers of the Chicago Exhibition of 1893 asked the Baroness to write a report on the philanthropic work of British women, which she produced under the title of *Woman's Mission*. But since, with her usual modesty, she scarcely mentioned her own work, the American President of the Ladies Committee asked the Duchess to set the record straight. Accordingly a slim volume was produced 'by a competent and accurate hand'.[44] In her introduction the Duchess wrote that she was overwhelmed by 'the Baroness' vast work', which was 'one of which no living hand can write the history, and she herself would probably be the first to desire that it should remain unwritten'.[45]

The people of Westminster too recognised her unique position. When she attended her St Stephen's Church, the congregation stood as for The Queen. And she was received like a queen when in 1894 she presented prizes to working boys at the Westminster Technical Institute, which she herself had founded. The *Strand Magazine* reported:

When Her Ladyship stood up to commence, the ovation was simply tremendous. . . . When at length it did subside the immense audience (and hundreds had been turned away) although the hour was late, sat and stood in perfect silence eager to catch every word that fell from her lips. The entire affair . . . had resolved itself into an unmistakable tribute of affectionate regard; for when the Baroness had entered the hall . . . everyone present had sprung to his feet and continued standing until she herself was seated. No greater respect could have been paid to majesty itself. . . .

Henry Furniss was among the crowds that surged past her window in Piccadilly at Queen Victoria's Diamond Jubilee:

Suddenly a hush spread over the vast sea of people. A slim form, supported by several ladies and men, was seen silhouetted against the light; it stepped on the balcony and stood there leaning tremulously against the window. A great hoarse roar spread over the night, cheers, snatches of songs and wild cries of welcome and delight . . . in the tiniest of tiny barrows a fat woman struggled to her feet . . . and yelled above all the clamour – 'The best woman in London – God bless her!'[46]

There had been no self-abasement. Angela Burdett-Coutts had, with great dignity, survived scandal. The partners at the Bank need not have worried; her extraordinary marriage had no more lowered their prestige than her grandfather's had done long years before.

45

Coutts & Co.:
The End of an Era

At the end of the eighteenth century Thomas Coutts had warned the young Edward Marjoribanks that 'a Banker's life is not a bed of roses'. At the end of the nineteenth century the partners at Coutts & Co. might well have echoed his words.

The second centenary of the Bank in the Strand marked the close of an exceptionally troubled period. There had been repeated crises in their domestic affairs. The failure of Edward Marjoribanks and the breakdown of the partnership; the death of Coulthurst and the retirement of his nephew; the scandal of the Baroness's marriage bringing a danger of collapse of confidence; the problem of the future succession and the need for new blood and new direction. All this was peculiar to Coutts & Co. But in addition this was a time when the financial world was in a state of turmoil and the affairs at the Bank in the Strand mirrored the general economic turbulence of the time.

Throughout the century there had been repeated panics in a ten-year cycle. Each 'Black Monday' was, according to contemporaries, the worst ever known. But the threatened collapse of Barings in 1890, one of the most respected banks in the City, sent an exceptional shockwave throughout the country. If Barings, the 'Sixth Estate', the symbol of banking probity, collapsed, so could half the banks in the City.

Edward Baring, the first Lord Revelstoke, like Edward Marjoribanks junior, had become over-extended in rash investments. This was a period of speculation at home and abroad, when bankers and their customers were led into risky projects – particularly in South America. Marjoribanks had foundered over the Colne Valley Water Company and Russian Railways. In November 1890 Baring was sinking with the Buenos Aires Water Supply & Drainage Company and other Argentine fiascos. It was ironical that the very cause, pure water for the cities, that had so inspired the Baroness more than thirty years earlier, should have been one of the reasons for the present trouble.

Now Barings needed around £9 million to save it from bankruptcy (£¼ billion in modern money). On 10 November 1890, William Lidderdale, Governor of the Bank of England, sent for George Goschen, the Chancellor of the Exchequer, in a state of complete panic. Barings, he told Goschen, 'was in such danger, that unless aid is given, they must stop and all Houses would tumble one after another'.[1] During a week of rising apprehension, Lidderdale and Bertram Currie, chief partner of Glyn Mills, persuaded Nathan Rothschild to come to the rescue. He coaxed £3 million in gold out of the Bank of France, the Bank of England lent a further £1 million, and all the leading banks rallied round.

Lord Revelstoke was partially saved, but he was forced to sell his house and much of his personal property and had to undergo a strict period of retrenchment. But a general collapse of confidence had been prevented. The Baring crisis had reminded Coutts & Co., if it needed such a reminder, that if banks of such size and prestige could sink, small private banks needed to safeguard their future.

The partnership in 1892 had been considerably strengthened, but the old guard could not go on for ever and when they died their fortunes would be taken out of the Bank. George Robinson, who died in September 1886, had left his capital in the Bank to Antrobus and Frank Money-Coutts, but others with families could not be expected to do the same. In the next year Henry Ryder, who was now increasingly frail, brought in his son, John Herbert Dudley Ryder.

In 1892 Hugh Lindsay Antrobus was the senior partner and his fellow partners were Henry Ryder, Robert Ruthven Pym, William Rolle Malcolm, Lord Archibald Campbell, George Marjoribanks and John Herbert Dudley Ryder.

Antrobus and Henry Ryder were the most experienced in the affairs of Coutts & Co. and their friendly relaxed relationship is reflected in their letters. Antrobus was often abroad and there were periods when Ryder took most of the responsibility of the Bank on his shoulders. Pym brought financial experience from the Bank of England, but his handling of his own affairs was becoming a matter of some concern. Campbell had charm, but again he himself was in some financial difficulty and his poor health meant that he was away from the Bank for long periods. Marjoribanks and John Ryder were still inexperienced. The Baroness herself was seventy-eight and could not be expected to live for many more years.

At last the partners decided to make the change they had so long avoided. In 1892 it was decided that Coutts & Co. should become an unlimited liability company.

There was little change in the organisation: the working partners were divided between managing partners and junior managing partners. The direction remained as it always had been in the hands of the managing partners. But in 1892 one man was emerging who was to dominate the history of the Bank until his death: William Rolle Malcolm, though not of the family, was to work for the rest of his life for Coutts & Co. with a dedication that would have delighted Thomas Coutts.

A contemporary described the gentlemen who now directed the affairs of Coutts & Co. He remembered

Lindsay Antrobus – no man of kinder heart in London than Mr H.L.A. – the father of the House. Seated in the middle of the large inner room, jovial faced and silvery headed he is treasurer of at least half the charitable institutions in the country. More the beau ideal of a gentleman farmer than one's preconceived idea of a banker, he appropriately spends all his spare time at his delightful spick and span farm at Cheam.[2]

According to the same observer Archibald Campbell, the second son of the Duke of Argyll, bore a 'striking resemblance to Napoleon Bonaparte in face and figure. This patriotic Scotsman has a close sympathy with all and knows the little troubles and worries of every man which made him a great favourite with all in the Bank.'[3]

John Dudley Ryder was described as being

very much like his father, Henry Dudley Ryder. He had the same tall slim figure, the same small side whiskers, the same carefully clean shaven upper lip and chin, and, more marked than any, the same always to be recognised Ryder nose. His quick, swinging walk on the tips of his toes was inherited from his father who gets it in turn from his grand and great-grandfather.[4]

John Ryder was apparently 'a kind hearted generous highminded man, though shy and self-effacing. He became a useful painstaking MP but was too nervous ever to become a great speaker.'[5] He was married to Mabel, the daughter of W. H. Smith, which gave him some influence in Parliament and was a useful contact for the Bank.

George Marjoribanks, son of the disgraced Edward, more than redeemed the family reputation. Tall and athletic, with dark wavy hair and ruddy cheeks, he was a striking figure. And, according to an observer, was 'a master of business to which he devotes his undivided attention'.[6]

Of William Rolle Malcolm he wrote that he was 'difficult to find, hidden away in a secluded corner . . . a small, neat side-whiskered man, very silent, more in his element amid the fruit trees and flowers of his Elizabethan manor house in Surrey. The *morale* of the bank occupies a great deal of his attention.'[7]

'So long as a certain number of quiet men of business watch its investments,' wrote Bagehot, 'and a responsible manager under fair supervision guides its routine, a bank, however large, may easily be safe. But everything depends on that manager and those few quiet men of business, especially on the latter. It is for the shareholders of the joint stock banks . . . to satisfy themselves ... that such persons ... have on all needful matters due authority and sufficient power.'[8]

Coutts & Co. was to flourish for the next 100 years because it was directed mainly by 'quiet men of business', supported by dedicated and responsible managers.

Part 4

1892–1992

46

The New Bank

The year 1892 not only marked the second centenary of Coutts & Co., it was also a watershed in the history of the Bank. After the change of 1892, much of the romance and drama of the old Bank disappeared. As Coutts & Co. became more public, the private lives of the people directing it became of less importance. Gone were the days when the great banker, Francis Child, could walk through the city with a long face and set stocks tumbling; or when the unconventional marriages of Thomas Coutts and later of his granddaughter could be of such importance to the history of the Bank. Coutts & Co., under William Malcolm, was a business, dealing not only with personalities, but also with institutions, governments and corporate bodies.

There were still eccentric figures on the board like Archibald Campbell, who kept alive the links with the Bank's Scottish past. In a quixotic gesture of repentance for the massacre of 1692, he sent his Argyll Pipers through Glencoe, their bagpipes wailing a lament loud enough to awaken the dead John Campbell in his goldsmith's shop in the Strand, or the Earl of Argyll and the Earl of Stair, who had ordered the slaughter 200 years before. But Archie retired in 1907 and died on 29 March 1913. He was piped to his last resting-place in traditional style. No Scot could have had a grander funeral.

Banking in the Victorian age had seen many changes: the accumulation of capital in an increasingly prosperous nation and the new opportunities to invest in an expanding economy, in railways, in mining for gold, silver, coal and copper. Fortunes were made, bringing wealthy new customers to banks.

In this climate private banks found it increasingly difficult to survive, threatened as they were by the flourishing joint stock banks, which could call on unlimited capital from a wide range of stockholders. Their published accounts advertised their success in a way that the secretive private banks could not do. By the end of the nineteenth century 'the circumstances that had favoured private banks had largely passed away'.[1]

In Thomas Coutts's day, as Bagehot wrote in 1873,

the name, London banker, was supposed to represent a certain union of pecuniary sagacity and educated refinement which was scarcely to be found in any other part of society ... the calling is hereditary; the credit of the bank descends from father to son; this inherited wealth soon brings inherited refinement.[2]

Society was smaller, more closely connected.

Thomas and his customers knew each other's circumstances and family histories, visited each other, and even intermarried. But in the developing world, the new rich were not disposed to risk the huge liabilities of private banking. 'No new private bank is founded in England', wrote Bagehot in 1873, 'because men of first rate wealth will not found one, and men not of absolutely first rate wealth cannot.'[3]

Private banks could survive only by becoming joint stock or by amalgamating. When even private banks with the highest reputations like Overend & Gurney and Barings went under, it was time for Coutts & Co. to change. After considering amalgamation with other banks, the partners chose to become a joint stock bank.

The first problem was whether to amalgamate or to choose limited or unlimited liability. That a bank with royal and aristocratic customers should accept unlimited liability was the best signal of confidence. For, once more in Bagehot's words, 'A bank ... lives on its credit. Till it is trusted it is nothing; and when it ceases to be trusted it returns to nothing.'[4] So, the credit of Coutts & Co. was shown to be 'unlimited'. Bankers to the Queen and to many members of the royal family, Coutts & Co. could well face the future with confidence.

The Queen was the first to be informed of the proposed change and, on 22 April 1892, Henry Ryder sent their first balance sheet to her Private Secretary, Sir Henry Ponsonby, with a letter of explanation:

You will observe that no change will be brought about in the conduct of affairs here; & the conversion of the House into an *un*limited Coy has been decided upon with a view to ensuring the maintenance intact of its Capital under all contingencies, whilst defining the relative positions & interests of the existing Partners who own shares in the business in a more satisfactory manner than hitherto.

We trust that this explanation may enable you to convey such information as you may think proper with our humble duty to Her Majesty whose Gracious patronage of our House has ever been our most cherished privilege. It is very possible that Lady Burdett-Coutts may think it incumbent upon her to write to you, but I have thought that it would be satisfactory to you to receive a business communication upon the subject.

signed H. D. Ryder[5]

On 27 June 1892, with Ryder in the chair and in the presence of Pym and Malcolm, Antrobus was elected Chairman of the new board and Ryder his Deputy. Shannon was appointed Secretary at an additional salary of £100 a year. Their first decision, proposed by Pym and seconded by

Malcolm, was 'that the firm of Coutts & Co. be wound up . . . and that repayment of capital be made'.[6] Antrobus and Ryder, as Trustees of the Duchess of St Albans's estate, were repaid £212,000; the Baroness £20,000; Antrobus £78,555; Ryder £91,000; Pym £40,000; Malcolm £58,435; Lord Archibald Campbell £30,000; Marjoribanks £40,000; and John Herbert Ryder £30,000.

The partners were asked 'forthwith to pay up the stock to the full nominal amount'.[7] The old partners reinvested their capital as stock in the new company, which, for a short time, was called Messrs Coutts & Co. On 15 July 1892 they reverted to the old name – Coutts & Co.

Paradoxically, under the new system the Baroness, as a stockholder, could now legitimately play a part in the direction of the Bank. It was she who proposed at the first General Ordinary Meeting on 21 October that remuneration of the managing partners be fixed at £4,000 per annum – 'to be divided in equal proportions and backdated to June 24th'.[8] In November it was decided that the junior managing partners should receive £500 a year. Decisions were to be taken by managing partners – a quorum of one was to be sufficient. Later this was changed to two.

In the following years Antrobus and Ryder were still active and the Baroness, now reconciled to her 'friends in the Strand', kept an eagle eye on them and on the Bank, but they belonged to an age that was passing. The future of Coutts & Co. was to be in the hands of a few 'quiet men', who understood the changing world.

In April 1893 Coutts & Co. was required to publish its accounts. The partners had always avoided publicity, but the newspaper reports which followed were for once welcomed.

The *Bankers' Magazine* printed with approval the first balance sheet that Coutts & Co. had ever published. It showed that Messrs Coutts 'had nothing to conceal while there was everything to court the publicity'. A 'representative' of the same magazine was taken through the offices and vaults of the Bank, sketched the premises and reported with approval:

[They] seem to occupy almost acres of ground in the middle of the Strand. The back premises run among and under the arches on which the Strand is built. From one illustration in this number an idea will be got of the piled-up records and family valuables which fill the vaults of Messrs. Coutts & Co. Coming to the partners' room, we are confronted with a curious and probably unique instance of what may be called the patriarchal form of banking. The partners do not rail themselves off or sit in a private room, impervious to staff or customers, but stand among their confidential clerks ready to answer questions, to consult with customers, or to direct the doings of their well-organised staff, as the case may be. While such a system continues it is of itself almost a guarantee of the continued vitality of the firm.[9]

Another paper congratulated Coutts & Co. on 'the splendid showing of their balance sheet':

Messrs Coutts & Co.'s balance sheet to 9th April will stand comparison with that of any joint stock bank which we know. It is a very simple one, and its analysis is an easy matter. The liabilities to the public amount to £6,365,927 and of this total only £3,560,531, or about fifty-six per cent, is employed in ordinary banking advances. The remainder, together with the capital and reserve, amounting to £1,000,000 is more or less liquid, and is scientifically distributed between cash in hand, cash available at call or short notice, and investments which could be turned into cash in the unlikely event of an emergency in Coutts's Bank. These items together amount to about sixty per cent of the liabilities to the public.[10]

It was, however, pointed out that the Bank's position was exceptional – many of its clients could afford to keep enormous balances.

The index of Messrs Coutts & Company's current account ledgers would be found to contain a more distinguished list of names than that of any other bank in the world – the Bank of England not excepted. If a big City firm keeps forty thousand pounds at its bankers it is because its needs are uncertain, and the banker has to keep a large proportion of it in hand. But if the Duke of ---- keeps a similar amount with Coutts the chances are that thirty-five thousand of it may safely be locked away by the bankers in advances or in Consols, producing an income which enormously exceeds the cost of working the account.[11]

For the rest of the decade, although nominally Antrobus and Ryder were Chairman and Vice-Chairman of Coutts & Co., it was Malcolm who was emerging as the driving force in the Bank. In the new world Malcolm was in his element. He had brought from his Civil Service days experience in running a department, and in committees and chairmanship; his clear, cool mind cut through the intricacies of the increasingly complicated banking world. Impatient with inefficiency, he insisted on high standards; somewhat brusque in manner and unsmiling, even dour in appearance, he did not suffer fools gladly and rogues not at all. No Duchess of Devonshire would ever be able to beguile him.

Pym, who got into financial difficulty, was quickly and quietly removed. Antrobus and Ryder held a discreet meeting – not at 59 Strand but at 65 Eaton Square, Antrobus's house – and, as the minutes recorded, 'The resignation of Ruthven Pym was accepted on the grounds of ill-health.'[12] On 14 June 1893 Malcolm sent a letter to the Chief Accountant of the Bank of England informing him that

Mr Robert Ruthven Pym, while retaining his interest in the Stock of our House, has been compelled by continued ill-health to resign his position as one of our Managing Partners. Consequently, he will no longer sign for the House and his name in future should be removed from our Powers of Attorney.[13]

Pym had shown himself unable to deal with his own financial affairs and, therefore, must go. The reason for his retirement had been given as ill-health, but in fact he had not measured up to the high standards demanded by Coutts & Co. George Robinson's instinct had been sound. Nevertheless, the *Westminster Gazette* gave Pym every credit for his philanthropic work, in which he was supported by the Baroness. He had been treasurer of the Middlesex Hospital and a contributor to many charities. He was 'a capital companion, an inimitable raconteur and the kindest of friends'. However, the *Gazette* concluded, 'woe betide the man who attempted to deceive him'.

When, in the autumn of 1896 Fitzroy Farquhar, who was brought in as a partner in April 1894, got into financial trouble, he too was quickly removed. He resigned on 17 November 1896. 'We are not in any way concerned with Mr Fitzroy Farquhar's affairs,' Malcolm wrote to a creditor. 'His position here under the articles of the company was simply that of a junior managing partner, at a salary. He is also a stockholder to a small extent in the company.'[14] On 25 November 1896 Malcolm informed a guarantor, Cosmo Bonsor MP, that 'Mr Fitzroy Farquhar's £3000 stock has today been purchased by Mr Malcolm . . . we propose, with your consent, to appropriate the purchase money (£7,590) in repayment of the balance of Mr Farquhar's indebtedness to us, & thereby to release you from your liability to us under your guarantee.'[15] In February 1897 he told a correspondent that he had no knowledge of Farquhar's affairs as he was no longer a member of the firm.

Malcolm applied the same high standards to himself. For a time he became seriously ill and, concerned that he might become a liability to the Bank, he asked his doctor to write directly to Ryder to explain exactly the state of his mental and physical health so that Ryder could decide whether he should retire. In fact he recovered and continued to work ceaselessly until his death. But he felt his position needed strengthening and on 11 December 1895 he brought in his son, Ronald, as a junior managing partner at a salary of £500 a year. Ronald, like his father, was a quiet man, conscientious and extremely hardworking. The Baroness welcomed his appointment for his own and for his father's sake. Though few would now remember how close she had been to Ronald's great-grandfather, the Duke of Wellington.

Hugh Lindsay Antrobus died on 18 March 1899, aged eighty, leaving a considerable fortune to his wife and four daughters. He recommended that his stock in the capital of Coutts & Co. of £82,900 should be left there during the lifetime of his wife. In 1900 his old friend, now Lord Harrowby, became ill and took a cruise to recuperate, but died while abroad. Antrobus and Harrowby were sadly missed: their unfailing kindness and courtesy, Antrobus's relaxed good humour and Harrowby's gentle consideration for all, had left a standard of behaviour which gave Coutts & Co. its distinctive tone. Harrowby was succeeded by his son, John Ryder, who had been a partner in the Bank since 1887. The Bank also needed the firmness and crispness of Malcolm's management, though he too wished to work in the traditional framework.

However, there was no question of bringing in members of the Coutts family merely for sentiment's sake. On 21 March 1899 Frank's son, Hugh Burdett Money-Coutts, then a student at Oxford, had written to Malcolm explaining that there was an understanding with his father that he was to be taken into the Bank as a partner on leaving Oxford. He thought that 'Owing to the sad death of Mr Antrobus and the illness of Mr Ryder . . . you can I imagine scarcely fail to be extremely shorthanded'.[16] He would like to offer his services, even though it might mean giving up his last term at Oxford. Malcolm, the Fellow of All Souls, advised him to finish his course at Oxford and then consult his father and Lady Burdett-Coutts.

To Frank, who was annoyed that Hugh had approached the partners without consulting him, Malcolm explained that they did not 'require assistance among our senior partners but amongst our juniors'. If his son came in, he must be 'prepared for three or four years of rather disagreeable drudgery',[17] and he would have to keep long office hours. Hugh did finish his course and entered the Bank that same year. When, early in 1903, Hugh wished to resign, Malcolm wrote about a date for his departure: '[We] don't think we will ask you to stay beyond the end of the year.'[18] Hugh, however, remained as a partner in the Bank until 1914.

In spite of repeated requests to the partners, Frank Money-Coutts was always quietly but firmly excluded from the partnership, although, as the representative of the Trust of the Duchess of St Albans, he was a stockholder. In 1913 the Barony of Latymer was called out of abeyance in his favour, and presumably he considered this a sufficient recompense for his exclusion from the Bank. His son, Hugh, was followed by his son, the Hon. Thomas Money-Coutts, and in 1958 by the present Chairman, David Money-Coutts, as active partners in the Bank.

Malcolm was now the senior partner at Coutts & Co. and it was he who presented the Bank's condolences to King Edward VII on the death of Queen Victoria in 1901. As Thomas Coutts would have done, the partners moved swiftly to secure the continued patronage of the new King. Malcolm called on General Sir Dighton Probyn, the new King's Comptroller and Treasurer, with a letter expressing the

profound grief at the sad calamity which has befallen His Majesty and the whole Empire in the death of his beloved Mother. . . . Our sentiment of sorrow is united with a grateful recollection of the confidence placed in us by her late revered Majesty, by two of her predecessors on the throne as well as by His Majesty for so many years. But we should leave deferred the expression of these feelings had we not felt that at the present moment we might perhaps have the power to afford some convenience to His Majesty. A little time may elapse before the forms of office will permit of our receiving the sums voted to the Privy Purse, and we therefore hope that his Majesty will be pleased to allow us to obviate any inconvenience which might arise from such delay by advancing, as we have on former similar occasions, such sums as may be required, until the necessary fresh arrangements can be completed.[19]

The new century brought problems that needed all Malcolm's management skills. The year 1892 had marked the end of one era. In 1904 another long chapter in the Bank's history closed: Coutts & Co. moved its premises from 59 Strand, where it had been established since 1739, and crossed the street to No. 440. The partners had not wished to move, but as early as 1891 they decided that they needed to expand their premises; and in any case their leases were running out. Their rival bank, Drummonds, owned the lease of their offices in John Street and James Street, and they leased the premises at 56–9 Strand from the Marquess of Salisbury.

George Drummond, Malcolm complained, 'practically obliged us to quit our present premises'. The lease of the rear portion, which according to him was 'the larger portion', was also due to end on Lady Day 1903, and the lease from the Marquess of Salisbury would run out in 1904. So they decided to move.

'It is sorely against our will to move,' Malcolm wrote to the Marquess's agent, Sir Richard Nicholson; 'personally it makes me miserable to think of leaving the place where the House has been for two hundred years.'[20] Malcolm, for all his brisk efficiency, had a feeling for the history of Coutts & Co. On 21 October 1903 he wrote again to Nicholson: 'We have a sentimental regard for old Mr Thomas Coutts' rooms at No. 59 and we should like to take with us the doors and mantelpieces of his sitting room and dining room.'[21] Not only that, he arranged for the transfer of the legendary Chinese wallpaper, the gift of Lord Macartney at the end of the eighteenth century, to the new premises.

Thomas's furniture was easily moved, but the Chinese wallpaper in his drawing-room presented greater problems. The British Museum was prepared to undertake the removal of the paper for £500, but the builders offered to tackle the difficult job for £50. The work was supervised by Holland & Hannen of 12 Hyde Street, Bloomsbury, assisted by the foreman, F. J. Copper, of 3 Wandsworth Bridge Road, Fulham. In a letter to the *Morning Leader* of 12 September 1905, Mr J. Howard explained that he had been mainly responsible for undertaking this difficult and delicate work:

The method of stripping the paper was not by removing blocks of plaster (which method was tried but failed) but by stripping with pallette knives, thus removing the paper from the lining paper which was left on the wall. This was done at the suggestion of T. L. Howard of Hammersmith (son of J. T. Howard). It was afterwards cleaned off at the back by scraping, and glasspapering. It was then mounted on strong brown lining paper, powdered with French chalk and compressed by being laid between heavy boards, being frequently attended to until rehung at 440 Strand by W. Gibbons and A. Day. After being hung it was varnished [with] white of eggs. The damaged portions were touched up and made good by Hoydenck of Mount St Berkely Sq, artist.[22]

There was practically no damage to the paper – only two strips, 12in. and 5in. wide respectively, at the top and bottom of one section, were too blackened by smoke to be used. They were cut out, mounted on a piece of wood (1½ft by 2ft) and kept as a picture by Mr Howard.

So after more than 170 years the Bank left 59 Strand, which, according to a contemporary writer,

is not only an institution, it is a metropolitan eccentricity. It is the only house in the Strand that is without a number or any indication outside as to who lives and works within and the nature of the business carried on during 'office hours'. It is the only house that has never been defiled on the outside by a gas-lamp, and (with a little deference to the spirit of the day) it still preserves that old banking tradition that a dull, sullen front, not over-clean windows, and just the suspicion of latent cobwebs, are the outward and visible signs of commercial stability and solvency. Kings have been welcomed at its dingy counters, and poor, honest Dr. Johnson stopped there to pay in his hard-earned dole when he 'walked down Fleet-street' to get a sniff of the 'country' about Pimlico.[23]

In fact Dr Johnson was never a customer, but many men and women of letters brought their 'dole' to Coutts & Co.

The site chosen for the new bank was the Lowther Arcade, a children's paradise where toys of all kinds were sold. It ran diagonally through a triangular block on the north side of the Strand, the block being bounded by the Strand to the south, Adelaide Street to the west and King William Street to the north-east.

The design for the triangular block had been originally drawn by John Nash, architect to the Crown Commissioners of Woods and Forests, as part of his grand design for a new London. According to his plan a wide road was to be built from the elegant crescents of Regent's Park to the sweeping curve of pillared Regent Street, through a new square and down to Carlton Terrace and the Prince of Wales's palace, Carlton House. In 1830 a handsome square, named after the Battle of Trafalgar, was laid out where, in John Campbell's day, there had been a maze of mean streets and the Royal Mews.

The design for the triangle east of St Martin's-in-the-Fields was part of Nash's other thoroughfare, designed to run west to east and to link St James's Palace through the square to the Strand and beyond to the British Museum. In 1830 the Commissioners divided the triangle into lots, which were leased by various shopkeepers, and building began. Nash designed the overall plan including that of the Arcade. He drew three elegant façades to enclose the triangle with turrets, which became known as the 'pepperpots', at the angles – a skilful architectural device to round the corners. But most of the actual building work was carried out by a competent builder, William Herbert. There was, however, an interesting exception. By a strange coincidence, No. 446, one of the shops on the Strand front, was built by the tea merchant, Edward Edmund Antrobus, a cousin of Thomas Coutts's partner Edmund Antrobus, who appears in the earlier history of the Bank. He had originally owned 480 Strand, but now exchanged the lease for that of 446. He had an argument with Herbert over the difference in height between his shop and those on either side; Nash was called in to adjudicate, Antrobus gave way and the frontage was made uniform.

According to the *Mirror* on 17 April 1832, the shops on the exterior had been designed to have the appearance of one great whole. 'The architecture is Grecian and the order employed Corinthian; the angles are finished in a novel manner, with circular buildings, the roof domed, with an ornament as a finish to the top of the dome.'

The West Strand improvements had been grandly conceived and even originally included educational galleries, where visitors could observe scientific experiments. As for the Lowther Arcade, its splendid design with the high-domed glass roof may have given the Baroness ideas when she planned Columbia Market, though her taste was Gothic, whereas Nash was inspired by classical architecture.

By the end of the nineteenth century, however, the area had deteriorated: leases ran out and stalls and shops became sad shadows of their former tinselled glory. It was perhaps to prevent a complete disintegration, when it became known that the Arcade was to be sold, that Malcolm denied the rumours in 1900 that Coutts & Co. was to buy the site. In fact he began negotiations for a lease in January 1900; the stallholders were given notice to quit in January 1901, and Coutts & Co. acquired the lease of the Arcade. On 17 March 1902 Malcolm informed the Crown Commissioners that their architect, MacVicar Anderson, had been given orders to prepare the plans, and that £3,250 caution money had been deposited with the Bank of England. Five days later the agreements were signed. By the autumn of 1903 the new bank was ready to receive Thomas Coutts's old doors and chimney-pieces, and by July 1904 the building was finished, furnished and ready for business.

MacVicar Anderson demolished the Lowther Arcade, leaving the rest of the triangle untouched, and built the new bank on the site. Gradually the Bank bought up the leases of the small shops surrounding the Arcade. It had been a comparatively speedy operation; but even more remarkable was that the builders did not exceed their original estimate of £99,000. In July 1904 Malcolm could report to the Baroness with some satisfaction that the cost had been 'up to date £87,098'.[24]

The actual move in 1904 caused much interested speculation. How would Coutts & Co. transfer its boxes of treasure across the Strand? The answer was, with its usual discretion and ingenuity. According to the *Daily Chronicle*, 'At 12 p.m. Whitsunday night the flitting began.'[25] Apparently a four-wheeled, two-horse builder's cart appeared at a secret entrance on James Street. It was driven by an ordinary working man with an unwashed face, who was, in fact, a 'highly respected bank clerk'.[26] At the corner of the street a plain-clothes detective idly lounged: Scotland Yard was well prepared and there were many such disguised officers along the route. Iron-bound boxes were loaded on to the wagon, but instead of crossing the Strand directly, it slowly trundled down to the Embankment, along to Blackfriars and back across the Strand to the Adelaide Street entrance. The idle stroller followed the wagon keeping a sharp lookout.

The last of the trunks and boxes were moved on the weekend before the August Bank Holiday. The clerks came to prepare for the opening and Ronald Malcolm explained to them the new layout; they were then given their stations.

The clerks, like the *Chronicle* reporter, were doubtless suitably impressed by the spacious building, the 'excellent library' and the '3 suites of rooms with bathrooms and sitting rooms for the 3 residential clerks'.[27] It was all 'typical Coutts'. Another newspaper thought highly of the imposing entrance 250 feet in length. 'Coutts', it added, 'has a tender regard for the creature comforts of its clerical staff and its kitchen and dining rooms and residential quarters for clerks on duty are not to be surpassed.'[28]

The doors veneered in rosewood and the carved marble fireplaces removed from the old bank were much admired, as was the 'ventilation by electric fan' and the orderly arrangement of avenues of double-lined rooms on the upper floor, floor to ceiling with red ledgers. A fumed oak screen 'divided the floor space into two parts, following the original plan', and the managers' desks still 'commanded a bird's eye view of all departments'.[29]

On 27 July 1905 William Malcolm was able to write to the Baroness with pride that

the figures show the largest amount of business we have ever had. The increase over July last year is more than a million and a quarter pounds, (£9,691,335 as against £8,337,884). I cannot help thinking that our new buildings have something to do with this unprecedented growth.[30]

Malcolm was too modest. There is no doubt that he was mainly responsible for the efficiency with which the operation had been arranged and carried out. There was a bonus for the Baroness: the rent of the building, which at 59 she had always paid, was now settled by the Bank.

At 59 Strand the old buildings were left deserted and silent except for the strange whirring of a broken electric fan – the ghost, some said, of Thomas Coutts, wailing for his lost home.

47

The Baroness – Last Years

The Baroness had survived the scandal of her marriage, and indeed Malcolm, who regarded her with respect and affection, treated her once more as head of the House. A builder herself, she had taken the greatest interest in the progress of the new bank. Although she was sad to see the end of Thomas Coutts's old home, where her mother had grown up, she enjoyed the challenge of change. She made a thorough tour of inspection, leaning on Shannon's arm; and though she was obviously tired and her voice was faint, she spoke to many of the clerks, asking them about their homes and families.

She had outlived many of her young friends: Cecil Rhodes, who had fascinated her on his visit to England, died in 1902 at the age of forty-nine. Stanley, whom she had welcomed on his return from Africa, finished his extraordinary career in 1904.

One by one even her friends in the Strand were disappearing. With the death of George Robinson the last link with her grandfather had been broken, but she had been deeply distressed by the death of Hugh Lindsay Antrobus. The loss of Henry Ryder was also painful: he had been her strong right hand for so many years. Loyal and courteous, he had nevertheless always had the courage to tell her unpalatable truths.

The royal ranks were thinning too. Mary Adelaide, Duchess of Teck, who had stood by her in the difficult year of her marriage, died in 1897. Now the Baroness lavished the same kind affection on her children, her godson Prince Francis of Teck, and Princess May, her particular favourite. In 1901 Queen Victoria's long reign ended, but Angela Burdett-Coutts had still five more years of active service.

Her strange marriage had proved unexpectedly successful. Bartlett's fellow MP, T. P. O'Connor, who knew them both well, reported that

her attitude remained to the end one of blind and open devotion. . . . You couldn't help liking her, and her soft, low voice had a music and even a charm, as well as a sweetness that drew you to her. You might be tempted to laugh at this love of December for May, but you couldn't do it once you were brought into the charm of her personality.[1]

Some of the memorabilia in the archives at Coutts & Co.: the famous golden guinea, given to Thomas Coutts by a well-wisher under the illusion that the frail old man was in need, displayed in a case specially made by Angela Burdett-Coutts; the gold snuffbox presented to Andrew Dickie by Louis Philippe; a display case in the garden court recalling Victorian life in the Bank

Top: The 1871 Christmas card from Baroness Burdett-Coutts and Mrs Brown

Bottom: Photo from the *Walrus* album, 1879, showing the Baroness with her future husband Ashmead Bartlett, Henry Irving, Mr Tennant and Admiral and Mrs Gordon

Partners in the Bank in the Strand: *(top left)* Lord Archibald Campbell in Highland dress, 1873–1907; *(top right)* Henry Ryder, fourth Earl of Harrowby, 1864–1900; *(bottom left)* William Rolle Malcolm, 1878–1923; *(bottom right)* Sir George Marjoribanks, 1877–1931

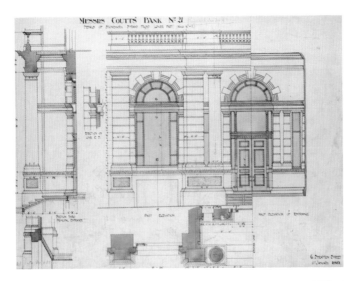

Top: An architectural drawing for the new Bank at 440 Strand, 1903

Bottom: The banking hall of 440 Strand in the early twentieth century

Charles Cockman *(top left)* and Charles Adcock *(top right)*, two twentieth-century members of staff who wrote their reminiscences of working for Coutts & Co.

Bottom: Lord Sandon and Sir Seymour Egerton sitting side by side at their desks at Coutts & Co. A young David Money-Coutts appears in the background.

Top left: Edith and Osbert Sitwell, grateful customers of the Bank

Top right: Sir Jasper Ridley by Leonard Applebee, director of the Bank from 1921 to 1951

Bottom: A. J. Robarts, the present Managing Director and a descendant of the Robarts banking family

"I TOLD YOU NOT TO PULL THE CORD TOO HARD MA'AM. — THE CEMENT'S STILL WET."

Top: Sir David Money-Coutts, the present Chairman of the Bank, standing in the boardroom at Coutts & Co. with the Macartney wallpaper in the background

Bottom: Cartoon of the Queen opening the new bank at 440 Strand, 1978

The atrium and garden court of the new bank, with Chantrey's statue of Thomas Coutts taking pride of place

As an MP Bartlett, as O'Connor claimed, 'in a modest way did some very important things'.[2] And there was one parliamentary occasion when the Baroness could claim her judgment of him was vindicated. She had sent him to South Africa to investigate the reports of the scandalous treatment of the wounded in the Boer War. His speech in that debate had a profound effect on the House: 'it was a moderate statement; but the facts were so terrible that the very simplicity of the language added to their effect'.[3] For once the Prime Minister, Arthur Balfour, lost his temper and 'Mr Burdett-Coutts, whom Mr Balfour had tried to belittle, was regarded as the hero of the occasion'.[4]

The Baroness invited O'Connor to Stratton Street and told him in her soft, quiet voice how she had worried about her husband while he had been absent in South Africa; 'this with a gentle, almost fluttering, smile on her reserved face,' O'Connor wrote. 'I saw the proof then of the fact that, however Mr Burdett-Coutts had been criticised, he had fulfilled his part of the contract by giving beautiful and unbroken happiness to the woman to whom he owed so much.'[5]

Bartlett certainly kept her young. In 1896, at the age of eighty-two, she travelled with him to Corsica and returned the next year for three months. Her English friends were amazed at her energy and noticed that she looked 'wonderfully young for her 82 years'.[6]

However, as she approached her ninetieth birthday, her days of foreign travel were over, though she still journeyed to Brighton in her famous great lumbering coach. Harry Preston, manager of the Royal York Hotel, remembered how she would take the whole first floor for herself and her suite, where she entertained guests. 'Every night she enjoyed a specially prepared four-course dinner . . . it was an epicurean repast. With the fish she would take a half bottle of excellent old vintage champagne. Later on she would take a pot of strong black tea, and then retire for the night and sleep like a baby.'[7] O'Connor had also remembered how every afternoon she took a dish of tea strong enough to shake ordinary nerves, and made stronger by a little dash of brandy.

In her last years she was reconciled to Frank Money-Coutts's family. Clara had died on 22 December 1899 and in the following years she invited Frank's daughters Clara and Nora to stay with her, first in Genoa, then in Stratton Street and Holly Lodge.

Clara later wrote her great-aunt's life and remembered her: 'Her hair was dark, not white, and she gave no suggestion of fragility. She was more like some old rock jutting out of the sea, storm worn but untroubled still.'[8] Clara recalled how overwhelmed they had been when they stayed at 1 Stratton Street. The major-domo, Mr Terry, and two footmen in livery greeted them and ushered them up to the great drawing-room, filled with priceless objets d'art and dominated by Chantrey's marble statue of Thomas Coutts.

On 24 April 1904 Bartlett gave her a birthday party. There were familiar names among the guests, but now they were descendants of her old friends: Prince Francis of Teck, the Duchess of St Albans, Mr and Mrs Herbert Gladstone, and Archdeacon and Mrs Wilberforce. Coutts & Co. was represented by George Marjoribanks, grandson of Edward Marjoribanks who had first introduced her to the Bank so many years before. The room was filled with flowers from the most distinguished in the land, but she gave pride of place on the dining-table to two silver vases inscribed 'To the Baroness Burdett-Coutts the best mistress and kindest friend in all the world, with the respect and affection of her household'.[9]

In 1905 she became very deaf and a little blind. In October she was deeply saddened by the death of Sir Henry Irving. Mrs Brown's 'brave boy' had died in harness on Friday the 13th after a performance of Tennyson's *Becket* at the Theatre Royal, Bradford. 'It's a pity,' he had said after his last appearance as Shylock, 'just as one is beginning to know a little about this work of ours it's time to leave it.'[10] He was to be buried in Westminster Abbey and his body was brought to Stratton Street for the lying-in-state in the great dining-room, under Edwin Long's portrait of Mrs Brown. The Baroness was now beginning to believe it was time for her too to leave her work.

One last blow came to her and to the Bank in the Strand with the death of Frederick Shannon in 1906. She had come to rely on him increasingly since the death of Henry Ryder. He had shared her love of France. When in 1879 on her way back from the Mediterranean cruise she had visited St Malo in order to present the citizens with a lifeboat, it was Shannon she chose to accompany her. He had been glad, however, to be excused making a speech, although he would have done so impeccably in his elegant French. The clerks at the Bank mourned the loss of Shannon, the 'courtly gentleman' who commanded their respect and affection.

The partners were to miss his deep knowledge of bank affairs acquired by long years of dedicated service to Coutts & Co. In the last years he had undertaken many delicate missions abroad and not only to royal customers overseas. Late in life he went to America to deal with the Bank's affairs there and arranged with the Metropolitan Museum of Art the sale of sculptures belonging to Coutts & Co.

Malcolm wrote with unaccustomed tenderness to his widow of the loss of their old and valued friend, who had been

in the service of Messrs Coutts for fifty-four years, and during that long period he devoted himself with unwearied zeal and conspicuous ability. To unusual attainments he added a grace and charm of manner which gained him the affection of all with whom he came in contact. There are none among the partners who can recollect the House without his presence to brighten it, and the thought that we have lost him is very grievous to us all.[11]

His letter, replied his widow, 'touched to the heart by your expression of the affection and esteem in which you held him we love. . . . The honour and love which my dear Husband felt for your House will live on in our hearts till we too die. . . . I am Sirs most gratefully yours, Emma Shannon.'[12]

Angela Burdett-Coutts had once recalled how Christmas had always brought a mingling of joy and sadness. So many of her friends and family, from the Duchess of St Albans to Mrs Brown and her sister Clara, had died at the turn of the year. The snowy December of 1906 when she was ninety-two was to defeat her too. When the 'day of sad remembrance',[13] the anniversary of Mrs Brown's death, came round again, she was seriously ill with bronchitis and she prepared for the end. She received her friends for a last farewell with that simple dignity that had distinguished her life. She gave to the Bishop of London a kind message for the vicar of St Stephen's: 'Tell the vicar and Mrs Twining I am so grievously sorry for what I did over the schools and to the Church and that I behaved so badly to the vicar who did all in his power to help me. They were both such true and good friends to me.'[14]

On Saturday 29 December she received her household, 'giving them each her hand', as Bartlett remembered.[15] Her gardener from Holly Lodge brought a bunch of sweet herbs which he always presented to her on Sundays. But at 10.30 on Sunday morning, the 30th, quite peacefully, she died. Bartlett placed the simple bunch on her coffin with his last message – 'To my dearest and best, from the Garden on the Hill'.[16]

She lay in state in the great dining-room beneath Long's portrait. For two days queues of mourners, 25,000 people of all ranks, followed the purple drugget to the catafalque beneath the great chandelier. The last rare honour was given to her: the Dean of Westminster offered interment in the Abbey, the first woman to be buried there in her own right. But, as she had been from the beginning 'cradled in conflict', so at her end there was acrimony. The Dean had stipulated, and Bartlett agreed, that she should be cremated. But the day before the funeral Bartlett withdrew his permission. The Dean, furious, refused to attend the ceremony, so it was the sub-Dean, Canon Duckworth, who finally officiated.*

The Baroness had outlived her age, but Londoners had not forgotten her. On 5 January at 11 o'clock the open funeral carriage was drawn by four black horses through the slush of Piccadilly. A passing omnibus driver, his whip tied with black crêpe, saluted. In Victoria Street the crowds were

---

* Mrs Twining in her journal claims there was a macabre sequel. The three-foot square space was prepared for a casket, not a coffin. Therefore after the burial, at the dead of night, the three coffin shells of elm, metal and oak, were removed, the body covered in quicklime and returned to the tomb. Mrs Twining's account is unconfirmed, but the details are convincing.

six deep, among them working men in black ties and their wives with black ribbons on their bonnets.

Outside the Abbey, a pearly king and queen and a procession of coster-mongers waited behind their great banner. Inside, only the dark purple and gold capes of Canon Duckworth and Archdeacon Wilberforce relieved the mourning black of an immense congregation. The King and Queen, the Prince and Princess of Wales and the Prime Minister were represented, the Lord Mayor of London and the Mayor of Westminster were there, but so were the flower girls from Bermondsey and working men and women from Westminster and Bethnal Green.

She was buried just inside the west door of the Abbey, 'in a position', Bartlett wrote, 'she herself would have chosen, close to what is really the People's door'.[17] Only a plain stone with letters of brass marks her grave, but the epitaph to Shaftesbury on the wall above, that she herself unveiled, might well have been her own: 'A long life spent in the cause of the helpless and suffering. Love and serve.'[18]

Angela Burdett-Coutts's will, dated 7 August 1883, was as simple as her grandfather's had been. 'She left personal estate to the value of £63,325 1s 8d and estate of the gross value of £78,937 13s 5d'[19] and she bequeathed it all to her husband and appointed him her sole Executor. She had trusted him to carry out her wishes as Thomas had trusted Harriot.

But she added directives concerning the colonial bishoprics she had established: 'In the event of the Church being disestablished all such endowments shall be nullified and revert to the residuary personal estate.'[20] It was a last shot in a battle she had waged with Gladstone almost half a century before.

Letters of sympathy poured into Stratton Street. Long articles in the press celebrated her years of public work. Malcolm wrote on behalf of the Bank with genuine respect and affection. She had outlived the scandal of her marriage and was at the end, as she had been ever since 1837, the public face of Coutts & Co. Among all her other interests, the Bank, its success and its honour had been her prime concern.

She had been the epitome of the Victorian age with all the energy, the enterprise and the wide-ranging interests of that most explosive period. Forward-looking, she relished the challenges of the new world of science, of railways and electricity, exploration and discovery. Her father's motto was her own: 'Man's eyes were given to him to look forward not back-ward.'[21] But at the same time her roots were deep in tradition. She looked back with some nostalgia to the best of the great country houses of her childhood, where 'noblesse oblige' was the motto. As she wrote in her preface to 'Woman's Mission', in the libraries of the country houses there was a source of learning denied to town dwellers. So she furnished a library in her block of workers' flats and paid for one for the clerks in the Bank in the Strand. Her aim in life was to bring back the old links between rich and poor, between town and country, and to recreate man's sense of responsibility to man and beast.

She came to believe that she had inherited not only a fortune, but also a great estate for which she had been given responsibility. It might well be said that in London and in the wider world she took on the role and duty of a second queen.

After the death of the Baroness, Bartlett dwindled into obscurity. He continued to work as an MP, but, as O'Connor reported,

the robust and distinguished man had a little of the phantom about him, as of a man who had lost his way somewhat in life. He wandered through the House a remote and isolated figure, and there was a certain brooding expression in the face. What he thought in the inner tabernacle of his soul I cannot tell. . . . For myself, I have to testify that I always found him a modest, agreeable, kindly man.[22]

In 1921 he became a Privy Councillor, but on 28 July in the same year he died at Holly Lodge. He was buried at Frant in Sussex, where Rudyard Kipling was among his mourners; and King George V was represented at his memorial service in St Margaret's, Westminster.

48

The Clerks' Tale

Until the outbreak of the First World War in 1914 Coutts & Co. ran smoothly under sound management and with an efficient and disciplined staff. The voice of the clerks had scarcely been heard in the last two centuries. Dickie, alas, left no memoirs, neither did Robinson nor Shannon. Only their letters reveal the value of their work. They worked long hours, had few holidays, and, since there was no retirement age, often died in harness. They had no time to write memoirs. When Mr Charles Turner, the Chief Clerk, died in March 1904, he had been in the service of Coutts & Co. for fifty-four years, but unfortunately left no record of his life.

In the twentieth century, however, some of the members of the staff were persuaded to write down their reminiscences and we are glad to hear the voices of Herbert E. Rowe, Charles Adcock and Charles H. Cockman.

Rowe entered the Bank on 17 March 1902 at the age of twenty-one with a total salary of £112 10s 0d. Eight years later he was described in the Staff Report Book as 'A floater who fills vacancies in the loan department' and earned high praise as 'one of the best men I have ever had to work with as far as [his] capacity for work is concerned'.[1] Apparently he was reluctant 'to act on his own initiative, ... probably through being in the loan department for some time where that virtue is rather discouraged'.[2] By 1915 he was in charge of 'Chief Warrants' in the Securities Department and 'has taken up these duties with much aptitude. A quiet painstaking reserved man, but an excellent painstaking unseen worker ... can be relied on'.[3] In 1945 Rowe was appointed Principal Officer and retired in October 1946 as head of the Stock Department. Fortunately the quiet reserved man was persuaded to write his *Edwardian Reminiscences*:

The reminiscences of one who entered Banking in the last years of the 19th Century, and Coutts' in the second year of the 20th Century, may not be entirely valueless as times have probably changed more profoundly and more suddenly in the years since 1912 than perhaps in any other period of recent history.[4]

When Rowe began he recalled that there were 125 clerks compared with 22 in 1801, 56 in 1849, 63 in 1859, 78 in 1869, 97 in 1879 and 101 in 1889.

In 1901 Shannon, then Secretary, had encouraged him to apply for a position as a clerk and greeted him on his first interview on 17 March 1902. 'He was a very courtly gentleman of pleasant manners and address; he spoke French like a Frenchman of high quality and breeding'; but, he later added, 'he could be magisterial'. Shannon immediately put him at his ease by 'introducing a bond of union in the fact that fifty years previously he had come to the Strand from the same source, viz the old London Joint Stock Bank'. Shannon had also told him how to dress: 'Black Frock-coat, Top Hat, White Linen Shirt with high collar stiff with starch were "de rigueur". If a member of the staff had the temerity to sport a coloured or striped shirt he would be sure of some sharp comment, perhaps from high quarters.' A clerk who ventured to appear in trousers with turn-ups was once asked sardonically whether he expected it to be muddy in the Bank.

Rowe's first years were spent in the old bank at 59 Strand, which had

no dignity of appearance but was spacious inside, as the front office (called the Shop) communicated with the large premises at the back by a bridge of pleasing design. . . . In the back office the partners (as they were then called) sat close to the wall on the East Side. Commencing from the left (north side) they were Hugh B. Money Coutts, the 5th Earl of Harrowby, Ronald Malcolm, George John Marjoribanks, William Rolle Malcolm, F. A. Shannon (then Secretary) and Lord Archibald Campbell.

It was important, Rowe emphasised, that in the old bank the partners were always visible and accessible. So they were to remain until the new bank was built in 1978.

Rowe was shown where to hang his hat in the dingy basement and supplied with pen, pencil, indiarubber and 'digger'. This was a sharp little knife, with which a skilled clerk could scratch out mistakes. He was taken to the luncheon room for a surprisingly good and free meal, thanks to the generosity of Angela Burdett-Coutts. For the first week he worked in a 'little cubby hole leading out of the Strong Room'. Here, 'surrounded by ledgers of the eighteenth century', he learned the

gentle art of writing up pass-books, which in those days were copied from the great leather-bound ledgers. Like old port the new man matured in these surroundings for about a month and then he went on to the 'Junior Post', the runner for the Corresponding Department, the deliverer of the Clerks' letters and the sticker-up of the post at night. In due time followed Cash Books, Walks, Rough Posting and all the other routine. The City Walk was the most interesting but also the hardest as it frequently meant being out nearly all day. It is noteworthy how much 'coupons' were a feature in those pre-war days, cutting them off the bonds, listing them, lodging them at paying-agents and collecting the cheques – all these operations became for a time part of the life of every junior clerk. Coutts, with their main business among the aristocracy and more wealthy members of the general population, had very large holdings of securities in their charge. Their lodgments were impressive in size compared with others.

Rowe vividly recalled the bonds and certificates of the American railways, 'Baltimore & Ohio, New York Central, Pennsylvania, etc.', and he remembered the intriguing illustrations on the bonds and certificates, 'of old-fashioned engines with cow-catchers, Indians chasing buffaloes, scantily dressed females seated on thrones handing out grapes, flowers, or may-be dollars'.

There was, as all clerks were warned on arrival, a great deal of drudgery. He found the Coutts system of bookkeeping somewhat antiquated: it 'included a double set of ledgers rough and fair, the pass books being copied from the fair ledgers'. The 'Walks', which were an important part of the clerk's life, were a welcome break from their close confinement. They were allotted an area in the City to which they walked, carrying documents from bank to bank.

The hours were long; much work was done 'after closing time by the juniors who stayed until their stint was finished, sometimes up to 6.30 and at the quarters, much later'. Then clerks might well stay all night, taking their breakfast nearby and returning to work in the morning.

In 1902 Rowe was allowed a fortnight's holiday, but in his early years he usually had to take it in March. The holiday rota for the Bank was decided by Shannon:

What happened was that Mr Shannon, J. F. Hamilton, who was head of the Loan Dept, and P. H. Michôd spent a Saturday afternoon and evening at Shannon's house in Westbourne Terrace and, with the Holiday Record Book before them, wrestled with the problem. The result would be copied fair on the Monday morning following and at 4 p.m. that day Mr Shannon would walk from his seat to the 'Shop' and deposit the Holiday List on the desk of the Chief Cashier, who, after a glance at it, for I do not think he was much interested in the subject himself, threw it behind him on to the desk whither a wild rush took place and a 'scrum' by younger and more virile personalities. Shannon rather enjoyed this spectacle and watched the proceedings from afar.

Rowe noted the working hours and numbers of clerks from 1801 to 1901:

At this point perhaps it would be convenient to say something of Banking Hours. It is as long ago as 1848 that the Banks in London decided to close to the public at 4 p.m. instead of 5 p.m., but there was no half-day on Saturdays until 1860. From 1860 the closing time on Saturdays was 3 p.m.; from 1886 2 p.m. In 1902, very soon after I came to the Strand, 1 p.m. was fixed, and from 1919 12 noon. Since 1961 the closing time on Saturday has been 11.30.

But Rowe appeared not to resent the drudgery. '. . . the training thereby acquired was thorough. An intelligent man had the opportunity of acquiring a wide acquaintance with the details of an important banking business conducted with a high class clientele.' It was this that added a gloss to their dull lives: 'The business was mostly among the upper classes, county families, titled gentry, large landowners, and predominantly of the Private Account nature.'

Most of the work and the prestige still came from the private accounts; as W. S. Gilbert, a customer himself, wrote in *The Gondoliers*:

> The aristocrat who hunts and shoots.
> The aristocrat who banks with Coutts.

As Rowe observed there were also some business concerns with

leading London solicitors, together with such institutions as Queen Anne's Bounty, the Duchy of Cornwall, the Duchy of Lancaster, the Society of Arts, some of the leading Clubs, the Cardiff Railway and John Murray the Publisher, but, except for some tradesmen of the immediate neighbourhood, not many commercial concerns, except that at the opening of the century there was already the Harmsworth Newspaper connection destined to be ever-growing in importance and value to the business of the Bank.

In his old age Rowe looked back with some nostalgia to the old bank with its

atmosphere of the 18th Century – the days of Lord North & Horace Walpole. Important looking desks, an air of quietness and dignity – the large ledgers fully-bound in sweet smelling Russia leather, tables provided with quill pens – more perhaps for show than practical use, pass-books of a pleasing design, free access to the desks of the staff, the partners sitting with the staff – all these features created an ethos, or genius of the institution, which was unlike any other in the same line of business, so far as has come within my observation.

Many clerks undoubtedly complained of the long hours and the drudgery, but there were many like Rowe who considered it a privilege to work at Coutts & Co. The Bank had, as he claimed, an 'ethos' of its own. 'Nostalgia', he concluded, 'some would say, but those old desks partook of the genius of the place. May the 21st century be able to look back with similar affectionate reflections and may that "genius of the place" never die.' Other members of the staff would later write their memoirs, but none perhaps is more evocative of Coutts & Co. at the turn of the century than Rowe's reminiscences.

In his memoirs *Long Playing Record*, Peter Boulton recalled another member of the staff, Charles Cockman, who made a particular impact:

he was one of those characters who gives such a flavour to Coutts. . . . He was universally liked and respected by Directors and Staff alike. He was tall, with large turned out feet and in appearance had the deadpan look of a tortoise, not very complimentary you may think, but . . . it would quickly vanish and be replaced with a twinkle and a charming smile. Most of his days were spent counselling old ladies about their investments at which he was very good.[5]

A talented actor and a good friend, he also had a remarkable career in the Second World War.

He came to Coutts & Co. on 19 September 1921 from University College School, where both his grandfathers had been masters. Between the wars he worked in the Correspondence, Indian, Foreign, Tax, Loan and Stock departments. His call-up was delayed because of ill-health, but finally he embarked for Arromanches as a captain in the Pay Corps on the staff of Brigadier Sir John Barraclough. He helped to set up the Military Government HQ and became a lieutenant-colonel with the responsibility of Controller of Public Finance for the North Rhine Province. Working under Sir Paul Chambers he helped to produce Germany's first post-war budget.

His wartime experience was of immense value to Coutts & Co. and on his return he started the Bank's first training school. In 1965 he was made Principal Officer and two years later Head Office Investment Manager. He retired in 1967 after forty-six years' service to the Bank. His memoirs written in retirement are a lively and informative record of his years at the Strand and will be quoted at length in the following pages.

Another voice worth hearing is that of Charles Adcock, whose forty-five years of service gave to the Bank continuity and stability which were two of the secrets of the success of Coutts & Co. over the years. Unlike Cockman, Adcock disliked change, as Boulton recorded in his notes:

He could not understand ... the mind of post war youth and its questionings of the old disciplines. This led later to trouble in the Chief Cashiers Dept ... not prepared to fight any decision of the Board. Adcock's mastery of invective made him a number of enemies.

President of the '59 Club' and at a tentative suggestion that ladies joined, his reply, 'Not while I am President.'

... a brilliant man in many respects, a prizeman of the Institute of Bankers, he was consulted on many points of the laws relating to banking, particularly on bills of exchange, by members of the Discount Market. Had an agile brain and a devastating wit considerable literary and composing skill and exquisite handwriting.[6]

He came to the Strand in 1915 and, according to his interviewer, he was 'rather undersized & young in appearance but is a sharp boy. He has passed the Junior & Senior Oxford Local, both with first-class honours & the London Matriculation. He understands French quite well but has had no practice in conversation.'[7] The sharp little boy began with a salary of £84 a year and ended his career in 1961 as the manager of Lombard Street earning £950 a year. Adcock was a shrewd man, an acute observer and devoted to the Bank.

49

Amalgamation

As the world rolled towards the war of 1914, private banks began to feel
the chill wind. In 1913, a sharp fall in the value of gilts cost Coutts & Co.
over £170,000.

Once again there were rumours in the City of possible amalgamations,
as there had been after the Baroness's marriage and again after her death
in December 1906. At that time the National Provincial had been eager to
buy the Bank, and the Union Bank, which cleared for Coutts & Co., had
also been interested. On 6 January 1907 W. Buxton had written on their
behalf suggesting that they should establish a closer connection, but the
Chairman, W. R. Malcolm, was not to be seduced. Courteously but firmly
he rejected their offer, although he did not deny that the situation might
change in the future.

Some of Malcolm's colleagues, however, were eager to consider these
offers seriously and there had been some acrimony in the debate in the
following years. Francis Money-Coutts was annoyed that the managing
partners were not prepared to take up good offers and in June 1913
strongly urged Malcolm to begin negotiations with Lloyds at once. His
son, Hugh Money-Coutts, who was more conciliatory than Francis, also
believed, as he wrote to Malcolm, that the time had come to take
seriously the question of amalgamation with one of the big joint stock
banks.

However, Malcolm was not a man to be rushed. It was not until 17 July
1914 that the financial press reported with much interest the statement
issued by Coutts & Co.: 'An amalgamation of Coutts & Co. and Robarts,
Lubbock & Co. has been arranged subject to confirmation by the Stock
Holders.'

Undoubtedly Malcolm had carefully considered the advantages of the
Robarts, Lubbock connection. He had known the Robarts family for a long
time and as early as 1889 he and his daughter, Angela, had been among
the guests at a house party at A. J. Robarts's country house.

The Times listed the partners of both firms:

The present partners [i.e. stockholders] are Lord Latymer; Messrs. William R. Malcolm and George J. Marjoribanks, Lord Harrowby, and Messrs Ronald Malcolm and Fredk. W. Stephenson who act as managing partners; Messrs Hugh Burdett Money-Coutts and Charles Augustus Phillimore, who are junior managing partners; Viscount Hambledon, the Marquess of Bute, Messrs John Wm. Coulthurst and John Berrill Fortescue; the Hon. Archibald D. Ryder, the Hon. A. D. Ryder, the Hon. Robt. N. Dudley Ryder, the executors of Lord Archibald Campbell, and others.

The present partners of Robarts, Lubbock and Co. are: Abraham John Robarts, Lord Avebury, Thomas Edward Robarts, Edward Beaumont Cotton Curtis, John Robarts, Frank Chaplin, Geoffrey Lubbock, Gerald Robarts, and the Hon. Harold Fox-Pitt Lubbock.

The history of both banks was outlined and their relative resources described. *The Times* reminded its readers that 'Coutts & Co. became a joint stock company with unlimited liability in 1892'. The *Financial Times* pointed out that 'As Messrs Robarts Lubbock & Company rank as a private enterprise, it is only necessary for the members of that house to pass a resolution sanctioning the amalgamation. Messrs Coutts & Company will, however, need to hold a special meeting of stockholders.'

It was acknowledged that Coutts & Co. was the larger and more famous of the two banks. While Robarts, Lubbock & Co. had nine partners with a capital reserve of £500,000 and deposits and current accounts of £4,130,850, Coutts & Co. had sixteen stockholders (according to the *The Times*) in July 1914, they had current and deposit accounts of £8,792,298 and at call to £2,299,200 and investments to £2,791,000. Lubbock had £3,873,820 in deposit and current accounts, £940,565 cash in hand and investments to £661,067.[1] In short the amalgamation represented a capital and reserve of £1½ million and current and deposit accounts of over £12½ million, with Coutts & Co. the dominant partner.

The *Evening News* thought it surprising that Robarts, Lubbock had 'never touched any Londoners' imagination in view of the eminent position which the late Lord Avebury held for so long in the banking and commercial world'.

The *Financial News* regretted that the 'Union of London and Smiths', the bankers Coutts & Co. had hitherto used, would now be denied the privilege of clearing for them. Until now, because it was based outside the City boundaries, Coutts & Co. had to rely on other banks for this service. Now it not only had a seat in the Clearing House, but it also had the advantage of the wide-ranging Robarts connections among country banks and in the City itself.

The news was welcomed in the City and in the press – only *John Bull* was doubtful, fearing 'the loss of competition'. But there was much fulsome praise for Coutts & Co., the 'most aristocratic of banks'.[2] 'In the City', *The*

World wrote, 'we only know Coutts by name and reputation, a glorious name and a glorious reputation. It is one of the happiest of acquisitions and amalgamations. The City welcomes Coutts with open arms. Long live Coutts!'[3] The *Money Market Review* was equally enthusiastic: 'Nothing has ever been lost at Coutts, it has always stood for everything that is solid and enduring.'

The *Daily Mail* joined the chorus: 'We hope that Coutts will always be Coutts, as unique and independent in AD 2014 as it is today.'

Few records have survived of the activities of Robarts, Lubbock & Co. so that in the accounts of the amalgamation they have been overshadowed by the royal bankers, Coutts & Co. But in fact they had a distinguished history, and among their predecessors were a number of outstanding bankers. They were themselves the product of an amalgamation. The Lubbock side was founded in the City in February 1772 under the name of Sir William Lemon, Buller, Edward Forster and John Lubbock. There were many changes in the partnership, but between 1800 and 1810 Lubbock and Forster were mainly in control. Robarts, Curtis & Co. had been founded in 1791 and based at 15 Lombard Street since 1795. The two banks represented by Robarts and Lubbock amalgamated in 1860, made their headquarters at 15 Lombard Street and were known as Robarts, Lubbock & Co. When they amalgamated with the Bank in the Strand, they lost their original title and the bank in Lombard Street took the name of Coutts & Co.

There were many who regretted the omission of the names Robarts and Lubbock from the style of the amalgamated bank. For there had been a Lubbock among the partners when the business began in 1772, and throughout the many changes and amalgamations that name had always been there. To keep it now would have been a fitting memorial to Sir John Lubbock, the first Baron Avebury, who had died in the previous year and had been one of the greatest figures in the history of nineteenth-century banking.

John Lubbock, the son of Sir John William Lubbock, another exceptional banker, left Eton to join his father's bank at the age of fourteen. A brilliant mathematician and scientist and treasurer of the Royal Society, much of his life was spent at Downe in Kent, where he was inspired and encouraged in his love of natural science by his neighbour, Charles Darwin. He quickly learned the principles of banking and was given an important share in the management at an early age. On his father's death in 1865 he inherited his title and his role in the bank. Had he confined his interests to banking, he would have been remarkable in any age, but with his wide-ranging, powerful mind he excelled in every subject he studied – science, archaeology, literature and education. He had an extraordinary grasp of detail and an ability to hold diverse subjects in his mind at the same time. The mere list of his titles illustrates the breadth of his work: first President of the Anthropological Institute, Vice-Chancellor of London University, Vice-President of the Royal Society, first President of the International Institute of Sociology, President of the British Association in its Jubilee Year, President of the London Chamber of Commerce 1888–93, a member of the London County Council 1889–92, Vice-Chairman 1889–90, Chairman 1890–2 and Alderman 1892. To these and many other achievements he added his *Hundred Best Books*, a popular aid to education. He became a Liberal Member of Parliament for Maidstone in 1870 and in 1880 for the University of London.

His most famous work as an MP was as the pioneer of the Bank Holiday Bill in 1871, which made compulsory by law four national holidays, for which service a grateful nation called August Bank Holiday, 'St Lubbock's Day'. He carried a number of important bills through the House, among them the Bills of Exchange Act, which codified the law relating to bills of exchange, promissory notes and cheques.

However, it was as a banker that he was best known. On his death the *Bankers' Magazine* said, 'he had come to be regarded almost in the light of the father of banking in the City'.[4] He was Honorary Secretary of London Bankers in 1863; from 1893 to 1913 Chairman of the Committee of London Clearing Bankers; from 1898 to 1913 President of the Central Association of Bankers; and from 1879 to 1913 first President of the Institute of Bankers. With all his brilliance and extraordinary range of achievement he had an exceptionally kindly and affectionate nature. In his way he was as remarkable as Thomas Coutts and Angela Burdett-Coutts. It is not surprising that the absence of his name from the new bank was regretted.

The Robarts family had also produced bankers of distinction. Abraham Robarts, in partnership with Sir William Curtis, had developed a flourishing business at 15 Lombard Street in the early nineteenth century. Their bank was well placed in the City, on the site of the old Lloyd's Coffee House, and thus well informed of movements in the banking world.

Robarts's son, Abraham Wildey Robarts, began his career in 1794 as a writer for the East India Company in China and remained there for seven years, returning to join his father in the banking partnership in Lombard Street in 1801. His father died in 1816, leaving Abraham his interest in the bank and his estates; to his younger son, William Tierney, he bequeathed £10,000, having already given him £20,000.

The two brothers both became Members of Parliament in 1818. Abraham was MP for Maidstone from 1818 to 1837, and William Tierney represented St Albans from 1818 until his death in 1820. Their uncle was the Whig, George Tierney, who in 1817 was the acknowledged leader of the opposition. Both brothers supported him throughout their careers, with the exception that they were against Catholic Emancipation. Both would have known and, on many issues, sympathised with, Sir Francis Burdett.

Abraham managed to combine an active life as an MP with a successful banking career and on his death in 1858 left his son, Abraham John, a considerable fortune, his share of the bank at 15 Lombard Street and a country estate. Two years later Abraham John Robarts, Curtis & Co. joined Sir John William Lubbock, Forster & Co. and became Robarts, Lubbock & Co. of 15 Lombard Street.

The marriage of Coutts & Co. and Robarts, Lubbock & Co. had its difficulties; indeed, there was considerable jealousy and even hostility between the men of 440 Strand and those of 15 Lombard Street. They sprang from different traditions. Lubbock and Robarts were country gentlemen for whom banking was an interest and provided the income for their way of life. For Thomas Coutts and many of his successors banking was life itself.

When the men from the Strand were sent to do a spell of service at 15 Lombard Street they undoubtedly felt superior – as their memoirs show. Cockman wrote:

The advent of the incorporation in 1914 must have come as a shock to all the Staff concerned. There is no doubt that if there was not open hostility or jealousy there was very definite segregation. In fact there was no attempt at integration for a long time. The Lombard Street Staff regarded themselves as 'Robarts Men'.[5]

The staff of Coutts & Co. had some reason to feel superior. A list drawn up of the 'privileges and peculiarities existing previous to amalgamation'[6] showed that compared with Robarts, Lubbock & Co. they had many advantages. Free lunches, originally provided by the Baroness, were still offered, as were free teas in the first weeks of January and July. The clerks' fund and the widows' fund set up by Coulthurst were now moribund, but porters and head messengers received a £10 and a £15 bonus at Christmas, and each married man was given a Christmas turkey. Thanks again to the Baroness, the clerks had the use of a permanent library and the Bank paid a subscription to W. H. Smith to enable their staff to borrow books. Sports and athletics were encouraged and subsidised and the Territorials had their expenses paid with one week's additional leave for camp. A man with ten to fifteen years' service was allowed two weeks' holiday with three extra days; after thirty to forty years he could have four weeks' holiday and nine extra days. The list ended with two 'peculiarities': every clerk should wear a black frock-coat, black boots or shoes and a starched white collar, and every clerk and messenger must be clean-shaven.

The immaculately dressed Coutts men, in their frock-coats and top hats, accustomed to discipline and order, found Lombard Street very different.

The choice of garb varied from shabby morning coats green with age to tattered 'office jackets' eminently suitable for a scarecrow. One aged gentleman, clad in the latter, was in the habit of roasting himself on a bench in the vaults before a large open fire connected with the hot water system. Upon being tickled with a feather to rouse him from his slumbers, he exclaimed, 'this damned coat is full of nits', and flung it on the fire.[7]

This story may have been apocryphal, but it would have been accepted with relish in the Strand.

Nevertheless, they undoubtedly relaxed in the easier atmosphere and accepted the horseplay. 'Whatever picture you may paint of 15 Lombard Street with the extraordinary changes it experienced, the loyalty and friendship within the Staff was quite an amazing feature.'[8]

Among the directors now brought from Robarts, Lubbock & Co. on to the board of Coutts & Co., Frank Chaplin seems to have been a favourite. As Cockman wrote,

Always kind, courteous and friendly in his dealings with the Staff (whose functions he invariably attended with his Sister), he was regarded with equal esteem by Directors and Staff at 440 Strand. In spite of his unfortunate limp he was an enthusiastic and prominent member of the Royal Yacht Squadron. He was very proud of his scarlet-lined overcoat – part of the 'uniform' of that eminent body. During the reign of King George V he was equally proud to have won outright the King's Cup. Mr Chaplin had an intense dislike of tobacco and would reprove any visiting Messengers in no uncertain terms. . . . The Staff who would smoke if they wished before and after Banking hours as in every Office (except 440 Strand for some unaccountable reason, since a small fire in a waste-paper basket) would respect his feelings over this, but as soon as he passed through the door in the afternoon a loud cry of 'All clear' went up.[9]

It has taken years and the determined efforts of David Money-Coutts and A. J. Robarts to achieve real unity between Lombard Street and the Strand.

50

War and Aftermath

The amalgamation was signed in July 1914. On 4 August England declared war, which many expected would be 'all over by Christmas'. Some in the banking world were taken by surprise. Sir Richard Martin, speaking at a meeting of Martin's Bank, said that he had just come back from Germany and that he had no idea in Hamburg or Cologne that England would be involved. He said that, 'although the trade of the country was in a sound position . . . the difficulty now was to obtain cash', and he urged everyone to 'use cheques if possible instead of gold . . . the credit of the country would stand the strain and they would manage all right in the end but . . . they would have a difficult time for weeks if not months'.[1]

In fact it was a difficult time for four years, not least for Coutts & Co. Many of its young men volunteered and were released on half salary. The Bank encouraged men to serve in the Territorials, receiving an annual bounty of £5.

Clerks like Mr Bird, who exchanged his frock-coat for the blood and sweat of Gallipoli, wrote moving accounts of their experiences. When Bird returned to England he showed great initiative, learning to fly a Sopwith aeroplane. Like many others he found it difficult to adjust to the discipline of the Bank after the war, and to the autocratic old guard among the directors. Those who remained in the Strand spent many hours lugging ledgers and boxes to the strongrooms during alerts, and often had make-shift luncheons there or in the vaults under the arches of Hungerford Bridge.

The First World War brought another disruption to life at Coutts & Co. Cockman, in his brief history of the Bank, wrote that

It came to our notice that one of the other Private Banks had broken with all tradition and engaged lady clerks apart from typists and who, it had been observed, were even more deft than the male species in the removal of coupons from Bearer Bonds. Thus started the invasion which was to grow quite rapidly as the War continued and more of the male Staff were called to the Colours. These five or six original lady clerks were paid a guinea a week and were handed a golden sovereign and a shilling on the familiar copper shovel by one of the Cashiers. Some time after recovering from the initial shock of this feminine intrusion, serious consideration was given to the question of entitlement to increase in the weekly wage and it was decided that the standard rise should be 2/6d a week and for very special recognition 5/-. Even after the First World War there was still some reluctance to admit that we had lady clerks. It so happened, however, that the return of the serving members of the Forces coincided with a rapid expansion of the banking business generally. So the ladies had not only retained their foothold but were here to stay and in increasing numbers. The typists were now to be seen in the public office and occupied the rooms on either side of the Adelaide Street entrance. Their cloakrooms, however, were at the extreme other end of the building and it was a rule for some years that they were not to be seen walking through the main banking hall to pass from one set of rooms to the other. This entailed quite a journey over the top floor of the building.[2]

There had been 'lady typists' as early at 1911,

the chief of whom always typed with her gloves on, possessed a very scanty knowledge of shorthand and would produce her own rather liberal interpretation of your dictation. Contact with the male species was forbidden, and dictation was carried out by use of an internal phone, mouth and earpiece in one, reminiscent of the tubes used to convey a message up and down a lift shaft. Perhaps the lady may be excused for her variation in the text![3]

Women were gradually accepted and were no longer required to be invisible and, as Cockman primly observed, 'the tradition of the Bank and pride of being in its service were quickly absorbed by all who entered its portals'.[4]

One lady clerk, Miss Pauline Hailey (later Mrs Geoffrey Norman), who joined the Bank in 1915, reminisced in old age:[5] 'When I went there first I had a guinea a week ... and I paid nothing at home, and I did quite well. Then I got a double rise every year I was there, which was ten bob a week extra.' Her guinea a week did not buy a great deal. 'It was enough', she remembered, to pay the railway fare from her home in Surbiton and enough 'to do my clothes with a little help from my mother'. Even so she managed to save something.

Balancing the ledgers was obviously a nightmare. She sat on a slippery high stool at a tall desk and, at the end of each day, 'when the Clearing was done, they used to bring the cheques up and put them in slots in a drawer beside you and then you'd enter them in a ledger and ... balance it in pencil at the side'. They often worked late until a father complained. Then it was agreed that the lady clerks should not stay after 9 p.m.

The City Walks had traditionally been done by clerks, but during the war women took their turn, as Mrs Norman remembered:

I had to go on the City walk with Mr Whichelo, and we went in a cab. Now whether it was their own cab or a hired cab I can't remember, but we went to the

City and you walked in the front door of one bank and you walked out of the back door of that bank and walked in the front door of another bank. You did that the entire morning, not even stopping for coffee. It poured with rain the entire morning and I got back soaked to the skin and I said, 'I'm not going to do it any more', and I didn't.

Mrs Norman was one of the first lady clerks to work at Coutts & Co. and had to remain invisible at the back. She had

a very nice man to work with. He had an elderly father working there. I seem to remember one or two occasions he had to go down with the money from the tills down to the safes down below with the messengers with a big barrow thing and I went down with him once or twice.

She had no happy memories of Ronald Malcolm, who was apparently 'unpopular with everybody ... he always looked as if he had an iron rod down his back ... and if you saw him coming ... you kept your eyes down and went on with your work'. She left the Bank when she married in 1918 and, since married women were not employed at Coutts & Co., she never went back. But in spite of the long hours and hard work she remembered her years there as some of the happiest in her life. When she retired she became a pensioner and, in her opinion, was 'treated very well. I felt I really belonged to a family, which you do there. I still feel I belong to Coutts although I left it all those years ago.'

Life in post-war Britain was even more difficult than before for the smaller banks. Even the amalgamation with Roberts, Lubbock & Co. had not given Coutts & Co. the secure base it needed. So it was decided to amalgamate with the National Provincial & Union Bank.

On 24 December 1919 customers received a somewhat startling communication:

Sir or Madam,

We beg to inform you that we have entered into an arrangement whereby we shall in future be associated with

    The National Provincial
      & Union Bank of England Ltd.,

We trust that this arrangement, under which the management will remain as at present, will meet with the approval of our customers, and be to their advantage.[6]

In a memorandum, drafted by Ronald Malcolm, a fuller explanation was given. Until recently, it stated, amalgamation meant complete fusion,

the Directors of the smaller Bank frequently remained connected ... but gradually such a connection ceased.

In the last year or two a totally different kind of arrangement had been made in several cases, in which the two Banks remain separate Companies, each with its own identity unimpaired. The community of interest is arranged by an exchange of the ownership of stock or shares, and the addition of a few Directors to the Boards. This scheme has been adopted where it has been considered essential for the prosperity of the business that no loss of special characteristics should ever take place. As examples one may quote the alliance between the London Joint City & Midland Bank, and the Clydesdale Bank and the Belfast Banking Company, or that between Barclays Bank, and the British Linen Bank and the Union Bank of Manchester; or again, that between Lloyds Bank and the National Bank of Scotland and the London & River Plate Bank.

In the case of Coutts & Co. it was stated:

It is more important in our case than in any of those mentioned that our special and separate identity should be kept intact for all time and our scheme is devised with the object of attaining that end. The National Provincial Bank will purchase our Stock, and our change of proprietorship will not affect the constitution of our Company in any way whatever. We shall have our separate Board, our separate Seal, our separate existence, and retain our present form of cheque exactly as now, and the regular management and supervision of the business will continue permanently to be conducted as hitherto. The name of Coutts & Co. stands high not only at home but also on the Continent, in India, and in America. The only efficient way of maintaining that position is as above stated to continue our existence as a separate Company, and therefore there can be no doubt of the permanence of this arrangement.

Finally, and with a touch of cynicism, the memorandum concluded: 'The most effective way of binding one's successors is to take care that their interests shall lead them to do what one wishes, and that we are certain we have done.'[7]

Many of the old customers of Coutts & Co. were uneasy at the amalgamation; some were downright hostile. At the end of 1919 William Malcolm had given Lord Northcliffe advance notice of the circular to be sent to customers:

Dear Lord Northcliffe.

We have appreciated so much the confidence you have reposed in Coutts Bank, and the very kind feelings you have always expressed to us, that I feel it right to give you early information of the fact that we have decided to fuse our business with that of the National Provincial Bank.

It is the desire of everyone that this fusion shall make no difference whatever in the manner of conducting our business. The Partners, & Clerks *will* remain in their present positions, and it is intended that the name of Coutts should be preserved. We hope & believe that to our customers the change will make no difference, except in those cases where the wide connections now obtained may enable us to offer them increased facilities.

I myself have been for some time taking less part than formerly in the management of business, and my partners feel that the trend of modern affairs would make some such step inevitable in time. We have thought it therefore right to accept a very favourable offer and to bring our Old Bank into line with the best, most progressive institutions.

I sincerely trust that we may count upon the continuation of your good will which we so highly value.

I am, Yours very truly.[8]

On 23 December Northcliffe replied in high dudgeon from *The Times* in a pungent letter marked '*Not Private*':

Dear Mr. Malcolm,

I am much obliged for your letter of last night, and Mr. Duguid has shown me your further letter.

I cannot say that I like the transaction, nor have I met anyone today who does.

We shall very carefully consider what to do about our accounts. I think that people so deeply concerned as we are should have been at least allowed to know the terms of the arrangement.

The Public are getting very anxious about these so-called fusions. There is an American touch about them that is un-English, and the American Government has, as you know, set its face against these gigantic trusts.

One thing I do hope, and that is, that Messrs. Coutts' Directors will do something to cause these big banks to pay their servants properly. Considering the gigantic profits that are made, the rate of wages is scandalous, and if the wages are not improved my newspapers will take the matter in hand as they did that of the Army & Navy Stores.

With kind regards and happy recollections of many years' association,

Yours sincerely
[signed] Northcliffe

Malcolm wrote back with his customary elegance and dignity:

24th Dec 1919

Dear Lord Northcliffe,

I have to acknowledge your letter of yesterday's date.

In making our arrangements with the NP bank we took into consideration the interests of two classes, our Stockholders, and our customers.

As to our Stockholders we made a good settlement – In exchange for our £800,000 capital we have got £1,000,000 shares of the NP fully paid and £200,000 War Stock.

As to our customers, the Bank will be carried on as before, by the same people and under the same management. We are to retain our name and individuality, with the advantage that we shall have behind us the strength of one of the best managed Banks in London.

You very rightly raise a question about the Staff. The NP have always enjoyed the reputation of treating their people well, & so I think have Messrs Coutts, & lately both they and we have given considerable augmentations of pay. I think you may be assured that this liberal policy will be continued in the future.

You are kind enough to refer to our happy associations of the past. At my age

413

I have only the past to look back upon, you have still the future. We have endeavoured to the utmost of our ability to serve your interests, holding you to be among our most valued customers, & I should be indeed sorry to think that anything should occur to diminish our mutual regard.

> Yours sincerely
> [signed] WRM[10]

In fact, as Malcolm might have pointed out, the clerks at Coutts were well paid by the standards of the day.

The greatest concern of the partners was to keep the confidence and custom of the royal family. So Malcolm wrote to Buckingham Palace. General Sir Dighton Probyn replied immediately on behalf of Queen Alexandra:

> SANDRINGHAM
> December 23rd 1919

Dear Mr. Malcolm

Thanks many for your letter of the 20th, telling me for Queen Alexandra's information, that Messrs Coutts & Co. are making an arrangement with the National Provincial & Union Bank of England for a fusion of the business.

I can answer for Queen Alexandra & Princess Victoria, that so long as the accounts of Her Majesty & Her Royal Highness are kept, as you say they will be, 'precisely as at present', it will make no difference to them what other Banking Firms Messrs Coutts may like to honour and trust by taking into partnership –

Let me now, please, avail myself of this opportunity, through you their Chairman, of thanking Messrs Coutts & Co. for the kind trouble they have invariably taken in anything and everything I have had to do with the Royal Accounts and their (Messrs Coutts) Bank during my tenure of office in our late King's and our Beloved Queen Alexandra's service, and that has now been for a period considerably over 2 score years –

With every possible good wish for the continued success and high reputation of Messrs Coutts in the Banking world.

> Very faithfully
> [signed] Dighton Probyn, General
> Comptroller
> to her Majesty Queen Alexandra[11]

The King, however, needed a little more convincing. He needed considerable reassurance that the customary discretion would be maintained. A memorandum kept by Malcolm recorded that he gave the King the firmest assurances:

H.M. would not obtain any greater guarantee of secrecy from the B of E [Bank of England] than from Messrs Coutts & Co.

The B of E is managed by a paid manager who is subject to the Govr of the B of E.

The Governor is changed every two years (as a rule) and is a member of a large Court of Directors who have a large body of Stockholders.

Messrs Coutts' Office management will be conducted by a *separate* Board of Directors. They will be the same as the present Directors & will employ the *same* staff. The present Directors have been in the management for many years and there is to be no change – they would resent and resist any attempt at inquisition into H.M.'s affairs.

The late Duc d'Aumale once said to the present senior partner '*Messrs Coutts – c'est le confessional*'. H.M. may be sure that there will be no change in this respect.

Should any person in the future be added to Messrs C & Co. Directors who have charge of H.M.'s affairs, Messrs C & Co. will be pleased to submit his name for H.M.'s approval.

WRM[12]

Discussions continued between the Keeper of the Privy Purse and the partners until well into February 1920. In February Sir George Marjoribanks, who was arranging to meet the Keeper of the Privy Purse, wrote suggesting that two of the directors of the National Provincial Bank should be present.

With reference to my interview with you yesterday and your kind consent to come to the Bank & make the acquaintance of my Partners so as to hear all explanations how they could meet his Majesty's wishes in the future – in the event of his graciously electing to continue to keep his a/cs with us – I now write to inquire if you could possibly make it convenient to come to 440 Strand on Monday about 3.30 p.m. The reason that I mention this hour is that I have already referred to the Directors of the N.P. Bk those points which you mentioned so seriously affected his Majesty's aspect of Messrs Coutts future separate individuality. They have held a special meeting today and two of their number Mr Colin Campbell and Mr F. Eley would be very grateful of the privilege of meeting you & assuring you of how it is their desire to maintain & their determination to perpetuate the individuality of Messrs C and their present system of control. They also very much wish to hear in what further way they can meet the King's wishes.

The Lawyers are consulting me on the ways and means of keeping the Cheque Form exactly as it is, and I have little doubt it will be so maintained.[13]

To which Sir Frederick Ponsonby replied in no uncertain terms; he saw

no object in seeing any of the Directors of the National Provincial. That would be exceeding my instructions from the King. After all, you will be able to tell me all that they have arranged, and my object in seeing you and your partners is to thrash the question out so that I can put the whole matter clearly before the King.

I therefore hope you will explain to Mr Colin Campbell that for the present I must confine my discussion to you and your partners.[14]

The King was finally persuaded and the finances of the royal family remained as they had been for more than 150 years: in the safe hands of Messrs Coutts & Co.

If the marriage of Robarts, Lubbock & Co. and Coutts & Co. had been difficult, the marriage *à trois* presented even greater problems.

The National Provincial had the temerity to send its inspectors to A. J. Robarts at 15 Lombard Street, as Cockman remembered:

... one of their Inspectors who was horrified by the prevailing system – one that has been described as neither double nor single entry. Alas, poor wretch, he did not know what he was up against. The Senior Partner then was Mr A. J. Robarts who, like his Grandson of the same initials, was not a man to be trifled with. The Wretch was summoned to the Partners Room by a Messenger and the following conversation is reported to have taken place:

NP 'Good morning, Sir, I understand you wish to see me.'
AJR 'Are you the Man from the other Bank?'
NP 'I am a National Provincial Bank Inspector and I am making an inspection on behalf of your parent company.'
AJR 'I understand that my books are not to your liking. They were good enough for my Grandfather, they were good enough for my Father, they are good enough for me and they will be good enough for you. Good morning.'[15]

Lord Northcliffe was not the only one to worry about the increasing number of amalgamations. There were many in Parliament, in the City and in the Bank of England who watched the growing concentration with alarm. There had been bank amalgamations throughout the nineteenth century – it was one of the ways small banks could survive in a competitive world – but at the end of the century there had been a merger boom: from 1888 to 1894 there were sixty-nine mergers in all, 'more than had taken place in the whole of the previous eighteen years'.[16] This movement continued and increased during the First World War until by 1918 the 'Big Five' – Barclays, Lloyds, the National Provincial, the Midland and the Westminster – had emerged, and by 1920 were holding four-fifths of deposits and dominating the banking world.

Distrusting monopoly of power and what was called a 'money trust', Members of Parliament began asking questions and in February 1918 Andrew Bonar Law, the Chancellor, appointed a committee of enquiry under the chairmanship of Lord Colwyn, which reported on 1 May. It recommended that a law be passed recommending that any further amalgamations be approved by the Treasury, the Board of Trade and an advisory committee. A Bill was drafted and given its first reading on 14 April 1919, but after much discussion it was finally withdrawn in December 1919.

A new President, Sir Eric Geddes, had taken over the Board of Trade and was more sympathetic to the bankers. He accepted their strong protest that 'special legislation apparently based upon the assumption that the Banks are a danger to the nation is a slur upon them which they are in no way conscious of having deserved'.[17] Instead of legislation it was now proposed that the 'Big Five' should in future refer any amalgamation to the Treasury: the only check would be after discussion with the Governor of the Bank of England. During this period of argument and consultation the 'Big Five' undertook not to propose further amalgamations. So there had been great surprise when the merger of the National Provincial and Coutts & Co. was allowed. Their case had been heard by Lord Colwyn alone and for some reason had been accepted. Childs, an old bank like Coutts & Co, was not so fortunate; when in 1923 it was proposed that it should merge with Lloyds, the Chancellor referred the proposal to the advisory committee and the project was disallowed.

Amalgamation was not the only method used by Coutts & Co. for expansion. The Bank had acquired wider contacts in the country and City through its mergers with Robarts, Lubbock & Co. and now with the National Provincial. But it also extended by opening up new branches for the convenience of customers. Its business was still mainly concerned with deposit gathering and in providing facilities for money transactions.

The first branch was opened in 1921 appropriately at 1 Park Lane. The premises had actually been acquired in 1914, but the war had delayed the opening. It was a few minutes' walk from 1 Stratton Street and near the Duke of Wellington's home, Apsley House. The second branch was opened in Cavendish Square in 1927 in an eighteenth-century house, once the home of Princess Amelia, daughter of George II. Further London branches followed: Cadogan Place, Sloane Street, in 1929 and Mayfair in 1932.

It was not until 1961 that Coutts & Co. opened its branch at Eton, the first outside London. As we have seen, Coutts & Co. had a long and close association with Eton, ever since the days when Sir Edmund Antrobus sent his young nephews, Edmund and Gibbs, to school there. In the following years further branches were opened: 188 Fleet Street in 1967, Brompton Road in 1978 and 32 Sloane Street in 1982. Bristol branch opened in November 1976 and was followed by offices in Norwich in 1978, Winchester in 1979 and Bath in 1990.

There were many problems for bankers generally in the years after the First World War, but there were also problems peculiar to Coutts & Co. The Bank had to maintain its own identity and traditions within the partnerships with Robarts, Lubbock & Co. and the National Provincial Bank, and in the increasingly complex modern world. It was fortunate that Coutts & Co. had strengthened its position by merging with the National

Provincial in 1920, for the next two decades were to plunge the world into financial crises and industrial unrest culminating in the Second World War.

On 3 May 1926, the eve of the General Strike, twelve mattresses, pillows and twenty-four blankets were delivered to the Strand for the nine members of staff who were to sleep in the Bank. On the first day of the strike, all except four of the staff reported for duty and, as the strike continued, 'there was little, if any, falling off of the general work', or so it was recorded;[18] 'with only one or two exceptions staff worked splendidly and were willing to assist in whatever manner they could. The Messengers, to a man, displayed a fine spirit and Lady members of staff showed great courage and determination in getting to the Bank.'[19] Charabancs were commissioned to bring staff to and from work. The closing of the Clearing House made their work difficult and post arrived late, but work was usually finished in time to catch the charabanc at 4 p.m. During the strike sixty-three members of staff joined the special constabulary, police stations were manned, buildings guarded and the streets patrolled. 'In all some 1,059 hours of duty were carried out not including the many hours spent just standing by.'[20]

The General Strike lasted only nine days and left deep wounds in the trades union movement. But it was remembered by many of the clerks of Coutts & Co. as a period of high excitement when, like many white-collared workers, they doffed their frock-coats and drove buses and lorries, or signed up with the Commissioner of Police as 'capable citizens under forty-five with the requisite health, strength and vigour'[21] and became special constables. A company was formed from the staff of the Bank and attached to Bow Street Station. As Cockman recalled,

The complete disruption aimed at by the Strike was brilliantly countered by an amazing volunteer force of men and women from all walks of life under skilled and well planned management and leadership. The steam trains, underground railways, bus services &c., were soon running thanks to this army of enthusiastic amateurs. They even produced a daily newspaper from the offices of The Morning Post.

The Specials were on call 24 hours a day and being conveniently grouped at 440 Strand, where they had sleeping quarters in the Board Room (mattresses on the floor), they became attached to Scotland Yard and formed a 'flying squad'. It was not unusual for a fleet of cars to come dashing up the Strand and whisk them off to some spot of emergency – the Produce Markets, factories, Railway Yards, Strike meetings. One met with considerable jeers and catcalls when carrying out these various jobs and I remember early one morning, on my way to take up duty in Covent Garden market, receiving the contents of a certain receptacle from an upstairs window.

There was practically nothing doing in the Banks, Insurance Offices, Stock Exchange or other financial institutions as the Strike went on for about 9 or 10 days. The coal strike, however, was to continue into the winter.[22]

While the strike was on little work was done since all the financial institutions were at a standstill. For the clerks it was a nine days' holiday with all the fun of the fair.

There was no such pleasurable excitement as the news from New York on 24 October 1929 reached the Bank. On that black Thursday, thirteen million shares changed hands on the New York Stock Exchange as Wall Street crashed.

It was a prelude to a turbulent decade. In 1931 the collapse of the German mark was followed by financial crisis in Britain. Cockman remembered the effect on Coutts & Co:

1931 was a disastrous year internationally, with unemployment, Bank failures abroad and the suspension of the Gold Standard by the British Government. In terms of gold the £ fell in value to 16/- and to 14/- by the end of the year – when a National Government had been formed. 1932 saw the Conversion offer of the first War issue of £2,085 million War 5% stock, and only 8% of the holders declined to accept the 3½% issue which was on offer. We were now in a period of cheap money. The following year, by agreement, the Banks received only a ⅓ share of Commission from Brokers instead of ½. Cheap money rates continued and the Government was able to issue Treasury 1 per cent Bonds 1939/41. In spite of the reduction in the division of Commission, our share was over £29,600 in 1936 – a year of great activity.[23]

Over the next years growing unemployment and the slump bred unrest at home. Europe saw the rise of Mussolini in Italy, Hitler in Germany, and Franco in Spain. The Civil War which tore Spain apart in 1936 ended with Franco's victory in 1939. Nazis and Fascists were on the march, threatening the whole of Europe with totalitarianism.

In January 1936 King George V died, to be succeeded for a short reign by Edward VIII, who abdicated on 12 December. The following year brought a brief interlude of celebration with the Coronation of King George VI on 12 May, but the world was moving inexorably towards war. At noon on 3 September 1939, the Prime Minister Neville Chamberlain stood grim-faced in the House of Commons and announced: 'This country is now at war with Germany. We are ready.'

The First World War had taken the banking world by surprise; the declaration of war against Germany in 1939 had been long foreshadowed and long feared, and lessons had been learned. During the six years of conflict the Government took more control of the economy than it had in 1914–18. There were direct controls – 'rationing, licensing, requisitions, prohibitions, the conscription of labour . . . price and rent controls, subsidies and the physical management of the coal and steel industries'.[24]

Coutts & Co., like all banks, was affected by these restrictions as it was by the regulations introduced in 1939 and 1940 to control the export of gold and foreign currencies. It too had to accept control of lending and agreed to limit advances to those which aided the national interest, for example defence, coal mining, agriculture and exports. But Coutts & Co. also had particular difficulties because of the extent of its overseas connections.

However, it had experience in organising the Bank in wartime. Ronald Malcolm had been his father's right hand during the First World War, when the ageing William was Chairman. After his father's death in 1923 George Marjoribanks succeeded as Chairman, and saw to it that the Bank continued to function throughout the Second World War with the minimum of disruption. Valuables were removed for safety, which was especially necessary during the intensity of the Blitz. Ledgers and other documents were taken to Welders, a house bought by Coutts & Co. in Buckinghamshire.

When 440 Strand was built it had been considered as rock-safe as a fortress, but the intensity of the aerial bombardment in the Second World War put it at risk, as recorded in this bank memorandum:

It would seem reasonable to assume that the present scale of bombing in London will continue indefinitely and this memorandum is written upon such an assumption turning out to be correct.

The building at 440 Strand is a particularly vulnerable one. It has a thin flat roof in which are placed large glass sky-lights, and nowhere is there more than one story over the main Banking hall except at the very ends of the building. The basement has been re-inforced, and is said to be capable of withstanding the collapse of the building, but not a direct hit from a high explosive bomb. A falling bomb if it hit the Bank at all would be very likely to explode in the main Banking hall. In this case the whole of the inside of the Bank would be shattered and would be unfit for further occupation.[25]

In May 1940 a detailed memorandum gave instructions for the removal of some of the most valuable documents to houses and buildings already prepared at Roehampton, while a small staff and one director would work at the premises in Hungerford Lane, Charing Cross, known as 'The Arches'. The same memorandum noted:

There are employed at the Strand 138 men and 97 women.
There are some 13,000 accounts.
In 1939 nearly 250,000 dividends were credited.
1,175,000 coupons were collected.
The cards recording registered securities number about 150,000.[26]

The blackout, which was strictly enforced, made work in the late winter afternoons almost impossible. Transport to and from work was hampered by bombing. Yet many braved the Blitz and arrived at the Strand armed with their gasmasks, though after a while many found the cases more convenient for the carrying of sandwiches than masks.

But, as Cockman found, 'As in all major conflicts facing a common enemy breaks down social barriers, brings the people very close together in sharing discomfort or sorrow.'[27] The experience of war played a great part in changing the attitudes of management to staff in Coutts & Co. as elsewhere.

One might have thought, Cockman wrote in his memoirs, that Coutts's men

Brought up to obey instructions implicitly ... one might have regarded them as good ground troops ... trained to the nth degree in accuracy and giving a service, they were suddenly given the opportunity to become leaders. ... How did they react? In a way that Mr. Thomas Coutts would have been proud of. The essential attention to detail, the happy spirit in which they had worked together as clerks, the abnegation of self in a job to be done, and done correctly, these surely provide some of the qualities of leadership, and overcoming the first reaction of slight shock, they eagerly seized their new found role of accepting responsibility.[28]

Although conscription was brought in, there were occupations, banking among them, which were considered vital to the running of the Home Front. Firms were allowed to state their claim for personnel essential to the business. Cockman recalled:

Here comes the laugh. The appointments or titles attributed to the members of the Staff had, until then, purposely been kept to the minimum – the Secretary, Heads of Departments and occasionally the Seconds. But now, mirabile dictu, strange and high sounding titles were attached to individual clerks in an attempt to retain their services at home. Some surprise was naturally in evidence that their importance and essential duties had hitherto not been marked or financially recognised.[29]

The Blitz on 16 April 1940 did much damage to the Bank at 440 Strand. Landmines fell on the George Inn nearby and blew out most of the windows. Fires from two incendiaries on the lower roof were promptly put out by firewatchers, but several more destroyed some of the shops in the block in spite of the efforts of the fire team. 'Just too many fires all round; altogether a very nasty night,' reported one of the firewatchers. The next morning an unexploded landmine on Charing Cross Station kept the staff underground until the mine was made safe. Throughout the autumn and winter, windows at 440 Strand were shattered again and again by high-explosive bombs on neighbouring shops and offices. In 1949 Coutts & Co. put in a claim for £8,091 3s 4d to the War Damage Commission for repairs to bank premises at 440 Strand, Lombard Street, Park Lane and Upper Brook Street. Of this sum only £375 10s 1d was disallowed.

51

Five Chairmen Remembered

During the next decades of profound and lasting change Coutts & Co. was fortunate to be directed by five successive Chairmen, each of exceptional ability, each creating confidence and stability in a turbulent world. From the end of the First World War until 1949 the direction of the Bank was still mainly in the hands of the 'quiet men', like William Rolle Malcolm and his son, Ronald. They were remembered by Charles Adcock, who served in the Bank under them all.[1]

Adcock was appointed as a clerk in the Bank on 25 January 1915. When he came to the Bank William Rolle Malcolm was, as he wrote, 'in the seat of the mighty'. Malcolm was seventy-five at this time, but was still very much in control. And although, as the years went by, he occasionally enjoyed 'a post prandial nap' at his desk, he remained alert until his death. It was he who guided the Bank through the difficult days after the amalgamation with the National Provincial. Adcock recalled how Malcolm called the staff together in 1919 to explain the change, telling them that he had informed the King and that 'the privileges and interests of the staff had been permanently safeguarded'. The *Vanity Fair* cartoon, 'The King's Banker', portrayed him exactly as Adcock remembered him: 'a stocky man of medium height and dignified presence, wearing the wing collar and bow tie that was his characteristic, his heavy jowl adding weight to his words'.

Malcolm was succeeded as Chairman by George Marjoribanks, a man of great presence who could in no way be counted among the 'quiet men'. His voice was unforgettable, booming through the banking hall 'like the voice of doom', striking terror among the young clerks. 'George,' Adcock once heard Malcolm say, 'that thing you've got in your hand is a telephone, not a speaking tube.' There was an occasion, long remembered, when Marjoribanks, 'bending low over a drawer ... received a slap on his posterior from a member of the staff who mistook him for a colleague. Profuse apologies followed, whereupon Sir George smiled and said, "That's all right Mr ----- but why so damned hard?"' Usually he was not noted for his sense of humour. No one was more jealous of the reputation of Coutts & Co. and he was quite seriously affronted 'by the suggestion, facetiously made, that a banner be displayed outside the premises, with the caption "All the best people bank here – why don't YOU?"'

Marjoribanks had long since lived down his father's disgrace, but the memory made him perhaps excessively anxious to preserve his own dignity and the prestige of the Bank his family had served since the end of the eighteenth century. Tall, handsome, with aquiline features, he was always impeccably dressed. 'Twelve inches of white silk handkerchief always hung from the breast pocket of his frock-coat, which in winter was black, but in summer time was Ascot grey, immaculately smart.' The memory of Marjoribanks and his silk handkerchief was indelibly fixed in the minds of many other members of the staff.

Coutts & Co. had always prided itself on the easy relations between directors and customers, but Marjoribanks was more regal than the King himself. A customer, displeased with Adcock's refusal to grant an overdraft, once said, '"I appeal unto Caesar." "Meaning what?" I asked. "I wish to see the chairman," he replied. I informed Sir George ... "Tell him", he said with the hint of a smile, "that Caesar does not see customers; he employs clerks for that duty."' Nevertheless, when Marjoribanks was knighted, the staff shared his delight in an honour all felt he richly deserved. He had been unflagging in his work for the Bank's prosperity. After his death in 1931 *The Times* recorded that

a rather abrupt and hasty manner concealed one of the kindest and most human personalities imaginable. No claim on his sympathy from any of those below him was ever disregarded, and whether kindly advice or financial help was in question he was equally ready to give. He had his reward ... in the real affection with which all who had to do with him regarded him. He was a great gentleman.

Ronald Malcolm, who succeeded him, was, like his father, a 'quiet man'. A distinguished mathematician, he had come to Coutts & Co. in 1896 at the age of twenty, after gaining his degree at New College, Oxford. Adcock came to know him well, since, when he became a manager, he had a working lunch with him every Monday. 'He was', he said, 'like Thomas Coutts, of whom it was written, "His main and sole point was his business and he hated idleness. He did not hate society but he did not court it."' As his son, Colin Malcolm, wrote to Adcock, 'the Bank was the core of his life'. Like his father he was rather forbidding in appearance, and only rarely showed signs of a sense of humour. 'Are you settling down?' he once asked Adcock, and allowed himself to laugh at the reply: 'Yes sir, thank you, and trying to get the customers to settle up.' He was, like Thomas Coutts, 'an exact man', impatient with carelessness, fastidious about details. Adcock remembered the distaste with which he removed pins from papers and documents. He brought his mathematical mind to bear on the new problems of banking and devised 'formulae for departmental costing and the allocation of profits as between departments and branches'. During his father's lifetime he shouldered much of the responsibility of the Bank and steered the Bank through the Second World War with the same efficiency as his father had shown in the First. Ronald Malcolm retired as Chairman in 1946, but he remained on the board until his death in 1949.

Both father and son were in close touch with the Government through Malcolm's younger son Dougal (later Sir Dougal), who, like his father, had gained a double first at Oxford and became a Fellow of All Souls. He was a very distinguished civil servant and, as one of Milner's 'young men', was an expert on colonial affairs – particularly South Africa. William Malcolm had been assisted by his nephew, Frederick Walter Stephenson; together with Ronald they spanned seventy years of service to Coutts & Co., guiding the Bank through the Boer War and two world wars, through the fundamental change of 1892, the move across the Strand in 1904 and through the amalgamations of 1914 and 1920. Ronald in particular, with his mathematical brilliance, had prepared the way for the banking of the modern world. If only his ancestor, the Duke of Wellington, as he talked with Babbage in Angela Burdett-Coutts's drawing-room so long ago, could have looked in the glass and seen his descendant preparing for the computerised future!

Ronald Malcolm was followed as Chairman in 1946 by Sir Jasper Ridley, who also had links with the past. He was the son of Mary Marjoribanks, daughter of Dudley, second son of Edward Marjoribanks senior. So, at long last, one of Dudley's family became not only a partner, but Chairman of the Bank which had excluded Dudley for decades. Ridley came to Coutts & Co. in 1920 at the age of twenty-three, after an education at Eton and Balliol College, Oxford. He served with great distinction in the First World War, was mentioned in dispatches and awarded the Legion of Honour. He worked for a year after the war as Secretary of the Ministry of Labour Training Grants Commission and then joined Coutts & Co.

Adcock recalled his 'spontaneous and infectious charm'. His talents were extraordinarily varied, ranging from farming – he was a member of the wartime Pig Board in Suffolk – to Chairman of the Trustees of the Tate Gallery and a Trustee of the British Museum. From 1950 to 1951 he was also the Chairman of the National Provincial. One of his co-directors once suggested to Adcock that 'it was impossible to be a good banker ... and have an artistic temperament. When I quoted Sir Jasper, he conceded that "he was the exception that proved the rule".' Adcock remembered him standing with his back to the fire in the 'preposterous Victorian marble fireplace in Lombard Street and ... saying ... "Mr Adcock you look more like a city banker every day" ... I stammered out, "And what, sir, does a city banker look like?" With that disarming smile of his he just said, "You."' Ridley took great pride in Coutts & Co., the Bank with which his family had been so long connected, and was delighted when Osbert Sitwell in his autobiography called it a bank with a soul, remembering how when he was eighteen Messrs Coutts & Co. had shown him more kindness and comprehension than his own father.[2]

Ridley was a Fellow of Eton and was mainly responsible for the selection of Evie Hone to design and make the new east window in Eton College Chapel, which replaced the old one destroyed by a bomb during the war. He was a personal friend of George VI, whom he usually visited at Windsor after the Provost and Fellows' meetings at Eton. It was perhaps because of this friendship that the King invited the Provost to tutor Princess Elizabeth.

It was much regretted that one who had such good taste in paintings should have been so badly portrayed in the posthumous portrait of him. Ridley died on 1 October 1951 at the age of sixty-four. He was much mourned by the staff and directors of Coutts & Co. A correspondent in *The Times* recalled that he had 'no trace of precocity or priggishness' and remembered his balanced judgment, his common sense and that he kept the humour of a boy even in his last illness. 'He grew up maturely wise: he died eternally young.' He could not have had a finer epitaph.

Ridley was succeeded by Seymour John Louis Egerton (later Sir Seymour), who, like many of the directors at Coutts & Co., was an Old Etonian. His father had considered university a waste of time and instead sent him at the age of eighteen on a 'public schoolboy tour' of India, which he always considered a 'most wonderful experience'[3] – probably more useful to him than university. He had some business experience in a discount house until the war, in which he served in the Grenadier Guards. After the war David Robarts approached him and asked, as he remembers, ' "Would I be prepared to consider coming to Coutts?" "Would I consider?" I liked that so I said, "I won't need to consider".'[4] Egerton, in his humorous self-deprecating way, was even more surprised at the speed with which Ronald Malcolm asked him to be a director. 'I said to him', he recalled, ' "I couldn't be a director because I didn't know the first thing about taxes." He said, "That don't matter." '[5] He remained a director from 1947 until his retirement in 1985, and was Chairman for twenty-five years from 1951 to 1976, during one of the most critical periods in the history of the Bank.

Adcock remembered his many kindnesses and that

it has been his responsibility to direct the Bank through the 'wind of change' into the age of computers and other electronic devices, of advertising and of internal administrative reorganisation. To do this while still preserving the 'soul' of the Bank . . . is no mean achievement.[6]

With disarming modesty Egerton refused to accept any credit for the vital changes made in the Bank during his term as Chairman. In a conversation after his retirement, he assured the author that 'it was Sandon [now Lord Harrowby], he's the wonderful fellow who did the whole thing'. As for computerisation – 'Isn't it a hoot! I didn't understand it.' He was, he insisted, 'the chap with the oil can – pouring oil on troubled waters sometimes – defuse the thing, you know. I tried to do a bit of that.'[7] For all his understatement, Egerton played an important role during a difficult decade when tempers were frayed and there was sometimes acrimony and jealousy between the amalgamated banks. At such a critical period in any organisation, 'the chap with the oil can' is indispensable. But there was also talent behind the jolly exterior, as the shrewd Ronald Malcolm had early seen.

Lord Harrowby remembered how Egerton had guided the Bank through difficult years: 'He smoothed the troubles over, was very popular and very good with customers. He was a very nice man; I can't think of anybody that I would have preferred to have sat next to for twenty years.'[8]

52

'A New Breed'

The 1960s brought fundamental changes in the banking world in general and in Coutts & Co. in particular.

When the Radcliffe Committee reported in 1957 there had been little change since the years between the two world wars. But in the 1960s there was a new boom in mergers. In 1957 there had been eleven members of the Committee of London Clearing Bankers including the 'Big Five'. By 1977, when the Wilson Committee reported, there were only six London Clearing Banks: Barclays, Coutts, Lloyds, the Midland, National Westminster and Williams & Glyn's. Coutts & National Westminster were allied. So power was concentrated: 'Barclays and National Westminster between them were responsible for almost 60 per cent of total liabilities; Lloyds and the Midland together accounted for just less than 40 per cent; and Williams & Glyn's for under 3 per cent.'[1]

In the 1960s it was necessary for the banks to be large enough to provide the immense loans increasingly requested by national and multinational companies. At the same time the proliferation of branches was not cost effective. A larger group could be rationalised, and the increased size made it possible to introduce the new techniques of computers and credit cards necessary in the modern world.

Accepting the new situation, the Government no longer hindered mergers; and the Prices and Incomes Board in 1966 announced, 'the Bank of England and the Treasury have made it plain that they would not obstruct some further amalgamation if the banks were willing to contemplate such a development'. Accordingly in 1968 it was proposed to merge the Westminster Bank with the National Provincial – the whole business becoming the National Westminster Bank in January 1969. Coutts & Co., as a subsidiary of the National Provincial, was now part of a huge organisation.

In this situation, Coutts & Co. was in danger of being smothered. How could a small bank, steeped in tradition, maintain its identity in the shadow of these great giants? That it has done so is to a large part due to the determination, dedication and enterprise of what one of the staff has called 'the new breed of directors'. Under this leadership the directors of Coutts

& Co. were not dragged unwillingly into the new world of electronics and large-scale management; they accepted the challenge with energy and enthusiasm.

The 1960s and 1970s brought great changes to Coutts & Co. and it was fortunate that there was a 'new breed of directors'. In some ways they were still the 'old breed', predominantly Old Etonians drawn from a privileged class. But they had mostly undergone the gruelling experience either of war service, in which some were wounded, or, in the case of the younger men, of national service. They returned with a better understanding of a world outside the magic circle, with practical and technical training and with a realisation of the importance of organisation. They had also learned that men returning from battle would not be prepared as before to accept the old authoritarian attitudes, however benevolent. Caesar no longer ruled.

It was important that many of the directors were working for a business that had been in their families for generations; this gave them an extra determination to make Coutts & Co. succeed in the changing world of banking.

The family of Thomas Coutts was represented by Lord Latymer and David Money-Coutts, both of whom were descended from Sophia and Sir Francis Burdett. Dudley, Viscount Sandon, traced his descent back to the bewitching Fanny, whose daughter, Frances, had married Lord Sandon, so bringing an alliance with a family with a long parliamentary history. Under the names of Ryder, Sandon and Harrowby they had made their mark as ministers and Members of Parliament. Lord Sandon was the first member of his family for seven generations not to be a Member of Parliament.

Like most of the directors of Coutts & Co., Viscount Sandon was educated at Eton, but had learned much from his war service in the 5th Parachute Brigade. He saw service in north-west Europe, India and Java, where he was seriously wounded. After the war he became a director of Coutts & Co. and in 1970 was appointed as Deputy Chairman. He also became a director of the parent company NatWest and from 1971 onwards was its Deputy Chairman. In the following years he was Chairman of all the operations involved in the international side. During this critical time he was therefore an invaluable link between NatWest and Coutts & Co.

Sandon's reserved, almost austere manner conceals a steely determination and drive. It was he who insisted that if Coutts & Co. wanted to survive in the new age, it must pay more attention to making profits. He also inherited from his mother a tradition of service to the community. Mabel, daughter of W. H. Smith, was renowned in Staffordshire for her philanthropic work. Sandon, in his turn, became a Governor and then Chairman of the Bethlem Royal and Maudsley Hospitals, and of the Institute of Psychiatry and a Trustee of the Psychiatry Research Trust. Although he has not followed his ancestors into national politics, he was a member of Kensington Borough Council from 1950 to 1965. After 1971 he was more directly involved with the parent company, but still retained his influence at Coutts & Co.

Julian Robarts brought in the different but long and distinguished tradition of the Robarts, Lubbock Bank. His uncle, David John Robarts, whose grandfather had taken Robarts, Lubbock into the amalgamation with Coutts & Co. in 1914, had joined Coutts in 1927 and the Board in 1931, and had become Chairman of the National Provincial Bank from 1954 to 1968, Chairman of the London Clearing Banks and President of the British Bankers Association from 1956 to 1960 and from 1968 to 1970. As the first Deputy Chairman and second Chairman of National Westminster Bank he must have had a considerable influence on the preservation of Coutts's independence.

Yet another family bank with a long history was represented by John Smith. Smith's Bank, once the largest private bank in Britain, had been absorbed into the National Provincial and so had been brought into affiliation with Coutts & Co. in the amalgamation of 1920. Smith's Bank traced its history back to 1658, when one Thomas Smith, a mercer and banker, set up his shop in Nottingham. There, in the eighteenth century, his grandsons, George and John Abel, founded one of the first branch banks in Britain. In 1758 the London branch of the family bank was established in Lombard Street and flourished in true nineteenth-century style. Successive marriages brought in wealthy nonconformists like the father of the famous William Wilberforce, the banker John Thornton, founder of the Clapham Sect, and the Derbyshire Baptist, Thomas Cook, who built up the world's first travel agency in the 1840s. It was Abel Smith MP who was at Angela Burdett-Coutts's right hand during the 1860s. John Smith also inherited considerable wealth and Shottesbrooke Park in Berkshire from ancestors who made and married fortunes from the East India Company.

To the rich, interwoven tapestry of these historic banks was now added the royal purple. Three of the present Queen's cousins, the Marquess of Cambridge, Earl Granville and the Hon. Michael Albemarle Bowes-Lyon became working directors. All took their duties seriously for, as contemporaries frequently remarked, there was no room at Coutts & Co. for those who did not work their passage. However distinguished their family, men were not invited to become directors, and were certainly never made Chairmen, through nepotism.

Lord James Crichton Stuart, who was of the Bute family, for example, was responsible in the late 1960s for setting up the international banking division. 'The only way that could be built', David Money-Coutts recorded, 'was by moving it into the City and getting it out of Head Office and making it a proper set-up and not just an ancillary nodule.'[2]

John Smith was considered a great asset to Coutts & Co. Forward-looking and, according to contemporaries, a great 'ideas man', he also had a passionate interest in the past, in conservation and the National Trust. He too was educated at Eton and Oxford and served in the RNVR from 1942 to 1946. After the war he became a full-time director of Coutts & Co. and as such set up and directed the Investment Management Department in the City in the early 1960s. He became Conservative MP for the Cities of London and Westminster from 1965 to 1970, when he ceased to be an executive director.

There was one director at this time, who had great influence and long experience. Charles Musk was neither an Etonian nor an Oxford graduate, nor did he have war experience. But he was that rare bird at Coutts & Co. – a director who rose from the ranks, though others came after him. Late in life Musk remembered with some pride that, whereas his two immediate predecessors from the ranks had been elevated to the Board after their retirement, he had been appointed in 1956 at the age of fifty-three.

Musk had joined the Bank in 1920 on his seventeenth birthday straight from his local grammar school. His father was the manager of a small advertising group agency who banked at Coutts & Co., and the owner of the group introduced young Charles. He began in the reign of Sir George Marjoribanks, who dazzled the new clerk with his sartorial splendour and famous breast-pocket handkerchief. An ambitious young man, determined to get to the top, Musk studied in his spare time and in three years, when he was twenty, passed the bankers' examinations and became an Associate Member of the Institute of Bankers. He had set his sights on becoming Secretary, one of the most prestigious positions in the Bank, which carried the privilege of signing 'Coutts & Co.' As a young clerk he practised at home signing a flourishing 'Coutts & Co.' ready for the great day. His talents were spotted and he was early pro-moted into the Loan Department, which was always regarded as the most important section of the Bank.

In 1952 he finally became Secretary and could at last sign for the Bank. In that capacity he dealt with the royal accounts, succeeding George King, whose telephone conversations with His Majesty were legendary – 'Is that George King? This is King George.'

When the deaths of Ronald Malcolm and Jasper Ridley left the board of directors weakened, Musk approached Lord Latymer and expressed his concern at the lack of men of weight on the board. Lord Latymer, who was the son of the Hugh Money-Coutts who had been rebuffed by William Malcolm, was a hardworking and much respected member of the Board. In 1956 Charles Musk was invited to become a director, a position he filled with total loyalty and dedication until he was seventy, even after his retirement from the Bank at sixty-five.

Rooted as he was in tradition, he watched the younger men moving into the electronic world with approval. Seymour Egerton, then Chairman of the Bank, shared Musk's ignorance about computers. 'I reckon he and I were a couple of old-fashioned bankers,' Musk remembered, 'and these young boys who we'd trained in the basics were now in control, and they had taken advantage of all the modern developments.'[3] He was particularly proud of his 'two boys', Julian Robarts and David Money-Coutts, and watched, with fatherly affection, their progress through three decades till they reached the highest positions in the Bank. It was Robarts's particular aim to see the amalgamated banks united in a seamless whole. This was difficult, but he was to work to that end with dogged determination and, after many years' effort, with success.

A handsome man, fresh-faced and youthful in appearance, easy and unaffected in manner, Julian Robarts dispelled the old image of the formal, frock-coated banker. His genuine interest in staff and customers certainly helped to maintain the family atmosphere so valued at Coutts & Co. But in the early days a certain brusqueness of manner and a hot temper quickly aroused often broke through his natural charm. In time, he mellowed, but the stresses of modern banking can try the most courteous and good-humoured, and there were times when the staff learned to keep their heads down in the onset of a sudden storm.

David Money-Coutts's intellectual ability was acknowledged from his earliest days at Coutts & Co. His father had not gone into the Bank but spent his career in the tobacco industry, retiring as a director of the Imperial Tobacco Company. His son chose to join Coutts & Co., believing that it offered a wider basic business training, and never regretted his decision. Like other directors he went to Eton at the age of thirteen and always valued his education there. His years of national service with the 1st Royal Dragoons in England, Germany and Egypt widened his experience of life and the subsequent years with the Territorial Army encouraged his fascination with all things mechanical. At Oxford he read Philosophy, Politics and Economics, which added yet another facet to a many-sided education. As one contemporary in his early days at Coutts & Co. remembers: 'He got on easily with everyone and his special skills led him towards the study of computers and other technical aspects of banking. With a brilliant brain and plenty of ideas I think he often felt frustrated'[4] – a judgment which Money-Coutts himself denies.

Like others of the 'new breed of directors' he went the rounds of the branches and departments of the Bank, listening, watching and learning, as he was to do throughout his career. Later in life he regretted that, unlike Robarts, he had taken his meals with the other directors instead of the staff. He not only spent time as a resident director at Lombard Street, but also worked at the National Provincial Bank in its Advance Department and with the National Provincial inspectors. A period with James Capel & Co., Coutts's stockbrokers, who had been associated with the Bank in the Strand since the days of Edmund Antrobus and Thomas Coutts, widened his education still further. Therefore, when after four years' general training he joined the Bank as a director, he brought with him an unusually wide and deep experience and not only of banking.

Somewhat donnish in appearance, he shows a remarkable resemblance to his ancestor, Thomas Coutts, with the same slight spare figure, the same wary eyes and humorous mouth. From the beginning of his career at Coutts & Co. he showed a determination to hold on to the old traditions but also to keep the Bank ahead of the changing times. A shy, slightly brusque manner sometimes conceals his genuine kindness and interest; and, a perfectionist in all things, he does not always suffer fools gladly: he himself confesses that he can be 'pernickety'. A practical man, he has been known to mend an out-of-action machine he noticed on his rounds, leaving a note from 'the Chairman'.

David Money-Coutts and Julian Robarts have worked in friendship together for more than thirty years, and though they were supported by the old and new directors, it was chiefly they who steered the Bank through the rough waters ahead.

In the period after the Second World War Coutts & Co. maintained its reputation for old world courtesy and discretion. The arrival of the horse-drawn brougham carrying The Queen's messenger from Buckingham Palace reminded passers-by that this was the royal bank. Customers were greeted by dignified gentlemen wearing frock-coats; distinguished customers still signed the visitors' book with quill pens; at the polished mahogany counters all was stability and security.

To some the old traditions at Coutts & Co. were a source of amusement, to rivals perhaps of envy. Some time in the early nineteenth century it had been decreed that all who worked at the Bank, from the hall porter to the Chairman, should be clean-shaven. In 1959 even Sir Kenneth Peppiatt, the distinguished Chief Cashier at the Bank of England, whose signature for many years graced our bank notes, shaved off a famous moustache, cherished for thirty years, when he became a director. *The Times* reported with sympathy: 'Sir Kenneth Peppiatt has to remove his fine dark moustache, the product of more than thirty years' careful cultivation. I am told his sense of bereavement is acute.'

The beardless bankers at Coutts & Co. provoked much facetious comment. 'I know a bank whereon no lip moss grows,' wrote one contemporary. The frock-coats too were targets for the humorists. The *Financial and*

Bullionist of 18 July 1914 had considered that the black frock-coats gave 'the staff the appearance of a collection of decorous deacons from the Chapels of Little Bethel'.

But anyone who assumed that Coutts & Co. was buried in the past was profoundly mistaken. In the autumn of 1960 a grave gentleman in a frock-coat was commissioned by the directors to 'investigate the possible use of electronic computers for Bank accounting purposes'. Mr G. Sterling, the Coutts representative on the electronics sub-committee of the Committee of London Clearing Bankers, then began months of work, researching and evaluating the use of the few computers then available for commercial use. At that time no bank was yet using computers. Coutts & Co. had also been in the 1920s one of the first banks to introduce machine-posted ledgers.

It was particularly appropriate that Coutts & Co. should have been among the forerunners in that field. For, more than a hundred years earlier, Charles Babbage had invited Angela Burdett-Coutts to see his calculating engine. The friend of Faraday, she was fascinated by the new scientific discoveries and with customary foresight saw something of its potential and encouraged him. Although the Bank could not claim him as a customer, Angela herself undoubtedly gave him some financial assistance. Whatever modern critics may say of Babbage, there is no doubt of his importance in the origin and development of the modern computer: but neither he nor Angela could have dreamt of the revolution his calculating engine would bring about in the world of banking.

In May 1961 Sterling and his staff of three decided, after seven months of careful research, that the magnetic tape computer, Univac SS80, then working in a bank in West Germany, was the most suitable. Premises were found in Marshall Street, an air-conditioning plant was installed, and the machine was set up in November 1961. During the testing period the Mayfair branch of Coutts & Co. ran a parallel programme using the old manual system of ledger posting. On 15 December 1962 this branch began its computer system and by the end of 1963 all the branches were using it, making Coutts & Co. the first British bank to be fully computerised. A school for punch-card operators run by Miss P. Hosegood provided two or three hundred trained girls in the first seven years.

In the past, 'Balance Nights' had been a dreaded twice-yearly ordeal, when clerks were sustained through the night by free beer and sandwiches provided by the Baroness. The new computers brought much relief, though the new equipment would also bring new problems.

As *The Statist* reported, the directors claimed

that the rewards for installing its Univac Solid State 80, bought at an original price of £150,000, will outweigh the costs eight years after coming into service in early 1963. These rewards will take the form of a saving in labour costs, of increased efficiency in transcription and finally of increased business and customer goodwill through the retention of detailed description of statements.[5]

And this was achieved without redundancy. 'The girls at the branches who had been working conventional (Burroughs) posting machines were merely trained to become punch-card operators.'[6] *The Statist* continued with approval:

What gives the Coutts computer system its special quality is the service which it performs for its customers in providing them with full alphabetical descriptions of amounts listed on their statements. It is hard to estimate exactly what effect this has on the bank's goodwill, but the favourable publicity which the Coutts system has received makes it worth asking why other banks have not been able or willing to follow its lead. The essential reason lies in the difference in size between Coutts and the Big Five. The major headache for the latter is the business of sorting the mass of cheques which they have to deal with.

... Beause of its smaller size, it is easier for Coutts to use a system of punch cards on which the branches are able to put all the details required.

... They have however managed to make one very big saving not made by many other financial institutions which are in the process of switching over to a computer. This is the fact that Coutts have refrained from running the computer system simultaneously with the previously existing system until the change-over process is completed. Coutts did in fact do this in its initial pilot scheme carried out in the Mayfair branch in December 1962, but this parallel system only lasted for a fortnight and was not repeated as the computer system was expanded. What happened in practice is that the staff have been trained in their tasks until the point where they can switch over at once.

Beneath their black tail-coats – worn even by the gentlemen who tend the computers – and in spite of the oldy-worldy home in the heart of Soho which they have found for their Univac SS80, the staff of Coutts are well geared to the needs of the second half of the 20th century. Even the antiquated house was settled for because it was cheap to rent and suitable for air conditioning.[7]

At the end of 1969 Mr Horace Cath wrote a memorandum for the directors on the installation of the early computers at the Bank. Well before then all the accounts at the branches, head office and the Lombard Street office had been passed to the computer. In June 1969 the Univac SS80 computer was replaced by a Univac 9300.

The Bank moved into the 1970s not only ahead of other banks but also with an improved computer. In the autumn of 1967 an IBM 3979 Reader-Sorter machine had been installed at 32 Lombard Street in the head office Clearing Department. Cath described it in his memorandum:

It has two main functions. The first is to list, sort and agree the cheques, drawn on ourselves, received from the Clearing House every day. Cheques are sorted into

Branches and into account number order for each Branch. . . . All Coutts Branches have adopted the Random Remittance system for their Out Clearings. In this system the cheques paid in by customers for the credit of their accounts are listed and agreed on specially adapted Olivetti Encoding machines, but further sorting into Clearing and other Banks and subsequent re-machining are not required. Instead, the cheques, in random order, are forwarded to the Clearing Department. There they are passed through the Reader-Sorter which sorts, lists and agrees them ready for distribution at the Clearing House. Cheques on non-clearing banks are also sorted on the machine. Not unnaturally, Coutts are proud of being the pioneers in the promotion and adoption of Random Remittance procedures, and full acknowledgement is made to the staff of the Head Office Clearing Department for their enthusiastic work which has placed the Bank in the forefront in this field.[8]

In 1972 the *Computer Weekly* could claim: 'In spite of the aura of the past at Coutts & Co., it has always been in the forefront of the introduction of modern devices.' In the next twenty years advances were made in the world of computers that revolutionised banking methods.

The new age demanded not only new techniques but also a new kind of organisation, with new attitudes and new relations between the directors and staff. Again Coutts & Co. adapted to the social changes.

After the Second World War neither the directors nor the staff were prepared to return to the autocratic rule that had characterised the first half of the century. The new directors returned to the old tradition of Coutts & Co. and were, unlike Caesar, accessible.

It was remembered that in the 1960s there was a changed attitude

between the Directors and the Senior Clerks in so far as the daily management of the Bank's affairs was concerned. This does not mean that the Directors had hitherto been unapproachable – far from it, but now, before election to the Board, a trainee Director spent at least three years working, lunching and sharing the discipline of the Staff. During that time he not only learned the complicated system in detail very thoroughly but came to know and assess the value of individual members of the Staff.

The daily routine was almost entirely in the hands of the Heads of Departments at 440 Strand and the Branch Managers, but these people were at regular intervals gathered together in the Board Room, addressed by the Chairman, informed of the Bank's policy and invited to enquire of almost any matter and to express views of common interest.

The Principal Officers and other Senior Officials were now openly expressing their opinions in a manner which would have been unthinkable in their early days. This was to lead in the second half of the decade to a complete reorganisation of the administration.[9]

By 1970 the National Westminster Bank had acquired so many subsidiaries, including Coutts & Co., that it was in danger of becoming unwieldy. It was time for a major reorganisation of the whole complex.

The Earl of Harrowby, who as Viscount Sandon was Deputy Chairman of Coutts & Co., looking back on that period considered that the face of banking at that time was changed dramatically by the Bank of England's introduction of Competition and Credit Control, which made banks compete. 'For the first time their shares became genuine equities with growth prospects and it led to many mergers.'[10]

It was clear that there must be a major review of policy and practice at Coutts & Co., especially in the light of the Westminster Bank's proposed merger with the National Provincial, which with Coutts & Co. would produce an even larger conglomerate.

In 1965 Associated Industrial Consultants had carried out for Coutts & Co. a major study of operating methods. Management consultancy was at this time an American concept and comparatively new in Britain and only accepted with some reservation especially by old-established firms. There were many who resented the intrusion of advisers and some who were to resent the changes; but Cockman remembered the AIC's visits without rancour:

The consultants wisely took cognisance of the tradition and service of the Bank; otherwise their report would have made very different reading. They set out, however, to examine in minute detail the tasks of each individual and department, calculated the man hours for almost every operation and the cost or profit attached to it. To many this might have appeared an irritating intrusion, but high praise is due to the manner in which it was conducted and to the thoughtful and considerate manner in which it was brought to a successful conclusion. It is significant that in the final outcome many of their proposals were accepted unanimously, while others, after lengthy consideration and debate, were rejected. Out of all this came a new and better understanding of our problems and a clearer picture of our future administration.[11]

In 1969 Coutts & Co., on the advice of NatWest, called in McKinsey & Co. to make proposals for 'organising for profitable growth'. Harrowby records that the parent bank had called in McKinsey & Co. prior to the merger in order

to fit them for the competitive future and it was very fortunate that they were in when the merger took place because they were able to give a great deal of guidance. . . . So many mergers end up with acrimony over individual's postings, individual's opportunities, and so forth. . . .[12]

Harrowby recalls the amalgamation of the Westminster with the National Provincial as being 'as smooth a merger as I know of personally'. This was because the joint top management appointed

two chief executives, one to put the Bank together and one to run the Bank. And the very wise personnel general manager, Mr Hopps, drew up the specifications, the job descriptions, job specification for each job, and then to a large extent left it to McKinseys to choose the top people, and that is why the Bank got away without a lot of in-fighting.[13]

McKinsey & Co. presented its report in February 1970. It analysed the position of Coutts & Co. and the need to make changes to meet the increasing pressure of the time. Banking, it stated, was becoming increasingly competitive: the Clearing Banks were beginning to be outstripped by the non-Clearing Banks, and within the group of Clearing Banks, Coutts & Co. was now at the bottom of the league.

Apart from the general constraints which affected all Clearing Banks, that is, costs rising faster than deposits and profitability dependent on the bank rate, Coutts & Co. had its own particular problems. Its high income customers were subject now to higher income tax. And the cost of the work of the Securities and Trustee Departments, according to the consultants, offset their higher-than-average balances. Like National Westminster, it too was now dependent on commercial business, but it was too small to get economies of any size in administration.

It was decided that in order to survive as an independent member of the group, Coutts & Co. must be as profitable as National Westminster and should show that it had a unique capability to serve a distinct section of the market. Coutts & Co. was almost as heavily involved in commercial business as the parent company. So how was Coutts & Co. to become more efficient and achieve a higher rate of growth? According to McKinsey it should target markets and provide new services. And, dread words, it should advertise. Sir George Marjoribanks must have turned in his grave.

Now the cold eye of the consultants turned its gaze on the salaries of the staff, which were, they stated, on average higher than those at National Westminster. Though they did not suggest cutting salaries, they did insist that in order to become more efficient, it would be necessary to have clearer accountability in all branches and a full-time cost reduction project.

To meet these needs four organisational changes were suggested. Firstly, top management should be encouraged to pay more attention to strategic planning. Then there should be greater individual profit accountability with a clear definition of responsibilities and a supporting information system. Thirdly, there must be close guidance and control of branch and service department managers by setting targets and measuring results, and fourthly, full-time cost reduction effort in branches and at head office.

In summary, the board of directors should

direct the Bank's affairs in the best long-term interest of the shareholder; while balancing the interests of staff, customers and the community in general. So it is they who should decide what kind of bank Coutts & Co. should be, how its assets should be mixed, and what market sectors should be targeted. The Board should set priorities, should concentrate on end results not operating detail. That should be the business of the single chief executive who should be fully accountable to the Board for results.

The business itself should be divided into five 'profit accountable' divisions – Branch Banking, Related Services, International Operations, Investment Operations and Coutts Finance.

In order to work effectively the Board and chief executives need to be supported by the analyses they need for strategic planning. This should be supplied by a department 'Business Development', just as 'Financial Control' should provide the regular information needed at each level.

Each staff group should be headed by a single executive reporting to the chief executive who should be fully accountable for planning his department and the resulting profit contribution or costs.[14]

They emphasised the importance of marketing and of communicating their aim to the staff through a regular review of progress. The first step, they insisted, in planning was the setting up of the 'Business Development' and 'Financial Control' groups. Then planning and control should be established by each manager agreeing his targets with his line superior. Finally, Coutts & Co. should make full use of the facilities of National Westminster in, for example, economic forecasting, training courses, property and cost reduction techniques. These proposals were accepted and changes made with a resulting potential 17 per cent increase in profitability, as estimated by McKinsey.

Not all the staff were enthusiastic about the reorganisation; there were those who felt that the aim of increasing profit for the shareholders now superseded the old tradition of service to the customer. Thomas Coutts had always given this priority, believing that whether financial profit followed or not, there were other kinds of profit just as valuable. But in many ways his banking practice would have gained the approval of McKinseys: his efficient organisation, clearly defined job specifications, the delegation of responsibility, were all in line with the consultants' recommendations. And none targeted his high profile customers with more skill or pursued them with more determination.

The review of the reorganisation of the Bank was timely because during the period of the investigation the directors were engaged in a long battle over the proposed new premises at 440 Strand. So the structure of management and the structure of the new building were discussed at the same time.

53

A Modern Image

Coutts & Co. entered the 1970s with an efficient modern organisation and an advanced computer system, but modern times demanded a modern image and a modern business needed more space.

In the past, John Campbell, George Middleton, Thomas Coutts and Angela Burdett-Coutts had been in turn the public face of Coutts & Co. Their reputation and prestige had gilded the reputation of the Bank and the building itself had been of less consequence. Indeed the ungarnished exterior of 59 Strand, with its hint of dust and cobwebs, had a certain cachet. Good wine had matured in that crusted old bottle.

Back in the 1950s the directors had realised that the 1904 building at 440 Strand would soon be inadequate and, in any case, their lease was due to expire in 1982. So in 1958 the decision was taken to build a new bank on the same site in the Strand. On 7 January 1959 Mr Fletcher Watson and Mr Leslie Chackett were appointed joint architects for the building, and so the marathon began. At the end of 1959 the architects produced four schemes for complete redevelopment, of which one, a plan for a sixteen-storey tower block, with a bell tower 230 feet high which would have towered above St Martin's-in-the-Fields, was smartly dismissed by the planning authorities.

Year after year the arguments continued, the architects producing thirty schemes which turned out to be unacceptable either to Coutts & Co. or to the London County Council. Part of the difficulty was the indecision at County Hall over the route of the planned new roads in the area – one of which was drawn to run straight through the triangle of land and thus through the middle of the Bank. Moreover, parts of the building were listed as of special historic interest, which meant that it was impossible to start with a clean slate. Then in 1965 an act was passed controlling the building of offices in London and requiring a licence – renewable yearly. Coutts & Co. applied for a permit, which was obtained in December 1965.

There followed four more years of delay; more schemes were submitted to solve the problem of the link road that the Council wanted to cut through the area. In vain the architects tried to accommodate the new road in their plans and, at the same time, to preserve the listed parts of the existing bank.

In 1961, while the directors were still battling over the plans for the Bank in the Strand, a new building at 15 Lombard Street was completed on the site of the old Robarts, Lubbock Bank. This was part of a larger building which included the Bankers' Clearing House, the Committee of London Clearing Bankers, the Institute of Bankers and the General Post Office. When the site was developed in 1938, the old Clearing House had been demolished, but on the outbreak of war in 1939 building was halted, and after the war scarcity of materials delayed the rebuilding of Coutts' Lombard Street premises until February 1958.

The new Lombard Street bank opened in the spring of 1961, and the first sight of the banking hall sent a shock wave through the City. Behind the conventional pseudo-Georgian exterior a stunning transformation had taken place. On 21 March the editor of the *Financial Times* reflected the general astonishment:

Bill-brokers showed genial bewilderment yesterday as they called with their wares for the first time at the new City office of Coutts. Well they might. The outside of the building at 15, Lombard Street – shared with the Bankers' Clearing House and other institutions – is, it is true, perfectly conventional pseudo-Georgian.

But the interior of Coutts' premises, designed by Mr. Lionel Brett, must have the most exotic decor that the brokers (or I) have ever seen in a bank or perhaps anywhere else outside the Brighton Pavilion or the late Cecil B. de Mille's visions of medieval Baghdad.

From the entrance you go through an almost oppressively low-ceilinged lift vestibule, done mainly in peacock blue. Then, suddenly, you emerge into the main banking hall. You are in a tall colonnade of golden arches interspersed with silver, culminating in a statue of founder Thomas Coutts, bathed in light as he sits in Byronic pose.

Outside the colonnade to your left, over a large open floor, the clerks sit at their desks in the traditional Coutts frock-coats, with a mahogany staircase rising behind them to a peacock blue gallery where there are more clerks.

Plainly, bank architecture will never be quite the same again. I for one applaud Coutts' adventurous spirit. But Coutts' City office manager, 64-year-old Mr. Charles Adcock, who has been with the bank for 46 years, still did not seem quite convinced yesterday of the aesthetic advantages of modernity.

The architect of this fantasy was the Hon. Lionel Brett, who explained his aim:

The basic idea of the design was that it should contain 18th century sculpture, 19th century furniture and frock coats and 20th century television sets and computing machines without dating or incongruity. The plan is therefore a classical axial one centred on a cast of the Chantrey statue of Thomas Coutts.[1]

Adcock, who was at this time the City Office Manager at 15 Lombard Street, loyally explained the architect's problem. He had to reconcile, he wrote, 'the traditional frock-coat with the year 1961. The basis of the design must be timeless, a mixture between the old and the new. We have tried to replace the drab Victoriana of the old building and yet at the same time be austere.'[2]

Adcock may have had his doubts, but the technical innovations at 15 Lombard Street impressed the City:

Coutts are only the second of the new City banking offices to install television. The camera of the television is on the second floor in the Ledger Department.

There are four screens in different parts of the building. And when the managers, or senior members of the staff, wish to check upon the account or creditworthiness of a customer, they telephone the ledger department, where the appropriate document is placed inside the top of the boxlike camera.[3]

There were many in the City who remembered Sir John Lubbock and who were pleased to see his statue, a bronze copy of the original, at the entrance. But it was the copy of Chantrey's statue of Thomas Coutts that looked down a long avenue of tall golden arches and dominated the banking hall.

It was Julian Robarts, a descendant of Abraham Robarts, who, in 1960, had laid the foundation-stone. 'It is curious', Cockman recalled, 'that the foundation-stone of 15 Lombard Street building, which was to be pulled down in 1958, was laid by Mr A. J. Robarts. In 1960 his great-grandson of the same initials laid the foundation-stone of the present building – and what a change from the previous frowsty place with its wooden plank floor.'[4]

There must have been some smug smiles of satisfaction at 15 Lombard Street that their new building had been so expeditiously finished. Meanwhile at the Strand the battle over the plans still raged.

Finally, in 1969, the directors parted amicably with their architects – all parties had now exhausted ideas and patience. Fletcher Watson retired and Frederick Gibberd & Partners were appointed, who proceeded with great energy and inspiration. Sir Frederick Gibberd's design, presented to the directors in the spring of 1970, was accepted.

Planning permission was applied for in April 1970, but four months later was refused, since the Greater London Council still demanded that a link road should run through the site. The idea of Coutts & Co. cut in two by a main road and spanned by a bridge appalled the directors, who appealed. The planning enquiry was held at County Hall on 31 March 1971, Sir Derek Walker Smith appearing for the Bank with Mr E. Vaughan-Neil as his junior. The Inspector ruled that the Bank's appeal should be upheld, but asked for detailed plans to be submitted which should include a pedestrian subway through the building. On 6 January 1972, Peter Walker, Secretary of State for the Environment, gave permission for the plans to be put into effect. Planning permission was finally granted in November 1973 and demolition began a year later. As Julian Robarts wryly recorded, the appeal cost the Bank around £150,000.

While the new building was in progress the 'branch' moved across the road back to the old address at No. 59, which luckily fell vacant at that time. The head office and archive department were moved to 1 Suffolk Street and the archives themselves to the National Westminster Bank at Lombard Street, where they had adequate strongrooms. Once more the staff faced the problems of moving and storing valuable treasures and documents. The Chinese wallpaper, which had once before been moved from Thomas Coutts's old apartments at 59 Strand to 440, was now carefully taken down again and restored, to be later skilfully replaced in the new boardroom.

The present archivist, Barbara Peters, remembers the difficulties of the move, which her predecessor, Veronica Stokes, organised and which gave them many a headache:

The overwhelming memories, for me, of the move in 1973 are heat and dirt. As part of head office the archives department was to move to Suffolk Street; no office move is trouble free but ours was simple when compared to the move of the archives and museum items. Everything from the prints on the walls to the contents, largely unknown, of obscure cupboards down in the bowels of the Strong Rooms had to be found a home – and everything but everything had to be *packed*!

Most of us have experienced at least one house move – picture our problem, a massive triangular 'house' with not just seventy years' accumulation of papers and 'things' but 270 years' worth. The transfer of items from the Muniment Room to safe storage at 21 Lombard Street was easy, neatly packaged and labelled boxes went effortlessly into tea chests; not so the contents of drawers and cupboards which had lain undisturbed, undusted and undiscovered since 1904. I remember the month of May in particular, it was unseasonably hot and I made an effort to get into work really early so that I could do a lot of the 'heavy' work before the real heat of the day. I spent what felt like years wrapping Victorian leather-bound Signature Books etc., their covers disintegrating into fine red dust. I sometimes wondered if I would ever be clean again. Many of the cupboards, like those below the display cases in the banking hall, had lost their keys so we became adept at forcing locks (a skill that was to prove very useful ten years on). On more than one occasion when we finally broke the lock the doors would burst open with the accumulated weight of the bundles of old documents, so carefully brought across from 59 Strand.

The department was situated at 449 Strand at this time, consequently we were amongst the last to vacate the West Strand site. I remember wandering through the deserted bank, my footsteps echoing back at me from the walls and ceilings. We had stripped out as many Edwardian fittings as we could as well as the counter and older items, but we had to leave behind the Voucher Room with its spiral staircase, beautifully fashioned curved cupboards in the gallery with their bone labels and in the depths a faint aroma of sherry. In the banking hall the display cases that had housed many an exhibition of archives under Mr Brooke-Caws and Veronica Stokes looked shabby and rather forlorn. One vivid picture stays in my mind to this day – one of Rogers & Co.'s men manhandling the Chantrey statue of Thomas Coutts down from his pedestal through the impressive Main Screen that divided the 'Shop' from the offices beyond and out into the sunlight of Adelaide Street.[5]

When the new building was completed, it aroused quite strong feelings. In an unusually intemperate and unjust article, the *Guardian* described the entrance as 'like some second-rate three-star hotel' and the pool in the garden court as a 'small pool of stagnant water in which float fag ends'.[6] But *The Times* praised the 'distinguished solution to a present-day planning problem',[7] and many agreed that the sense of space and light was 'exhilarating'. Whatever critics might say of the entrance to the Bank, it was impossible to deny the success of the banking hall in the garden court. The best proof was the speed with which other business houses followed the example of this, the first atrium building in London.

Indoor gardens in public buildings are now commonplace, but at this time there were many problems to be solved concerning the cultivation of trees, shrubs and plants in an artificial environment. However, Sir Frederick Gibberd, himself an enthusiastic gardener, enjoyed the challenge. In the pool, recessed areas were designed to give the carp shelter from the constant light. Full-grown trees were imported from Italy and Belgium, and planted in tubs, one of which revolves by electricity to ensure vertical growth. Trees and shrubs are watered by a trickle irrigation system with specially de-ionised water, and the climate is controlled by computer. It was an imaginative and original blend of modern technology with graceful gardening.

Now, after fourteen years the garden has grown lush and leafy. Ivy trails over the balconies, softening the marble and concrete. The white-stemmed *Ficus Nitrida* has grown to a great height at the entrance and the olive tree flourishes by the pool. Here customers can rest on comfortable seats and, watching the gliding carp, forget for the moment their financial concerns. Chantrey would have been delighted that his statue of Thomas Coutts takes the place of honour.

Thomas Coutts too would have been glad to be for ever remembered in a garden in his Bank.

Sparkling and modern though the new bank was, there were reminders of the past in the banking hall. Around the walls were portraits of the men who had played a part in the history of Coutts & Co. An old desk which probably belonged to Harriot, brought from 59 Strand, and one of the old mahogany counters, linked the new with the old.

Showcases were designed to be placed in the garden court and on the fourth floor, where old letters, memorabilia and treasures were displayed. The small exhibitions, frequently changed, are of riveting interest, reminding customers of the deep roots and traditions of Coutts & Co.

There have been many particularly memorable displays bringing to life past wars: the Crimean War, with portraits of customers such as Lord Lucan, Alfred Lord Tennyson and William Howard Russell, and the American War of Independence, including contemporary letters from America and tobacco leaves and the Bank's small collection of snuffboxes. Other exhibitions recalled both world wars and the RFC and RAF as seen by the clerks of Coutts & Co. One of the most charming exhibits was the illustrated diary of a bank clerk, Nieman Smith, who with his friends spent the new bank holidays on long walking tours.

Some exhibitions have dealt with interesting customers like Lord Elgin, who brought the Greek marbles to Britain; Sir Walter Scott; the philosopher, David Hume – friend of James and Thomas Coutts; and the artist, Allan Ramsay. In one showcase were the sad relics of Joseph Roman, who, having spent his life in the service of the East India Company, died within days of landing in England. His personal effects were left with the Bank with his household accounts and details of his last illness and funeral. The little collection of his portrait, seal, watch, spectacles, Indian gold coins and heavy Spanish pillar dollars is poignant and evocative of the period and the man.

There have been displays of priceless, delicate objects: a painted fan, the elaborate Valentine card sent by the Duke of St Albans to Harriot, a pretty cameo and diamond ring, Susannah Coutts's cosmetic box, her daughter's ivory card case, and the gold snuffbox given to Andrew Dickie by King Louis Philippe.

Over the years customers and staff have given or bequeathed many fascinating objects and documents, enough to fill a museum. These, together with the vast collection of documents in the archives, make a treasure that is beyond price.

Other customers' valuables have been discovered in the Bank's *Oubliettes*. Barbara Peters describes one treasure hunt at Coutts & Co.:

Space is always a problem in central London and our Strong Rooms were no exception, added to which the Bank had over a number of years been considering the tricky question of Customer *Oubliette*, i.e. items deposited by customers in Safe Custody and then simply forgotten. In 1985 the Bank finally decided to act and appointed James Gillespie (ex-inspector and ex-Archives department) to tackle the matter. His job would be to find out what the relevant boxes/envelopes/plate chests etc. contained and then track down the current legal heir/heirs. This was not as simple as it might appear because the items form part of an individual's residuary estate, which means that the hunt has to be via wills rather than following straightforward descendants.

The directors took the decision that if no legal heirs could be found, the items were to be passed to the care of the Archivist and could be used for display and research purposes. At *no time* has the Bank considered the *Oubliette* to be the possession of the Bank; it is held as a completely separate collection.

Several thousand items (an item being anything from a single document to several plate chests) were opened and a vast range of material uncovered. In terms of bulk, papers were to form the largest group; a few examples will suffice – manuscript books of music composed by an eighteenth-century Italian court musician, letters from J. J. Rousseau, the complete archive of a general trader out of St Petersburg at the turn of the eighteenth and nineteenth centuries, details of the British hospitals in North America during the War of Independence and household accounts from India.

We did not find any real skeletons though I am sure that in time the boxes of papers will throw up some metaphorical ones! Apart from papers the boxes included such things as large quantities of silver, twenty-four gold dinner plates, diamond necklaces, sapphire tiaras, Indian miniatures and an early nineteenth-century guitar.

Amongst the most intriguing are the more bizarre finds – seven adult teeth, each one individually housed in a small pouch; the nails from a loved wife's coffin; a pair of black silk stockings left in an eighteenth-century hotel bedroom; and last but not least half a pound of government margarine as issued during the Second World War. We have our own theory about the last item: it was found securely wrapped and sealed in the Jewel Room and, not believing that *anyone* would deposit such a thing, we assumed it contained uncut diamonds or something similar; consequently we carefully 'spread' the margarine (it had kept very well) out on to a large sheet of newspaper hoping with every move of the knife to find a hard rough lump. Nothing, absolutely nothing! It later came to light that the Trustee under whose name the parcel had been deposited had left the UK to seek the warmer climes of South America.[8]

Coutts & Co. was now splendidly housed. After twenty years of frustration, the dream had become reality.

On 14 December 1978 Queen Elizabeth II stood by the statue of Thomas Coutts in the garden court of the banking hall and declared the new building open. In welcoming Her Majesty, the Chairman, David Money-Coutts, reminded his audience that his ancestor had been made a Gentleman of the Privy Chamber by King George III:

As he sits there now on his pedestal looking down at us I hope that he is proud that the great-great-great-great-granddaughter of his most important customer should be opening this new building at a time when both the Deputy Chairman and the Chairman, Lord Sandon and myself, are *his* great-great-great-great-grandsons.[9]

The Queen replied:

Mr Chairman,

With all those 'greats' on both sides, I do indeed agree that this is very much a family occasion. Members of my family, for generations, have had to acknowledge the wisdom and prudence of the advice they have received from Coutts . . . even if they have not *always* been grateful for it.

Advice is however always easier to accept if it is delivered with that old-fashioned courtesy for which this institution is renowned – and backed up by authority and expertise. That combination of courtesy and business efficiency is symbolised in this building – whose old walls encase this new Central Hall, and every modern aid.[10]

After the opening David Money-Coutts wrote a message to the Bank in its magazine, *The Three Crowns*:

I am writing this sitting in one of the Pepperpots and it seems hard to believe that, after so many years of frustration and effort, we have completed the rebuilding of 440 Strand, but finish it we have. Those who are in it now enjoy excellent working conditions and I sense that we all take pride in our new home – as we did in the honour of having it opened by The Queen.

1979 does not promise to be an easy year. As I write we face road haulage and rail strikes and have been grappling with the coldest winter for some fifteen years. These difficulties challenge our ingenuity and resolve, and it is easy to allow them to wear us down if they go on too long, but they do also bring out a characteristic of good humour in adversity and, when they are over, we get much satisfaction from having overcome them.

One of the main tasks of the year will be implementing the decision to transfer our clearing and data-processing work to our parent bank. This was not an easy decision, nor will the implementation of it be easy, but I do believe that, in the end, we will be glad to have taken it. There is no intention, nor is there any need, for it to affect the quality of our service to our customers and it certainly will improve Group profits and so give us renewed strength to face the future.

We can now look to 1979 and the years beyond with the confidence that we have a role to play in providing a quality service to the top end of the banking market, both personal and corporate, that we have a principal office suited to that task and that we will have the means to provide that service at an acceptable cost.[11]

The new premises would provide the right background for the achievement of this double aim. There was no doubt that Coutts & Co. could only survive in the shadow of the vast conglomeration, National Westminster, by offering a quality service to a specialised clientele.

But above all the Chairman, directors and staff faced a daunting challenge as they settled into their new bank at 440 Strand. How could they maintain in a world of electronics that special 'ethos' that had distinguished Coutts & Co. over the past centuries, a quality difficult to describe but deeply felt by all who have worked there?

As with the adoption of computers, Coutts & Co. had not only accepted change, it had anticipated it, and before 1992 it had prepared for a new role in the wider world.

54

Coutts & Co.
in the Global Village

As the Chairman and directors stood beside the Queen at the opening of the Bank in the Strand they could indeed look to the future with confidence. The new building presented a handsome, modern face to the world. Her Majesty's presence was a powerful reminder of more than two centuries of royal patronage and of the stability and confidence created by long tradition. Coutts & Co. had come surprisingly well through a difficult decade. In the 1970s its rebuilding and reorganisation had coincided with a period of industrial unrest and of financial crises at home and abroad, which can only be briefly outlined here.

The economic crisis of 1973 had been followed by the miners' strike and the three-day week, which brought down Edward Heath's Conservative Government in February 1974. The advent of a Labour Government with no overall majority under Harold Wilson alarmed the City and caused a spectacular drop in share prices. It was an unsettled year, since a second election was called in October, at which Labour gained a majority of just three seats.

The massive jump in oil prices, engineered by OPEC, had begun to dislocate the world economy. Britain's own North Sea oil had only started to come on stream in November. Inflation soared worldwide and so did pay rises in Britain, since Heath's Government had indexed them to prices. As Chancellor Denis Healey said, 1974 saw 'a madman's merry-go-round of inflation'[1] and Coutts & Co., like other banks, suffered from the resulting bad and doubtful debts. In September 1975 the TUC agreed to accept a voluntary pay restraint, limiting pay rises to £6. Wilson resigned in March 1976 and was succeeded by James Callaghan, who faced a deepening economic crisis culminating in the collapse of the pound in September 1976. A £2.3 billion loan from the International Monetary Fund restored confidence and almost immediately the economy began to improve. As Healey recorded, 'the pound grew stronger month by month. Interest rates began to fall even faster than we wanted.'² Only half the IMF loan was drawn and that was paid back in 1978.

The economy improved and many of the Bank's bad debts were recovered, but industrial relations worsened. The trade unions had accepted three years of pay restraint, but when the Government tightened the screw still further, limiting pay increases to 5 per cent, a fuse was lit that exploded in the bitter 'winter of discontent'.

The Labour Government fell on 3 May 1979 and the Conservatives, led by Mrs Margaret Thatcher, won the election and were to remain in power for more than a decade.

The 1980s were a decade of great turbulence, framed at its beginning and end by two major wars, in the Falklands in 1982 and in the Gulf in 1990. In Britain it was a period of urban riots and demonstrations and, in 1984, a twelve-week miners' strike with violent confrontation between police and miners. The IRA kept up its murderous campaign in Northern Ireland and on the mainland and in October 1984 killed and wounded leaders of the Conservative Party in a bomb attack on the Brighton hotel where they were staying for their annual conference.

Nevertheless, Britain was swept up, as well as down, on the roller-coaster of the 1980s. At home, the Conservative Government was strengthened by the bonus of North Sea oil, which added £62 billion to the Government's revenues in its first nine years as well as massive assistance to Britain's balance of payments. In 1986 and 1987 a boom in the property market brought a phenomenal rise in house prices, affecting modest home owners and property moguls alike, and creating a sense of euphoria and prosperity which lasted until the down-turn came with the collapse of the property market in 1990.

In spite of wars and disasters the 1980s were a period that gave hope to the world. The arrival of Mikhail Gorbachev in the Kremlin brought a breakthrough in East-West relations and an end to the Cold War. In November 1989 the symbol of the old divisions, the Berlin Wall, was suddenly demolished. A wave of excitement swept Eastern Europe, as one country after another threw off its communist shackles. Freedom, however, brought new problems, and euphoria gradually diminished as reviving nationalism aroused old enmities. No one before had attempted to make the transformation from a communist to a capitalist economy – to turn an omelette into an egg, as they began to say in Moscow.

In the Far East, the Agreement signed between the United Kingdom and China for the return of Hong Kong, followed by the massacre of Tiananmen Square, created considerable nervousness in the financial world.

The oil crisis of the early 1970s had been the prologue to a period of fundamental change in the economies of the world. Oil producers had funds to lend which the Third World countries were desperate to borrow through the commercial banks where they were deposited. As a result, countries like Mexico, Brazil and Argentina borrowed so deeply that they could never hope to service their debts, let alone repay them.

The oil and debt crises were only part of a revolution which was shaking the whole world economy. The introduction of computers and information technology had produced a single global financial market, making it possible to move billions of dollars in microseconds twenty-four hours a day. It was a world in which John Law would have been completely at home, but in which small private banks like Coutts & Co. might have been swamped had it not been for the financial and technological backing of the powerful NatWest Bank.

For all the euphoria of the 1980s this was a very destabilising period for financial markets. Deregulation, which allowed financial institutions to invade each other's markets, culminating in 'Big Bang', which threw stock markets open to all in 1986, led to much fiercer competition, and off-the-shelf computer programmes made entry to the banking market much easier for newcomers. 'Black Monday', the worldwide collapse of stock markets in October 1987, was an inevitable consequence of 'Big Bang' and inflated markets. It paved the way to a worldwide recession which brought the collapse of the Savings and Loan institutions in the USA. Meanwhile many of the US banks were under great strain and some collapsed through unwise investment.

At the same time, lower tax rates and the removal of exchange control regulations around the world had made it possible for more individuals to accumulate wealth and to spread their risk by investing it in different countries. With interest margins squeezed by the growth in competition, the accounts of these wealthy individuals and the fee income they could generate suddenly became more attractive to the banks. This created an opportunity for a private bank like Coutts, with the benefit of its own long traditions and the security provided by its membership of the National Westminster Bank Group. In October 1990, in recognition of the growing importance of cross-border banking, NatWest and Coutts decided to strengthen their representation in this international field. Coutts & Co. had already opened subsidiaries in Geneva, the Isle of Man and Nassau; and NatWest provided off-shore banking, trustee and investment services, and company management, through NatWest International Trust Corporation. NatWest also owned HandelsBank, a major private Swiss bank with branches in Geneva, Zurich and Chiasso. In October 1990 NatWest decided to bring all these international operations together to form a new group under the name of Coutts & Co. 'The new group', it was explained, 'will provide our customers with worldwide asset management and private banking from over 30 offices in 13 jurisdictions: England; Guernsey; Jersey; Isle of Man; Gibraltar; Switzerland; Singapore; Hong Kong; Tokyo; USA; Bahamas; Cayman Islands; and Uruguay.'[3]

David Money-Coutts, as Chairman of the new Coutts & Co. Group, aimed to maintain Coutts's high standards, stressing that they did not intend

to grow beyond a size at which we are able to continue to deliver existing standards of service. As the distinct private banking arm of the NatWest Group, we aim to exploit the strength of that Group's resources, whilst retaining the character of a much smaller private bank.[4]

It is a far cry from John Campbell's goldsmith's shop. Yet the principles which helped to create the Coutts ethos are the same. Campbell travelled to Norwich's cattle fair to meet the Scottish drovers and his farming customers. Sir David Money-Coutts jets across the globe to make and keep good personal relationships, especially important in the age of impersonal electronic communication. Thomas Coutts, who travelled through Europe listening and making influential friends, established links which have endured, and Angela Burdett-Coutts, whose interests spanned the globe, would have relished the new international venture. The Coutts brothers of Montrose, who sailed across their seventeenth-century world, would doubtless have drunk a deep dram in celebration.

Expansion abroad made it even more important to keep Coutts's distinctive quality at home. For in its long history it had often seen financial hurricanes strike out of a clear blue sky and uproot even the stoutest oaks. A series of natural and manmade disasters on both sides of the Atlantic have severely strained insurance companies – even historic institutions like Lloyds have suffered. It is now that deep roots are of the greatest value.

It was important to avoid the mistakes of other banks in England and America who moved into areas they did not understand and had to be rescued by government intervention. The directors of Coutts & Co. decided to continue, as they had done for 300 years, to concentrate on 'providing private banking of quality to the "high net worth" customer'.[5]

'Private banking' had always meant the private ownership of banks by their partners. Hoare's in London, Brown Brothers Harriman in New York and Lombard Odier in Geneva were private banks in that sense. But, as David Money-Coutts wrote, the term has now 'come to mean the delivery of financial services in a particular style to customers whose needs are not only more sophisticated, but are also constantly changing'.[6] The 'style', as he emphasised, is of importance, but the frock-coats and the traditional courtesy are only the outward signs of a bank that cares 'about relationships and the quality of understanding of individual needs'.[7] This is only possible in a small bank that limits the number of its customers.

Style alone has not produced the special Coutts ethos, which is quickly recognised but difficult to define. In Thomas Coutts's day, that astute observer, the Reverend William Bagshaw Stevens, had noted that '*Esse quam videre*', 'To be rather than to seem', was the motto of Mr Coutts. 'Being' meant identifying their principles and philosophy, and it is significant that, whereas other businesses might speak of their policy, at Coutts & Co. they refer to their 'philosophy'. David Money-Coutts explained it:

First, the commitment stems from the top.

Secondly, the way in which the organisation treats its own staff will directly influence the way in which they, in turn, will treat their customers.

Thirdly, I believe that senior management must be freely accessible to staff and managers alike – and by the same token to customers when so required.[8]

There is no doubt that the emphasis on good human relations between staff and management is partly a legacy from Angela Burdett-Coutts; certainly it has been felt by staff and customers for at least a century. Again and again they have emphasised in their memoirs that at Coutts they felt that they belonged to a family.

Julian Robarts and David Money-Coutts have conscientiously worked to foster this sense of family, keeping constantly in touch with staff at all levels, not only attending their office celebrations but also showing a genuine interest in and knowledge of their personal problems. A visiting French author was astonished that the Chairman of the Bank did not send down his secretary to meet him but came down himself; and particularly noticed his friendly relationship with the staff as they walked through the Bank.

Osbert Sitwell called it a 'bank with a soul'. But in the harsh world of finance, 'soul' is not enough. 'To provide services in that manner', as David Money-Coutts wrote, 'is expensive.' He believes the Bank

indeed can be more profitable than in the past for various reasons.

First, in their efforts to reduce costs and to serve the mass market the bigger banks have destroyed most of the personality of their service.

Second, computer technology can now provide information in a way which both reduces costs and enhances services.

Third, customers are better off than they have been for a long time and are now willing to pay more for a service that gives them added benefit – true private banking.[9]

The principles which have guided Coutts & Co. through the centuries are, in his opinion, 'The key elements of a private banking relationship . . . trust, professionalism and understanding.'[10]

'A Snob Bank', 'paternalistic', so say the critics of Coutts & Co. – with some truth. The Chairman, however, claims that 'we are not snobs, though some of our customers are'. But, if it were only that, the Bank would not have survived for 300 years, nor would it have retained the lifetime service and devotion of so many of its staff throughout three centuries and the patronage of so many distinguished customers.

The chief secret of its success lies, as it has always done, in good human relations. 'I do not treat my apprentices as they do in Scotland,' goldsmith John Campbell had said in the early eighteenth century, 'but as gentlemen's sons ought to be treated.'

Successful banking, after all, depends on mutual trust and confidence between directors, staff and customers. It also depends on the competence and the discipline set up by that 'exact' man, Thomas Coutts, which was transmitted through the centuries by a series of exceptional managers from Andrew Dickie and George Robinson to men like Frederick Shannon and Charles Musk.

Thomas Coutts left other legacies which have survived today: the value of meeting the customer on his home ground, whether in Britain or abroad, the importance of understanding world affairs and the readiness to seize opportunities.

Each generation added its own contribution. Angela Burdett-Coutts encouraged the partners to take care of the welfare of the staff, and to regard service to the community as part of their duty. This remains one of the Bank's principles emphasised by the Chairman today. She encouraged enterprise and foresight, quoting her father's phrase, 'man's eyes were given him to look forward', a precept which Coutts and Co. put into practice when it progressed into the electronic age and moved into the international field.

But, in spite of technological advance, banking will be in the future as it has essentially been in the past, deeply dependent on human beings, on their energy and enterprise and, above all, on the trust and confidence they inspire.

Let one of its famous customers have the last word on Messrs Coutts and Co. In his autobiography Osbert Sitwell wrote:

When businesses were content to lose everything except their profits, this great institution kept its soul alive. Throughout three centuries, those who work in it have maintained the same name for personal kindness and personal contact and, no doubt for that reason, have numbered among their clients many grateful artists and writers. In a day when it seems popular to attack the present methods of banking, I must state my opinion and experience, and add that, to my belief, there is more of character and rectitude, enterprise and independence contained in this one ancient house than in the whole of the attacking body. Not only the chiefs, but every one of Messrs Coutts' clerks and employees, understands and takes pride in its traditions.[11]

Partners and Directors of the Bank

1. John Campbell, 1692–1712
2. George Middleton, 1708–47
3. George Campbell, 1727–60
4. David Bruce, 1744–51
5. James Coutts, 1755–75
6. Thomas Coutts, 1761–1822
7. Adam Drummond, 1775–80
8. Edmund Antrobus, 1777–1826
9. John Antrobus, 1783–94
10. Coutts Trotter, 1793–1837
11. Edward Marjoribanks, 1798–1868
12. Edmund Antrobus junior, 1816–70
13. Mrs Harriot Coutts, 1822–37
14. Andrew Dickie, 1827–34   [Clerk]
15. William Matthew Coulthurst, 1827–77
16. Edward Marjoribanks junior, 1838–77
17. Hugh Lindsay Antrobus, 1843–99
18. Edmund Coulthurst, 1857–77
19. Hon. Henry D. Ryder (*later* 4th Earl of Harrowby), 1865–1900
20. George Robinson, 1869–86   [Clerk]
21. Lord Archibald Campbell (Argyll), 1873–1907
22. Sir George John Marjoribanks, KVCO, 1877–1931   [Chairman]
23. Robert Ruthven Pym, 1878–93
24. William Rolle Malcolm, 1878–1923   [Chairman]
25. Robert Lindsay Antrobus, 1878–91
26. John H. Dudley Ryder (*later* 5th Earl of Harrowby), 1887–1948
27. FitzRoy J. W. Farquhar, 1894–6
28. Ronald Malcolm, 1896–1946   [Chairman]
29. Hugh Burdett Money-Coutts (*later* 6th Lord Latymer), 1899–1914
30. F. W. Stephenson, 1902–44
31. Charles A. Phillimore, 1904–35
32. Major J. W. A. Drummond, 1914–26

In August 1914, on the amalgamation with Robarts, Lubbock & Co., the following partners in that firm became managing partners of Coutts & Co.:

33. Abraham J. Robarts, 1914–26
34. John Birkbeck, 2nd Lord Avebury, 1914–29
35. John Robarts, 1914–54
36. Frank Chaplin, 1914–47

Directors subsequently elected:

37. Gerald Robarts, 1920–31
38. Colin F. Campbell (*later* Lord Colgrain), 1920–54
39. Charles G. Hamilton, OBE, 1920–53
40. Hon. Sir Jasper N. Ridley, KVCO, OBE, 1921–51   [Chairman]
41. Sir Alfred E. Dunphie, KVCO, 1926–38   [Clerk]
42. Hon. Thomas B. Money-Coutts (*later* 7th Lord Latymer), 1927–72
43. Hon. George F. H., 2nd Marquess of Cambridge, 1929–51
44. David John Robarts, 1931–76
45. Colin Ronald Malcolm, 1935–59
46. Henry Brougham Loch, 1945–50   [Clerk]
47. Sir Seymour John Louis Egerton, GCVO, 1947–85   [Chairman]
48. Dudley D. G. C. Ryder, (*later* 7th Earl of Harrowby, TD), 1948–89
49. The Rt Hon. Granville J., Earl Granville, MC, 1950–65
50. Sir John Lindsay Eric Smith, CBE, 1951–
51. The Rt Hon. Ralph, Lord Clitheroe, PC, 1955–71
52. Albert C. E. Musk, MVO, 1955–73   [Clerk]
53. Sir Kenneth Oswald Peppiatt, KBE, MC, 1958–69
54. Sir David Burdett Money-Coutts, KCVO, 1958–
        [Chairman from 1976]
55. Sir John Rupert Colville, CB, CVO, 1960–80
56. Anthony Julian Robarts, 1963–
57. David Victor Bonsor, 1963–80
58. Lord James C. Crichton-Stuart, 1964–82
59. Charles John Leslie Hibberd, CVO, 1966–74   [Clerk]
60. Richard Alfred Robertson, 1968–71   [Clerk]
61. Hon. Michael Albemarle Bowes-Lyon, 1969–
62. Hon. Richard G. Lyon-Dalberg-Acton, 1970–4
63. Alastair Campbell Davidson, 1972–80   [Clerk]
64. George Dawson Burnett, 1972–80
65. Peter Leslie Boulton, 1973–80   [Clerk]
66. John Francis Acheson, 1974–85   [Clerk]
67. Thomas McMillan 1978–85
68. David Buxton, 1978–89   [Clerk]
69. Sir Philip William Wilkinson, 1980–2

70. David Cameron Macdonald, 1980–
71. Carel Maurits Mosselmans, TD, 1981–
72. John Roderick Cunningham, 1982–7   [Clerk]
73. Denis Marsden Child, CBE, 1985–
74. Gerald Cavendish Grosvenor, 6th Duke of Westminster, 1985
75. Gerald Anthony Davies, 1986–   [Clerk]
76. Roger Flemington, 1986–
77. Hon. Nicholas Assheton, 1987–
78. Stuart Walter Marshall, 1989–   [Clerk]
79. Geoffrey Thomas Spencer, 1989–90   [Clerk]
80. Edward William Barron (alternate for R. Flemington), 1989–90
81. John Tugwell, 1990–1
82. Bernard Philip Horn, 1991–
83. Ian Ross Farnsworth (alternate for B. P. Horn), 1991–

Source Notes

1: At the Sign of the Three Crowns, London 1692
1. Lord Macaulay, *The History of England* (ed. T. F. Henderson); 2. Dorothy Middleton, *The Life of Charles, Second Earl of Middleton 1650–1719*; 3–4. Macaulay, *op. cit.*

2: Scotland 1692: Edinburgh, Aberdeen and Montrose
1–2. Daniel Defoe, *A Tour through the Whole Island of Great Britain*; 3–4. *Aberdeen Journal*, Notes and Queries, vol. I (Aberdeen University Library, 1908); 5. Defoe, *op. cit.*; 6. *Aberdeen Journal, op. cit.*; 7. Provost Thomas of Montrose's speech, August 1913, quoted in the booklet, 'The Coutts Room', Montrose Old Kirk Museum; 8. Montrose Burgh Minutes

3: John Campbell: Goldsmith Banker
1. Sir William Forbes, *Memoirs of a Banking House*; 2–3. Daniel Defoe, *Essay on Projects*, chapter 'On Banking'; 4–5. Veronica Stokes on John Campbell, 'Scotch Mist & London Fog', *The Three Crowns*, Coutts & Co. staff magazine; 6. Coutts & Co. Archives, Barbara Peters, unpublished description of exhibition model; 7–13. Coutts & Co. Archives; 14. Lockhart Papers, ii 10, quoted in *Dictionary of National Biography*, vol. VIII, p. 372; 15. John Macky, *Memoirs of the Secret Services of John Macky, Esq* (1733); 16. Forbes, *op. cit.*; 17. Coutts & Co. Archives; 18. Note from Professor Roseveare to the author, 1991; 19–35. Coutts & Co. Archives

4: Early Banking: Enterprise and Adventure
1. Bank of Scotland Archives, Adven-turers Ledger; 2–3. Quoted in John Prebble, *The Darien Disaster*

5: Middleton and the Jacobites
1–7. Coutts & Co. Archives

6: The Fiery Trial
1. H. Montgomery Hyde, *The Amazing Story of John Law*; 2–3. Adolphe Thiers, *The Mississippi Bubble – A Memoir of John Law*; 4. Mary Wortley Montagu, *Letters 1709–1762*; 5–6. Thiers, *op. cit.*; 7. Voltaire, quoted in *ibid*; 8–21. Coutts & Co. Archives; 22–4. Thiers, *op. cit.*; 25–49. Coutts & Co. Archives; 50. Unidentified MP; 51–69. Coutts & Co. Archives; 70. Montgomery Hyde, *op. cit.*; 71–7. Coutts & Co. Archives; 78. Thiers, *op. cit.*; 79–109. Coutts & Co. Archives

7: Middleton: Quiet Journey's End
1–5. Coutts & Co. Archives; 6. Royal Bank of Scotland Archives, 6 December 1745; 7. Royal Bank of Scotland Archives, Court of Directors of the Royal Bank of Scotland, Friday, 22 November 1745; 8. *Ibid.*, pp. 298/299, Friday, 28 November 1746; 9. *Ibid.*, p. 310, Friday, 27 February 1747; 10–14. Coutts & Co. Archives; 15. Thiers, *op. cit.*, p. 210

8: Provost John Coutts of Edinburgh
1–2. Forbes, *op. cit.*, p. 10; 3. Duncan Fraser, *Montrose before 1700*; 4–6. Forbes, *op. cit.*; 7–8. Coutts & Co. Archives; 9. S. G. Checkland, *Scottish Banking, A History 1695–1973*; 10. Antrobus MSS; 11. Royal Archives, Windsor, RA 10234, 9 June 1801; 12. Coutts & Co. Archives; 13.

National Library of Scotland, 11004, f. 68; 14–15. Royal Bank of Scotland Archives, Minutes of the Court of Directors, 4 September 1745, f. 223; 16–18. Royal Bank of Scotland Archives, John Campbell, *Leaves from the Diary of an Edinburgh Banker*, p. 1; 19–20. Minutes of the Court of Directors, ff. 225, 227; 21–2. Campbell, *op. cit.*, pp. 18, 19; 23–5. Minutes of the Court of Directors, ff. 233, 234, 235; 26–9. National Library of Scotland, 11003, f. 19; 30. Royal Archives, Windsor, Cumberland Papers, RA CP Box 12, 17/117, James Coutts to Sir Everard Fawkener, 7 July 1746; 31. RA CP 18/82, Report of the Managers of Montrose to the Duke of Cumberland, 16 and 17 August 1746; 32–3. RA CP 12/144, James Coutts to Sir Everard Fawkener, 17 March 1746; 34. RA CP 16/323A (undated); 35. RA CP 17/192, James Coutts to Sir Everard Fawkener, 12 July 1746; 36. RA CP 17/320, James Coutts to Sir Everard Fawkener, 18 July 1746; 37–8. RA CP 18/82, Report of the Managers of Montrose to the Duke of Cumberland, 16 August 1746; 39. Forbes, *op. cit.*; 40. RA CP; 41. Saltoun Papers, John Coutts to Lord Milton, 11 August 1749; 42. Forbes, *op. cit.*; 43. National Library of Scotland, 14225.260, f. 5, Archibald Trotter to William Chalmers, 26 April 1750

9: The Coutts Brothers

1–3. Forbes, *op. cit.*; 4–6. Coutts & Co. Archives; 7–8. Forbes, *op. cit.*, p. 10; 9–10. W. A. S. Hewins (ed.), *The Whitefoord Papers*, Whitefoord to the Earl of Stair, 1752; 11–12. *Ibid.*, Whitefoord to James Coutts, 1 September 1753; 13. *Ibid.*, Adam Smith on Caleb Whitefoord; 14. Goldsmith epitaph, from 'Retaliation', quoted in Ernest H. Coleridge, *The Life of Thomas Coutts, Banker*, vol. 1, p. 64; 15. National Library of Scotland, 11003, f. 60, Thomas Coutts to Lord Minto, 22 April 1760

10: Early Years in the Strand

1. Coutts & Co. Archives; 2–3. Forbes, *op. cit.*; 4–8. Coutts & Co. Archives; 9–10. John Brooke, *King George III*, p. 202; 11. Coutts & Co. Archives

11: Public Service and Private Affairs

1. Saltoun Papers, John Coutts to Lord Milton, 11 August 1749; 2. Coutts & Co. Archives; 3. *Who's Who – British Members of Parliament*, James Coutts to William Mure; 4–5. British Library, Whitefoord Papers, Add. 36595, f. 283; 6. National Library of Scotland, 4942, f. 219, James Coutts to William Mure, 9 August 1763, quoted in *Who's Who – British Members of Parliament*; 7. *Ibid.*, James Coutts to David Hume, 1762; 8–11. National Library of Scotland, 4942, f. 225, James Coutts to William Mure, 9 September 1763; 12–16. James Boswell, *Boswell's London Journal 1762–1763*; 17. British Library, Whitefoord Papers, Add. 36595, f. 65; 18. Coutts & Co. Archives; 19. Letter from Lord Dundonald to *Morning Post*, 25 March 1822, quoted in Coleridge, *op. cit.*; 20. Galbraith, Georgina (ed.), *The Journal of the Reverend Bagshaw Stevens*; 21. Lord Dundonald, *op. cit.*; 22. National Library of Scotland, folder 1767–69, Robert Herries to Sir William Forbes; 23–4. Oliver Goldsmith, *Men and Manners*, quoted in Wheatley and Cunningham, *London Past and Present*

12: Banking 1762–73

1–3. Coutts & Co. Archives; 4–6. Forbes, *op. cit.*; 7. Scott's epitaph, quoted in *ibid.*

13: The Separation

1. Coutts & Co. Archives; 2. *Who's Who – British Members of Parliament*; 3–20. Coutts & Co. Archives

14: New Partners

1–2. Coutts & Co. Archives; 3. Huntington MSS, HA 1651; 4–8. Coutts & Co. Archives

15: Friends and Correspondents

1. Coutts & Co. Archives; 2. British Library, Whitefoord Papers; 3. *Town & Country Magazine*; 4–12. Coutts & Co. Archives; 13. Brooke, *op. cit.*, p. 187; 14–25. Coutts & Co. Archives; 26. Carl van Dorens, *Benjamin Franklin*, p. 671; 27–8. Coutts & Co. Archives

16: Thomas Coutts, Banker, 1777–88

1–9. Coutts & Co. Archives

17: Of Princes, Painters and a Lovely Duchess
1–4. Coutts & Co. Archives; 5. Shane Leslie (ed.), *Letters of Mrs Fitzherbert & Connected Papers*, p. 141; 6–8. Coutts & Co. Archives; 9. Box G. C. 1803, Blair Adam MSS; 10. Brooke, *op. cit.*; 11–12. Christopher Hibbert, *The French Revolution*; 13–14. Malcolm Elwin (ed.), *The Autobiography & Journals of Benjamin Robert Haydon*, p. 314; 15. Coutts & Co. Archives; 16. Joseph Farington, *The Farington Diary 1815–1821*, 24 February 1809, p. 119; 17–18. Coutts & Co. Archives; 19. Chatsworth MSS, quoted in The Earl of Bessborough (ed.), *Georgiana, Extracts from the Correspondence of Georgiana, Duchess of Devonshire*; 20–1. Chatsworth MSS, 1786, 1787; 22–5. Chatsworth MSS, 813.1

18: The Grand Tour
1–2. Coutts & Co. Archives; 3. Chatsworth MSS, to the Duchess of Devonshire, 24 December 1788; Coleridge, *op. cit.*, p. 263; 4. Lord Auckland, *Journals and Correspondence of Lord Auckland*, vol. II, p. 320; 5. Hewins (ed.), *op. cit.*, memorandum sent by Thomas Coutts to Caleb Whitefoord, 24 November 1788; 6–7. Chatsworth MSS, 926.2, 16 November 1788; 8. M. W. Patterson, *Francis Burdett and His Times*, vol. I, p. 11; 9. Galbraith (ed.), *op. cit.*, to the Revd William Bagshaw Stevens, p. 68; 10. Coutts & Co. Archives; 11. Antrobus Papers; 12–13. Coutts & Co. Archives, Historical Commission Report; 14–18. Coutts & Co. Archives

19: 1792: A Black Year
1. Coutts & Co. Archives; 2–3. Chatsworth MSS, 1127.3, 15 June 1792; 4. *Ibid.*, 1107.1, 13 January 1792; 5. *Ibid.*, 19 February 1792; 6. *Ibid.*, 1126.1, 25 May 1792; 7–8. *Ibid.*, 4 September 1792; 9–10. *Ibid.*, 2 November 1792; 11. *Ibid.*, 14 December 1792; Bessborough, *op. cit.*, pp. 196–7; 12–13. Coutts & Co. Archives; 14–16. Professor A. Aspinall (ed.) *Correspondence of George Prince of Wales, 1770–1812*, Thomas Coutts's memorandum, 22 December 1792, pp. 320–1; 17. Coutts & Co. Archives

20: 1793: A Year of Tragedy
1. Whitefoord Papers, *op. cit.*; 2.

Antrobus MSS; 3–9. Coutts & Co. Archives

21: Thomas Coutts and the French Revolution
1. Coutts & Co. Archives; 2. Craufurd Papers; 3–9. Coutts & Co. Archives

22: Francis Burdett
1–4. Galbraith (ed.), *op. cit.*; 5. Hewins (ed.), *op cit.*; 6. Galbraith (ed.), *op. cit.*; 7. Royal Archives, Windsor, RA 7339; 8–9. Hewins (ed.), *op. cit.*; 10–15. Galbraith (ed.), *op. cit*; 16–17. Hewins (ed.), *op. cit.*

23: The Rift
1. The letters in this chapter are taken from an unpublished *Short History of the Antrobus Family*, compiled in 1889 by Mary Egidia Antrobus, in the possession of Sir Philip Antrobus at Amesbury House, Wiltshire; 2. Ian Bruce, *The Nun of Lebanon*

24: Private and Public Affairs, 1794–1800
1. Coutts & Co. Archives; 2. All references in this section are from Bagshaw Stevens, quoted in Galbraith (ed.), *op. cit.*, unless otherwise stated; 3–4. Lord Holland, *Memoirs of the Whig Party*; 5–7. Davis, *op. cit.*; 8–20. Coutts & Co. Archives

25: 'A Banker's life is not a bed of roses'
1–3. Coutts & Co. Archives; 4. Coutts & Co. Archives, Historical Commission Report; 5. Coutts & Co. Archives; 6–8. Galbraith (ed.), *op. cit.*

26: New Century – New Problems
1. Coutts & Co. Archives; 2. Chatsworth MSS; 3–5. Coutts & Co. Archives; 6. Antrobus MSS; 7–10. Coutts & Co. Archives; 11–14. Ralph M. Robinson, *Coutts, The History of a Banking House*, pp. 40–1; 15. Blair Adam Papers, Box GC 1806 A–D; 16. Coutts & Co. Archives; 17. Farington, *op. cit.*, vol. IV, p. 196

27: Sir Francis Burdett – The 'Frantic Disturber'
1. Quoted in Patterson, *op. cit.*, vol. II, pp. 667, 668, and W. F. Moneypenny

and G. E. Buckle, *The Life of Benjamin Disraeli, Earl of Beaconsfield*; 2. Coutts & Co. Archives; 3–4. House of Commons Parliamentary Report, 12 April 1802; 5. Samuel Bamford, *Passages in the Life of a Radical*; 6–7. Aspinall (ed.), *op. cit.*, 16 July 1802; 8. *Ibid.*, 19 July 1802; 9. Royal Archives, Windsor, RA 10234, 9 June 1801; 10. Coleridge, *op. cit.*, vol. II, p. 133; Dropmore MSS, vol. VII; 11. Hector Bolitho and Derek Peel, *The Drummonds of Charing Cross*; 12. Coutts & Co. Archives; 13. Latymer Papers, f. L696; 14–15. Coutts & Co. Archives; 16–17. House of Commons, *Parliamentary Records*; 18–23. Patterson, *op. cit.*, vol. I, pp. 210–14; 24. *Ibid.*, pp. 215–17; 25. Henry Hunt, quoted in *ibid.*, p. 217; 26–7. House of Commons Report, quoted in *ibid.*, p. 246

28: Enter Miss Harriot Mellon
1–2. Mrs Cornwell Barron-Wilson, *Memoirs of Harriot Mellon, Duchess of St Albans*, p. 176; 3–5. *Ibid.* p. 197; 6. *Ibid.* p. 231; 7. Farington, *op. cit.*, 1807, vol. VII; 8–21. Coutts & Co. Archives

29: The Second Secret Marriage
1. Brooke, *op. cit.*; 2–4. Coutts & Co. Archives; 5. Barron-Wilson, *op. cit.*; 6–7. Leslie (ed.), *op. cit.*; 8–9. Coutts & Co. Archives; 10. Barron-Wilson, *op. cit.*; 11–21. Coutts & Co. Archives; 22. Disraeli, quoted in Moneypenny and Buckle, *op. cit.*; 23–8. Coutts & Co. Archives

30: The Antrobus Family
1. Elizabeth Longford, *Wellington*, vol. II; 2. Coutts & Co. Archives; 3. Mary Egidia Antrobus, *op. cit.*: all references in this section come from this source

31: Thomas Coutts, Finale
1. J. T. Smith, *Nollekens & His Times*, p. 234; 2. Harrowby MSS, LXII, ff. 39–40; 3–6. Coutts & Co. Archives; 7. Lady Holland, *Journal of Elizabeth Lady Holland 1791–1811*; 8–9. Coutts & Co. Archives; 10. *Brighton Patriot*, quoted in Coleridge, *op. cit.*, vol. II, p. 392; 11–13. Coutts & Co. Archives; 14–15. *Mrs Arbuthnot's Journal*, vol. I, p. 391; 16. Coutts & Co. Archives; 17–18. Robinson, *op. cit.*, pp. 155–6; 19–20. Antrobus MSS

32: The Partners, 1826–37
1. M. C. Reed, *A History of James Capel & Co.*, p. 21; 2–4. Leslie (ed.), *op. cit.*, vol. II; 5. Coutts & Co. Archives; 6. Wellington, quoted in Leslie, *op. cit.*; 7. Anon., *Secret Memoirs of Harriot Pumpkin*

33: Harriot, Duchess of St Albans
1. Quoted in Coleridge, *op. cit.*; 2. Anderson (ed.), *Journal of Sir Walter Scott*; 3–6. Coutts & Co. Archives; 7. Antrobus Papers; 8. Wilshere, quoted in Robinson, *op. cit.*, pp. 153–4; 9–10. Coutts & Co. Archives; 11. Lady Holland, *op. cit.*, 6 December 1826; 12–15. Coutts & Co. Archives; 16. Patterson, *op. cit.*, vol. II, p. 530; 17. Quoted in Edna Healey, *Lady Unknown, The Life of Angela Burdett-Coutts*; 18. Coutts & Co. Archives; 19. Burdett-Coutts Collection MSS, privately owned, quoted in Healey, *op cit.*; 20. *Brighton Patriot*, 15 August 1837; 21. Quoted in Robinson, *op. cit.*, p. 26; 22. Patterson, *op. cit.*, vol. II, p. 650; 23. *Ibid.*, p. 648; 24. Sir Francis Burdett to Lady Guilford, August 1837, quoted in *ibid.*, vol. II, p. 651

34: The Heiress
1. Patterson, *op. cit.*, vol. II, pp. 651–2; 2–5. Duchess of St Albans's will, printed in Barron-Wilson, *op. cit.*; 6. Harrowby MSS, LXI, f. 391, Lady Sandon to Dowager Marchioness of Bute, 14 June 1827; 7–8. *Ibid.*, LXII, f. 119, 17 June 1829; 9–10. Duchess of St Albans's will, printed in Barron-Wilson, *op. cit.*; 11. Bodleian MSS, English Letters cl. 98, Sir Francis Burdett to Angela Burdett-Coutts, 27 July 1838; 12. Lord Houghton, *Memoirs: Life, Letters of Richard Moncton Milnes, 1st Lord Houghton*, 2 vols (Cassell, 1890); 13. *Punch*, 21 November 1846; 14. *The Times*, Law Report of trial, 27 February 1847; 15. Pierpont Morgan Library, Dickens's Letters, Dickens to Angela Burdett-Coutts, 15 July 1856

35: The Marjoribanks Years
1. From the journals of B. R. Haydon, quoted in the *Faber Book of Diaries*, p. 34; 2. Elwin (ed.), *op. cit.*, p. 639; 3. Antrobus MSS, 29 June 1843; 4–5. *Ibid.*, f. 213, 19 June 1845; 6–7. Coutts & Co. Archives;

8. Norman St John-Stevas (ed.), *The Collected Works of Walter Bagehot*, vol. IX, p. 188; 9. RA, Queen Victoria's Journal, 15 March 1838, quoted in Elizabeth Longford, *Victoria RI*; 10. Coutts & Co. Archives

36: A World of Change

1–2. *The Times*, quoted in June Sampson, *All Change, Kingston, Surbiton and New Malden in the 19th Century*; 3. *Surrey Comet*, quoted in *ibid.*; 4. *The Times*, 8 August 1840; 5. *Ibid.*, 22 October 1840; 6. *Ibid.*, 8 August 1840; 7–8. Coutts & Co. Archives; 9–11. Sampson, *op. cit.*; 12. Patricia Ward, *From Tolworth Hamlet to Tolworth Tower*, 1871 census

37: Miss Coutts – Loving and Giving

1. Michael Faraday to Angela Burdett-Coutts, *c.* 1846, Burdett-Coutts Papers, quoted in Healey, *op. cit.*; 2. Julian Young, quoted in *ibid.*; 3. Pierpont Morgan Library MSS, quoted in *The Letters of Charles Dickens*, Pilgrim edn, vol. VI, 13 January 1852; 4. Pierpont Morgan Library MSS, Dickens to Mrs Brown, 3 November 1855, quoted in Edgar Johnson, *The Heart of Charles Dickens*, p. 310; 5. Dickens to Angela Burdett-Coutts, 19 May 1858, quoted in *ibid.*; 6. Wellington Archives, Stratfield Saye, 12 January 1847; 7. *Ibid.*, 5 January 1847; 8. Pierpont Morgan Library MSS, 5 September 1857, quoted in Johnson, *op. cit.*; 9. Dickens to Angela Burdett-Coutts, 16 August 1841, quoted in *ibid.*; 10. Pierpont Morgan Library MSS, Angela Burdett-Coutts to Charles Dickens, quoted in *The Letters of Charles Dickens*, vol. II; 11. Bodleian MSS, English Letters cl. 98, f. 147, Sir Francis Burdett to Angela Burdett-Coutts, 27 November 1838; 12. Pierpont Morgan Library MSS, Dickens to Edward Marjoribanks, 1 August 1840, quoted in *The Letters of Charles Dickens*, vol. II; 13. John Forster, *The Life of Charles Dickens*; 14. Pierpont Morgan Library MSS, Dickens to Angela Burdett-Coutts, 22 March 1842, from Baltimore, quoted in *The Letters of Charles Dickens*, vol. III; 15–16. Coutts & Co. Archives; 17. Pierpont Morgan Library MSS, Dickens to Angela Burdett-Coutts, 28 July 1843, quoted in

The Letters of Charles Dickens, vol. III; 18. Pierpont Morgan Library MSS, Dickens to Angela Burdett-Coutts, 5 January 1850, quoted in *ibid.*, vol VI; 19. Coutts & Co. Archives; 20. Harrowby MSS, LXIV, f. 200; 21. Dickens to W. H. Wills, 28 October 1855, quoted in Lehman, *Charles Dickens as Editor*, pp. 182–3; 22–3. Dickens to Angela Burdett-Coutts, 16 September 1857, quoted in Johnson, *op. cit.*; 24. Pierpont Morgan Library MSS, Dickens to Angela Burdett-Coutts, 28 October 1847, quoted in *The Letters of Charles Dickens*, vol. V; 25. Pierpont Morgan Library MSS, Dickens to Dr William Brown, 6 November 1849, quoted in *ibid.*; 26. Pierpont Morgan Library MSS, Dickens to Angela Burdett-Coutts, 15 November 1856, quoted in Johnson, *op. cit.*; 27. Burdett-Coutts Papers, quoted in Healey, *op. cit.*, p. 119

38: 'Miss Angela' and the Duke

1. Wellington Archives, Stratfield Saye, Angela Burdett-Coutts to Edward Marjoribanks, 19 November 1846, drafted by Wellington; 2. *Ibid.*, Wellington to Angela Burdett-Coutts, 24 November 1846; 3. 7th Duke of Wellington (ed.), *Wellington and His Friends*; 4. Wellington Archives, Stratfield Saye, 24 August 1846; 5. 5 January 1847, quoted in Wellington (ed.), *op. cit.*; 6. 5 June 1847, quoted in *ibid.*; 7. 8 February 1847, quoted in *ibid.*; 8. Wellington Archives, Stratfield Saye, 1847; 9. *Ibid.*, 8 February 1847; 10. *Ibid.*, June 1847; 11. Burdett-Coutts MSS, 10 August 1880, quoted in *Lady Unknown*, *op. cit.*; 12. Greville Memoirs, 13 July 1847, *Leaves from the Greville Diary*; 13–14. Wellington Archives, Stratfield Saye, 30 October 1847; 15. *Ibid.*, 30 December 1847; 16. *Ibid.*, 10 April 1848; 17. *Ibid.*, 1851; 18. *Ibid.*, 31 January 1851; 19. Pierpont Morgan Library MSS, Dr John Sutherland to Dickens, 10 July 1855, quoted in Johnson, *op. cit.*, p. 306; 20. Pierpont Morgan Library MSS, Dickens to Angela Burdett-Coutts, 1 April 1853, quoted in *ibid.*; 21–2. Quoted in Healey, *op. cit.*, p. 172; Bertram, *Les Belges à Londres*; 23. Pierpont Morgan Library MSS, Dickens to Angela Burdett-Coutts, 19 May 1858,

quoted in Johnson, *op. cit.*, p. 356; 24. Pierpont Morgan Library MSS, Dickens to Angela Burdett-Coutts and Mrs Brown, 11 June 1865, quoted in *ibid.*; 25. Pierpont Morgan Library MSS, Dickens to Angela Burdett-Coutts, 13 March 1860, quoted in *ibid.*

39: Miss Coutts and the Wider World
1. Owen Rutter, *Rajah Brooke and Baroness Burdett-Coutts*; all Brooke's letters come from the British Library, quoted in Rutter; 2. Pierpont Morgan Library MSS, Dickens to Angela Burdett-Coutts, 30 January 1860, quoted in Johnson, *op. cit.*; 3. Rutter, *op. cit.*; 4–9. Quoted in *ibid.*; 10–11. Duchess of Teck, *The Baroness Burdett-Coutts*; 12. Pierpont Morgan Library MSS, Dickens to Angela Burdett-Coutts, 3 February 1857, quoted in Johnson, *op. cit.*

40: The Bank in the Strand
1–14. Coutts & Co. Archives; 15. Harrowby MSS, LXVI, 11 and 12; 16–18. Coutts & Co. Archives; 19–21. Harrowby MSS, ff. 32–5, vol. 66, 6 January 1866; 22. *Ibid.*, f. 34, 12 January 1865; 23. *Ibid.*, f. 52, 5 December 1865; 24. St John-Stevas (ed.), *op. cit.*, vol. IX, chapter VIII; 25. *Ibid.*, p. 128; 26–9. *Ibid.*, p. 186; 30–4. Coutts & Co. Archives

41: Years of Honour
1. Duchess of Teck, *op. cit.*; 2–3. *The Times*, 29 April 1869; 4. Duchess of Teck, *op. cit.*; 5–6. A. S. Gay *History of the Burdett-Coutts' Lodge* (London, 1869); 7. British Library, Gladstone Papers, 44,430; 8–9. Queen Victoria's Journal, 7 May 1871; 10. Gladstone Papers, Angela Burdett-Coutts to Gladstone, 12 May 1871; 11. *The Scotsman*, 16 January 1874, quoted in Healey, *op. cit.*, p. 180; 12. Harrowby MSS, Angela Burdett-Coutts to Ryder, 1874

42: Years of Stress
1. Harrowby MSS, LXVI, f. 402, Angela Burdett-Coutts to Ryder, 5 February 1878; 2. *Ibid.*, f. 120, 4 February 1878; 3. *Ibid.*, f. 160, 8 February 1875; 4–5. *Ibid.*, LXVI, f. 199, 3 July 1877; 6. *Ibid.*, f. 221, Angela Burdett-Coutts to

Ouvry, 26 July 1877; 7. *Ibid.*, ff. 223, 225; 8. *Ibid.*, f. 227, July 1877 (undated); 9. St John-Stevas (ed.), *op. cit.*; 10. Harrowby MSS, LXVI, f. 77, 22 July 1872; 11. *Ibid.*, f. 78, 23 July 1872; 12. *Ibid.*, f. 88, 4 April 1873; 13. *Ibid.*, f. 92–5, 11 April 1873; 14. *Ibid.*, ff. 181–3, Marjoribanks to Robinson, 17 June 1875; 15–16. *Ibid.*, f. 230, Marjoribanks to George Robinson, 18 August 1877; 17. *Ibid.*, ff. 234–9, Ryder memorandum, 27 August 1877; 18. *Ibid.*, f. 221, 8 September 1877; 19. Harrowby MSS, LXVI, ff. 313 and 307–822, 22 October 1877; 20. Ward, *op. cit.*; 21. Coutts & Co. Archives

43: New Hands at the Helm
1. Harrowby MSS, HLA, vol. LXVI, f. 522, 24 November 1878; 2–3. *Ibid.*, LXVI, ff. 324–7, 3 November 1877; 4–5. *Ibid.*, f. 325, 5 November 1877; 6. *Ibid.*, f. 488, 2 July 1878; 7–10. *Ibid.*, f. 347; 11–13. *Ibid.*, ff. 349–54, 26 December 1877; 14. *Ibid.*, ff. 355–8, Angela Burdett-Coutts to Lord Harrowby, 27 December 1877; 15–17. *Ibid.*, LXVI, f. 359, 28 December 1877; 18. *Ibid.*, ff. 367–70, 31 December 1877; 19. *Ibid.*, f. 383, 29 December 1877; 20. *Ibid.*, ff. 494-5, 13 July 1878; 21–2. *Ibid.*, ff. 398–9, 25 January 1878; 23–4. *Ibid.*, f. 401, 27 January 1878; 25–7. *Ibid.*, ff. 402–3, 5 February 1878; 28–9. Coutts & Co. Archives; 30. Harrowby MSS, f. 422, 16 April 1878; 31. *Ibid.*, LXVI, f. 424, Robinson to Ouvry to Pym, 22 April 1878; 32–3. *Ibid.*, f. 502, 16 August 1878; 34. *Ibid.*, f. 498, Robinson to Ryder, 24 July 1878; 35–8. *Ibid.*, f. 488, 22 June 1878; 39. *Ibid.*, f. 492, 2 July 1878; 40. *Ibid.*, ff. 483–6, 22 June 1878

44: 'The Mad Marriage'
1. Quoted in Healey, *op. cit.*, p. 188; 2. Laurence Irving, *Life of Henry Irving*; 3. Wagner Papers (in possession of Sir Anthony Wagner), William Sinclair to Henry Wagner, quoted in Healey, *op. cit.*, p. 188; 4. British Library, Layard Papers, 39012, Angela Burdett-Coutts to A. H. Layard, 30 August 1877; 5. *Ibid.*, 39017, 7 January 1878; 6. Wagner Papers, 27 December 1878; 7. Layard Papers, 39025, 21 February 1879; 8. Royal Archives, Windsor, RA 512/1, Angela Burdett-

Coutts to Queen Victoria; 9. Harrowby MSS, LXVI, f. 120, 25 October 1873; 10. Quoted in Clara Burdett Patterson, *Angela Burdett-Coutts and the Victorians*; 11. *Ibid.*, 2 October 1879; 12. Harrowby MSS, LXVII, f. 143, 25 July 1880; 13–14. *Ibid.*, f. 84, July 1880; 15. Royal Archives, Windsor, Add. L14/56, Queen Victoria to Sir H. Ponsonby, 10 July 1880; 16. *Ibid.*, vol. LI, f. 270, 18 July 1880; 17. Harrowby MSS, LXVII, ff. 88 and 89, 11 July 1880; 18. *Ibid.*, f. 109, 11 July 1880; 19. *Ibid.*, ff. 95–6, 12 July 1880, quoted in Healey, *op. cit.*, p. 198; 20–1. *Ibid.*, LXVII, 13 July 1880; 22. *Ibid.*, LXVII, f. 109; 23. *Ibid.*, f. 143; 24. *Ibid.*, LXVII, f. 107, 16 July 1880; 25. *Ibid.*, f. 109, 18 July 1880; 26. *Ibid.*, ff. 126–7, Malcolm to Ryder, 20 July 1880; 27–8. *Ibid.*, f. 82, July 1880; 29–30. Coutts & Co. Archives; 31–2. Gladstone Papers, quoted in Healey, *op. cit.*, p. 201; 33. *Disraeli: Letters to Queen Victoria*, vol. III, p. 146, 22 September 1880; 34. Queen Victoria to Sir Theodore Martin, 17 January 1881, quoted in Healey, *op. cit.*, p. 235; 35. Harrowby MSS, LXVII, ff. 230–1, 11 September 1880; 36. *Ibid.*, f. 353, 11 July 1881; 37. British Library, Osborne Papers, 46,404; 38. Harrowby MSS, LXVII, f. 107, 22 November 1881; 39. *Ibid.*, f. 389, 25 July 1880; 40. Quoted in Healey, *op. cit.*; 41. *Thomas Moore, Memoirs, Journals & Correspondence*; 42. Duchess of Teck, *op. cit.*; 43–4. *Ibid.*, p. 156; 45. Introduction to *ibid.*; 46. Henry Furniss, *Some Victorian Women*

45: Coutts & Co.: The End of an Era
1. Philip Ziegler, *The Sixth Great Power*; 2–7. Identity unknown; 8. St John-Stevas (ed.), *op. cit.*, vol. IX, p. 391: 'Joint Stock Banks' (first published in *Economist*, 17 August 1861)

46: The New Bank
1. St John-Stevas, *op. cit.*, p. 184 (from 'Lombard Street 1873'); 2. *Ibid.*, p. 183; 3–4. *Ibid.*, p. 184; 5–8. Coutts & Co. Archives; 9. *Bankers' Magazine*, pp. 150–2; 10–24. Coutts & Co. Archives; 25–9. *Daily Chronicle*, Whit Monday 1904; 30. Coutts & Co. Archives

47: The Baroness – Last Years
1–5. *The Times*, obituary by T. P. O'Connor, 12 January 1907; 6. Quoted in Healey, *op. cit.*, p. 223; 7. Quoted in *ibid.*; Clifford Musgrave, *Life in Brighton*; 8. Clara Patterson, *op. cit.*; 9. Quoted in Healey, *op. cit.*; 10. Irving, *op. cit.*; 11–12. Coutts & Co. Archives; 13–15. Quoted in Healey, *op. cit.*, p. 224; 16. *Ibid.*, p. 226; 17. Davidson Papers, vol. 124, ff. 156–9, Lambeth Palace Library, W. Burdett-Coutts to Davidson; 18. Quoted in Healey, *op. cit.*; 19–20. Coutts & Co. Archives; 21. Quoted in Angela Burdett-Coutts, *Woman's Mission*; 22. *The Times*, obituary by T. P. O'Connor, 1921

48: The Clerks' Tale
1–3. Coutts & Co. Archives; 4. All quotes on pp. 398–401 are from H. E. Rowe's papers in Coutts & Co. Archives; 5–6. Peter Boulton, *Long Playing Record*; 7. Coutts & Co. Archives

49: Amalgamation
1. *Daily Telegraph*, 17 July 1914; 2–3. *The World*, 21 July 1914; 4. *Bankers' Magazine*, 1913; 5–9. Coutts & Co. Archives

50: War and Aftermath
1. *Financial Times*, 5 August 1914; 2–15. Coutts & Co. Archives; 16. Michael Collins, *Money & Banking in the UK, A History*, p. 79; 17. Hill, *Bank of England*, vol. I; 18–23. Coutts & Co. Archives; 24. Collins, *op. cit.*; 25–9. Coutts & Co. Archives

51: Five Chairmen Remembered
1. All quotes on pp. 422–4 are from Charles Adcock's MSS, Coutts & Co. Archives; 2. Osbert Sitwell, *Left Hand, Right Hand, An Autobiography*; 3–5. Author's recorded interview with Sir Seymour Egerton; 6. Coutts & Co. Archives; 7. Author's recorded interview with Sir Seymour Egerton; 8. Author's recorded interview with Lord Harrowby

52: 'A New Breed'
1. Collins, *op. cit.*; 2. Author's

recorded interview with Sir David Money-Coutts; 3. Author's recorded interview with Charles Musk; 4. Boulton, *op. cit.*; 5–7. 'The Computer in the Office' and 'Magnetic Tape in Soho', *The Statist*, 19 February 1965; 8–9. Coutts & Co. Archives; 10. Author's recorded interview with Lord Harrowby; 11. Coutts & Co. Archives; 12–13. Author's recorded interview with Lord Harrowby; 14. Coutts & Co. Archives, author's summary of McKinsey Report

53: A Modern Image

1. *Financial Times*, 21 March 1961; 2. Coutts & Co. Archives; 3. *City Press*, 14 April 1961; 4–5. Coutts & Co. Archives; 6. *Guardian*, 22 February 1979; 7. *The Times*, December 1978; 8–11. Coutts & Co. Archives

54: Coutts & Co. in the Global Village

1–2. Denis Healey, *The Time of My Life*; 3–10. Coutts & Co. Archives; 11. Sitwell, *op. cit.*

Bibliography

Manuscript Sources
Aberdeen Archive Department,
    Aberdeen Museum
Aberdeen Burgh Records
Aberdeen University Library (Aberdeen
    Journals)
Sir Philip Antrobus:
  Family Papers
  Short History of the Antrobus Family
    (unpublished) by Mary Egidia
    Antrobus (wife of John, son of
    Gibbs Antrobus)
Bank of Scotland:
  Records
  Adventurers Ledger
Blair Adam Papers, Blair Adam, Scotland
Bodleian Library, Oxford – Department
    of Western Manuscripts:
  Burdett Family Papers
British Library:
  Babbage Papers
  Burdett-Coutts Papers
  Dropmore MSS
  Gladstone Papers
  Layard Papers
  Whitefoord Papers
Burdett Family Papers:
  Bodleian Library, Oxford
  County Record Office, Wiltshire
Bute Papers, Mount Stuart, Rothesay
Cardiff Castle Records
Coutts & Co.:
  Archives
  Dutens Papers
  'History of the Triangular Site Known
    as the West Strand Improvements of
    1831 including the Lowther
    Arcade', prepared for Messrs Farrer
    & Co. by Miss V. Stokes, Archivist,
    Coutts & Co.

Lawrence Papers
Latymer Papers
Marjoribanks Papers
Major Broadfoot's Notes (1601.a)
Staff Memoirs
Internal Memoranda
Craufurd Family Papers – Miss Deirdre
    Craufurd and General Tuzo
    (direct descendants of John
    Campbell by his daughter, Mary
    Middleton)
Devonshire Collection – Duke of
    Devonshire's Archives,
    Chatsworth
Edinburgh Burgesses, Roll of
Edinburgh Burgh Record Office
Edinburgh City Archives
Harrowby MSS, Sandon Hall, Stafford
Huntington Museum, California, USA:
  Stowe Collection
Lambeth Palace Library:
  Davidson Papers
Montrose Burgh Court Claims, Series I,
    1707–1820
Montrose Burgh Records
Montrose Museum Records
Montrose Old Kirk Records
Montrose Town Council Minutes
Museum of Scotland, Edinburgh
National Archives, Paris
National Library of Scotland:
  Liston Papers
  Minto Papers
  Saltoun Papers
New York Public Library
Pierpont Morgan Library, New York:
  Dickens's Letters
Royal Archives, Windsor
Royal Bank of Scotland:
  Archives

Minutes of the Court of Directors, vol. 4, 2 October 1741–25 March 1748

Scottish Church Records

Scottish Record Office:
General Register House
Leven and Melville MSS
Stair MSS
Treasury Sederunt Books

Scottish United Services Museum, Edinburgh Castle

Tower of London, Records of the Jewel House

University Library, Edinburgh

Wellington MSS, Stratford Saye

Public Libraries and Local Record Offices

Brighton Reference Library
British Library
Cheshire Record Office
Gloucestershire Archives Department
Highgate Literary Institute
London Borough of Sutton and Cheam Reference Library
The London Library
Norwich Public Library
Surrey Record Office
Westminster Public Library
Wiltshire Record Office

Newspapers and Magazines

Bankers' Magazine
Brighton Patriot
The Bullionist
Daily Chronicle
The Economist
Financial Times
Guardian
Punch
The Statist
Telegraph
The Times

Published Sources

Anderson (ed.), *Journal of Sir Walter Scott*

Anon., *The Life of the Late Thomas Coutts by a Person of the First Respectability* (London, 1822)

Anon., *The Secret Memoirs of Harriot Pumpkin* (J. Cahuac, London, 1825)

Ashton, T. S., and Sayers, R. F. (eds), *Papers in English Monetary History* (Clarendon Press, Oxford, 1953)

Aspinall, Professor A. (ed.), *George IV's Letters from the Royal Archives* (Cambridge University Press, Cambridge, 1966)

Aspinall, Professor A. (ed.), *Correspondence of George Prince of Wales, 1770–1812* (Cassell, London, 1963–7)

Bamford, Francis, and the Duke of Wellington (eds.), *Mrs Arbuthnot's Journal* (Macmillan, London, 1950)

Bamford, Samuel, *Passages in the Life of a Radical*, 2 vols (London, 1844)

Barron-Wilson, Mrs Cornwell, *Memoirs of Harriot Mellon, Duchess of St Albans*, 2 vols (Remington & Co., London, 1844 and 1886)

Beresford, John (ed.), *Adventures of an Eighteenth Century Footman* (Routledge, London, 1927)

Bertram, *Les Belges à Londres* (Ghent, 1867; translated by E. Healey)

Bessborough, The Earl of, *Georgiana, Extracts from the Correspondence of Georgiana, Duchess of Devonshire* (John Murray, London, 1955)

Biscoe, A. G., *The Earls of Middleton* (London, 1876)

Bolitho, Hector, and Peel, Derek, *The Drummonds of Charing Cross* (Allen & Unwin, London, 1967)

Boswell, James, *Boswell's London Journal 1762–1763* (Heinemann, London, 1950)

Briggs, Asa, *The Age of Improvement, 1793–1867* (Longman, London, 1959)

Brooke, John, *King George III* (Constable, London, 1972)

Bruce, Ian, *The Nun of Lebanon* (Collins, London, 1951)

Buckle (ed.), *Letters of Queen Victoria*, 2 vols (John Murray, London, 1930)

Burdett-Coutts, Angela, *The Ambulatory Schoolmaster* (London, 1865)

Burdett-Coutts, Angela, *Woman's Mission* (written for the Chicago Exhibition, London, 1893)

Burdett-Coutts, Angela, *Noble Workers* (London, undated)

Burnett, Charles J., and Bennett, Helen, *The Green Mantle* (National Museums of Scotland, 1989)

Campbell, John, *Leaves from the Diary of an Edinburgh Banker from 14 September 1845 to 23 November 1845* (privately printed, 1881, Royal Bank of Scotland Archives)

Checkland, S. G., *Scottish Banking, A History 1695–1973* (Collins for The Institute of Bankers, London, 1975)

Clapham, Sir John, *The Bank of England, A History,* 2 vols (Cambridge University Press, Cambridge, 1944)

Clarke, Philip, *Child & Co. 1673–1973* (Perivall Williams Group, London, 1973)

Cobb, Richard and Jones, *The French Revolution* (Simon & Schuster, London, 1988)

Cobham, Alfred, *A History of Modern France,* 2 vols (Penguin Books, London, 1961)

Coleridge, Ernest H., *The Life of Thomas Coutts, Banker,* 2 vols (John Lane, The Bodley Head, London, 1920)

Collins, Michael, *Money & Banking in the UK, A History* (Croom Helm Ltd, Collins, London, 1988)

Coutts & Co., *The Three Crowns,* staff magazine of Coutts & Co.

Coutts, Herbert, *Edinburgh – An Illustrated History* (City of Edinburgh Museums & Art Galleries Publication, 1977; second edition, 1981)

Dalgleish, George, and Maxwell, Stuart, *The Lovable Craft* (Royal Museums of Scotland, 1987)

Davis, T. M., *The Harlot & the Statesman* (Kensal Press, London, 1986)

Defoe, Daniel, *A Tour through England and Wales,* 2 vols (introduced by G. D. H. Cole, Dent, London, 1927)

Defoe, Daniel, *A Tour through the Whole Island of Great Britain* (Michael Joseph, London, 1989)

Defoe, Daniel, *Essay on Projects* (chapter 'On Banking'), 1693

Dictionary of National Biography

Dickson, P., *The Financial Revolution in England* (Macmillan, London, 1967)

Dickens, Charles, *The Letters of Charles Dickens,* Pilgrim edn, vols I–VI, eds: M. House, G. Storey, K. Tillotsen and N. Burgess (Clarendon Press, Oxford, 1965–88)

Dorens, Carl van, *Benjamin Franklin* (Putnam, London, 1939)

Elwin, Malcolm (ed.), *The Autobiography & Journals of Benjamin Robert Haydon* (Macdonald, London, 1853; republished 1950)

Farington, Joseph, *The Farington Diary 1815–1821,* 8 vols (Hutchinson, London, 1922)

Forbes, Sir William, Bart, *Memoirs of a Banking House* (second edition, Chambers, London, 1860)

Forster, John, *The Life of Charles Dickens,* 3 vols (London, 1872–4)

Foster, Sir W., *John Company* (John Lane, London, 1926)

Fowl, Nicholas (ed.), *Fuseli, The Nightmare* (Viking Press, New York, 1973)

Fraser, Duncan, *Montrose before 1700* (Standard Press, Montrose, 1967)

Fraser, Duncan, *The Smugglers* (Standard Press, Montrose, 1978)

Fulford, Roger, *The Royal Dukes* (Pan Books, Duckworth, London, 1935)

Furniss, Henry, *Some Victorian Women* (London, 1923)

Galbraith, Georgina (ed.), *The Journal of the Reverend Bagshaw Stevens* (Clarendon Press, Oxford, 1965)

Galbraith, John Kenneth, *Money* (André Deutsch, London, 1975)

Galbraith, John Kenneth, *A Short History of Financial Euphoria* (Whittle Direct Books, Knoxville, Tennessee, USA, 1990)

Goldsmith, Oliver, *Men and Manners* (Cooke, London, 1802)

Gower, Iris Levison, *A Face without a Frown* (Frederick Muller, London, 1944)

Hahn, Emily, *James Brooke of Sarawak* (Arthur Barker, London, 1953)

Healey, Denis, *The Time of My Life* (Michael Joseph, London, 1989)

Healey, Edna, *Lady Unknown, The Life of Angela Burdett-Coutts* (Sidgwick & Jackson, London, 1978)

Hewins, W. A. S. (ed.), *The Whitefoord Papers* (Clarendon Press, Oxford, 1898)

Hibbert, Christopher, *George IV* (Longman, London, 1972)

Hibbert, Christopher, *The French Revolution* (Penguin Books, London, 1980)

Hilton Price, F. G., *A Handbook of London Bankers* (Leadenhall, London, 1891)

Hoare's Bank, *Hoare's Bank, A Record 1673–1932* (London, 1932)

Holland, Lady, *Journal of Elizabeth Lady Holland 1791–1811* (Fox Strangeways, Longman, London, 1909)

Holland, Lord, *Memoirs of the Whig Party*, 2 vols (London, 1854)

Hunt, Leigh, *Men Women & Books* (1847)

Hyde, H. Montgomery, *The Amazing Story of John Law* (Home & Van Thal, London, 1948)

Insh, George Pratt, *Company of Scotland Trading to Africa and the Indies* (Charles Scribner's & Sons, London & New York, 1932)

Irving, Lawrence, *Henry Irving* (Faber & Faber, London, 1951)

Jenkins, Alan, *The Stock Exchange Story* (Heinemann, London, 1973)

Jennings, L. J. (ed.), *The Croker Papers, 1808–1857*, 3 vols (London, 1884)

Johnson, Edgar, *The Heart of Charles Dickens* (Duell, Sloane & Pearce, New York, 1952)

Joslin, D. M., *Economic History Review* (London Private Bankers)

Kriegel, Abraham D. (ed.), *The Holland House Diaries 1831–1840, The Diary of Henry Vassall Fox, Third Lord Holland, with extracts from the Diary of Dr John Allen* (Routledge & Kegan Paul, London, 1977)

Layard, George (ed.), *Sir Thomas Lawrence Letterbag* (George Allen, London, 1906)

Lenman, Bruce, *The Jacobite Risings in Britain 1689–1746* (Methuen, London, 1980)

Leslie, Shane (ed.), *Letters of Mrs Fitzherbert & Connected Papers*, 2 vols (Hollis & Carter, London, 1944)

Lockhart, J. G., *Memoirs of the Life of Sir Walter Scott*, 7 vols (Black, London, 1882)

Louis Philippe, *Mes Mémoires*, 2 vols (Librairie Plon, Paris, 1974)

Longford, Elizabeth, *Victoria RI* (Weidenfeld & Nicolson, London, 1964)

Longford, Elizabeth, *Wellington*, 2 vols (Weidenfeld & Nicolson, London, 1969)

Lucas, C. B. (ed.), *The Letters of Horace Walpole* (Simkin Marshall, London, 1904)

Macaulay, Lord, *The History of England*, edited by T. F. Henderson (Routledge, London, 1907)

MacKay, Charles, *The Extraordinary Popular Delusions and the Madness of Crowds* (Farrar Strauss & Giroux, New York, 1932, from the 1841 edition)

Macklynn, Frank, *The Jacobites* (Routledge & Kegan Paul, London, 1985)

Maclean, Fitzroy, *A Concise History of Scotland* (Thames & Hudson, London, 1970)

Macky, John, *Memoirs of the Secret Services of John Macky, Esq* (London, 1733)

Malcolm, Charles A., *The Bank of Scotland 1695–1945* (R & R Clerk, Edinburgh, undated, c. 1946–8)

Marshall, C. J., *History of Sutton & Cheam* (1936; revised edition, 1971)

Mercer, Derrick (ed.), *The Chronicle of the Twentieth Century* (Jacques Legrand, Paris)

Middleton, Dorothy, *The Life of Charles, Second Earl of Middleton 1650–1719* (Staples Press, London, 1957)

Mingay, G. E., *English Landed Society in the Eighteenth Century* (Routledge & Kegan Paul, London, 1963)

Moneypenny, W. F., and Buckle, G. E., *The Life of Benjamin Disraeli, Earl of Beaconsfield*, 2 vols (London, 1929)

Montagu, Mary Wortley, *Letters 1709–1762* (Dent, London, 1906)

Morrell, Phillip (ed.), *Leaves from the Greville Diary* (London, 1929)

Morris, The Rev. David, *A Class-Book History of England* (Longman, Green & Co., London, 1894)

Musgrave, Clifford, *Life in Brighton* (Roch, London, 1981)

Napier, Lewis, and Brooke, John (eds), *House of Commons 1754–1790* (Historical Publications Trust, HMSO, London, 1964)

Osborne, Charles, *Letters of Charles Dickens to the Baroness Burdett-Coutts* (John Murray, London, 1931)

Patterson, Clara Burdett, *Angela Burdett-Coutts and the Victorians* (John Murray, London, 1953)

Patterson, M. W., *Francis Burdett and His Times*, 2 vols (Macmillan, London, 1931)

Pearce, Charles E., *The Jolly Duchess* (Stanley Paul, London, 1915)

Poisson, Georges, *Cette Curieuse Famille d'Orléans* (Librairie Académique Perrin, Paris, 1976)

Pope-Hennessy, James, *Queen Mary* (Allen & Unwin, London, 1959)

Prebble, John, *The Darien Disaster* (Secker & Warburg, London, 1968)

Prior, Felix (ed.), *Faber Book of Diaries: Journals of B. R. Haydon* (Faber & Faber, London, 1987)

Reed, M. C., *A History of James Capel & Co.* (private circulation, Longman Group, London, 1975; reprinted, 1984)

Richardson, Ralph, *Coutts & Co.*, (London, 1900)

Robinson, Ralph M., *Coutts, The History of a Banking House* (John Murray, London, 1929)

Rogers, The Rev Charles, *Genealogical Memoirs of the Families of Colt and Coutts* (The Royal Historical Society, London, 1879)

The Royal Bank of Scotland, *The Royal Bank of Scotland 1727-1977* (published May 1977 for The Royal Bank of Scotland)

Rutter, Owen (ed.), *Rajah Brooke and Baroness Burdett-Coutts* (Hutchinson & Co., London, 1935)

St John-Stevas, Norman (ed.), *Bagehot's Historical Essays* (Dobson, London, 1965)

St John-Stevas, Norman (ed.), *The Collected Works of Walter Bagehot*, 10 vols (*Economist*, London, 1978)

Sampson, June, *All Change: Kingston, Surbiton and New Malden in the 19th Century* (St Luke's Church, Kingston-upon-Thames, 1985)

Sayers, R. F., *The Bank of England 1891-1944*, 2 vols (Cambridge University Press, Cambridge, 1976)

Schama, Simon, *The Embarrassment of Riches* (Fontana, London, 1987)

Selected Statutes: Documents Relating to British Banking 1832-1928, 2 vols (Oxford University Press, Oxford, 1929)

Seton of Abercorn, Walter, 'Some Stuart Papers belonging to Messrs Coutts & Co.', *Scottish Historical Review*, June 1976

Sharpe, W. (ed.), *Recollections of Samuel Rogers* (London, 1859)

Sichell, Walter, *Life of Sheridan* (Constable, London, 1906)

Sitwell, Osbert, *Left Hand, Right Hand: An Autobiography*, vol. III: *Great Morning* (Macmillan, London, 1948)

Smith, Adam, *The Wealth of Nations* (Ward Lock & Co. Ltd, London)

Smith, J. T., *Nollekens & His Times* (Trunstile Press, 1828; republished 1949)

Sparrow, Elizabeth, 'The Alien Office 1792-1806', *The Historical Journal*, 33/2, 1990, 361-84

Stokes, Veronica, 'Scotch Mist & London Fog', *The Three Crowns*, Coutts & Co. staff magazine, 1968

J. G. Tait (ed.), *Journals of Sir Walter Scott Bart*, 3 vols (1939-46)

Taylor, T., *Benjamin Robert: The Life of Benjamin Robert Haydon from his Autobiography and Letters* (MacDonal, London, 1853)

Teck, Duchess of, *The Baroness Burdett-Coutts* (prepared for the World Columbian Exposition, Chicago, 1893)

Thiers, Adolphe, *The Mississippi Bubble - A Memoir of John Law* (New York, 1864)

Thompson, J. M., *The French Revolution* (Basil Blackwell, Oxford, 1944)

Thorne, R. G., (ed.), *House of Commons 1790-1820* (Secker & Warburg, London, 1986)

Trevelyan, G. M., *English Social History, Chaucer to Queen Victoria* (Longman, Green & Co., London, third edition, April 1946)

Ward, Patricia, *From Tolworth Hamlet to Tolworth Tower* (London, 1975)

Wellington, 7th Duke of (ed.), *Wellington*

Bibliography

& His Friends (Macmillan, London, 1965)

Wheatley and Cunningham, London Past and Present (John Murray, London, 1891)

Who's Who (various years)

Who's Who – British Members of Parliament

Who Was Who

Woodward, Sir Llewellyn, The Age of Reform 1815–1821 (Clarendon Press, Oxford, 1938)

Young, Julian, A Memoir of Charles Mayne Young, Tragedian, with Extracts from his Son's Journal (London, 1971)

Ziegler, Philip, The Sixth Great Power (Collins, London, 1988)

Index